Seasonal Charts for Futures Traders

A Sourcebook

COURTNEY SMITH

JOHN WILEY & SONS

New York • Chichester • Brisbane • Toronto • Singapore

Library of Congress Cataloging in Publication Data:

Smith, Courtney.
Seasonal charts for futures traders.

Bibliography: p.
1. Commodity exchanges. 2. Commodity exchanges—Charts, diagrams, etc. I. Title

HG6046.S57 1986 332.63′28 86-15980
ISBN 0-471-84888-3

Printed in the United States of America

10 9 8 7 6 5 4 3 2 1

To

Ken, Jack, John, and Malcolm

Preface

The purpose of this book is to be the most complete guide to seasonal price movement available for commodity futures traders and hedgers. This book will be a valuable aid in developing a profitable trading strategy to suit your personal market approach. It details dozens of seasonal price trends in the futures market with over 80% reliability. Several commodities have seasonal periods with 100% reliability.

The percent reliability is only one factor that can be used to locate profitable seasonal price tendencies. This book contains statistics that allow you to time entry and exit points, set stop-loss orders, and establish realistic goals for a given trade. Combinations of these unique statistics can isolate the relative risk/reward ratio for a given trade at a particular time of year.

Don't be intimidated by the statistics in this book. Ignorance is not bliss in commodity trading. More knowledge increases your chances of being successful. As a result, a great deal of time and effort has been expended to make this study as complete and useful as possible.

The ability to use this book to its full potential rests with the reader. Those who take the time to understand how the graphs are produced and what they reveal about seasonality will find their efforts well rewarded.

Trading commodities using seasonal tendencies can be used profitably only if used wisely. This is not the Holy Grail of commodity trading systems, but it is a powerful tool for increasing profits and minimizing losses. Throughout I will point out ways to use this information to maximum advantage and also show its limitations.

All futures traders will find the charts and tables extremely useful in their trading program. Traders will have the "odds" for profit before they put on the trade. No longer will they be trading against the seasonals without knowing it. The first rule of commodity trading is to trade with the trend and seasonal tendencies are very powerful trends. I will show you seasonal moves that have occurred 100% of the time under study—true profitability!

This book is intended as a reference guide for traders who wish to be fully informed before they make a trade. It should not be followed slavishly. It should be used as an additional information source in analyzing a potential trade. Traders have their own reasons for taking positions in the market. The purpose of this book is to help traders and hedgers get a sense of the profit potential and risk involved for a given trade at a given time of year. It is meant to augment, not replace, whatever guides you use to trade in the market, whether they are technical or fundamental. Be aware of any fixed system, for the nature of the market is change. Remember the words of the wise skeptic who said: "Even a broken clock works twice a day!"

This book reviews and analyzes what past prices have already shown us. If it helps you to profit, or saves you a loss, its purpose will have been well served.

I hope this book teaches you enough to pay for its cost many times over. This book was written to be used and referred to constantly. I want you to wear it out.

COURTNEY SMITH

New York, New York
October 1986

Acknowledgments

I'd like to especially thank Jason P. Gillard and Renee Karpiel for their help. Thanks to my editor at John Wiley & Sons, Nettie Bleich, and publisher, Stephen Kippur, for their support.

C. S.

Contents

1 The Nature of Seasonal Tendencies 1

2 Using the Charts to Trade Seasonal Tendencies 5

3 Interest Rates 17

4 Currencies 37

5 Metals 81

6 Grains 131

7 Meats 213

8 Softs 269

9 Miscellaneous Commodities 319

10 Seasonal Calendar 345

11 Further Reading 357

ONE

The Nature of Seasonal Tendencies

Seasonal price tendencies are the cyclical fluctuations in commodity prices during a year. This book examines the month-to-month movement of futures prices to find the reliability and magnitude of these moves. In some cases, great magnitude and reliability was found; in other cases, no consistent cycle was found.

Seasonals occur because periodic events in the real world affect commodity prices. A classic example is wheat. The low price for wheat typically comes at harvest time. Farmers rarely have the space to store their entire crop after harvest, and they have cash-flow problems as well. These problems force farmers to sell their excess wheat, which in turn causes a vast increase in market supplies and the market price responds by falling. After farmers have sold this excess wheat, they are in a position to hold their remaining stocks until the price improves. They have greater control of the supply of wheat because they are not forced to sell due to a lack of storage space and cash. The wheat charts in this book clearly show what happens to wheat prices after farmers stop their "distress" wheat sales. Wheat prices reach their harvest low in May then rise sharply to September.

The copper market is another classic seasonal market. Each spring, copper users restock their inventories in preparation for extra summer demand caused largely by increased building of houses and automobiles during this period. House and car building require large amounts of copper. Many people think the high price of copper should occur in the summer at the peak of copper demand. However, the high price occurs much earlier because the suppliers stock up in anticipation of the rush to ensure adequate supplies. The copper charts in this book reveal this trend as the price advances steadily from January to April.

Even the strongest seasonal may not happen at the exact time it has in the past and, in fact, may not happen at all in a given year. Events can interrupt the seasonal cycle: events such as large Soviet grain purchases or freezes in Florida may be the catalyst for contraseasonal behavior. Traders must keep abreast of current market developments to spot possible moves against established seasonal trends.

Some markets may have no strong seasonals. In some cases this is because there are no overriding supply and demand considerations at any one time in the year. These commodities may have supply and demand evenly balanced for the whole year. This happens most frequently with commodities like corn. As a rule, commodities that can be stored for long periods have a smaller supply/demand swing than perishable commodities.

There are seasonal patterns where the commodity price will have a sharp up move, followed by a month of trendless activity, and culminating in a sharp down move (or vice versa). These months of trendless activity occur at seasonal turning points. They are the months where, for instance, the market is making its first judgment of the new crop and futures prices. These are influenced by both old and new crop fundamentals. You can see this clearly in the wheat charts.

Seasonal tendencies also change over time as conditions change. An example is the well-known hog cycle. Let's enter the hog cycle when hog prices are fairly high. Farmers reason that they will make higher profits if they increase their pig production. The number of hogs that are bred begins to increase, since many farmers feel the same way about high pork prices. Over the period of a year or two, more and more pigs reach the slaughterhouse. There is a time lag between the day farmers decide to increase the size of their pig crops and when available pork supplies increase. It takes roughly a year for a young pig to reach maturation and appear beside our apple sauce. Eventually, the supply of pork increases to the point that the price softens and farmers become less anxious to raise pigs at current prices. After another year or so has passed, the supply of pork decreases and, once again, the price begins to firm. So goes a complete "revolution" of the hog cycle.

Until recently, the hog cycle had been one of the most consistent and best documented of all cycles. The cycle can be clearly seen in hog prices as far back as 1900 yet we find little seasonality in the recent price history of hogs. This is a major example of how a change in production technology can alter a once-reliable price cycle. In the past, the majority of hogs were produced on farms by small individual suppliers. Now, most pork comes from full confinement operations where sows produce young three times a year instead of twice. This increased breeding capacity is attributed to better feed programs and healthier livestock conditions. The high overhead of these operations also demands continuous pork production to maintain cash flow. These changes in pork supply characteristics have played a major role in altering a once-regular price cycle.

The seasonal behavior of commodity prices owes its nature to the periodicity of events in the outside world. Crop commodities have seasonals that result directly from their production cycles, from spring planting to fall harvest. Lumber, corn, and other commodities experience seasonal fluctuations of supply and demand for reasons such as a preferred time of year to build houses or the presence of ice-free shipping lanes. Even currencies experience a certain ebb and flow based on such factors as seasonal demand for foreign oil. This, however, is only one ingredient that goes into to the final price behavior with which commodity traders have to contend.

The calm, comparatively regular seasonality that forms part of the characteristics of commodity prices is superimposed on the backdrop of irregular events that encompass all human action. Occasional large purchases or sales, market psychology, and ever advancing technology are just a few of the factors that disguise and distort seasonal price behavior. This book attempts to filter out the background noise of the market and locate seasonal patterns that can be used profitably. The graphs in this book are structured with this dual nature of commodity prices in mind and hope to reveal seasonal trends that have previously gone unnoticed and most certainly have gone unquantified.

Chapters 2 and 3 are the keys in which to gain the most value from this book. Chapter 2 explains how the statistics were calculated and Chapter 3 details how to interpret these statistics and use them to locate profitable trends.

TWO

Using the Charts to Trade Seasonal Tendencies

This chapter is divided into two sections. The first section describes the charts and tables used in this book and shows how they were constructed. The second section describes how to use and interpret the charts and tables to discover profitable information.

HOW TO READ THE CHARTS AND TABLES

There are three charts, two tables, and two different methods of determining seasonality for each commodity futures contract in this book. The two methods of seasonal determination were selected because each method has unique advantages and disadvantages that make them complementary. Their differences will be highlighted as we explore the tables and charts.

With the exception of the seasonal index calculated using the link relative method, the charts and tables are easily understood. Let's look at the construction of the charts and tables, first the tables.

Table 2.1 contains the information for using seasonals in trading or hedging. The charts illustrate the information in the table. The table is divided into sections and each section, except the first, has a subtitle. Let's use March Treasury bonds as an example.

The top section contains the basic information for the seasonal study. The year of contract expiration is given on the far left column. In this example, the first contract expiration is the March 1979 contract. Across the top of the table are the names of the months preceding the expiration of the contract. Thus the last month listed will be the last month the commodity trades. Each number in the table is the average settlement price for that month. The numbers are shown with two decimal places but all calculations use three decimal places. The last column in the table is the average of all entries for that year. Occasionally there were situations where a commodity did not trade for the first month in the table. In this case, the average for the remaining months was inserted as the entry for that particular month. There rare circumstances are identified by the first month and the yearly average having the same value.

TABLE 2.1. TREASURY BONDS—MARCH

Year of Expiration	May	Jun	Jul	Aug	Sep	Oct	Nov	Dec	Jan	Feb	Mar	May-Mar Average
1979	93.78	92.99	92.00	94.26	94.82	92.88	92.62	91.38	90.61	90.20	89.91	92.31
1980	89.23	91.30	90.99	90.62	88.49	82.97	80.68	82.13	78.22	68.60	67.78	82.82
1981	80.05	82.69	78.88	74.69	72.75	71.76	68.83	69.03	70.16	65.97	66.81	72.87
1982	64.92	67.60	64.44	61.68	58.99	58.36	63.39	62.77	59.23	59.44	62.53	62.12
1983	64.66	61.25	62.70	65.81	68.84	74.67	76.93	75.85	75.81	74.64	76.67	70.71
1984	76.16	73.86	71.21	69.50	70.86	71.32	70.45	69.82	70.88	69.90	67.77	71.07
1985	60.72	60.04	61.45	64.53	66.42	68.13	70.79	71.44	71.79	71.28	69.14	66.88
AVERAGE MOVE												
All Years		0.03	-1.15	-0.08	0.01	-0.15	0.51	-0.18	-0.82	-2.38	0.08	
Less Extremes		0.19	-1.14	0.10	-0.05	-0.28	0.30	-0.30	-0.59	-1.45	-0.07	
Ave Up - All Years		2.47	1.43	2.82	1.71	2.67	3.32	0.77	0.85	0.21	1.99	
Ave Down - All Years		-1.80	-2.19	-2.25	-2.26	-2.27	-1.59	-0.89	-2.06	-2.81	-1.34	
COUNT												
Number Up		3	2	3	4	3	3	3	3	1	3	
Number Down		4	5	4	3	4	4	4	4	6	4	
Pct Up		42.9%	28.6%	42.9%	57.1%	42.9%	42.9%	42.9%	42.9%	14.3%	42.9%	
Pct Down		57.1%	71.4%	57.1%	42.9%	57.1%	57.1%	57.1%	57.1%	85.7%	57.1%	
EXTREMES												
Greatest Up		2.69	1.45	3.10	3.03	5.83	5.03	1.44	1.13	0.21	3.09	
Greatest Down		-3.41	-3.82	-4.18	-2.69	-5.51	-2.93	-1.24	-3.91	-9.62	-2.13	
SEASONAL INDEX : AVERAGE PERCENTAGE METHOD												
All Years	101.9	101.9	100.3	100.1	100.1	100.1	101.1	100.9	99.8	96.7	97.0	
Less Extremes	102.5	102.7	100.7	99.6	99.8	100.3	101.0	100.8	99.3	97.6	97.7	
SEASONAL INDEX : LINK RELATIVE METHOD												
All Years		99.9	98.9	99.3	99.8	100.3	101.7	101.8	101.1	98.3	98.9	
Less Extremes		100.3	99.2	99.6	100.0	100.1	101.0	101.0	100.6	98.9	99.2	

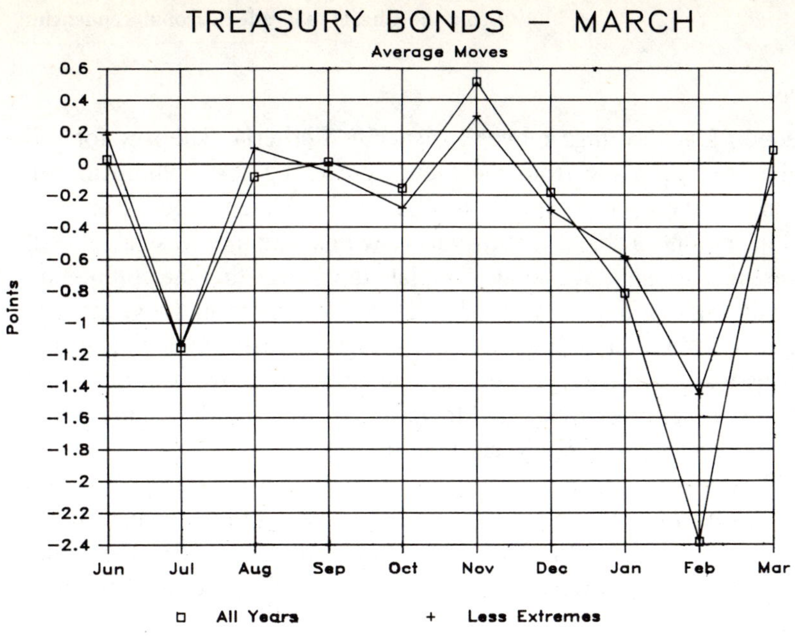
TREASURY BONDS — MARCH
Average Moves
Points
0.6
0.4
0.2
0
−0.2
−0.4
−0.6
−0.8
−1
−1.2
−1.4
−1.6
−1.8
−2
−2.2
−2.4
Jun
Jul
Aug
Sep
Oct
Nov
Dec
Jan
Feb
Mar
All Years
Less Extremes

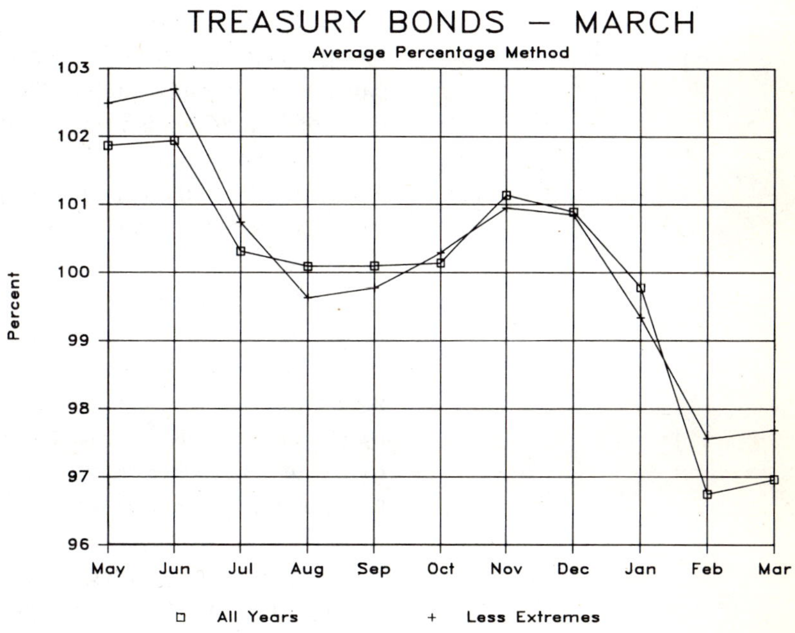
TREASURY BONDS — MARCH
Average Percentage Method
Percent
103
102
101
100
99
98
97
96
May
Jun
Jul
Aug
Sep
Oct
Nov
Dec
Jan
Feb
Mar
All Years
Less Extremes

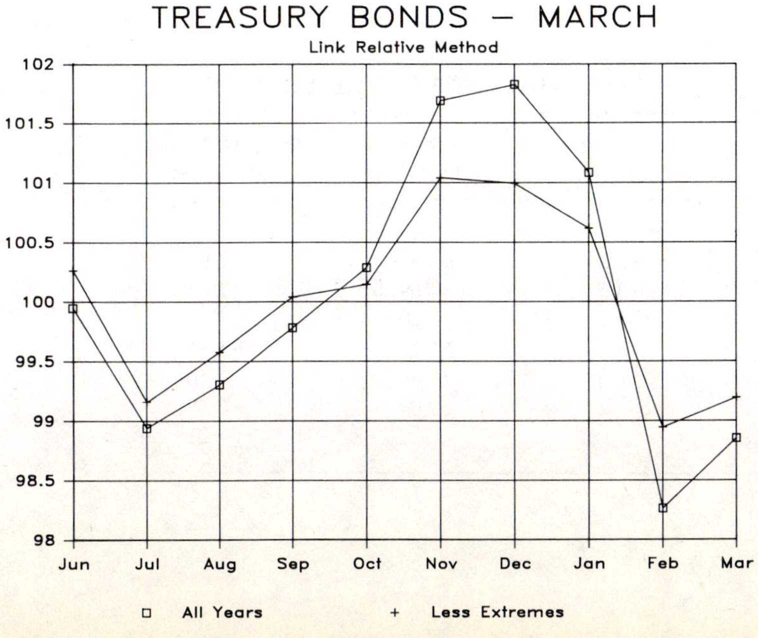
TREASURY BONDS — MARCH
Link Relative Method
102
101.5
101
100.5
100
99.5
99
98.5
98
Jun
Jul
Aug
Sep
Oct
Nov
Dec
Jan
Feb
Mar
All Years
Less Extremes

Average Move

The second section gives average moves for specified criteria. The row for "all years" gives the average move from the month preceding that column to that month. For example, the average move for all years for March bonds from May to June is 0.03 of a point. Table 2.2 shows us how this example was calculated.

To determine the average move, first, calculate the moves that the commodity made each year during that month. Second, sum the moves for all the years. The net total will reflect both up and down moves during the years studied. The sum of all price moves was only +0.21, showing a small net up move over the seven years. The tug of war between higher and lower prices was won by higher prices even though there were more down years than up years.

Finally, divide the net total price change by the number of years examined. Our example uses seven years of prices, so we divide the net total move, +0.21, by the number of years, seven, to derive the average move, +0.03. We would therefore expect March bond prices to rise an average of 0.03 points from May to June.

The next row shows the average move for all years except the two years that had the extreme up and down moves. Those two years are removed from the calculation. In our example, the largest up move was in 1982 when the average price of March bonds moved from 64.92 to 67.60, a total move of +2.68. The largest down was the −3.41 that occurred in 1983. These two values are then eliminated from the calculation of the average move and the result is entered in the spot for the Average Move Less Extremes. This procedure helps eliminate those extraordinary years that can distort the underlying seasonal. The two measures, the average move for all years and the average move less extremes, will sometimes give different pictures of seasonality.

The information presented up to this point, while useful, does not tell the whole story. Most seasonal studies go only this far. Basing decisions on these figures alone could be misleading. Using only the average move could hide the true nature of prices because the average move is the result of combining and averaging a series of price changes. The following section helps confirm the validity of the average move.

Our example has three up years and four down years yet the average move was up. The average move is suggesting that traders go long but the reliability

TABLE 2.2. CALCULATION OF THE AVERAGE MOVE

Year	Average Price in May	Average Price in June	Price Difference May–June
1979	93.78	92.99	−0.79
1980	89.23	91.30	+2.07
1981	80.05	82.69	+2.64
1982	64.92	67.60	+2.68
1983	64.66	61.25	−3.41
1984	76.16	73.86	−2.30
1985	60.72	60.04	−0.68
Total			+0.21

is suggesting a short position. This risk is mitigated by using the "Average Up" and "Down" lines.

The next two rows show the average move in only those years when the market was up or down. For example, March bonds were up from May to June in three of the last seven years. The average move during those three years was +2.47 points. March bonds were lower in four of those years with an average decline in 1.80 points.

The Average Up and Down figures give traders a better estimate on future prices. Let's say you are bearish and want to short the bonds in May. A reasonable objective would be the average down move of 1.80 points. You can use the Average Up to help determine the trade risk.

Count

The Count section gives the number of years the market was up and down and the percentage of up and down years. This is used in the calculation of the preceding section. Its major value is determining seasonal reliability. This is a crucial tool for seasonal traders.

Extremes

The extreme up and down moves for that month are highlighted in the next section. March bonds had their extreme up move in 1982 and extreme down move in 1983. Note that we are talking of their extreme move in terms of the average price of one month versus the average price of the previous month, not the actual extreme price move. Actual extreme price moves will be greater than the average move given in this study.

These figures are found by looking through the top section of Table 2.1 and selecting the greatest up and down moves. We can now see the greatest increase and decrease of the average prices for that month.

We have now looked at the average movement of March bond prices from May to June. The probability of prices moving higher or lower has been examined and is referred to as the reliability. We gained more insight into the nature of the average seasonal move by examining the average up and down moves. These figures show us how the price has behaved in the past given a bull or bear trend. The Extremes section shows the extreme price moves that have occurred in both types of markets and will allow us to plan out better trading, risk, and money mangement plans.

SEASONAL INDEX: AVERAGE PERCENTAGE METHOD

The seasonal index calculated using the average percentage method is shown for each month in the next section. This is found by simply calculating what percent of the annual average is represented by each month's price and averaging the results to find the seasonal index. First, find what percent each entry is of the year's average. For example, Table 2.3 illustrates this.

TABLE 2.3. CALCULATION OF THE SEASONAL INDEX USING THE AVRAGE PERCENTAGE METHOD

	June Price	Average Yearly Price	Percent of Average Yearly
1979	92.99	92.31	100.74
1980	91.30	82.82	110.24
1981	82.69	72.87	113.48
1982	67.60	62.12	108.82
1983	61.25	70.71	86.62
1984	73.86	71.07	103.93
1985	60.04	66.88	89.77
			713.60

Thus the total of the percents, 713.60, is divided by the number of years, seven, to derive the average percentage move for that month, 101.9.

SEASONAL INDEX: LINK RELATIVE METHOD

The final section gives the seasonal index using the link relative method. This method is more complex to calculate:

1. Calculate each month as a percent of the previous month's price.
2. Average the results for each month.
3. Calculate all monthly figures as a percentage relative to the first month's figure after setting the first month to 100.0.
4. Detrend the result by subtracting one from each month from the second month on using the following equation:

$$\frac{\text{month \#} - 1}{\text{number of months in study}} \times \text{difference between the first and last month}$$

   In other words, detrend the result by dividing one by the number of months in the study. Multiply the answer by the difference between the first and last months and subtract this result from the second month. For the third month, divide by *two* the number of months in the study. Multiply the answer by the difference between the first and last months and subtract this result from the third month, and so on.
5. Make the total of the resulting figures total to 100 times the number of months in the study by multiplying each figure by an appropriate factor. The result is the seasonal index.

Let's take a look at an example to clarify the calculations: First, take the monthly average prices (Table 2.4) and express them as a percentage of the previous month's price. Table 2.5 shows this with the average of each month listed at the bottom.

TABLE 2.4. LUMBER—MARCH—MONTHLY AVERAGE PRICE

Year of Expiration	May	Jun	Jul	Aug	Sep	Oct	Nov	Dec	Jan	Feb	Mar	May-Mar Average
1976	152.56	159.18	158.57	147.35	137.59	135.09	150.77	155.40	161.79	163.97	155.95	152.56
1977	177.20	173.15	164.90	162.21	171.06	173.65	185.63	192.44	182.82	185.20	180.90	177.20
1978	199.92	199.35	195.91	193.59	192.68	189.93	194.61	209.58	209.92	216.64	214.33	201.50
1979	183.03	183.80	186.16	189.34	198.22	207.01	195.68	207.56	221.25	236.60	221.97	202.78
1980	209.26	209.71	211.59	221.82	232.95	219.03	212.26	218.61	222.64	223.75	213.02	217.69
1981	204.71	211.67	215.69	204.47	194.99	195.22	197.94	178.65	181.30	166.27	149.33	190.93
1982	211.32	211.15	204.38	187.56	170.63	158.75	162.16	164.01	151.96	140.92	134.85	172.51
1983	167.86	155.32	155.64	154.75	155.97	163.04	177.12	180.67	191.25	184.37	177.08	169.37
1984	231.32	228.70	218.17	202.55	196.98	201.18	192.41	186.85	177.39	181.87	180.33	199.79
1985	171.04	166.34	152.16	155.63	148.83	153.80	162.34	160.06	161.04	146.88	129.45	155.23

Next, set the first month to a value of 100.0 and express all subsequent values as a percent of that value. Table 2.6 shows the result. For example, the average for all years in July is 98.1% of the June average so its value becomes 98.1. August is 97.8% of July so its value becomes 95.9 (98.1 times .978 equals 95.9), and so on.

Then detrend the results. The final entry in Table 2.6, 92.6, is less than the beginning value, 100.0. This means that the long-term trend of March lumber prices has been down during the study period. This trend obscures the underlying seasonality.

The trend is eliminated by finding a numeric constant that detrends the data. The constant will be a number that stimulates a constant monthly decline that eliminates the decline to 92.6 in the final entry. The numeric constant can be found using logarithms or can be closely approximated through simple math. The charts and tables in this book were calculated using logarithms, however, the explanation of their use is beyond the scope of this book. (For more details on the use of logarithms in the link relative method, write to me at the address in Chapter 11.)

TABLE 2.5. MARCH LUMBER—AVERAGE OF EACH MONTH

Year of Expiration	Jun	Jul	Aug	Sep	Oct	Nov	Dec	Jan	Feb	Mar
1976	104.3	99.6	92.9	93.4	98.2	111.6	103.1	104.1	101.3	95.1
1977	97.7	95.2	98.4	105.5	101.5	106.9	103.7	95.0	101.3	97.9
1978	99.7	98.3	98.8	99.5	98.6	102.5	107.7	100.2	103.2	98.9
1979	100.4	101.3	101.7	104.7	104.4	94.5	106.1	106.6	106.9	93.8
1980	100.2	100.9	104.8	105.0	94.0	96.9	103.0	101.8	100.5	95.2
1981	103.4	101.9	94.8	95.4	100.1	101.4	90.3	101.5	91.7	89.8
1982	99.9	96.8	91.8	91.0	93.0	102.1	101.1	92.7	92.7	95.7
1983	92.5	100.2	99.4	100.8	104.5	108.6	102.0	105.9	96.4	96.0
1984	98.9	95.4	92.8	97.2	102.1	95.6	97.1	94.9	102.5	99.2
1985	97.3	91.5	102.3	95.6	103.3	105.6	98.6	100.6	91.2	88.1
AVERAGE All Years	99.4	98.1	97.8	98.8	100.0	102.6	101.3	100.3	98.8	95.0

TABLE 2.6. MARCH LUMBER—RESULTS

	Jun	Jul	Aug	Sep	Oct	Nov	Dec	Jan	Feb	Mar
All Years	100.0	98.1	95.9	94.8	94.8	97.2	98.4	98.8	97.6	92.6

The second method gives a close approximation and takes several simple steps. First, take the difference between the first and last values in Table 2.6, 100.0 and 92.6. The difference in this example is 7.4. Calculate 1/10 of the difference. (The calculation is not always 1/10. Use 1 over the number of months in the study. Thus a study of 12 months would use 1/12.) In this case that is .74. Since this is an uptrend, add .74 to the first month following the initial month. Add two times .74 to the subsequent month, three time .74 in the following month, and so on. If the case had been in a downtrend, subtract .74 from the first month, two times .74 from the second month, and so on.

We can go further and make sure that, for purposes of uniformity and convenience, the sum of the entries equals 100 times the number of months in the study, in this case 1000. This is done simply by adding the monthly results just calculated and finding a multiplier that will adjust all the months so they add to 1000.

The two methods have different uses. The average percentage method is easier to calculate and update and shows the major underlying trend. The link relative method better shows the underlying seasonal, because it eliminates the major underlying trend.

MONTH OF HIGH AND LOW

Table 2.7 shows which month the high and low occurred that year. Once again, the high and low refer to the highest and lowest monthly average price. This table is particularly useful in determining if current prices are coming near a time when prices are usually making peaks and troughs. In addition, historical comparison analysis becomes much better using this table. Historical comparison analysis is a style of analysis that tries to find a year in the past with similar fundamental and/or technical conditions. Table 2.7 will help identify when highs and lows will be set after you have identified the analogous years.

TABLE 2.7. MONTH OF HIGH AND LOW

Year of Expiration	May	Jun	Jul	Aug	Sep	Oct	Nov	Dec	Jan	Feb	Mar
1979	H										L
1980		H									L
1981		H								L	
1982		H				L					
1983		L					H				
1984	H										L
1985		L							H		

THE CHARTS

Turning back to Table 2.1, the three charts illustrate six of the data series. The average move, average percentage move seasonal index, and the link relative seasonal index are graphed. All three charts show the information for all years and all years less extremes. One way to use the charts is to quickly spot long or powerful seasonal trends and then refer to the tables for details.

IDENTIFYING PROFITABLE TRADES

Your approach to trading futures is unique. Your experience, available specualtive capital, time available, and financial commitments all play an important part in the trading strategy you adopt. One trader's comfortable level of risk could cause another trader's heart to fail. This principle also applies to the use and interpretation of this book.

Several major criteria can be used to isolate potentially profitable trading situations. Unfortunately, there is no clear line between what an acceptable level of risk would be or what constitutes a reliable trend, since each of us has our own level of assumable risk and our own ideas of when the noise stops and the trend begins. By the end of this chapter, the interpretation of the charts and tables should be clear enough so that you will be able to select positions that suit your own market approach. One of the advantages of having all these statistics available is that traders can evaluate market positions and personalize their investment decisions based on potential risk/reward ratios, set realistic stop-loss orders, and improve their trade timing. With your own special needs in mind, let's examine how you can use the charts to spot potential profit opportunites.

The first and most obvious step in looking at seasonal trends is to find instances when the price has trended in one direction more times than not. This would be a percent reliability of greater than 50%.

The more often a price has moved either up or down at a given time of year, the more likely we are to believe a valid trend is in evidence. As a result, the higher the reliability the stronger the signal that a reliable seasonal move has been found. This study shows many trends that have performed over 80% of the time under study. Some trends have occurred 10 years in a row. Even the most avid proponent of the random walk theory would have trouble explaining this and other seasonals, especially in those cases with powerful fundamental explanations for consistent behavior. Traders can examine these charts and tables with their own levels of risk in mind and select the trends that most interest them. The percent reliability can be used as a gauge of the likelihood of the market trending. The greater the reliability, the smaller the relative risk of being on the wrong side of the market.

If trade selection were solely a function of reliability, we would approach the market armed only with Chapter 10. A high reliability is not the only factor that determines a good trade. We also want to know how large a price swing might occur.

Live cattle is a good example of what to watch for. There are many excellent reliable seasonal trends but the average moves are miniscule. You will often be right but won't profit enough to cover the commissions. Your broker might love you for putting on this trade, but unless he or she makes a habit of buying you expensive lunches, this one is not worth following up.

The key is to examine the average move and the average up and down moves. This gives you the extra dimensions of determining if the reward is worth the risk. The principle of comparing these factors is a good habit to acquire.

Traders can establish a relative risk/reward ratio for a position by using the average up and down move figures. There are many cases when a commodity exhibits a strong tendency to move explosively, either up or down, several times during the years under study. This is seen when a chart with an unexciting reliability shows a much stronger figure for the average up move versus the average down move or vice versa. Given a 50% chance of the market trending with your position, if the average move in one direction has been 10 times the average move in the opposite direction, many traders will look at this situation favorably.

The average up and down moves can be used to gain greater insight into average seasonal moves, occasionally revealing seasonals that would have gone unnoticed. The relative magnitude of the average up versus the average down moves also allow traders to establish realistic risk/reward ratios for specific trades at specific times of the year.

Separately, the average move, the reliability, and the average up and down moves give valuable hints to the seasonal behavior of a commodity, but the real power of the charts is that they allow you to select a trade based on the total picture revealed by these statistics in concert. None of these statistics taken alone can benefit traders as powerfully as several together. An average move may be large but a low reliability may show there is little profit opportunity. This could happen in a case where the price change in one direction had been large relative to previous moves. This could cause the average move to be large but the percent reliability will be low, alerting us to the existence of a rare explosive move. A quick glance at the greatest up and down moves will verify this by showing a greatest move in one direction many times as large as the greatest move in the opposite direction.

The longer the time frame you examine, the more accurate the picture your analysis can show, since a larger time period of examination will tend to average out these unusually large moves. Occasionally, there will be explosive years like 1973.

This shows an advantage of using the link relative method versus the aveage percentage move method. The link relative method will not be affected by the extreme move to the extent of the average percentage move method.

Whenever you are interested in a commodity at a given time of year, check to see if there are several consecutive months of prices moving in the same direction. For example, prices move lower in every month from May to August in September soybean meal. This is a good indication of a strong seasonal, since it shows the market reacting for several consecutive months. This usually adds greater profitability to trades, since it has greater time to work. Time is on the trader's side.

Consecutive repetition in average price, percent reliability, or average up or down moves gives added support ot the existence of a seasonal trend. Any occurrence of a statistic that encourages traders to take market positions is good; several in succession are excellent.

Table 2.7, showing the high and low average price for the year, is another useful tool. Examine the table to see if the highs and lows of the year occurr at about the same time. The table can be used to help determine if the high or the low of the year has been made during the current year. Traders using the historical comparison analysis (see Smith, *Commodity Spreads,* 1982, Wiley for more details) can use the table to help make timing decisions.

THREE

Interest Rates

Interest rate futures have not been traded long enough to make definitive statements about their seasonality. However, some preliminary seasonal patterns have developed. Note the sharp down move in February. Unfortunately, the rest of the year has weak seasonality.

Interest rates are affected by such factors as credit demands, inflation, and the state of the economy. However, it appears that most strongly seasonal fundamental factors tend to be seasonal at different times of the year, essentially canceling each other's effect. For example, the federal government typically borrows the heaviest during the fourth quarter, yet unseasonally adjusted industrial production is weakest in the same quarter. The two forces cancel each other out leading to weak seasonal trends.

HIGHEST RELIABLE TRENDS

Commodity	Contract	Month	Position	Reliability	Average Move
T-bonds	Mar	Mar	Short	71.4	−2.19
	Mar	Feb	Short	85.7	−2.81
	Jun	Feb	Short	85.7	−2.86
	Jun	Jun	Long	71.4	+2.79
	Sep	Feb	Short	85.7	−2.88
	Sep	Jul	Short	71.4	−2.18
	Sep	Aug	Short	71.4	−1.85
	Dec	Jul	Short	71.4	−2.16
	Dec	Aug	Short	71.4	−1.86
T-bills	Mar	Jul	Short	71.4	−0.38
	Mar	Dec	Short	71.4	−0.36
	Mar	Feb	Short	85.7	−0.65
	Mar	Mar	Short	71.4	−0.61
	Jun	Oct	Long	71.4	+0.42
	Jun	Feb	Short	85.7	−0.61
	Jun	Mar	Short	71.4	−0.62
	Jun	Apr	Long	71.4	+0.79
	Jun	Jun	Long	71.4	+0.83
	Sep	Feb	Short	85.7	−0.55
	Sep	Apr	Long	71.4	+0.76
	Sep	May	Long	71.4	+0.92

(*Continued on next page.*)

Commodity	Contract	Month	Position	Reliability	Average Move
T-bills	Sep	Jun	Long	71.4	+0.78
	Sep	Sep	Long	71.4	+0.42
	Dec	Apr	Long	71.4	+0.70
	Dec	May	Long	71.4	+0.81
	Dec	Oct	Long	71.4	+0.77
	Dec	Nov	Long	71.4	+0.82

TREASURY BONDS - MARCH - MONTHLY AVERAGE PRICE

Year of Expiration	May	Jun	Jul	Aug	Sep	Oct	Nov	Dec	Jan	Feb	Mar	May-Mar Average
1979	93.78	92.99	92.00	94.26	94.82	92.88	92.62	91.38	90.61	90.20	89.91	92.31
1980	89.23	91.30	90.99	90.62	88.49	82.97	80.68	82.13	78.22	68.60	67.78	82.82
1981	80.05	82.69	78.88	74.69	72.75	71.76	68.83	69.03	70.16	65.97	66.81	72.87
1982	64.92	67.60	64.44	61.68	58.99	58.36	63.39	62.77	59.23	59.44	62.53	62.12
1983	64.66	61.25	62.70	65.81	68.84	74.67	76.93	75.85	75.81	74.64	76.67	70.71
1984	76.16	73.86	71.21	69.50	70.86	71.32	70.45	69.82	70.88	69.90	67.77	71.07
1985	60.72	60.04	61.45	64.53	66.42	68.13	70.79	71.44	71.79	71.28	69.14	66.88

AVERAGE MOVE											
All Years		0.03	-1.15	-0.08	0.01	-0.15	0.51	-0.18	-0.82	-2.38	0.08
Less Extremes		0.19	-1.14	0.10	-0.05	-0.28	0.30	-0.30	-0.59	-1.45	-0.07
Ave Up - All Years		2.47	1.43	2.82	1.71	2.67	3.32	0.77	0.85	0.21	1.99
Ave Down - All Years		-1.80	-2.19	-2.25	-2.26	-2.27	-1.59	-0.89	-2.06	-2.81	-1.34
COUNT											
Number Up		3	2	3	4	3	3	3	3	1	3
Number Down		4	5	4	3	4	4	4	4	6	4
Pct Up		42.9%	28.6%	42.9%	57.1%	42.9%	42.9%	42.9%	42.9%	14.3%	42.9%
Pct Down		57.1%	71.4%	57.1%	42.9%	57.1%	57.1%	57.1%	57.1%	85.7%	57.1%
EXTREMES											
Greatest Up		2.69	1.45	3.10	3.03	5.83	5.03	1.44	1.13	0.21	3.09
Greatest Down		-3.41	-3.82	-4.18	-2.69	-5.51	-2.93	-1.24	-3.91	-9.62	-2.13
SEASONAL INDEX : AVERAGE PERCENTAGE METHOD											
All Years	101.9	101.9	100.3	100.1	100.1	100.1	101.1	100.9	99.8	96.7	97.0
Less Extremes	102.5	102.7	100.7	99.6	99.8	100.3	101.0	100.8	99.3	97.6	97.7
SEASONAL INDEX : LINK RELATIVE METHOD											
All Years		99.9	98.9	99.3	99.8	100.3	101.7	101.8	101.1	98.3	98.9
Less Extremes		100.3	99.2	99.6	100.0	100.1	101.0	101.0	100.6	98.9	99.2

TREASURY BONDS - MARCH - MONTH OF HIGH AND LOW

Year of Expiration	May	Jun	Jul	Aug	Sep	Oct	Nov	Dec	Jan	Feb	Mar
1979	H										L
1980		H									L
1981		H								L	
1982		H				L					
1983		L					H				
1984	H										L
1985		L							H		

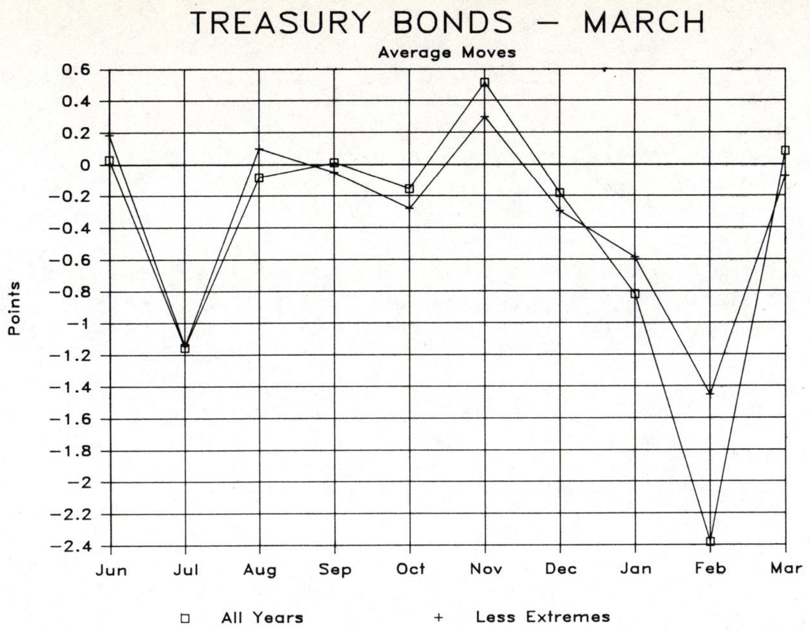
TREASURY BONDS — MARCH
Average Moves
Points
0.6
0.4
0.2
0
−0.2
−0.4
−0.6
−0.8
−1
−1.2
−1.4
−1.6
−1.8
−2
−2.2
−2.4
Jun
Jul
Aug
Sep
Oct
Nov
Dec
Jan
Feb
Mar
All Years
Less Extremes

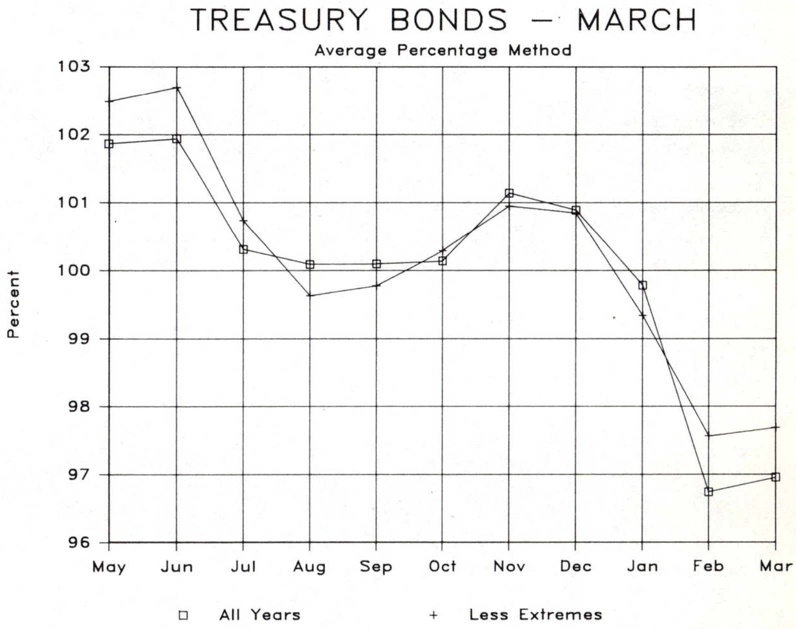
TREASURY BONDS — MARCH
Average Percentage Method
Percent
103
102
101
100
99
98
97
96
May
Jun
Jul
Aug
Sep
Oct
Nov
Dec
Jan
Feb
Mar
All Years
Less Extremes

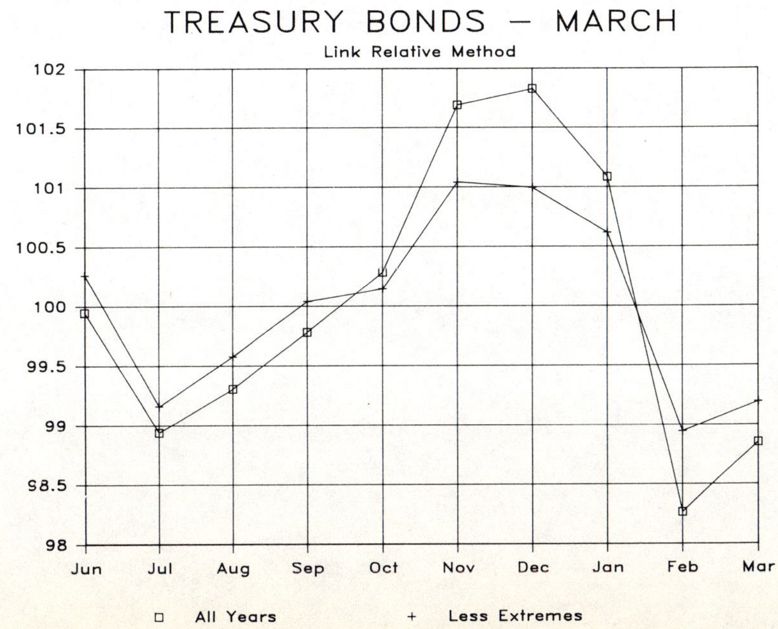
TREASURY BONDS — MARCH
Link Relative Method
102
101.5
101
100.5
100
99.5
99
98.5
98
Jun
Jul
Aug
Sep
Oct
Nov
Dec
Jan
Feb
Mar
All Years
Less Extremes

TREASURY BONDS - JUNE - MONTHLY AVERAGE PRICE

Year of Expiration	Aug	Sep	Oct	Nov	Dec	Jan	Feb	Mar	Apr	May	Jun	Aug-Jun Average
1979	93.97	94.76	92.98	92.93	91.67	90.83	90.39	90.19	89.50	88.75	90.94	91.54
1980	90.56	88.44	83.01	81.29	82.75	78.92	69.17	68.15	73.95	80.04	83.49	79.98
1981	74.73	72.99	72.03	69.45	69.98	71.15	67.04	67.26	64.26	62.34	65.55	68.80
1982	62.24	59.49	58.76	63.48	62.92	59.51	59.85	62.61	63.17	63.91	61.01	61.54
1983	65.94	68.91	74.42	76.54	75.29	75.14	73.93	76.06	77.79	77.68	75.61	74.30
1984	69.10	70.44	70.83	69.92	69.25	70.30	69.28	66.89	65.71	62.17	62.27	67.83
1985	64.09	65.93	67.59	70.15	70.74	70.92	70.27	68.43	70.64	73.91	78.89	70.14

	Aug	Sep	Oct	Nov	Dec	Jan	Feb	Mar	Apr	May	Jun
AVERAGE MOVE											
All Years		0.05	-0.19	0.59	-0.17	-0.84	-2.41	-0.05	0.78	0.54	1.28
Less Extremes		0.02	-0.29	0.40	-0.27	-0.64	-1.49	-0.14	0.53	0.24	1.38
Ave Up - All Years		1.74	2.52	3.13	0.86	0.80	0.34	1.70	2.57	3.36	2.79
Ave Down - All Years		-2.20	-2.22	-1.31	-0.93	-2.06	-2.86	-1.36	-1.62	-1.58	-2.48
COUNT											
Number Up		4	3	3	3	3	1	3	4	3	5
Number Down		3	4	4	4	4	6	4	3	4	2
Pct Up		57.1%	42.9%	42.9%	42.9%	42.9%	14.3%	42.9%	57.1%	42.9%	71.4%
Pct Down		42.9%	57.1%	57.1%	57.1%	57.1%	85.7%	57.1%	42.9%	57.1%	28.6%
EXTREMES											
Greatest Up		2.97	5.52	4.72	1.46	1.17	0.34	2.76	5.80	6.08	4.99
Greatest Down		-2.75	-5.43	-2.57	-1.26	-3.84	-9.75	-2.38	-2.99	-3.54	-2.90
SEASONAL INDEX : AVERAGE PERCENTAGE METHOD											
All Years	101.1	101.1	100.9	101.9	101.7	100.6	97.4	97.4	98.4	99.0	100.6
Less Extremes	101.1	100.8	101.3	102.0	101.6	100.7	98.6	98.8	98.3	99.4	100.0
SEASONAL INDEX : LINK RELATIVE METHOD											
All Years		100.9	100.9	102.0	101.8	100.7	97.5	97.5	98.6	99.2	100.9
Less Extremes		101.0	100.8	101.4	101.1	100.3	98.3	98.0	98.8	99.2	101.0

TREASURY BONDS - JUNE - MONTH OF HIGH AND LOW

Year of Expiration	Aug	Sep	Oct	Nov	Dec	Jan	Feb	Mar	Apr	May	Jun
1979		H								L	
1980	H							L			
1981	H									L	
1982			L							H	
1983	L								H		
1984			H							L	
1985	L										H

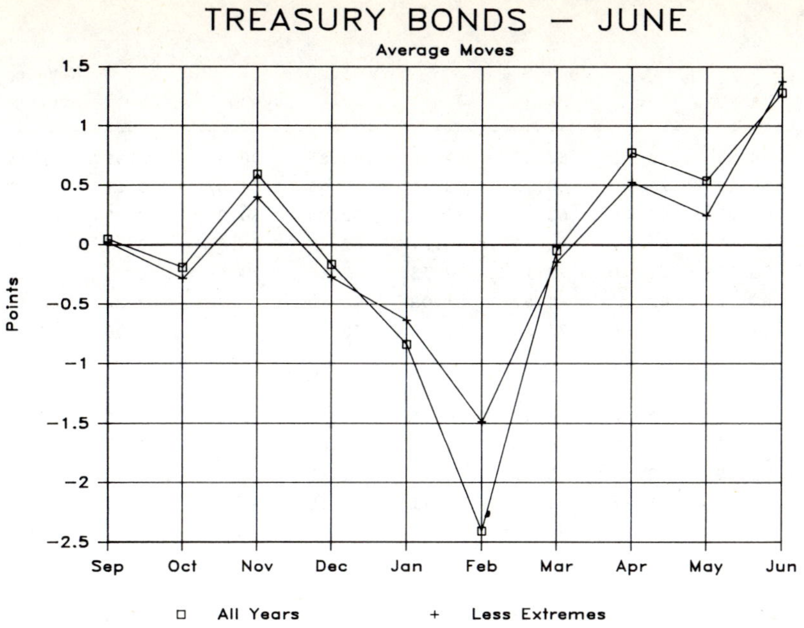
TREASURY BONDS – JUNE
Average Moves
Points
1.5
1
0.5
0
-0.5
-1
-1.5
-2
-2.5
Sep
Oct
Nov
Dec
Jan
Feb
Mar
Apr
May
Jun
All Years
Less Extremes

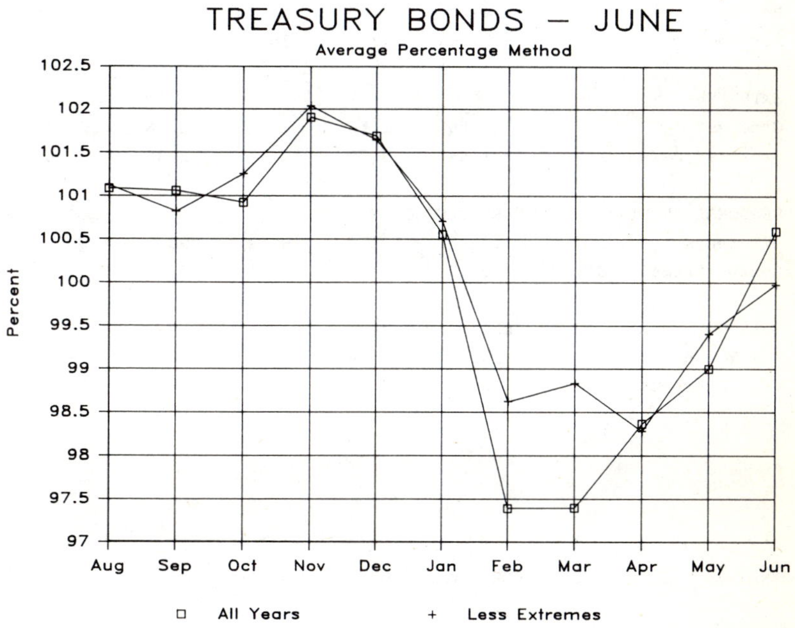
TREASURY BONDS – JUNE
Average Percentage Method
Percent
102.5
102
101.5
101
100.5
100
99.5
99
98.5
98
97.5
97
Aug
Sep
Oct
Nov
Dec
Jan
Feb
Mar
Apr
May
Jun
All Years
Less Extremes

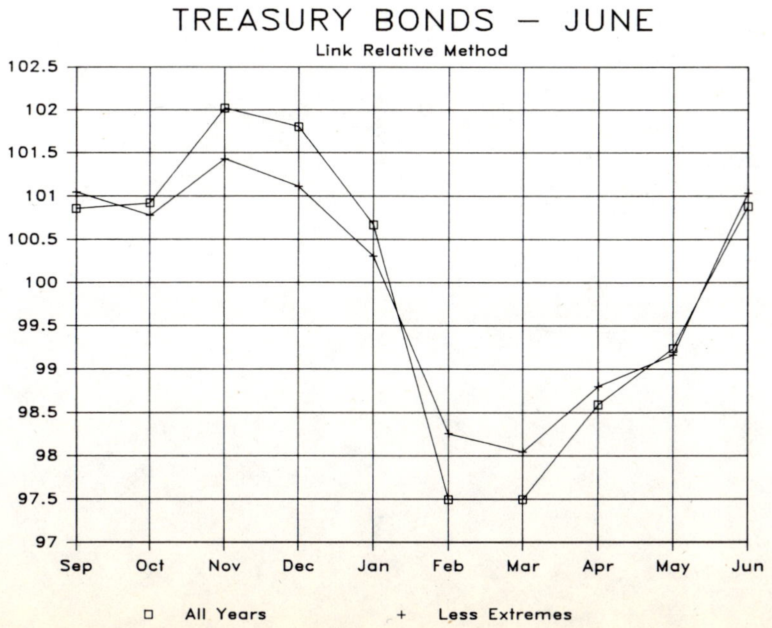
TREASURY BONDS – JUNE
Link Relative Method
102.5
102
101.5
101
100.5
100
99.5
99
98.5
98
97.5
97
Sep
Oct
Nov
Dec
Jan
Feb
Mar
Apr
May
Jun
All Years
Less Extremes

TREASURY BONDS - SEPTEMBER - MONTHLY AVERAGE PRICE

Year of Expiration	Nov	Dec	Jan	Feb	Mar	Apr	May	Jun	Jul	Aug	Sep	Nov-Sep Average
1979	93.23	91.99	91.12	90.60	90.39	89.74	88.93	91.18	90.85	90.63	88.96	90.69
1980	81.68	83.25	79.55	69.84	69.12	74.76	80.15	83.21	79.06	74.67	73.61	77.17
1981	69.82	70.52	71.68	67.61	67.82	64.92	63.41	66.31	62.95	60.03	58.28	65.76
1982	63.57	63.09	59.82	60.23	62.91	63.45	64.16	60.71	62.28	65.87	68.65	63.16
1983	76.28	74.84	74.62	73.35	75.53	77.23	77.10	74.73	72.15	70.56	71.34	74.34
1984	69.46	68.74	69.74	68.71	66.35	65.15	61.52	61.02	62.50	65.73	67.32	66.02
1985	69.59	70.13	70.19	69.49	67.61	69.64	72.88	77.25	76.76	76.65	76.30	72.41

	Nov	Dec	Jan	Feb	Mar	Apr	May	Jun	Jul	Aug	Sep
AVERAGE MOVE											
All Years		-0.15	-0.83	-2.41	-0.01	0.74	0.47	0.89	-1.12	-0.35	0.05
Less Extremes		-0.24	-0.66	-1.52	-0.08	0.48	0.30	1.07	-1.05	-0.33	-0.14
Ave Up - All Years		0.94	0.74	0.41	1.69	2.48	3.11	3.15	1.53	3.40	1.72
Ave Down - All Years		-0.97	-2.01	-2.88	-1.29	-1.59	-1.52	-2.11	-2.18	-1.85	-1.21
COUNT											
Number Up		3	3	1	3	4	3	4	2	2	3
Number Down		4	4	6	4	3	4	3	5	5	4
Pct Up		42.9%	42.9%	14.3%	42.9%	57.1%	42.9%	57.1%	28.6%	28.6%	42.9%
Pct Down		57.1%	57.1%	85.7%	57.1%	42.9%	57.1%	42.9%	71.4%	71.4%	57.1%
EXTREMES											
Greatest Up		1.56	1.16	0.41	2.68	5.64	5.39	4.37	1.58	3.58	2.78
Greatest Down		-1.44	-3.70	-9.71	-2.36	-2.90	-3.63	-3.45	-4.14	-4.39	-1.75
SEASONAL INDEX : AVERAGE PERCENTAGE METHOD											
All Years	102.8	102.6	101.5	98.2	98.2	99.1	99.6	100.7	99.2	98.9	99.2
Less Extremes	103.4	102.7	101.3	98.5	99.0	98.7	100.1	100.9	98.8	99.1	99.4
SEASONAL INDEX : LINK RELATIVE METHOD											
All Years		101.5	100.6	97.7	98.0	99.3	100.1	101.5	100.3	100.3	100.7
Less Extremes		100.9	100.3	98.4	98.5	99.4	100.0	101.6	100.4	100.2	100.3

TREASURY BONDS - SEPTEMBER - MONTH OF HIGH AND LOW

Year of Expiration	Nov	Dec	Jan	Feb	Mar	Apr	May	Jun	Jul	Aug	Sep
1979	H						L				
1980		H									L
1981			H								L
1982			L								H
1983						H				L	
1984			H					L			
1985					L			H			

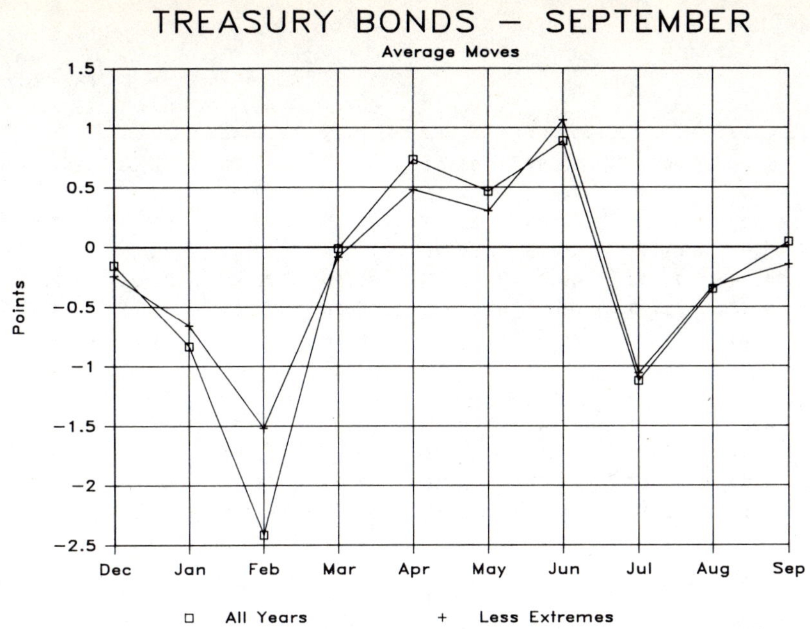
TREASURY BONDS — SEPTEMBER
Average Moves
Points
1.5
1
0.5
0
-0.5
-1
-1.5
-2
-2.5
Dec
Jan
Feb
Mar
Apr
May
Jun
Jul
Aug
Sep
□ All Years
+ Less Extremes

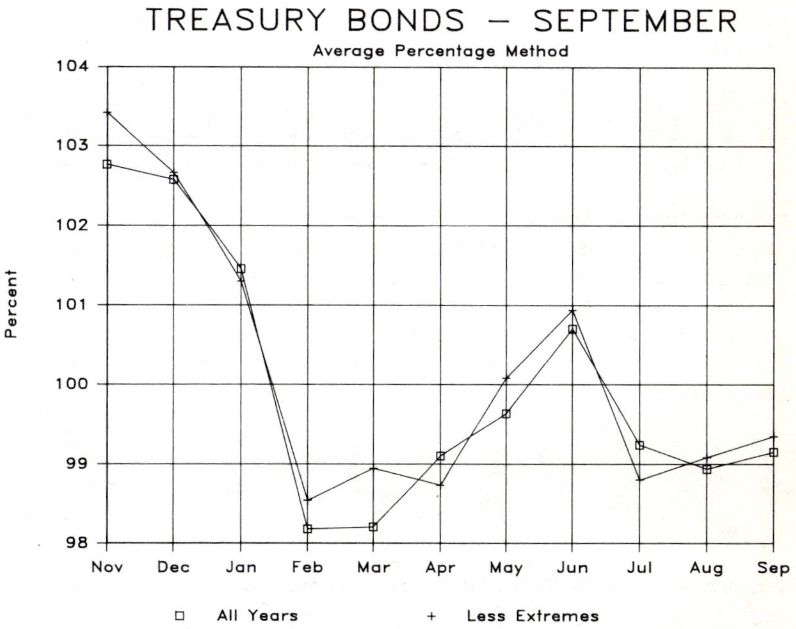
TREASURY BONDS — SEPTEMBER
Average Percentage Method
Percent
104
103
102
101
100
99
98
Nov
Dec
Jan
Feb
Mar
Apr
May
Jun
Jul
Aug
Sep
□ All Years
+ Less Extremes

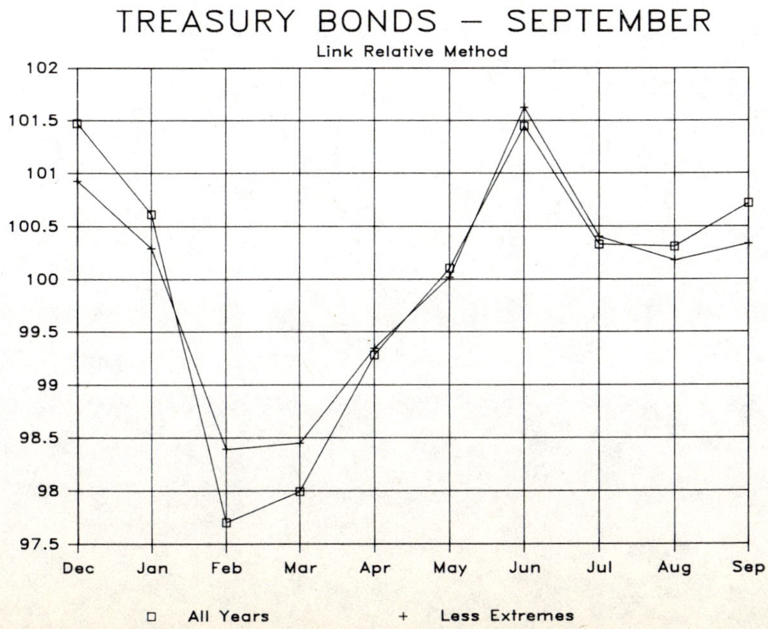
TREASURY BONDS — SEPTEMBER
Link Relative Method
102
101.5
101
100.5
100
99.5
99
98.5
98
97.5
Dec
Jan
Feb
Mar
Apr
May
Jun
Jul
Aug
Sep
□ All Years
+ Less Extremes

TREASURY BONDS - DECEMBER - MONTHLY AVERAGE PRICE

Year of Expiration	Feb	Mar	Apr	May	Jun	Jul	Aug	Sep	Oct	Nov	Dec	Feb-Dec Average
1979	90.72	90.55	89.94	89.11	91.27	90.93	90.57	88.53	82.96	80.15	81.68	87.86
1980	70.42	70.05	75.43	80.13	82.96	78.98	74.66	72.51	71.48	68.01	66.40	73.73
1981	67.95	68.14	65.38	64.27	67.07	63.78	60.94	58.39	57.89	63.28	63.44	63.68
1982	60.60	63.24	63.77	64.40	60.97	62.48	65.75	69.01	75.34	77.42	76.29	67.20
1983	72.92	75.10	76.75	76.60	74.26	71.62	69.97	71.39	71.90	71.03	70.36	72.90
1984	68.19	65.87	64.70	61.06	60.46	61.90	65.05	67.00	68.76	71.54	72.03	66.05
1985	68.85	66.91	68.77	71.95	76.24	75.69	75.55	75.22	76.16	80.19	83.30	74.44

	Feb	Mar	Apr	May	Jun	Jul	Aug	Sep	Oct	Nov	Dec
AVERAGE MOVE											
All Years		0.03	0.70	0.40	0.81	-1.12	-0.41	-0.06	0.35	1.02	0.27
Less Extremes		-0.02	0.45	0.35	0.97	-1.07	-0.37	-0.23	0.34	1.04	0.08
Ave Up - All Years		1.67	2.36	2.84	3.02	1.47	3.21	2.21	2.39	3.57	1.32
Ave Down - All Years		-1.20	-1.51	-1.43	-2.13	-2.16	-1.86	-1.77	-2.37	-2.38	-1.14
COUNT											
Number Up		3	4	3	4	2	2	3	4	4	4
Number Down		4	3	4	3	5	5	4	3	3	3
Pct Up		42.9%	57.1%	42.9%	57.1%	28.6%	28.6%	42.9%	57.1%	57.1%	57.1%
Pct Down		57.1%	42.9%	57.1%	42.9%	71.4%	71.4%	57.1%	42.9%	42.9%	42.9%
EXTREMES											
Greatest Up		2.64	5.38	4.71	4.29	1.51	3.27	3.26	6.33	5.39	3.11
Greatest Down		-2.31	-2.76	-3.64	-3.43	-3.98	-4.33	-2.56	-5.57	-3.47	-1.61
SEASONAL INDEX : AVERAGE PERCENTAGE METHOD											
All Years	98.8	98.8	99.7	100.1	101.2	99.6	99.1	99.1	99.9	101.6	101.9
Less Extremes	98.9	99.0	100.0	100.0	101.0	99.5	99.0	99.9	99.3	101.0	102.0
SEASONAL INDEX : LINK RELATIVE METHOD											
All Years		99.7	100.4	100.6	101.3	99.7	99.0	98.8	99.2	100.6	100.6
Less Extremes		99.7	100.2	100.5	101.6	99.9	99.3	98.9	99.2	100.5	100.3

TREASURY BONDS - DECEMBER - MONTH OF HIGH AND LOW

Year of Expiration	Feb	Mar	Apr	May	Jun	Jul	Aug	Sep	Oct	Nov	Dec
1979					H					L	
1980					H						L
1981		H							L		
1982	L									H	
1983			H				L				
1984					L						H
1985		L									H

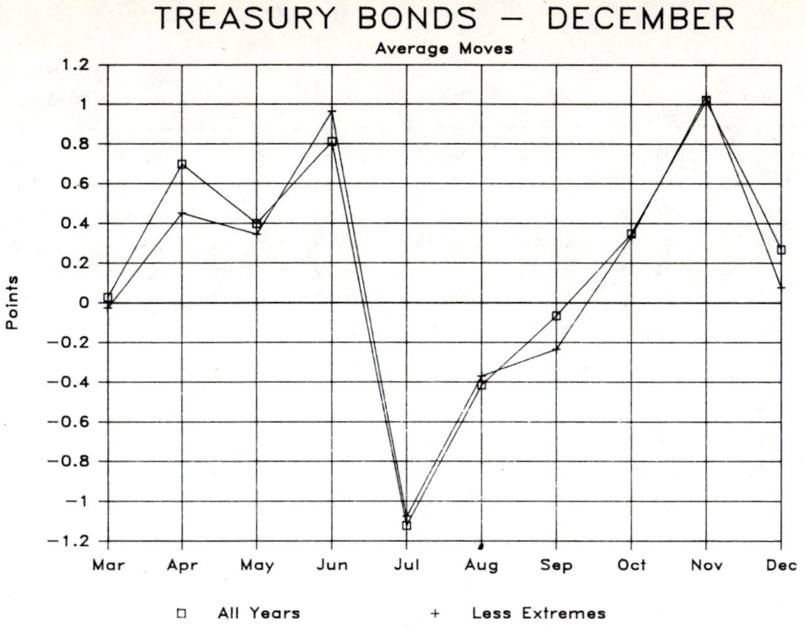
TREASURY BONDS – DECEMBER
Average Moves
Points
1.2
1
0.8
0.6
0.4
0.2
0
−0.2
−0.4
−0.6
−0.8
−1
−1.2
Mar
Apr
May
Jun
Jul
Aug
Sep
Oct
Nov
Dec
□ All Years
+ Less Extremes

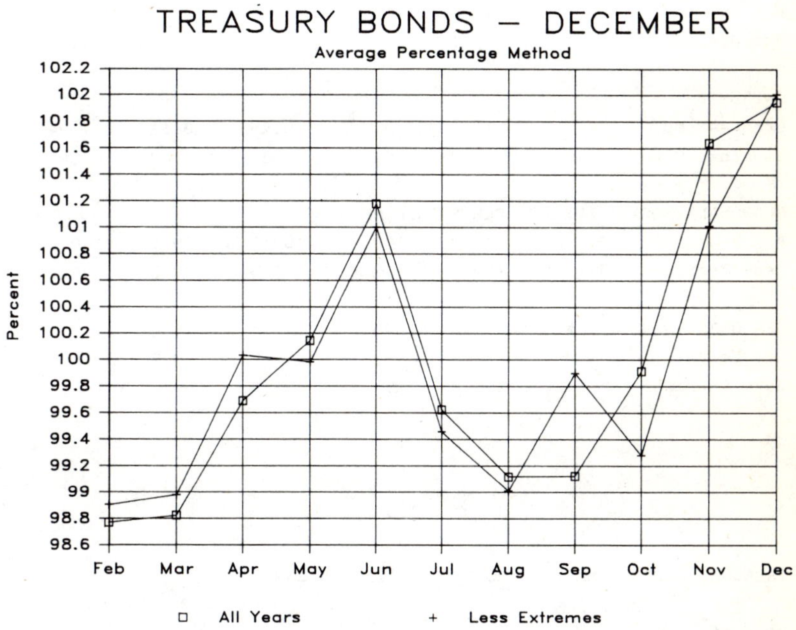
TREASURY BONDS – DECEMBER
Average Percentage Method
Percent
102.2
102
101.8
101.6
101.4
101.2
101
100.8
100.6
100.4
100.2
100
99.8
99.6
99.4
99.2
99
98.8
98.6
Feb
Mar
Apr
May
Jun
Jul
Aug
Sep
Oct
Nov
Dec
□ All Years
+ Less Extremes

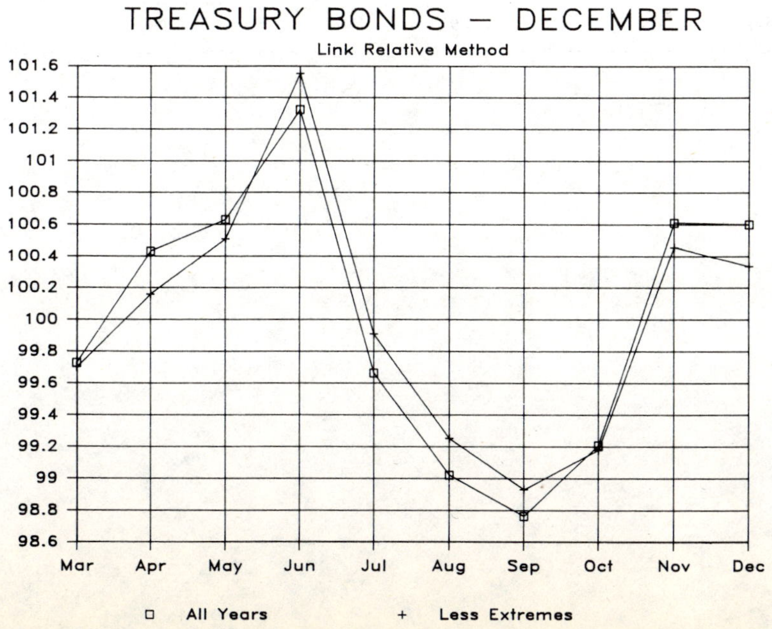
TREASURY BONDS – DECEMBER
Link Relative Method
101.6
101.4
101.2
101
100.8
100.6
100.4
100.2
100
99.8
99.6
99.4
99.2
99
98.8
98.6
Mar
Apr
May
Jun
Jul
Aug
Sep
Oct
Nov
Dec
□ All Years
+ Less Extremes

TREASURY BILLS - MARCH - MONTHLY AVERAGE PRICE

Year of Expiration	May	Jun	Jul	Aug	Sep	Oct	Nov	Dec	Jan	Feb	Mar	May-Mar Average
1979	91.99	91.97	91.88	92.17	91.90	91.35	90.72	90.60	90.53	90.73	90.58	91.31
1980	90.82	91.92	91.82	91.21	90.55	88.92	89.23	89.12	88.64	87.06	84.77	89.46
1981	91.55	92.21	91.61	90.29	88.83	88.68	87.25	86.30	87.08	86.09	86.26	88.74
1982	86.66	87.88	87.17	86.39	85.97	86.62	88.88	88.35	86.99	86.31	87.61	87.17
1983	87.61	86.82	87.52	88.47	89.10	91.04	91.54	91.90	92.22	91.91	91.79	89.99
1984	91.20	90.48	90.08	89.83	90.36	90.74	90.66	90.57	90.95	90.89	90.72	90.59
1985	88.13	87.84	88.20	88.93	89.33	89.88	91.02	91.53	91.96	91.69	91.37	89.99
AVERAGE MOVE												
All Years		0.17	-0.12	-0.14	-0.18	0.17	0.29	-0.13	.00	-0.53	-0.23	
Less Extremes		0.15	-0.17	-0.12	-0.09	0.18	0.25	-0.10	0.12	-0.46	-0.12	
Ave Up - All Years		0.99	0.53	0.66	0.52	0.88	1.05	0.43	0.48	0.19	0.74	
Ave Down - All Years		-0.46	-0.38	-0.74	-0.70	-0.77	-0.71	-0.36	-0.64	-0.65	-0.61	
COUNT												
Number Up		3	2	3	3	4	4	2	4	1	2	
Number Down		4	5	4	4	3	3	5	3	6	5	
Pct Up		42.9%	28.6%	42.9%	42.9%	57.1%	57.1%	28.6%	57.1%	14.3%	28.6%	
Pct Down		57.1%	71.4%	57.1%	57.1%	42.9%	42.9%	71.4%	42.9%	85.7%	71.4%	
EXTREMES												
Greatest Up		1.22	0.70	0.95	0.63	1.94	2.25	0.51	0.78	0.19	1.30	
Greatest Down		-0.79	-0.72	-1.31	-1.47	-1.63	-1.43	-0.95	-1.37	-1.58	-2.30	
SEASONAL INDEX : AVERAGE PERCENTAGE METHOD												
All Years	100.1	100.3	100.2	100.0	99.8	100.0	100.3	100.2	100.2	99.6	99.3	
Less Extremes	100.1	100.4	100.1	100.0	99.8	99.9	100.4	100.4	100.1	99.6	99.7	
SEASONAL INDEX : LINK RELATIVE METHOD												
All Years		99.9	99.9	99.8	99.7	100.0	100.4	100.3	100.4	99.9	99.7	
Less Extremes		100.0	99.9	99.8	99.7	100.0	100.3	100.2	100.4	99.9	99.8	

TREASURY BILLS - MARCH - MONTH OF HIGH AND LOW

Year of Expiration	May	Jun	Jul	Aug	Sep	Oct	Nov	Dec	Jan	Feb	Mar
1979				H					L		
1980		H									L
1981		H								L	
1982					L		H				
1983		L							H		
1984	H			L							
1985		L							H		

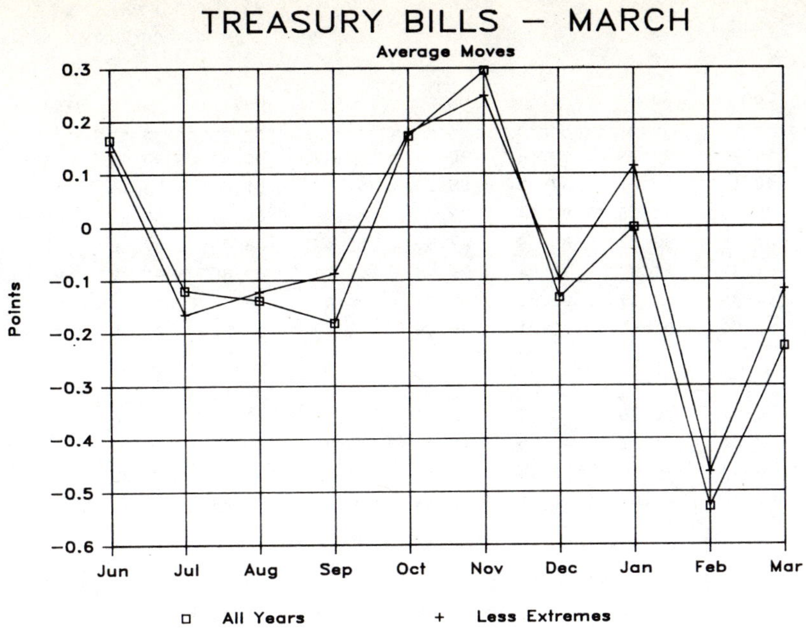
TREASURY BILLS – MARCH
Average Moves
Points
0.3
0.2
0.1
0
–0.1
–0.2
–0.3
–0.4
–0.5
–0.6
Jun
Jul
Aug
Sep
Oct
Nov
Dec
Jan
Feb
Mar
All Years
Less Extremes

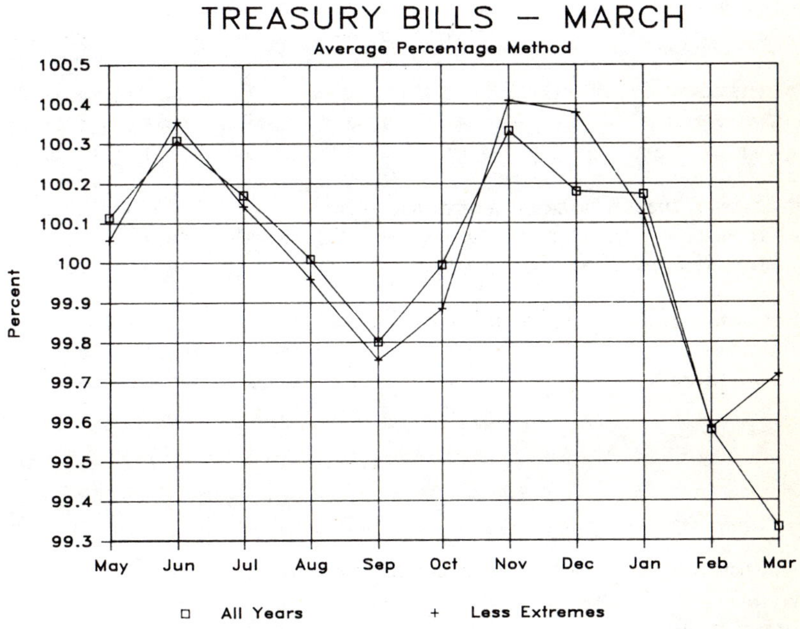
TREASURY BILLS – MARCH
Average Percentage Method
Percent
100.5
100.4
100.3
100.2
100.1
100
99.9
99.8
99.7
99.6
99.5
99.4
99.3
May
Jun
Jul
Aug
Sep
Oct
Nov
Dec
Jan
Feb
Mar
All Years
Less Extremes

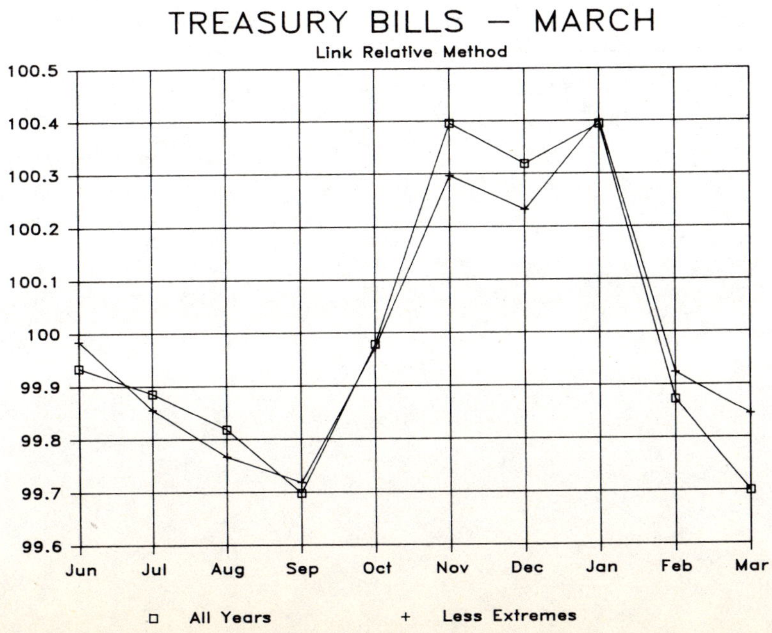
TREASURY BILLS – MARCH
Link Relative Method
100.5
100.4
100.3
100.2
100.1
100
99.9
99.8
99.7
99.6
Jun
Jul
Aug
Sep
Oct
Nov
Dec
Jan
Feb
Mar
All Years
Less Extremes

TREASURY BILLS - JUNE - MONTHLY AVERAGE PRICE

Year of Expiration	Aug	Sep	Oct	Nov	Dec	Jan	Feb	Mar	Apr	May	Jun	Aug-Jun Average
1979	91.88	91.80	91.22	90.67	90.49	90.39	90.56	90.55	90.57	90.50	90.96	90.87
1980	91.59	91.01	89.69	89.97	90.13	89.61	87.45	85.26	87.92	91.48	93.19	89.75
1981	90.14	88.73	88.78	87.69	87.23	88.25	87.64	88.21	86.96	84.32	85.33	87.57
1982	86.75	86.21	86.77	88.68	87.98	86.73	86.36	87.35	87.48	88.25	87.76	87.30
1983	88.25	88.68	90.50	91.09	91.46	91.87	91.74	91.59	91.79	91.80	91.37	90.92
1984	89.65	90.12	90.48	90.36	90.26	90.62	90.52	90.14	90.01	89.79	90.24	90.20
1985	88.69	89.06	89.55	90.61	91.06	91.49	91.21	90.85	91.82	92.52	93.05	90.90
AVERAGE MOVE												
All Years		-0.19	0.20	0.30	-0.07	0.05	-0.50	-0.22	0.37	0.30	0.46	
Less Extremes		-0.08	0.18	0.25	-0.04	0.12	-0.30	-0.07	0.24	0.24	0.40	
Ave Up - All Years		0.42	0.66	0.96	0.33	0.56	0.18	0.78	0.79	1.26	0.83	
Ave Down - All Years		-0.65	-0.95	-0.59	-0.36	-0.63	-0.61	-0.62	-0.69	-0.98	-0.46	
COUNT												
Number Up		3	5	4	3	4	1	2	5	4	5	
Number Down		4	2	3	4	3	6	5	2	3	2	
Pct Up		42.9%	71.4%	57.1%	42.9%	57.1%	14.3%	28.6%	71.4%	57.1%	71.4%	
Pct Down		57.1%	28.6%	42.9%	57.1%	42.9%	85.7%	71.4%	28.6%	42.9%	28.6%	
EXTREMES												
Greatest Up		0.47	1.83	1.91	0.45	1.02	0.18	0.99	2.65	3.56	1.71	
Greatest Down		-1.41	-1.32	-1.09	-0.70	-1.26	-2.16	-2.18	-1.25	-2.64	-0.49	
SEASONAL INDEX : AVERAGE PERCENTAGE METHOD												
All Years	99.9	99.7	99.9	100.3	100.2	100.2	99.7	99.4	99.8	100.2	100.7	
Less Extremes	99.9	99.8	99.9	100.1	100.2	100.2	99.9	100.1	100.0	100.6	100.7	
SEASONAL INDEX : LINK RELATIVE METHOD												
All Years		100.1	100.2	100.5	100.3	100.3	99.6	99.3	99.6	99.9	100.3	
Less Extremes		100.0	100.1	100.3	100.1	100.2	99.7	99.6	99.7	99.9	100.3	

TREASURY BILLS - JUNE - MONTH OF HIGH AND LOW

Year of Expiration	Aug	Sep	Oct	Nov	Dec	Jan	Feb	Mar	Apr	May	Jun
1979	H					L					
1980								L			H
1981	H									L	
1982		L		H							
1983	L					H					
1984	L					H					
1985	L										H

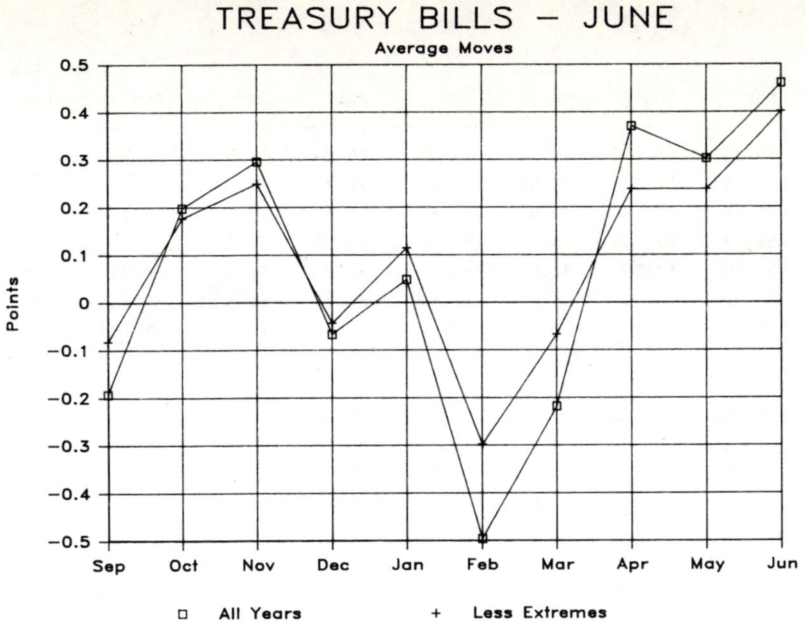
TREASURY BILLS — JUNE
Average Moves
Points
0.5
0.4
0.3
0.2
0.1
0
−0.1
−0.2
−0.3
−0.4
−0.5
Sep
Oct
Nov
Dec
Jan
Feb
Mar
Apr
May
Jun
□ All Years
+ Less Extremes

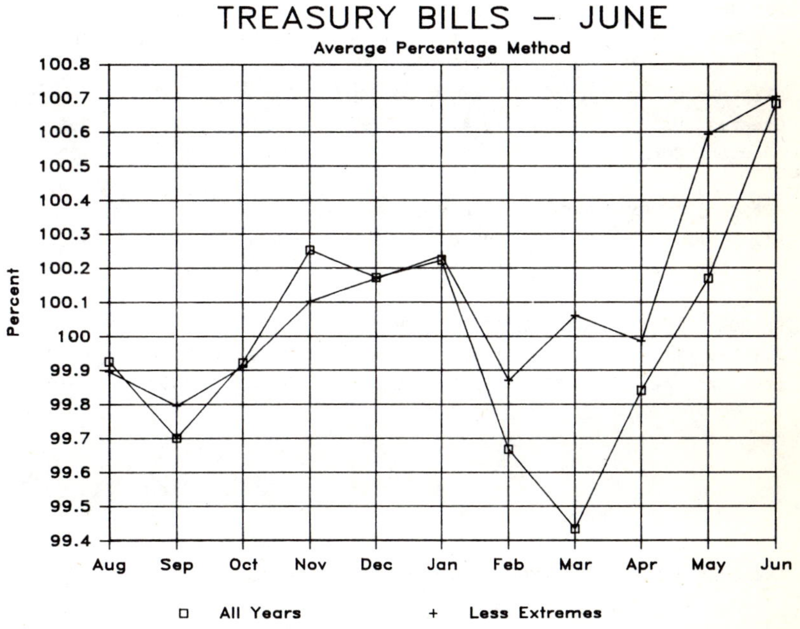
TREASURY BILLS — JUNE
Average Percentage Method
Percent
100.8
100.7
100.6
100.5
100.4
100.3
100.2
100.1
100
99.9
99.8
99.7
99.6
99.5
99.4
Aug
Sep
Oct
Nov
Dec
Jan
Feb
Mar
Apr
May
Jun
□ All Years
+ Less Extremes

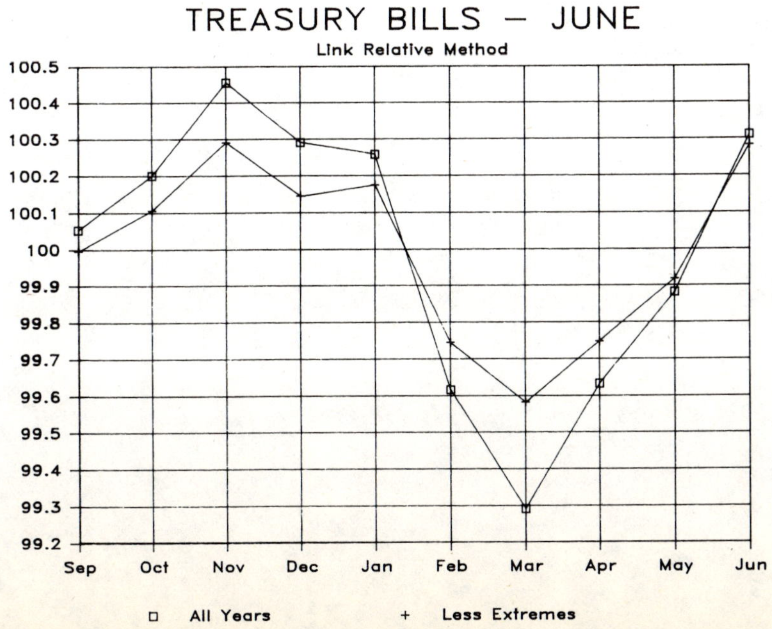
TREASURY BILLS — JUNE
Link Relative Method
100.5
100.4
100.3
100.2
100.1
100
99.9
99.8
99.7
99.6
99.5
99.4
99.3
99.2
Sep
Oct
Nov
Dec
Jan
Feb
Mar
Apr
May
Jun
□ All Years
+ Less Extremes

TREASURY BILLS - SEPTEMBER - MONTHLY AVERAGE PRICE

Year of Expiration	Nov	Dec	Jan	Feb	Mar	Apr	May	Jun	Jul	Aug	Sep	Nov-Sep Average
1979	90.75	90.52	90.37	90.49	90.54	90.55	90.61	91.35	90.98	90.49	89.71	90.58
1980	90.43	90.68	90.24	88.06	86.14	88.81	91.61	92.83	91.95	90.64	89.88	90.11
1981	87.89	87.80	88.70	88.22	88.82	87.56	85.89	86.94	85.98	85.09	85.35	87.11
1982	88.47	87.74	86.56	86.40	87.14	87.21	88.06	87.13	88.06	90.22	91.73	88.06
1983	90.77	91.05	91.54	91.45	91.40	91.51	91.61	90.87	90.61	90.57	90.74	91.10
1984	90.11	90.02	90.34	90.23	89.80	89.58	88.90	88.99	89.34	89.65	89.75	89.70
1985	90.23	90.65	91.00	90.73	90.37	91.31	92.09	92.88	92.90	92.90	92.98	91.64

	Nov	Dec	Jan	Feb	Mar	Apr	May	Jun	Jul	Aug	Sep
AVERAGE MOVE											
All Years		-0.03	0.04	-0.45	-0.20	0.33	0.32	0.32	-0.17	-0.04	0.08
Less Extremes		0.02	0.11	-0.22	-0.04	0.18	0.22	0.39	-0.23	-0.22	-0.03
Ave Up - All Years		0.31	0.52	0.12	0.46	0.76	0.92	0.78	0.43	0.83	0.42
Ave Down - All Years		-0.28	-0.59	-0.55	-0.69	-0.74	-1.17	-0.84	-0.62	-0.68	-0.77
COUNT											
Number Up		3	4	1	3	5	5	5	3	3	5
Number Down		4	3	6	4	2	2	2	4	4	2
Pct Up		42.9%	57.1%	14.3%	42.9%	71.4%	71.4%	71.4%	42.9%	42.9%	71.4%
Pct Down		57.1%	42.9%	85.7%	57.1%	28.6%	28.6%	28.6%	57.1%	57.1%	28.6%
EXTREMES											
Greatest Up		0.41	0.91	0.12	0.74	2.67	2.80	1.22	0.94	2.16	1.51
Greatest Down		-0.73	-1.18	-2.18	-1.92	-1.26	-1.67	-0.93	-0.95	-1.31	-0.79
SEASONAL INDEX : AVERAGE PERCENTAGE METHOD											
All Years	100.1	100.0	100.1	99.6	99.4	99.7	100.1	100.4	100.2	100.2	100.3
Less Extremes	100.2	100.1	100.1	99.6	99.6	99.8	100.0	100.2	100.2	100.2	100.0
SEASONAL INDEX : LINK RELATIVE METHOD											
All Years		100.1	100.1	99.6	99.4	99.7	100.1	100.4	100.2	100.1	100.2
Less Extremes		99.9	100.0	99.7	99.7	99.9	100.1	100.5	100.3	100.0	99.9

TREASURY BILLS - SEPTEMBER - MONTH OF HIGH AND LOW

Year of Expiration	Nov	Dec	Jan	Feb	Mar	Apr	May	Jun	Jul	Aug	Sep
1979								H			L
1980					L			H			
1981			H							L	
1982				L							H
1983							H			L	
1984			H				L				
1985	L										H

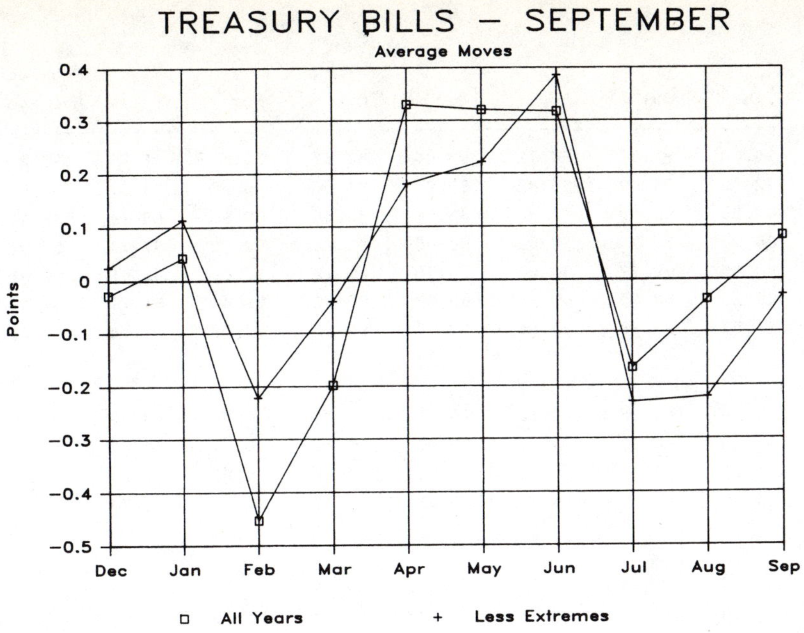
TREASURY BILLS — SEPTEMBER
Average Moves
Points
0.4
0.3
0.2
0.1
0
−0.1
−0.2
−0.3
−0.4
−0.5
Dec
Jan
Feb
Mar
Apr
May
Jun
Jul
Aug
Sep
All Years
Less Extremes

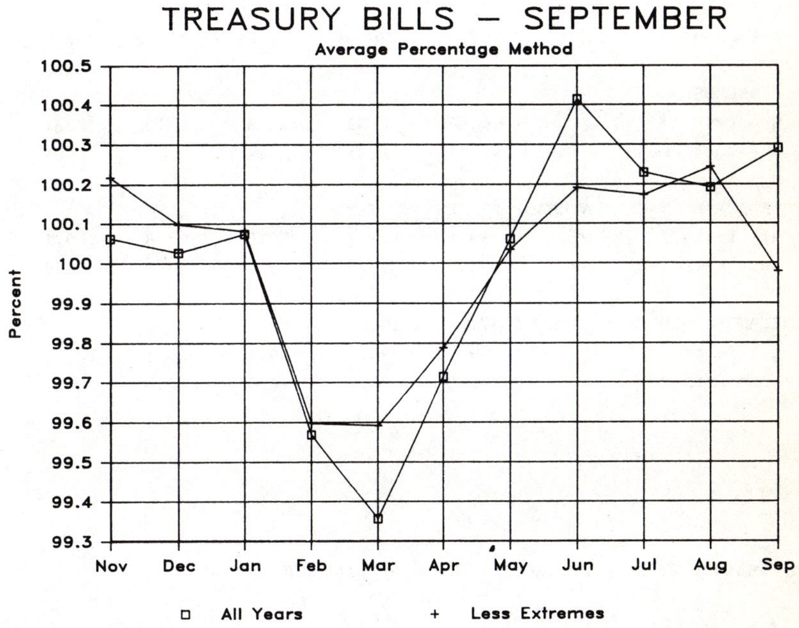
TREASURY BILLS — SEPTEMBER
Average Percentage Method
Percent
100.5
100.4
100.3
100.2
100.1
100
99.9
99.8
99.7
99.6
99.5
99.4
99.3
Nov
Dec
Jan
Feb
Mar
Apr
May
Jun
Jul
Aug
Sep
All Years
Less Extremes

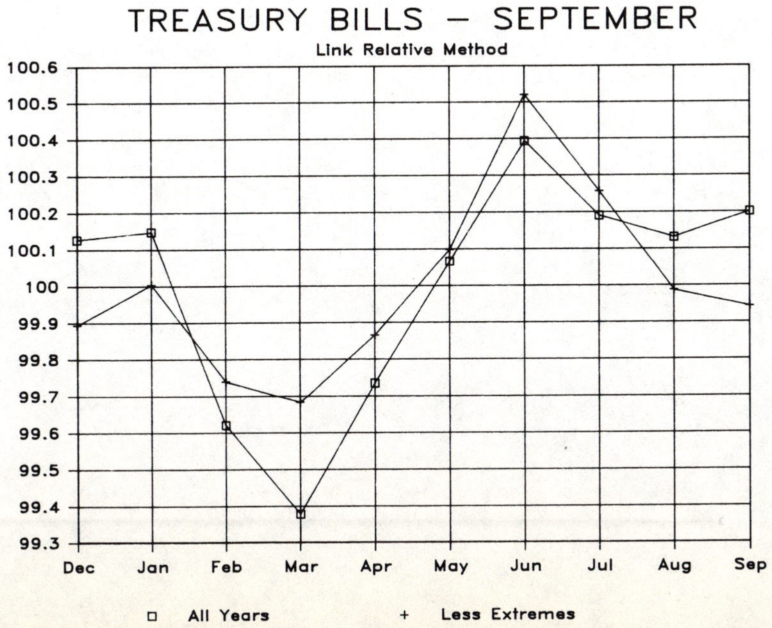
TREASURY BILLS — SEPTEMBER
Link Relative Method
100.6
100.5
100.4
100.3
100.2
100.1
100
99.9
99.8
99.7
99.6
99.5
99.4
99.3
Dec
Jan
Feb
Mar
Apr
May
Jun
Jul
Aug
Sep
All Years
Less Extremes

TREASURY BILLS - DECEMBER - MONTHLY AVERAGE PRICE

Year of Expiration	Feb	Mar	Apr	May	Jun	Jul	Aug	Sep	Oct	Nov	Dec	Feb-Dec Average
1979	90.50	90.56	90.60	90.73	91.68	91.37	90.71	90.04	88.37	88.57	88.09	90.11
1980	88.49	86.88	89.39	91.62	92.52	91.80	90.42	89.07	88.56	86.60	84.27	89.06
1981	88.38	88.92	87.69	86.45	87.58	86.69	85.86	85.68	86.48	88.95	89.14	87.44
1982	86.45	87.02	87.05	87.79	86.90	87.72	89.04	90.08	91.94	92.08	92.16	88.93
1983	91.16	91.20	91.29	91.39	90.65	90.27	90.09	90.70	91.13	91.08	91.02	90.91
1984	89.98	89.54	89.22	88.44	88.28	88.65	89.26	89.63	90.22	91.41	91.77	89.67
1985	90.35	90.04	90.88	91.72	92.53	92.58	92.59	92.70	92.87	92.96	92.94	92.01

	Feb	Mar	Apr	May	Jun	Jul	Aug	Sep	Oct	Nov	Dec
AVERAGE MOVE											
All Years		-0.16	0.28	0.29	0.29	-0.15	-0.16	-0.01	0.24	0.30	-0.32
Less Extremes		-0.02	0.14	0.21	0.35	-0.20	-0.21	0.05	0.30	0.31	-0.06
Ave Up - All Years		0.30	0.70	0.81	0.95	0.41	0.65	0.53	0.77	0.82	0.21
Ave Down - All Years		-0.78	-0.77	-1.01	-0.59	-0.57	-0.77	-0.73	-1.09	-1.00	-0.72
COUNT											
Number Up		4	5	5	4	3	3	4	5	5	3
Number Down		3	2	2	3	4	4	3	2	2	4
Pct Up		57.1%	71.4%	71.4%	57.1%	42.9%	42.9%	57.1%	71.4%	71.4%	42.9%
Pct Down		42.9%	28.6%	28.6%	42.9%	57.1%	57.1%	42.9%	28.6%	28.6%	57.1%
EXTREMES											
Greatest Up		0.57	2.51	2.23	1.13	0.81	1.33	1.03	1.86	2.46	0.36
Greatest Down		-1.61	-1.23	-1.24	-0.88	-0.89	-1.39	-1.35	-1.67	-1.96	-2.33
SEASONAL INDEX : AVERAGE PERCENTAGE METHOD											
All Years	99.6	99.4	99.7	100.0	100.3	100.1	100.0	100.0	100.2	100.6	100.2
Less Extremes	99.7	99.3	99.9	99.7	100.1	99.9	100.0	100.1	100.0	100.6	100.6
SEASONAL INDEX : LINK RELATIVE METHOD											
All Years		99.6	99.9	100.1	100.4	100.1	99.9	99.8	100.0	100.3	99.8
Less Extremes		99.8	99.9	100.1	100.4	100.1	99.7	99.7	100.0	100.2	100.1

TREASURY BILLS - DECEMBER - MONTH OF HIGH AND LOW

Year of Expiration	Feb	Mar	Apr	May	Jun	Jul	Aug	Sep	Oct	Nov	Dec
1979					H						L
1980					H						L
1981								L			H
1982	L										H
1983				H			L				
1984					L						H
1985		L								H	

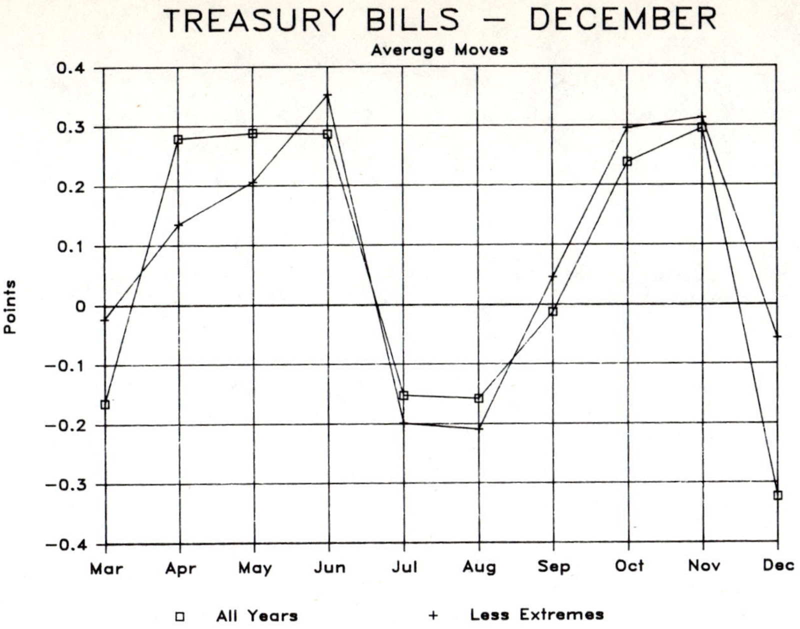
TREASURY BILLS – DECEMBER
Average Moves
Points
0.4
0.3
0.2
0.1
0
−0.1
−0.2
−0.3
−0.4
Mar
Apr
May
Jun
Jul
Aug
Sep
Oct
Nov
Dec
All Years
Less Extremes

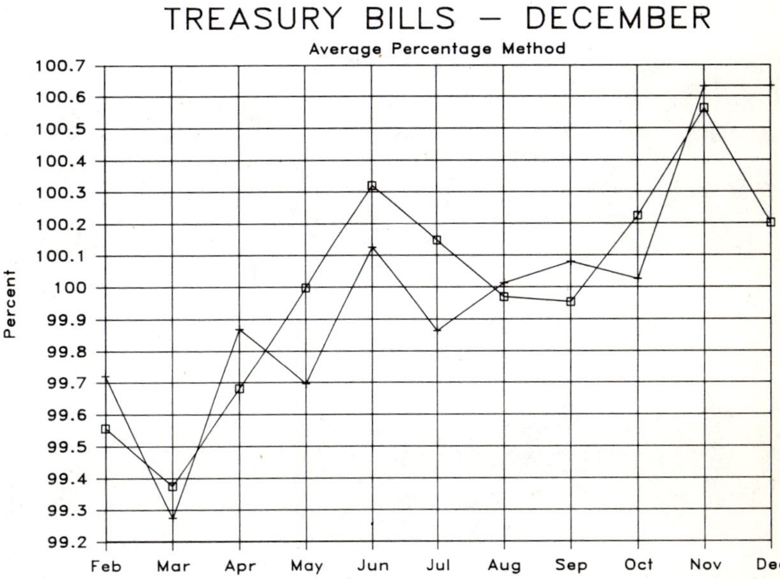
TREASURY BILLS – DECEMBER
Average Percentage Method
Percent
100.7
100.6
100.5
100.4
100.3
100.2
100.1
100
99.9
99.8
99.7
99.6
99.5
99.4
99.3
99.2
Feb
Mar
Apr
May
Jun
Jul
Aug
Sep
Oct
Nov
Dec

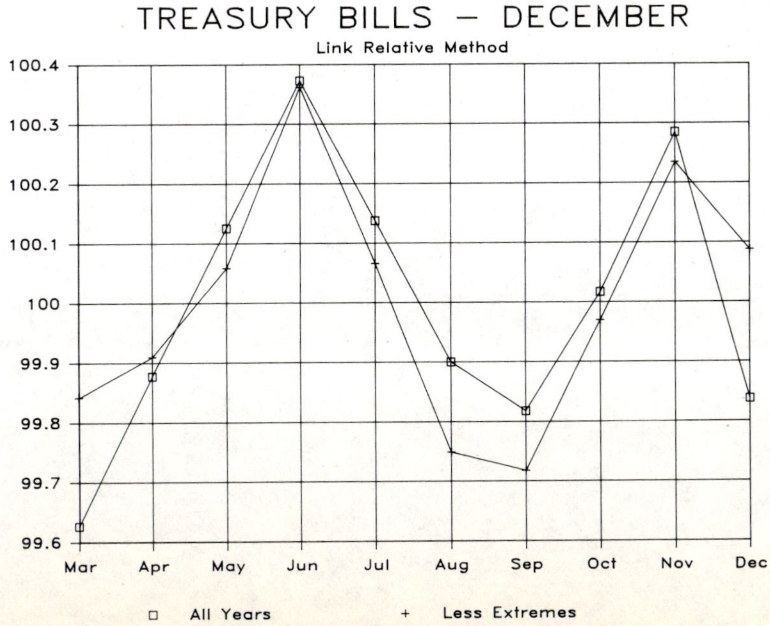
TREASURY BILLS – DECEMBER
Link Relative Method
100.4
100.3
100.2
100.1
100
99.9
99.8
99.7
99.6
Mar
Apr
May
Jun
Jul
Aug
Sep
Oct
Nov
Dec
All Years
Less Extremes

FOUR

Currencies

Currencies are one of the better seasonal commodities. There are several seasonal tendencies with reliabilties of greater than 70%. Currency seasonals exist because of the ebb and flow of such key economic indicators as trade flows and capital flows.

In *Profits Through Seasonal Trading* (Grushcow & Smith, 1980, Wiley) the problems of trading the currencies from a seasonal perspective because of the limited trading history and because most of the currencies had only been in bull trends during their trading history were mentioned. However, most currencies have reversed their bull trends since 1980. Traders should have more confidence in the seasonal tendencies because of the additional years of trading. However, the British pound and Canadian dollar have remained in bear trends throughout most of the study period and that has distorted the average percentage method of isolating seasonality.

HIGHEST RELIABLE TRENDS

Commodity	Contract	Month	Position	Reliability	Average Move
British pound	Mar	Jun	Short	80.0	−4.15
	Mar	Aug	Short	70.0	−2.71
	Mar	Sep	Short	70.0	−2.98
	Mar	Mar	Short	70.0	−4.17
	Jun	Oct	Short	70.0	−3.05
	Sep	Sep	Short	70.0	−2.08
	Dec	Mar	Short	70.0	−5.72
	Dec	Sep	Short	70.0	−3.03
Canadian dollar	Mar	Oct	Short	75.0	−0.53
	Mar	Jan	Short	75.0	−0.28
	Jun	Jun	Short	75.0	−0.64
	Sep	Apr	Short	75.0	−0.68
	Sep	Jun	Short	75.0	−0.90
	Sep	Aug	Short	75.0	−0.50
	Dec	Dec	Short	75.0	−0.63
Deutsche mark	Mar	Jun	Long	70.0	+0.54
	Mar	Aug	Short	80.0	−0.86
	Mar	Oct	Long	70.0	+1.22
	Mar	Feb	Short	70.0	−1.27

(Continued on next page.)

Commodity	Contract	Month	Position	Reliability	Average Move
Deutsche mark	Jun	Feb	Short	70.0	−1.29
	Jun	Apr	Short	70.0	−0.88
	Jun	May	Short	70.0	−1.10
	Sep	Feb	Short	70.0	−1.30
	Sep	Apr	Short	70.0	−0.92
	Sep	May	Short	70.0	−1.07
	Sep	Aug	Short	70.0	−0.86
	Dec	Apr	Short	70.0	−0.95
	Dec	May	Short	70.0	−1.05
	Dec	Aug	Short	70.0	−0.83
Japanese yen	Mar	Dec	Long	75.0	+1.00
	Mar	Feb	Short	100.0	−0.98
	Mar	Mar	Short	75.0	−0.69
	Jun	Feb	Short	100.0	−1.00
	Jun	Apr	Short	75.0	−0.88
	Sep	Aug	Short	75.0	−0.52
	Sep	Sep	Short	75.0	−0.63
	Dec	Aug	Short	75.0	−0.52
Swiss franc	Mar	Aug	Short	80.0	−0.94
	Mar	Nov	Short	70.0	−1.61
	Mar	Jan	Short	70.0	−1.02
	Mar	Feb	Short	70.0	−1.81
	Mar	Mar	Short	70.0	−1.08
	Jun	Nov	Short	70.0	−1.61
	Jun	Jan	Short	70.0	−0.99
	Jun	Feb	Short	70.0	−1.83
	Jun	Mar	Short	90.0	−0.87
	Jun	Apr	Short	70.0	−1.11
	Jun	May	Short	80.0	−0.99
	Sep	Jan	Short	70.0	−1.02
	Sep	Feb	Short	70.0	−1.82
	Sep	Apr	Short	70.0	−1.13
	Sep	May	Short	80.0	−0.99
	Sep	Aug	Short	80.0	−0.86
	Dec	Apr	Short	70.0	−1.23
	Dec	May	Short	70.0	−1.13
	Dec	Aug	Short	70.0	−0.96

BRITISH POUND - MARCH - MONTHLY AVERAGE PRICE

Year of Expiration	May	Jun	Jul	Aug	Sep	Oct	Nov	Dec	Jan	Feb	Mar	May-Mar Average
1976	220.28	218.56	212.74	205.87	204.68	202.02	201.89	199.70	201.30	201.97	196.52	205.96
1977	166.43	169.80	171.12	170.71	165.00	155.55	158.44	163.56	168.78	169.88	171.49	166.43
1978	167.55	167.06	167.81	172.35	174.24	178.35	182.61	185.79	193.77	194.12	192.72	179.67
1979	177.59	179.69	186.76	191.55	193.11	198.60	194.73	197.93	199.86	200.03	202.99	192.98
1980	219.40	209.99	222.77	221.15	218.12	214.46	212.58	219.04	225.46	228.28	222.19	219.40
1981	226.51	225.69	230.97	231.69	237.19	240.25	239.79	237.62	242.03	229.94	220.81	232.95
1982	217.78	202.10	191.69	186.83	184.11	184.82	189.56	189.65	188.37	184.96	181.38	191.02
1983	181.10	178.96	176.48	174.03	172.64	170.43	163.84	161.60	157.04	152.87	150.66	167.24
1984	156.47	154.85	153.13	150.82	150.14	150.06	148.16	143.87	140.85	144.18	146.77	149.03
1985	141.72	140.42	132.99	132.50	126.35	122.35	124.19	118.32	112.19	108.94	107.62	124.33

	May	Jun	Jul	Aug	Sep	Oct	Nov	Dec	Jan	Feb	Mar
AVERAGE MOVE											
All Years		-2.77	-0.07	-0.90	-1.19	-0.87	-0.11	0.13	1.26	-1.45	-2.20
Less Extremes		-1.92	-0.38	-0.86	-1.41	-0.59	0.09	0.09	1.34	-0.71	-1.98
Ave Up - All Years		2.74	5.44	3.35	2.98	3.34	3.43	3.61	4.59	1.41	2.39
Ave Down - All Years		-4.15	-5.57	-2.71	-2.98	-3.68	-2.47	-3.35	-3.74	-5.73	-4.17
COUNT											
Number Up		2	5	3	3	4	4	5	6	6	3
Number Down		8	5	7	7	6	6	5	4	4	7
Pct Up		20.0%	50.0%	30.0%	30.0%	40.0%	40.0%	50.0%	60.0%	60.0%	30.0%
Pct Down		80.0%	50.0%	70.0%	70.0%	60.0%	60.0%	50.0%	40.0%	40.0%	70.0%
EXTREMES											
Greatest Up		3.37	12.78	4.79	5.50	5.49	4.74	6.46	7.98	3.33	2.95
Greatest Down		-15.68	-10.40	-6.87	-6.15	-9.45	-6.58	-5.88	-6.12	-12.09	-9.14
SEASONAL INDEX : AVERAGE PERCENTAGE METHOD											
All Years	103.1	101.6	101.3	100.8	99.9	99.2	99.2	99.1	99.4	98.7	97.7
Less Extremes	103.1	101.3	101.5	100.6	99.9	99.5	99.2	99.0	99.5	98.9	97.9
SEASONAL INDEX : LINK RELATIVE METHOD											
All Years		100.3	100.4	100.3	99.8	99.4	99.8	99.9	100.6	100.1	99.4
Less Extremes		100.4	100.3	100.0	99.5	99.3	99.7	100.0	100.8	100.4	99.6

BRITISH POUND - MARCH - MONTH OF HIGH AND LOW

Year of Expiration	May	Jun	Jul	Aug	Sep	Oct	Nov	Dec	Jan	Feb	Mar
1976	H										L
1977			H			L					
1978		L								H	
1979	L										H
1980		L								H	
1981									H		L
1982	H										L
1983	H										L
1984	H								L		
1985	H										L

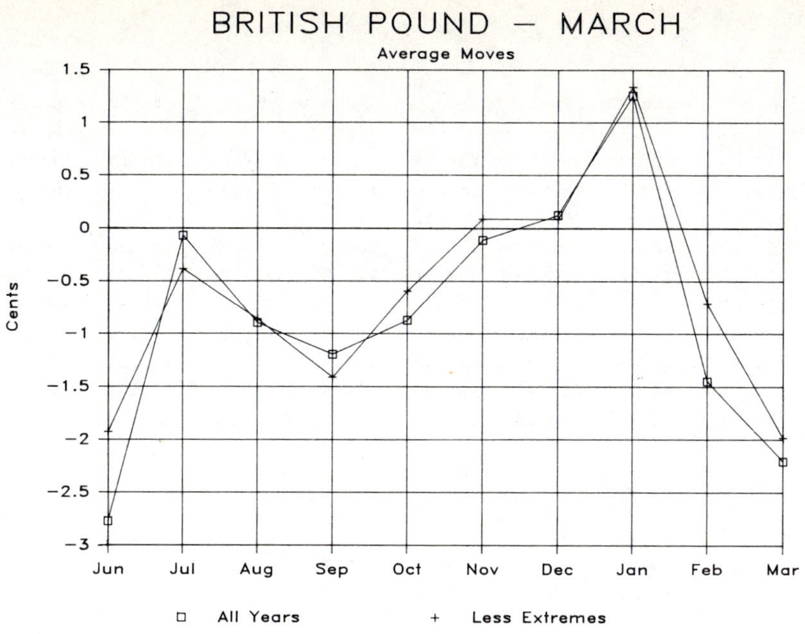
BRITISH POUND – MARCH
Average Moves
Cents
1.5
1
0.5
0
−0.5
−1
−1.5
−2
−2.5
−3
Jun
Jul
Aug
Sep
Oct
Nov
Dec
Jan
Feb
Mar
All Years
Less Extremes

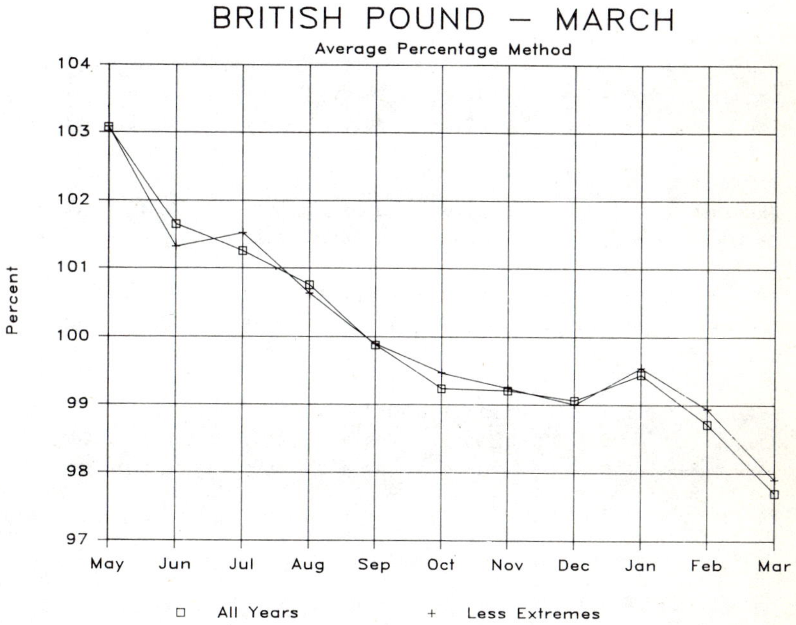
BRITISH POUND – MARCH
Average Percentage Method
Percent
104
103
102
101
100
99
98
97
May
Jun
Jul
Aug
Sep
Oct
Nov
Dec
Jan
Feb
Mar
All Years
Less Extremes

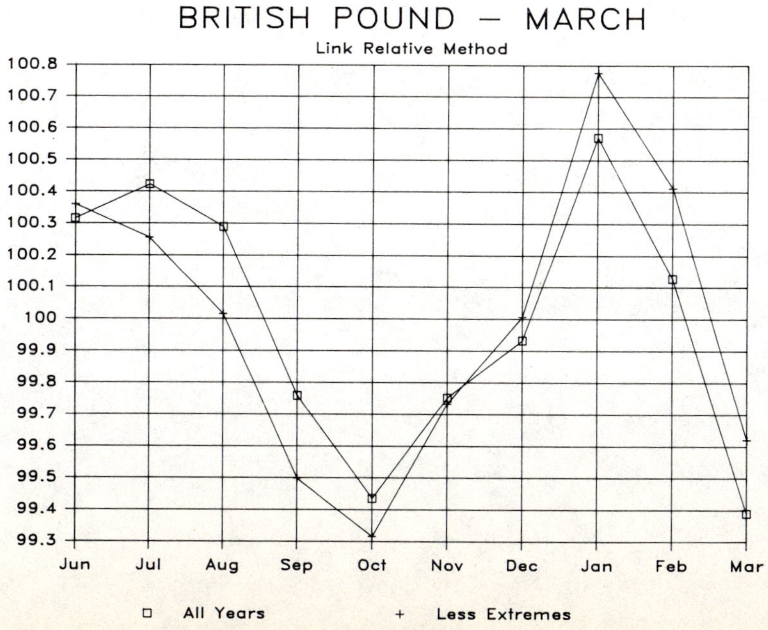
BRITISH POUND – MARCH
Link Relative Method
100.8
100.7
100.6
100.5
100.4
100.3
100.2
100.1
100
99.9
99.8
99.7
99.6
99.5
99.4
99.3
Jun
Jul
Aug
Sep
Oct
Nov
Dec
Jan
Feb
Mar
All Years
Less Extremes

BRITISH POUND - JUNE - MONTHLY AVERAGE PRICE

Year of Expiration	Aug	Sep	Oct	Nov	Dec	Jan	Feb	Mar	Apr	May	Jun	Aug-Jun Average
1976	203.86	203.03	199.86	199.87	197.60	199.09	199.98	191.98	182.96	179.97	175.16	193.94
1977	164.34	160.79	151.85	154.85	160.21	165.87	166.57	169.20	170.88	171.45	171.71	164.34
1978	171.47	174.06	178.60	182.62	185.67	194.16	194.04	190.42	184.64	181.39	182.64	183.61
1979	190.21	191.90	197.19	193.72	197.03	198.95	198.88	203.13	206.97	205.69	208.50	199.29
1980	220.04	217.22	214.29	212.03	218.07	224.66	227.23	220.51	221.56	229.24	232.69	221.59
1981	228.24	236.64	240.00	239.93	238.42	243.57	232.63	224.62	218.83	210.25	197.51	228.24
1982	188.05	185.22	185.06	189.31	189.40	188.58	185.61	181.19	178.01	181.28	178.34	184.55
1983	176.50	173.69	171.05	164.24	161.44	156.42	152.26	148.53	153.90	157.23	157.31	161.14
1984	150.90	150.35	150.25	148.46	144.14	141.02	144.47	146.25	142.64	139.25	139.02	145.16
1985	119.75	126.11	122.71	124.38	118.34	111.63	108.00	111.61	123.33	124.44	127.00	119.75

	Aug	Sep	Oct	Nov	Dec	Jan	Feb	Mar	Apr	May	Jun
AVERAGE MOVE											
All Years		0.57	-0.82	-0.14	0.09	1.37	-1.43	-2.22	-0.37	-0.35	-1.03
Less Extremes		0.10	-0.56	0.14	0.11	1.49	-0.85	-2.31	-0.80	-0.33	-0.13
Ave Up - All Years		4.76	4.40	2.59	3.57	4.89	1.90	3.07	4.73	3.19	1.73
Ave Down - All Years		-2.23	-3.05	-2.88	-3.39	-3.92	-3.65	-5.75	-5.48	-3.90	-5.18
COUNT											
Number Up		4	3	5	5	6	4	4	5	5	6
Number Down		6	7	5	5	4	6	6	5	5	4
Pct Up		40.0%	30.0%	50.0%	50.0%	60.0%	40.0%	40.0%	50.0%	50.0%	60.0%
Pct Down		60.0%	70.0%	50.0%	50.0%	40.0%	60.0%	60.0%	50.0%	50.0%	40.0%
EXTREMES											
Greatest Up		8.40	5.29	4.25	6.04	8.49	3.45	4.24	11.72	7.68	3.45
Greatest Down		-3.55	-8.94	-6.81	-6.04	-6.71	-10.95	-8.01	-9.01	-8.57	-12.75
SEASONAL INDEX : AVERAGE PERCENTAGE METHOD											
All Years	100.9	101.2	100.6	100.5	100.3	100.7	99.9	99.0	99.2	99.0	98.7
Less Extremes	100.7	101.2	100.9	100.8	100.2	100.9	100.4	99.2	99.2	99.2	99.2
SEASONAL INDEX : LINK RELATIVE METHOD											
All Years		100.3	99.9	100.1	100.1	100.7	100.1	99.4	99.9	99.9	99.7
Less Extremes		100.0	99.8	100.2	100.3	101.1	100.5	99.7	99.5	99.5	99.6

BRITISH POUND - JUNE - MONTH OF HIGH AND LOW

Year of Expiration	Aug	Sep	Oct	Nov	Dec	Jan	Feb	Mar	Apr	May	Jun
1976	H										L
1977			L								H
1978	L					H					
1979	L										H
1980				L							H
1981						H					L
1982					H				L		
1983	H							L			
1984	H										L
1985							L				H

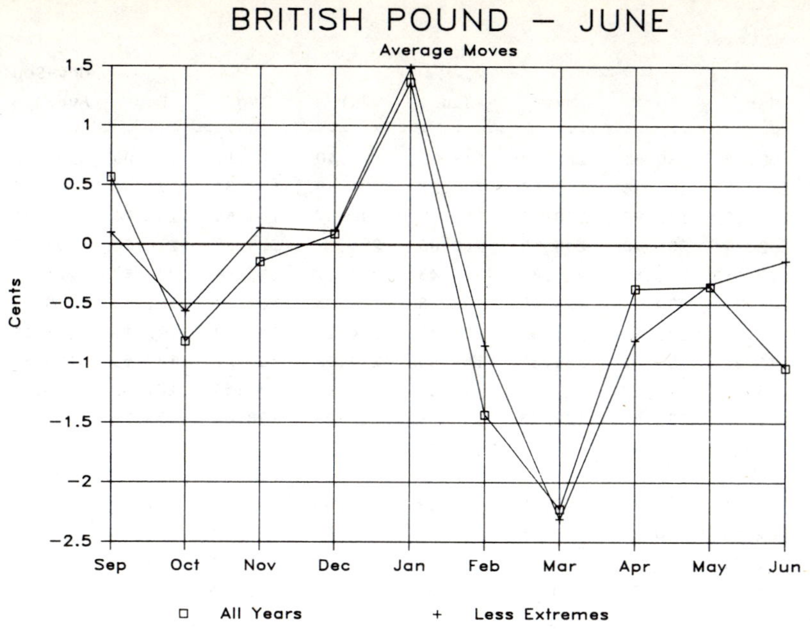
BRITISH POUND — JUNE
Average Moves
Cents
1.5
1
0.5
0
−0.5
−1
−1.5
−2
−2.5
Sep
Oct
Nov
Dec
Jan
Feb
Mar
Apr
May
Jun
□ All Years
+ Less Extremes

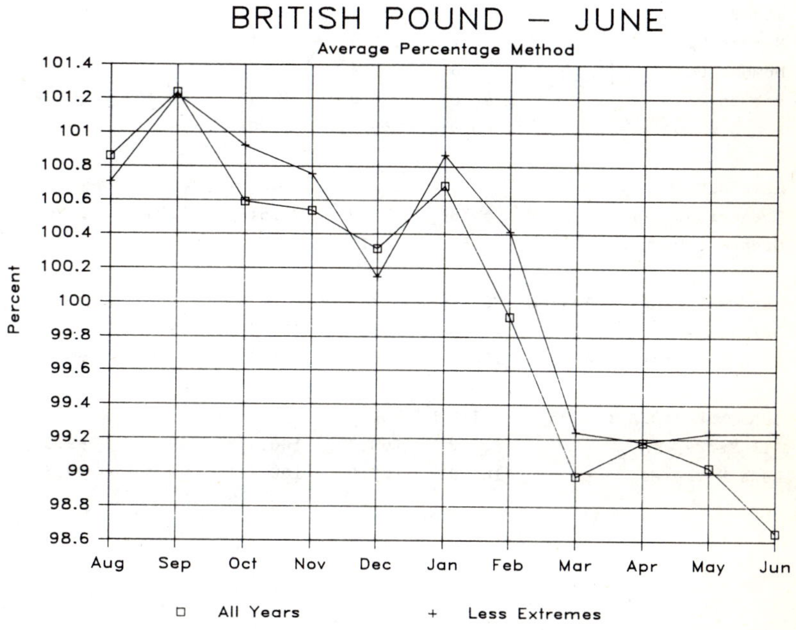
BRITISH POUND — JUNE
Average Percentage Method
Percent
101.4
101.2
101
100.8
100.6
100.4
100.2
100
99.8
99.6
99.4
99.2
99
98.8
98.6
Aug
Sep
Oct
Nov
Dec
Jan
Feb
Mar
Apr
May
Jun
□ All Years
+ Less Extremes

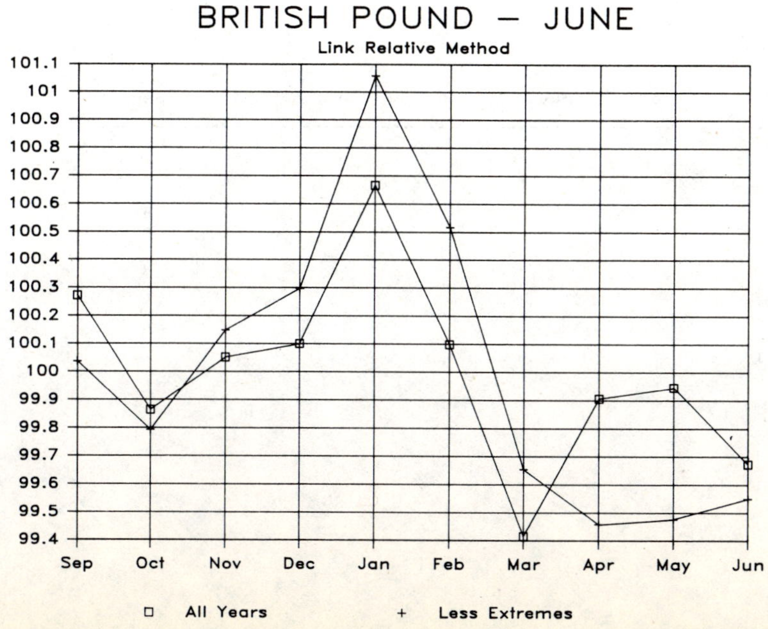
BRITISH POUND — JUNE
Link Relative Method
101.1
101
100.9
100.8
100.7
100.6
100.5
100.4
100.3
100.2
100.1
100
99.9
99.8
99.7
99.6
99.5
99.4
Sep
Oct
Nov
Dec
Jan
Feb
Mar
Apr
May
Jun
□ All Years
+ Less Extremes

BRITISH POUND - SEPTEMBER - MONTHLY AVERAGE PRICE

Year of Expiration	Nov	Dec	Jan	Feb	Mar	Apr	May	Jun	Jul	Aug	Sep	Nov-Sep Average
1976	197.05	195.15	196.93	198.01	190.03	180.81	177.73	173.63	176.40	177.14	176.09	185.36
1977	168.05	158.23	163.09	164.10	166.40	168.94	170.08	170.17	171.35	173.84	174.28	168.05
1978	182.57	185.61	194.41	193.86	190.29	183.98	180.06	182.23	188.87	193.64	194.74	188.21
1979	192.56	195.95	197.98	197.71	202.74	206.70	205.19	210.06	224.67	223.37	221.74	207.15
1980	211.32	216.90	223.90	226.38	220.61	221.58	226.77	229.43	234.61	235.86	240.82	226.20
1981	240.06	238.70	244.16	234.65	226.26	220.93	213.45	199.65	188.93	182.94	181.34	215.55
1982	190.71	189.22	188.71	186.23	181.90	178.60	181.81	176.89	174.22	172.58	172.16	181.19
1983	161.29	161.73	156.06	151.91	148.27	153.71	156.87	154.65	152.92	150.39	149.59	154.31
1984	147.03	144.42	141.23	144.74	146.95	143.37	140.04	138.51	131.98	131.54	127.33	139.74
1985	124.54	118.42	111.26	107.61	111.32	122.57	123.23	126.68	137.29	138.05	133.18	123.10

	Nov	Dec	Jan	Feb	Mar	Apr	May	Jun	Jul	Aug	Sep
AVERAGE MOVE											
All Years		-1.09	1.34	-1.26	-2.04	-0.36	-0.59	-1.33	1.93	-0.19	-0.81
Less Extremes		-0.83	1.47	-0.82	-2.14	-0.70	-0.46	-0.55	1.93	-0.08	-1.02
Ave Up - All Years		3.11	4.99	2.02	3.31	4.83	2.67	2.65	6.83	2.00	2.16
Ave Down - All Years		-3.88	-4.13	-3.44	-5.61	-5.55	-3.86	-5.31	-5.41	-2.38	-2.08
COUNT											
Number Up		4	6	4	4	5	5	5	6	5	3
Number Down		6	4	6	6	5	5	5	4	5	7
Pct Up		40.0%	60.0%	40.0%	40.0%	50.0%	50.0%	50.0%	60.0%	50.0%	30.0%
Pct Down		60.0%	40.0%	60.0%	60.0%	50.0%	50.0%	50.0%	40.0%	50.0%	70.0%
EXTREMES											
Greatest Up		5.58	8.80	3.51	5.03	11.26	5.19	4.87	14.61	4.78	4.95
Greatest Down		-9.82	-7.15	-9.52	-8.39	-9.22	-7.48	-13.80	-10.72	-5.99	-4.87
SEASONAL INDEX : AVERAGE PERCENTAGE METHOD											
All Years	101.7	100.8	101.1	100.4	99.5	99.6	99.3	98.7	99.9	99.8	99.1
Less Extremes	101.6	100.4	100.9	101.0	99.9	99.5	99.5	98.9	99.9	100.1	99.8
SEASONAL INDEX : LINK RELATIVE METHOD											
All Years		100.2	100.7	100.1	99.5	99.9	99.7	99.2	100.4	100.4	99.9
Less Extremes		100.3	101.0	100.4	99.7	99.5	99.4	99.2	100.3	100.4	99.9

BRITISH POUND - SEPTEMBER - MONTH OF HIGH AND LOW

Year of Expiration	Nov	Dec	Jan	Feb	Mar	Apr	May	Jun	Jul	Aug	Sep
1976				H				L			
1977		L									H
1978							L				H
1979	L								H		
1980	L										H
1981			H								L
1982	H										L
1983		H			L						
1984	H										L
1985				L						H	

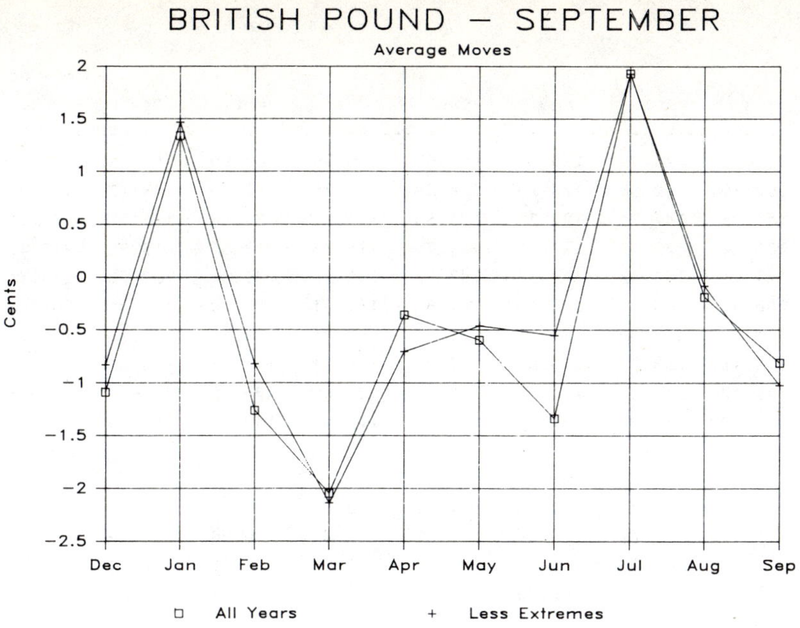
BRITISH POUND — SEPTEMBER
Average Moves
Cents
2
1.5
1
0.5
0
-0.5
-1
-1.5
-2
-2.5
Dec
Jan
Feb
Mar
Apr
May
Jun
Jul
Aug
Sep
All Years
Less Extremes

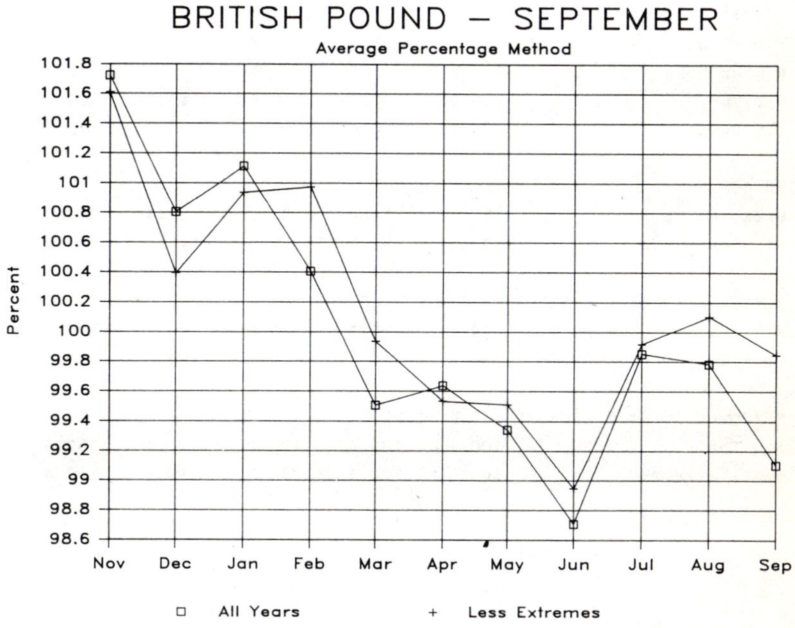
BRITISH POUND — SEPTEMBER
Average Percentage Method
Percent
101.8
101.6
101.4
101.2
101
100.8
100.6
100.4
100.2
100
99.8
99.6
99.4
99.2
99
98.8
98.6
Nov
Dec
Jan
Feb
Mar
Apr
May
Jun
Jul
Aug
Sep
All Years
Less Extremes

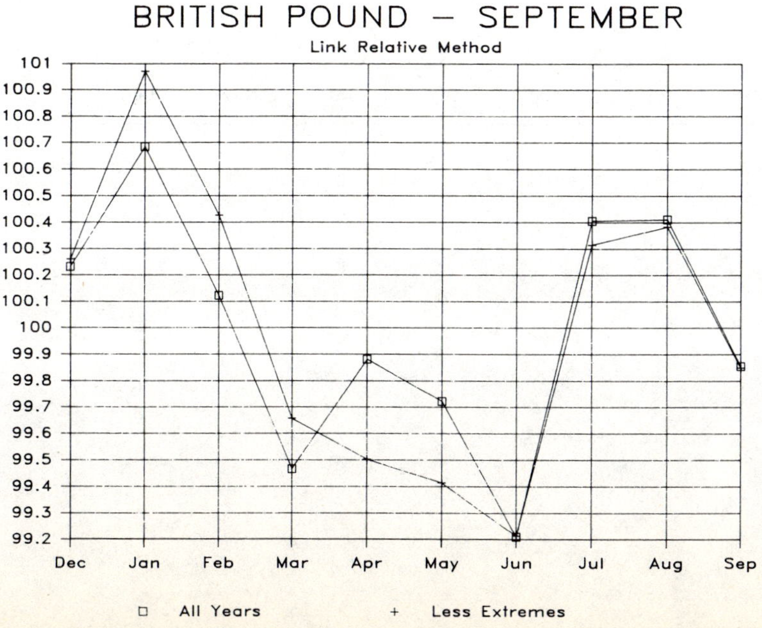
BRITISH POUND — SEPTEMBER
Link Relative Method
101
100.9
100.8
100.7
100.6
100.5
100.4
100.3
100.2
100.1
100
99.9
99.8
99.7
99.6
99.5
99.4
99.3
99.2
Dec
Jan
Feb
Mar
Apr
May
Jun
Jul
Aug
Sep
All Years
Less Extremes

BRITISH POUND - DECEMBER - MONTHLY AVERAGE PRICE

Year of Expiration	Feb	Mar	Apr	May	Jun	Jul	Aug	Sep	Oct	Nov	Dec	Feb-Dec Average
1976	195.98	188.22	178.95	175.57	171.38	173.63	174.03	168.81	160.20	162.66	166.63	174.19
1977	161.83	164.24	167.09	168.70	168.30	169.38	173.16	174.39	177.75	182.05	183.73	171.87
1978	193.81	190.02	183.30	178.74	180.98	187.74	192.57	194.55	199.99	195.76	196.60	190.37
1979	213.41	202.97	206.37	204.70	209.18	223.67	222.19	218.73	214.33	213.06	218.95	213.41
1980	226.00	220.56	221.27	225.11	227.21	232.43	233.19	237.97	240.76	239.38	233.92	230.71
1981	232.33	227.51	222.59	215.51	200.98	190.76	185.16	182.82	184.51	189.99	191.85	202.18
1982	186.65	182.47	179.02	182.20	178.05	175.39	173.18	171.62	169.86	163.55	162.41	174.94
1983	151.68	148.06	153.60	156.65	154.75	153.02	150.61	149.93	149.94	147.93	143.52	150.88
1984	145.11	147.69	144.15	140.88	139.42	132.41	131.98	125.90	122.09	124.15	119.99	133.98
1985	107.39	111.25	122.30	122.44	125.60	136.22	137.08	135.22	141.43	143.58	145.65	129.83

	Feb	Mar	Apr	May	Jun	Jul	Aug	Sep	Oct	Nov	Dec
AVERAGE MOVE											
All Years		-3.12	-0.44	-0.81	-1.47	1.88	-0.15	-1.32	0.09	0.12	0.12
Less Extremes		-3.08	-0.77	-0.61	-0.58	1.82	-0.09	-1.49	0.41	0.26	0.09
Ave Up - All Years		2.95	4.71	2.37	2.99	6.74	2.13	2.66	3.25	3.29	2.72
Ave Down - All Years		-5.72	-5.58	-3.99	-4.44	-5.40	-2.43	-3.03	-4.65	-3.04	-3.79
COUNT											
Number Up		3	5	5	4	6	5	3	6	5	6
Number Down		7	5	5	6	4	5	7	4	5	4
Pct Up		30.0%	50.0%	50.0%	40.0%	60.0%	50.0%	30.0%	60.0%	50.0%	60.0%
Pct Down		70.0%	50.0%	50.0%	60.0%	40.0%	50.0%	70.0%	40.0%	50.0%	40.0%
EXTREMES											
Greatest Up		3.86	11.04	3.85	4.48	14.50	4.83	4.78	6.21	5.49	5.89
Greatest Down		-10.45	-9.27	-7.08	-14.53	-10.22	-5.60	-6.08	-8.61	-6.31	-5.46
SEASONAL INDEX : AVERAGE PERCENTAGE METHOD											
All Years	102.0	100.5	100.5	100.0	99.2	100.2	100.1	99.2	99.3	99.4	99.4
Less Extremes	102.7	100.9	100.1	100.0	99.2	100.4	100.5	99.7	99.1	98.9	99.1
SEASONAL INDEX : LINK RELATIVE METHOD											
All Years		100.1	100.4	100.0	99.4	100.5	100.5	99.6	99.7	99.9	99.9
Less Extremes		100.3	100.1	99.7	99.4	100.4	100.4	99.6	99.7	100.1	100.2

BRITISH POUND - DECEMBER - MONTH OF HIGH AND LOW

Year of Expiration	Feb	Mar	Apr	May	Jun	Jul	Aug	Sep	Oct	Nov	Dec
1976	H								L		
1977	L								H		
1978				L					H		
1979	L					H					
1980		L							H		
1981	H							L			
1982	H										L
1983				H							L
1984		H									L
1985	L										H

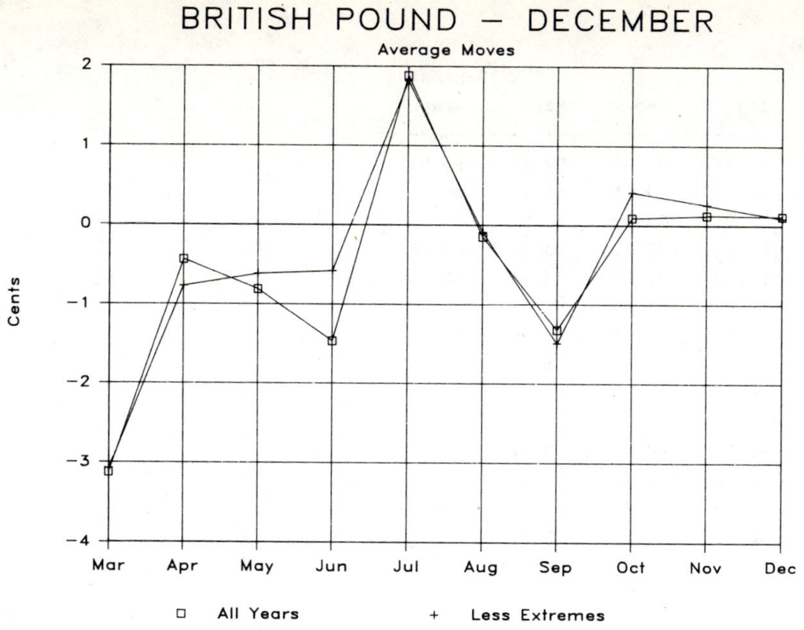
BRITISH POUND – DECEMBER
Average Moves
Cents
2
1
0
−1
−2
−3
−4
Mar
Apr
May
Jun
Jul
Aug
Sep
Oct
Nov
Dec
All Years
Less Extremes

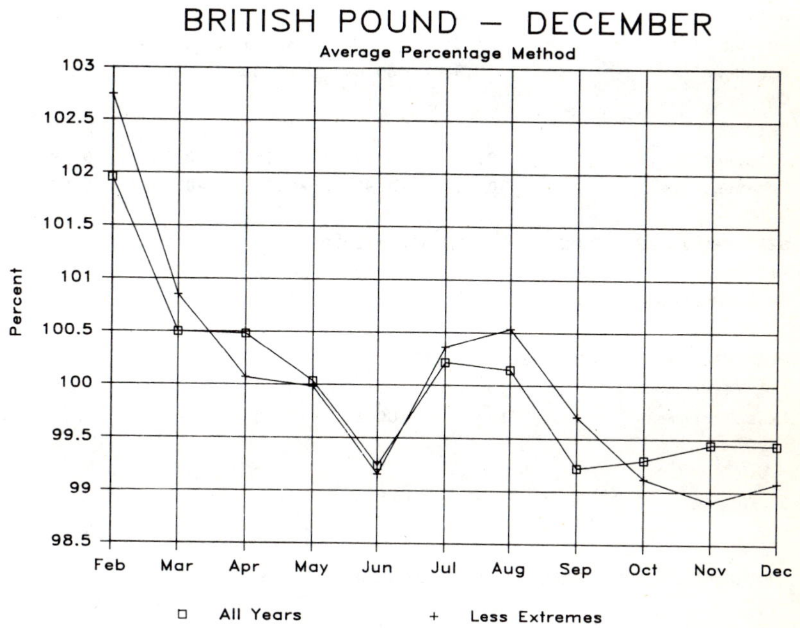
BRITISH POUND – DECEMBER
Average Percentage Method
Percent
103
102.5
102
101.5
101
100.5
100
99.5
99
98.5
Feb
Mar
Apr
May
Jun
Jul
Aug
Sep
Oct
Nov
Dec
All Years
Less Extremes

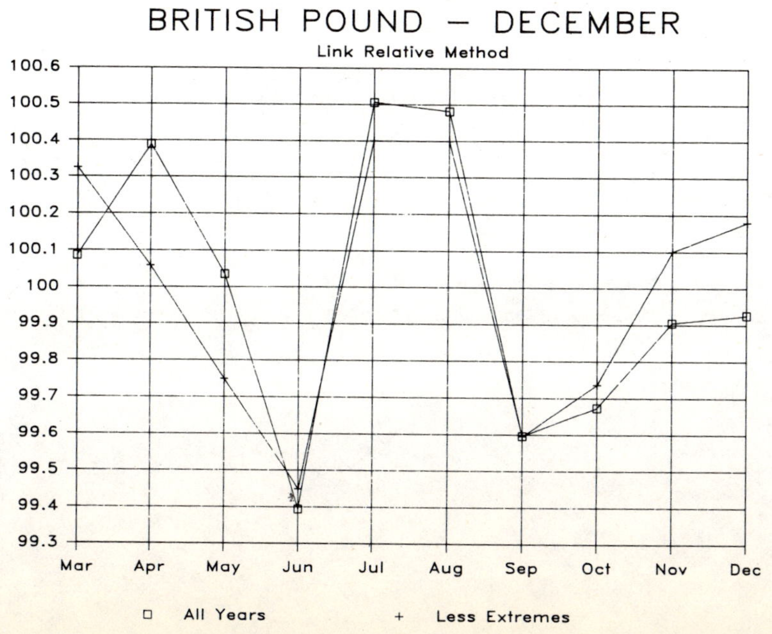
BRITISH POUND – DECEMBER
Link Relative Method
100.6
100.5
100.4
100.3
100.2
100.1
100
99.9
99.8
99.7
99.6
99.5
99.4
99.3
Mar
Apr
May
Jun
Jul
Aug
Sep
Oct
Nov
Dec
All Years
Less Extremes

CANADIAN DOLLAR - MARCH - MONTHLY AVERAGE PRICE

Year of Expiration	Sep	Oct	Nov	Dec	Jan	Feb	Mar	Sep-Mar Average
1978	91.79	90.85	90.01	91.15	90.81	89.84	89.13	90.51
1979	85.56	84.82	85.65	84.92	84.06	83.64	84.85	84.78
1980	86.16	85.45	85.02	85.68	86.01	86.59	85.87	85.83
1981	86.31	86.01	85.11	84.14	84.12	83.37	83.41	84.64
1982	82.37	82.42	83.44	83.83	83.72	82.37	82.14	82.90
1983	80.40	80.85	81.20	80.53	81.27	81.44	81.61	81.04
1984	81.34	81.26	80.98	80.29	80.11	80.14	79.09	80.46
1985	75.92	75.52	75.60	75.51	75.36	73.79	71.84	74.79

	Sep	Oct	Nov	Dec	Jan	Feb	Mar
AVERAGE MOVE							
All Years		-0.33	-0.02	-0.12	-0.07	-0.53	-0.41
Less Extremes		-0.37	-0.05	-0.19	-0.08	-0.55	-0.42
Ave Up - All Years		0.25	0.57	0.73	0.53	0.26	0.47
Ave Down - All Years		-0.53	-0.61	-0.63	-0.28	-1.01	-0.93
COUNT							
Number Up		2	4	3	2	3	3
Number Down		6	4	5	6	5	5
Pct Up		25.0%	50.0%	37.5%	25.0%	37.5%	37.5%
Pct Down		75.0%	50.0%	62.5%	75.0%	62.5%	62.5%
EXTREMES							
Greatest Up		0.46	1.02	1.14	0.74	0.59	1.21
Greatest Down		-0.94	-0.90	-0.97	-0.85	-1.57	-1.95
SEASONAL INDEX : AVERAGE PERCENTAGE METHOD							
All Years	100.7	100.3	100.3	100.2	100.1	99.4	98.9
Less Extremes	100.8	100.3	100.4	100.1	100.1	99.3	99.1
SEASONAL INDEX : LINK RELATIVE METHOD							
All Years		100.3	100.0	100.2	100.2	100.2	99.7
Less Extremes		100.3	100.1	100.2	100.1	100.2	99.7

CANADIAN DOLLAR - MARCH - MONTH OF HIGH AND LOW

Year of Expiration	Sep	Oct	Nov	Dec	Jan	Feb	Mar
1978	H						L
1979			H			L	
1980			L			H	
1981	H					L	
1982				H			L
1983	L						H
1984	H						L
1985	H						L

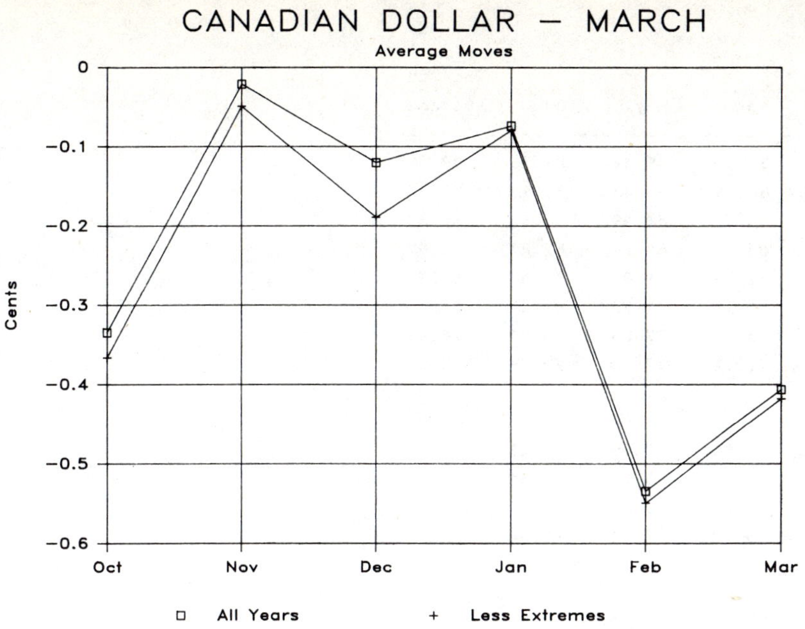
CANADIAN DOLLAR – MARCH
Average Moves
Cents
0
–0.1
–0.2
–0.3
–0.4
–0.5
–0.6
Oct
Nov
Dec
Jan
Feb
Mar
All Years
Less Extremes

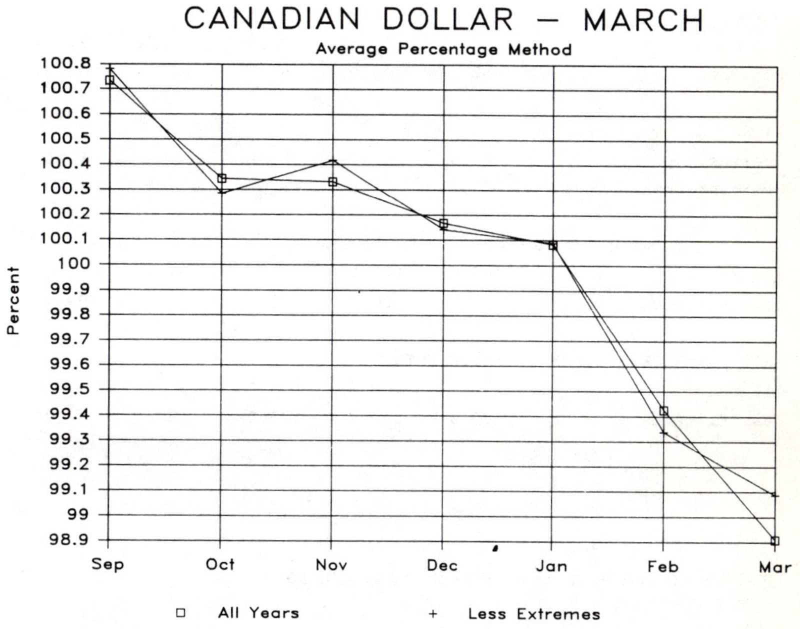
CANADIAN DOLLAR – MARCH
Average Percentage Method
Percent
100.8
100.7
100.6
100.5
100.4
100.3
100.2
100.1
100
99.9
99.8
99.7
99.6
99.5
99.4
99.3
99.2
99.1
99
98.9
Sep
Oct
Nov
Dec
Jan
Feb
Mar
All Years
Less Extremes

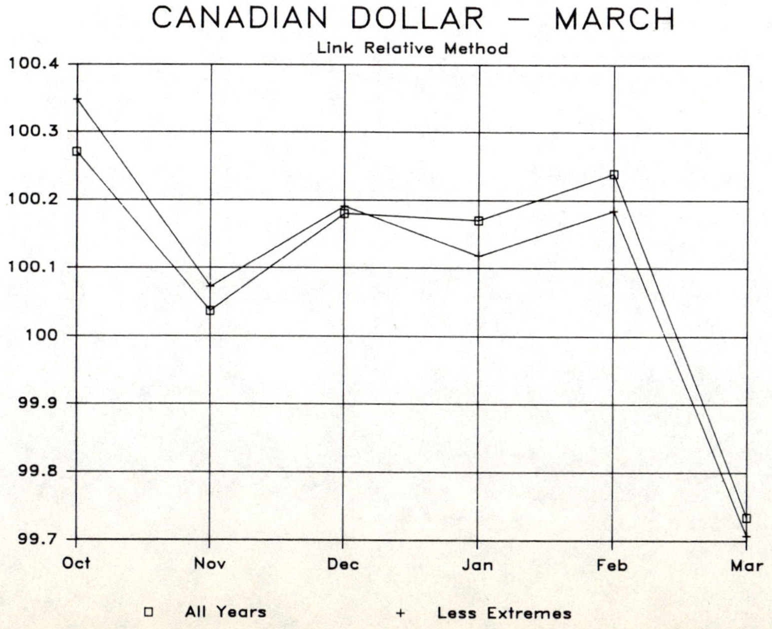
CANADIAN DOLLAR – MARCH
Link Relative Method
100.4
100.3
100.2
100.1
100
99.9
99.8
99.7
Oct
Nov
Dec
Jan
Feb
Mar
All Years
Less Extremes

CANADIAN DOLLAR - JUNE - MONTHLY AVERAGE PRICE

Year of Expiration	Dec	Jan	Feb	Mar	Apr	May	Jun	Dec-Jun Average
1978	91.13	90.85	89.82	88.71	87.45	89.39	89.29	89.52
1979	85.28	84.30	83.67	85.18	87.19	86.45	85.17	85.32
1980	85.84	86.20	86.97	85.97	84.57	84.99	86.65	85.88
1981	84.41	84.30	83.45	83.68	83.73	83.26	82.83	83.67
1982	83.47	83.58	82.38	81.70	81.59	81.01	79.57	81.90
1983	80.33	81.08	81.35	81.50	81.18	81.33	81.07	81.12
1984	80.35	80.13	80.17	78.76	78.18	77.29	76.93	78.83
1985	75.39	75.21	73.53	71.96	73.12	72.60	72.98	73.54

	Dec	Jan	Feb	Mar	Apr	May	Jun
AVERAGE MOVE							
All Years		-0.07	-0.54	-0.48	-0.06	-0.09	-0.23
Less Extremes		-0.05	-0.57	-0.64	-0.18	-0.29	-0.34
Ave Up - All Years		0.41	0.36	0.63	1.07	0.84	1.02
Ave Down - All Years		-0.35	-1.08	-1.15	-0.73	-0.64	-0.64
COUNT							
Number Up		3	3	3	3	3	2
Number Down		5	5	5	5	5	6
Pct Up		37.5%	37.5%	37.5%	37.5%	37.5%	25.0%
Pct Down		62.5%	62.5%	62.5%	62.5%	62.5%	75.0%
EXTREMES							
Greatest Up		0.76	0.77	1.52	2.01	1.94	1.66
Greatest Down		-0.98	-1.68	-1.57	-1.40	-0.89	-1.44
SEASONAL INDEX : AVERAGE PERCENTAGE METHOD							
All Years	101.0	100.9	100.2	99.6	99.6	99.4	99.2
Less Extremes	101.1	101.0	100.4	99.8	99.5	99.4	99.2
SEASONAL INDEX : LINK RELATIVE METHOD							
All Years		100.5	100.6	100.1	99.6	99.7	99.8
Less Extremes		100.6	100.7	100.3	99.7	99.7	99.6

CANADIAN DOLLAR - JUNE - MONTH OF HIGH AND LOW

Year of Expiration	Dec	Jan	Feb	Mar	Apr	May	Jun
1978	H				L		
1979			L		H		
1980			H		L		
1981	H						L
1982		H					L
1983	L			H			
1984	H						L
1985	H			L			

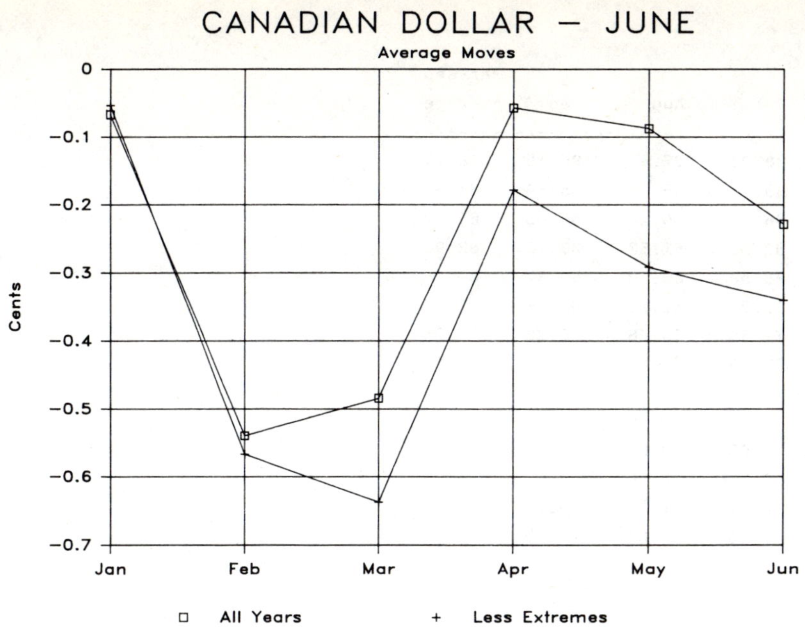
CANADIAN DOLLAR — JUNE
Average Moves
Cents
0
-0.1
-0.2
-0.3
-0.4
-0.5
-0.6
-0.7
Jan
Feb
Mar
Apr
May
Jun
All Years
Less Extremes

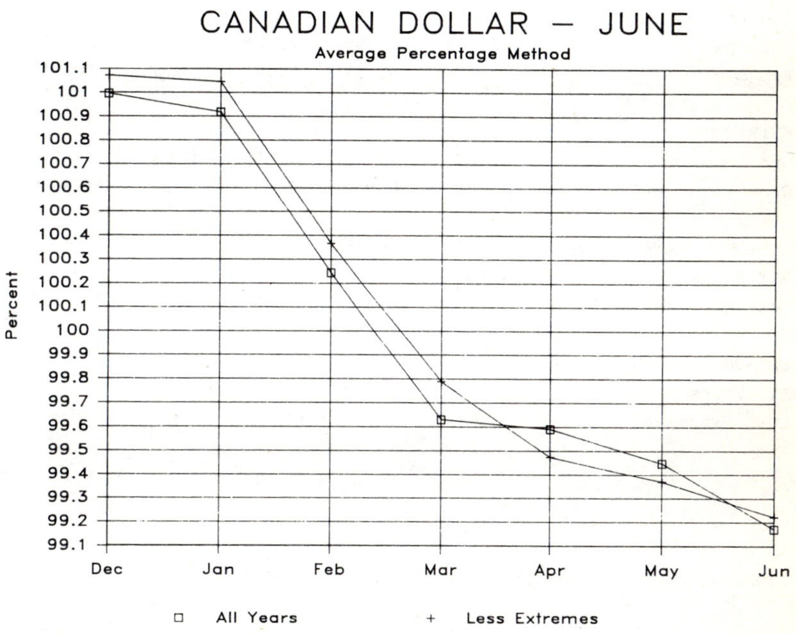
CANADIAN DOLLAR — JUNE
Average Percentage Method
Percent
101.1
101
100.9
100.8
100.7
100.6
100.5
100.4
100.3
100.2
100.1
100
99.9
99.8
99.7
99.6
99.5
99.4
99.3
99.2
99.1
Dec
Jan
Feb
Mar
Apr
May
Jun
All Years
Less Extremes

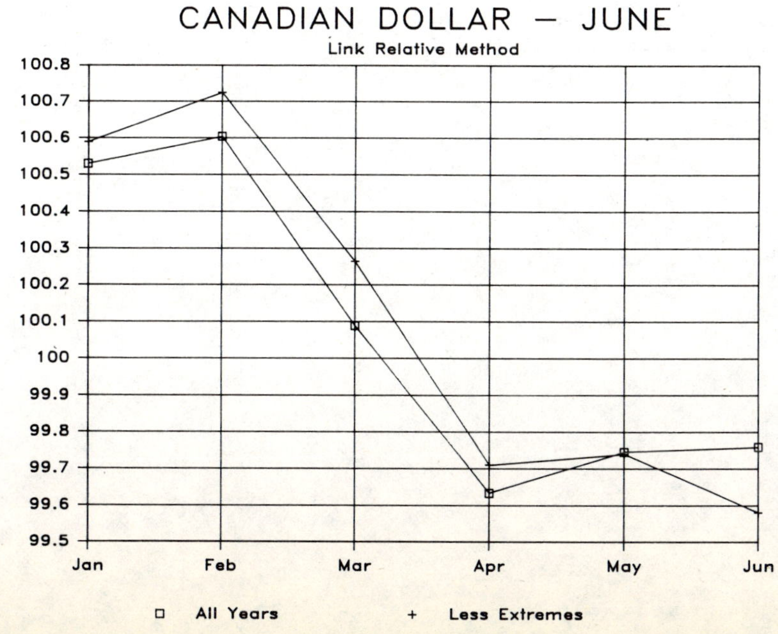
CANADIAN DOLLAR — JUNE
Link Relative Method
100.8
100.7
100.6
100.5
100.4
100.3
100.2
100.1
100
99.9
99.8
99.7
99.6
99.5
Jan
Feb
Mar
Apr
May
Jun
All Years
Less Extremes

CANADIAN DOLLAR - SEPTEMBER - MONTHLY AVERAGE PRICE

Year of Expiration	Mar	Apr	May	Jun	Jul	Aug	Sep	Mar-Sep Average
1978	88.63	87.27	89.35	89.13	88.93	87.63	86.15	88.16
1979	85.27	87.26	86.43	85.20	85.85	85.42	85.84	85.90
1980	86.51	84.79	84.90	86.40	86.51	86.26	86.05	85.92
1981	83.71	83.66	83.29	82.80	82.35	81.57	83.18	82.94
1982	81.47	81.40	80.80	78.04	78.58	80.10	80.87	80.18
1983	81.44	81.13	81.28	81.23	81.23	81.13	81.16	81.23
1984	78.79	78.20	77.31	76.67	75.46	76.68	76.20	77.04
1985	71.69	72.94	72.33	72.81	73.78	73.63	72.91	72.87

	Mar	Apr	May	Jun	Jul	Aug	Sep
AVERAGE MOVE							
All Years		-0.11	-0.12	-0.43	0.05	-0.03	-0.01
Less Extremes		-0.19	-0.36	-0.36	0.11	-0.08	-0.03
Ave Up - All Years		1.62	0.78	0.99	0.57	1.37	0.71
Ave Down - All Years		-0.68	-0.66	-0.90	-0.46	-0.50	-0.72
COUNT							
Number Up		2	3	2	4	2	4
Number Down		6	5	6	4	6	4
Pct Up		25.0%	37.5%	25.0%	50.0%	25.0%	50.0%
Pct Down		75.0%	62.5%	75.0%	50.0%	75.0%	50.0%
EXTREMES							
Greatest Up		1.99	2.09	1.49	0.96	1.52	1.61
Greatest Down		-1.71	-0.88	-2.76	-1.21	-1.30	-1.47
SEASONAL INDEX : AVERAGE PERCENTAGE METHOD							
All Years	100.5	100.4	100.2	99.7	99.8	99.7	99.7
Less Extremes	100.6	100.5	100.2	99.8	99.8	99.8	99.9
SEASONAL INDEX : LINK RELATIVE METHOD							
All Years		100.3	100.3	100.1	99.7	99.8	99.9
Less Extremes		100.4	100.3	100.0	99.6	99.9	99.9

CANADIAN DOLLAR - SEPTEMBER - MONTH OF HIGH AND LOW

Year of Expiration	Mar	Apr	May	Jun	Jul	Aug	Sep
1978			H				L
1979		H		L			
1980		L			H		
1981	H					L	
1982	H			L			
1983	H					L	
1984	H				L		
1985	L				H		

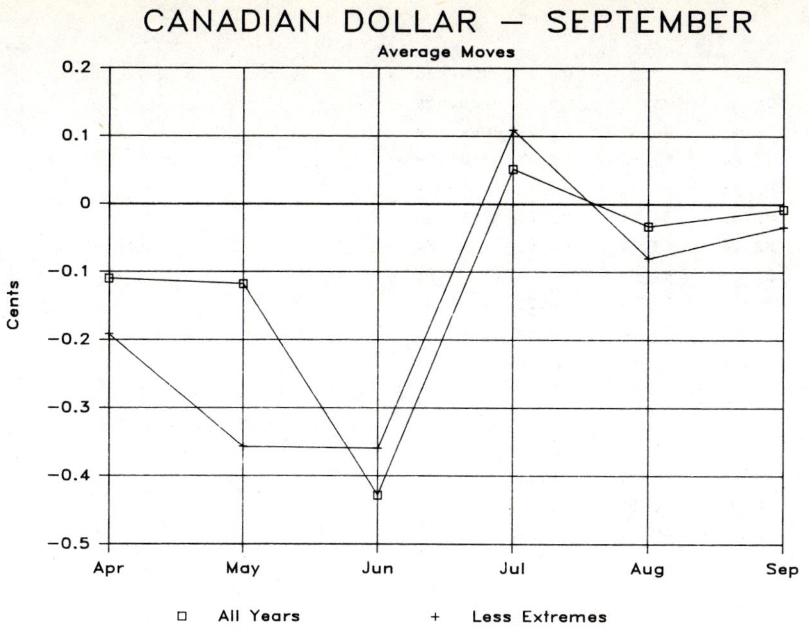
CANADIAN DOLLAR — SEPTEMBER
Average Moves
Cents
0.2
0.1
0
−0.1
−0.2
−0.3
−0.4
−0.5
Apr
May
Jun
Jul
Aug
Sep
All Years
Less Extremes

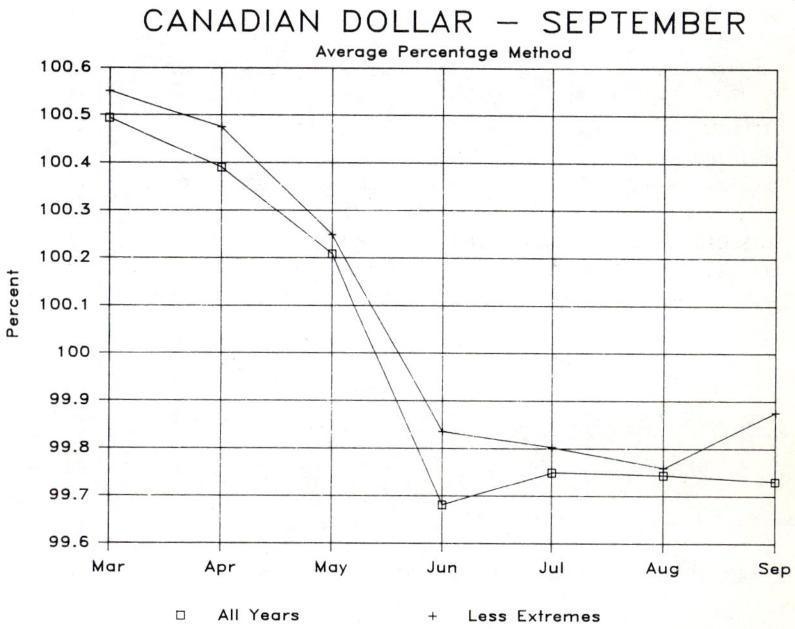
CANADIAN DOLLAR — SEPTEMBER
Average Percentage Method
Percent
100.6
100.5
100.4
100.3
100.2
100.1
100
99.9
99.8
99.7
99.6
Mar
Apr
May
Jun
Jul
Aug
Sep
All Years
Less Extremes

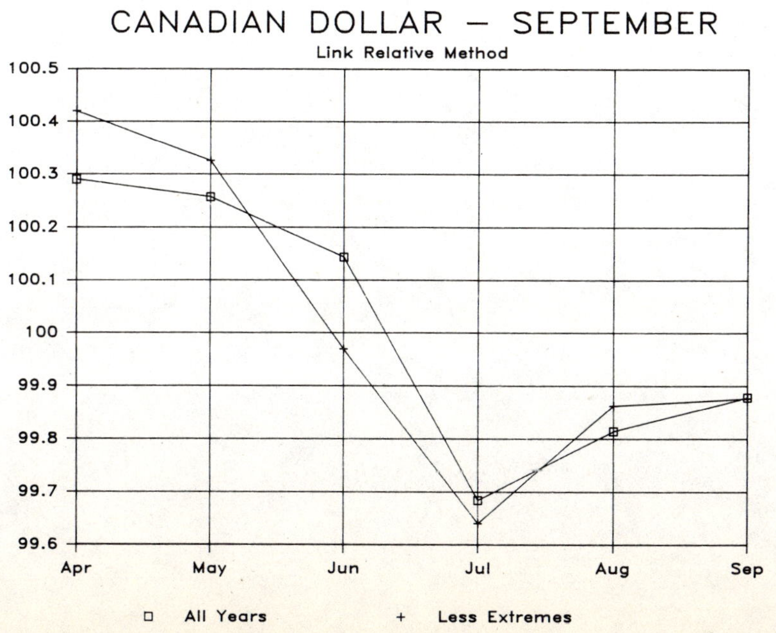
CANADIAN DOLLAR — SEPTEMBER
Link Relative Method
100.5
100.4
100.3
100.2
100.1
100
99.9
99.8
99.7
99.6
Apr
May
Jun
Jul
Aug
Sep
All Years
Less Extremes

CANADIAN DOLLAR - DECEMBER - MONTHLY AVERAGE PRICE

Year of Expiration	Jun	Jul	Aug	Sep	Oct	Nov	Dec	Jun-Dec Average
1978	89.12	88.96	87.54	85.61	84.67	85.30	84.88	86.58
1979	85.18	85.87	85.41	86.01	85.20	84.81	85.72	85.46
1980	86.27	86.34	86.36	86.12	85.83	84.51	83.55	85.57
1981	82.62	82.15	81.11	82.74	82.79	83.94	84.37	82.82
1982	77.81	78.25	79.56	80.67	81.09	81.44	80.73	79.93
1983	81.24	81.29	81.27	81.26	81.23	80.89	80.21	81.06
1984	76.67	75.32	76.62	75.97	75.65	75.81	75.66	75.96
1985	72.54	73.56	73.45	72.82	73.10	72.60	71.78	72.83

	Jun	Jul	Aug	Sep	Oct	Nov	Dec
AVERAGE MOVE							
All Years		0.04	-0.05	-0.01	-0.21	-0.03	-0.30
Less Extremes		0.11	-0.05	0.03	-0.19	-0.01	-0.39
Ave Up - All Years		0.46	0.88	1.12	0.25	0.58	0.67
Ave Down - All Years		-0.66	-0.61	-0.69	-0.48	-0.64	-0.63
COUNT							
Number Up		5	3	3	3	4	2
Number Down		3	5	5	5	4	6
Pct Up		62.5%	37.5%	37.5%	37.5%	50.0%	25.0%
Pct Down		37.5%	62.5%	62.5%	62.5%	50.0%	75.0%
EXTREMES							
Greatest Up		1.03	1.31	1.64	0.41	1.15	0.91
Greatest Down		-1.35	-1.42	-1.92	-0.95	-1.33	-0.96
SEASONAL INDEX : AVERAGE PERCENTAGE METHOD							
All Years	100.2	100.2	100.2	100.2	99.9	99.9	99.5
Less Extremes	100.2	100.2	100.4	100.2	100.0	99.8	99.4
SEASONAL INDEX : LINK RELATIVE METHOD							
All Years		100.0	100.1	100.1	100.2	100.0	100.0
Less Extremes		99.9	100.1	100.1	100.2	100.0	100.1

CANADIAN DOLLAR - DECEMBER - MONTH OF HIGH AND LOW

Year of Expiration	Jun	Jul	Aug	Sep	Oct	Nov	Dec
1978	H				L		
1979				H		L	
1980			H				L
1981			L				H
1982	L					H	
1983		H					L
1984	H				L		
1985		H					L

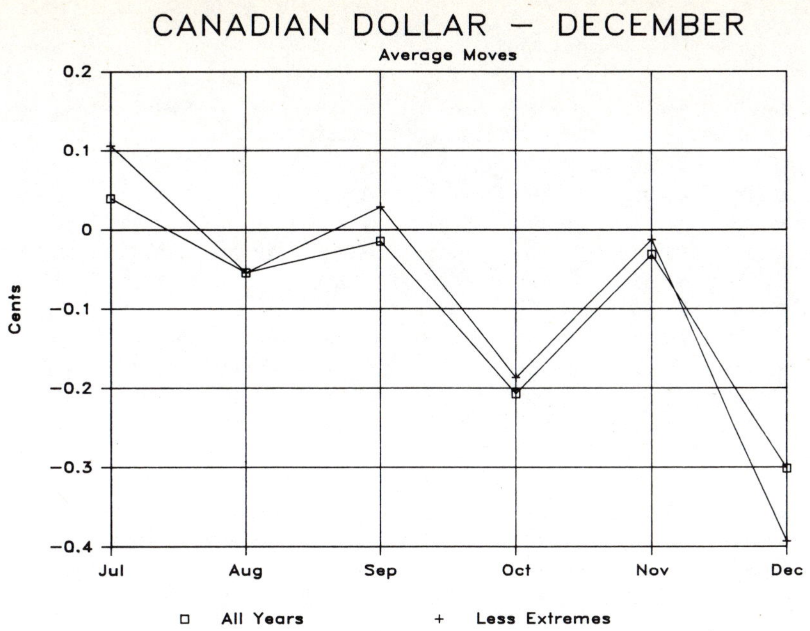
CANADIAN DOLLAR — DECEMBER
Average Moves
Cents
0.2
0.1
0
−0.1
−0.2
−0.3
−0.4
Jul
Aug
Sep
Oct
Nov
Dec
All Years
Less Extremes

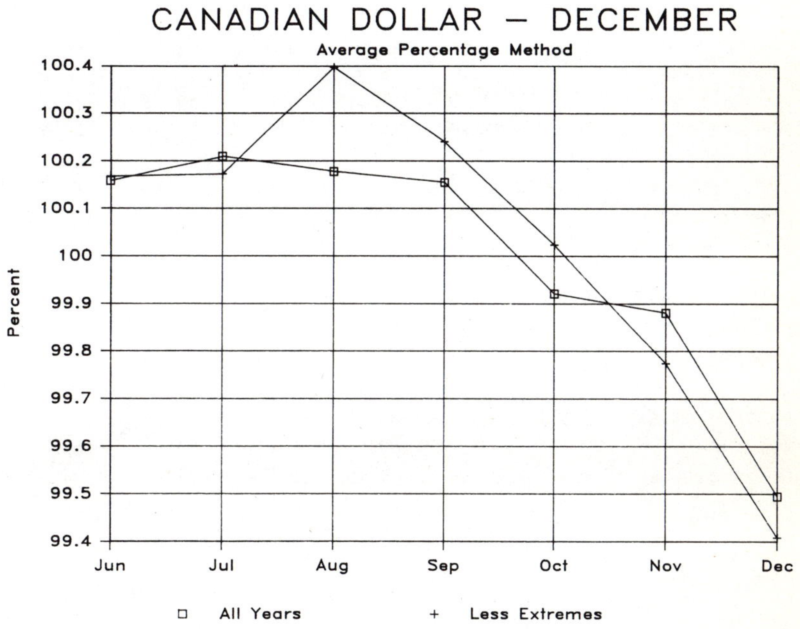
CANADIAN DOLLAR — DECEMBER
Average Percentage Method
Percent
100.4
100.3
100.2
100.1
100
99.9
99.8
99.7
99.6
99.5
99.4
Jun
Jul
Aug
Sep
Oct
Nov
Dec
All Years
Less Extremes

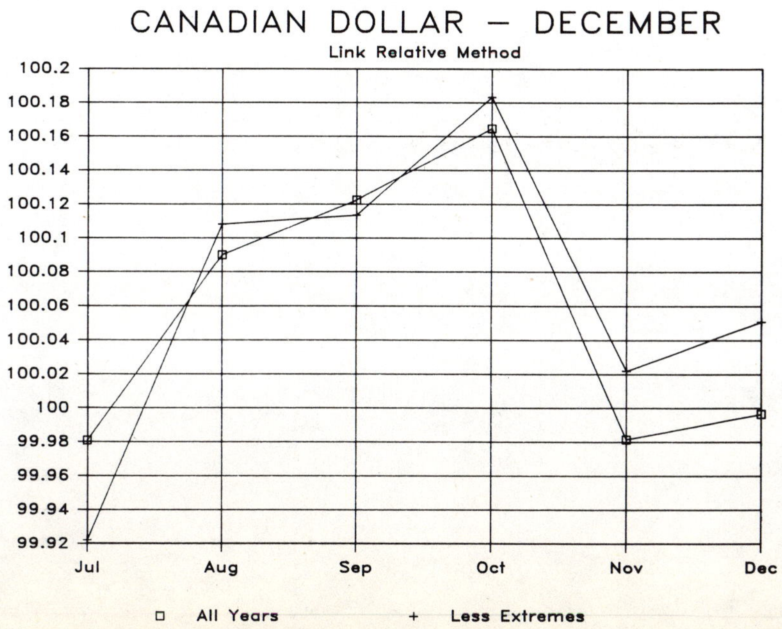
CANADIAN DOLLAR — DECEMBER
Link Relative Method
100.2
100.18
100.16
100.14
100.12
100.1
100.08
100.06
100.04
100.02
100
99.98
99.96
99.94
99.92
Jul
Aug
Sep
Oct
Nov
Dec
All Years
Less Extremes

DEUTSCHE MARK - MARCH - MONTHLY AVERAGE PRICE

Year of Expiration	May	Jun	Jul	Aug	Sep	Oct	Nov	Dec	Jan	Feb	Mar	May-Mar Average
1976	43.36	43.34	41.07	39.66	38.86	39.35	39.02	38.38	38.54	39.14	38.87	39.96
1977	39.95	39.53	39.34	39.92	40.42	41.35	41.58	41.98	41.82	41.61	41.77	40.84
1978	43.06	43.15	44.46	43.84	43.63	44.54	45.09	46.95	47.54	48.30	49.33	45.44
1979	49.35	49.88	50.45	51.66	52.27	55.98	54.18	54.34	54.75	54.23	53.88	52.81
1980	54.29	54.70	56.20	56.11	57.25	57.33	57.59	58.50	58.55	57.48	55.28	56.66
1981	56.84	57.03	57.72	56.87	56.93	55.35	53.35	51.93	50.48	46.95	47.10	53.69
1982	45.06	43.24	42.25	41.33	43.75	45.37	45.36	44.61	43.85	42.44	42.28	43.59
1983	41.14	41.14	42.14	41.19	40.75	40.06	39.52	41.69	42.07	41.27	41.60	41.14
1984	38.27	40.80	39.86	38.46	38.28	39.06	37.78	36.76	35.80	37.20	38.71	38.27
1985	38.24	38.24	36.57	35.90	33.96	33.28	33.84	32.48	31.70	30.38	29.62	34.02
AVERAGE MOVE												
All Years		0.15	-0.10	-0.51	0.12	0.56	-0.44	0.03	-0.25	-0.61	-0.06	
Less Extremes		0.10	-0.03	-0.62	0.08	0.43	-0.36	-0.06	-0.21	-0.50	0.01	
Ave Up - All Years		0.54	1.01	0.90	0.95	1.22	0.40	1.10	0.32	0.92	0.63	
Ave Down - All Years		-0.75	-1.21	-0.86	-0.71	-0.98	-0.99	-1.04	-0.82	-1.27	-0.75	
COUNT												
Number Up		7	5	2	5	7	4	5	5	3	5	
Number Down		3	5	8	5	3	6	5	5	7	5	
Pct Up		70.0%	50.0%	20.0%	50.0%	70.0%	40.0%	50.0%	50.0%	30.0%	50.0%	
Pct Down		30.0%	50.0%	80.0%	50.0%	30.0%	60.0%	50.0%	50.0%	70.0%	50.0%	
EXTREMES												
Greatest Up		2.53	1.50	1.22	2.42	3.71	0.56	2.17	0.59	1.40	1.51	
Greatest Down		-1.82	-2.28	-1.41	-1.94	-1.57	-2.00	-1.42	-1.45	-3.53	-2.20	
SEASONAL INDEX : AVERAGE PERCENTAGE METHOD												
All Years	101.2	101.6	101.0	99.7	99.8	100.9	100.1	100.0	99.4	98.2	98.2	
Less Extremes	100.8	101.1	100.9	99.6	99.4	100.7	100.1	100.2	99.5	98.5	98.3	
SEASONAL INDEX : LINK RELATIVE METHOD												
All Years		100.3	100.1	99.1	99.5	101.0	100.4	100.6	100.2	99.3	99.5	
Less Extremes		100.3	100.4	99.2	99.6	100.9	100.4	100.4	100.1	99.2	99.4	

DEUTSCHE MARK - MARCH - MONTH OF HIGH AND LOW

Year of Expiration	May	Jun	Jul	Aug	Sep	Oct	Nov	Dec	Jan	Feb	Mar
1976	H							L			
1977			L					H			
1978	H										H
1979	L					H					
1980	L								H		
1981			H							L	
1982				L		H					
1983			H				L				
1984		H							L		
1985		H									L

DEUTSCHE MARK – MARCH
Average Moves

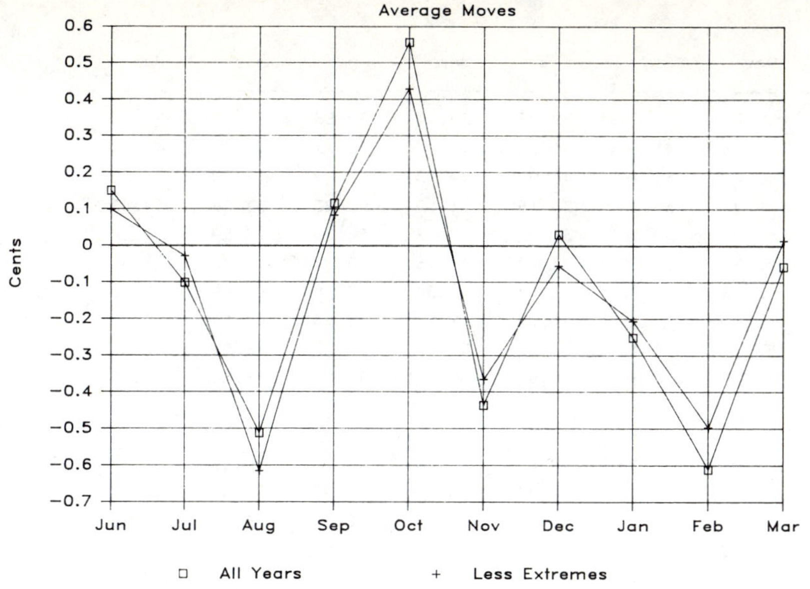

DEUTSCHE MARK – MARCH
Average Percentage Method

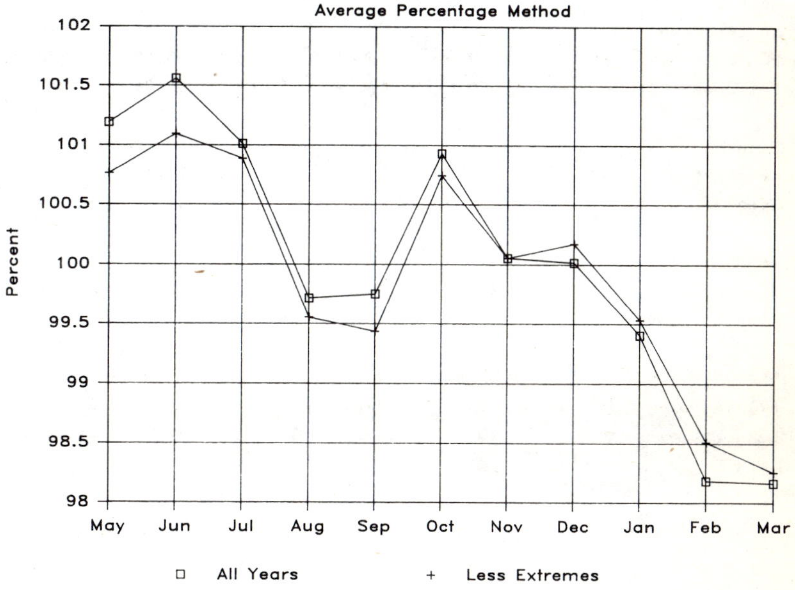

DEUTSCHE MARK – MARCH
Link Relative Method

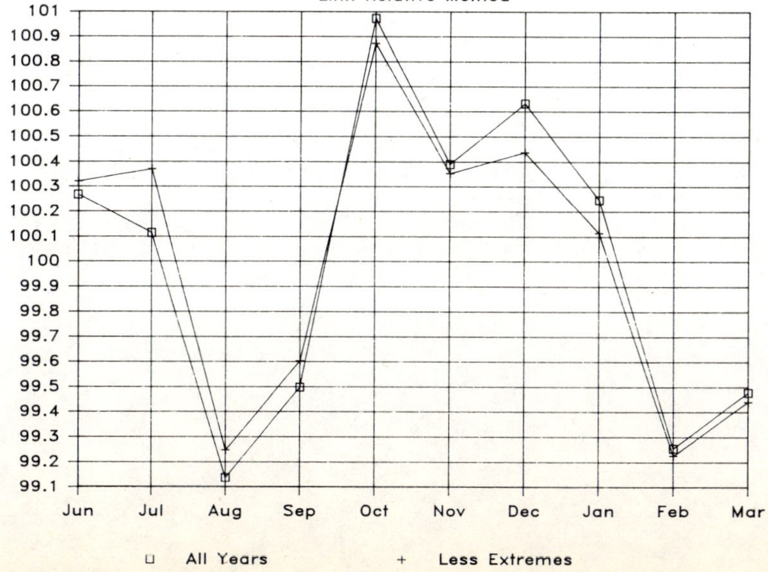

DEUTSCHE MARK - JUNE - MONTHLY AVERAGE PRICE

Year of Expiration	Aug	Sep	Oct	Nov	Dec	Jan	Feb	Mar	Apr	May	Jun	Aug-Jun Average
1976	39.86	39.17	39.63	39.27	38.66	38.76	39.37	39.31	39.55	39.09	38.80	39.22
1977	41.82	40.54	41.43	41.68	42.05	41.90	41.71	41.87	42.21	42.45	42.41	41.82
1978	47.73	47.73	44.97	45.54	47.42	48.13	48.90	49.73	49.32	47.70	47.92	47.73
1979	52.28	52.95	56.86	55.11	55.40	55.83	55.18	54.60	53.25	52.68	52.45	54.24
1980	56.56	57.83	58.09	58.34	59.35	59.42	58.42	55.27	54.20	55.89	56.54	57.26
1981	57.10	57.50	55.95	54.08	52.75	51.38	47.69	47.85	46.50	43.92	41.97	50.61
1982	41.87	44.26	45.84	45.71	45.03	44.38	43.02	42.58	42.19	43.46	41.91	43.66
1983	41.63	41.09	40.48	39.84	42.05	42.45	41.67	41.96	41.26	40.68	39.12	41.11
1984	38.78	38.64	39.43	38.17	37.13	36.12	37.59	39.00	38.12	36.57	36.97	37.87
1985	36.43	34.49	33.74	34.22	32.80	31.94	30.62	30.62	32.57	32.24	32.55	32.93

	Aug	Sep	Oct	Nov	Dec	Jan	Feb	Mar	Apr	May	Jun
AVERAGE MOVE											
All Years		0.01	0.22	-0.45	0.07	-0.23	-0.62	-0.14	-0.36	-0.45	-0.40
Less Extremes		-0.04	0.13	-0.40	-0.01	-0.21	-0.49	0.05	-0.53	-0.45	-0.34
Ave Up - All Years		0.95	1.32	0.39	1.16	0.34	0.95	0.48	0.84	1.07	0.39
Ave Down - All Years		-0.92	-1.42	-1.00	-1.02	-0.81	-1.29	-1.06	-0.88	-1.10	-0.94
COUNT											
Number Up		5	6	4	5	5	3	6	3	3	4
Number Down		5	4	6	5	5	7	4	7	7	6
Pct Up		50.0%	60.0%	40.0%	50.0%	50.0%	30.0%	60.0%	30.0%	30.0%	40.0%
Pct Down		50.0%	40.0%	60.0%	50.0%	50.0%	70.0%	40.0%	70.0%	70.0%	60.0%
EXTREMES											
Greatest Up		2.39	3.91	0.57	2.21	0.70	1.47	1.41	1.95	1.69	0.64
Greatest Down		-1.95	-2.77	-1.87	-1.42	-1.37	-3.69	-3.15	-1.36	-2.58	-1.95
SEASONAL INDEX : AVERAGE PERCENTAGE METHOD											
All Years	102.0	101.7	102.1	101.2	101.2	100.5	99.3	99.2	98.6	97.6	96.7
Less Extremes	101.4	100.8	102.1	101.2	101.2	100.8	99.7	99.3	98.9	98.4	97.8
SEASONAL INDEX : LINK RELATIVE METHOD											
All Years		99.9	100.8	100.3	100.8	100.6	99.7	100.0	99.9	99.3	98.7
Less Extremes		100.0	100.8	100.4	100.7	100.5	99.8	100.3	99.7	99.1	98.7

DEUTSCHE MARK - JUNE - MONTH OF HIGH AND LOW

Year of Expiration	Aug	Sep	Oct	Nov	Dec	Jan	Feb	Mar	Apr	May	Jun
1976	H				L						
1977	L									H	
1978	L							H			
1979	L		H								
1980						H			L		
1981		H									L
1982	L		H								
1983						H					L
1984			H			L					
1985	H						L				

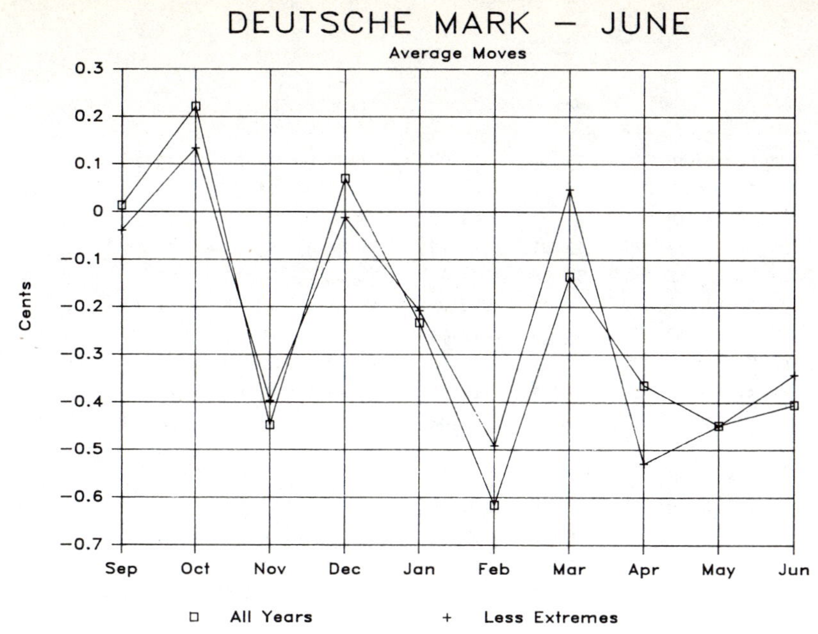
DEUTSCHE MARK – JUNE
Average Moves
0.3
0.2
0.1
0
–0.1
–0.2
–0.3
–0.4
–0.5
–0.6
–0.7
Cents
Sep
Oct
Nov
Dec
Jan
Feb
Mar
Apr
May
Jun
All Years
Less Extremes

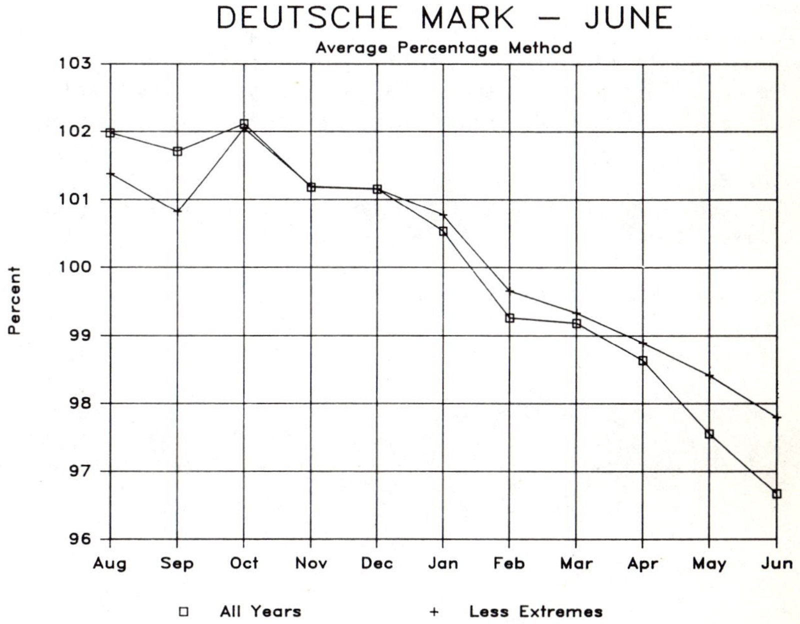
DEUTSCHE MARK – JUNE
Average Percentage Method
103
102
101
100
99
98
97
96
Percent
Aug
Sep
Oct
Nov
Dec
Jan
Feb
Mar
Apr
May
Jun
All Years
Less Extremes

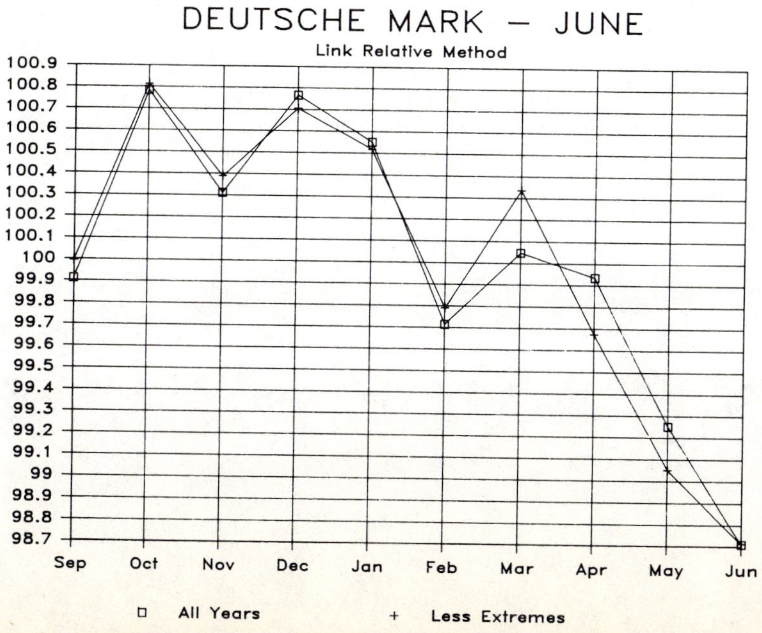
DEUTSCHE MARK – JUNE
Link Relative Method
100.9
100.8
100.7
100.6
100.5
100.4
100.3
100.2
100.1
100
99.9
99.8
99.7
99.6
99.5
99.4
99.3
99.2
99.1
99
98.9
98.8
98.7
Sep
Oct
Nov
Dec
Jan
Feb
Mar
Apr
May
Jun
All Years
Less Extremes

DEUTSCHE MARK - SEPTEMBER - MONTHLY AVERAGE PRICE

Year of Expiration	Nov	Dec	Jan	Feb	Mar	Apr	May	Jun	Jul	Aug	Sep	Nov-Sep Average
1976	39.48	38.90	38.98	39.62	39.60	39.81	39.34	39.04	38.93	39.58	39.74	39.36
1977	41.90	42.16	42.02	41.81	41.98	42.35	42.67	42.70	43.99	43.26	43.04	42.53
1978	45.49	47.85	48.70	49.47	50.33	49.86	48.26	48.60	49.13	50.32	50.38	48.94
1979	56.15	56.44	56.82	56.04	55.38	53.92	53.31	53.72	55.24	54.90	55.16	55.19
1980	57.30	60.03	60.13	59.26	56.30	55.13	56.15	56.60	57.22	55.94	56.21	57.30
1981	54.80	53.48	52.09	48.28	48.28	46.86	44.49	42.57	41.38	40.17	41.39	46.71
1982	46.05	45.35	44.91	43.59	43.18	42.83	44.09	41.84	40.92	40.41	40.20	43.03
1983	40.68	43.14	42.84	42.06	42.41	41.72	41.11	39.68	38.94	37.57	37.34	40.68
1984	38.55	37.51	36.47	37.97	39.48	38.61	37.11	37.05	35.44	34.86	33.39	36.95
1985	34.65	33.19	32.22	30.88	30.93	32.82	32.46	32.83	34.59	35.95	34.35	33.17
AVERAGE MOVE												
All Years		0.30	-0.29	-0.62	-0.11	-0.40	-0.49	-0.44	0.11	-0.28	-0.17	
Less Extremes		0.22	-0.29	-0.49	0.04	-0.55	-0.48	-0.32	0.12	-0.35	-0.17	
Ave Up - All Years		1.62	0.35	0.97	0.59	0.82	0.87	0.32	1.14	1.07	0.39	
Ave Down - All Years		-1.02	-0.71	-1.30	-0.81	-0.92	-1.07	-1.19	-0.92	-0.86	-0.74	
COUNT												
Number Up		5	4	3	5	3	3	5	5	3	5	
Number Down		5	6	7	5	7	7	5	5	7	5	
Pct Up		50.0%	40.0%	30.0%	50.0%	30.0%	30.0%	50.0%	50.0%	30.0%	50.0%	
Pct Down		50.0%	60.0%	70.0%	50.0%	70.0%	70.0%	50.0%	50.0%	70.0%	50.0%	
EXTREMES												
Greatest Up		2.74	0.85	1.50	1.51	1.90	1.27	0.45	1.76	1.36	1.22	
Greatest Down		-1.46	-1.40	-3.81	-2.96	-1.46	-2.38	-2.26	-1.62	-1.37	-1.60	
SEASONAL INDEX : AVERAGE PERCENTAGE METHOD												
All Years	102.7	103.0	102.2	100.9	100.9	100.2	99.1	98.0	98.2	97.7	97.1	
Less Extremes	102.0	102.2	101.7	101.5	101.1	100.2	99.1	98.6	98.7	97.8	97.3	
SEASONAL INDEX : LINK RELATIVE METHOD												
All Years		101.0	100.7	99.9	100.4	100.3	99.6	99.1	99.7	99.6	99.5	
Less Extremes		101.0	100.7	100.1	100.7	100.1	99.4	99.2	99.8	99.5	99.5	

DEUTSCHE MARK - SEPTEMBER - MONTH OF HIGH AND LOW

Year of Expiration	Nov	Dec	Jan	Feb	Mar	Apr	May	Jun	Jul	Aug	Sep
1976		L				H					
1977				L					H		
1978	L										H
1979			H				L				
1980			H			L					
1981	H									L	
1982	H										L
1983	H										L
1984					H						L
1985				L						H	

DEUTSCHE MARK – SEPTEMBER

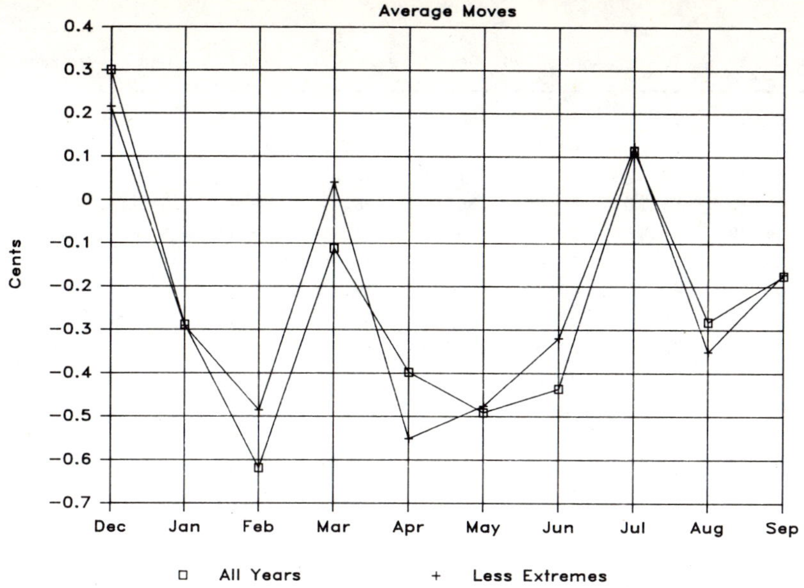

DEUTSCHE MARK – SEPTEMBER

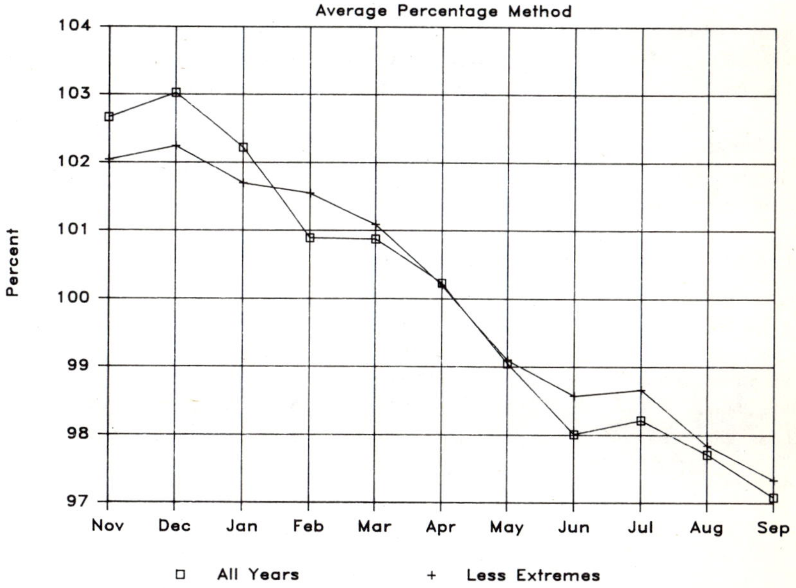

DEUTSCHE MARK – SEPTEMBER

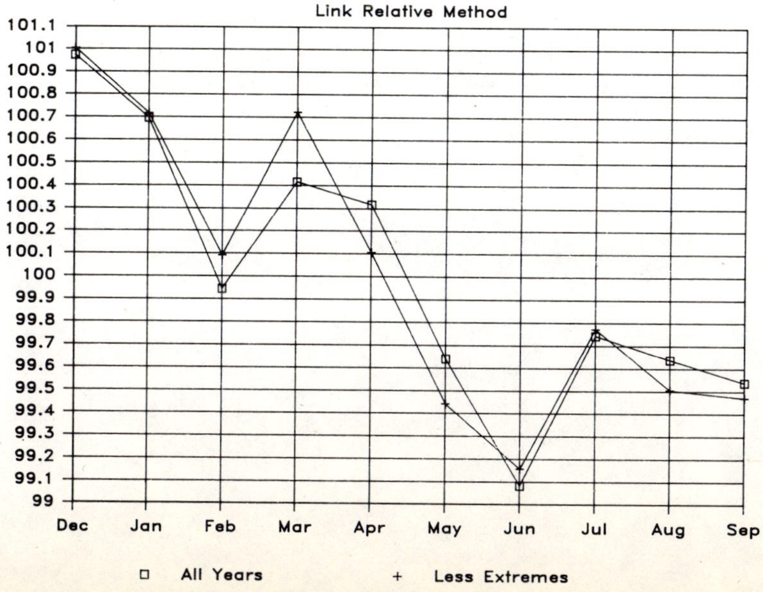

DEUTSCHE MARK - DECEMBER - MONTHLY AVERAGE PRICE

Year of Expiration	Feb	Mar	Apr	May	Jun	Jul	Aug	Sep	Oct	Nov	Dec	Feb-Dec Average
1976	39.84	39.82	40.06	39.63	39.28	39.11	39.73	40.32	41.26	41.47	41.64	40.19
1977	41.93	42.10	42.51	42.89	42.93	44.25	43.56	43.34	44.16	44.73	46.19	43.51
1978	50.00	50.87	50.37	48.81	49.27	49.80	50.99	51.53	55.02	53.08	52.57	51.12
1979	56.83	56.09	54.46	53.81	54.20	55.77	55.55	56.54	56.49	56.71	57.60	55.82
1980	60.02	57.08	55.88	56.47	56.80	57.43	56.35	56.32	54.69	52.47	50.78	55.84
1981	48.79	48.66	47.16	44.95	42.95	41.91	40.80	43.16	44.78	45.01	44.57	44.79
1982	44.24	43.71	43.36	44.72	42.51	41.50	40.78	40.31	39.72	39.24	40.92	41.91
1983	42.53	42.83	42.16	41.53	40.11	39.40	38.01	37.89	38.69	37.42	36.44	39.73
1984	38.37	39.96	39.12	37.67	37.64	35.99	35.39	33.50	32.87	33.51	32.39	36.04
1985	31.20	31.27	33.14	32.72	33.03	34.85	36.27	35.61	38.05	38.67	39.61	34.95
AVERAGE MOVE												
All Years		-0.14	-0.42	-0.50	-0.45	0.13	-0.26	0.11	0.72	-0.34	0.04	
Less Extremes		.00	-0.55	-0.52	-0.34	0.14	-0.33	0.08	0.67	-0.23	0.05	
Ave Up - All Years		0.60	0.84	0.78	0.31	1.17	1.07	1.12	1.69	0.41	1.03	
Ave Down - All Years		-0.87	-0.95	-1.05	-1.20	-0.92	-0.83	-0.57	-0.72	-1.48	-0.95	
COUNT												
Number Up		5	3	3	5	5	3	4	6	6	5	
Number Down		5	7	7	5	5	7	6	4	4	5	
Pct Up		50.0%	30.0%	30.0%	50.0%	50.0%	30.0%	40.0%	60.0%	60.0%	50.0%	
Pct Down		50.0%	70.0%	70.0%	50.0%	50.0%	70.0%	60.0%	40.0%	40.0%	50.0%	
EXTREMES												
Greatest Up		1.59	1.87	1.36	0.46	1.82	1.42	2.36	3.49	0.64	1.69	
Greatest Down		-2.94	-1.63	-2.21	-2.21	-1.64	-1.39	-1.89	-1.62	-2.23	-1.69	
SEASONAL INDEX : AVERAGE PERCENTAGE METHOD												
All Years	102.0	101.9	101.2	100.0	98.9	99.1	98.5	98.6	100.3	99.7	99.9	
Less Extremes	102.7	102.3	101.0	99.9	98.7	99.3	98.8	98.8	100.4	99.2	99.4	
SEASONAL INDEX : LINK RELATIVE METHOD												
All Years		101.2	100.8	99.8	98.9	99.2	98.8	99.1	101.0	100.5	100.8	
Less Extremes		101.5	100.6	99.5	98.9	99.3	98.8	99.0	100.9	100.6	100.8	

DEUTSCHE MARK - DECEMBER - MONTH OF HIGH AND LOW

Year of Expiration	Feb	Mar	Apr	May	Jun	Jul	Aug	Sep	Oct	Nov	Dec
1976						L					H
1977	L										H
1978				L					H		
1979				L							H
1980	H										L
1981	H						L				
1982				H						L	
1983		H									L
1984		H									L
1985	L										H

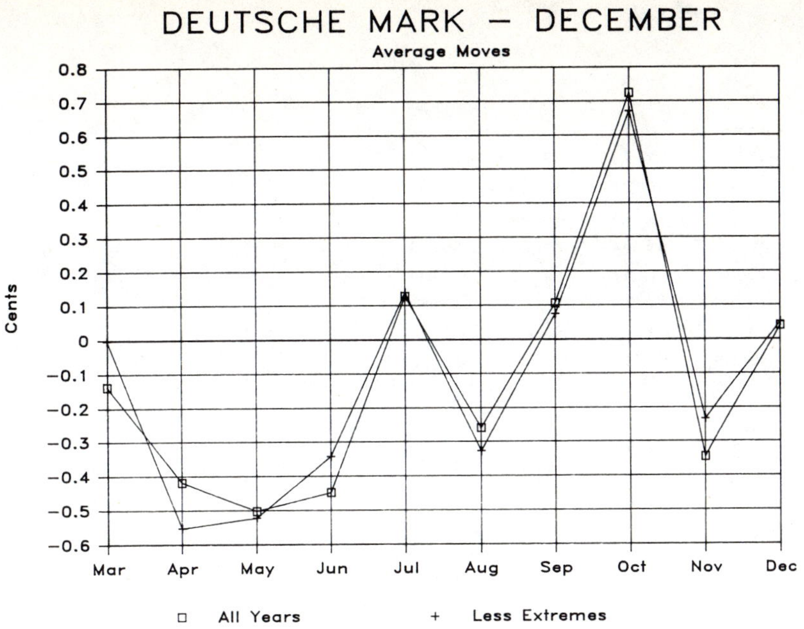
DEUTSCHE MARK – DECEMBER
Average Moves
Cents
0.8
0.7
0.6
0.5
0.4
0.3
0.2
0.1
0
−0.1
−0.2
−0.3
−0.4
−0.5
−0.6
Mar
Apr
May
Jun
Jul
Aug
Sep
Oct
Nov
Dec
□ All Years
+ Less Extremes

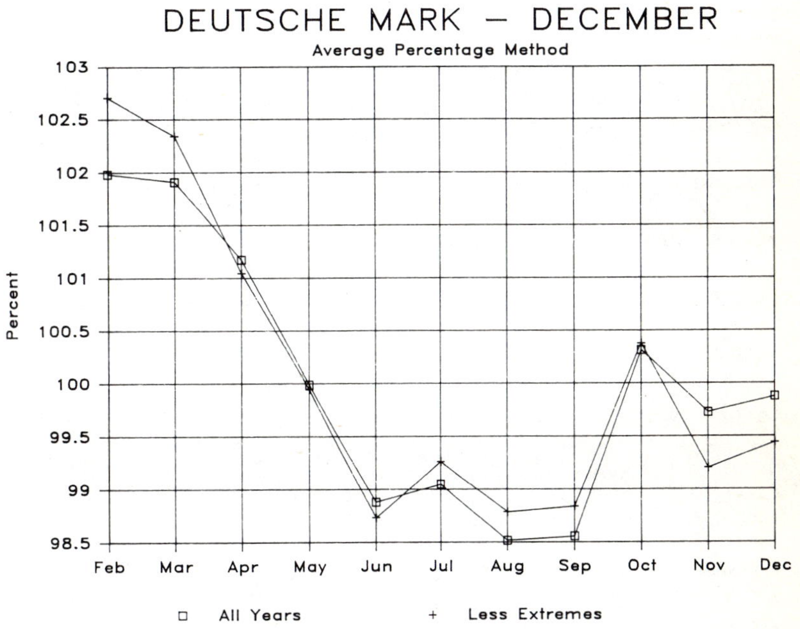
DEUTSCHE MARK – DECEMBER
Average Percentage Method
Percent
103
102.5
102
101.5
101
100.5
100
99.5
99
98.5
Feb
Mar
Apr
May
Jun
Jul
Aug
Sep
Oct
Nov
Dec
□ All Years
+ Less Extremes

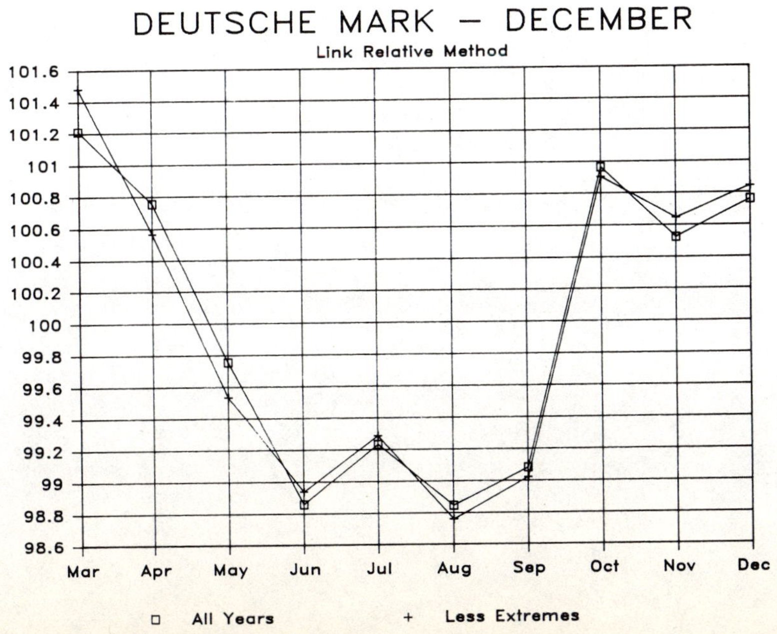
DEUTSCHE MARK – DECEMBER
Link Relative Method
101.6
101.4
101.2
101
100.8
100.6
100.4
100.2
100
99.8
99.6
99.4
99.2
99
98.8
98.6
Mar
Apr
May
Jun
Jul
Aug
Sep
Oct
Nov
Dec
□ All Years
+ Less Extremes

JAPANESE YEN - MARCH - MONTHLY AVERAGE PRICE

Year of Expiration	Sep	Oct	Nov	Dec	Jan	Feb	Mar	Sep-Mar Average
1978	41.49	39.98	41.36	41.88	41.79	41.75	42.34	41.51
1979	54.33	56.05	53.77	52.38	51.43	50.29	48.69	52.42
1980	46.22	44.62	41.77	42.18	42.51	41.15	40.38	42.69
1981	46.99	48.48	47.91	48.89	50.20	48.96	48.13	48.51
1982	45.80	44.81	45.77	46.42	45.04	42.82	42.16	44.69
1983	38.90	37.42	38.21	41.62	43.13	42.38	42.15	40.54
1984	41.95	43.51	43.04	43.09	43.01	42.94	44.44	43.14
1985	41.82	41.33	41.53	40.59	39.49	38.48	38.40	40.23

	Sep	Oct	Nov	Dec	Jan	Feb	Mar
AVERAGE MOVE							
All Years		-0.16	-0.35	0.46	-0.06	-0.98	-0.26
Less Extremes		-0.24	-0.23	0.28	-0.10	-0.93	-0.33
Ave Up - All Years		1.59	0.83	1.00	1.05	NONE	1.05
Ave Down - All Years		-1.22	-1.54	-1.17	-0.72	-0.98	-0.69
COUNT							
Number Up		3	4	6	3	0	2
Number Down		5	4	2	5	8	6
Pct Up		37.5%	50.0%	75.0%	37.5%	0.0%	25.0%
Pct Down		62.5%	50.0%	25.0%	62.5%	100.0%	75.0%
EXTREMES							
Greatest Up		1.72	1.38	3.41	1.51	0.00	1.51
Greatest Down		-1.60	-2.85	-1.39	-1.38	-2.22	-1.61
SEASONAL INDEX : AVERAGE PERCENTAGE METHOD							
All Years	101.0	100.5	99.8	101.0	100.9	98.7	98.2
Less Extremes	100.7	100.8	100.2	100.8	100.4	98.2	98.1
SEASONAL INDEX : LINK RELATIVE METHOD							
All Years		100.2	99.9	99.6	101.0	101.2	99.2
Less Extremes		100.4	100.0	100.0	100.9	100.9	99.1

JAPANESE YEN - MARCH - MONTH OF HIGH AND LOW

Year of Expiration	Sep	Oct	Nov	Dec	Jan	Feb	Mar
1978		L					H
1979		H					L
1980	H						L
1981	L				H		
1982				H			L
1983		L			H		
1984	L						H
1985	H						L

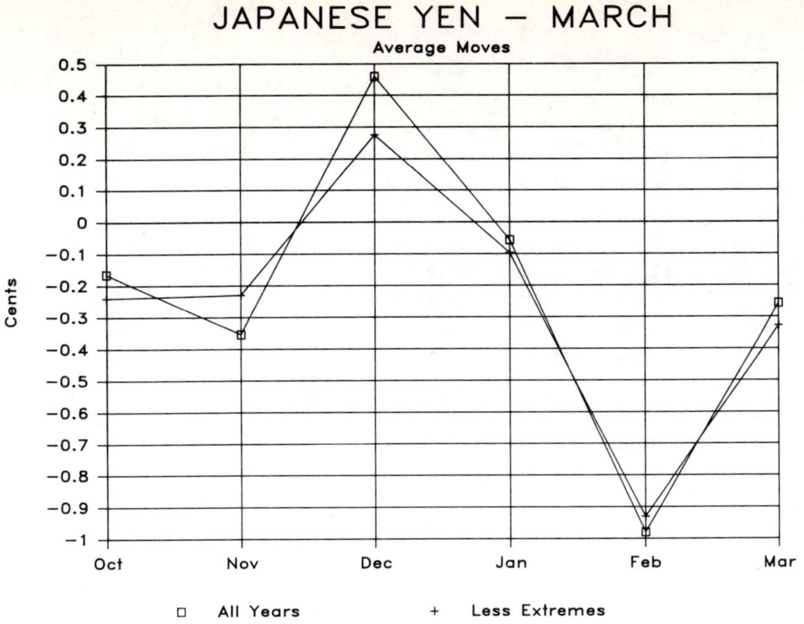
JAPANESE YEN — MARCH
Average Moves
Cents
0.5
0.4
0.3
0.2
0.1
0
-0.1
-0.2
-0.3
-0.4
-0.5
-0.6
-0.7
-0.8
-0.9
-1
Oct
Nov
Dec
Jan
Feb
Mar
All Years
Less Extremes

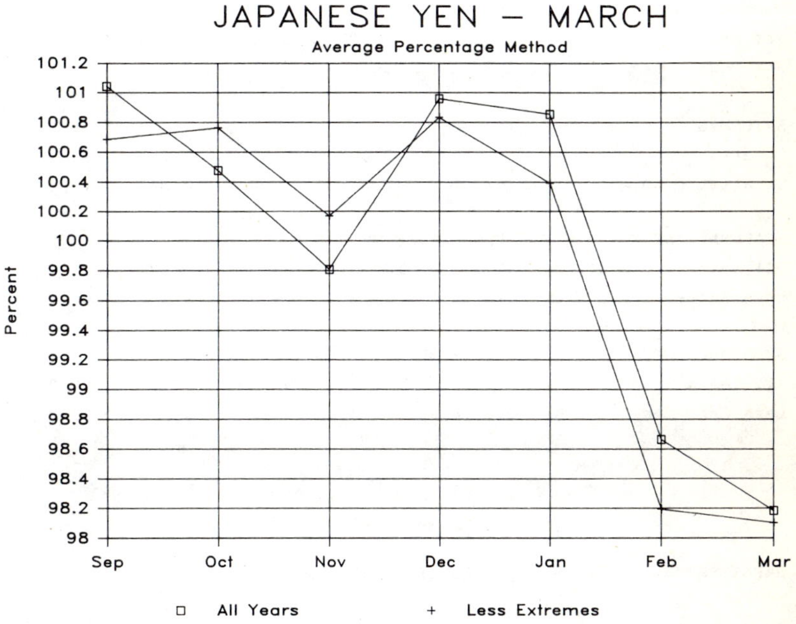
JAPANESE YEN — MARCH
Average Percentage Method
Percent
101.2
101
100.8
100.6
100.4
100.2
100
99.8
99.6
99.4
99.2
99
98.8
98.6
98.4
98.2
98
Sep
Oct
Nov
Dec
Jan
Feb
Mar
All Years
Less Extremes

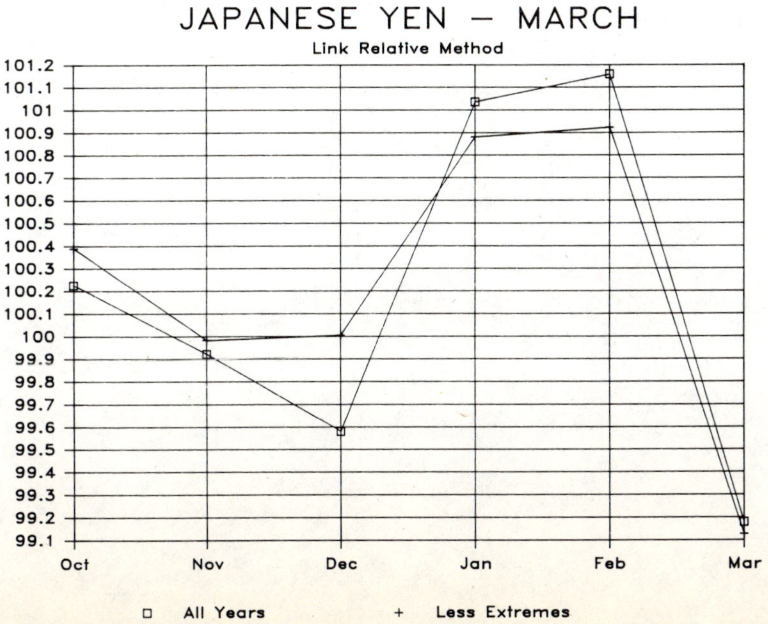
JAPANESE YEN — MARCH
Link Relative Method
101.2
101.1
101
100.9
100.8
100.7
100.6
100.5
100.4
100.3
100.2
100.1
100
99.9
99.8
99.7
99.6
99.5
99.4
99.3
99.2
99.1
Oct
Nov
Dec
Jan
Feb
Mar
All Years
Less Extremes

JAPANESE YEN - JUNE - MONTHLY AVERAGE PRICE

Year of Expiration	Dec	Jan	Feb	Mar	Apr	May	Jun	Dec-Jun Average
1978	42.24	42.32	42.21	43.91	45.57	44.48	45.79	43.79
1979	53.56	52.55	51.17	49.17	46.63	46.05	45.55	49.24
1980	42.74	43.11	41.74	40.68	40.34	43.76	45.72	42.58
1981	49.62	51.09	49.95	48.76	47.17	45.80	44.51	48.13
1982	47.24	45.94	43.77	42.31	41.60	42.48	40.65	43.43
1983	41.93	43.44	42.69	42.28	42.28	42.71	41.52	42.40
1984	43.48	43.41	43.33	44.88	44.76	43.58	43.21	43.80
1985	40.96	39.77	38.77	39.08	39.91	39.79	40.11	39.77

	Dec	Jan	Feb	Mar	Apr	May	Jun
AVERAGE MOVE							
All Years		-0.02	-1.00	-0.32	-0.35	0.05	-0.20
Less Extremes		-0.06	-0.96	-0.38	-0.32	-0.28	-0.29
Ave Up - All Years		0.86	NONE	1.19	1.25	1.58	1.19
Ave Down - All Years		-0.89	-1.00	-1.23	-0.88	-0.87	-1.04
COUNT							
Number Up		4	0	3	2	3	3
Number Down		4	8	5	6	5	5
Pct Up		50.0%	0.0%	37.5%	25.0%	37.5%	37.5%
Pct Down		50.0%	100.0%	62.5%	75.0%	62.5%	62.5%
EXTREMES							
Greatest Up		1.51	0.00	1.70	1.66	3.42	1.95
Greatest Down		-1.30	-2.16	-2.00	-2.54	-1.36	-1.83
SEASONAL INDEX : AVERAGE PERCENTAGE METHOD							
All Years	102.3	102.3	100.0	99.3	98.7	98.9	98.5
Less Extremes	102.2	102.5	99.9	99.5	98.5	99.1	98.0
SEASONAL INDEX : LINK RELATIVE METHOD							
All Years		101.3	101.6	99.7	99.4	99.0	99.6
Less Extremes		101.4	101.7	100.0	99.6	99.3	99.2

JAPANESE YEN - JUNE - MONTH OF HIGH AND LOW

Year of Expiration	Dec	Jan	Feb	Mar	Apr	May	Jun
1978			L				H
1979	H						L
1980					L		H
1981		H					L
1982	H						L
1983		H					L
1984				H			L
1985	H		L				

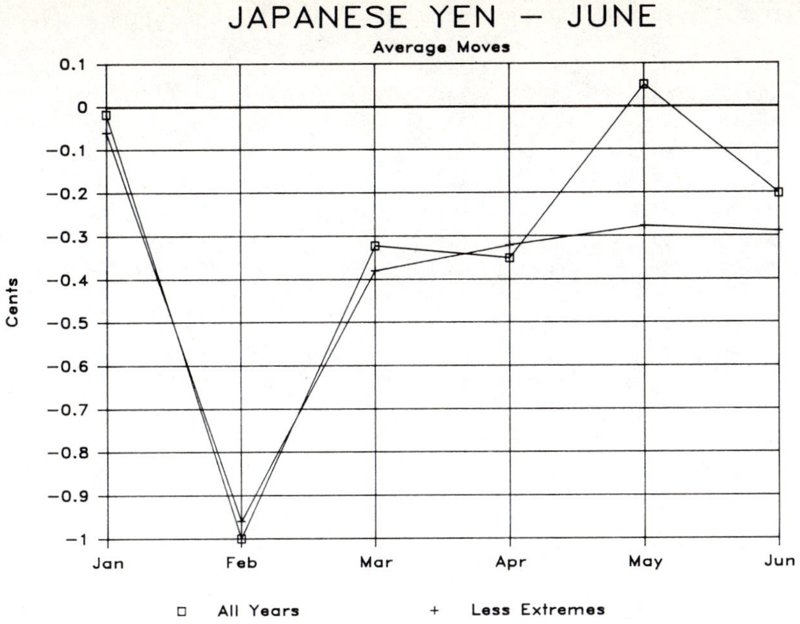
JAPANESE YEN — JUNE
Average Moves
Cents
0.1
0
−0.1
−0.2
−0.3
−0.4
−0.5
−0.6
−0.7
−0.8
−0.9
−1
Jan
Feb
Mar
Apr
May
Jun
□ All Years
+ Less Extremes

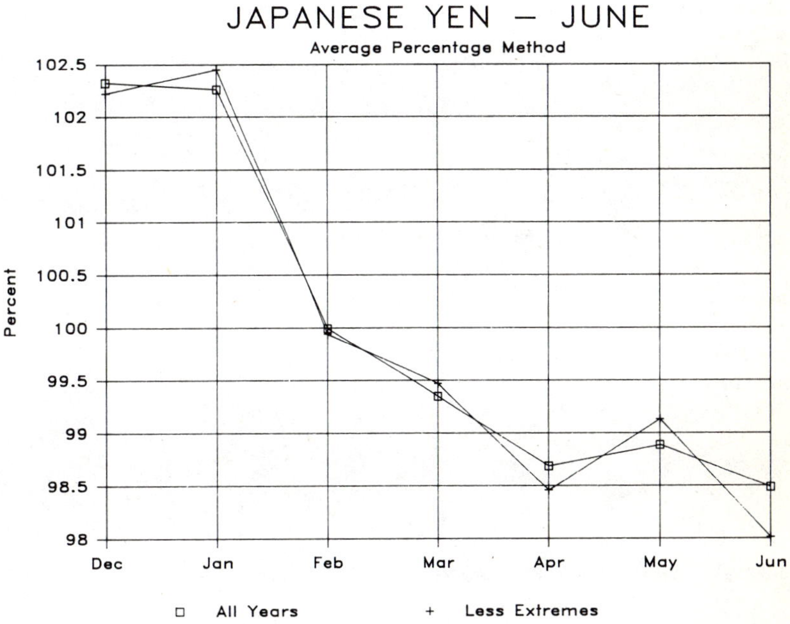
JAPANESE YEN — JUNE
Average Percentage Method
Percent
102.5
102
101.5
101
100.5
100
99.5
99
98.5
98
Dec
Jan
Feb
Mar
Apr
May
Jun
□ All Years
+ Less Extremes

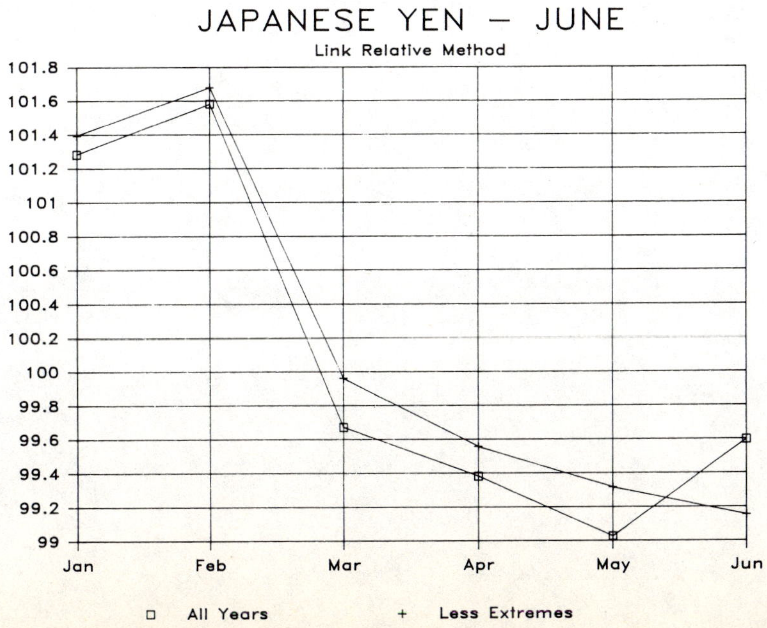
JAPANESE YEN — JUNE
Link Relative Method
101.8
101.6
101.4
101.2
101
100.8
100.6
100.4
100.2
100
99.8
99.6
99.4
99.2
99
Jan
Feb
Mar
Apr
May
Jun
□ All Years
+ Less Extremes

JAPANESE YEN - SEPTEMBER - MONTHLY AVERAGE PRICE

Year of Expiration	Mar	Apr	May	Jun	Jul	Aug	Sep	Mar-Sep Average
1978	44.40	46.09	44.99	47.40	50.66	53.30	52.45	48.47
1979	49.91	47.17	46.65	46.34	46.63	46.09	45.08	46.84
1980	41.11	40.67	43.69	45.67	44.94	44.61	46.34	43.86
1981	49.55	48.08	46.97	45.70	43.79	43.28	43.37	45.82
1982	43.15	42.46	43.23	40.62	39.67	38.75	38.55	40.92
1983	42.61	42.63	43.03	42.00	41.83	41.03	40.87	42.00
1984	45.39	45.30	44.18	43.42	41.52	41.50	40.79	43.16
1985	39.48	40.18	40.00	40.34	41.60	42.19	41.33	40.73

	Mar	Apr	May	Jun	Jul	Aug	Sep
AVERAGE MOVE							
All Years		-0.38	0.02	-0.16	-0.11	0.01	-0.25
Less Extremes		-0.33	-0.29	-0.18	-0.37	-0.27	-0.45
Ave Up - All Years		0.80	1.40	1.57	1.60	1.62	0.91
Ave Down - All Years		-1.09	-0.80	-1.20	-1.13	-0.52	-0.63
COUNT							
Number Up		3	3	3	3	2	2
Number Down		5	5	5	5	6	6
Pct Up		37.5%	37.5%	37.5%	37.5%	25.0%	25.0%
Pct Down		62.5%	62.5%	62.5%	62.5%	75.0%	75.0%
EXTREMES							
Greatest Up		1.69	3.03	2.41	3.26	2.64	1.73
Greatest Down		-2.74	-1.13	-2.62	-1.91	-0.92	-1.01
SEASONAL INDEX : AVERAGE PERCENTAGE METHOD							
All Years	101.1	100.3	100.4	99.9	99.6	99.6	99.0
Less Extremes	101.5	100.8	100.8	99.6	99.5	98.7	98.3
SEASONAL INDEX : LINK RELATIVE METHOD							
All Years		100.5	99.9	100.2	100.0	99.9	100.0
Less Extremes		100.8	100.5	100.3	100.2	99.8	99.5

JAPANESE YEN - SEPTEMBER - MONTH OF HIGH AND LOW

Year of Expiration	Mar	Apr	May	Jun	Jul	Aug	Sep
1978	L					H	
1979	H						L
1980		L					H
1981	H					L	
1982			H				L
1983			H				L
1984	H						L
1985	L					H	

JAPANESE YEN – SEPTEMBER

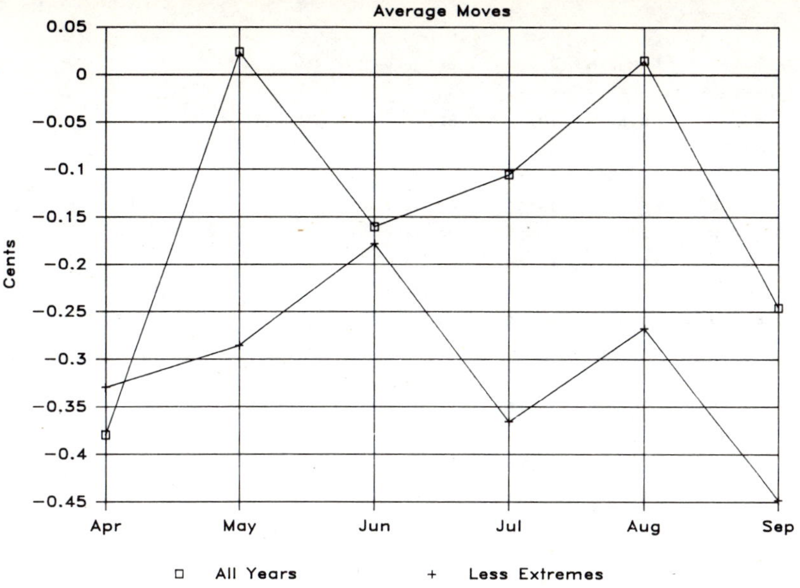

JAPANESE YEN – SEPTEMBER

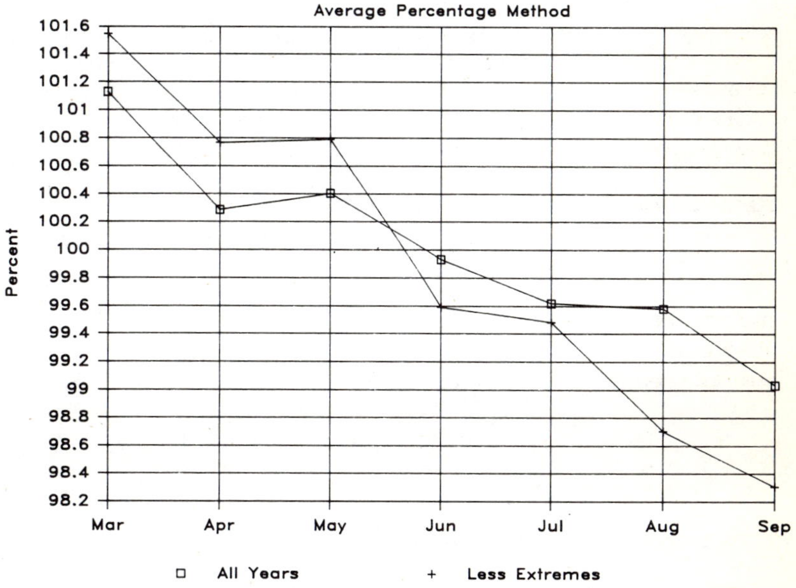

JAPANESE YEN – SEPTEMBER

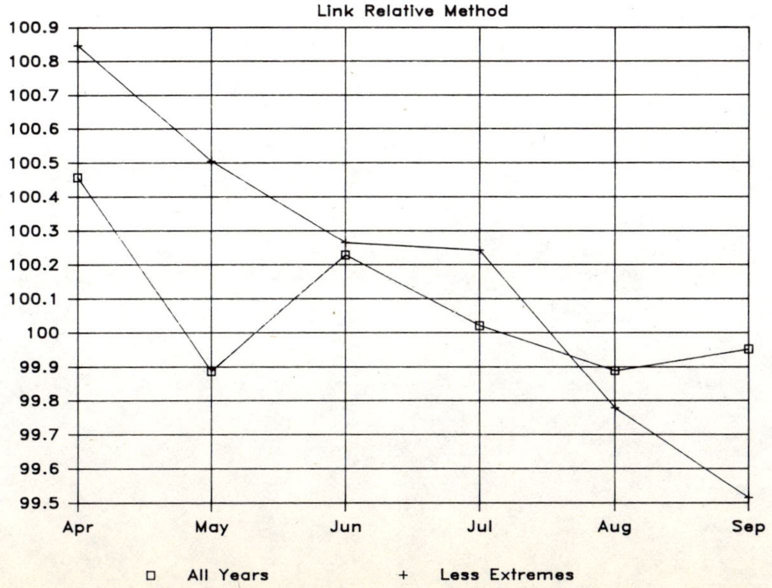

JAPANESE YEN - DECEMBER - MONTHLY AVERAGE PRICE

Year of Expiration	Jun	Jul	Aug	Sep	Oct	Nov	Dec	Jun-Dec Average
1978	48.01	51.36	54.14	53.55	55.10	52.62	50.88	52.24
1979	46.84	47.14	46.65	45.56	43.95	41.10	41.43	44.67
1980	45.73	44.85	44.62	46.65	48.04	47.19	47.40	46.35
1981	46.57	44.82	44.51	44.70	43.84	45.05	45.95	45.06
1982	41.42	40.39	39.20	38.39	37.08	37.93	40.75	39.31
1983	42.37	42.24	41.43	41.61	43.18	42.67	42.60	42.30
1984	44.09	42.15	42.08	41.26	40.84	41.19	40.46	41.72
1985	40.53	41.80	42.40	42.62	46.72	49.06	49.20	44.62

	Jun	Jul	Aug	Sep	Oct	Nov	Dec
AVERAGE MOVE							
All Years		-0.10	0.03	-0.09	0.55	-0.24	0.23
Less Extremes		-0.37	-0.22	-0.27	0.32	-0.24	0.13
Ave Up - All Years		1.64	1.69	0.65	2.15	1.19	0.88
Ave Down - All Years		-1.14	-0.52	-0.83	-1.05	-1.67	-0.84
COUNT							
Number Up		3	2	4	4	4	5
Number Down		5	6	4	4	4	3
Pct Up		37.5%	25.0%	50.0%	50.0%	50.0%	62.5%
Pct Down		62.5%	75.0%	50.0%	50.0%	50.0%	37.5%
EXTREMES							
Greatest Up		3.35	2.78	2.03	4.10	2.34	2.82
Greatest Down		-1.94	-1.20	-1.09	-1.61	-2.86	-1.74
SEASONAL INDEX : AVERAGE PERCENTAGE METHOD							
All Years	100.1	99.7	99.6	99.3	100.5	100.1	100.8
Less Extremes	100.7	99.7	99.5	99.5	100.7	99.8	100.5
SEASONAL INDEX : LINK RELATIVE METHOD							
All Years		100.1	99.8	99.6	99.4	100.5	100.0
Less Extremes		100.8	100.2	99.8	99.3	99.9	99.8

JAPANESE YEN - DECEMBER - MONTH OF HIGH AND LOW

Year of Expiration	Jun	Jul	Aug	Sep	Oct	Nov	Dec
1978	L				H		
1979		H				L	
1980			L		H		
1981	H				L		
1982	H				L		
1983			L		H		
1984	H						L
1985	L						H

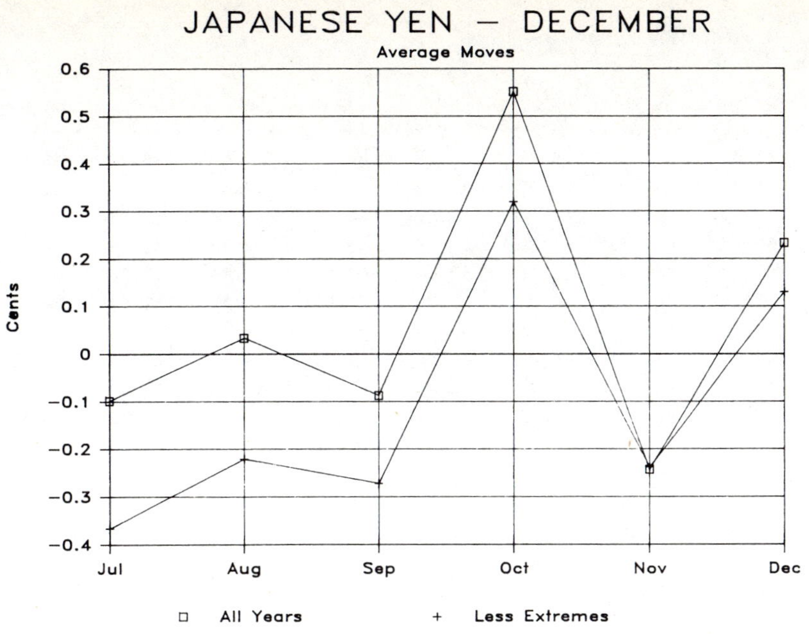
JAPANESE YEN – DECEMBER
Average Moves
Cents
0.6
0.5
0.4
0.3
0.2
0.1
0
–0.1
–0.2
–0.3
–0.4
Jul
Aug
Sep
Oct
Nov
Dec
□ All Years
+ Less Extremes

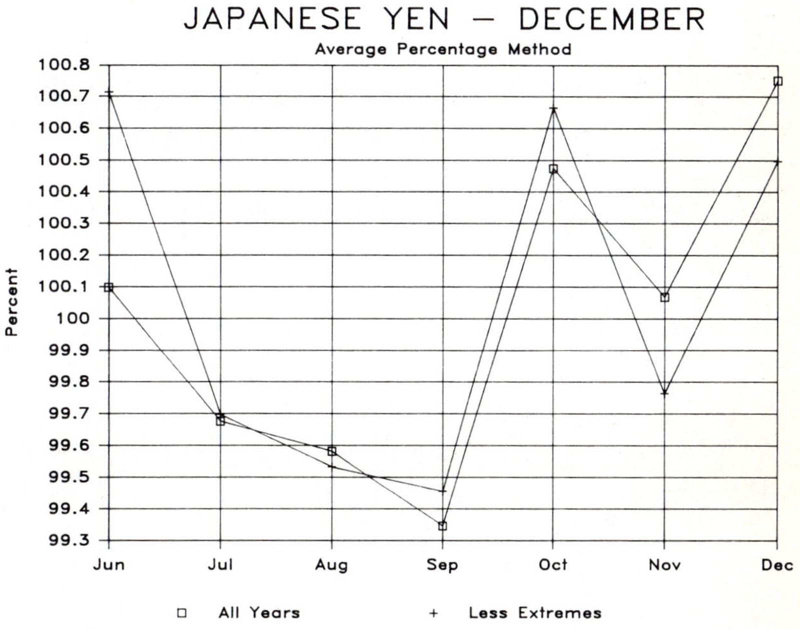
JAPANESE YEN – DECEMBER
Average Percentage Method
Percent
100.8
100.7
100.6
100.5
100.4
100.3
100.2
100.1
100
99.9
99.8
99.7
99.6
99.5
99.4
99.3
Jun
Jul
Aug
Sep
Oct
Nov
Dec
□ All Years
+ Less Extremes

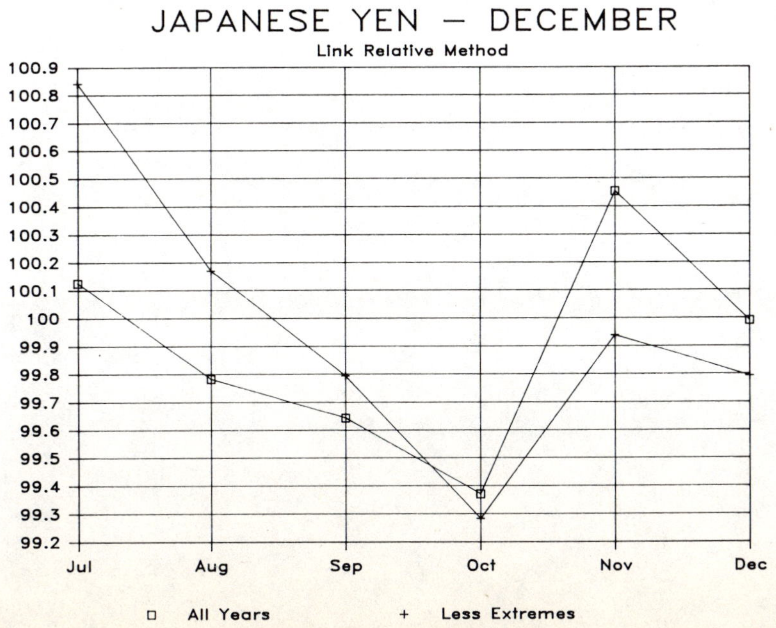
JAPANESE YEN – DECEMBER
Link Relative Method
100.9
100.8
100.7
100.6
100.5
100.4
100.3
100.2
100.1
100
99.9
99.8
99.7
99.6
99.5
99.4
99.3
99.2
Jul
Aug
Sep
Oct
Nov
Dec
□ All Years
+ Less Extremes

SWISS FRANC - MARCH - MONTHLY AVERAGE PRICE

Year of Expiration	May	Jun	Jul	Aug	Sep	Oct	Nov	Dec	Jan	Feb	Mar	May-Mar Average
1976	40.58	40.74	38.76	38.08	37.64	38.26	38.13	38.26	38.68	39.07	38.72	38.81
1977	41.68	42.03	41.45	41.29	41.23	41.52	41.39	41.14	40.39	39.76	39.14	41.00
1978	40.29	40.93	42.24	42.37	42.93	44.83	46.19	48.80	50.76	52.78	53.07	45.93
1979	53.64	55.92	58.15	62.73	66.45	67.98	62.60	61.58	60.95	60.35	59.75	60.92
1980	61.57	62.46	64.42	63.67	65.47	64.39	63.06	63.94	63.58	61.49	57.76	62.89
1981	62.57	63.03	63.96	62.58	62.99	62.16	60.05	57.78	56.00	51.85	51.57	59.50
1982	51.64	50.67	50.05	48.40	51.15	54.39	56.74	55.63	54.70	53.20	53.62	52.74
1983	55.09	51.64	50.83	49.53	48.45	47.29	46.46	49.50	51.35	49.70	48.72	49.87
1984	50.51	49.12	48.87	47.74	47.50	48.44	47.03	46.24	45.15	45.63	46.82	47.55
1985	46.86	46.41	43.59	43.12	41.25	40.59	41.18	39.41	37.81	35.78	34.77	40.98

	May	Jun	Jul	Aug	Sep	Oct	Nov	Dec	Jan	Feb	Mar
AVERAGE MOVE											
All Years		-0.15	-0.06	-0.28	0.55	0.48	-0.70	-0.06	-0.29	-0.97	-0.57
Less Extremes		-0.04	-0.01	-0.71	0.46	0.34	-0.50	-0.17	-0.38	-0.95	-0.39
Ave Up - All Years		0.80	1.61	2.36	1.85	1.42	1.43	1.67	1.41	0.97	0.64
Ave Down - All Years		-1.57	-1.18	-0.94	-0.74	-0.93	-1.61	-1.20	-1.02	-1.81	-1.08
COUNT											
Number Up		6	4	2	5	6	3	4	3	3	3
Number Down		4	6	8	5	4	7	6	7	7	7
Pct Up		60.0%	40.0%	20.0%	50.0%	60.0%	30.0%	40.0%	30.0%	30.0%	30.0%
Pct Down		40.0%	60.0%	80.0%	50.0%	40.0%	70.0%	60.0%	70.0%	70.0%	70.0%
EXTREMES											
Greatest Up		2.28	2.23	4.58	3.72	3.24	2.35	3.04	1.96	2.02	1.19
Greatest Down		-3.45	-2.82	-1.65	-1.87	-1.17	-5.37	-2.27	-1.78	-4.15	-3.74
SEASONAL INDEX : AVERAGE PERCENTAGE METHOD											
All Years	101.4	101.0	100.4	99.7	100.5	101.5	100.4	100.3	99.8	98.0	97.0
Less Extremes	101.5	100.9	100.6	100.0	100.3	101.0	100.4	100.1	99.4	97.3	96.2
SEASONAL INDEX : LINK RELATIVE METHOD											
All Years		99.4	99.4	99.0	100.1	101.5	100.8	101.1	100.8	99.3	98.5
Less Extremes		99.7	99.9	98.9	100.1	101.3	100.9	101.0	100.6	99.1	98.6

SWISS FRANC - MARCH - MONTH OF HIGH AND LOW

Year of Expiration	May	Jun	Jul	Aug	Sep	Oct	Nov	Dec	Jan	Feb	Mar
1976		H			L						
1977		H									L
1978	L										H
1979	L					H					
1980					H						L
1981			H								L
1982				L			H				
1983	H						L				
1984	H								L		
1985	H										L

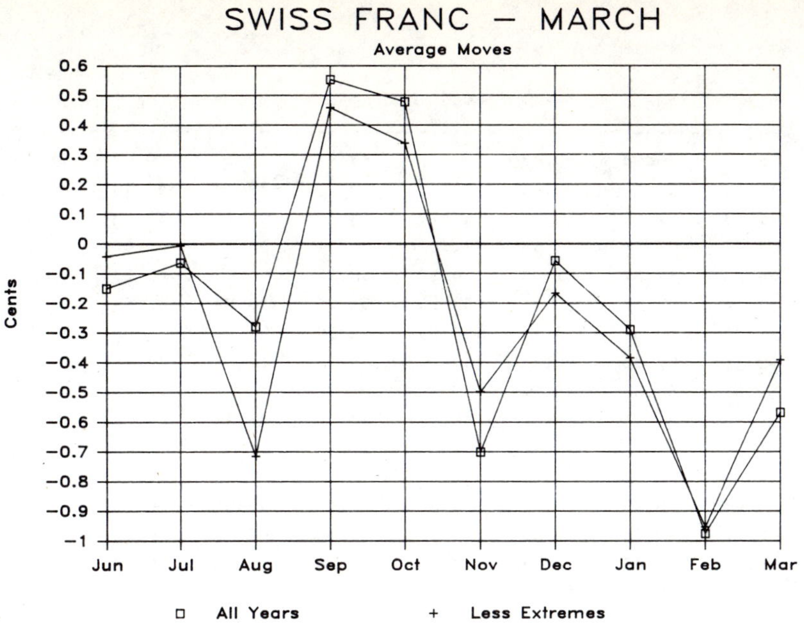
SWISS FRANC — MARCH
Average Moves
Cents
0.6
0.5
0.4
0.3
0.2
0.1
0
−0.1
−0.2
−0.3
−0.4
−0.5
−0.6
−0.7
−0.8
−0.9
−1
Jun
Jul
Aug
Sep
Oct
Nov
Dec
Jan
Feb
Mar
All Years
Less Extremes

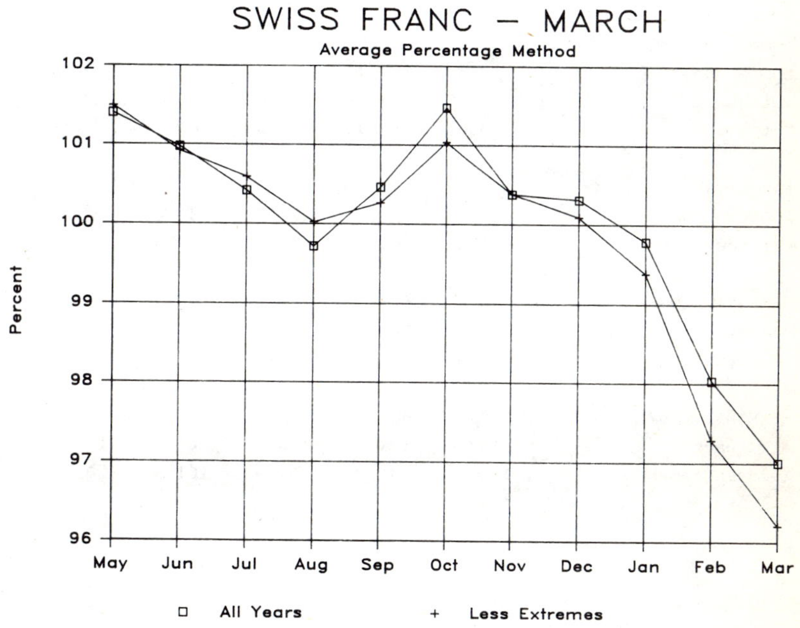
SWISS FRANC — MARCH
Average Percentage Method
Percent
102
101
100
99
98
97
96
May
Jun
Jul
Aug
Sep
Oct
Nov
Dec
Jan
Feb
Mar
All Years
Less Extremes

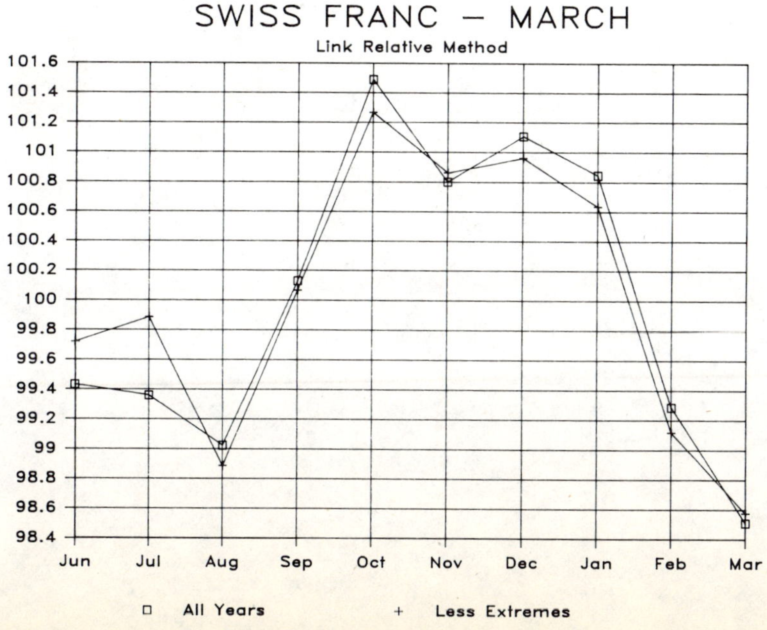
SWISS FRANC — MARCH
Link Relative Method
101.6
101.4
101.2
101
100.8
100.6
100.4
100.2
100
99.8
99.6
99.4
99.2
99
98.8
98.6
98.4
Jun
Jul
Aug
Sep
Oct
Nov
Dec
Jan
Feb
Mar
All Years
Less Extremes

SWISS FRANC - JUNE - MONTHLY AVERAGE PRICE

Year of Expiration	Aug	Sep	Oct	Nov	Dec	Jan	Feb	Mar	Apr	May	Jun	Aug-Jun Average
1976	38.31	37.93	38.57	38.45	38.59	38.98	39.47	39.39	39.83	40.37	40.63	39.14
1977	40.67	41.73	41.93	41.71	41.43	40.75	40.10	39.43	39.77	39.75	40.16	40.67
1978	50.18	44.04	45.36	46.77	49.43	51.58	53.74	53.70	53.19	51.24	52.76	50.18
1979	63.86	67.77	69.53	64.24	63.38	62.79	61.98	61.07	59.21	58.41	58.07	62.75
1980	64.88	66.84	65.87	64.32	65.25	64.92	62.99	58.37	58.19	60.42	61.23	63.02
1981	63.68	64.09	63.30	61.38	59.14	57.37	53.06	52.95	51.26	48.84	47.59	56.61
1982	49.16	51.77	54.85	57.22	56.30	55.51	54.10	54.09	51.90	51.76	49.09	53.25
1983	49.07	48.79	47.91	47.08	50.21	52.10	50.46	49.14	49.02	48.76	47.19	49.07
1984	48.38	48.11	48.95	47.63	46.87	45.80	46.36	47.38	46.21	44.41	44.38	46.77
1985	43.92	41.98	41.14	41.68	39.87	38.17	36.11	36.08	38.89	38.36	38.72	39.54

	Aug	Sep	Oct	Nov	Dec	Jan	Feb	Mar	Apr	May	Jun
AVERAGE MOVE											
All Years		0.09	0.44	-0.70	.00	-0.25	-0.96	-0.68	-0.41	-0.51	-0.25
Less Extremes		0.39	0.28	-0.50	-0.11	-0.36	-0.93	-0.40	-0.60	-0.62	-0.17
Ave Up - All Years		1.99	1.31	1.44	1.72	1.48	1.07	1.03	1.20	1.38	0.67
Ave Down - All Years		-1.80	-0.87	-1.61	-1.14	-0.99	-1.83	-0.87	-1.11	-0.99	-1.17
COUNT											
Number Up		5	6	3	4	3	3	1	3	2	5
Number Down		5	4	7	6	7	7	9	7	8	5
Pct Up		50.0%	60.0%	30.0%	40.0%	30.0%	30.0%	10.0%	30.0%	20.0%	50.0%
Pct Down		50.0%	40.0%	70.0%	60.0%	70.0%	70.0%	90.0%	70.0%	80.0%	50.0%
EXTREMES											
Greatest Up		3.92	3.09	2.37	3.14	2.16	2.16	1.03	2.81	2.23	1.51
Greatest Down		-6.14	-0.97	-5.30	-2.23	-1.77	-4.31	-4.61	-2.19	-2.42	-2.67
SEASONAL INDEX : AVERAGE PERCENTAGE METHOD											
All Years	102.2	102.0	102.9	101.7	101.7	101.2	99.4	98.2	97.7	96.7	96.3
Less Extremes	102.1	102.4	103.3	102.0	101.6	101.1	99.4	98.0	97.6	97.2	96.7
SEASONAL INDEX : LINK RELATIVE METHOD											
All Years		99.9	101.3	100.8	101.3	101.3	99.9	99.2	99.2	98.6	98.6
Less Extremes		100.1	101.2	100.9	101.3	101.2	99.8	99.6	99.0	98.3	98.5

SWISS FRANC - JUNE - MONTH OF HIGH AND LOW

Year of Expiration	Aug	Sep	Oct	Nov	Dec	Jan	Feb	Mar	Apr	May	Jun
1976		L									H
1977			H					L			
1978		L					H				
1979			H								L
1980		H							L		
1981		H									L
1982				H							L
1983				L		H					
1984			H								L
1985	H							L			

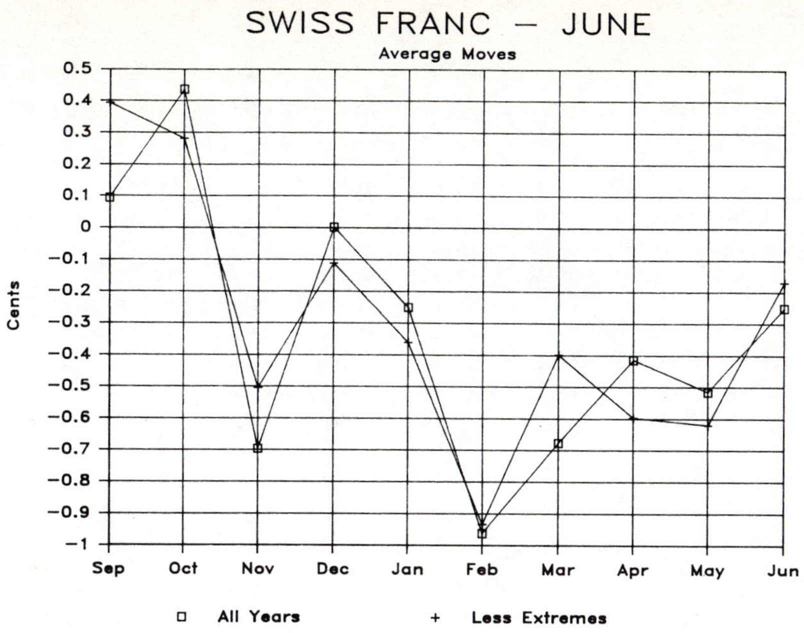
SWISS FRANC — JUNE
Average Moves
Cents
0.5
0.4
0.3
0.2
0.1
0
−0.1
−0.2
−0.3
−0.4
−0.5
−0.6
−0.7
−0.8
−0.9
−1
Sep
Oct
Nov
Dec
Jan
Feb
Mar
Apr
May
Jun
All Years
Less Extremes

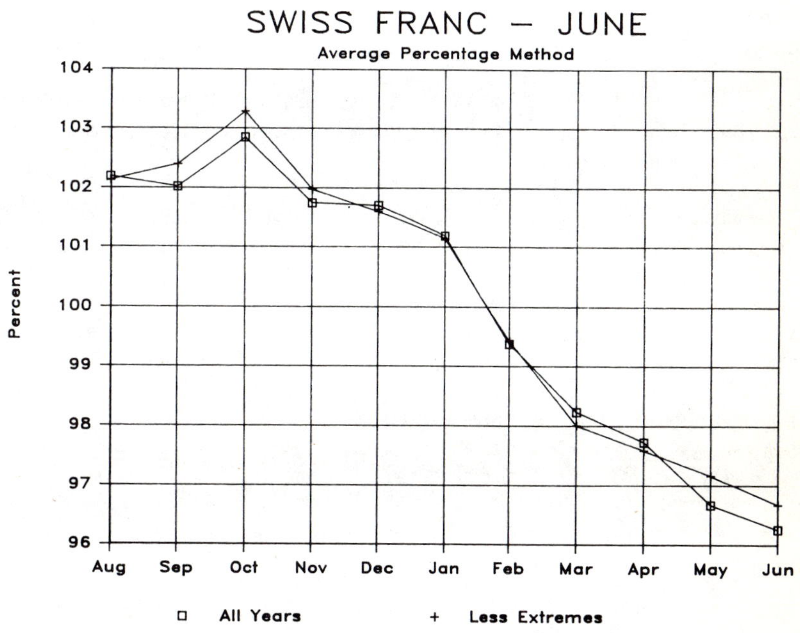
SWISS FRANC — JUNE
Average Percentage Method
Percent
104
103
102
101
100
99
98
97
96
Aug
Sep
Oct
Nov
Dec
Jan
Feb
Mar
Apr
May
Jun
All Years
Less Extremes

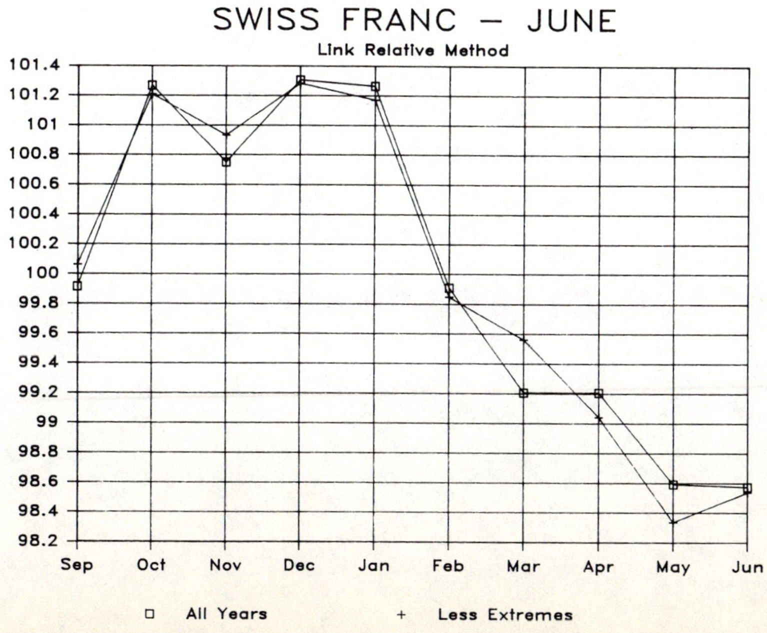
SWISS FRANC — JUNE
Link Relative Method
101.4
101.2
101
100.8
100.6
100.4
100.2
100
99.8
99.6
99.4
99.2
99
98.8
98.6
98.4
98.2
Sep
Oct
Nov
Dec
Jan
Feb
Mar
Apr
May
Jun
All Years
Less Extremes

SWISS FRANC - SEPTEMBER - MONTHLY AVERAGE PRICE

Year of Expiration	Nov	Dec	Jan	Feb	Mar	Apr	May	Jun	Jul	Aug	Sep	Nov-Sep Average
1976	38.77	38.88	39.29	39.83	39.77	40.24	40.84	41.02	40.53	40.43	40.32	39.99
1977	40.86	41.74	41.06	40.50	39.67	40.02	39.93	40.42	41.70	41.68	41.91	40.86
1978	47.26	50.03	52.27	54.53	54.60	54.11	52.08	54.04	56.15	60.37	62.19	54.33
1979	65.89	65.09	64.47	63.56	62.54	60.49	59.69	60.31	61.65	60.87	61.15	62.34
1980	66.03	66.58	66.21	64.42	59.91	59.50	61.30	61.82	62.61	60.78	61.31	62.77
1981	62.88	60.54	58.55	54.08	53.78	52.13	49.87	49.14	48.35	46.48	47.84	53.06
1982	57.52	56.89	56.21	54.88	55.07	53.07	53.02	49.35	48.49	47.66	47.19	52.67
1983	47.64	50.95	52.78	51.17	49.83	49.69	49.37	47.94	47.66	46.44	46.00	49.04
1984	48.28	47.44	46.40	46.99	48.18	47.02	45.27	44.66	41.95	41.68	40.23	45.28
1985	42.18	40.33	38.54	36.46	36.48	39.23	38.65	39.16	41.86	43.75	41.69	39.85

	Nov	Dec	Jan	Feb	Mar	Apr	May	Jun	Jul	Aug	Sep
AVERAGE MOVE											
All Years		0.12	-0.27	-0.94	-0.66	-0.43	-0.55	-0.22	0.31	-0.08	-0.03
Less Extremes		0.02	-0.37	-0.89	-0.41	-0.63	-0.63	-0.06	0.39	-0.39	-0.01
Ave Up - All Years		1.52	1.49	1.13	0.37	1.19	1.20	0.71	1.64	3.06	0.84
Ave Down - All Years		-1.29	-1.02	-1.82	-1.34	-1.13	-0.99	-1.61	-1.03	-0.86	-0.91
COUNT											
Number Up		5	3	3	4	3	2	6	5	2	5
Number Down		5	7	7	6	7	8	4	5	8	5
Pct Up		50.0%	30.0%	30.0%	40.0%	30.0%	20.0%	60.0%	50.0%	20.0%	50.0%
Pct Down		50.0%	70.0%	70.0%	60.0%	70.0%	80.0%	40.0%	50.0%	80.0%	50.0%
EXTREMES											
Greatest Up		3.31	2.24	2.26	1.18	2.75	1.80	1.96	2.70	4.22	1.82
Greatest Down		-2.34	-1.99	-4.48	-4.52	-2.05	-2.26	-3.66	-2.71	-1.87	-2.07
SEASONAL INDEX : AVERAGE PERCENTAGE METHOD											
All Years	103.2	103.4	102.8	100.9	99.8	99.3	98.1	97.7	98.3	98.3	98.1
Less Extremes	103.3	103.5	102.6	101.7	100.0	99.2	98.2	97.7	98.4	98.1	97.2
SEASONAL INDEX : LINK RELATIVE METHOD											
All Years		101.6	101.5	100.2	99.5	99.5	98.8	98.8	99.8	100.1	100.3
Less Extremes		101.7	101.5	100.2	99.9	99.3	98.5	98.9	100.0	99.9	100.2

SWISS FRANC - SEPTEMBER - MONTH OF HIGH AND LOW

Year of Expiration	Nov	Dec	Jan	Feb	Mar	Apr	May	Jun	Jul	Aug	Sep
1976	L							H			
1977					L						H
1978	L										H
1979	H						L				
1980		H				L					
1981	H									L	
1982	H										L
1983			H								L
1984	H										L
1985				L						H	

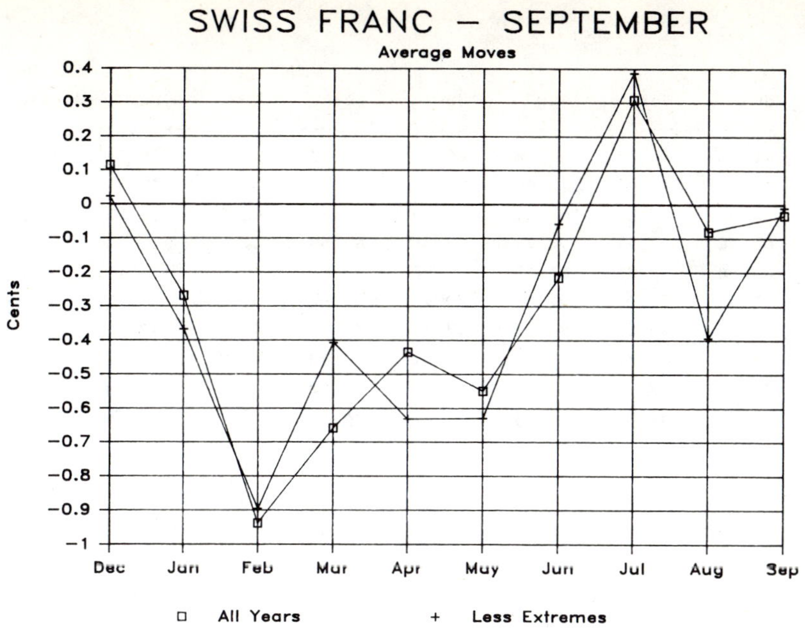
SWISS FRANC — SEPTEMBER
Average Moves
Cents
0.4
0.3
0.2
0.1
0
−0.1
−0.2
−0.3
−0.4
−0.5
−0.6
−0.7
−0.8
−0.9
−1
Dec
Jan
Feb
Mar
Apr
May
Jun
Jul
Aug
Sep
□ All Years
+ Less Extremes

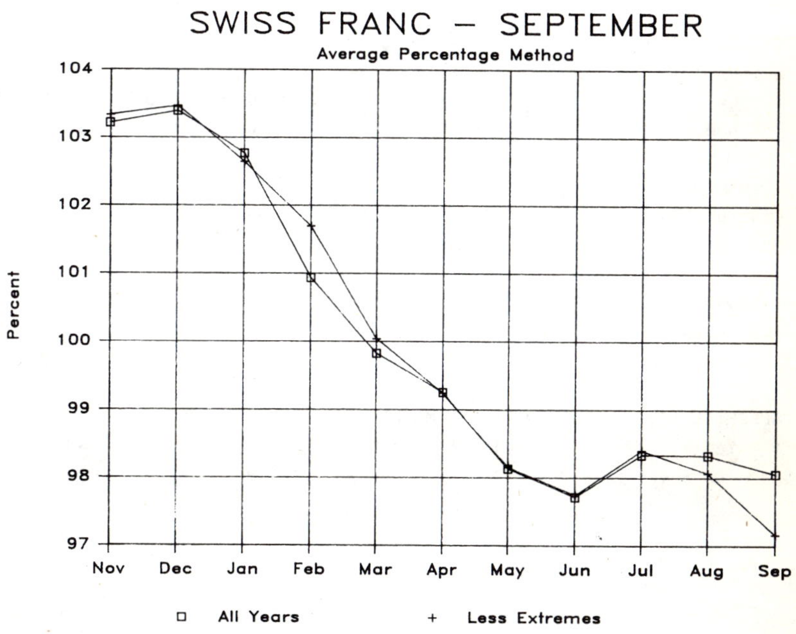
SWISS FRANC — SEPTEMBER
Average Percentage Method
Percent
104
103
102
101
100
99
98
97
Nov
Dec
Jan
Feb
Mar
Apr
May
Jun
Jul
Aug
Sep
□ All Years
+ Less Extremes

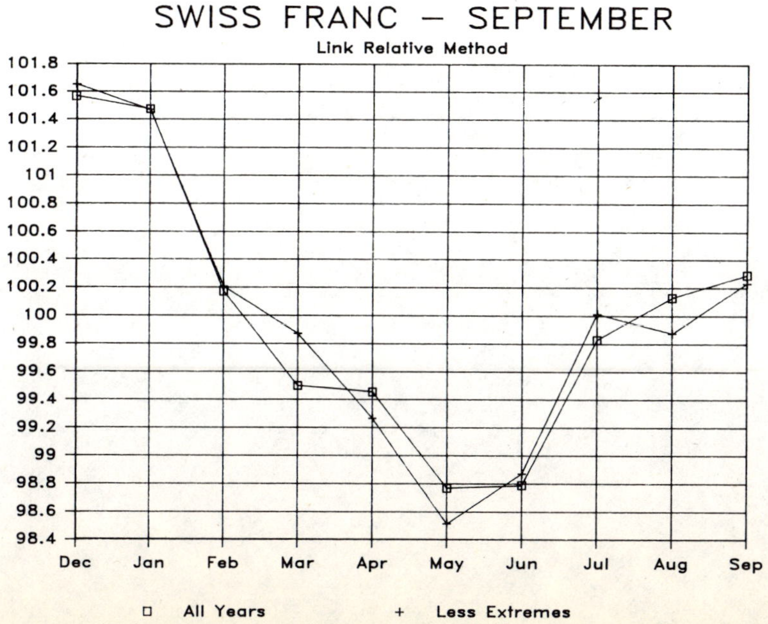
SWISS FRANC — SEPTEMBER
Link Relative Method
101.8
101.6
101.4
101.2
101
100.8
100.6
100.4
100.2
100
99.8
99.6
99.4
99.2
99
98.8
98.6
98.4
Dec
Jan
Feb
Mar
Apr
May
Jun
Jul
Aug
Sep
□ All Years
+ Less Extremes

SWISS FRANC - DECEMBER - MONTHLY AVERAGE PRICE

Year of Expiration	Feb	Mar	Apr	May	Jun	Jul	Aug	Sep	Oct	Nov	Dec	Feb-Dec Average
1976	40.16	40.12	40.64	41.28	41.53	40.97	40.88	40.85	41.17	41.07	40.79	40.86
1977	40.87	39.93	40.30	40.14	40.64	41.99	42.06	42.56	44.33	45.67	47.56	42.37
1978	55.31	55.57	54.91	52.90	54.99	57.16	61.51	65.07	66.29	60.86	59.03	58.51
1979	65.04	63.91	61.60	60.75	61.46	62.96	62.29	63.85	62.59	61.40	62.57	62.58
1980	65.70	61.29	60.59	62.18	62.48	63.30	61.65	61.96	61.02	58.51	56.16	61.35
1981	55.05	54.68	52.88	50.73	49.91	49.22	47.52	50.43	53.67	56.22	55.17	52.32
1982	55.75	56.00	54.16	54.21	50.53	49.63	48.56	47.60	46.56	45.80	47.99	50.62
1983	51.95	50.47	50.33	49.97	48.55	48.32	47.11	46.92	47.83	46.39	45.57	48.49
1984	47.61	48.90	47.76	46.10	45.53	42.76	42.41	40.57	40.03	40.72	39.23	43.78
1985	36.87	36.90	39.67	38.97	39.42	42.19	44.14	43.29	46.45	47.15	47.45	42.05

	Feb	Mar	Apr	May	Jun	Jul	Aug	Sep	Oct	Nov	Dec
AVERAGE MOVE											
All Years		-0.65	-0.49	-0.56	-0.22	0.35	-0.04	0.50	0.68	-0.62	-0.23
Less Extremes		-0.43	-0.67	-0.63	-0.08	0.43	-0.38	0.41	0.61	-0.41	-0.26
Ave Up - All Years		0.46	1.22	0.76	0.72	1.72	2.12	1.77	1.77	1.32	1.38
Ave Down - All Years		-1.39	-1.23	-1.13	-1.62	-1.03	-0.96	-0.77	-0.94	-1.90	-1.30
COUNT											
Number Up		4	3	3	6	5	3	5	6	4	4
Number Down		6	7	7	4	5	7	5	4	6	6
Pct Up		40.0%	30.0%	30.0%	60.0%	50.0%	30.0%	50.0%	60.0%	40.0%	40.0%
Pct Down		60.0%	70.0%	70.0%	40.0%	50.0%	70.0%	50.0%	40.0%	60.0%	60.0%
EXTREMES											
Greatest Up		1.29	2.77	1.59	2.09	2.76	4.35	3.56	3.24	2.54	2.19
Greatest Down		-4.41	-2.31	-2.16	-3.68	-2.77	-1.70	-1.84	-1.26	-5.43	-2.35
SEASONAL INDEX : AVERAGE PERCENTAGE METHOD											
All Years	101.9	100.8	100.1	99.0	98.5	99.1	99.0	99.7	101.3	100.5	100.1
Less Extremes	102.7	101.1	99.8	99.0	98.4	99.2	99.3	99.2	101.1	100.2	99.8
SEASONAL INDEX : LINK RELATIVE METHOD											
All Years		100.6	100.1	99.0	98.6	99.3	99.3	100.1	101.6	100.8	100.5
Less Extremes		100.9	99.9	98.8	98.8	99.6	99.2	100.0	101.4	101.0	100.5

SWISS FRANC - DECEMBER - MONTH OF HIGH AND LOW

Year of Expiration	Feb	Mar	Apr	May	Jun	Jul	Aug	Sep	Oct	Nov	Dec
1976		L			H						
1977		L									H
1978				L					H		
1979	H			L							
1980	H		L								
1981							L			H	
1982		H								L	
1983	H										L
1984		H									L
1985	L										H

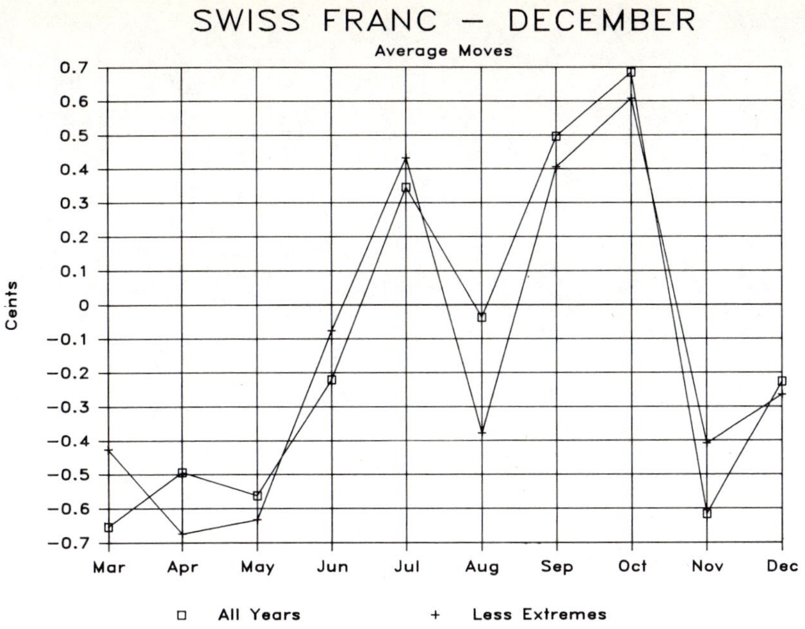
SWISS FRANC — DECEMBER
Average Moves
Cents
0.7
0.6
0.5
0.4
0.3
0.2
0.1
0
-0.1
-0.2
-0.3
-0.4
-0.5
-0.6
-0.7
Mar
Apr
May
Jun
Jul
Aug
Sep
Oct
Nov
Dec
All Years
Less Extremes

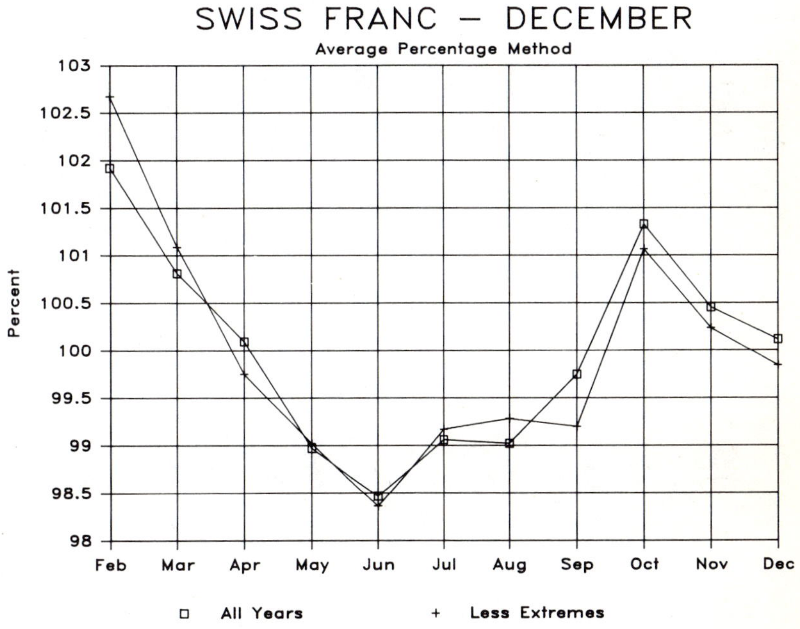
SWISS FRANC — DECEMBER
Average Percentage Method
Percent
103
102.5
102
101.5
101
100.5
100
99.5
99
98.5
98
Feb
Mar
Apr
May
Jun
Jul
Aug
Sep
Oct
Nov
Dec
All Years
Less Extremes

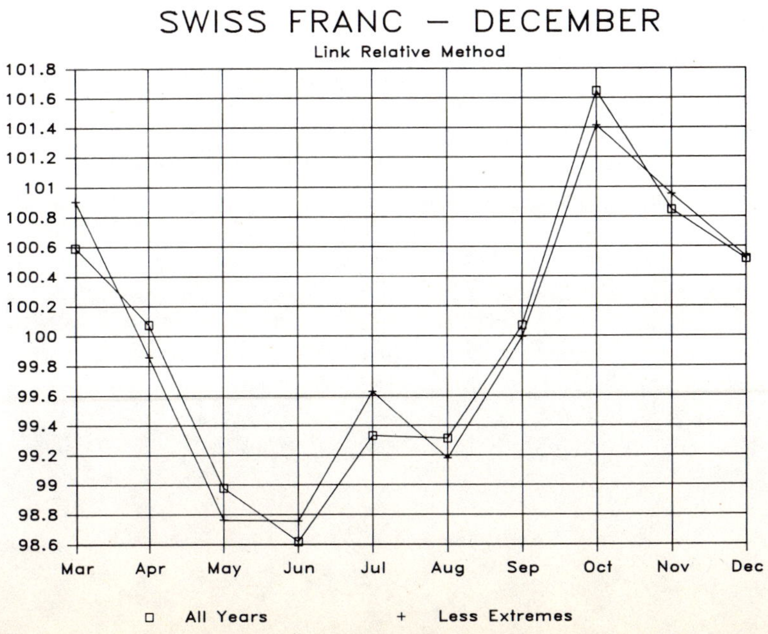
SWISS FRANC — DECEMBER
Link Relative Method
101.8
101.6
101.4
101.2
101
100.8
100.6
100.4
100.2
100
99.8
99.6
99.4
99.2
99
98.8
98.6
Mar
Apr
May
Jun
Jul
Aug
Sep
Oct
Nov
Dec
All Years
Less Extremes

FIVE

Metals

GOLD

Gold has some excellent seasonal trades though much of the seasonal information is distorted by the explosive move of 1980. The excellence of several of the months is surprising.

World production of gold is steady throughout the year. Production in North America slumps during the winter, but it is summer in the southern hemisphere and mining is increasing in such countries as South Africa. The two production cycles essentially cancel each other.

Demand is largely based on investment demand. It is doubtful that this is seasonal. It may be that the industrial and jewelry demand, which is seasonal, is the prime mover behind the seasonal moves in gold.

Ten years of gold history suggests several months with a strong seasonal bias. For example, gold futures prices have declined from October to November in 8 of 10 years with an average drop of almost $17. Another excellent period is May when there is also a 70 to 80% chance of a down move, depending on the contract month being traded.

PLATINUM

The seasonal tendency trader will not find platinum to be a good prospect. The moves in platinum are reasonably strong, but the reliability is mediocre.

Platinum follows a pattern similar to copper, since the two are used in many of the same industries. For example, platinum is used in the catalytic converters installed in cars made in the United States. Users purchase platinum in the winter and spring for use in the summer. This ensures that they will not be short of the metal during the actual manufacturing period. Platinum's role as a precious metal dampens these effects and provides a partial offset to the pattern of industrial use.

Platinum is also a very illiquid market. In other words, there are few traders in the platinum markert. This creates situations in which a small group of traders can exert a disproportionate influence; very wide price swings and distorted seasonal patterns may result.

Nontheless, platinum does have some attractive time periods. Bulls will particularly like the September period with its high reliability and strong moves. Bears will likely focus on November. October platinum appears to offer the best prospects. Note the strong reliability in March, June, and September. March and September have strong moves combined with high reliability.

SILVER

Silver is a mediocre seasonal performer. Although there are several months of reasonable reliability, there are no runs of good seasonal months. In other words, there is no run of several months with high seasonal reliability in a row. The patterns that exist tend to be weak shadows of copper seasonality.

The demand for silver follows much the same pattern as the demand for copper. The late winter/early spring price rise of silver is a result of its use as an industrial commodity. The price also tends to be dragged up in sympathy with the winter run-up in copper prices. (Traders should note in their analysis of the seasonal charts the influence of the 1980 bull market in silver.)

After the early spring price rise, the silver price settles into a vacillating pattern for the rest of the year. This is a result of silver's nature as a processed commodity that can be stored and sold at any time of the year. This means that when demand is high the supply can also be high. Silver, however, is still influenced strongly by the price action of other precious metals. Much of the explosive price action of 1974 and 1980 was caused by factors outside of silver's use as an industrial commodity. It was largely the demand for silver as an inflation or monetary hedge that led to those explosive moves.

COPPER

Copper is one of the best seasonal commodities. It has two periods of incredible reliability, combined with long and strong moves, that make it ideal for the seasonal tendency trader. There are many periods of 80% and even 90% reliability.

The largest users of copper are in the housing and automobile industries. Peak production of automobiles is in the summer. It is then that automobile manufacturers produce the new cars for unveiling in the fall. They purchase massive quantities of copper during the late winter and early spring to ensure an adequate supply for their summer production season.

The construction industry also makes heavy purchases of copper in late winter and early spring. Summer is the season of greatest construction. Obviously, it is extremely difficult to construct houses, apartments, and commercial properties in much of North America during the winter. Only in southern regions is there a significant amount of construction during winter. A large pecentage of electrical wiring is done with copper. Once again, to avoid a shortage of copper during the summer construction season, the construction industry purchases its copper in advance. This contributes to heavy demand during the winter and spring preceeding the construction season. During the actual construction season, contractors buy little copper because they have already satisfied their needs with early purchasing. This period of peak demand can be seen clearly on the charts that follow.

HIGHEST RELIABLE TRENDS

Commodity	Contract	Month	Position	Reliability	Average Move
Gold	Feb	May	Short	80.0	−9.85
	Feb	Jun	Short	70.0	−14.26
	Feb	Jul	Long	70.0	+13.51

Commodity	Contract	Month	Position	Reliability	Average Move
	Feb	Sep	Long	70.0	+31.64
	Feb	Nov	Short	80.0	−16.91
	Apr	Jul	Long	70.0	+14.00
	Apr	Sep	Long	70.0	+32.74
	Apr	Nov	Short	80.0	−17.30
	Jun	Sep	Long	70.0	+33.84
	Jun	Nov	Short	80.0	−17.74
	Jun	Apr	Short	70.0	−13.28
	Jun	May	Short	70.0	−9.99
	Jun	Jun	Short	70.0	−10.45
	Aug	Nov	Short	80.0	−18.25
	Aug	Apr	Short	70.0	−13.91
	Aug	May	Short	70.0	−10.73
	Aug	Jun	Short	70.0	−13.11
	Oct	Apr	Short	70.0	−14.50
	Oct	May	Short	70.0	−11.42
	Oct	Jun	Short	70.0	−13.48
	Oct	Sep	Long	70.0	+29.09
	Dec	Apr	Short	70.0	−15.14
	Dec	May	Short	70.0	−12.09
	Dec	Jun	Short	70.0	−13.80
	Dec	Sep	Long	70.0	+30.58
	Dec	Nov	Short	80.0	−16.91
Platinum	Jan	Apr	Short	70.0	−39.49
	Jan	Jun	Short	70.0	−16.13
	Jan	Sep	Long	70.0	+25.83
	Jan	Nov	Short	70.0	−15.89
	Apr	Sep	Long	70.0	+26.77
	Apr	Nov	Short	70.0	−16.35
	Jul	Nov	Short	70.0	−16.86
	Jul	Jun	Short	70.0	−16.65
	Oct	Mar	Short	70.0	−40.77
	Oct	Jun	Short	70.0	−16.27
	Oct	Sep	Long	70.0	+24.75
Silver	Jan	Apr	Short	70.0	−238.81
	Jan	Jul	Long	70.0	+32.87
	Jan	Sep	Long	70.0	+163.32
	Mar	Jul	Long	70.0	+33.98
	Mar	Sep	Long	70.0	+166.39
	May	Sep	Long	70.0	+169.07
	May	Dec	Short	70.0	−58.56
	May	May	Short	70.0	−58.30
	Jul	Dec	Short	70.0	−59.89
	Jul	May	Short	70.0	−67.87
	Sep	Dec	Short	70.0	−61.28
	Sep	May	Short	70.0	−71.39
	Sep	Sep	Long	70.0	+160.93

(Continued on next page.)

Commodity	Contract	Month	Position	Reliability	Average Move
Silver	Dec	May	Short	70.0	−75.64
	Dec	Sep	Long	70.0	+161.87
Copper	Jan	May	Short	80.0	−3.16
	Jan	Jun	Short	80.0	−4.42
	Jan	Sep	Short	70.0	−2.99
	Jan	Nov	Short	80.0	−1.64
	Jan	Jan	Long	70.0	+4.36
	Mar	Jun	Short	80.0	−4.41
	Mar	Sep	Short	70.0	−3.03
	Mar	Nov	Short	80.0	−1.57
	Mar	Feb	Long	70.0	+4.28
	May	Sep	Short	70.0	−3.05
	May	Nov	Short	80.0	−1.59
	May	Feb	Long	70.0	+4.61
	May	May	Short	80.0	−2.57
	Jul	Nov	Short	80.0	−1.60
	Jul	Feb	Long	70.0	+4.70
	Jul	Apr	Long	70.0	+2.13
	Jul	May	Short	80.0	−3.10
	Jul	Jun	Short	90.0	−3.88
	Sep	Feb	Long	70.0	+4.70
	Sep	Apr	Long	70.0	+2.11
	Sep	May	Short	80.0	−2.98
	Sep	Jun	Short	80.0	−4.40
	Dec	Apr	Long	70.0	+2.02
	Dec	May	Short	80.0	−2.83
	Dec	Jun	Short	80.0	−4.38
	Dec	Sep	Short	70.0	−2.62
	Dec	Nov	Short	80.0	−1.70
	Dec	Dec	Long	70.0	+2.32

GOLD - FEBRUARY - MONTHLY AVERAGE PRICE

Year of Expiration	Apr	May	Jun	Jul	Aug	Sep	Oct	Nov	Dec	Jan	Feb	May-Mar Average
1976	179.31	176.76	173.16	175.10	170.45	147.73	145.62	143.99	140.11	131.54	130.43	155.84
1977	132.89	131.98	131.51	120.97	110.89	114.68	116.91	132.39	134.92	132.64	135.85	126.87
1978	156.31	152.68	146.03	147.74	148.91	153.75	162.90	164.97	162.32	174.02	177.79	158.86
1979	185.16	186.57	194.30	199.40	214.20	220.20	234.39	209.22	211.89	228.06	245.75	211.74
1980	259.07	277.42	296.52	312.67	316.97	373.18	405.91	404.15	475.90	677.09	669.87	406.25
1981	583.83	557.21	645.25	684.26	660.89	714.42	687.30	643.47	607.25	560.05	499.69	622.15
1982	554.02	538.72	502.40	442.19	441.87	471.99	455.46	421.66	414.66	385.37	376.14	454.95
1983	389.05	365.29	343.00	365.03	384.77	451.78	434.20	422.82	449.85	483.97	497.79	417.05
1984	465.74	465.58	438.70	447.34	436.84	426.55	404.68	389.67	391.05	371.65	385.14	420.27
1985	416.07	410.24	406.62	368.44	366.91	355.42	350.13	347.39	321.94	303.30	299.83	358.75

	Apr	May	Jun	Jul	Aug	Sep	Oct	Nov	Dec	Jan	Feb
AVERAGE MOVE											
All Years		-5.90	1.51	-1.44	-1.04	17.70	-3.22	-11.78	3.02	13.78	-2.94
Less Extremes		-6.34	-4.59	0.86	-0.85	16.59	-4.73	-11.18	-0.67	-2.02	1.66
Ave Up - All Years		9.89	38.29	13.51	10.00	31.64	14.58	8.78	21.07	65.80	10.40
Ave Down - All Years		-9.85	-14.26	-36.31	-8.41	-14.83	-15.08	-16.91	-15.04	-20.90	-16.28
COUNT											
Number Up		2	3	7	4	7	4	2	5	4	5
Number Down		8	7	3	6	3	6	8	5	6	5
Pct Up		20.0%	30.0%	70.0%	40.0%	70.0%	40.0%	20.0%	50.0%	40.0%	50.0%
Pct Down		80.0%	70.0%	30.0%	60.0%	30.0%	60.0%	80.0%	50.0%	60.0%	50.0%
EXTREMES											
Greatest Up		18.35	88.05	39.00	19.74	67.01	32.73	15.48	71.74	201.20	17.69
Greatest Down		-26.63	-36.31	-60.22	-23.36	-22.72	-27.12	-43.83	-36.22	-47.20	-60.36
SEASONAL INDEX : AVERAGE PERCENTAGE METHOD											
All Years	100.5	99.1	98.6	97.6	97.2	100.5	100.7	98.6	99.5	103.7	104.1
Less Extremes	102.4	100.5	99.9	98.3	98.0	100.0	100.6	98.6	98.5	98.2	99.5
SEASONAL INDEX : LINK RELATIVE METHOD											
All Years		100.0	99.6	98.6	97.9	101.4	101.2	98.8	99.2	101.8	101.5
Less Extremes		99.7	98.6	98.7	98.4	102.8	102.8	100.0	99.7	99.3	99.9

GOLD - FEBRUARY - MONTH OF HIGH AND LOW

Year of Expiration	Apr	May	Jun	Jul	Aug	Sep	Oct	Nov	Dec	Jan	Feb
1976	H										L
1977					L						H
1978			L								H
1979	L										H
1980	L										H
1981						H					L
1982	H										L
1983			L								H
1984	H									L	
1985	H										L

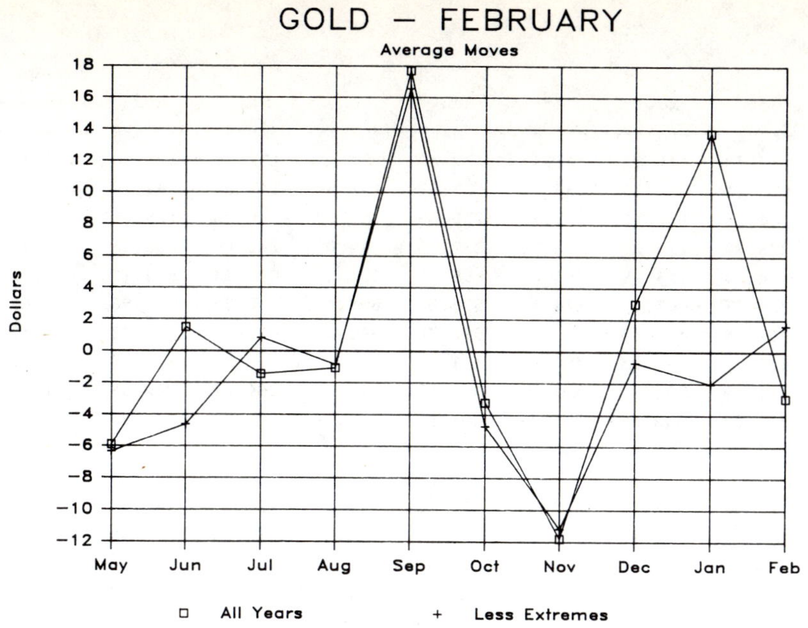
GOLD — FEBRUARY
Average Moves
Dollars
18
16
14
12
10
8
6
4
2
0
−2
−4
−6
−8
−10
−12
May
Jun
Jul
Aug
Sep
Oct
Nov
Dec
Jan
Feb
□ All Years
+ Less Extremes

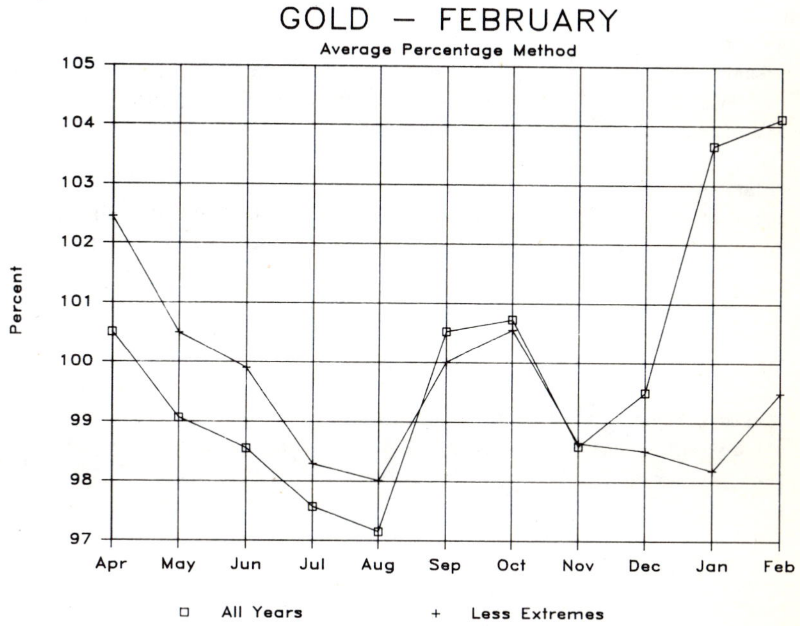
GOLD — FEBRUARY
Average Percentage Method
Percent
105
104
103
102
101
100
99
98
97
Apr
May
Jun
Jul
Aug
Sep
Oct
Nov
Dec
Jan
Feb
□ All Years
+ Less Extremes

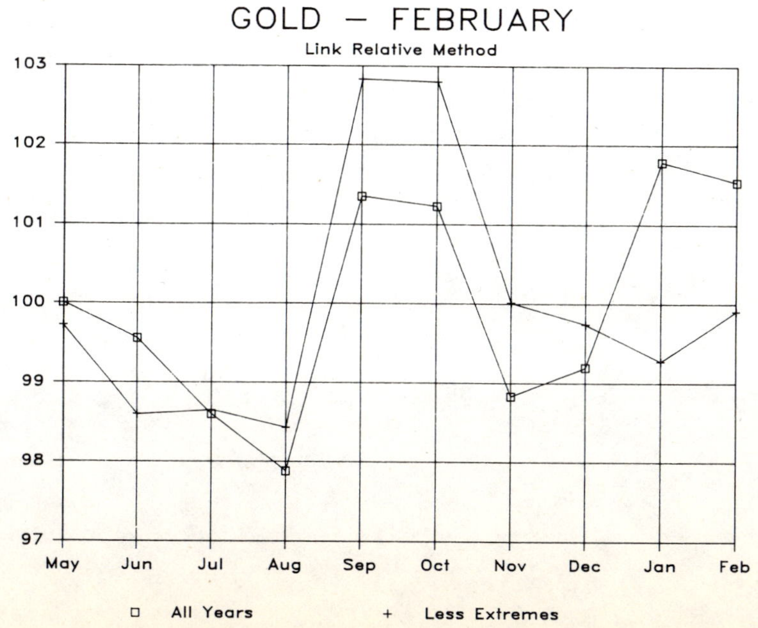
GOLD — FEBRUARY
Link Relative Method
103
102
101
100
99
98
97
May
Jun
Jul
Aug
Sep
Oct
Nov
Dec
Jan
Feb
□ All Years
+ Less Extremes

GOLD - APRIL - MONTHLY AVERAGE PRICE

Year of Expiration	Jun	Jul	Aug	Sep	Oct	Nov	Dec	Jan	Feb	Mar	Apr	Jun-Apr Average
1976	175.48	177.96	173.51	150.11	147.73	145.82	141.44	132.63	131.11	132.76	127.96	148.77
1977	133.07	122.32	111.90	115.30	117.31	133.36	135.93	133.57	137.54	149.09	149.64	130.82
1978	147.58	149.20	150.39	155.27	164.76	167.12	164.40	176.45	180.08	184.03	175.28	164.96
1979	197.31	202.59	217.47	223.67	238.20	213.21	215.70	232.30	249.01	242.06	238.35	224.53
1980	301.09	317.80	322.35	380.12	414.94	413.99	488.36	695.98	681.13	553.24	514.13	462.10
1981	656.65	697.58	674.58	731.87	704.27	661.04	624.96	575.51	506.40	500.24	496.56	620.88
1982	514.39	452.70	453.14	484.64	467.08	430.33	422.41	392.76	380.56	331.65	350.59	425.48
1983	350.80	372.84	392.16	460.31	441.20	429.23	456.58	491.23	495.15	422.21	433.65	431.40
1984	446.16	455.15	444.76	433.93	411.19	396.11	397.52	377.53	391.33	396.02	382.08	411.98
1985	415.03	375.89	373.92	361.96	356.07	352.55	326.33	306.96	301.16	305.78	324.83	345.50

	Jun	Jul	Aug	Sep	Oct	Nov	Dec	Jan	Feb	Mar	Apr
AVERAGE MOVE											
All Years		-1.36	-0.98	18.30	-3.44	-12.00	3.09	14.13	-6.15	-23.64	-2.40
Less Extremes		0.90	-0.77	17.28	-5.21	-11.60	-0.93	-2.11	-1.13	-15.01	-0.49
Ave Up - All Years		14.00	8.08	32.74	15.21	9.21	21.64	67.73	8.41	5.29	12.50
Ave Down - All Years		-37.20	-10.05	-15.39	-15.88	-17.30	-15.46	-21.61	-20.70	-52.57	-12.33
COUNT											
Number Up		7	5	7	4	2	5	4	5	5	4
Number Down		3	5	3	6	8	5	6	5	5	6
Pct Up		70.0%	50.0%	70.0%	40.0%	20.0%	50.0%	40.0%	50.0%	50.0%	40.0%
Pct Down		30.0%	50.0%	30.0%	60.0%	80.0%	50.0%	60.0%	50.0%	50.0%	60.0%
EXTREMES											
Greatest Up		40.93	19.32	68.16	34.81	16.05	74.38	207.62	16.70	11.55	19.06
Greatest Down		-61.69	-23.00	-23.40	-27.59	-43.24	-36.08	-49.46	-69.11	-127.89	-39.11
SEASONAL INDEX : AVERAGE PERCENTAGE METHOD											
All Years	99.9	98.7	98.2	101.4	101.3	99.1	99.7	103.2	102.9	98.3	97.4
Less Extremes	101.6	99.8	99.5	101.7	101.2	99.4	99.6	99.0	100.0	98.2	97.4
SEASONAL INDEX : LINK RELATIVE METHOD											
All Years		97.7	97.4	101.2	101.4	99.4	100.1	103.1	102.6	98.8	98.1
Less Extremes		98.1	98.2	102.9	103.1	100.6	100.6	100.4	100.8	97.8	97.4

GOLD - APRIL - MONTH OF HIGH AND LOW

Year of Expiration	Jun	Jul	Aug	Sep	Oct	Nov	Dec	Jan	Feb	Mar	Apr
1976		H									L
1977			L								H
1978	L									H	
1979	L								H		
1980	L							H			
1981				H							L
1982	H									L	
1983	L								H		
1984		H						L			
1985	H								L		

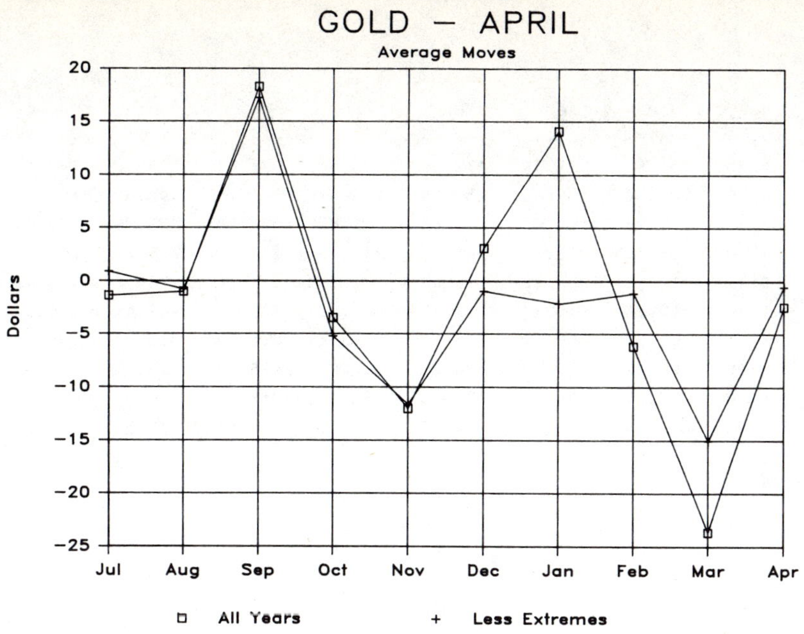

GOLD – APRIL
Average Moves
Dollars
Jul
Aug
Sep
Oct
Nov
Dec
Jan
Feb
Mar
Apr
All Years
Less Extremes

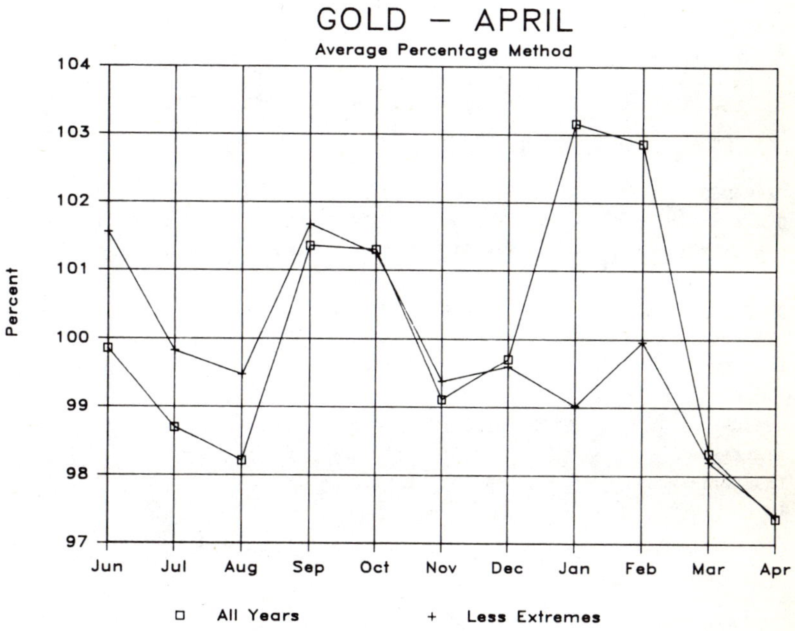

GOLD – APRIL
Average Percentage Method
Percent
Jun
Jul
Aug
Sep
Oct
Nov
Dec
Jan
Feb
Mar
Apr
All Years
Less Extremes

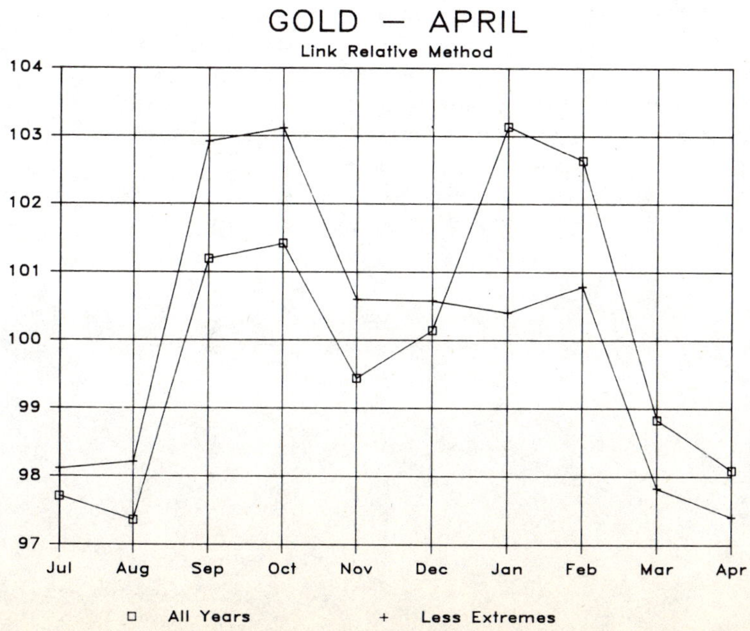

GOLD – APRIL
Link Relative Method
Jul
Aug
Sep
Oct
Nov
Dec
Jan
Feb
Mar
Apr
All Years
Less Extremes

GOLD - JUNE - MONTHLY AVERAGE PRICE

Year of Expiration	Aug	Sep	Oct	Nov	Dec	Jan	Feb	Mar	Apr	May	Jun	Aug-Jun Average
1976	176.53	152.52	149.85	147.69	142.88	133.80	132.03	132.90	128.52	127.52	126.52	140.98
1977	112.99	116.04	117.83	134.38	136.96	134.64	138.65	150.64	150.01	146.78	141.00	134.54
1978	151.90	156.83	166.66	169.33	166.54	178.98	182.65	186.63	175.82	176.74	183.86	172.36
1979	220.81	227.19	242.04	217.25	219.53	236.58	253.51	246.40	242.16	258.67	279.27	240.31
1980	327.60	386.58	423.67	423.03	500.43	714.93	704.28	572.30	524.36	517.55	596.92	517.42
1981	688.41	749.60	721.62	678.72	642.46	590.56	519.47	511.42	502.91	482.27	462.41	595.44
1982	464.50	497.43	478.87	439.44	431.24	401.32	389.57	338.80	356.28	335.82	316.00	404.48
1983	399.74	469.13	448.33	435.83	463.68	498.45	502.70	428.20	437.88	438.26	412.57	448.62
1984	452.90	441.43	417.96	402.71	404.30	383.62	397.75	402.78	386.30	379.21	378.53	404.32
1985	381.46	369.05	362.52	358.27	331.24	311.29	305.55	310.19	327.55	316.84	316.51	335.50

	Aug	Sep	Oct	Nov	Dec	Jan	Feb	Mar	Apr	May	Jun
AVERAGE MOVE											
All Years		18.90	-3.64	-12.27	3.26	14.49	-5.80	-24.59	-4.85	-5.21	3.39
Less Extremes		17.95	-5.69	-12.05	-1.06	-2.21	-0.48	-15.74	-2.25	-6.00	-2.47
Ave Up - All Years		33.84	15.89	9.61	22.34	69.69	8.60	5.30	14.84	5.94	35.70
Ave Down - All Years		-15.97	-16.67	-17.74	-15.82	-22.31	-20.20	-54.48	-13.28	-9.99	-10.45
COUNT											
Number Up		7	4	2	5	4	5	5	3	3	3
Number Down		3	6	8	5	6	5	5	7	7	7
Pct Up		70.0%	40.0%	20.0%	50.0%	40.0%	50.0%	50.0%	30.0%	30.0%	30.0%
Pct Down		30.0%	60.0%	80.0%	50.0%	60.0%	50.0%	50.0%	70.0%	70.0%	70.0%
EXTREMES											
Greatest Up		69.40	37.09	16.55	77.40	214.50	16.93	11.99	17.48	16.51	79.37
Greatest Down		-24.01	-27.97	-42.90	-36.26	-51.90	-71.09	-131.99	-47.94	-20.65	-25.69
SEASONAL INDEX : AVERAGE PERCENTAGE METHOD											
All Years	99.8	102.7	102.4	100.1	100.4	103.3	102.9	98.5	97.0	96.0	96.9
Less Extremes	101.2	103.3	102.6	100.7	100.6	100.2	100.7	98.6	96.8	96.2	96.8
SEASONAL INDEX : LINK RELATIVE METHOD											
All Years		99.6	100.2	98.7	99.8	103.2	103.2	99.7	98.8	97.9	98.8
Less Extremes		101.0	101.7	99.8	100.3	100.7	101.8	99.2	98.9	98.1	98.5

GOLD - JUNE - MONTH OF HIGH AND LOW

Year of Expiration	Aug	Sep	Oct	Nov	Dec	Jan	Feb	Mar	Apr	May	Jun
1976	H										L
1977	L							H			
1978	L							H			
1979				L							H
1980	L					H					
1981		H									L
1982		H									L
1983	L						H				
1984	H										L
1985	H						L				

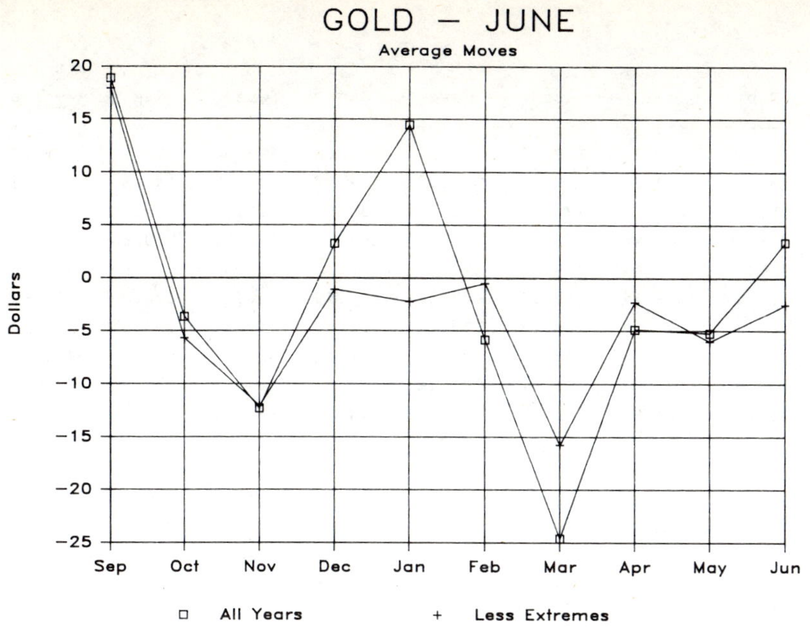
GOLD – JUNE
Average Moves
Dollars
20
15
10
5
0
-5
-10
-15
-20
-25
Sep
Oct
Nov
Dec
Jan
Feb
Mar
Apr
May
Jun
All Years
Less Extremes

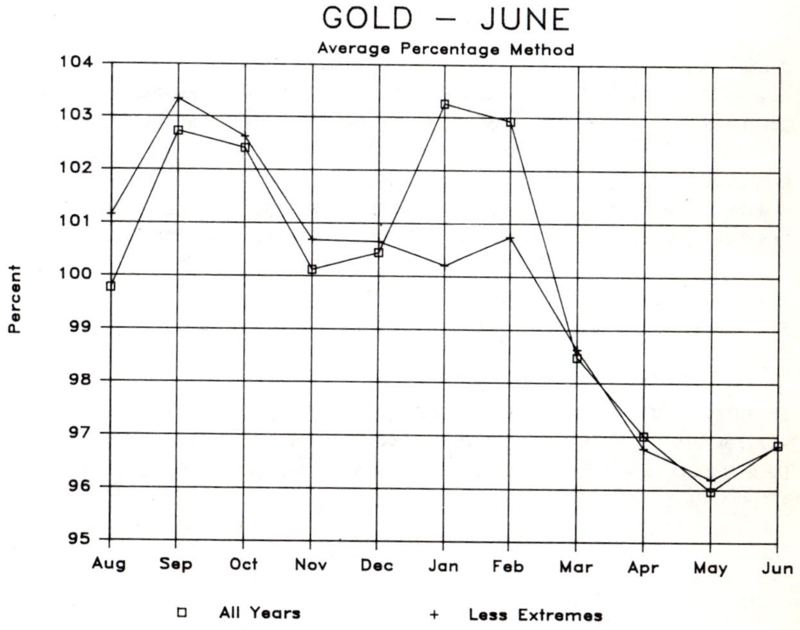
GOLD – JUNE
Average Percentage Method
Percent
104
103
102
101
100
99
98
97
96
95
Aug
Sep
Oct
Nov
Dec
Jan
Feb
Mar
Apr
May
Jun
All Years
Less Extremes

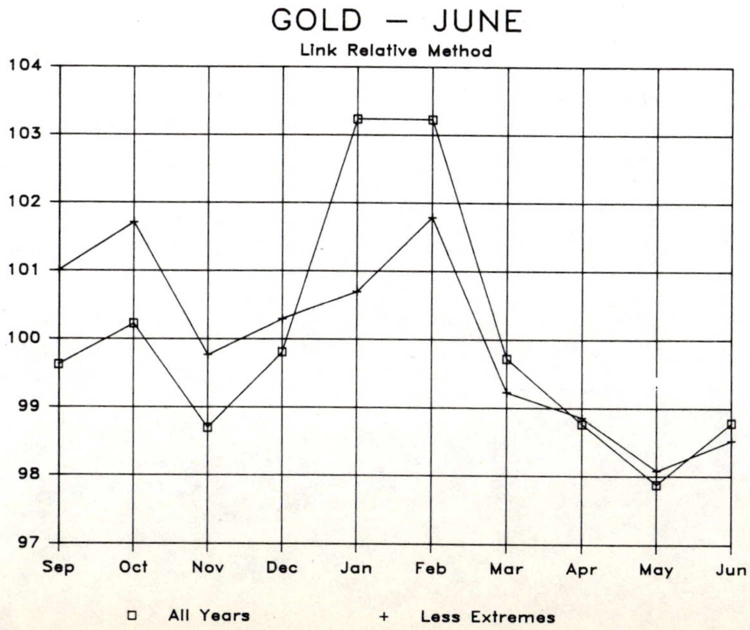
GOLD – JUNE
Link Relative Method
104
103
102
101
100
99
98
97
Sep
Oct
Nov
Dec
Jan
Feb
Mar
Apr
May
Jun
All Years
Less Extremes

GOLD - AUGUST - MONTHLY AVERAGE PRICE

Year of Expiration	Oct	Nov	Dec	Jan	Feb	Mar	Apr	May	Jun	Jul	Aug	Oct-Aug Average
1976	152.01	149.59	144.45	135.06	133.21	133.73	129.50	128.51	127.06	117.34	110.06	132.77
1977	118.53	135.52	138.11	135.81	139.91	152.20	151.49	148.07	142.07	144.08	145.55	141.03
1978	168.58	171.54	168.73	181.50	185.22	189.28	178.05	179.09	185.60	190.36	205.81	182.16
1979	245.91	221.32	223.39	240.89	258.00	250.76	246.29	263.30	282.51	296.56	299.88	257.16
1980	432.31	431.61	511.84	733.16	728.03	592.04	539.42	527.54	611.52	646.09	625.65	579.93
1981	739.54	696.77	659.81	605.37	532.47	523.14	515.58	496.36	467.09	410.72	410.09	550.63
1982	490.62	448.58	440.47	410.46	398.71	346.26	364.43	343.09	320.37	342.42	360.87	387.84
1983	455.68	442.50	470.81	506.05	510.77	434.58	444.49	444.87	417.41	424.89	416.73	451.71
1984	424.87	409.45	411.22	389.93	404.33	409.63	393.07	386.16	382.57	347.11	348.61	391.54
1985	368.96	364.06	336.28	315.70	310.05	314.90	331.89	320.54	319.25	318.71	330.25	330.05

	Oct	Nov	Dec	Jan	Feb	Mar	Apr	May	Jun	Jul	Aug
AVERAGE MOVE											
All Years		-12.61	3.42	14.88	-5.32	-25.42	-5.23	-5.67	1.79	-1.72	1.52
Less Extremes		-12.54	-1.14	-2.26	0.32	-16.31	-2.23	-6.54	-4.60	0.58	2.15
Ave Up - All Years		9.97	22.99	71.70	8.81	5.41	15.02	6.14	36.57	14.15	8.62
Ave Down - All Years		-18.25	-16.16	-23.00	-19.46	-56.24	-13.91	-10.73	-13.11	-25.52	-9.13
COUNT											
Number Up		2	5	4	5	5	3	3	3	6	6
Number Down		8	5	6	5	5	7	7	7	4	4
Pct Up		20.0%	50.0%	40.0%	50.0%	50.0%	30.0%	30.0%	30.0%	60.0%	60.0%
Pct Down		80.0%	50.0%	60.0%	50.0%	50.0%	70.0%	70.0%	70.0%	40.0%	40.0%
EXTREMES											
Greatest Up		16.98	80.23	221.31	17.10	12.29	18.17	17.01	83.98	34.56	18.45
Greatest Down		-42.76	-36.96	-54.44	-72.90	-135.98	-52.62	-21.34	-29.27	-56.37	-20.44
SEASONAL INDEX : AVERAGE PERCENTAGE METHOD											
All Years	104.3	101.8	101.9	104.1	103.7	99.3	97.8	96.6	96.8	96.4	97.2
Less Extremes	104.3	102.2	101.5	102.6	102.2	99.4	97.2	96.6	96.9	96.8	97.7
SEASONAL INDEX : LINK RELATIVE METHOD											
All Years		99.5	100.5	103.8	103.8	100.2	99.1	98.0	98.3	97.9	98.9
Less Extremes		101.3	101.6	101.7	102.7	99.8	99.2	98.1	97.7	98.2	99.6

GOLD - AUGUST - MONTH OF HIGH AND LOW

Year of Expiration	Oct	Nov	Dec	Jan	Feb	Mar	Apr	May	Jun	Jul	Aug
1976	H										L
1977	L					H					
1978	L										H
1979		L									H
1980		L		H							
1981	H										L
1982	H								L		
1983					H						L
1984	H									L	
1985	H				L						

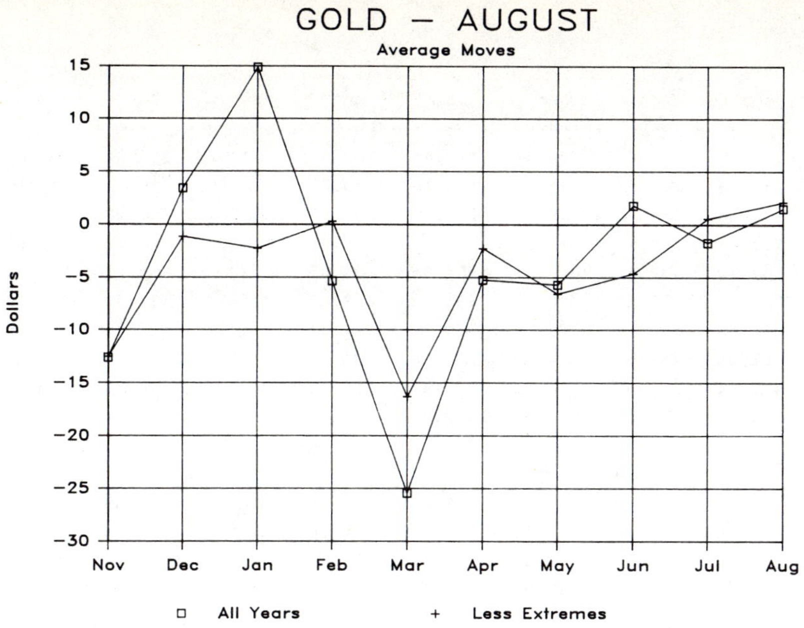
GOLD – AUGUST
Average Moves
15
10
5
0
−5
−10
−15
−20
−25
−30
Dollars
Nov
Dec
Jan
Feb
Mar
Apr
May
Jun
Jul
Aug
All Years
Less Extremes

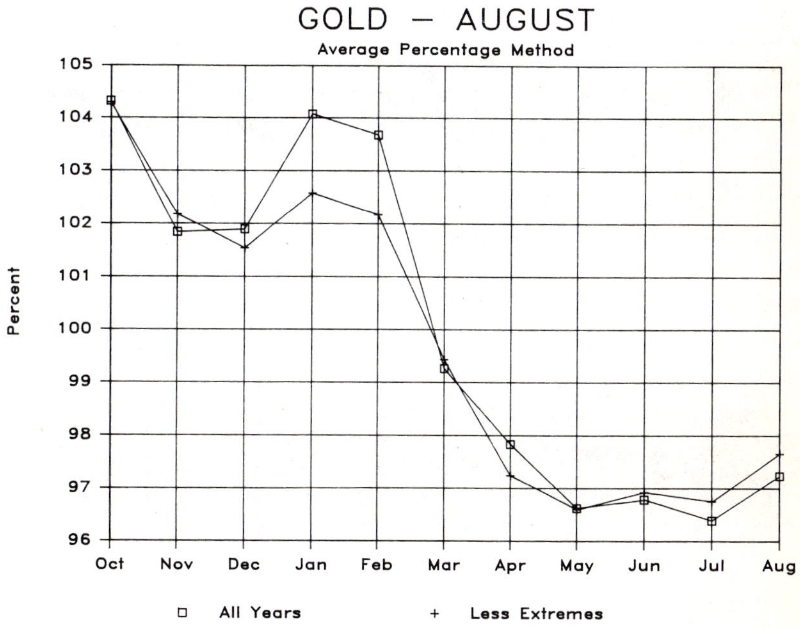
GOLD – AUGUST
Average Percentage Method
105
104
103
102
101
100
99
98
97
96
Percent
Oct
Nov
Dec
Jan
Feb
Mar
Apr
May
Jun
Jul
Aug
All Years
Less Extremes

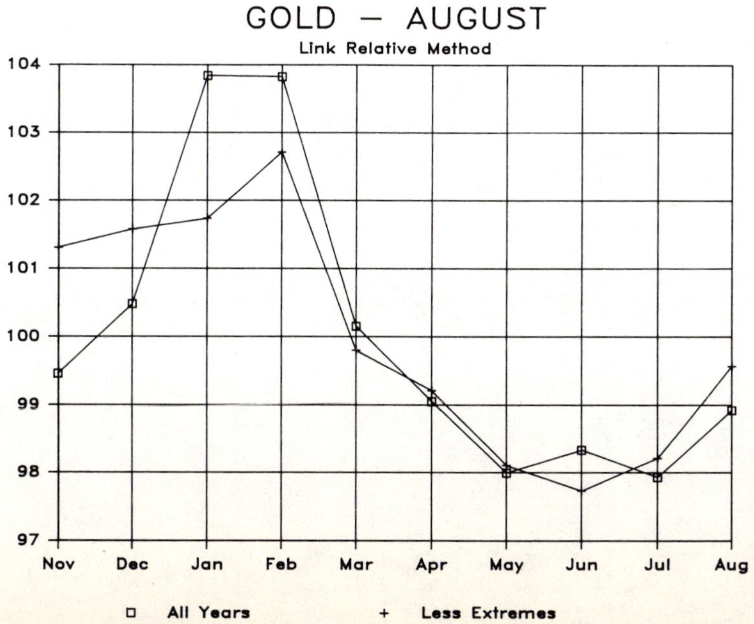
GOLD – AUGUST
Link Relative Method
104
103
102
101
100
99
98
97
Nov
Dec
Jan
Feb
Mar
Apr
May
Jun
Jul
Aug
All Years
Less Extremes

GOLD - OCTOBER - MONTHLY AVERAGE PRICE

Year of Expiration	Dec	Jan	Feb	Mar	Apr	May	Jun	Jul	Aug	Sep	Oct	Dec-Oct Average
1976	146.08	136.33	134.48	134.76	130.58	129.61	128.44	118.44	109.42	114.01	115.39	127.05
1977	139.36	137.01	141.21	153.79	153.03	149.54	143.31	145.18	146.27	150.65	159.42	147.16
1978	170.93	184.03	187.79	191.94	180.36	181.52	188.43	193.26	207.91	213.61	226.23	193.27
1979	227.25	245.24	262.51	255.15	250.51	267.98	287.25	302.01	305.78	358.45	390.77	286.63
1980	523.04	751.07	751.44	611.78	554.40	537.41	622.61	657.85	634.68	679.08	663.41	635.16
1981	677.03	620.13	545.46	534.96	528.31	510.41	478.67	421.22	419.65	446.77	438.52	511.01
1982	449.90	419.80	408.06	353.81	372.42	350.36	327.86	349.79	371.31	436.11	423.76	387.56
1983	478.22	513.95	519.08	441.22	451.34	451.63	424.40	432.26	421.84	412.73	396.04	449.34
1984	418.35	396.47	411.15	416.76	400.44	393.82	390.11	353.81	353.10	342.28	340.58	383.35
1985	341.58	320.31	314.82	319.90	336.61	324.65	322.86	322.29	333.75	323.35	326.17	326.02

	Dec	Jan	Feb	Mar	Apr	May	Jun	Jul	Aug	Sep	Oct
AVERAGE MOVE											
All Years		15.26	-4.83	-26.19	-5.61	-6.10	1.70	-1.78	0.76	17.33	0.33
Less Extremes		-2.32	1.13	-16.86	-2.16	-7.06	-4.56	0.55	1.16	14.92	-1.55
Ave Up - All Years		73.71	7.57	5.54	15.15	6.31	37.13	14.42	10.50	29.09	11.58
Ave Down - All Years		-23.71	-23.44	-57.93	-14.50	-11.42	-13.48	-26.08	-8.98	-10.11	-10.93
COUNT											
Number Up		4	6	5	3	3	3	6	5	7	5
Number Down		6	4	5	7	7	7	4	5	3	5
Pct Up		40.0%	60.0%	50.0%	30.0%	30.0%	30.0%	60.0%	50.0%	70.0%	50.0%
Pct Down		60.0%	40.0%	50.0%	70.0%	70.0%	70.0%	40.0%	50.0%	30.0%	50.0%
EXTREMES											
Greatest Up		228.03	17.27	12.58	18.61	17.48	85.20	35.24	21.52	64.79	32.32
Greatest Down		-56.90	-74.67	-139.65	-57.39	-22.06	-31.74	-57.45	-23.17	-10.82	-16.69
SEASONAL INDEX : AVERAGE PERCENTAGE METHOD											
All Years	102.9	104.5	104.0	99.6	98.2	96.9	96.8	96.1	96.6	101.5	102.9
Less Extremes	102.1	104.8	103.8	99.8	98.8	97.7	97.7	96.6	97.0	100.3	100.9
SEASONAL INDEX : LINK RELATIVE METHOD											
All Years		103.6	103.5	99.7	98.4	97.2	97.4	96.9	97.4	102.3	103.5
Less Extremes		103.2	103.8	100.3	99.3	97.6	96.8	96.8	97.5	101.9	102.8

GOLD - OCTOBER - MONTH OF HIGH AND LOW

Year of Expiration	Dec	Jan	Feb	Mar	Apr	May	Jun	Jul	Aug	Sep	Oct
1976	H								L		
1977		L									H
1978	L										H
1979	L										H
1980	L		H								
1981	H								L		
1982	H						L				
1983			H								L
1984	H										L
1985	H		L								

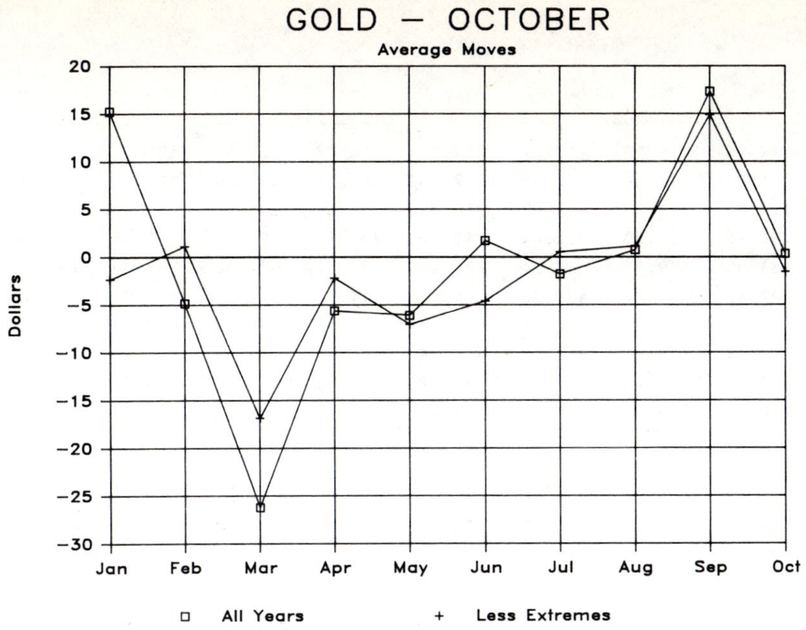
GOLD — OCTOBER
Average Moves
Dollars
20
15
10
5
0
-5
-10
-15
-20
-25
-30
Jan Feb Mar Apr May Jun Jul Aug Sep Oct
All Years
Less Extremes

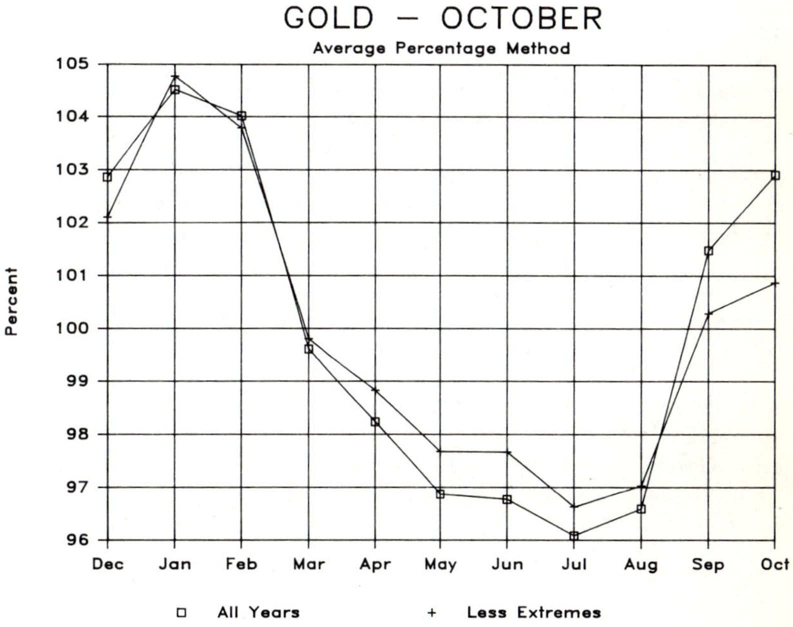
GOLD — OCTOBER
Average Percentage Method
Percent
105
104
103
102
101
100
99
98
97
96
Dec Jan Feb Mar Apr May Jun Jul Aug Sep Oct
All Years
Less Extremes

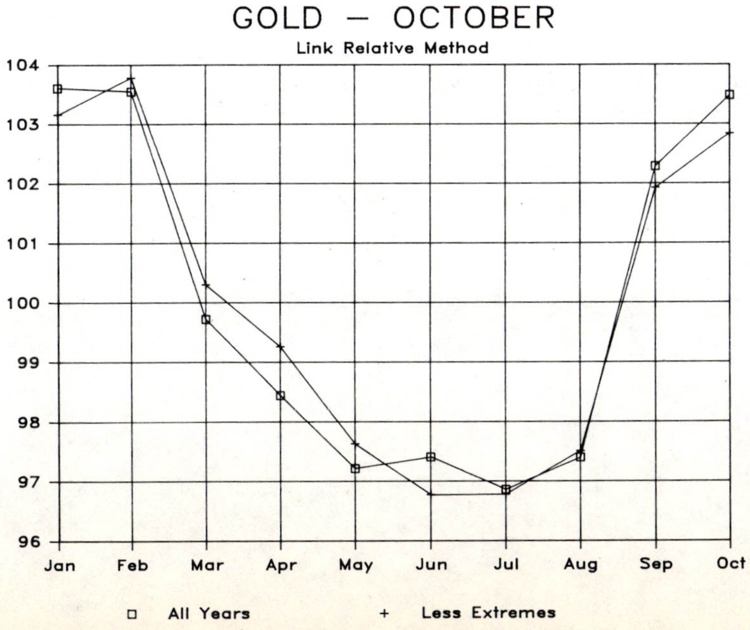
GOLD — OCTOBER
Link Relative Method
104
103
102
101
100
99
98
97
96
Jan Feb Mar Apr May Jun Jul Aug Sep Oct
All Years
Less Extremes

GOLD - DECEMBER - MONTHLY AVERAGE PRICE

Year of Expiration	Feb	Mar	Apr	May	Jun	Jul	Aug	Sep	Oct	Nov	Dec	Feb-Dec Average
1976	135.80	135.88	131.71	130.76	129.96	119.63	110.01	114.27	116.72	131.54	134.20	126.41
1977	142.53	155.45	154.63	151.10	144.63	146.44	147.58	152.29	161.11	162.86	160.04	152.60
1978	190.41	194.63	182.72	184.00	191.35	196.29	211.02	216.82	230.64	205.43	206.43	200.88
1979	267.05	259.57	254.77	272.71	291.95	307.50	311.52	366.16	396.71	393.67	455.94	325.23
1980	774.69	631.52	569.22	547.29	633.93	670.96	647.34	697.21	671.07	624.96	593.80	642.00
1981	558.45	546.84	541.12	524.54	490.47	431.67	430.71	459.45	444.15	413.75	410.99	477.47
1982	417.70	361.50	380.61	357.73	335.38	357.33	377.59	443.64	427.47	416.57	443.01	392.59
1983	527.58	448.04	458.43	458.52	431.41	439.65	429.09	419.34	398.31	383.49	387.40	434.66
1984	418.22	424.32	408.03	401.89	398.29	361.05	359.93	348.82	344.01	342.18	320.87	375.23
1985	319.92	325.41	341.64	329.00	326.80	326.27	338.02	327.70	329.22	326.31	322.04	328.39

	Feb	Mar	Apr	May	Jun	Jul	Aug	Sep	Oct	Nov	Dec
AVERAGE MOVE											
All Years		-26.92	-6.03	-6.54	1.67	-1.74	0.60	18.29	-2.63	-11.87	3.40
Less Extremes		-17.37	-2.14	-7.55	-4.49	0.55	1.17	15.99	-3.84	-10.92	0.36
Ave Up - All Years		5.76	15.24	6.43	37.75	14.92	10.38	30.58	11.43	8.28	19.26
Ave Down - All Years		-59.60	-15.14	-12.09	-13.80	-26.73	-9.18	-10.39	-16.69	-16.91	-12.46
COUNT											
Number Up		5	3	3	3	6	5	7	5	2	5
Number Down		5	7	7	7	4	5	3	5	8	5
Pct Up		50.0%	30.0%	30.0%	30.0%	60.0%	50.0%	70.0%	50.0%	20.0%	50.0%
Pct Down		50.0%	70.0%	70.0%	70.0%	40.0%	50.0%	30.0%	50.0%	80.0%	50.0%
EXTREMES											
Greatest Up		12.92	19.10	17.93	86.65	37.03	20.25	66.05	30.56	14.82	62.28
Greatest Down		-143.16	-62.30	-22.88	-34.07	-58.81	-23.62	-11.11	-26.14	-46.12	-31.16
SEASONAL INDEX : AVERAGE PERCENTAGE METHOD											
All Years	105.2	100.6	99.2	97.7	97.4	96.6	96.9	101.8	102.5	100.3	101.8
Less Extremes	106.1	101.5	100.0	97.9	97.9	96.3	97.2	101.8	101.4	99.4	99.1
SEASONAL INDEX : LINK RELATIVE METHOD											
All Years		101.2	99.6	98.1	98.2	97.4	97.7	102.5	102.9	100.8	101.7
Less Extremes		101.1	100.0	98.3	97.5	97.5	98.2	102.8	103.2	100.6	100.8

GOLD - DECEMBER - MONTH OF HIGH AND LOW

Year of Expiration	Feb	Mar	Apr	May	Jun	Jul	Aug	Sep	Oct	Nov	Dec
1976		H					L				
1977	L									H	
1978			L						H		
1979			L								H
1980	H			L							
1981	H										L
1982					L			H			
1983	H									L	
1984		H									L
1985	L		H								

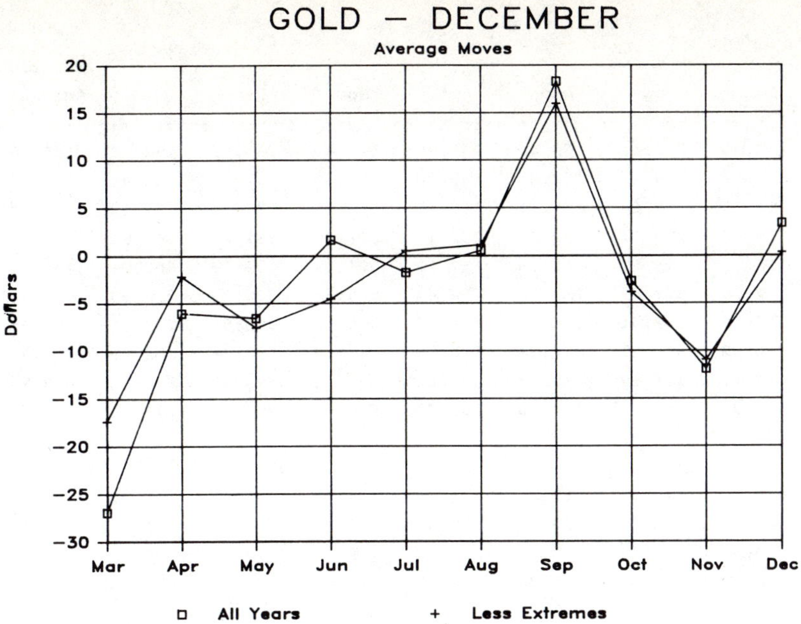
GOLD — DECEMBER
Average Moves
Dollars
20
15
10
5
0
−5
−10
−15
−20
−25
−30
Mar
Apr
May
Jun
Jul
Aug
Sep
Oct
Nov
Dec
All Years
Less Extremes

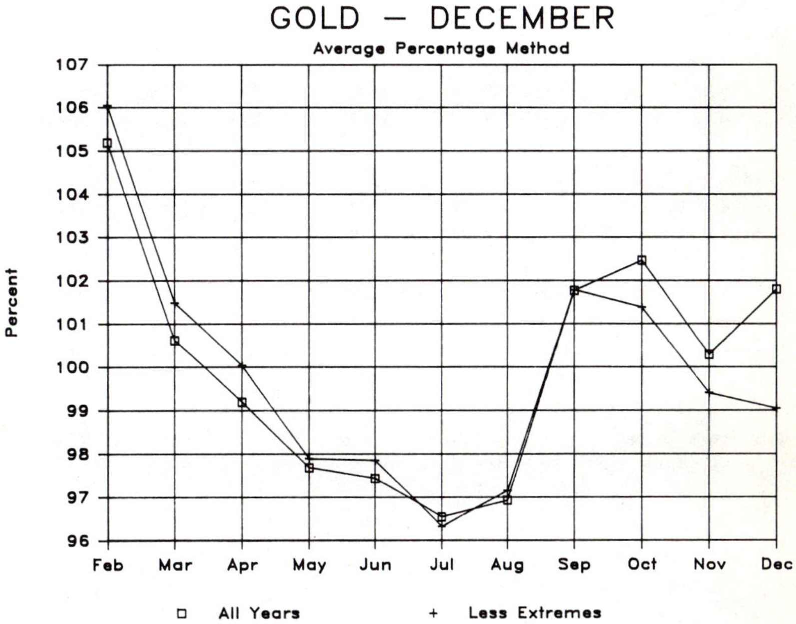
GOLD — DECEMBER
Average Percentage Method
Percent
107
106
105
104
103
102
101
100
99
98
97
96
Feb
Mar
Apr
May
Jun
Jul
Aug
Sep
Oct
Nov
Dec
All Years
Less Extremes

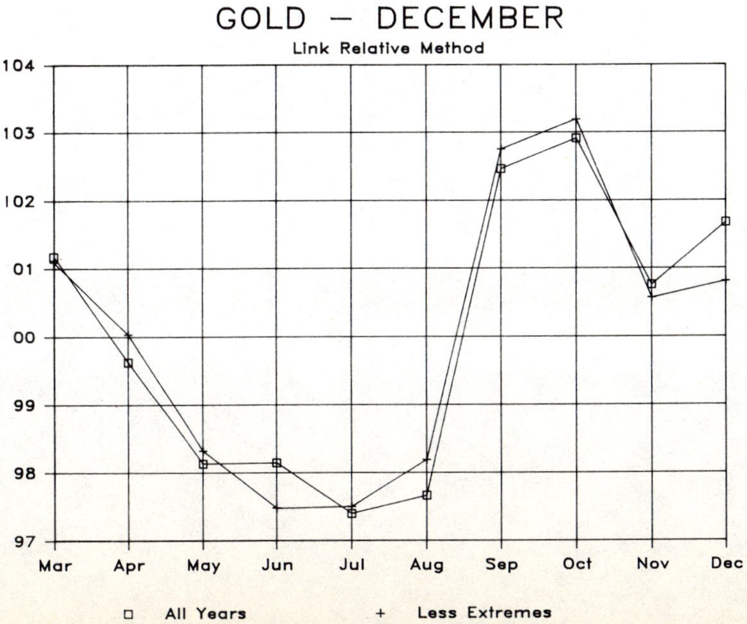
GOLD — DECEMBER
Link Relative Method
104
103
102
01
00
99
98
97
Mar
Apr
May
Jun
Jul
Aug
Sep
Oct
Nov
Dec
All Years
Less Extremes

PLATINUM - JANUARY - MONTHLY AVERAGE PRICE

Year of Expiration	Mar	Apr	May	Jun	Jul	Aug	Sep	Oct	Nov	Dec	Jan	Mar-Jan Average
1976	161.09	155.42	156.55	155.94	168.90	176.55	160.43	147.76	147.30	144.99	144.15	156.28
1977	144.12	159.77	164.13	177.41	177.81	159.25	162.53	159.58	157.86	152.61	150.44	160.50
1978	172.67	168.81	162.93	155.69	154.16	150.64	154.11	160.85	171.10	177.51	191.92	165.49
1979	238.89	222.15	235.56	249.92	254.73	269.57	272.28	332.17	327.01	339.77	347.16	280.84
1980	394.11	387.33	429.56	429.37	410.88	395.61	464.16	517.10	504.41	602.28	800.94	485.07
1981	865.79	647.81	584.12	675.71	697.78	671.01	733.35	692.84	640.57	590.39	536.89	666.93
1982	543.12	526.64	507.86	475.91	427.56	439.01	451.67	424.92	395.05	395.61	363.11	450.04
1983	347.49	365.26	329.69	292.67	301.92	305.15	332.94	340.95	347.57	370.74	452.68	344.28
1984	423.16	439.01	465.90	437.09	449.61	449.69	439.32	400.62	391.56	395.32	372.58	423.99
1985	425.71	416.79	410.20	403.08	359.06	353.53	333.90	328.37	330.65	302.72	271.30	357.75

	Mar	Apr	May	Jun	Jul	Aug	Sep	Oct	Nov	Dec	Jan
AVERAGE MOVE											
All Years		-22.72	-4.25	0.63	-5.04	-3.24	13.47	0.05	-9.21	5.89	15.92
Less Extremes		-3.37	-2.63	-6.03	-3.01	-2.56	10.72	-2.36	-6.26	1.40	1.76
Ave Up - All Years		16.42	17.60	39.75	10.33	7.45	25.83	31.90	6.38	24.09	75.60
Ave Down - All Years		-39.49	-26.10	-16.13	-28.10	-13.93	-15.37	-21.19	-15.89	-21.41	-23.86
COUNT											
Number Up		3	5	3	6	5	7	4	3	6	4
Number Down		7	5	7	4	5	3	6	7	4	6
Pct Up		30.0%	50.0%	30.0%	60.0%	50.0%	70.0%	40.0%	30.0%	60.0%	40.0%
Pct Down		70.0%	50.0%	70.0%	40.0%	50.0%	30.0%	60.0%	70.0%	40.0%	60.0%
EXTREMES											
Greatest Up		17.77	42.23	91.60	22.06	14.85	68.55	59.89	10.25	97.87	198.66
Greatest Down		-217.98	-63.69	-37.01	-48.35	-26.76	-19.63	-40.51	-52.27	-50.18	-53.50
SEASONAL INDEX : AVERAGE PERCENTAGE METHOD											
All Years	103.4	100.0	99.4	99.0	98.1	97.2	99.4	100.0	98.6	100.2	104.7
Less Extremes	102.8	100.5	99.4	99.0	98.2	97.2	98.8	98.7	97.7	99.2	100.8
SEASONAL INDEX : LINK RELATIVE METHOD											
All Years		101.1	100.5	100.1	99.0	97.8	100.1	100.5	98.8	99.7	102.3
Less Extremes		100.6	100.3	99.7	99.2	98.9	101.2	100.7	99.2	99.6	100.5

PLATINUM - JANUARY - MONTH OF HIGH AND LOW

Year of Expiration	Mar	Apr	May	Jun	Jul	Aug	Sep	Oct	Nov	Dec	Jan
1976						H					L
1977	L				H						
1978						L					H
1979		L									H
1980		L									H
1981	H										L
1982	H										L
1983				L							H
1984			H								L
1985	H										L

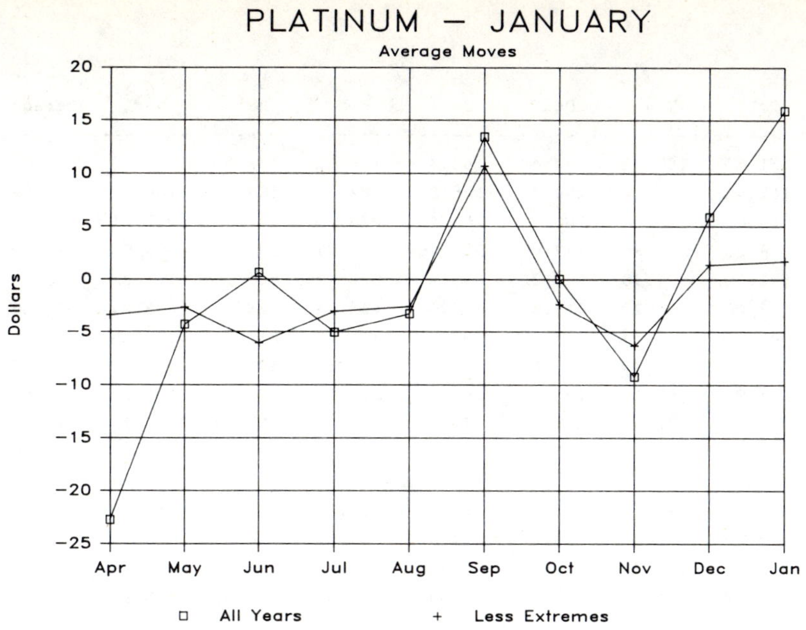
PLATINUM — JANUARY
Average Moves
Dollars
20
15
10
5
0
−5
−10
−15
−20
−25
Apr
May
Jun
Jul
Aug
Sep
Oct
Nov
Dec
Jan
All Years
Less Extremes

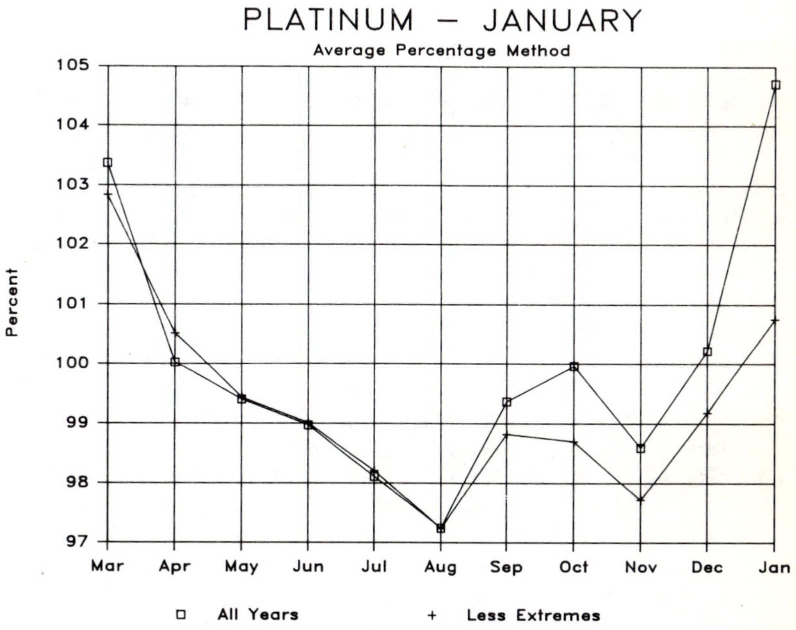
PLATINUM — JANUARY
Average Percentage Method
Percent
105
104
103
102
101
100
99
98
97
Mar
Apr
May
Jun
Jul
Aug
Sep
Oct
Nov
Dec
Jan
All Years
Less Extremes

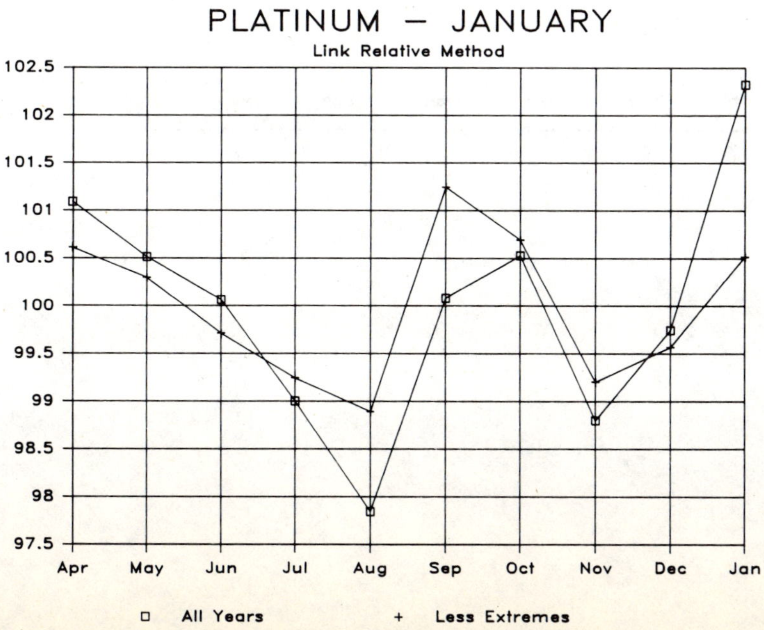
PLATINUM — JANUARY
Link Relative Method
102.5
102
101.5
101
100.5
100
99.5
99
98.5
98
97.5
Apr
May
Jun
Jul
Aug
Sep
Oct
Nov
Dec
Jan
All Years
Less Extremes

PLATINUM - APRIL - MONTHLY AVERAGE PRICE

Year of Expiration	Jun	Jul	Aug	Sep	Oct	Nov	Dec	Jan	Feb	Mar	Apr	Jun-Apr Average
1976	159.11	173.22	181.21	164.35	151.65	150.62	147.48	143.45	138.62	137.50	144.86	153.82
1977	180.81	181.12	162.08	165.52	162.43	160.12	154.71	156.88	162.84	163.84	160.93	164.66
1978	158.45	156.89	153.18	156.61	163.63	173.84	180.26	205.47	226.55	226.74	217.91	183.59
1979	252.35	258.29	272.47	275.17	333.86	329.29	343.07	363.75	411.97	391.35	386.94	328.95
1980	432.01	413.63	400.49	469.22	521.04	506.98	601.36	809.21	899.93	761.28	573.74	580.81
1981	692.14	716.81	691.61	760.49	717.00	668.29	617.87	544.69	483.34	488.05	478.24	623.50
1982	492.87	443.41	455.28	467.89	440.76	406.44	405.74	367.96	361.87	317.74	339.25	409.02
1983	301.39	310.63	312.48	340.08	347.96	353.49	377.66	463.71	466.86	402.61	415.65	372.05
1984	443.58	456.18	457.09	445.10	406.91	397.44	403.25	381.46	396.59	401.36	393.31	416.57
1985	412.56	368.44	362.84	343.07	336.43	337.89	309.11	275.82	270.02	259.38	285.76	323.76

	Jun	Jul	Aug	Sep	Oct	Nov	Dec	Jan	Feb	Mar	Apr
AVERAGE MOVE											
All Years		-4.66	-2.99	13.88	-0.58	-9.73	5.61	17.19	10.62	-26.87	-15.32
Less Extremes		-2.73	-2.36	11.21	-2.63	-7.35	1.52	4.65	9.60	-16.86	0.99
Ave Up - All Years		11.15	7.36	26.77	31.36	5.73	28.91	68.39	30.71	2.67	17.08
Ave Down - All Years		-28.38	-13.34	-16.20	-21.87	-16.35	-17.69	-34.01	-19.52	-46.57	-36.92
COUNT											
Number Up		6	5	7	4	3	5	5	6	4	4
Number Down		4	5	3	6	7	5	5	4	6	6
Pct Up		60.0%	50.0%	70.0%	40.0%	30.0%	50.0%	50.0%	60.0%	40.0%	40.0%
Pct Down		40.0%	50.0%	30.0%	60.0%	70.0%	50.0%	50.0%	40.0%	60.0%	60.0%
EXTREMES											
Greatest Up		24.67	14.18	68.89	58.69	10.21	94.38	207.86	90.71	4.78	26.39
Greatest Down		-49.46	-25.21	-19.76	-43.50	-48.70	-50.43	-73.18	-61.35	-138.65	-187.54
SEASONAL INDEX : AVERAGE PERCENTAGE METHOD											
All Years	99.7	98.8	97.9	99.8	99.5	97.9	98.8	102.9	106.3	100.3	98.1
Less Extremes	99.4	100.2	99.1	99.4	98.9	98.0	98.7	100.6	103.8	99.3	98.2
SEASONAL INDEX : LINK RELATIVE METHOD											
All Years		98.1	97.2	99.6	100.1	98.4	99.4	103.0	105.4	100.0	98.8
Less Extremes		99.3	98.9	101.1	100.4	98.6	98.9	100.8	103.6	99.1	99.5

PLATINUM - APRIL - MONTH OF HIGH AND LOW

Year of Expiration	Jun	Jul	Aug	Sep	Oct	Nov	Dec	Jan	Feb	Mar	Apr
1976			H							L	
1977		H					L				
1978			L							H	
1979	L								H		
1980			L						H		
1981				H							L
1982	H									L	
1983	L								H		
1984			H					L			
1985	H									L	

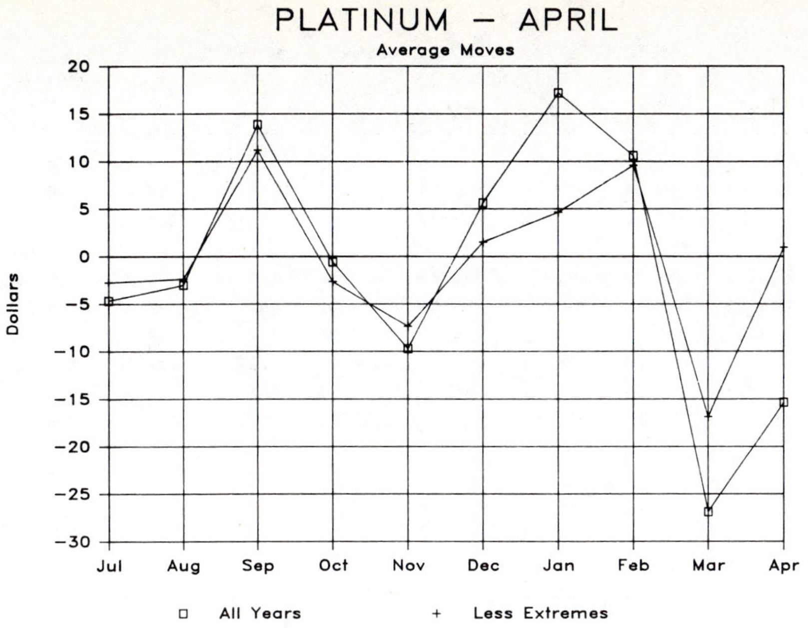
PLATINUM – APRIL
Average Moves
Dollars
20
15
10
5
0
−5
−10
−15
−20
−25
−30
Jul
Aug
Sep
Oct
Nov
Dec
Jan
Feb
Mar
Apr
All Years
Less Extremes

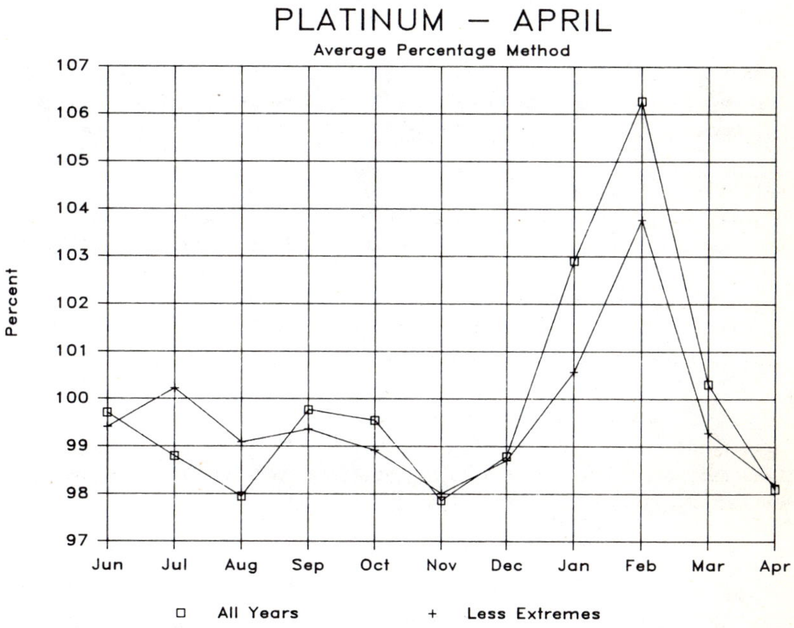
PLATINUM – APRIL
Average Percentage Method
Percent
107
106
105
104
103
102
101
100
99
98
97
Jun
Jul
Aug
Sep
Oct
Nov
Dec
Jan
Feb
Mar
Apr
All Years
Less Extremes

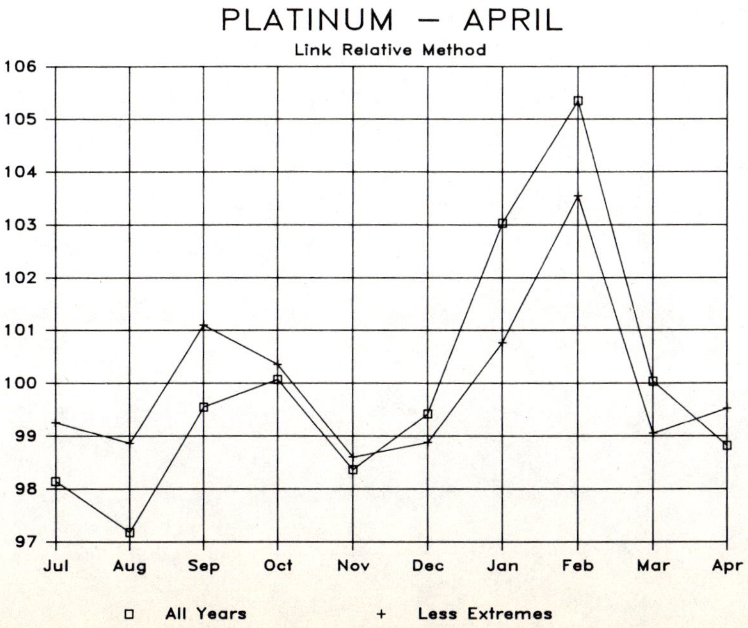
PLATINUM – APRIL
Link Relative Method
106
105
104
103
102
101
100
99
98
97
Jul
Aug
Sep
Oct
Nov
Dec
Jan
Feb
Mar
Apr
All Years
Less Extremes

PLATINUM - JULY - MONTHLY AVERAGE PRICE

Year of Expiration	Sep	Oct	Nov	Dec	Jan	Feb	Mar	Apr	May	Jun	Jul	Sep-Jul Average
1976	168.32	155.77	154.42	150.49	146.01	140.81	138.93	153.56	158.33	170.14	179.02	155.98
1977	168.62	165.37	162.89	157.19	159.51	165.54	166.75	162.89	157.37	150.43	147.38	160.36
1978	159.20	166.47	176.78	183.02	209.14	230.52	230.72	214.74	232.80	245.33	241.21	208.17
1979	278.23	336.68	332.23	345.73	366.88	413.25	391.54	385.90	428.92	427.24	418.89	375.04
1980	472.88	526.90	513.11	606.23	813.17	930.71	794.71	596.84	562.99	645.97	668.87	648.40
1981	789.17	743.67	697.07	645.34	566.01	503.85	505.52	489.55	468.02	441.58	399.77	568.14
1982	484.42	457.24	418.64	417.57	378.01	371.52	325.89	344.58	310.07	275.74	287.15	370.07
1983	347.57	354.96	360.17	385.09	469.97	471.46	408.74	423.69	454.00	422.71	432.68	411.91
1984	452.81	414.35	403.64	410.00	388.29	403.25	409.97	400.96	393.32	382.72	343.23	400.23
1985	352.41	344.66	645.23	316.29	281.14	275.38	264.01	287.51	272.35	267.07	267.95	324.91

	Sep	Oct	Nov	Dec	Jan	Feb	Mar	Apr	May	Jun	Jul
AVERAGE MOVE											
All Years		-0.75	19.81	-24.72	16.12	12.82	-26.95	-17.66	-2.21	-0.92	-4.28
Less Extremes		-2.56	-6.98	-1.43	4.20	9.10	-17.53	-0.27	-3.82	-7.23	-2.98
Ave Up - All Years		31.78	105.36	28.83	68.28	34.63	2.45	17.95	24.04	35.77	10.81
Ave Down - All Years		-22.45	-16.86	-78.28	-36.04	-19.90	-46.55	-41.39	-19.70	-16.65	-19.36
COUNT											
Number Up		4	3	5	5	6	4	4	4	3	5
Number Down		6	7	5	5	4	6	6	6	7	5
Pct Up		40.0%	30.0%	50.0%	50.0%	60.0%	40.0%	40.0%	40.0%	30.0%	50.0%
Pct Down		60.0%	70.0%	50.0%	50.0%	40.0%	60.0%	60.0%	60.0%	70.0%	50.0%
EXTREMES											
Greatest Up		58.45	300.57	93.12	206.94	117.53	6.72	23.51	43.02	82.98	22.90
Greatest Down		-45.50	-46.60	-328.94	-79.33	-62.16	-136.00	-197.87	-34.51	-34.33	-41.81
SEASONAL INDEX : AVERAGE PERCENTAGE METHOD											
All Years	101.2	100.4	107.6	98.8	101.6	104.7	99.1	96.9	97.1	96.7	95.9
Less Extremes	100.1	99.2	99.8	98.3	100.5	102.3	98.4	97.5	96.8	96.8	96.5
SEASONAL INDEX : LINK RELATIVE METHOD											
All Years		96.2	102.9	99.6	103.0	105.6	100.3	98.9	98.7	97.9	96.8
Less Extremes		99.3	98.5	99.0	101.0	104.2	99.8	100.2	100.1	99.2	98.8

PLATINUM - JULY - MONTH OF HIGH AND LOW

Year of Expiration	Sep	Oct	Nov	Dec	Jan	Feb	Mar	Apr	May	Jun	Jul
1976							L				H
1977	H										L
1978	L									H	
1979	L								H		
1980	L					H					
1981	H										L
1982	H									L	
1983	L					H					
1984	H										L
1985	H						L				

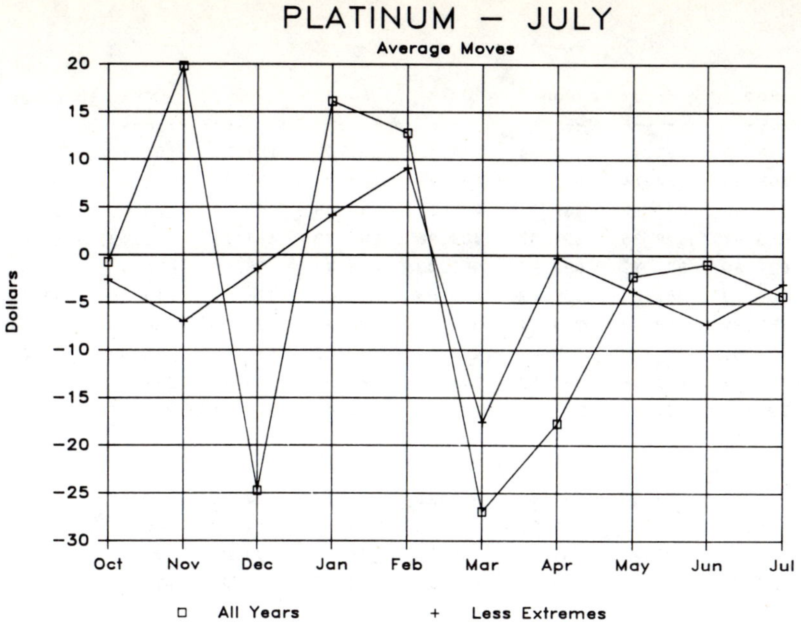
PLATINUM – JULY
Average Moves
Dollars
20
15
10
5
0
-5
-10
-15
-20
-25
-30
Oct
Nov
Dec
Jan
Feb
Mar
Apr
May
Jun
Jul
□ All Years
+ Less Extremes

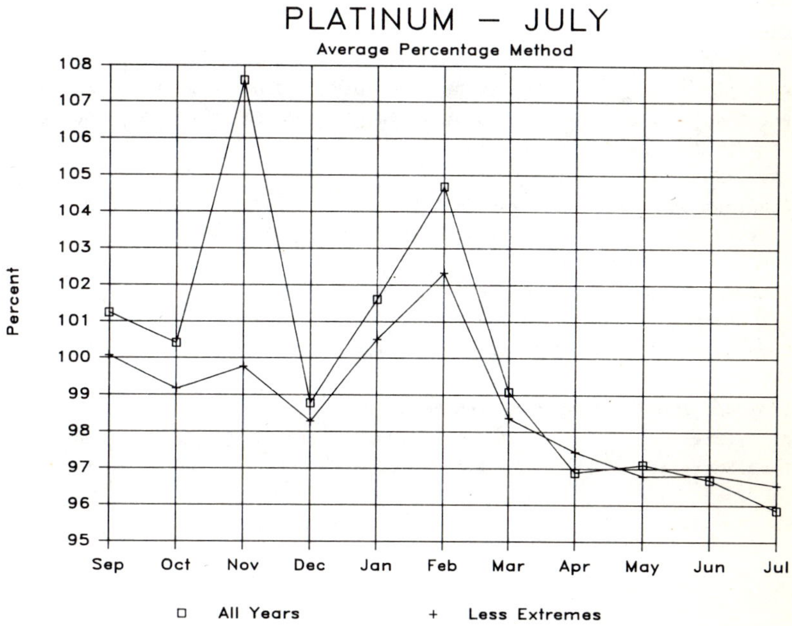
PLATINUM – JULY
Average Percentage Method
Percent
108
107
106
105
104
103
102
101
100
99
98
97
96
95
Sep
Oct
Nov
Dec
Jan
Feb
Mar
Apr
May
Jun
Jul
□ All Years
+ Less Extremes

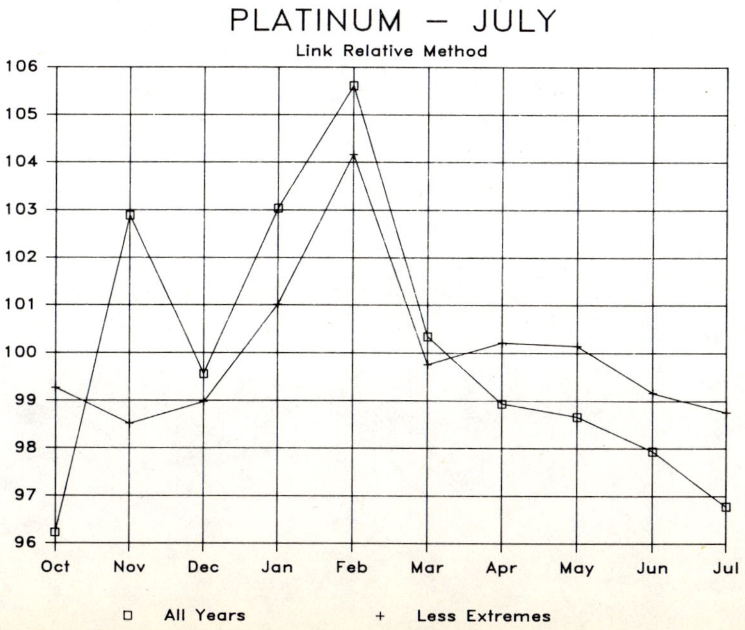
PLATINUM – JULY
Link Relative Method
106
105
104
103
102
101
100
99
98
97
96
Oct
Nov
Dec
Jan
Feb
Mar
Apr
May
Jun
Jul
□ All Years
+ Less Extremes

PLATINUM - OCTOBER - MONTHLY AVERAGE PRICE

Year of Expiration	Dec	Jan	Feb	Mar	Apr	May	Jun	Jul	Aug	Sep	Oct	Dec-Oct Average
1976	153.60	148.79	143.31	141.34	156.66	161.17	173.84	174.58	156.52	159.55	157.76	157.01
1977	159.72	162.20	168.28	169.69	165.83	160.14	153.06	151.45	148.27	151.73	153.82	158.56
1978	185.90	212.83	234.53	234.78	218.36	234.10	247.71	251.19	266.89	269.54	305.62	241.95
1979	348.44	370.00	414.97	392.49	385.81	428.36	427.37	409.88	395.93	464.74	522.49	414.59
1980	612.17	820.92	971.27	832.09	621.60	572.79	659.54	681.03	652.46	705.95	676.69	709.68
1981	673.08	587.60	524.28	524.27	507.79	487.64	459.22	412.06	423.23	436.17	414.96	495.48
1982	430.55	389.59	382.62	334.74	353.39	318.33	283.41	292.97	297.38	326.28	330.13	339.94
1983	392.56	477.51	478.35	415.72	430.31	459.19	430.61	443.05	442.33	431.86	395.39	436.08
1984	416.95	395.17	410.17	417.84	408.84	401.86	393.57	349.40	343.37	324.48	321.37	380.27
1985	323.73	287.03	281.01	269.79	292.96	277.15	271.49	270.73	311.65	310.21	322.33	292.55
AVERAGE MOVE												
All Years		15.49	15.71	-27.61	-19.12	-4.08	-0.09	-6.35	0.17	14.25	2.01	
Less Extremes		3.96	8.77	-18.07	-0.48	-4.32	-6.59	-4.73	-1.33	11.57	-0.15	
Ave Up - All Years		68.93	39.82	3.11	17.93	22.92	37.68	9.54	18.05	24.75	22.38	
Ave Down - All Years		-37.95	-20.45	-40.77	-43.82	-22.08	-16.27	-22.24	-11.75	-10.27	-18.37	
COUNT												
Number Up		5	6	3	4	4	3	5	4	7	5	
Number Down		5	4	7	6	6	7	5	6	3	5	
Pct Up		50.0%	60.0%	30.0%	40.0%	40.0%	30.0%	50.0%	40.0%	70.0%	50.0%	
Pct Down		50.0%	40.0%	70.0%	60.0%	60.0%	70.0%	50.0%	60.0%	30.0%	50.0%	
EXTREMES												
Greatest Up		208.76	150.35	7.67	23.17	42.55	86.75	21.49	40.91	68.82	57.75	
Greatest Down		-85.48	-63.32	-139.18	-210.49	-48.81	-34.92	-47.17	-28.57	-18.89	-36.47	
SEASONAL INDEX : AVERAGE PERCENTAGE METHOD												
All Years	101.9	103.5	106.3	100.8	98.8	98.2	97.7	96.1	96.2	99.5	101.1	
Less Extremes	100.7	103.5	104.4	100.1	99.1	99.5	97.8	95.8	95.8	99.7	100.2	
SEASONAL INDEX : LINK RELATIVE METHOD												
All Years		102.1	105.2	100.2	98.9	98.5	98.3	96.8	97.2	100.7	102.0	
Less Extremes		101.5	104.3	99.8	100.0	99.3	98.5	97.5	97.4	100.3	101.3	

PLATINUM - OCTOBER - MONTH OF HIGH AND LOW

Year of Expiration	Dec	Jan	Feb	Mar	Apr	May	Jun	Jul	Aug	Sep	Oct
1976				L				H			
1977				H					L		
1978	L										H
1979	L										H
1980			H			L					
1981	H							L			
1982	H						L				
1983	L		H								
1984				H							L
1985	H			L							

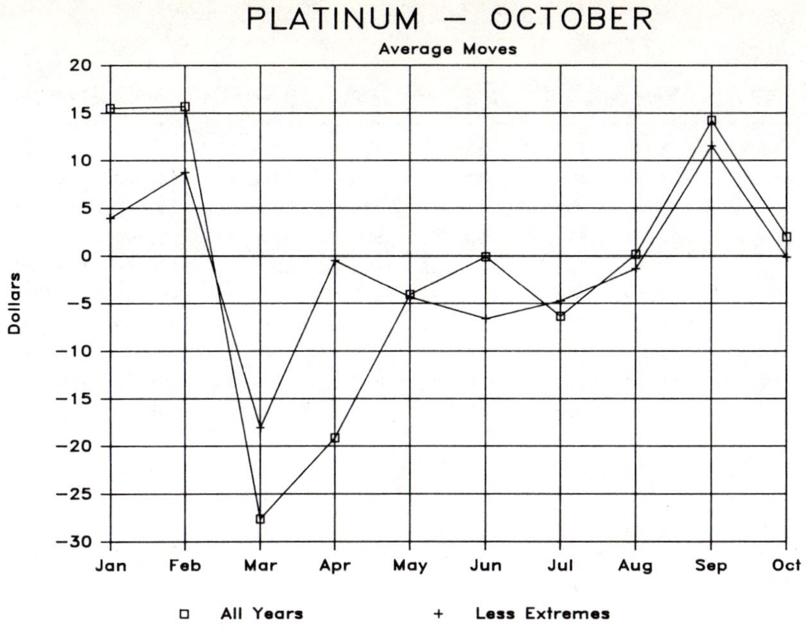
PLATINUM — OCTOBER
Average Moves
Dollars
20
15
10
5
0
−5
−10
−15
−20
−25
−30
Jan
Feb
Mar
Apr
May
Jun
Jul
Aug
Sep
Oct
□ All Years
+ Less Extremes

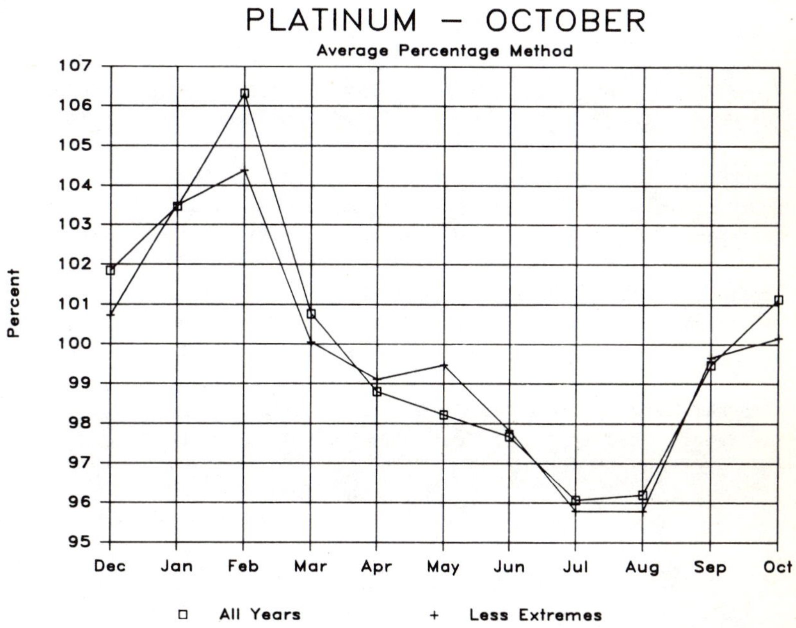
PLATINUM — OCTOBER
Average Percentage Method
Percent
107
106
105
104
103
102
101
100
99
98
97
96
95
Dec
Jan
Feb
Mar
Apr
May
Jun
Jul
Aug
Sep
Oct
□ All Years
+ Less Extremes

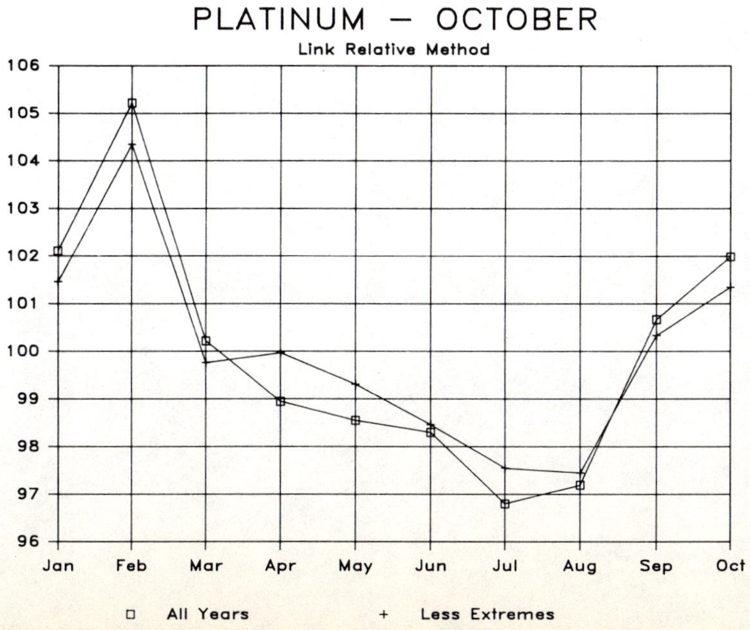
PLATINUM — OCTOBER
Link Relative Method
106
105
104
103
102
101
100
99
98
97
96
Jan
Feb
Mar
Apr
May
Jun
Jul
Aug
Sep
Oct
□ All Years
+ Less Extremes

SILVER - JANUARY - MONTHLY AVERAGE PRICE

Year of Expiration	Mar	Apr	May	Jun	Jul	Aug	Sep	Oct	Nov	Dec	Jan	Mar-Jan Average
1976	460.47	445.99	476.91	469.73	492.63	511.50	462.49	438.55	435.74	409.11	407.12	455.47
1977	441.63	458.10	467.77	495.96	487.49	432.70	435.48	425.52	439.21	436.68	440.57	451.01
1978	507.97	499.24	487.88	461.01	463.59	456.07	462.38	484.39	486.78	472.26	493.41	479.54
1979	564.41	543.63	439.77	555.24	556.40	566.54	570.82	602.08	594.16	595.48	618.40	564.27
1980	788.28	792.86	887.36	896.23	956.51	973.64	1422.06	1738.35	1681.58	2282.73	3870.05	1480.88
1981	3132.10	1668.60	1348.79	1672.62	1699.71	1672.69	2099.49	2079.48	1899.06	1658.05	1499.42	1857.27
1982	1387.07	1279.35	1214.94	1088.50	932.14	959.34	1060.04	955.72	867.85	851.09	800.57	1036.05
1983	808.23	805.04	727.13	607.33	693.04	742.46	896.38	966.49	992.41	1066.52	1229.25	866.75
1984	1148.85	1256.86	1378.18	1238.67	1269.05	1257.74	1223.48	1005.50	898.61	917.85	816.24	1128.28
1985	1051.94	998.69	965.18	932.17	783.08	797.43	752.10	745.91	758.07	667.43	608.30	823.66

	Mar	Apr	May	Jun	Jul	Aug	Sep	Oct	Nov	Dec	Jan
AVERAGE MOVE											
All Years		-154.26	-35.44	2.36	-8.38	3.65	101.46	5.73	-38.85	30.38	142.61
Less Extremes		-23.39	-19.49	-20.09	-1.65	5.23	76.90	-5.13	-29.25	-7.05	-0.32
Ave Up - All Years		43.02	64.10	119.09	32.87	22.85	163.32	109.92	13.54	173.96	359.60
Ave Down - All Years		-238.81	-101.81	-75.47	-104.64	-25.16	-42.86	-63.73	-73.78	-65.35	-74.38
COUNT											
Number Up		3	4	4	7	6	7	4	4	4	5
Number Down		7	6	6	3	4	3	6	6	6	5
Pct Up		30.0%	40.0%	40.0%	70.0%	60.0%	70.0%	40.0%	40.0%	40.0%	50.0%
Pct Down		70.0%	60.0%	60.0%	30.0%	40.0%	30.0%	60.0%	60.0%	60.0%	50.0%
EXTREMES											
Greatest Up		108.01	121.32	323.83	85.71	49.43	448.43	316.28	25.92	601.15	1587.32
Greatest Down		-1463.50	-319.81	-139.51	-156.36	-54.79	-49.01	-217.98	-180.42	-241.01	-158.63
SEASONAL INDEX : AVERAGE PERCENTAGE METHOD											
All Years	108.4	99.2	96.1	95.6	94.5	94.6	101.0	101.1	98.6	100.2	110.7
Less Extremes	107.7	101.9	97.4	97.8	96.0	96.0	100.7	100.6	98.9	95.8	96.7
SEASONAL INDEX : LINK RELATIVE METHOD											
All Years		101.5	97.7	97.8	96.7	96.2	103.7	103.1	99.5	99.5	104.3
Less Extremes		99.8	97.2	97.2	97.2	98.2	104.4	104.2	101.8	100.0	99.9

SILVER - JANUARY - MONTH OF HIGH AND LOW

Year of Expiration	Mar	Apr	May	Jun	Jul	Aug	Sep	Oct	Nov	Dec	Jan
1976						H					L
1977				H				L			
1978	H					L					
1979			L								H
1980	L										H
1981	H										L
1982	H										L
1983				L							H
1984			H								L
1985	H										L

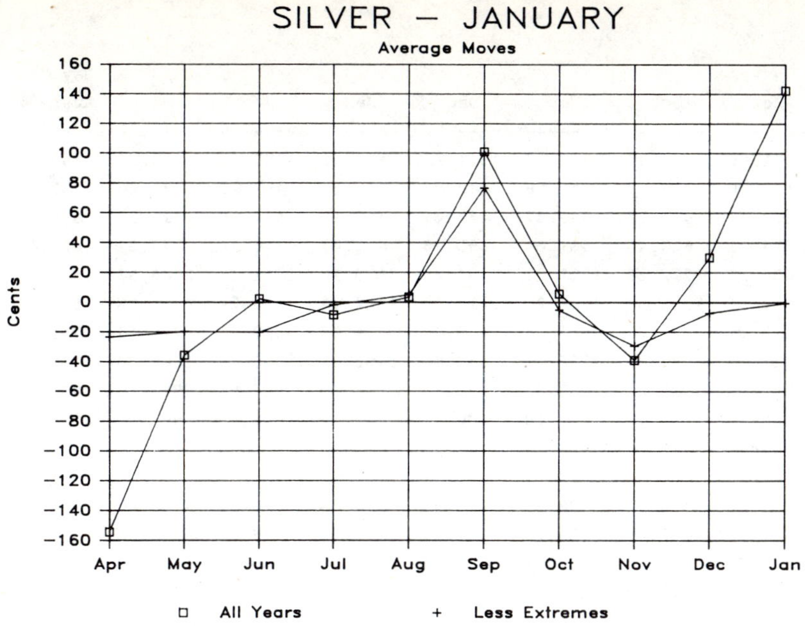
SILVER — JANUARY
Average Moves
Cents
160
140
120
100
80
60
40
20
0
−20
−40
−60
−80
−100
−120
−140
−160
Apr
May
Jun
Jul
Aug
Sep
Oct
Nov
Dec
Jan
All Years
Less Extremes

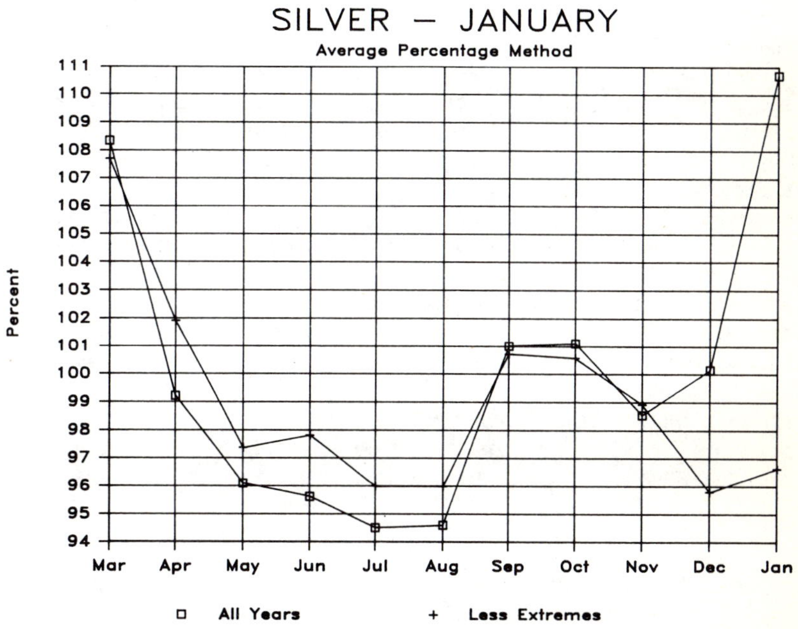
SILVER — JANUARY
Average Percentage Method
Percent
111
110
109
108
107
106
105
104
103
102
101
100
99
98
97
96
95
94
Mar
Apr
May
Jun
Jul
Aug
Sep
Oct
Nov
Dec
Jan
All Years
Less Extremes

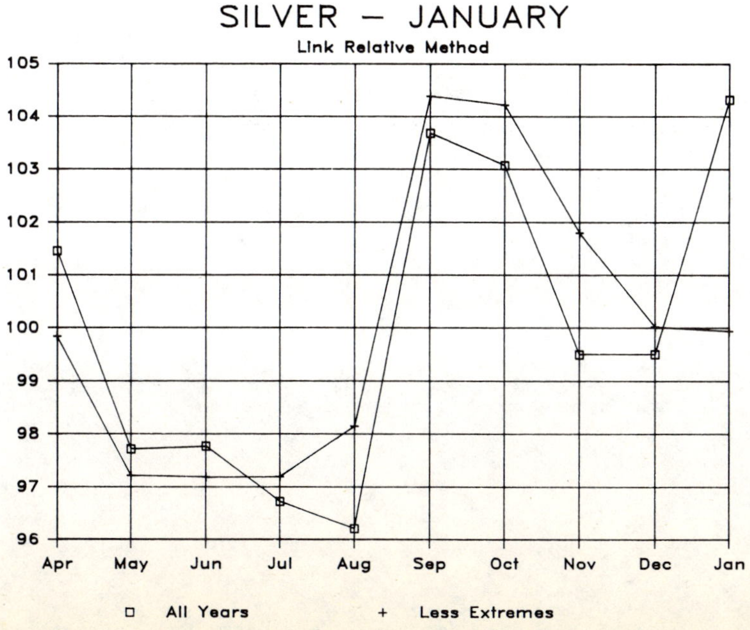
SILVER — JANUARY
Link Relative Method
105
104
103
102
101
100
99
98
97
96
Apr
May
Jun
Jul
Aug
Sep
Oct
Nov
Dec
Jan
All Years
Less Extremes

SILVER - MARCH - MONTHLY AVERAGE PRICE

Year of Expiration	May	Jun	Jul	Aug	Sep	Oct	Nov	Dec	Jan	Feb	Mar	May-Mar Average
1976	483.07	476.37	500.20	520.34	471.06	446.30	442.92	414.73	408.46	409.54	419.23	453.84
1977	473.60	501.11	492.11	437.69	439.70	429.48	442.98	440.84	443.59	454.22	485.56	458.26
1978	493.32	466.40	468.81	461.27	467.76	490.27	492.87	478.47	498.15	494.86	526.33	485.32
1979	547.85	563.52	564.61	574.87	579.21	610.45	601.64	602.28	631.47	744.16	740.52	614.60
1980	898.92	907.63	968.94	987.55	1436.42	1772.26	1723.24	2294.22	3628.18	3551.25	2588.33	1886.99
1981	1373.57	1700.14	1730.61	1708.17	2151.06	2132.59	1954.22	1710.29	1514.24	1303.74	1235.88	1683.14
1982	1248.26	1115.82	956.78	985.47	1090.01	981.79	886.74	868.30	814.83	832.50	725.12	955.05
1983	743.85	622.05	709.00	756.88	912.45	980.45	1007.61	1082.86	1262.67	1390.75	1065.78	957.67
1984	1399.10	1259.22	1291.02	1280.10	1245.02	1022.21	913.48	932.36	829.02	919.94	967.39	1096.26
1985	984.94	951.95	799.23	813.08	766.49	759.33	770.10	676.97	616.23	608.67	597.03	758.55

	May	Jun	Jul	Aug	Sep	Oct	Nov	Dec	Jan	Feb	Mar
AVERAGE MOVE											
All Years		-8.23	-8.29	4.41	103.38	6.60	-38.93	26.55	114.55	6.28	-135.85
Less Extremes		-33.62	-1.35	6.33	79.27	-5.89	-29.77	-7.69	0.95	18.15	-55.38
Ave Up - All Years		94.62	33.98	23.24	166.39	114.40	13.51	166.44	313.08	60.18	29.99
Ave Down - All Years		-76.79	-106.92	-23.83	-43.65	-65.27	-73.89	-66.70	-83.97	-74.57	-246.40
COUNT											
Number Up		4	7	6	7	4	4	4	5	6	4
Number Down		6	3	4	3	6	6	6	5	4	6
Pct Up		40.0%	70.0%	60.0%	70.0%	40.0%	40.0%	40.0%	50.0%	60.0%	40.0%
Pct Down		60.0%	30.0%	40.0%	30.0%	60.0%	60.0%	60.0%	50.0%	40.0%	60.0%
EXTREMES											
Greatest Up		326.57	86.95	47.88	448.87	335.85	27.16	570.98	1333.96	128.08	47.45
Greatest Down		-139.88	-159.04	-54.43	-49.29	-222.81	-178.37	-243.94	-196.05	-210.50	-962.92
SEASONAL INDEX : AVERAGE PERCENTAGE METHOD											
All Years	99.6	97.3	95.8	95.9	101.8	101.2	98.4	98.6	104.8	107.5	99.2
Less Extremes	102.2	100.0	98.6	98.7	101.8	99.0	98.1	97.4	97.6	101.1	97.7
SEASONAL INDEX : LINK RELATIVE METHOD											
All Years		96.8	95.9	95.6	103.2	102.8	99.4	99.3	103.0	104.9	98.9
Less Extremes		97.3	97.2	98.1	104.3	103.9	101.4	99.4	99.1	101.6	97.7

SILVER - MARCH - MONTH OF HIGH AND LOW

Year of Expiration	May	Jun	Jul	Aug	Sep	Oct	Nov	Dec	Jan	Feb	Mar
1976				H					L		
1977		H				L					
1978				L							H
1979	L									H	
1980	L								H		
1981					H						L
1982	H										L
1983		L								H	
1984	H								L		
1985	H										L

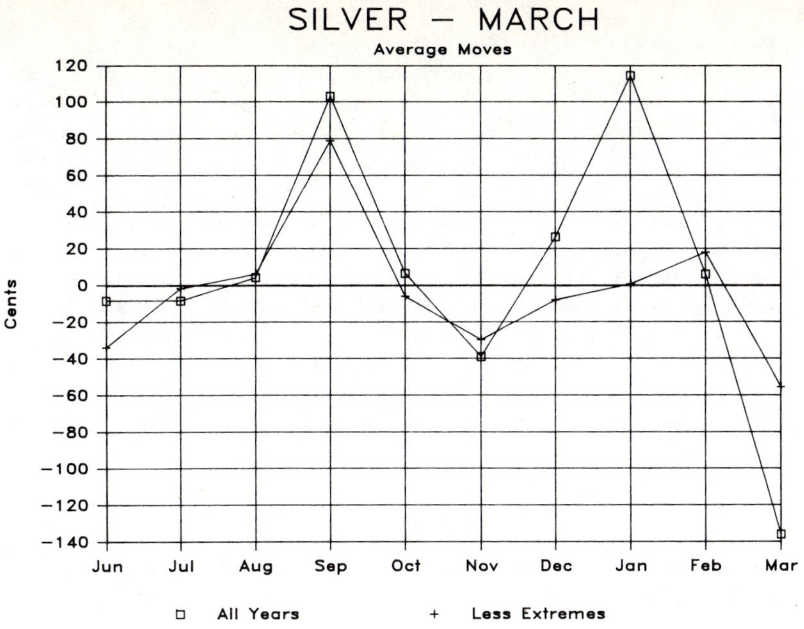

SILVER — MARCH
Average Moves
Cents
120
100
80
60
40
20
0
−20
−40
−60
−80
−100
−120
−140
Jun
Jul
Aug
Sep
Oct
Nov
Dec
Jan
Feb
Mar
All Years
Less Extremes

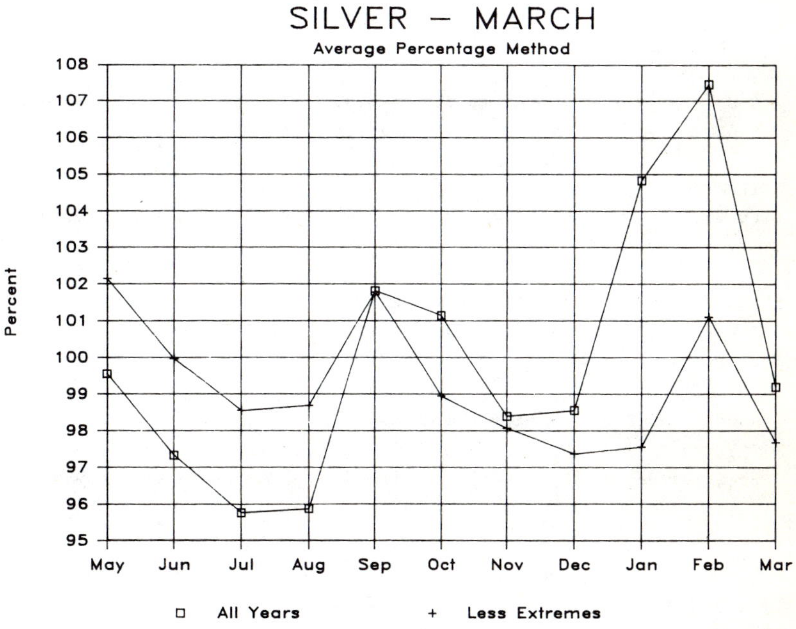

SILVER — MARCH
Average Percentage Method
Percent
108
107
106
105
104
103
102
101
100
99
98
97
96
95
May
Jun
Jul
Aug
Sep
Oct
Nov
Dec
Jan
Feb
Mar
All Years
Less Extremes

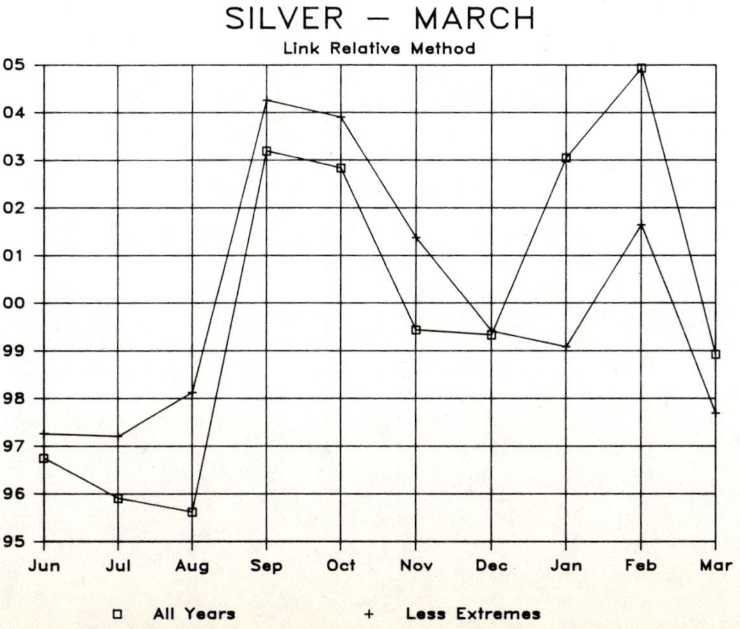

SILVER — MARCH
Link Relative Method
105
104
103
102
101
100
99
98
97
96
95
Jun
Jul
Aug
Sep
Oct
Nov
Dec
Jan
Feb
Mar
All Years
Less Extremes

SILVER - MAY - MONTHLY AVERAGE PRICE

Year of Expiration	Jul	Aug	Sep	Oct	Nov	Dec	Jan	Feb	Mar	Apr	May	Jul-May Average
1976	507.60	528.64	479.45	453.99	450.19	421.32	413.80	414.53	419.77	436.25	445.55	451.92
1977	496.87	442.76	444.04	433.67	447.11	444.91	447.96	458.96	488.15	478.99	470.91	459.48
1978	474.15	466.69	473.31	496.31	498.99	484.73	505.05	501.97	532.73	512.59	509.01	495.96
1979	573.29	583.35	587.91	618.92	609.82	609.62	638.58	753.65	751.11	751.71	835.63	664.87
1980	981.37	1000.54	1446.58	1791.26	1748.60	2329.40	3676.91	3620.33	2883.48	1482.33	1258.83	2019.96
1981	1761.66	1743.50	2203.36	2189.22	2009.75	1759.43	1558.29	1341.66	1259.32	1153.19	1092.97	1642.94
1982	981.41	1011.54	1118.65	1006.52	906.89	887.93	834.09	854.27	736.15	732.09	671.89	885.58
1983	724.96	771.33	929.36	995.24	1023.35	1100.21	1282.60	1422.23	1078.46	1180.24	1297.76	1073.25
1984	1313.07	1302.65	1267.02	1040.01	929.31	948.74	843.14	935.47	980.34	927.13	893.71	1034.60
1985	816.34	829.09	780.98	772.94	782.54	687.41	624.84	617.32	607.43	647.11	628.01	708.55

	Jul	Aug	Sep	Oct	Nov	Dec	Jan	Feb	Mar	Apr	May
AVERAGE MOVE											
All Years		4.94	105.06	6.74	-39.16	26.72	115.15	9.51	-118.35	-143.53	-19.74
Less Extremes		7.14	79.99	-6.28	-30.03	-7.91	0.65	21.52	-61.43	-16.99	-11.42
Ave Up - All Years		23.25	169.07	116.15	13.46	225.70	316.44	63.16	27.51	39.64	70.24
Ave Down - All Years		-22.54	-44.31	-66.19	-74.23	-58.56	-86.14	-70.95	-215.59	-265.64	-58.30
COUNT											
Number Up		6	7	4	4	3	5	6	4	4	3
Number Down		4	3	6	6	7	5	4	6	6	7
Pct Up		60.0%	70.0%	40.0%	40.0%	30.0%	50.0%	60.0%	40.0%	40.0%	30.0%
Pct Down		40.0%	30.0%	60.0%	60.0%	70.0%	50.0%	40.0%	60.0%	60.0%	70.0%
EXTREMES											
Greatest Up		46.37	459.86	344.68	28.11	580.80	1347.51	139.64	44.88	101.78	117.52
Greatest Down		-54.11	-49.19	-227.01	-179.47	-250.32	-201.14	-216.63	-736.85	-1401.14	-223.50
SEASONAL INDEX : AVERAGE PERCENTAGE METHOD											
All Years	97.9	98.0	103.8	102.6	99.6	99.3	104.7	107.4	100.3	93.4	93.0
Less Extremes	100.4	100.6	104.0	100.5	98.4	98.3	98.0	101.6	98.0	93.9	92.8
SEASONAL INDEX : LINK RELATIVE METHOD											
All Years		94.0	102.0	102.2	99.3	99.7	104.0	106.6	101.3	96.2	94.6
Less Extremes		97.1	103.5	103.4	101.2	99.5	99.4	102.5	98.8	97.8	96.7

SILVER - MAY - MONTH OF HIGH AND LOW

Year of Expiration	Jul	Aug	Sep	Oct	Nov	Dec	Jan	Feb	Mar	Apr	May
1976		H					L				
1977	H			L							
1978		L							H		
1979	L										H
1980	L						H				
1981			H								L
1982			H								L
1983	L							H			
1984	H						L				
1985		H							L		

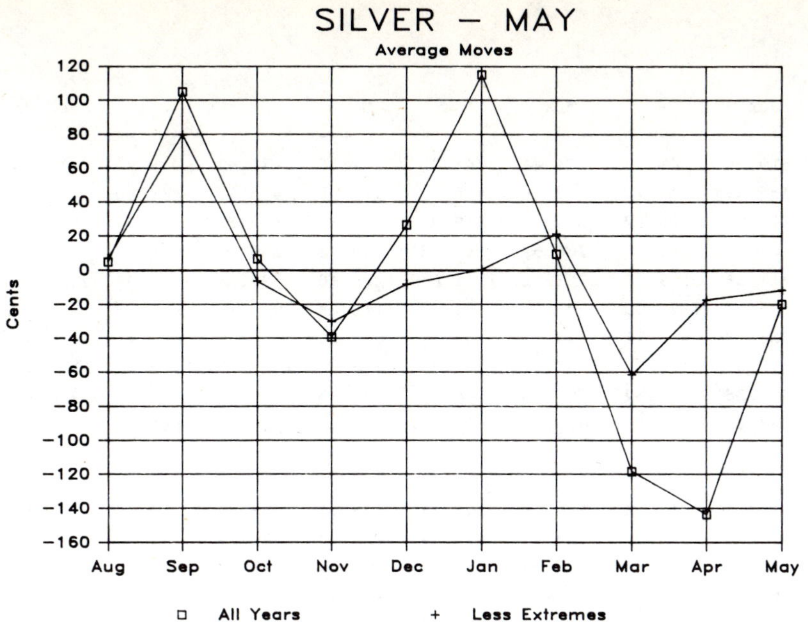
SILVER — MAY
Average Moves
Cents
120
100
80
60
40
20
0
−20
−40
−60
−80
−100
−120
−140
−160
Aug
Sep
Oct
Nov
Dec
Jan
Feb
Mar
Apr
May
All Years
Less Extremes

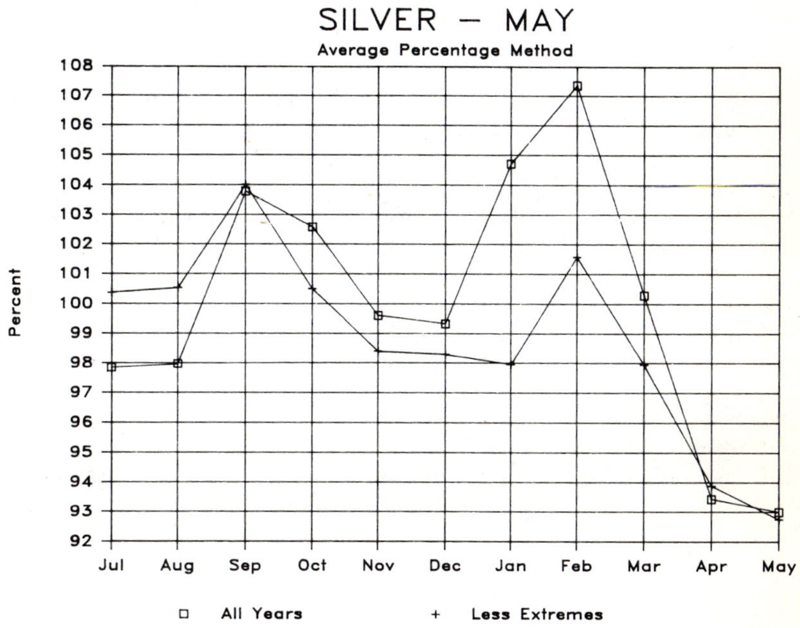
SILVER — MAY
Average Percentage Method
Percent
108
107
106
105
104
103
102
101
100
99
98
97
96
95
94
93
92
Jul
Aug
Sep
Oct
Nov
Dec
Jan
Feb
Mar
Apr
May
All Years
Less Extremes

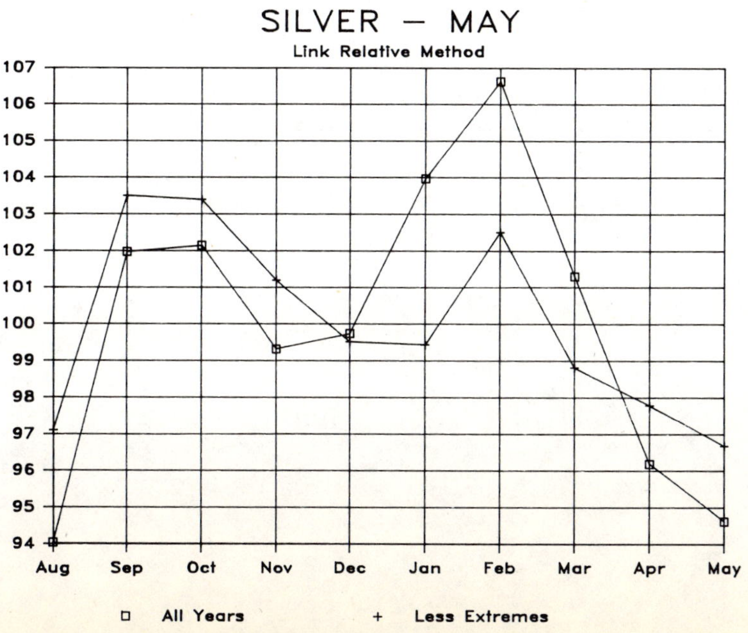
SILVER — MAY
Link Relative Method
107
106
105
104
103
102
101
100
99
98
97
96
95
94
Aug
Sep
Oct
Nov
Dec
Jan
Feb
Mar
Apr
May
All Years
Less Extremes

SILVER - JULY - MONTHLY AVERAGE PRICE

Year of Expiration	Sep	Oct	Nov	Dec	Jan	Feb	Mar	Apr	May	Jun	Jul	Sep-Jul Average
1976	487.49	461.48	457.39	427.89	419.34	419.97	424.44	441.01	451.56	481.61	479.75	450.17
1977	448.42	437.92	451.45	449.03	452.37	463.72	493.14	484.12	471.85	445.27	449.86	458.83
1978	478.95	502.41	505.15	491.03	512.00	509.17	540.46	519.94	517.25	532.23	530.97	512.69
1979	596.85	627.74	618.30	618.03	646.58	761.98	760.52	763.13	849.48	856.88	918.37	728.89
1980	1456.53	1810.23	1773.93	2363.62	3717.86	3679.28	2953.52	1531.64	1274.10	1591.95	1621.24	2161.26
1981	2255.48	2240.11	2065.17	1808.71	1601.31	1379.00	1291.07	1184.05	1113.08	1002.18	864.86	1527.73
1982	1147.30	1031.31	926.89	907.56	853.77	875.71	754.33	750.00	677.26	563.40	649.11	830.60
1983	946.26	1010.06	1039.14	1117.71	1302.89	1445.97	1095.91	1199.29	1316.88	1179.07	1213.00	1169.65
1984	1289.06	1057.91	945.20	965.23	857.38	951.34	997.76	944.43	908.96	876.35	747.29	958.26
1985	796.12	786.82	795.34	698.21	633.95	626.72	616.75	655.88	632.48	619.33	608.79	679.12
AVERAGE MOVE												
All Years		6.35	-38.80	26.91	115.04	11.54	-118.50	-145.44	-26.06	-6.46	-6.50	
Less Extremes		-7.38	-30.27	-8.02	0.44	24.33	-63.21	-16.99	-15.08	-30.59	-1.68	
Ave Up - All Years		117.96	13.47	229.43	318.46	64.40	27.90	40.42	71.50	92.57	43.00	
Ave Down - All Years		-68.05	-73.65	-59.89	-88.38	-67.74	-216.09	-269.35	-67.87	-72.49	-56.01	
COUNT												
Number Up		4	4	3	5	6	4	4	3	4	5	
Number Down		6	6	7	5	4	6	6	7	6	5	
Pct Up		40.0%	40.0%	30.0%	50.0%	60.0%	40.0%	40.0%	30.0%	40.0%	50.0%	
Pct Down		60.0%	60.0%	70.0%	50.0%	40.0%	60.0%	60.0%	70.0%	60.0%	50.0%	
EXTREMES												
Greatest Up		353.70	29.08	589.68	1354.25	143.09	46.43	103.38	117.60	317.86	85.71	
Greatest Down		-231.15	-174.94	-256.45	-207.40	-222.31	-725.75	-1421.88	-257.55	-137.81	-137.32	
SEASONAL INDEX : AVERAGE PERCENTAGE METHOD												
All Years	106.7	104.9	101.7	101.0	105.4	107.9	101.2	94.6	93.5	91.6	91.5	
Less Extremes	106.5	102.4	99.9	100.8	99.2	102.4	98.9	96.2	94.9	91.6	91.6	
SEASONAL INDEX : LINK RELATIVE METHOD												
All Years		99.3	97.4	98.7	103.7	107.4	103.0	98.7	97.5	96.9	97.3	
Less Extremes		101.2	99.8	98.9	99.6	103.6	100.7	100.4	99.6	97.9	98.4	

SILVER - JULY - MONTH OF HIGH AND LOW

Year of Expiration	Sep	Oct	Nov	Dec	Jan	Feb	Mar	Apr	May	Jun	Jul
1976	H				L						
1977		L					H				
1978	L						L				
1979	L										H
1980					H				L		
1981	H										L
1982	H									L	
1983	L					H					
1984	H										L
1985	H										L

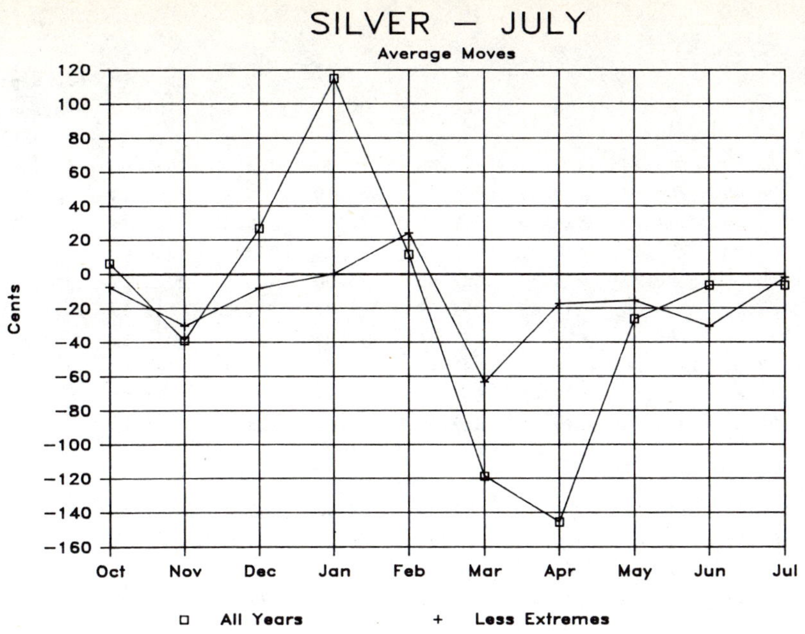
SILVER — JULY
Average Moves
Cents
120
100
80
60
40
20
0
−20
−40
−60
−80
−100
−120
−140
−160
Oct
Nov
Dec
Jan
Feb
Mar
Apr
May
Jun
Jul
□ All Years
+ Less Extremes

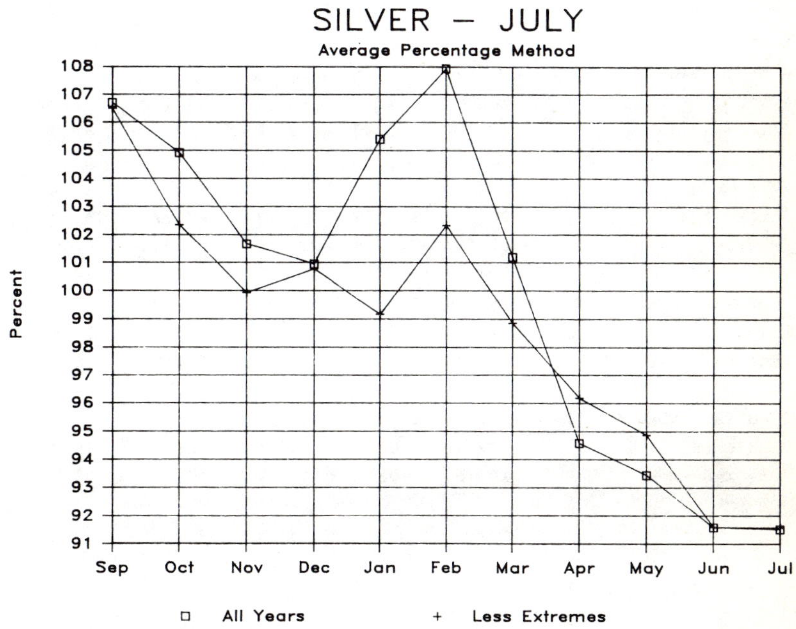
SILVER — JULY
Average Percentage Method
Percent
108
107
106
105
104
103
102
101
100
99
98
97
96
95
94
93
92
91
Sep
Oct
Nov
Dec
Jan
Feb
Mar
Apr
May
Jun
Jul
□ All Years
+ Less Extremes

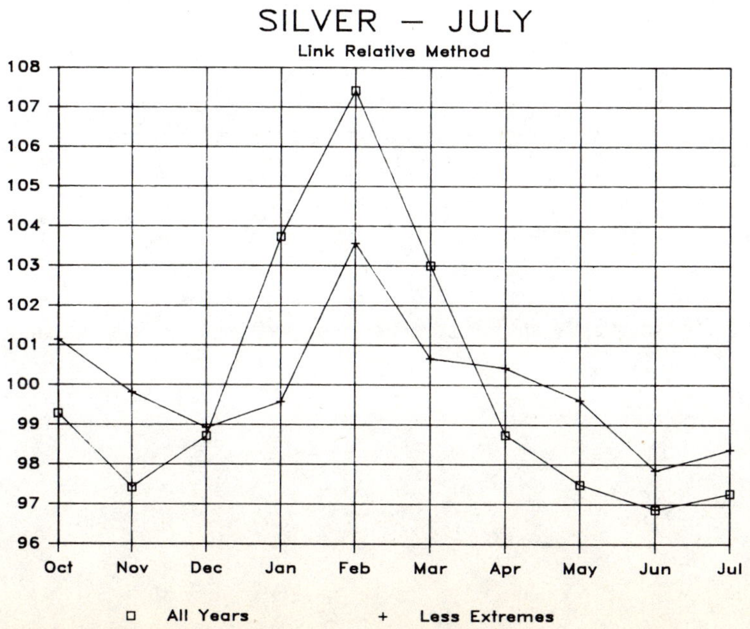
SILVER — JULY
Link Relative Method
108
107
106
105
104
103
102
101
100
99
98
97
96
Oct
Nov
Dec
Jan
Feb
Mar
Apr
May
Jun
Jul
□ All Years
+ Less Extremes

SILVER - SEPTEMBER - MONTHLY AVERAGE PRICE

Year of Expiration	Nov	Dec	Jan	Feb	Mar	Apr	May	Jun	Jul	Aug	Sep	Nov-Sep Average
1976	464.52	434.48	425.11	425.65	429.75	446.24	456.51	485.82	479.51	423.41	428.95	445.45
1977	455.98	453.21	456.81	468.47	498.05	489.13	477.25	450.40	453.10	445.76	452.49	463.70
1978	511.37	497.35	518.97	516.48	548.25	527.58	524.36	539.52	540.51	550.52	555.74	530.06
1979	626.86	626.52	654.67	770.41	769.90	773.55	863.06	871.49	928.84	943.67	1360.06	835.37
1980	1799.05	2397.41	3759.18	3740.33	3025.38	1580.79	1298.50	1617.88	1638.00	1605.62	2015.33	2225.22
1981	2120.61	1858.02	1644.14	1415.92	1323.25	1215.80	1147.43	1032.57	880.77	904.53	1022.07	1324.10
1982	946.87	927.20	873.45	897.12	772.42	768.24	693.90	577.94	661.23	716.21	881.59	792.38
1983	1054.96	1135.19	1323.19	1469.70	1113.55	1218.38	1336.90	1198.42	1225.90	1213.77	1197.86	1226.16
1984	961.20	982.12	871.95	967.47	1015.44	962.16	927.42	894.42	752.19	767.43	724.54	893.30
1985	809.37	709.83	643.86	636.90	627.43	665.78	640.88	627.27	616.67	627.77	604.53	655.48

	Nov	Dec	Jan	Feb	Mar	Apr	May	Jun	Jul	Aug	Sep
AVERAGE MOVE											
All Years		27.06	115.00	13.71	-118.50	-147.58	-28.14	-7.05	-11.90	2.20	104.45
Less Extremes		-8.15	0.26	27.35	-64.76	-17.00	-14.71	-31.42	-6.31	2.89	83.87
Ave Up - All Years		233.17	320.63	65.61	28.36	40.83	72.77	93.07	31.99	21.65	160.93
Ave Down - All Years		-61.28	-90.63	-64.13	-216.41	-273.18	-71.39	-73.79	-77.73	-26.99	-27.35
COUNT											
Number Up		3	5	6	4	4	3	4	6	6	7
Number Down		7	5	4	6	6	7	6	4	4	3
Pct Up		30.0%	50.0%	60.0%	40.0%	40.0%	30.0%	40.0%	60.0%	60.0%	70.0%
Pct Down		70.0%	50.0%	40.0%	60.0%	60.0%	70.0%	60.0%	40.0%	40.0%	30.0%
EXTREMES											
Greatest Up		598.35	1361.78	146.51	47.97	104.83	118.52	319.38	83.29	54.98	416.40
Greatest Down		-262.59	-213.88	-228.22	-714.94	-1444.60	-282.29	-138.48	-151.79	-56.11	-42.89
SEASONAL INDEX : AVERAGE PERCENTAGE METHOD											
All Years	105.2	104.0	107.7	110.0	103.3	96.6	95.1	92.9	92.0	92.0	101.2
Less Extremes	102.1	103.1	103.8	104.9	100.8	98.4	97.9	93.5	92.8	92.3	96.4
SEASONAL INDEX : LINK RELATIVE METHOD											
All Years		102.0	106.1	108.9	103.6	98.4	96.2	94.7	93.7	93.7	102.7
Less Extremes		102.6	102.2	105.4	101.5	100.3	98.6	95.9	95.0	95.6	102.8

SILVER - SEPTEMBER - MONTH OF HIGH AND LOW

Year of Expiration	Nov	Dec	Jan	Feb	Mar	Apr	May	Jun	Jul	Aug	Sep
1976			L					H			
1977					H					L	
1978		L									H
1979		L									H
1980			H				L				
1981	H								L		
1982	H							L			
1983	L			H							
1984					H						L
1985	H										L

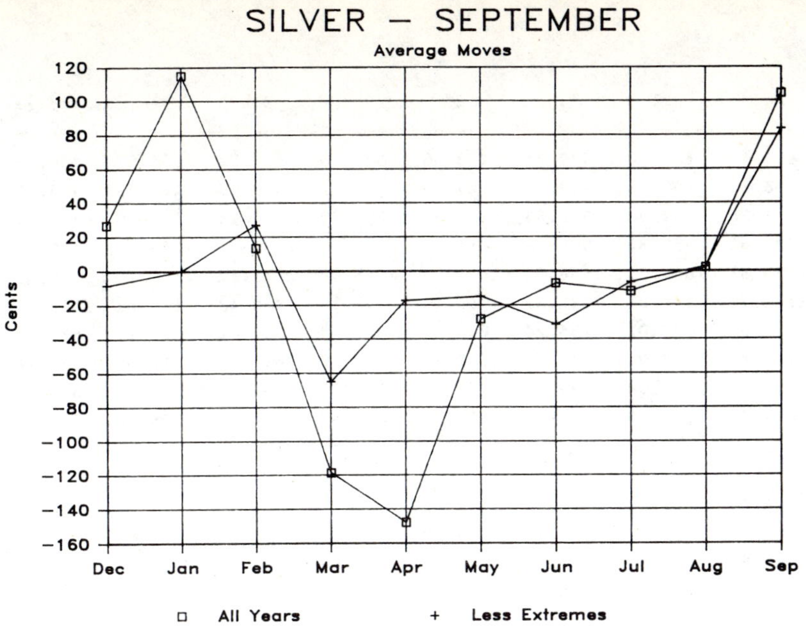
SILVER — SEPTEMBER
Average Moves
Cents
120
100
80
60
40
20
0
−20
−40
−60
−80
−100
−120
−140
−160
Dec
Jan
Feb
Mar
Apr
May
Jun
Jul
Aug
Sep
All Years
Less Extremes

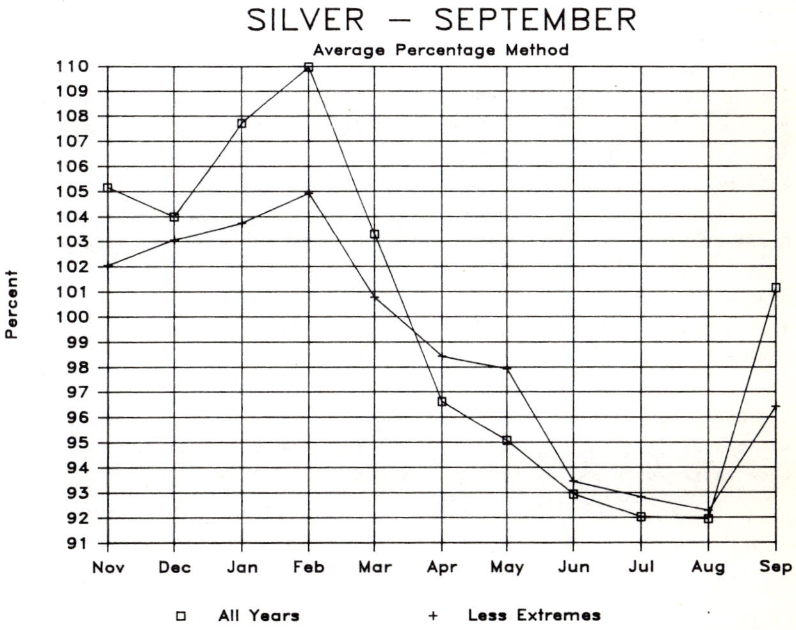
SILVER — SEPTEMBER
Average Percentage Method
Percent
110
109
108
107
106
105
104
103
102
101
100
99
98
97
96
95
94
93
92
91
Nov
Dec
Jan
Feb
Mar
Apr
May
Jun
Jul
Aug
Sep
All Years
Less Extremes

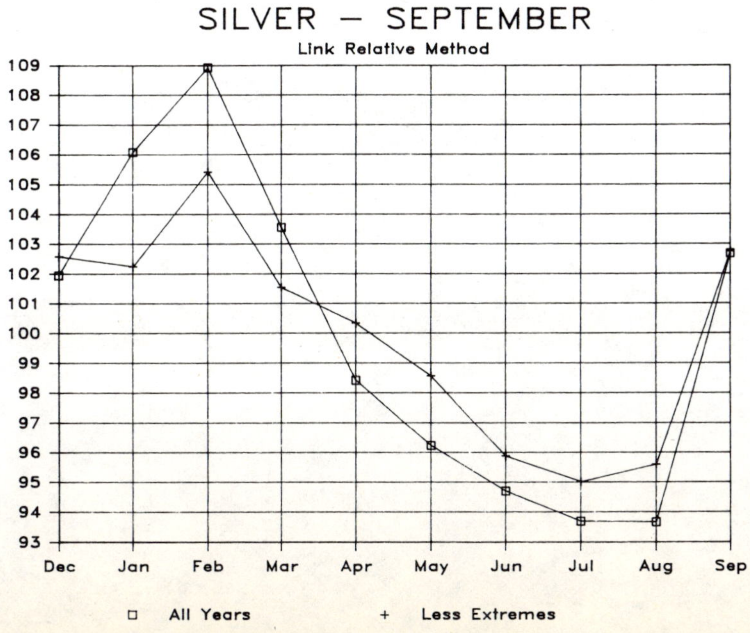
SILVER — SEPTEMBER
Link Relative Method
109
108
107
106
105
104
103
102
101
100
99
98
97
96
95
94
93
Dec
Jan
Feb
Mar
Apr
May
Jun
Jul
Aug
Sep
All Years
Less Extremes

SILVER - DECEMBER - MONTHLY AVERAGE PRICE

Year of Expiration	Feb	Mar	Apr	May	Jun	Jul	Aug	Sep	Oct	Nov	Dec	Feb-Dec Average
1976	434.57	438.65	455.12	464.90	493.40	485.30	430.24	433.86	424.16	437.25	435.57	448.46
1977	475.80	505.50	496.68	485.21	458.35	460.96	453.43	459.78	481.61	483.78	469.83	475.54
1978	527.81	560.39	539.56	535.76	551.26	552.38	562.66	566.87	597.90	590.15	591.30	561.46
1979	782.82	783.81	788.18	881.57	890.61	950.33	966.66	1414.79	1722.35	1668.45	2138.89	1180.77
1980	3809.40	3105.19	1646.83	1336.14	1658.83	1684.09	1654.93	2073.81	2053.09	1871.42	1640.11	2048.53
1981	1470.82	1371.18	1263.61	1198.16	1074.79	919.81	946.21	1045.10	942.36	858.43	852.77	1085.75
1982	928.98	799.28	795.82	718.83	599.96	685.07	735.24	888.24	959.38	985.42	1054.13	831.85
1983	1505.56	1140.10	1247.25	1367.87	1228.46	1258.06	1246.58	1212.76	997.10	891.07	917.58	1182.94
1984	992.30	1042.69	989.28	955.39	922.40	775.06	789.75	745.05	739.35	752.15	671.03	852.22
1985	653.55	644.54	681.69	654.47	639.23	628.83	640.50	614.73	625.87	614.70	588.68	635.16
AVERAGE MOVE												
All Years		-119.03	-148.73	-30.57	-8.10	-11.74	2.63	102.88	8.82	-39.04	20.71	
Less Extremes		-67.06	-17.02	-14.45	-33.04	-5.94	3.90	78.17	-0.46	-29.34	-4.00	
Ave Up - All Years		23.55	41.28	74.60	93.93	33.90	21.59	161.87	88.54	13.52	141.70	
Ave Down - All Years		-261.60	-275.41	-75.64	-76.12	-80.21	-25.81	-34.76	-70.91	-74.08	-59.95	
COUNT												
Number Up		5	4	3	4	6	6	7	5	4	4	
Number Down		5	6	7	6	4	4	3	5	6	6	
Pct Up		50.0%	40.0%	30.0%	40.0%	60.0%	60.0%	70.0%	50.0%	40.0%	40.0%	
Pct Down		50.0%	60.0%	70.0%	60.0%	40.0%	40.0%	30.0%	50.0%	60.0%	60.0%	
EXTREMES												
Greatest Up		50.39	107.15	120.62	322.69	85.11	50.16	448.13	307.56	26.03	470.44	
Greatest Down		-704.21	-1458.36	-310.69	-139.42	-154.98	-55.06	-44.70	-215.67	-181.67	-231.31	
SEASONAL INDEX : AVERAGE PERCENTAGE METHOD												
All Years	113.7	106.4	99.0	96.9	94.5	93.0	92.9	100.5	102.0	99.5	101.7	
Less Extremes	110.6	105.8	100.9	98.5	95.3	92.6	92.8	99.7	98.7	97.3	94.7	
SEASONAL INDEX : LINK RELATIVE METHOD												
All Years		103.5	98.8	96.9	95.6	94.9	95.1	104.1	105.2	102.5	103.3	
Less Extremes		101.4	100.5	98.9	96.4	95.8	96.7	103.2	104.2	101.9	100.9	

SILVER - DECEMBER - MONTH OF HIGH AND LOW

Year of Expiration	Feb	Mar	Apr	May	Jun	Jul	Aug	Sep	Oct	Nov	Dec
1976					H				L		
1977		H					L				
1978	L								H		
1979	L										L
1980	H			L							
1981	H										L
1982					L						H
1983	H									L	
1984		H									L
1985			H								L

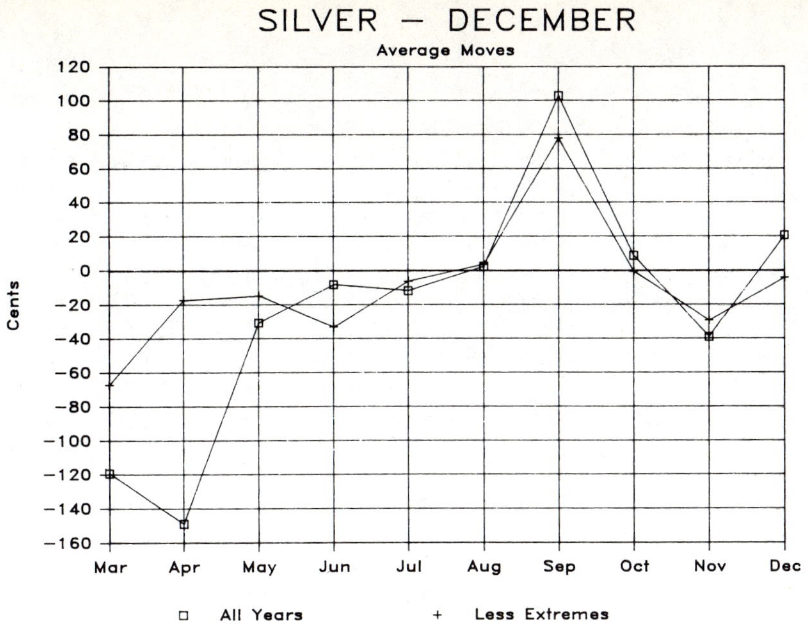
SILVER – DECEMBER
Average Moves
Cents
120
100
80
60
40
20
0
–20
–40
–60
–80
–100
–120
–140
–160
Mar
Apr
May
Jun
Jul
Aug
Sep
Oct
Nov
Dec
All Years
Less Extremes

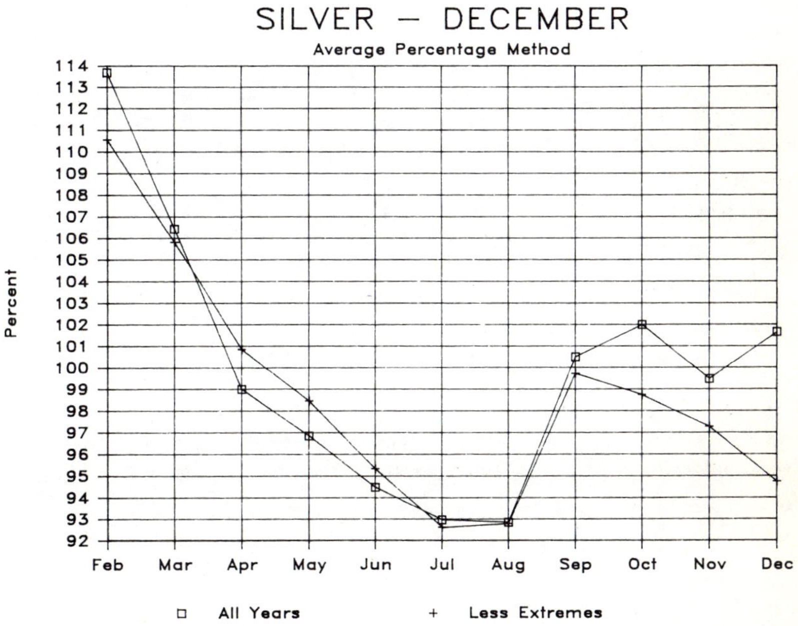
SILVER – DECEMBER
Average Percentage Method
Percent
114
113
112
111
110
109
108
107
106
105
104
103
102
101
100
99
98
97
96
95
94
93
92
Feb
Mar
Apr
May
Jun
Jul
Aug
Sep
Oct
Nov
Dec
All Years
Less Extremes

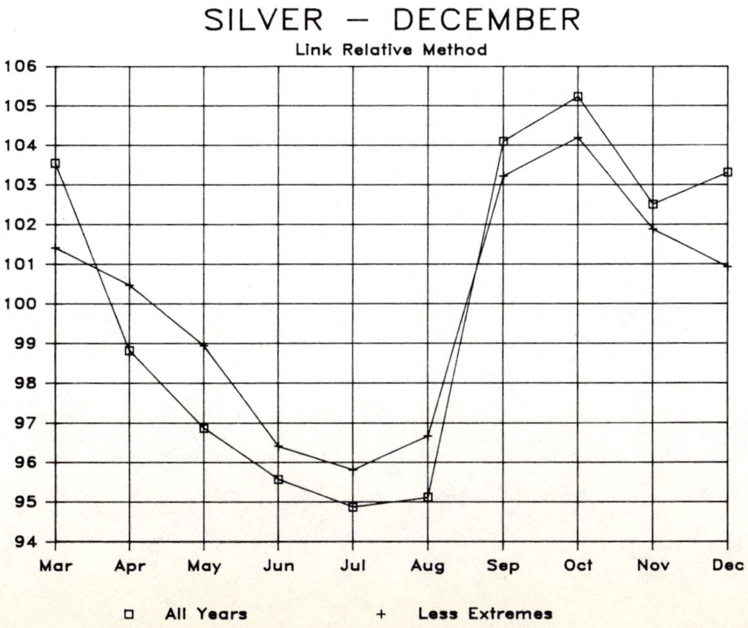
SILVER – DECEMBER
Link Relative Method
106
105
104
103
102
101
100
99
98
97
96
95
94
Mar
Apr
May
Jun
Jul
Aug
Sep
Oct
Nov
Dec
All Years
Less Extremes

COPPER - JANUARY - MONTHLY AVERAGE PRICE

Year of Expiration	Mar	Apr	May	Jun	Jul	Aug	Sep	Oct	Nov	Dec	Jan	Mar-Jan Average
1976	63.86	62.60	59.11	56.16	59.67	61.60	57.95	55.70	55.11	53.85	55.44	58.28
1977	65.02	72.32	72.26	74.12	78.07	71.93	67.73	59.32	59.05	59.60	63.97	67.58
1978	73.82	69.61	66.64	63.13	59.27	55.16	56.52	57.01	55.62	58.92	58.84	61.32
1979	63.34	63.97	64.36	64.60	64.49	66.71	66.54	68.94	66.81	68.24	72.09	66.37
1980	93.21	93.24	86.57	84.48	82.23	88.95	92.94	94.51	96.75	100.73	114.77	93.49
1981	109.26	97.61	94.84	91.58	100.26	95.61	96.22	96.01	93.29	84.38	84.68	94.89
1982	92.59	92.30	89.27	85.19	83.44	86.37	81.27	77.53	74.80	73.75	71.91	82.58
1983	75.79	76.36	75.81	63.44	67.50	65.07	64.59	65.51	64.85	66.92	72.39	68.93
1984	79.24	81.45	83.53	79.42	79.89	77.09	72.76	66.13	63.47	64.49	62.17	73.60
1985	73.93	74.14	68.41	65.38	61.83	62.17	59.15	57.79	60.33	57.69	58.58	63.58

	Mar	Apr	May	Jun	Jul	Aug	Sep	Oct	Nov	Dec	Jan
AVERAGE MOVE											
All Years		-0.65	-2.28	-3.33	0.91	-0.60	-1.50	-1.72	-0.84	-0.15	2.63
Less Extremes		-0.26	-2.28	-2.85	0.54	-0.82	-1.74	-1.40	-1.02	0.43	1.82
Ave Up - All Years		1.82	1.24	1.05	4.13	2.83	1.98	1.35	2.39	2.06	4.36
Ave Down - All Years		-4.35	-3.16	-4.42	-2.30	-4.03	-2.99	-3.77	-1.64	-3.47	-1.42
COUNT											
Number Up		6	2	2	5	5	3	4	2	6	7
Number Down		4	8	8	5	5	7	6	8	4	3
Pct Up		60.0%	20.0%	20.0%	50.0%	50.0%	30.0%	40.0%	20.0%	60.0%	70.0%
Pct Down		40.0%	80.0%	80.0%	50.0%	50.0%	70.0%	60.0%	80.0%	40.0%	30.0%
EXTREMES											
Greatest Up		7.30	2.09	1.87	8.68	6.72	3.99	2.40	2.54	3.98	14.04
Greatest Down		-11.64	-6.67	-12.37	-3.85	-6.14	-5.10	-8.41	-2.74	-8.92	-2.32
SEASONAL INDEX : AVERAGE PERCENTAGE METHOD											
All Years	108.2	107.7	104.6	99.9	101.0	100.0	97.7	95.2	94.1	94.1	97.5
Less Extremes	108.3	108.0	105.0	99.9	100.8	100.5	97.9	95.1	93.9	93.2	96.0
SEASONAL INDEX : LINK RELATIVE METHOD											
All Years		104.4	102.3	98.6	100.5	100.6	99.2	97.5	97.1	97.9	102.0
Less Extremes		104.2	102.0	99.0	100.8	100.6	98.8	97.6	96.9	98.2	101.8

COPPER - JANUARY - MONTH OF HIGH AND LOW

Year of Expiration	Mar	Apr	May	Jun	Jul	Aug	Sep	Oct	Nov	Dec	Jan
1976	H									L	
1977					H				L		
1978	H					L					
1979	L										H
1980					L						H
1981	H									L	
1982	H										L
1983		H		L							
1984			H								L
1985		H								L	

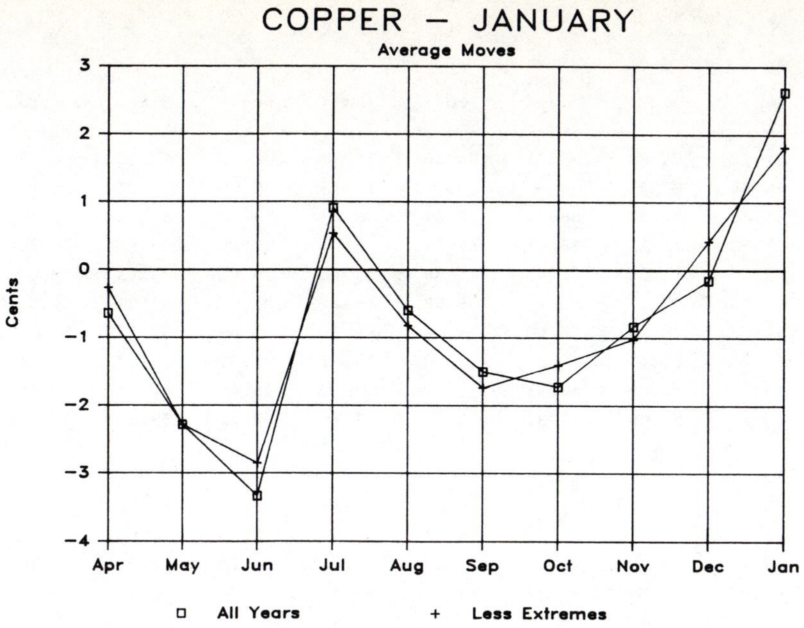
COPPER — JANUARY
Average Moves
3
2
1
0
−1
−2
−3
−4
Cents
Apr
May
Jun
Jul
Aug
Sep
Oct
Nov
Dec
Jan
□ All Years
+ Less Extremes

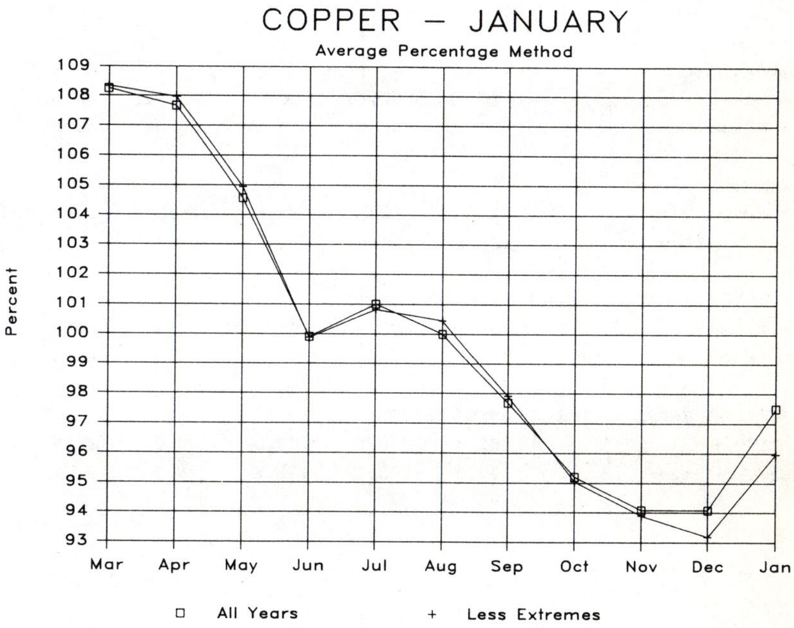
COPPER — JANUARY
Average Percentage Method
109
108
107
106
105
104
103
102
101
100
99
98
97
96
95
94
93
Percent
Mar
Apr
May
Jun
Jul
Aug
Sep
Oct
Nov
Dec
Jan
□ All Years
+ Less Extremes

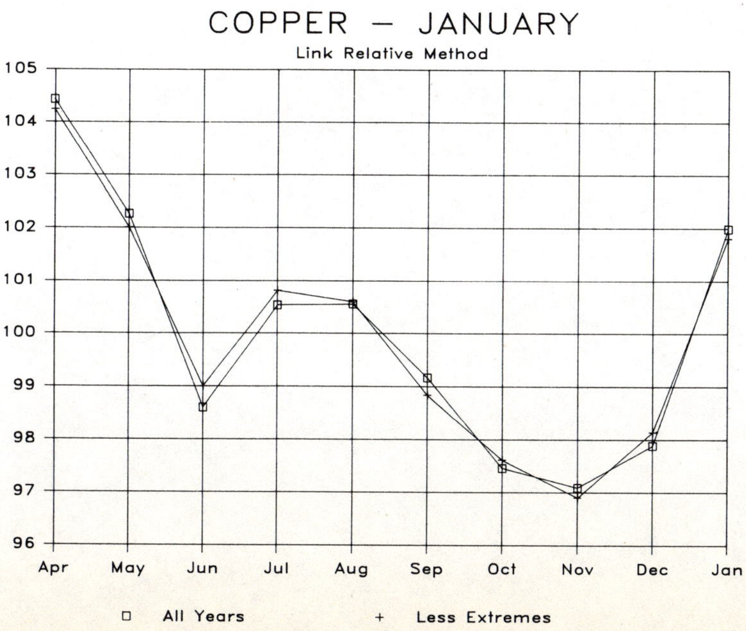
COPPER — JANUARY
Link Relative Method
105
104
103
102
101
100
99
98
97
96
Apr
May
Jun
Jul
Aug
Sep
Oct
Nov
Dec
Jan
□ All Years
+ Less Extremes

COPPER - MARCH - MONTHLY AVERAGE PRICE

Year of Expiration	May	Jun	Jul	Aug	Sep	Oct	Nov	Dec	Jan	Feb	Mar	May-Mar Average
1976	60.11	57.16	60.76	62.77	59.25	56.88	56.21	54.70	55.88	56.88	61.15	58.34
1977	72.83	74.99	79.16	73.10	68.84	60.27	60.02	60.38	64.73	65.60	69.71	68.15
1978	67.51	64.03	60.19	56.06	57.42	57.94	56.53	59.81	59.23	56.98	58.32	59.46
1979	65.37	65.61	65.57	67.75	67.53	70.11	68.31	69.79	73.71	86.30	90.64	71.88
1980	86.86	84.79	82.51	89.36	93.49	95.05	97.05	101.56	119.14	129.82	99.13	98.07
1981	96.04	92.85	101.27	96.73	97.84	97.69	95.45	86.98	86.24	81.67	82.09	92.26
1982	91.59	87.32	85.78	88.83	83.58	79.60	76.51	75.44	73.27	71.86	67.72	80.14
1983	77.39	65.04	69.00	66.26	65.76	66.48	66.03	68.19	73.59	76.01	73.07	69.71
1984	84.64	80.66	81.16	78.60	74.21	67.46	64.77	65.79	63.12	64.45	67.48	72.03
1985	69.73	66.74	63.05	63.39	60.36	58.99	61.32	58.52	59.71	60.78	59.91	62.05

	May	Jun	Jul	Aug	Sep	Oct	Nov	Dec	Jan	Feb	Mar
AVERAGE MOVE											
All Years		-3.29	0.93	-0.56	-1.46	-1.78	-0.83	-0.11	2.75	2.17	-2.11
Less Extremes		-2.83	0.59	-0.80	-1.68	-1.48	-0.94	0.36	1.57	1.71	0.65
Ave Up - All Years		1.19	4.13	2.88	2.20	1.35	2.16	2.13	5.60	4.28	2.92
Ave Down - All Years		-4.41	-2.28	-4.01	-3.03	-3.86	-1.57	-3.46	-1.54	-2.74	-9.66
COUNT											
Number Up		2	5	5	3	4	2	6	6	7	6
Number Down		8	5	5	7	6	8	4	4	3	4
Pct Up		20.0%	50.0%	50.0%	30.0%	40.0%	20.0%	60.0%	60.0%	70.0%	60.0%
Pct Down		80.0%	50.0%	50.0%	70.0%	60.0%	80.0%	40.0%	40.0%	30.0%	40.0%
EXTREMES											
Greatest Up		2.16	8.42	6.85	4.13	2.58	2.33	4.51	17.58	12.59	4.33
Greatest Down		-12.36	-3.84	-6.06	-5.24	-8.57	-3.09	-8.47	-2.66	-4.57	-30.69
SEASONAL INDEX : AVERAGE PERCENTAGE METHOD											
All Years	106.2	101.6	102.7	101.7	99.3	96.7	95.6	95.5	98.9	101.7	100.1
Less Extremes	107.0	102.2	103.3	101.8	99.2	96.6	95.5	95.4	97.5	99.5	98.8
SEASONAL INDEX : LINK RELATIVE METHOD											
All Years		101.5	102.7	102.0	100.0	97.5	96.4	96.5	99.7	102.3	101.4
Less Extremes		102.0	103.1	102.2	99.7	97.7	96.3	96.8	99.2	101.0	102.0

COPPER - MARCH - MONTH OF HIGH AND LOW

Year of Expiration	May	Jun	Jul	Aug	Sep	Oct	Nov	Dec	Jan	Feb	Mar
1976				H				L			
1977			H				L				
1978	H			L							
1979	L										H
1980			L							H	
1981			H							L	
1982	H										L
1983	H				L						
1984	H								L		
1985	H							L			

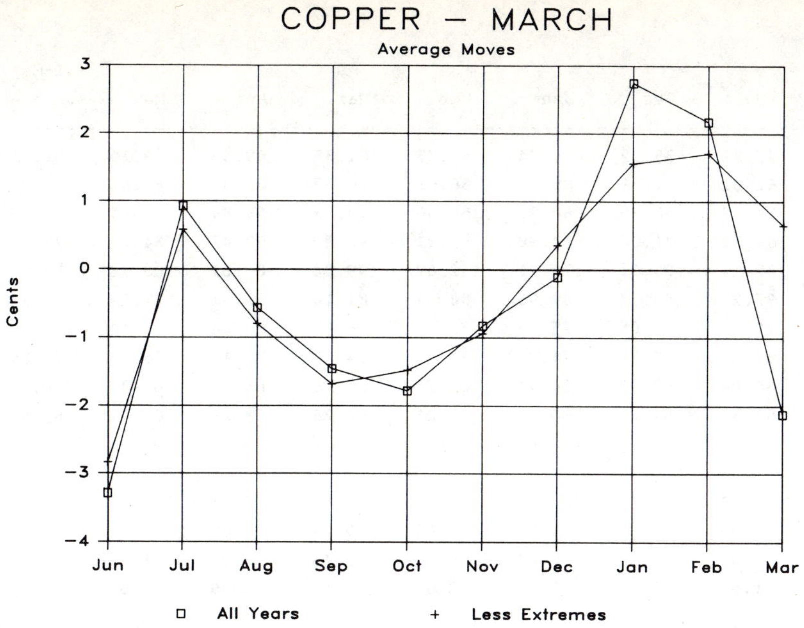
COPPER – MARCH
Average Moves
Cents
3
2
1
0
–1
–2
–3
–4
Jun
Jul
Aug
Sep
Oct
Nov
Dec
Jan
Feb
Mar
All Years
Less Extremes

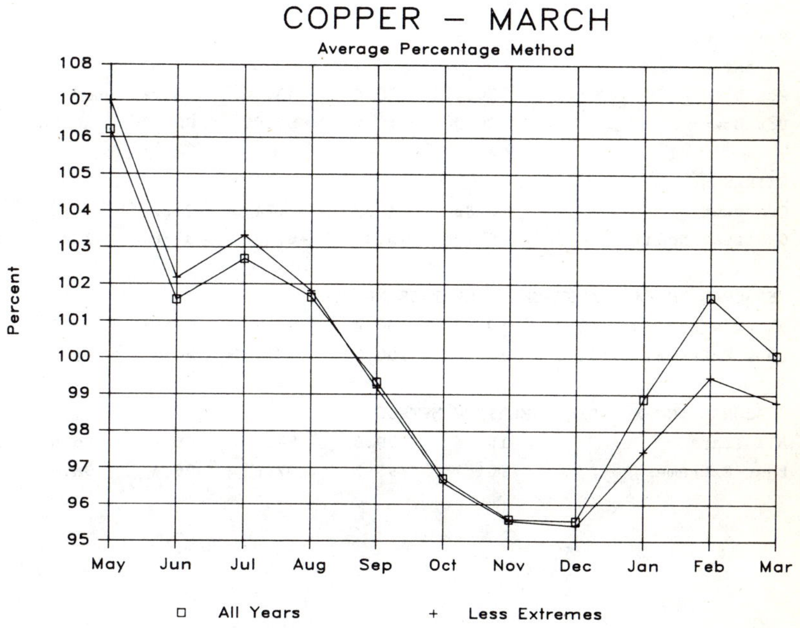
COPPER – MARCH
Average Percentage Method
Percent
108
107
106
105
104
103
102
101
100
99
98
97
96
95
May
Jun
Jul
Aug
Sep
Oct
Nov
Dec
Jan
Feb
Mar
All Years
Less Extremes

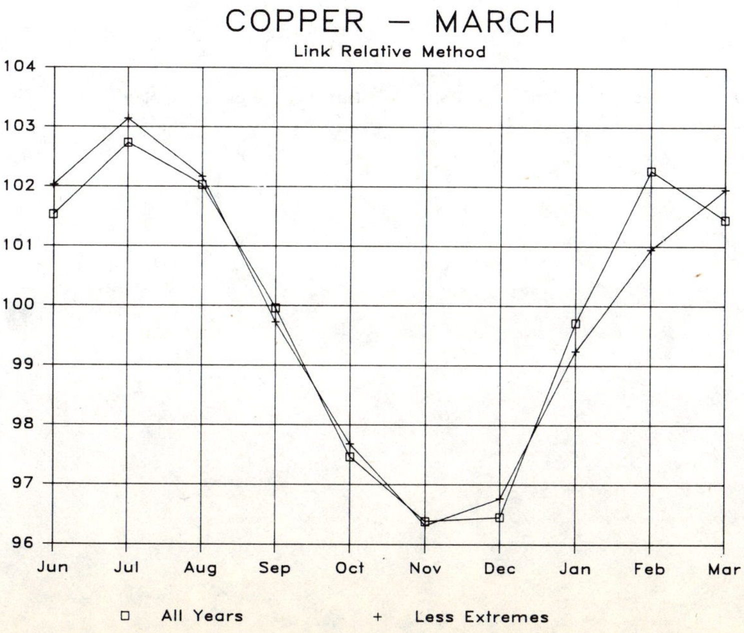
COPPER – MARCH
Link Relative Method
104
103
102
101
100
99
98
97
96
Jun
Jul
Aug
Sep
Oct
Nov
Dec
Jan
Feb
Mar
All Years
Less Extremes

COPPER - MAY - MONTHLY AVERAGE PRICE

Year of Expiration	Jul	Aug	Sep	Oct	Nov	Dec	Jan	Feb	Mar	Apr	May	Jul-May Average
1976	61.76	63.80	60.51	58.08	57.32	55.72	56.74	57.73	61.85	69.55	69.15	61.11
1977	80.03	74.24	69.94	61.27	61.02	61.31	65.68	66.63	70.33	65.80	63.84	67.28
1978	61.09	56.96	58.32	58.96	57.52	60.75	60.22	58.00	59.33	59.84	59.64	59.15
1979	66.59	68.65	68.41	71.15	69.51	71.06	74.98	87.31	92.31	92.47	84.67	77.01
1980	82.71	89.56	94.08	95.42	97.19	100.91	120.21	132.67	99.84	89.62	88.72	99.18
1981	102.28	97.92	99.39	99.26	97.21	89.34	88.96	84.34	84.10	82.91	79.59	91.39
1982	87.92	91.15	85.69	81.55	78.18	77.05	75.07	73.97	68.93	69.34	70.18	78.09
1983	70.48	67.48	66.93	67.52	67.03	69.21	74.74	77.50	74.22	76.17	78.96	71.84
1984	82.37	80.02	75.60	68.80	66.06	67.09	64.41	65.75	68.74	68.73	63.37	70.09
1985	64.35	64.58	61.50	60.13	62.36	59.26	60.16	61.61	60.76	63.85	63.21	61.98

	Jul	Aug	Sep	Oct	Nov	Dec	Jan	Feb	Mar	Apr	May
AVERAGE MOVE											
All Years		-0.52	-1.40	-1.82	-0.88	-0.17	2.95	2.43	-2.51	-0.21	-1.70
Less Extremes		-0.78	-1.63	-1.54	-0.95	0.31	1.61	2.06	0.34	0.05	-1.49
Ave Up - All Years		2.88	2.45	1.33	1.99	2.00	5.84	4.61	3.43	2.30	1.81
Ave Down - All Years		-3.92	-3.05	-3.92	-1.59	-3.43	-1.39	-2.65	-8.45	-3.99	-2.57
COUNT											
Number Up		5	3	4	2	6	6	7	5	6	2
Number Down		5	7	6	8	4	4	3	5	4	8
Pct Up		50.0%	30.0%	40.0%	20.0%	60.0%	60.0%	70.0%	50.0%	60.0%	20.0%
Pct Down		50.0%	70.0%	60.0%	80.0%	40.0%	40.0%	30.0%	50.0%	40.0%	80.0%
EXTREMES											
Greatest Up		6.85	4.53	2.74	2.22	3.72	19.31	12.46	5.00	7.70	2.79
Greatest Down		-5.79	-5.46	-8.67	-3.38	-7.88	-2.68	-4.62	-32.83	-10.21	-7.80
SEASONAL INDEX : AVERAGE PERCENTAGE METHOD											
All Years	103.7	102.7	100.4	97.7	96.5	96.3	99.7	102.7	100.6	101.0	98.8
Less Extremes	104.3	102.6	100.7	97.1	96.0	96.2	98.0	100.1	99.8	100.1	98.4
SEASONAL INDEX : LINK RELATIVE METHOD											
All Years		101.4	99.6	97.3	96.4	96.5	100.1	103.1	102.1	102.7	100.7
Less Extremes		101.7	99.5	97.6	96.4	96.9	99.5	101.7	102.6	103.0	101.1

COPPER - MAY - MONTH OF HIGH AND LOW

Year of Expiration	Jul	Aug	Sep	Oct	Nov	Dec	Jan	Feb	Mar	Apr	May
1976						L				H	
1977	H				L						
1978	H	L									
1979	L									H	
1980	L							H			
1981	H										L
1982		H							L		
1983			L								H
1984	H										L
1985		H				L					

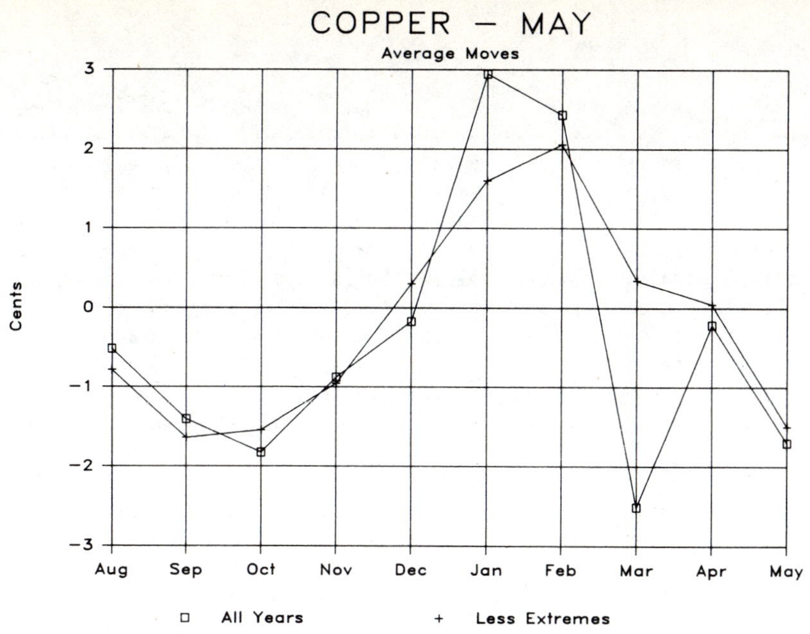
COPPER — MAY
Average Moves
Cents
3
2
1
0
−1
−2
−3
Aug
Sep
Oct
Nov
Dec
Jan
Feb
Mar
Apr
May
All Years
Less Extremes

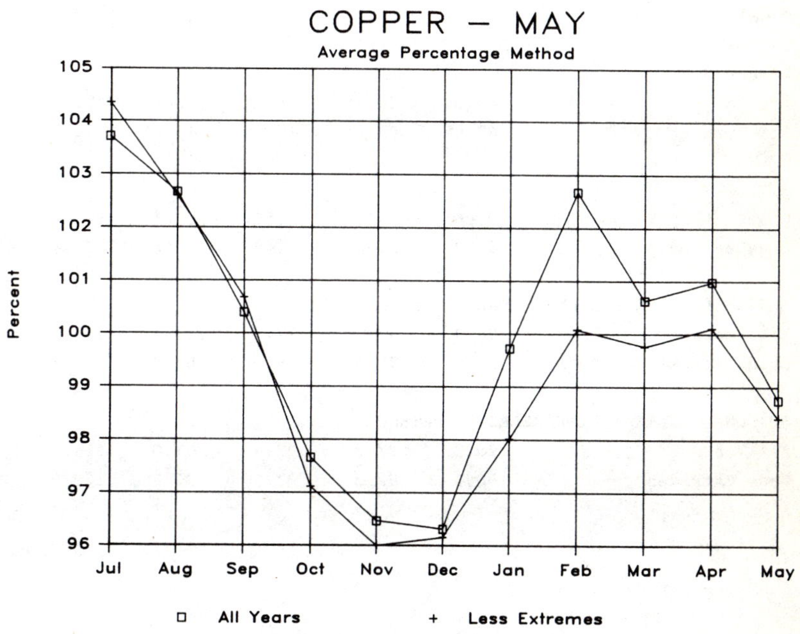
COPPER — MAY
Average Percentage Method
Percent
105
104
103
102
101
100
99
98
97
96
Jul
Aug
Sep
Oct
Nov
Dec
Jan
Feb
Mar
Apr
May
All Years
Less Extremes

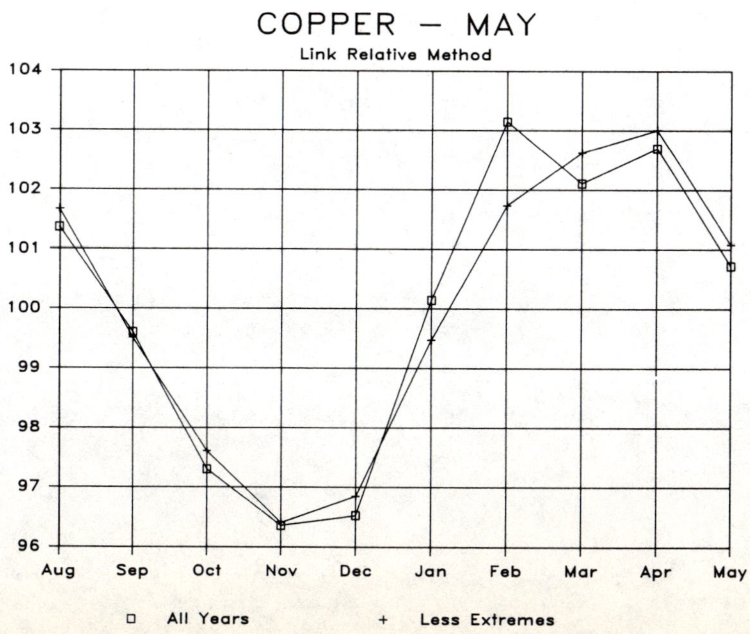
COPPER — MAY
Link Relative Method
104
103
102
101
100
99
98
97
96
Aug
Sep
Oct
Nov
Dec
Jan
Feb
Mar
Apr
May
All Years
Less Extremes

COPPER - JULY - MONTHLY AVERAGE PRICE

Year of Expiration	Sep	Oct	Nov	Dec	Jan	Feb	Mar	Apr	May	Jun	Jul	Sep-Jul Average
1976	61.69	59.24	58.39	56.75	57.59	58.61	62.65	70.37	69.83	70.83	74.93	63.72
1977	70.93	62.23	62.00	62.25	66.60	67.62	71.34	66.83	63.93	60.51	57.04	64.66
1978	59.21	59.89	58.52	61.68	61.20	59.00	60.35	60.94	61.22	61.20	60.96	60.38
1979	69.26	72.12	70.62	72.23	76.01	87.47	92.77	93.41	84.88	83.15	81.25	80.29
1980	94.23	95.74	97.35	100.91	121.15	134.49	102.86	92.39	90.69	87.59	98.02	101.40
1981	100.93	100.82	98.84	91.35	91.09	86.85	86.28	85.30	81.56	78.07	76.04	88.83
1982	87.77	83.44	79.84	78.66	76.84	75.92	70.74	71.31	70.79	58.43	63.44	74.29
1983	68.08	68.56	68.03	70.22	75.86	78.93	75.66	77.68	79.83	75.34	75.94	74.01
1984	76.97	70.16	67.38	68.42	65.73	67.07	70.03	70.12	64.36	61.31	58.79	67.30
1985	62.63	61.28	63.40	59.99	60.60	62.24	61.36	64.66	63.59	60.33	60.78	61.90

	Sep	Oct	Nov	Dec	Jan	Feb	Mar	Apr	May	Jun	Jul
AVERAGE MOVE											
All Years		-1.82	-0.91	-0.19	3.02	2.56	-2.42	-0.10	-2.23	-3.39	1.04
Less Extremes		-1.55	-0.95	0.25	1.58	2.06	0.27	0.21	-1.99	-2.82	0.44
Ave Up - All Years		1.38	1.86	1.97	5.91	4.70	3.47	2.13	1.22	1.01	4.12
Ave Down - All Years		-3.96	-1.60	-3.43	-1.31	-2.45	-8.31	-5.32	-3.10	-3.88	-2.03
COUNT											
Number Up		4	2	6	6	7	5	7	2	1	5
Number Down		6	8	4	4	3	5	3	8	9	5
Pct Up		40.0%	20.0%	60.0%	60.0%	70.0%	50.0%	70.0%	20.0%	10.0%	50.0%
Pct Down		60.0%	80.0%	40.0%	40.0%	30.0%	50.0%	30.0%	80.0%	90.0%	50.0%
EXTREMES											
Greatest Up		2.86	2.12	3.56	20.24	13.34	5.30	7.72	2.15	1.01	10.43
Greatest Down		-8.70	-3.60	-7.48	-2.68	-4.24	-31.63	-10.47	-8.53	-12.36	-3.47
SEASONAL INDEX : AVERAGE PERCENTAGE METHOD											
All Years	102.3	99.4	98.2	97.9	101.3	104.3	102.3	102.8	99.8	95.3	96.4
Less Extremes	102.3	98.9	97.8	98.0	100.4	102.3	101.6	102.5	99.9	95.4	95.1
SEASONAL INDEX : LINK RELATIVE METHOD											
All Years		98.3	97.3	97.4	101.0	104.0	103.0	103.7	101.0	96.5	97.8
Less Extremes		98.6	97.3	97.6	100.1	102.5	103.3	103.8	101.1	97.4	98.3

COPPER - JULY - MONTH OF HIGH AND LOW

Year of Expiration	Sep	Oct	Nov	Dec	Jan	Feb	Mar	Apr	May	Jun	Jul
1976				L							H
1977							H				L
1978			L	H							
1979		L						H			
1980						H				L	
1981	H										L
1982	H									L	
1983			L						H		
1984	H										L
1985				L				H			

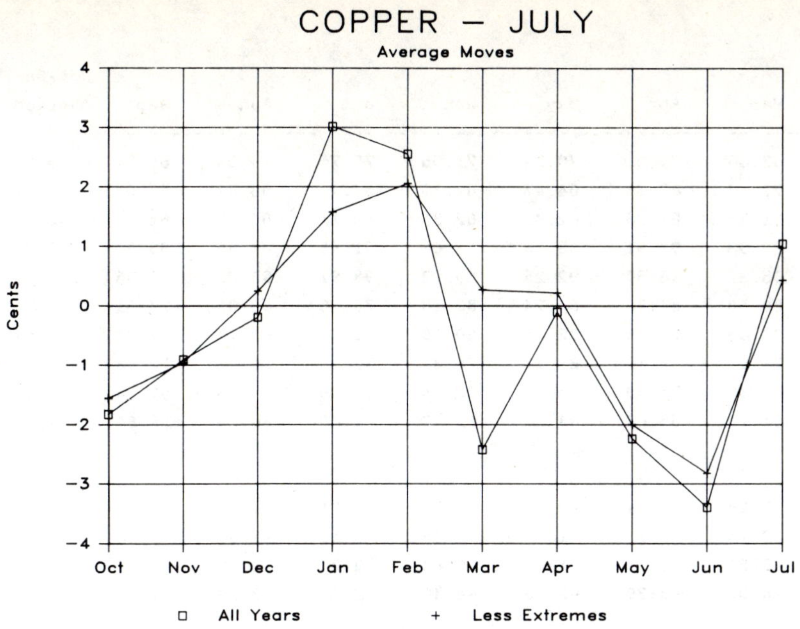
COPPER – JULY
Average Moves
4
3
2
1
0
–1
–2
–3
–4
Cents
Oct
Nov
Dec
Jan
Feb
Mar
Apr
May
Jun
Jul
All Years
Less Extremes

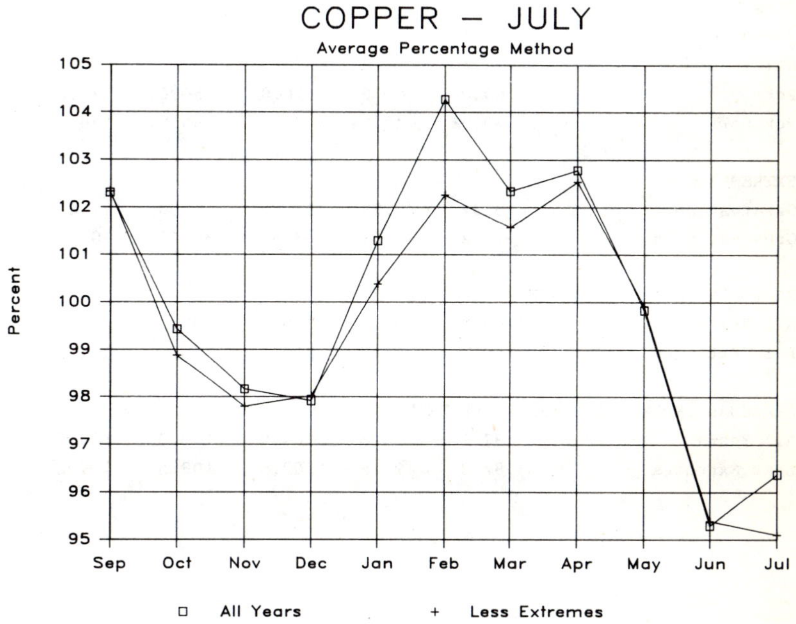
COPPER – JULY
Average Percentage Method
105
104
103
102
101
100
99
98
97
96
95
Percent
Sep
Oct
Nov
Dec
Jan
Feb
Mar
Apr
May
Jun
Jul
All Years
Less Extremes

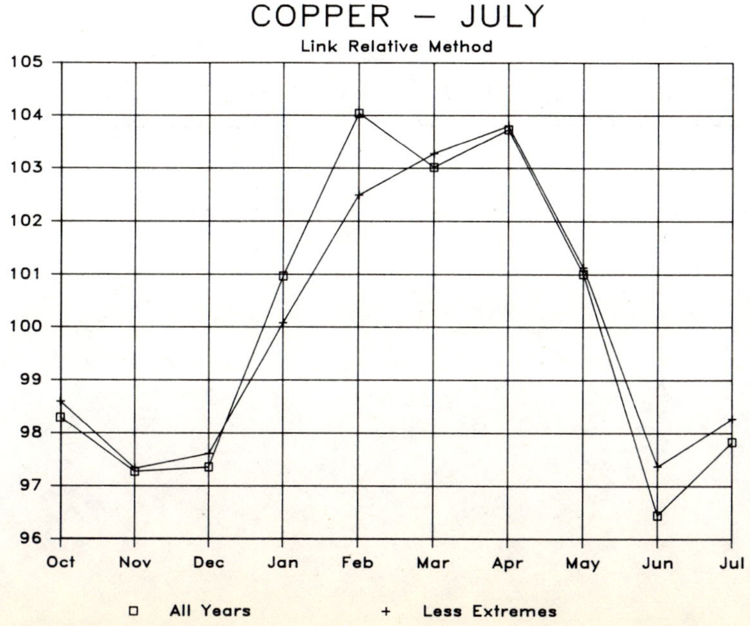
COPPER – JULY
Link Relative Method
105
104
103
102
101
100
99
98
97
96
Oct
Nov
Dec
Jan
Feb
Mar
Apr
May
Jun
Jul
All Years
Less Extremes

COPPER - SEPTEMBER - MONTHLY AVERAGE PRICE

Year of Expiration	Nov	Dec	Jan	Feb	Mar	Apr	May	Jun	Jul	Aug	Sep	Nov-Sep Average
1976	59.43	57.71	58.45	59.49	63.49	71.11	70.72	71.95	75.75	69.54	66.57	65.84
1977	62.86	63.13	67.51	68.53	72.30	67.83	64.87	61.38	57.47	53.41	55.04	63.12
1978	59.49	62.58	62.12	59.95	61.35	61.96	62.31	62.36	62.11	64.47	64.41	62.10
1979	71.68	73.24	76.86	87.43	92.93	93.31	85.66	83.66	81.65	87.65	88.84	83.90
1980	97.54	100.96	121.69	135.63	105.37	94.50	92.25	89.02	98.91	93.23	93.36	102.04
1981	100.46	93.35	93.09	89.23	88.58	87.76	84.24	80.58	78.58	81.06	77.61	86.78
1982	81.52	80.28	78.61	77.82	72.48	73.05	72.54	60.18	64.44	62.44	62.91	71.48
1983	69.02	71.22	76.88	80.12	77.01	79.10	81.17	76.81	77.17	74.01	70.98	75.77
1984	68.71	69.76	67.08	68.42	71.31	71.49	65.75	62.64	59.39	59.63	57.14	65.57
1985	64.44	60.73	61.01	62.81	61.78	65.08	64.25	61.23	61.40	60.39	59.66	62.07

	Nov	Dec	Jan	Feb	Mar	Apr	May	Jun	Jul	Aug	Sep
AVERAGE MOVE											
All Years		-0.22	3.04	2.61	-2.28	-0.14	-2.14	-3.39	0.71	-1.10	-0.93
Less Extremes		0.19	1.54	2.00	0.24	0.23	-1.98	-2.85	0.13	-1.35	-0.94
Ave Up - All Years		1.93	5.90	4.70	3.51	2.11	1.21	0.64	3.70	2.77	0.86
Ave Down - All Years		-3.45	-1.27	-2.28	-8.07	-5.39	-2.98	-4.40	-2.29	-3.69	-2.12
COUNT											
Number Up		6	6	7	5	7	2	2	5	4	4
Number Down		4	4	3	5	3	8	8	5	6	6
Pct Up		60.0%	60.0%	70.0%	50.0%	70.0%	20.0%	20.0%	50.0%	40.0%	40.0%
Pct Down		40.0%	40.0%	30.0%	50.0%	30.0%	80.0%	80.0%	50.0%	60.0%	60.0%
EXTREMES											
Greatest Up		3.42	20.73	13.93	5.50	7.62	2.07	1.23	9.89	6.00	1.63
Greatest Down		-7.12	-2.68	-3.87	-30.25	-10.87	-7.66	-12.36	-3.90	-6.21	-3.45
SEASONAL INDEX : AVERAGE PERCENTAGE METHOD											
All Years	99.6	99.3	102.6	105.6	103.7	104.1	101.2	96.7	97.2	95.7	94.4
Less Extremes	99.4	99.1	102.2	104.0	103.3	104.6	101.8	96.6	95.9	95.8	93.8
SEASONAL INDEX : LINK RELATIVE METHOD											
All Years		97.1	100.8	104.0	103.3	104.1	101.7	97.3	98.3	97.2	96.2
Less Extremes		97.2	99.8	102.5	103.5	104.2	101.8	98.3	98.9	97.4	96.3

COPPER - SEPTEMBER - MONTH OF HIGH AND LOW

Year of Expiration	Nov	Dec	Jan	Feb	Mar	Apr	May	Jun	Jul	Aug	Sep
1976		L							H		
1977					H					L	
1978	L									H	
1979	L					H					
1980				H				L			
1981	H										L
1982	H							L			
1983	L						H				
1984						H					L
1985						H					L

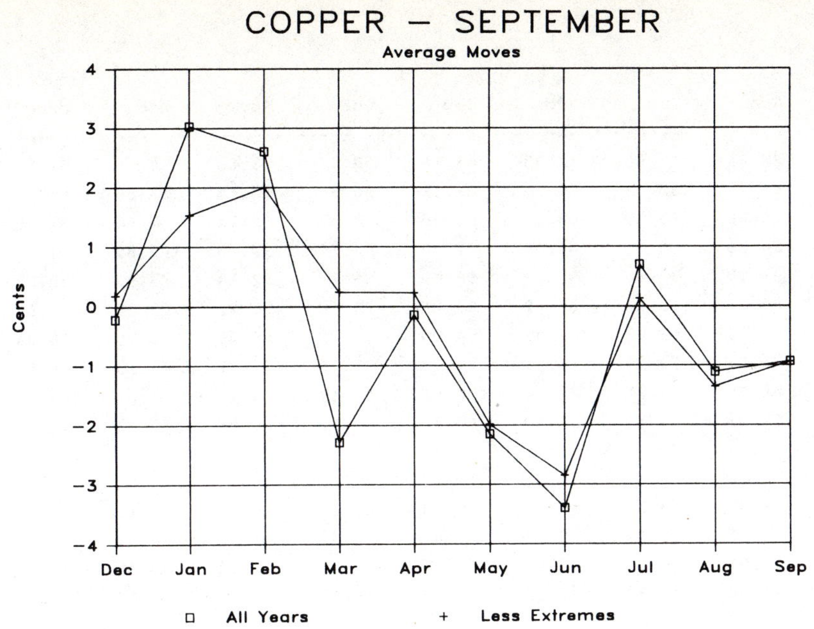

COPPER – SEPTEMBER
Average Moves
Cents
4
3
2
1
0
−1
−2
−3
−4
Dec
Jan
Feb
Mar
Apr
May
Jun
Jul
Aug
Sep
□ All Years
+ Less Extremes

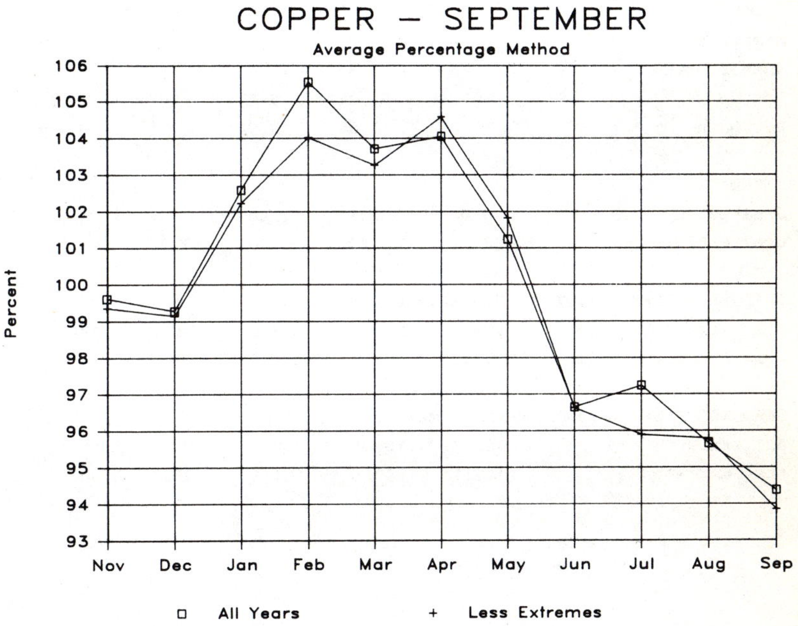

COPPER – SEPTEMBER
Average Percentage Method
Percent
106
105
104
103
102
101
100
99
98
97
96
95
94
93
Nov
Dec
Jan
Feb
Mar
Apr
May
Jun
Jul
Aug
Sep
□ All Years
+ Less Extremes

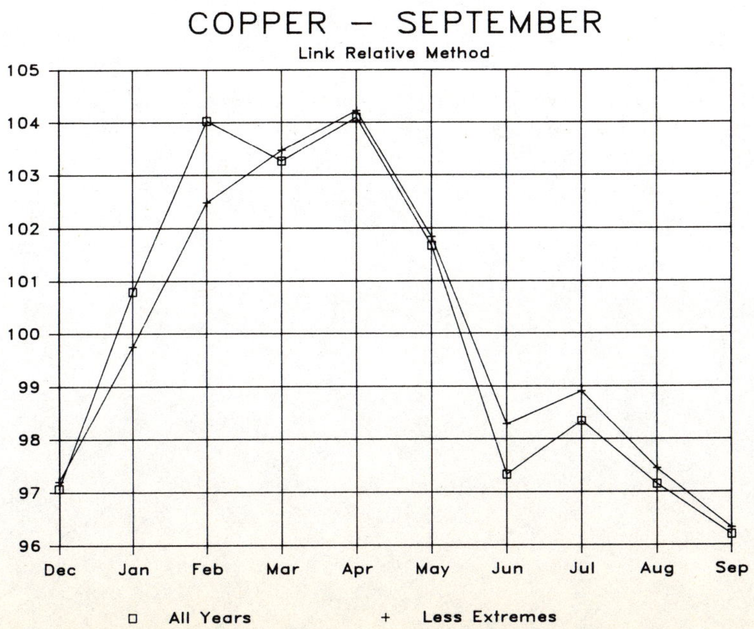

COPPER – SEPTEMBER
Link Relative Method
105
104
103
102
101
100
99
98
97
96
Dec
Jan
Feb
Mar
Apr
May
Jun
Jul
Aug
Sep
□ All Years
+ Less Extremes

COPPER - DECEMBER - MONTHLY AVERAGE PRICE

Year of Expiration	Feb	Mar	Apr	May	Jun	Jul	Aug	Sep	Oct	Nov	Dec	Feb-Dec Average
1976	60.70	64.64	72.08	71.91	73.63	77.56	71.33	67.18	58.87	58.64	58.96	66.86
1977	69.62	73.44	69.21	66.24	62.72	58.83	54.74	56.11	56.61	55.16	58.58	61.93
1978	61.36	62.84	63.47	63.86	64.06	63.90	66.22	66.06	68.35	66.11	67.64	64.90
1979	87.11	93.15	93.26	86.41	84.36	82.11	88.84	92.70	94.24	97.29	102.69	91.11
1980	137.08	108.34	96.89	94.23	90.95	99.78	95.07	95.40	95.17	92.24	83.67	98.98
1981	92.30	91.63	91.20	88.10	84.11	82.26	85.17	80.11	76.50	73.92	73.29	83.51
1982	80.48	75.01	75.57	75.01	62.66	66.75	64.48	64.00	65.05	64.29	66.18	69.04
1983	81.78	78.69	80.89	82.98	78.81	79.26	76.33	72.03	65.44	62.82	64.17	74.84
1984	70.45	73.28	73.49	67.75	64.69	61.21	61.54	58.54	57.19	59.82	54.25	63.84
1985	63.63	62.48	65.52	64.91	62.27	62.49	61.58	60.41	61.62	60.86	63.17	62.63

	Feb	Mar	Apr	May	Jun	Jul	Aug	Sep	Oct	Nov	Dec
AVERAGE MOVE											
All Years		-2.10	-0.19	-2.02	-3.31	0.59	-0.88	-1.28	-1.35	-0.79	0.15
Less Extremes		0.21	0.26	-1.93	-2.81	0.12	-1.17	-1.44	-0.93	-1.00	0.58
Ave Up - All Years		3.62	2.02	1.25	0.96	3.50	3.07	1.85	1.32	2.84	2.32
Ave Down - All Years		-7.82	-5.37	-2.83	-4.38	-2.33	-3.52	-2.62	-4.02	-1.70	-4.92
COUNT											
Number Up		5	7	2	2	5	4	3	5	2	7
Number Down		5	3	8	8	5	6	7	5	8	3
Pct Up		50.0%	70.0%	20.0%	20.0%	50.0%	40.0%	30.0%	50.0%	20.0%	70.0%
Pct Down		50.0%	30.0%	80.0%	80.0%	50.0%	60.0%	70.0%	50.0%	80.0%	30.0%
EXTREMES											
Greatest Up		6.04	7.44	2.10	1.72	8.83	6.73	3.86	2.29	3.05	5.40
Greatest Down		-28.74	-11.45	-6.86	-12.36	-3.90	-6.23	-5.06	-8.31	-2.93	-8.58
SEASONAL INDEX : AVERAGE PERCENTAGE METHOD											
All Years	108.0	106.2	106.4	103.8	99.2	99.7	98.3	96.4	94.6	93.5	93.9
Less Extremes	106.4	105.8	106.4	104.0	98.9	98.9	98.5	96.5	94.1	93.0	92.8
SEASONAL INDEX : LINK RELATIVE METHOD											
All Years		102.1	103.5	102.0	98.5	100.1	99.8	98.9	98.0	97.8	99.2
Less Extremes		102.1	103.5	101.9	99.1	100.3	99.6	98.5	98.1	97.6	99.3

COPPER - DECEMBER - MONTH OF HIGH AND LOW

Year of Expiration	Feb	Mar	Apr	May	Jun	Jul	Aug	Sep	Oct	Nov	Dec
1976						H				L	
1977		H					L				
1978	L								H		
1979						L					H
1980	H										L
1981	H										L
1982	H				L						
1983				H						L	
1984			H								L
1985			H					L			

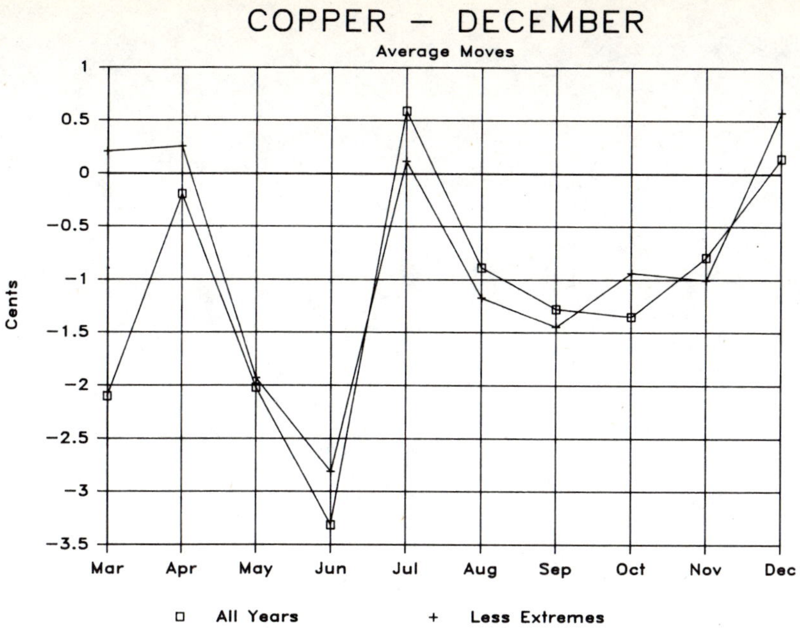
COPPER — DECEMBER
Average Moves
Cents
1
0.5
0
−0.5
−1
−1.5
−2
−2.5
−3
−3.5
Mar
Apr
May
Jun
Jul
Aug
Sep
Oct
Nov
Dec
All Years
+ Less Extremes

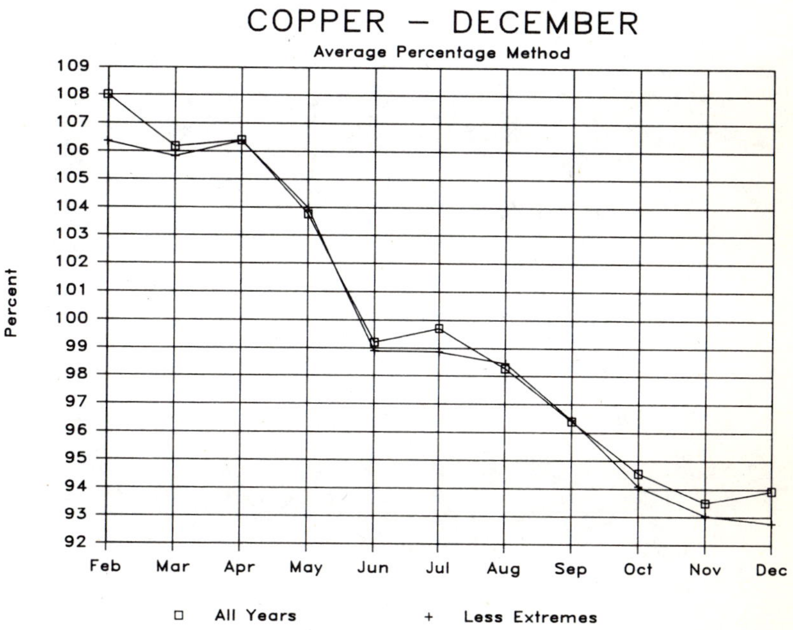
COPPER — DECEMBER
Average Percentage Method
Percent
109
108
107
106
105
104
103
102
101
100
99
98
97
96
95
94
93
92
Feb
Mar
Apr
May
Jun
Jul
Aug
Sep
Oct
Nov
Dec
All Years
+ Less Extremes

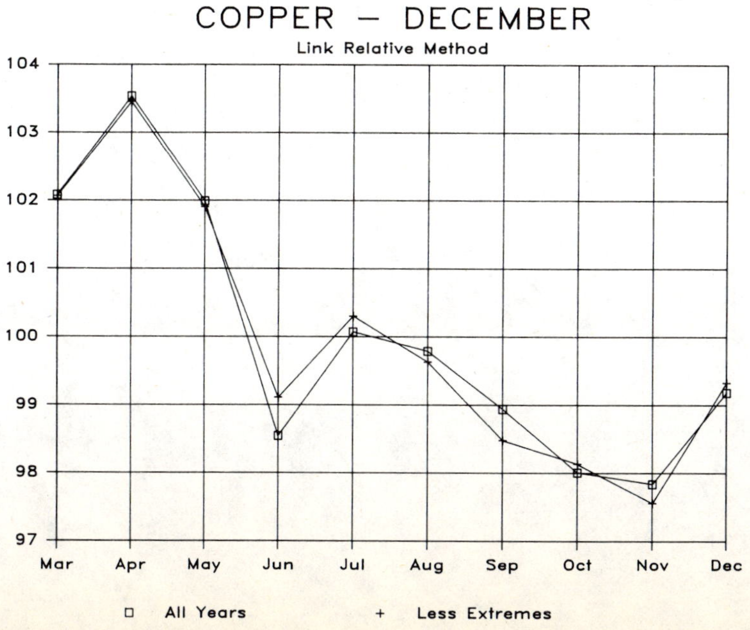
COPPER — DECEMBER
Link Relative Method
104
103
102
101
100
99
98
97
Mar
Apr
May
Jun
Jul
Aug
Sep
Oct
Nov
Dec
All Years
+ Less Extremes

SIX

Grains

The grains are classic seasonal markets because of the clearly seasonal nature of their production. However, they are a mixed bag for seasonal traders. Soybeans, for example, only have one month in all contracts with a reliability of greater than 70%!

CORN

Corn has been a favorite of seasonal trends traders for many years. The harvest lows in October and November have been traditional buying times for large professional traders. However, recent research suggests that the seasonals in corn are not as consistent as they have been in the past. The reemerging importance of government programs and the existence of two droughts in the last five years have probably reduced the importance of the planting/harvest cycle. Nonetheless, there remain good and long seasonal runs from which traders can profit.

Traders can look at the corn chart and see the pattern of corn prices. The first three months are a time of low export demand because the Great Lakes are frozen and the increased cost of shipping to the Gulf of Mexico makes the corn less competitive in the export markets. These three months are also a time of only moderate demand for corn for feed in the domestic market, since most feed users would have already bought the corn they need in the previous two months.

After this period of relatively flat price action, the price moves strongly upward to the summer highs. This is largely caused by the opening of the Great Lakes to shipping, which results in increased export demand, and by the decreasing amount of corn available for use.

The fall period is marked by a downturn in the price of corn. The price drops as the size of the new crop becomes known and as the new crop is harvested.

It is after the harvest that the peak demand for corn occurs. Export demand is heavy and corn feeders are buying extra feed to fatten their animals because of the winter cold. This winter period is typified by strong prices from November to January.

WHEAT

Wheat has many opportunites for the seasonal tendency trader. It has periods that have good moves and high reliability. Wheat should be considered an excellent trading vehicle for the average trader.

Wheat follows the classic pattern of harvest lows and late season highs. Most wheat is harvested during the months of May and June. This is also the time of the seasonal price low. Traders should note that the impending harvest is enough to turn the market bearish before the actual harvest. It is only after the harvest that the price beings to rise, which it does until it reaches its winter highs.

SOYBEANS

Soybeans have become one of the least reliable seasonal commodities. There is only one entry in the tables of highly reliable seasonals. This can be partially attributed to the conflicting seasonality of demand, particularly export demand, of the soybean products, meal and oil. Both products are better seasonal performers than the beans themselves. Nonetheless, there are seasonal patterns to exploit due to the strong moves.

The harvest lows in September and October are key buying times for professional traders. The price plummet from summer highs to harvest lows forces the small speculators to leap out of their long positions, which the large traders and export buyers willingly purchase.

After the harvest low, soybean prices begin a long steady uptrend that usually ends in mid-summer. This trend is brought about by an increase in demand for domestically used soybean meal. The meal is used through the winter as a food supplement, mainly for the poultry and hog industries. This seasonally high demand compensates for the generally reduced export demand. The price uptrend gains strength through the spring as soybeans become more scarce.

Late summer and early fall are marked by a strong downturn in the price of soybeans. As the size of the new crop becomes known and as the new crop is harvested, the price plunges.

SOYBEAN MEAL

Soybean meal presents excellent opportunites for the seasonal trader. It has a number of trades greater than 80% reliability. In addition to the high reliability, meal has strong and potentially profitable moves. It is also known as a relatively low risk commodity without high volatility. This is a good trading vehicle for most speculators.

Soybean meal prices are largely determined by the price of soybeans. The seasonal tendencies of meal are similar to the beans. However, meal provides a lower risk alternative to trading soybeans, yet traders can capitalize on essentially the same seasonal trends as the beans.

A key feature of soybean meal is the sharp rally following the November low. This is a result of a buying streak by meat producers in the late fall. The meat producers, mainly poultry and hog growers, are large consumers of soybeans because of its feed value. During the winter, the animals are placed under greater stress as a result of cold temperatures. Therefore, livestock producers purchase soybean meal, which is high in protein, to supplement their normal feed ration. They find that the extra protein of the soybean meal helps their animals through the winter.

From this point on, the meal seasonals essentially follow the same pattern as the soybeans. Alert traders may consider using the divergences between meal and oil versus soybeans as the basis for spreading the meal and oil against the beans.

SOYBEAN OIL

Soybean oil is not a good commodity for seasonal tendency traders. Both the supply and demand remain fairly constant throughout the year. As a result, little occurs in the way of an exceptional seasonal tendency.

More than 90% of the soybean oil produced is used for salad oil, margarine, and shortening. The demand for these products has no discernible seasonal pattern. The only time of high demand is during the summer months when export demand for soybean oil is heavy. This, in addition to the declining stocks of soybeans, creates the summer bulge in price. Notice, however, that the oncoming harvest of soybeans puts a damper on the price in the late summer and early fall.

Although soybean oil has become a more important component in the soybean complex, it is still the junior partner to soybean meal. This is particularly true in the fall and winter months when the soybeans are crushed largely to satisfy soybean meal demand. This increases the production of soybean oil beyond the amount necessary to satisfy the immeditate demand. The price of soybean oil, however, does not collapse because the oil may be stored and sold at other times of the year.

It is this ability to store the produce until needed, combined with even demand throughout the year, that gives soybean oil its relatively flat seasonal pattern. Even the summer price bulge is relatively weak.

The differences in seasonality of the various components of the soybean complex can provide good spread possibilities. For instance, soybean meal increases in price during the spring, while soybean oil remains steady. Traders can take advantage of this by buying meal and selling oil in the spring.

OATS

Oats have become better for seasonal traders over the past several years. The reliability has improved though the strength of the moves is still low as befits the lowest priced grain.

Oats follow the classic pattern of reaching their lows near harvest and rising in price throughout the rest of the year. The major demand for oats is as feed, especially for horses. The price is particularly strong during the fall months because of the heavy demand caused by the oncoming shortage of fresh forage for animals. For example, horse owners may put their horses out to pasture during the summer but find their pasture's grass dying when fall arrives and will buy oats to feed the horses. Once the winter purchasing season for oats is over, the oat price is determined largely by the size of the upcoming harvest. Thus the price decreases to a low point during harvest.

HIGHEST RELIABLE TRENDS

Commodity	Contract	Month	Position	Reliability	Average Move
Corn	May	May	Short	73.3	−5.40
	Jul	May	Short	73.3	−7.42
Wheat	Mar	Dec	Short	73.3	−19.18
	May	Dec	Short	73.3	−19.56
	May	May	Short	73.3	−18.27
	Jul	Mar	Short	73.3	−15.92
	Jul	May	Short	73.3	−16.33
	Sep	Mar	Short	73.3	−15.48
	Sep	May	Short	73.3	−15.87
	Dec	Mar	Short	73.3	−15.80
	Dec	May	Short	73.3	−15.36
	Dec	Dec	Short	73.3	−15.82
Soybeans	Jan	Dec	Short	73.3	−30.45
Soybean meal	Jan	May	Short	70.0	−6.65
	Jan	Oct	Short	70.0	−5.25
	Jan	Dec	Short	70.0	−11.47
	Mar	Dec	Short	80.0	−10.45
	Mar	Feb	Short	70.0	−7.87
	Mar	Mar	Short	70.0	−5.88
	May	Dec	Short	70.0	−11.08
	May	Feb	Short	70.0	−6.73
	May	May	Short	70.0	−6.78
	Jul	Dec	Short	70.0	−10.54
	Jul	May	Short	80.0	−7.29
	Jul	Jun	Short	80.0	−12.05
	Aug	Dec	Short	70.0	−8.98
	Aug	May	Short	80.0	−7.35
	Aug	Jun	Short	80.0	−11.04
	Aug	Aug	Short	80.0	−11.34
	Sep	Dec	Short	70.0	−6.75
	Sep	May	Short	70.0	−7.03
	Sep	Jun	Short	80.0	−7.29
	Sep	Aug	Short	80.0	−12.12
	Oct	Jun	Short	70.0	−5.96
	Oct	Aug	Short	80.0	−11.42
	Dec	May	Short	70.0	−6.52
	Dec	Aug	Short	70.0	−12.63
	Dec	Nov	Long	70.0	+8.35
Soybean oil	Jan	Dec	Short	80.0	−1.20
	Mar	Dec	Short	80.0	−1.13
	May	Dec	Short	80.0	−1.08
	Jul	Dec	Short	80.0	−1.07
	Aug	Dec	Short	73.3	−1.09
	Aug	Feb	Long	73.3	+1.04
	Sep	Dec	Short	86.7	−0.88
	Sep	Feb	Long	73.3	+0.96

Commodity	Contract	Month	Position	Reliability	Average Move
Oats	Mar	Jun	Short	70.0	−9.14
	Mar	Jul	Short	70.0	−6.77
	Mar	Aug	Short	70.0	−8.23
	Mar	Dec	Short	90.0	−4.56
	Mar	Jan	Short	70.0	−4.22
	May	Aug	Short	70.0	−7.87
	May	Dec	Short	90.0	−4.34
	May	Mar	Short	70.0	−6.61
	May	Apr	Long	70.0	+4.76
	Jul	Dec	Short	70.0	−4.44
	Jul	Jun	Short	70.0	−8.01
	Sep	Mar	Short	70.0	−6.43
	Sep	Jun	Short	70.0	−8.72
	Sep	Jul	Short	80.0	−8.50
	Sep	Aug	Short	90.0	−10.69
	Sep	Sep	Long	80.0	+5.93
	Dec	Mar	Short	80.0	−6.76
	Dec	Jun	Short	70.0	−9.52
	Dec	Jul	Short	80.0	−7.62
	Dec	Aug	Short	90.0	−8.68

CORN - MARCH - MONTHLY AVERAGE PRICE

Year of Expiration	May	Jun	Jul	Aug	Sep	Oct	Nov	Dec	Jan	Feb	Mar	May-Mar Average
1971	125.86	131.12	134.58	147.39	157.12	154.58	152.77	154.51	156.17	152.07	150.28	146.95
1972	143.01	157.33	143.62	126.68	120.68	120.31	119.57	122.90	121.43	119.55	120.10	128.65
1973	131.80	127.63	130.51	133.25	145.32	141.11	141.47	156.01	157.49	161.33	164.24	144.56
1974	177.54	202.66	222.52	282.29	251.38	250.70	256.38	269.48	286.76	313.26	302.14	255.92
1975	244.32	258.04	318.30	355.31	357.21	389.41	374.54	357.41	327.02	295.65	280.73	323.45
1976	250.96	248.70	268.16	315.70	309.19	298.46	276.21	267.89	267.49	268.62	267.94	276.30
1977	274.80	289.14	290.62	282.58	291.62	273.85	251.29	252.10	259.42	255.71	254.17	270.48
1978	257.58	249.06	228.24	206.09	209.70	217.55	229.18	225.12	224.23	226.26	235.57	228.05
1979	263.73	267.11	250.56	234.14	231.16	240.21	238.90	233.35	231.81	236.49	238.92	242.40
1980	280.01	306.08	318.94	291.49	290.61	293.58	285.79	287.40	274.30	271.79	262.86	287.53
1981	309.56	305.51	334.86	350.43	364.80	372.01	395.19	379.91	371.57	361.11	349.95	354.08
1982	380.64	367.66	369.81	332.24	313.43	309.15	295.15	272.18	272.73	267.95	258.47	312.67
1983	297.54	289.38	275.27	253.36	240.16	234.23	242.06	241.67	254.95	273.21	280.78	262.06
1984	300.06	285.98	310.88	363.83	365.08	347.67	349.12	335.54	330.23	324.79	343.32	332.41
1985	310.74	313.48	298.49	291.13	290.37	284.53	281.81	270.00	270.82	268.51	270.16	286.37

	May	Jun	Jul	Aug	Sep	Oct	Nov	Dec	Jan	Feb	Mar
AVERAGE MOVE											
All Years		3.38	6.43	4.70	-1.87	-0.70	-2.53	-4.26	-1.27	-0.67	-1.11
Less Extremes		2.98	4.39	3.72	-0.89	-1.92	-2.96	-4.27	-0.46	-0.40	-1.56
Ave Up - All Years		13.12	17.67	32.63	7.43	11.85	8.36	5.86	6.05	9.41	6.13
Ave Down - All Years		-7.75	-16.03	-19.73	-10.01	-6.98	-9.78	-11.01	-7.68	-7.40	-7.45
COUNT											
Number Up		8	10	7	7	5	6	6	7	6	7
Number Down		7	5	8	8	10	9	9	8	9	8
Pct Up		53.3%	66.7%	46.7%	46.7%	33.3%	40.0%	40.0%	46.7%	40.0%	46.7%
Pct Down		46.7%	33.3%	53.3%	53.3%	66.7%	60.0%	60.0%	53.3%	60.0%	53.3%
EXTREMES											
Greatest Up		26.07	60.26	59.77	14.37	32.20	23.18	14.55	17.28	26.50	18.53
Greatest Down		-14.08	-20.82	-37.57	-30.91	-17.77	-22.56	-22.97	-30.38	-31.38	-14.91
SEASONAL INDEX : AVERAGE PERCENTAGE METHOD											
All Years	97.7	99.4	100.9	102.1	101.6	101.2	100.3	99.4	99.2	99.2	99.0
Less Extremes	98.1	99.2	100.6	102.0	101.6	100.6	99.7	99.5	99.1	98.5	98.8
SEASONAL INDEX : LINK RELATIVE METHOD											
All Years		98.1	100.4	102.2	101.8	101.2	100.3	99.4	99.1	98.9	98.5
Less Extremes		98.9	100.6	101.7	101.5	100.9	100.1	99.1	99.2	99.1	98.8

CORN - MARCH - MONTH OF HIGH AND LOW

Year of Expiration	May	Jun	Jul	Aug	Sep	Oct	Nov	Dec	Jan	Feb	Mar
1971	L				H						
1972		H								L	
1973		L									H
1974	L									H	
1975	L					H					
1976		L		H							
1977					H		L				
1978	H			L							
1979		H			L						
1980			H								L
1981		L					H				
1982	H										L
1983	H					L					
1984		L			H						
1985		H								L	

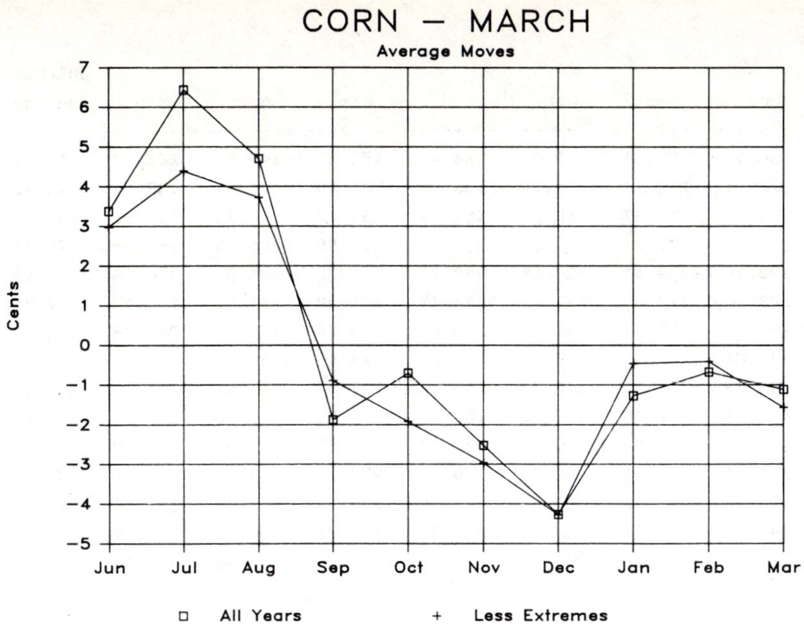
CORN — MARCH
Average Moves
Cents
7
6
5
4
3
2
1
0
−1
−2
−3
−4
−5
Jun
Jul
Aug
Sep
Oct
Nov
Dec
Jan
Feb
Mar
□ All Years
+ Less Extremes

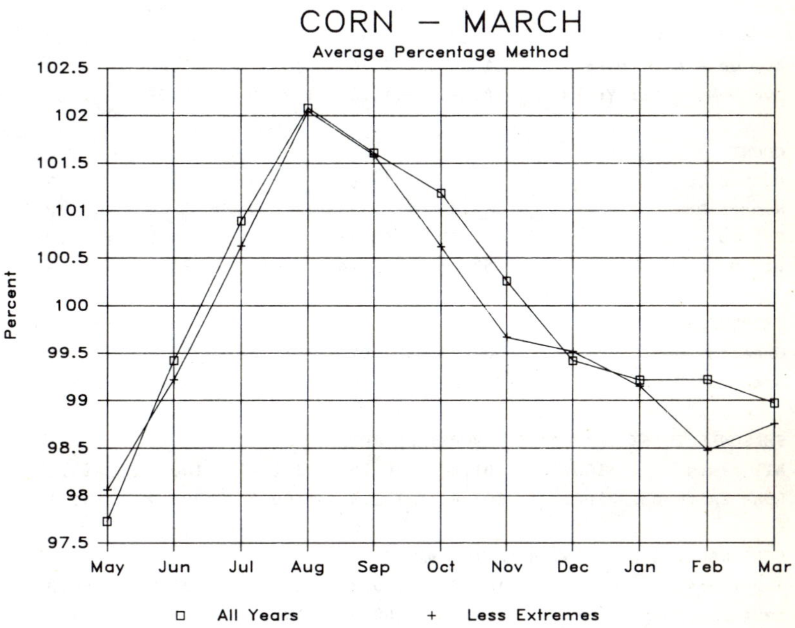
CORN — MARCH
Average Percentage Method
Percent
102.5
102
101.5
101
100.5
100
99.5
99
98.5
98
97.5
May
Jun
Jul
Aug
Sep
Oct
Nov
Dec
Jan
Feb
Mar
□ All Years
+ Less Extremes

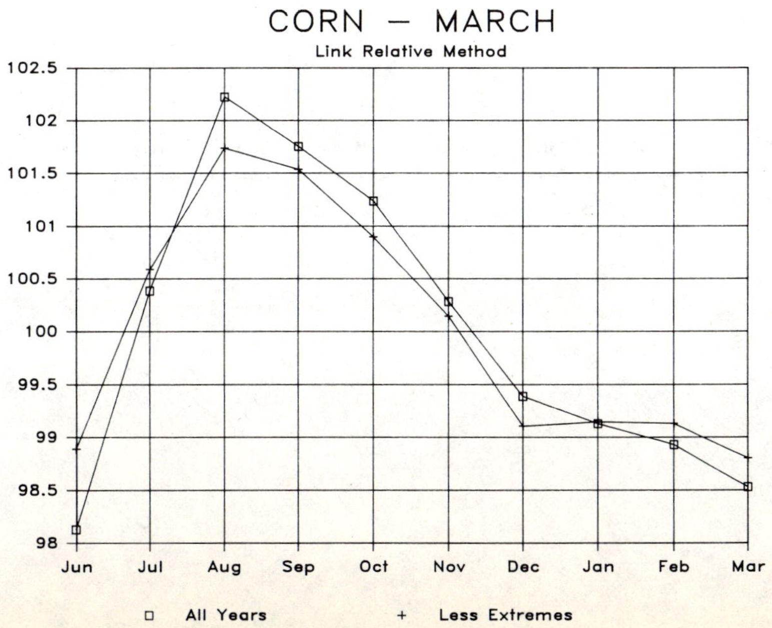
CORN — MARCH
Link Relative Method
102.5
102
101.5
101
100.5
100
99.5
99
98.5
98
Jun
Jul
Aug
Sep
Oct
Nov
Dec
Jan
Feb
Mar
□ All Years
+ Less Extremes

CORN - MAY - MONTHLY AVERAGE PRICE

Year of Expiration	Jul	Aug	Sep	Oct	Nov	Dec	Jan	Feb	Mar	Apr	May	Jul-May Average
1971	137.42	149.94	159.69	157.70	156.01	157.54	158.93	154.69	151.19	145.82	145.20	152.19
1972	145.88	129.65	123.75	123.36	122.54	126.14	124.79	123.30	123.85	124.33	123.02	126.42
1973	133.34	136.10	148.30	144.15	144.35	155.37	150.07	154.47	159.12	160.33	185.96	151.96
1974	220.90	279.57	253.11	254.29	259.44	272.21	290.22	318.19	300.96	266.35	264.05	270.84
1975	319.69	355.94	362.04	393.22	378.78	359.41	329.19	299.21	286.13	288.86	276.18	331.69
1976	272.39	319.64	311.42	301.88	280.20	272.69	273.42	274.49	271.58	267.14	281.42	284.21
1977	295.29	287.33	296.11	279.26	256.36	256.73	264.83	262.01	259.04	252.69	241.75	268.31
1978	233.29	211.01	214.46	222.41	233.04	227.61	228.37	230.04	243.91	256.60	255.43	232.38
1979	255.16	239.57	237.03	246.66	245.84	241.73	240.49	246.33	247.00	254.08	261.80	246.88
1980	321.45	296.77	297.83	303.50	297.36	298.86	287.20	285.15	269.75	267.98	271.38	290.66
1981	341.19	352.04	369.11	376.58	400.29	385.98	380.01	372.24	360.25	364.55	348.77	368.27
1982	377.94	344.35	324.52	320.86	306.68	282.21	282.80	279.95	270.77	278.24	270.75	303.55
1983	284.11	263.42	250.42	244.31	248.93	249.43	264.12	282.79	295.76	312.55	310.80	273.33
1984	317.04	367.85	368.62	348.14	348.60	337.35	333.02	328.28	346.73	354.01	349.77	345.40
1985	304.87	297.15	294.53	289.44	288.54	277.18	276.86	275.87	275.30	283.18	282.02	285.90

	Jul	Aug	Sep	Oct	Nov	Dec	Jan	Feb	Mar	Apr	May
AVERAGE MOVE											
All Years		4.69	-1.29	-0.34	-2.59	-4.44	-1.07	0.18	-1.71	1.02	-0.56
Less Extremes		3.48	-0.77	-1.22	-3.05	-4.22	-0.30	0.36	-2.07	2.55	-1.40
Ave Up - All Years		31.30	7.40	10.51	7.46	4.47	6.33	9.94	8.53	6.79	12.76
Ave Down - All Years		-18.59	-11.23	-7.58	-9.29	-12.23	-7.54	-6.33	-8.54	-10.51	-5.40
COUNT											
Number Up		7	8	6	6	7	7	6	6	10	4
Number Down		8	7	9	9	8	8	9	9	5	11
Pct Up		46.7%	53.3%	40.0%	40.0%	46.7%	46.7%	40.0%	40.0%	66.7%	26.7%
Pct Down		53.3%	46.7%	60.0%	60.0%	53.3%	53.3%	60.0%	60.0%	33.3%	73.3%
EXTREMES											
Greatest Up		58.67	17.07	31.18	23.72	12.77	18.00	27.98	18.45	16.79	25.63
Greatest Down		-33.60	-26.46	-20.48	-22.90	-24.47	-30.21	-29.98	-17.23	-34.62	-15.78
SEASONAL INDEX : AVERAGE PERCENTAGE METHOD											
All Years	100.7	101.8	101.5	101.2	100.2	99.2	98.9	99.2	98.7	99.0	99.5
Less Extremes	100.4	101.8	101.6	100.8	99.9	99.1	98.7	98.5	98.8	98.8	98.9
SEASONAL INDEX : LINK RELATIVE METHOD											
All Years		100.8	100.8	100.7	100.0	99.3	99.3	99.6	99.4	99.8	100.3
Less Extremes		100.7	100.8	100.5	99.9	99.1	99.3	99.7	99.4	100.4	100.1

CORN - MAY - MONTH OF HIGH AND LOW

Year of Expiration	Jul	Aug	Sep	Oct	Nov	Dec	Jan	Feb	Mar	Apr	May
1971	L		H								
1972	H				L						
1973	L										H
1974	L							H			
1975				H							L
1976		H								L	
1977			H								L
1978		L								H	
1979			L								H
1980	H									L	
1981	L				H						
1982	H										L
1983				L						H	
1984	L		H								
1985	H								L		

CORN — MAY

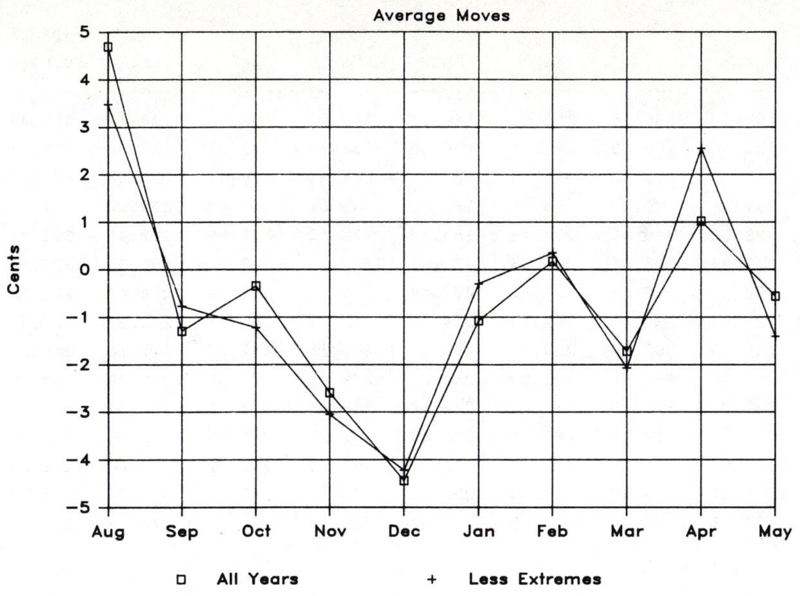

CORN — MAY

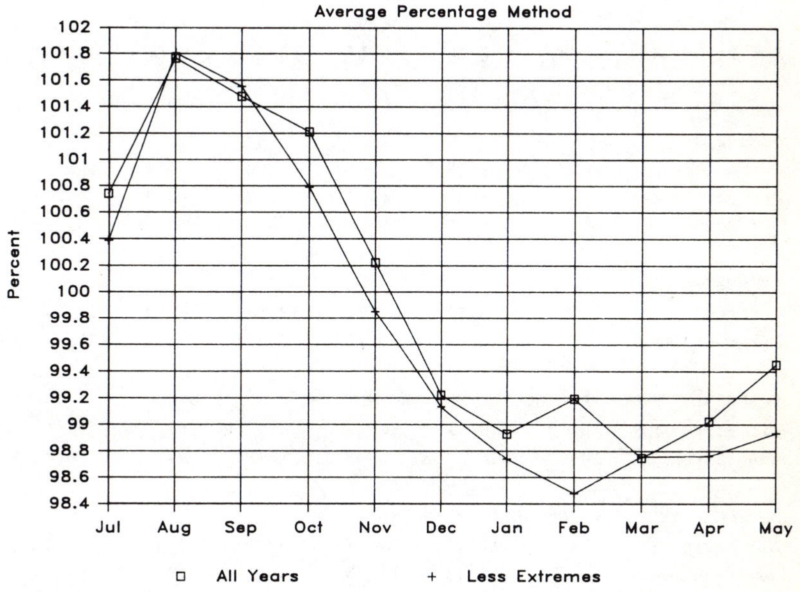

CORN — MAY

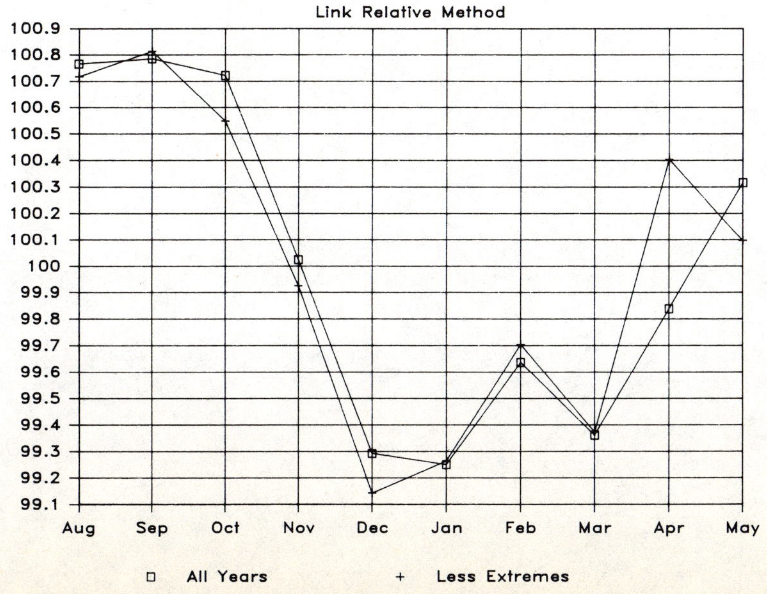

CORN - JULY - MONTHLY AVERAGE PRICE

Year of Expiration	Sep	Oct	Nov	Dec	Jan	Feb	Mar	Apr	May	Jun	Jul	Sep-Jul Average
1971	160.49	159.34	158.13	158.75	160.70	156.56	153.02	146.97	145.21	154.94	148.76	154.81
1972	125.82	125.38	124.90	128.25	127.06	125.89	127.26	128.38	126.74	121.91	123.96	125.96
1973	150.16	146.00	146.10	155.09	145.20	148.83	155.83	159.11	185.59	228.41	235.35	168.70
1974	253.54	255.76	260.71	273.72	292.26	320.60	303.52	267.92	263.44	283.28	319.22	281.27
1975	363.98	393.64	379.71	357.77	328.05	299.08	285.15	288.35	272.60	279.89	288.43	321.51
1976	310.94	302.48	281.88	275.55	277.24	278.26	275.48	271.37	283.55	297.99	301.80	286.96
1977	298.14	282.95	259.83	260.30	269.39	267.37	264.52	257.44	244.09	234.52	214.67	259.38
1978	218.01	225.82	234.54	228.31	229.74	229.87	245.63	254.39	256.07	256.61	235.92	237.72
1979	240.18	250.07	249.96	247.24	245.50	251.90	250.73	258.73	267.25	287.38	312.18	260.10
1980	301.95	309.19	303.68	306.26	296.14	295.48	282.05	280.30	279.91	278.95	306.70	294.60
1981	368.92	375.04	399.79	385.94	382.99	379.67	368.14	374.18	355.26	341.06	340.67	370.15
1982	332.52	328.84	314.33	287.85	288.33	289.21	280.01	288.66	279.21	272.75	266.20	293.45
1983	256.94	252.01	254.56	255.69	272.07	289.76	301.85	316.94	309.51	311.41	328.60	286.30
1984	367.79	345.44	345.10	336.33	333.07	328.80	343.63	351.85	348.97	349.20	350.16	345.48
1985	296.17	291.88	292.52	281.04	279.49	278.83	276.82	281.99	276.44	275.48	273.27	282.18

	Sep	Oct	Nov	Dec	Jan	Feb	Mar	Apr	May	Jun	Jul
AVERAGE MOVE											
All Years		-0.11	-2.54	-4.51	-0.73	0.86	-1.76	0.86	-2.18	5.33	4.81
Less Extremes		-0.69	-3.06	-4.17	0.02	1.04	-1.94	2.57	-3.10	3.95	4.37
Ave Up - All Years		10.49	6.95	4.31	7.08	8.30	10.21	6.75	12.22	12.99	14.22
Ave Down - All Years		-7.18	-8.87	-12.22	-7.56	-5.65	-7.75	-10.92	-7.42	-6.16	-9.31
COUNT											
Number Up		6	6	7	7	7	5	10	4	9	9
Number Down		9	9	8	8	8	10	5	11	6	6
Pct Up		40.0%	40.0%	46.7%	46.7%	46.7%	33.3%	66.7%	26.7%	60.0%	60.0%
Pct Down		60.0%	60.0%	53.3%	53.3%	53.3%	66.7%	33.3%	73.3%	40.0%	40.0%
EXTREMES											
Greatest Up		29.67	24.75	13.01	18.54	28.34	15.76	15.09	26.48	42.82	35.94
Greatest Down		-22.35	-23.13	-26.47	-29.73	-28.97	-17.07	-35.61	-18.92	-14.21	-20.69
SEASONAL INDEX : AVERAGE PERCENTAGE METHOD											
All Years	101.3	101.2	100.2	99.0	98.7	99.1	98.7	98.9	98.6	101.3	103.0
Less Extremes	101.2	100.7	99.8	98.8	99.3	98.8	98.7	98.7	98.8	99.8	101.7
SEASONAL INDEX : LINK RELATIVE METHOD											
All Years		101.7	100.7	99.5	99.1	99.4	98.9	99.0	98.6	100.9	102.2
Less Extremes		101.4	100.5	99.5	99.3	99.7	99.2	99.9	98.8	100.2	101.5

CORN - JULY - MONTH OF HIGH AND LOW

Year of Expiration	Sep	Oct	Nov	Dec	Jan	Feb	Mar	Apr	May	Jun	Jul
1971					H				L		
1972								H		L	
1973					L						H
1974	L					H					
1975		H							L		
1976	H							L			
1977	H										L
1978	L									H	
1979	L										H
1980		H								L	
1981			H								L
1982	H										L
1983		L									H
1984	H					L					
1985	H										L

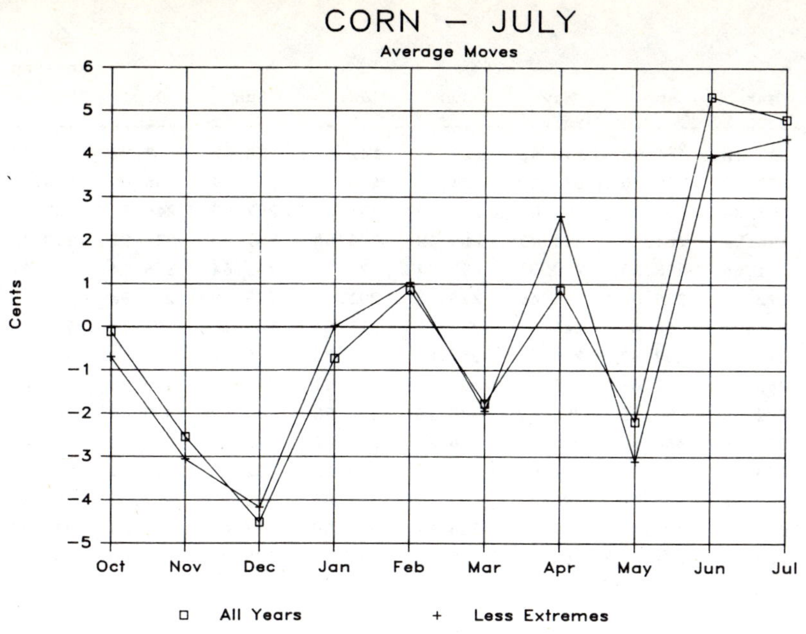
CORN – JULY
Average Moves
Cents
6
5
4
3
2
1
0
–1
–2
–3
–4
–5
Oct
Nov
Dec
Jan
Feb
Mar
Apr
May
Jun
Jul
All Years
Less Extremes

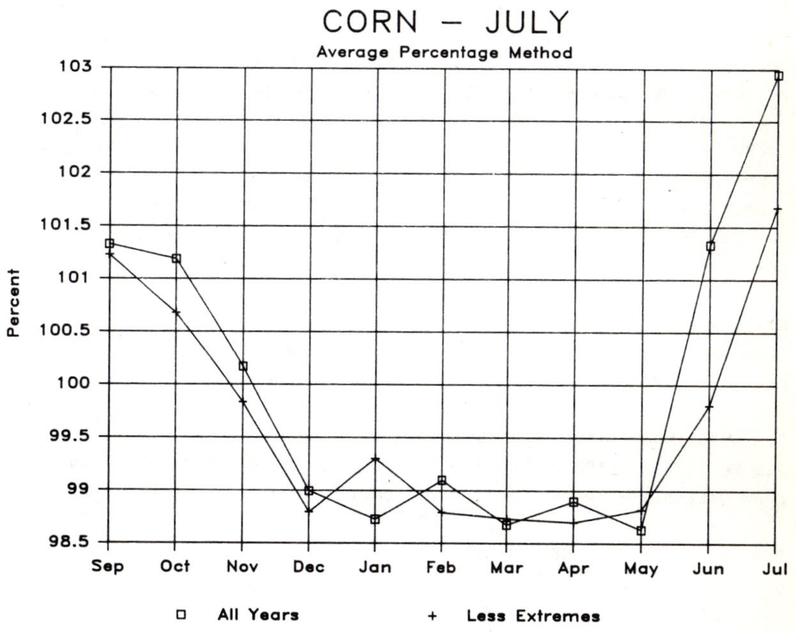
CORN – JULY
Average Percentage Method
Percent
103
102.5
102
101.5
101
100.5
100
99.5
99
98.5
Sep
Oct
Nov
Dec
Jan
Feb
Mar
Apr
May
Jun
Jul
All Years
Less Extremes

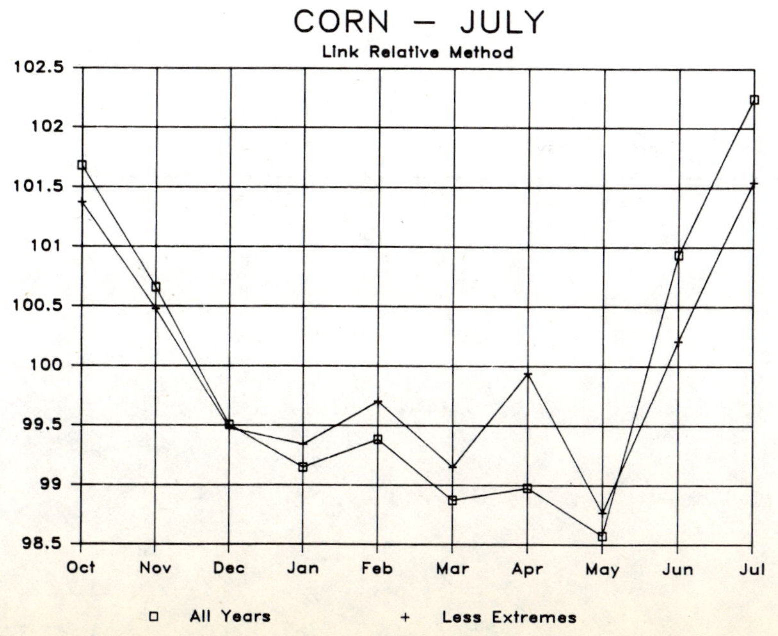
CORN – JULY
Link Relative Method
102.5
102
101.5
101
100.5
100
99.5
99
98.5
Oct
Nov
Dec
Jan
Feb
Mar
Apr
May
Jun
Jul
All Years
Less Extremes

CORN - SEPTEMBER - MONTHLY AVERAGE PRICE

Year of Expiration	Nov	Dec	Jan	Feb	Mar	Apr	May	Jun	Jul	Aug	Sep	Nov-Sep Average
1971	158.00	158.41	159.88	155.59	152.42	146.00	142.65	153.95	142.82	123.82	117.22	146.43
1972	125.60	129.22	127.82	126.53	128.89	130.00	128.42	124.13	126.19	128.04	136.80	128.33
1973	143.68	152.37	140.46	143.80	152.24	157.93	181.06	216.02	235.55	297.65	246.31	187.92
1974	255.96	267.38	285.13	313.92	296.92	261.18	254.49	269.69	326.08	357.63	339.92	293.48
1975	367.28	338.21	309.90	286.22	274.66	278.53	260.01	257.94	272.26	311.64	306.14	296.62
1976	274.62	272.08	274.21	276.30	272.38	268.50	274.46	290.33	291.64	278.59	291.98	278.65
1977	258.20	259.64	269.32	270.09	267.05	260.40	246.91	237.76	213.81	189.26	192.11	242.23
1978	232.51	224.87	228.73	227.42	245.26	252.39	254.91	257.83	236.83	219.37	212.81	235.72
1979	251.00	249.08	247.53	254.78	253.65	261.66	270.17	292.33	306.41	281.91	275.98	267.68
1980	307.20	310.54	302.73	303.85	292.30	290.25	289.88	286.25	316.75	342.49	353.45	308.70
1981	386.40	375.33	376.25	376.80	368.38	380.48	363.65	348.35	346.66	311.12	282.84	356.02
1982	319.58	290.05	290.54	293.63	283.78	292.38	281.09	271.48	259.12	232.78	223.21	276.15
1983	258.24	261.12	275.58	288.37	297.90	309.40	299.85	293.64	312.46	352.90	356.27	300.52
1984	314.99	309.57	306.85	301.96	314.58	322.46	322.88	324.87	307.50	297.46	306.04	311.74
1985	288.35	277.98	273.48	271.84	269.00	271.88	264.41	259.23	247.34	229.90	226.56	261.81

	Nov	Dec	Jan	Feb	Mar	Apr	May	Jun	Jul	Aug	Sep
AVERAGE MOVE											
All Years		-4.38	-0.50	1.51	-1.45	0.94	-3.24	3.26	3.84	0.88	-5.79
Less Extremes		-3.66	0.24	1.35	-1.73	2.90	-4.09	2.25	1.94	-1.03	-3.77
Ave Up - All Years		4.54	6.35	6.64	10.16	6.88	8.11	14.92	19.63	33.51	7.98
Ave Down - All Years		-12.19	-8.31	-6.18	-7.25	-10.95	-8.91	-6.93	-14.20	-20.88	-14.98
COUNT											
Number Up		7	8	9	5	10	5	7	8	6	6
Number Down		8	7	6	10	5	10	8	7	9	9
Pct Up		46.7%	53.3%	60.0%	33.3%	66.7%	33.3%	46.7%	53.3%	40.0%	40.0%
Pct Down		53.3%	46.7%	40.0%	66.7%	33.3%	66.7%	53.3%	46.7%	60.0%	60.0%
EXTREMES											
Greatest Up		11.42	17.74	28.79	17.84	12.10	23.13	34.96	56.39	62.10	13.39
Greatest Down		-29.53	-28.32	-23.67	-17.00	-35.74	-18.52	-15.30	-23.95	-35.54	-51.34
SEASONAL INDEX : AVERAGE PERCENTAGE METHOD											
All Years	100.8	99.5	99.2	99.6	99.3	99.6	98.7	100.4	101.5	102.0	99.5
Less Extremes	100.9	99.7	100.1	100.5	99.9	100.2	98.8	100.3	100.7	99.5	98.6
SEASONAL INDEX : LINK RELATIVE METHOD											
All Years		99.4	99.1	99.6	99.4	99.7	98.9	100.7	101.9	101.7	99.6
Less Extremes		99.3	99.4	99.9	99.7	100.9	99.5	100.6	101.4	100.3	99.0

CORN - SEPTEMBER - MONTH OF HIGH AND LOW

Year of Expiration	Nov	Dec	Jan	Feb	Mar	Apr	May	Jun	Jul	Aug	Sep
1971			H								L
1972								L			H
1973			L							H	
1974							L			H	
1975	H							L			
1976						L					H
1977				H						L	
1978								H			L
1979			L						H		
1980								L			H
1981	H										L
1982	H										L
1983	L										H
1984								H		L	
1985	H										L

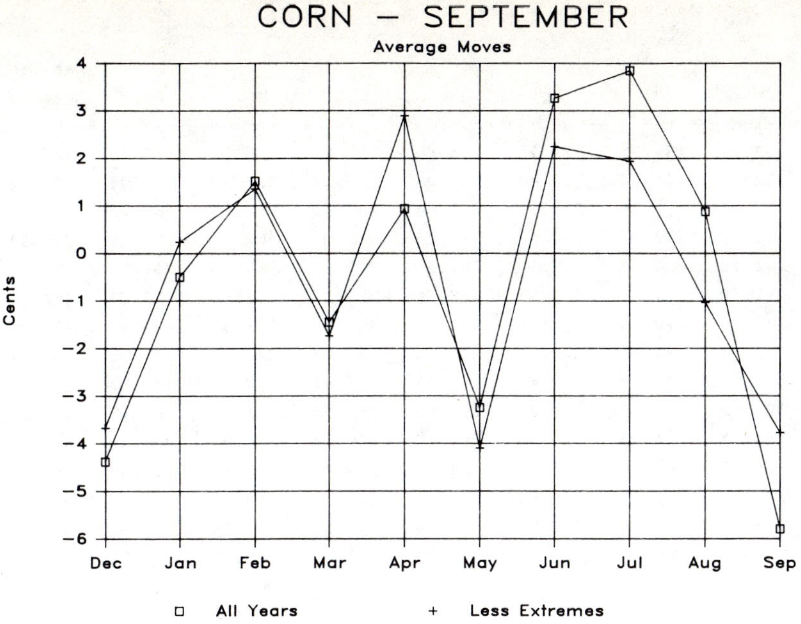
CORN — SEPTEMBER
Average Moves
Cents
4
3
2
1
0
-1
-2
-3
-4
-5
-6
Dec
Jan
Feb
Mar
Apr
May
Jun
Jul
Aug
Sep
□ All Years
+ Less Extremes

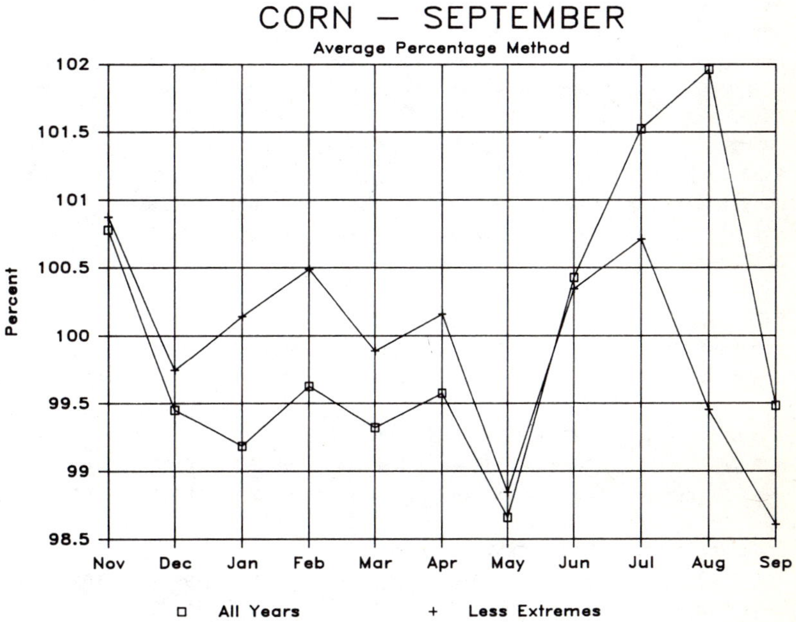
CORN — SEPTEMBER
Average Percentage Method
Percent
102
101.5
101
100.5
100
99.5
99
98.5
Nov
Dec
Jan
Feb
Mar
Apr
May
Jun
Jul
Aug
Sep
□ All Years
+ Less Extremes

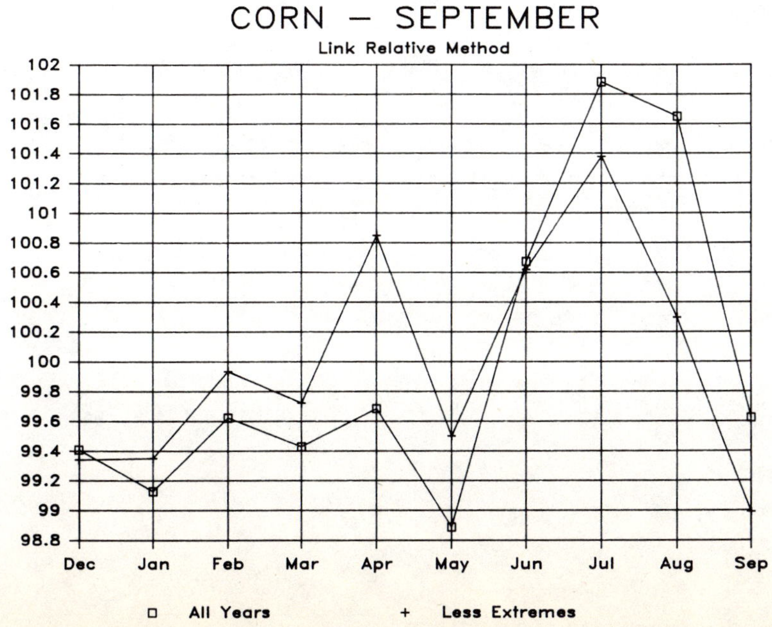
CORN — SEPTEMBER
Link Relative Method
102
101.8
101.6
101.4
101.2
101
100.8
100.6
100.4
100.2
100
99.8
99.6
99.4
99.2
99
98.8
Dec
Jan
Feb
Mar
Apr
May
Jun
Jul
Aug
Sep
□ All Years
+ Less Extremes

CORN - DECEMBER - MONTHLY AVERAGE PRICE

Year of Expiration	Feb	Mar	Apr	May	Jun	Jul	Aug	Sep	Oct	Nov	Dec	Feb-Dec Average
1971	153.26	150.06	143.01	138.77	153.08	139.35	121.90	115.88	115.51	115.12	117.81	133.07
1972	124.33	127.10	128.98	127.09	123.23	126.04	128.44	139.96	135.37	136.92	155.04	132.04
1973	138.42	146.82	155.55	175.72	203.08	221.96	283.64	247.84	245.84	252.55	263.21	212.24
1974	289.25	278.35	248.02	239.77	252.40	313.94	350.55	349.26	380.24	364.87	357.64	311.30
1975	271.71	259.81	263.16	245.54	242.58	260.81	307.92	301.49	290.49	268.96	261.50	270.36
1976	271.72	266.48	264.64	267.24	281.08	281.57	273.73	283.36	265.17	242.81	243.02	267.35
1977	273.47	270.33	263.86	249.66	241.40	220.19	198.23	201.13	208.51	221.67	217.39	233.26
1978	226.93	246.58	253.66	256.96	260.48	242.45	225.52	221.78	230.63	228.78	221.96	237.79
1979	258.96	258.94	265.76	271.99	297.54	310.14	281.33	278.12	277.94	268.35	270.17	276.29
1980	312.26	301.49	295.77	297.46	293.52	324.71	343.21	353.80	360.95	381.40	367.11	330.15
1981	376.55	368.81	383.23	368.24	354.65	356.23	316.86	295.20	290.71	276.99	255.32	331.16
1982	300.25	288.97	297.00	284.46	275.13	260.76	237.44	224.23	219.86	233.06	233.89	259.55
1983	288.32	296.09	302.79	291.62	278.63	302.70	355.64	358.04	347.54	349.29	331.43	318.37
1984	285.93	294.09	301.95	301.53	303.87	288.99	283.65	285.84	278.38	273.16	257.96	286.85
1985	266.34	263.12	266.44	260.10	254.43	240.50	223.05	219.93	223.44	238.19	246.05	245.60

	Feb	Mar	Apr	May	Jun	Jul	Aug	Sep	Oct	Nov	Dec
AVERAGE MOVE											
All Years		-1.38	1.12	-3.85	2.60	5.02	2.72	-3.68	-0.35	-1.23	-3.51
Less Extremes		-2.19	2.52	-4.63	1.94	2.69	1.42	-2.38	-1.39	-1.27	-3.77
Ave Up - All Years		9.35	6.82	6.79	14.22	19.04	36.54	6.54	11.57	10.23	6.03
Ave Down - All Years		-6.74	-10.28	-9.17	-7.58	-16.02	-19.83	-10.50	-6.32	-11.25	-11.85
COUNT											
Number Up		5	10	5	7	9	6	6	5	7	7
Number Down		10	5	10	8	6	9	9	10	8	8
Pct Up		33.3%	66.7%	33.3%	46.7%	60.0%	40.0%	40.0%	33.3%	46.7%	46.7%
Pct Down		66.7%	33.3%	66.7%	53.3%	40.0%	60.0%	60.0%	66.7%	53.3%	53.3%
EXTREMES											
Greatest Up		19.65	14.42	20.17	27.36	61.54	61.68	11.52	30.98	20.46	18.12
Greatest Down		-11.90	-30.32	-17.62	-13.59	-21.21	-39.37	-35.80	-18.19	-22.35	-21.67
SEASONAL INDEX : AVERAGE PERCENTAGE METHOD											
All Years	99.9	99.6	99.9	98.5	100.0	101.1	101.7	100.3	100.0	99.7	99.3
Less Extremes	101.2	100.6	100.8	99.2	100.3	100.7	100.5	100.1	99.5	99.5	99.1
SEASONAL INDEX : LINK RELATIVE METHOD											
All Years		99.0	99.3	98.1	99.7	101.4	102.0	100.7	100.3	100.0	99.4
Less Extremes		99.5	100.5	98.9	100.1	101.2	101.1	100.1	99.8	99.9	99.0

CORN - DECEMBER - MONTH OF HIGH AND LOW

Year of Expiration	Feb	Mar	Apr	May	Jun	Jul	Aug	Sep	Oct	Nov	Dec
1971	H									L	
1972					L						H
1973	L										H
1974				L					H		
1975					L		H				
1976								H		L	
1977	H						L				
1978					H			L			
1979		L				H					
1980					L					H	
1981			H								L
1982	H								L		
1983					L			H			
1984					H						L
1985			H					L			

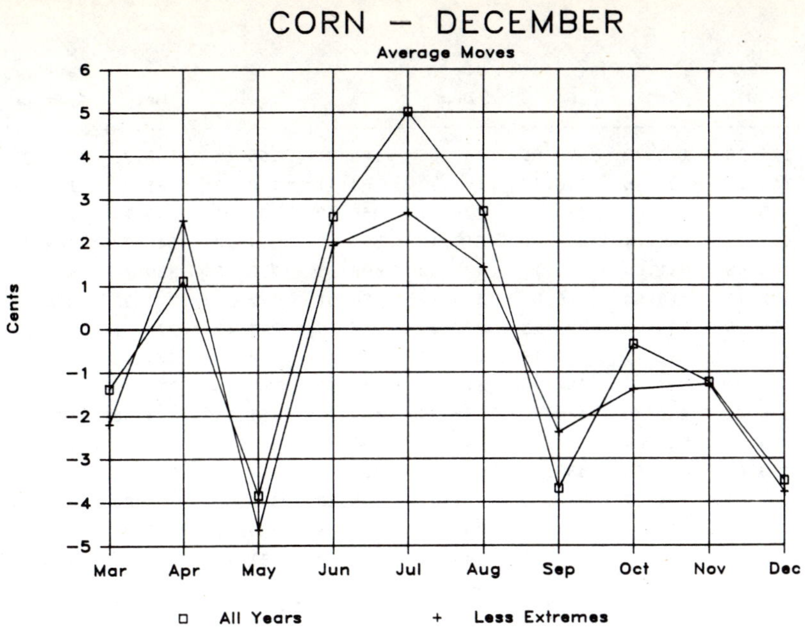
CORN — DECEMBER
Average Moves
Cents
6
5
4
3
2
1
0
−1
−2
−3
−4
−5
Mar
Apr
May
Jun
Jul
Aug
Sep
Oct
Nov
Dec
□ All Years
+ Less Extremes

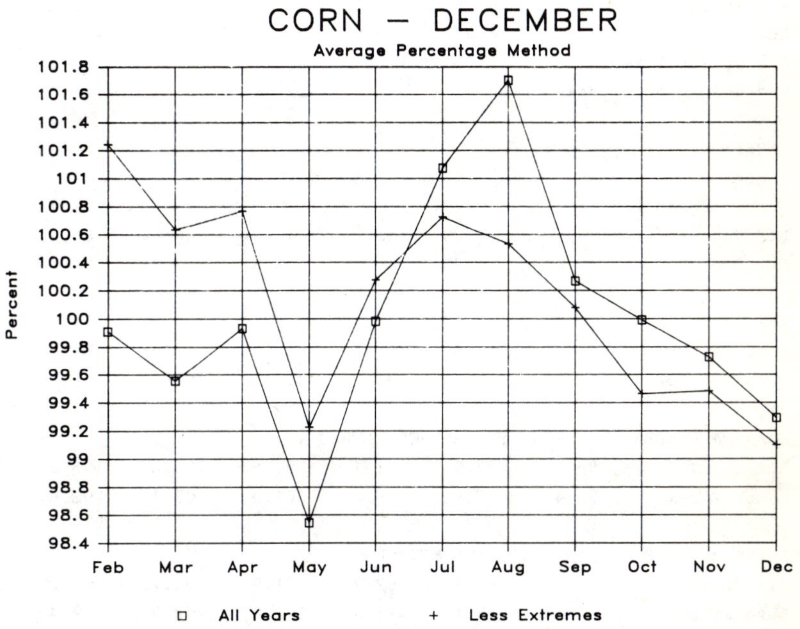
CORN — DECEMBER
Average Percentage Method
Percent
101.8
101.6
101.4
101.2
101
100.8
100.6
100.4
100.2
100
99.8
99.6
99.4
99.2
99
98.8
98.6
98.4
Feb
Mar
Apr
May
Jun
Jul
Aug
Sep
Oct
Nov
Dec
□ All Years
+ Less Extremes

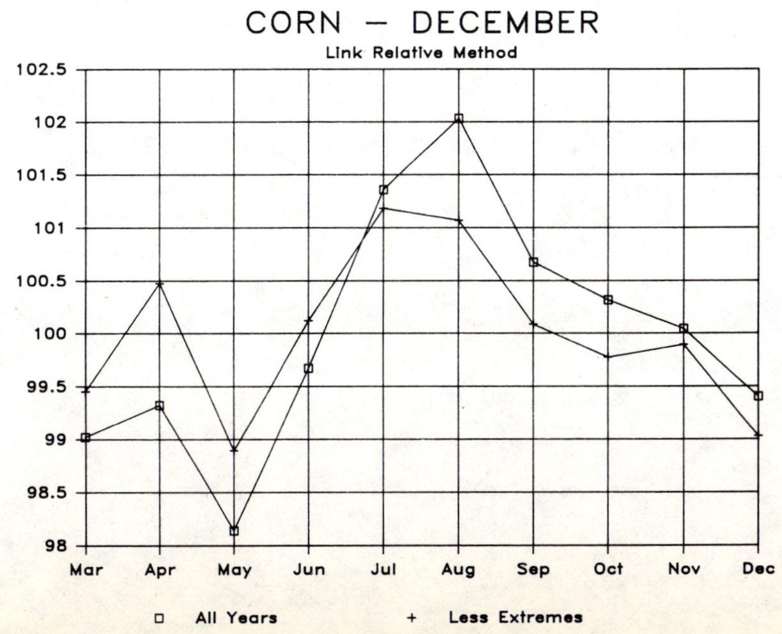
CORN — DECEMBER
Link Relative Method
102.5
102
101.5
101
100.5
100
99.5
99
98.5
98
Mar
Apr
May
Jun
Jul
Aug
Sep
Oct
Nov
Dec
□ All Years
+ Less Extremes

WHEAT - MARCH - MONTHLY AVERAGE PRICE

Year of Expiration	May	Jun	Jul	Aug	Sep	Oct	Nov	Dec	Jan	Feb	Mar	May-Mar Average
1971	145.70	147.50	151.87	160.13	171.18	173.73	174.89	169.05	168.71	168.64	165.70	163.37
1972	158.26	167.10	158.08	150.12	148.54	152.86	156.44	161.50	164.47	160.63	161.34	158.12
1973	152.81	150.32	160.87	189.03	213.74	218.68	230.93	259.41	258.40	238.91	235.73	209.89
1974	253.32	272.29	289.23	440.92	494.21	444.74	442.32	519.40	569.59	597.28	548.73	442.91
1975	370.61	420.95	455.75	461.91	464.48	531.00	511.11	475.88	408.58	388.05	359.98	440.75
1976	335.80	330.98	374.22	435.61	442.10	418.64	368.00	343.64	350.91	372.91	370.36	376.65
1977	378.54	399.98	391.60	349.17	328.18	299.93	273.13	272.00	277.70	279.42	273.34	320.27
1978	274.98	268.06	254.25	240.52	254.91	262.21	280.66	271.43	273.85	264.45	276.40	265.61
1979	327.82	328.22	323.74	316.67	332.06	344.56	354.20	348.14	347.97	362.78	379.38	342.32
1980	383.31	454.49	457.37	449.26	456.71	459.86	448.74	448.90	444.70	451.24	428.68	443.93
1981	462.56	453.54	476.36	489.67	515.31	541.44	544.71	495.11	490.75	460.92	428.17	487.14
1982	484.66	461.30	460.30	454.69	450.02	458.68	453.26	404.77	386.95	364.50	352.44	430.14
1983	413.48	394.19	387.29	382.28	361.51	331.07	348.79	336.02	335.55	338.90	322.80	359.26
1984	390.76	380.56	382.68	414.82	403.69	379.41	361.20	357.39	348.58	329.79	350.92	372.71
1985	377.74	383.62	373.20	372.65	358.16	359.55	360.45	345.98	347.99	351.18	352.09	362.06

	May	Jun	Jul	Aug	Sep	Oct	Nov	Dec	Jan	Feb	Mar
AVERAGE MOVE											
All Years		6.85	5.58	14.04	5.82	-1.23	-4.50	-6.68	-2.26	-3.01	-8.24
Less Extremes		4.22	4.18	7.80	4.23	-2.73	-2.72	-9.82	-1.29	-3.30	-7.39
Ave Up - All Years		22.35	17.22	43.01	17.89	13.75	8.37	27.69	11.76	11.33	10.26
Ave Down - All Years		-10.87	-7.72	-11.31	-12.27	-31.18	-19.21	-19.18	-11.61	-15.55	-17.48
COUNT											
Number Up		8	8	7	9	10	8	4	6	7	5
Number Down		7	7	8	6	5	7	11	9	8	10
Pct Up		53.3%	53.3%	46.7%	60.0%	66.7%	53.3%	26.7%	40.0%	46.7%	33.3%
Pct Down		46.7%	46.7%	53.3%	40.0%	33.3%	46.7%	73.3%	60.0%	53.3%	66.7%
EXTREMES											
Greatest Up		71.18	43.24	151.69	53.29	66.52	18.44	77.07	50.20	27.69	21.13
Greatest Down		-23.37	-13.81	-42.43	-20.99	-49.47	-50.64	-49.60	-67.30	-29.83	-48.55
SEASONAL INDEX : AVERAGE PERCENTAGE METHOD											
All Years	95.2	97.0	98.1	101.5	103.4	103.1	102.4	101.1	100.7	99.6	97.8
Less Extremes	96.4	97.6	98.8	101.3	103.1	102.6	102.7	100.6	99.6	98.0	97.1
SEASONAL INDEX : LINK RELATIVE METHOD											
All Years		95.8	97.2	101.8	103.7	103.2	102.3	100.7	100.0	98.6	96.7
Less Extremes		97.1	98.4	101.0	102.9	102.4	102.1	100.2	100.0	98.9	97.1

WHEAT - MARCH - MONTH OF HIGH AND LOW

Year of Expiration	May	Jun	Jul	Aug	Sep	Oct	Nov	Dec	Jan	Feb	Mar
1971	L						H				
1972		H			L						
1973		L						H			
1974	L									H	
1975						H					L
1976		L			H						
1977		H						L			
1978				L			H				
1979				L							H
1980	L					H					
1981							H				L
1982	H										L
1983	H										L
1984				H						L	
1985		H						L			

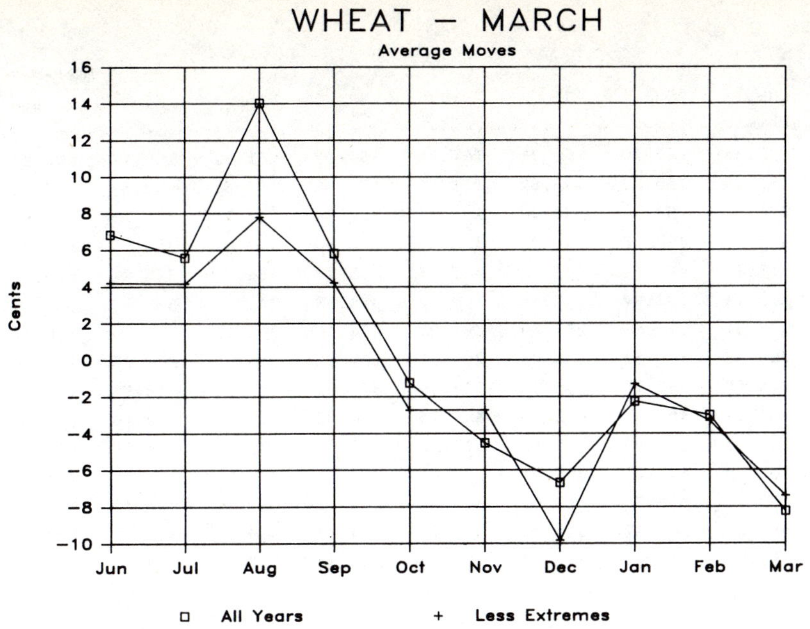
WHEAT — MARCH
Average Moves
Cents
16
14
12
10
8
6
4
2
0
−2
−4
−6
−8
−10
Jun
Jul
Aug
Sep
Oct
Nov
Dec
Jan
Feb
Mar
All Years
+ Less Extremes

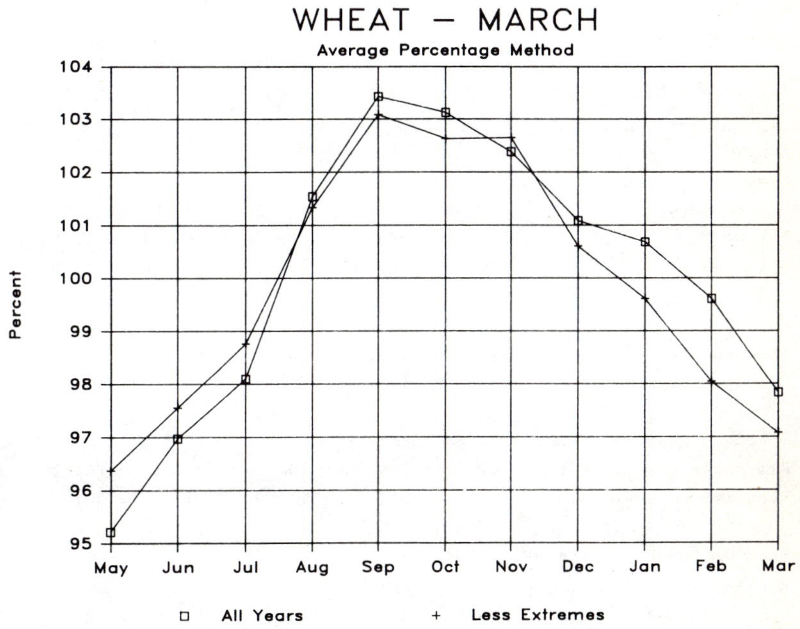
WHEAT — MARCH
Average Percentage Method
Percent
104
103
102
101
100
99
98
97
96
95
May
Jun
Jul
Aug
Sep
Oct
Nov
Dec
Jan
Feb
Mar
All Years
+ Less Extremes

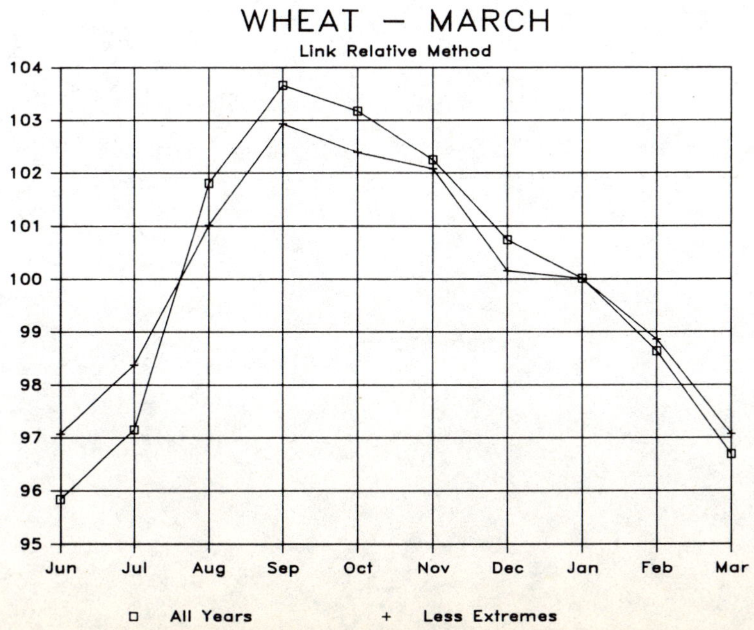
WHEAT — MARCH
Link Relative Method
104
103
102
101
100
99
98
97
96
95
Jun
Jul
Aug
Sep
Oct
Nov
Dec
Jan
Feb
Mar
All Years
+ Less Extremes

WHEAT - MAY - MONTHLY AVERAGE PRICE

Year of Expiration	Jul	Aug	Sep	Oct	Nov	Dec	Jan	Feb	Mar	Apr	May	Mar-May Average
1971	150.81	158.35	168.47	171.26	173.44	167.70	166.79	164.50	160.89	161.12	160.18	163.95
1972	156.47	148.91	147.02	150.13	151.69	155.23	155.82	152.16	156.52	159.81	162.57	154.21
1973	159.91	187.83	212.13	215.88	226.26	254.34	250.48	231.39	227.64	236.25	246.53	222.60
1974	282.10	419.51	477.34	426.13	413.33	498.38	546.05	575.65	510.38	417.64	353.27	447.25
1975	450.83	457.73	461.29	529.47	513.40	475.45	404.63	384.86	363.73	356.36	318.07	428.71
1976	375.60	438.04	443.87	422.13	373.24	348.94	357.46	380.32	370.80	344.50	339.33	381.29
1977	290.92	350.79	334.38	306.30	277.13	276.86	283.89	287.24	278.80	265.31	248.50	290.92
1978	258.95	245.38	260.33	268.43	285.58	275.61	280.05	269.21	287.82	316.85	308.28	277.86
1979	320.83	313.65	328.06	339.92	344.60	338.73	331.92	343.26	346.07	340.33	365.58	337.54
1980	451.57	447.51	460.22	467.69	454.17	455.07	453.26	463.28	430.05	396.81	410.46	444.55
1981	480.23	493.69	521.46	547.62	551.99	502.89	499.61	471.07	433.55	437.77	411.08	486.45
1982	473.82	467.21	457.10	468.08	462.80	412.28	397.51	378.40	363.16	370.51	349.65	418.23
1983	393.75	389.13	369.77	339.66	353.76	343.37	343.81	349.47	342.12	351.56	350.41	356.98
1984	383.35	415.76	409.49	381.10	362.35	355.37	347.48	331.70	354.17	366.54	365.57	370.26
1985	376.00	372.70	356.25	356.66	354.52	340.44	341.47	342.12	345.86	357.27	340.13	353.04

	Jul	Aug	Sep	Oct	Nov	Dec	Jan	Feb	Mar	Apr	May
AVERAGE MOVE											
All Years		20.07	6.74	-1.12	-6.15	-6.51	-2.70	-2.37	-10.20	-6.19	-9.94
Less Extremes		13.63	4.81	-2.59	-4.65	-10.16	-1.33	-2.82	-8.48	-2.25	-8.45
Ave Up - All Years		43.49	19.06	14.28	7.78	29.39	9.96	11.93	10.40	9.55	12.99
Ave Down - All Years		-6.70	-11.75	-31.91	-18.33	-19.56	-13.77	-14.88	-20.50	-29.81	-18.27
COUNT											
Number Up		8	9	10	7	4	7	7	5	9	4
Number Down		7	6	5	8	11	8	8	10	6	11
Pct Up		53.3%	60.0%	66.7%	46.7%	26.7%	46.7%	46.7%	33.3%	60.0%	26.7%
Pct Down		46.7%	40.0%	33.3%	53.3%	73.3%	53.3%	53.3%	66.7%	40.0%	73.3%
EXTREMES											
Greatest Up		137.41	57.84	68.18	17.15	85.05	47.66	29.61	22.47	29.03	25.26
Greatest Down		-13.57	-19.35	-51.22	-48.89	-50.52	-70.83	-28.54	-65.27	-92.74	-64.38
SEASONAL INDEX : AVERAGE PERCENTAGE METHOD											
All Years	96.9	102.4	104.3	104.0	102.6	101.2	100.6	99.6	97.5	96.5	94.3
Less Extremes	98.3	102.3	104.2	103.2	102.1	101.0	99.5	98.2	97.2	96.2	94.6
SEASONAL INDEX : LINK RELATIVE METHOD											
All Years		98.6	101.5	101.9	101.3	100.8	100.8	100.4	99.1	98.8	96.9
Less Extremes		99.1	101.8	101.8	101.5	100.2	100.5	100.0	98.8	99.0	97.3

WHEAT - MAY - MONTH OF HIGH AND LOW

Year of Expiration	Jul	Aug	Sep	Oct	Nov	Dec	Jan	Feb	Mar	Apr	May
1971	L				H						
1972			L								H
1973	L					H					
1974	L							H			
1975				H							L
1976			H								L
1977		H									L
1978		L								H	
1979		L									H
1980				H						L	
1981					H						L
1982	H										L
1983	H								L		
1984		H						L			
1985	H										L

WHEAT — MAY
Average Moves

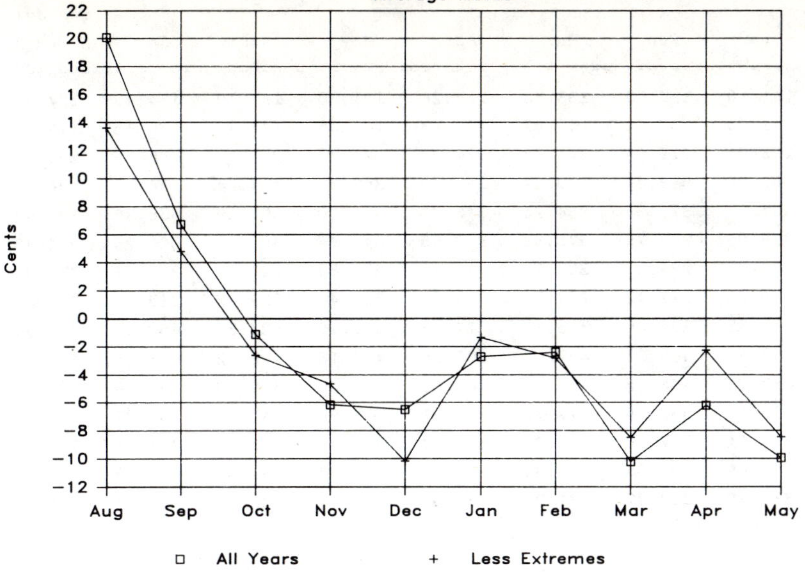

WHEAT — MAY
Average Percentage Method

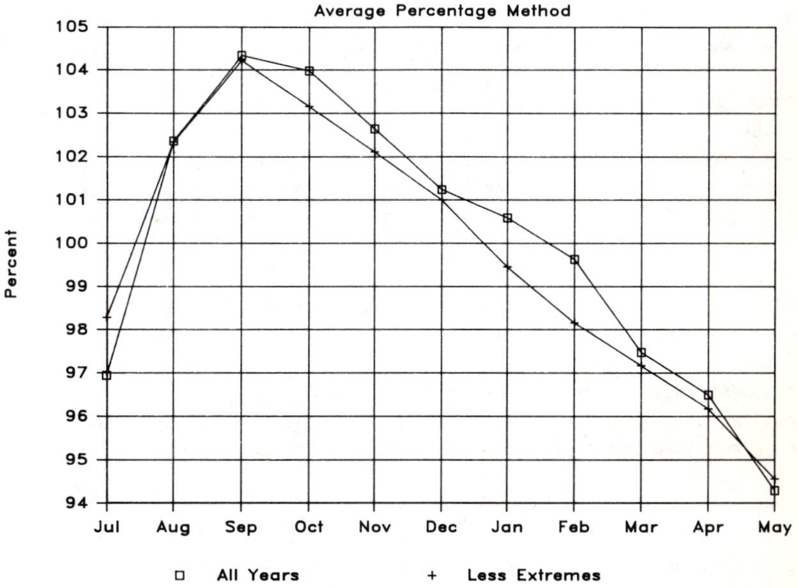

WHEAT — MAY
Link Relative Method

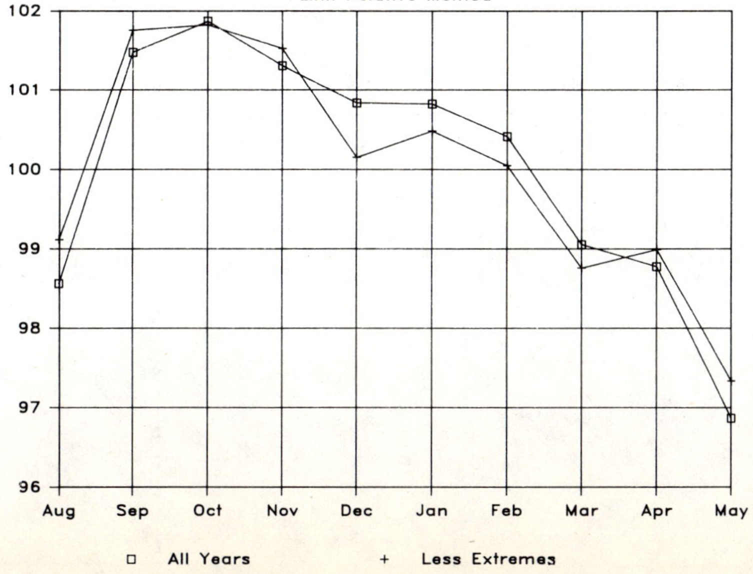

WHEAT - JULY - MONTHLY AVERAGE PRICE

Year of Expiration	Sep	Oct	Nov	Dec	Jan	Feb	Mar	Apr	May	Jun	Jul	Sep-Jul Average
1971	158.07	160.09	162.87	159.14	161.10	157.22	153.55	154.26	151.30	160.19	154.49	157.48
1972	138.97	139.71	139.49	145.05	145.06	142.04	147.82	148.43	145.08	142.82	150.65	144.10
1973	187.97	189.35	204.86	236.84	236.91	219.18	214.78	224.29	254.70	277.27	285.58	230.16
1974	412.22	381.57	364.43	442.70	482.66	519.38	470.81	399.79	351.53	403.64	436.30	424.09
1975	438.58	489.23	477.54	439.07	387.65	372.61	354.25	345.93	314.50	306.30	335.98	387.42
1976	425.62	416.49	370.97	351.29	359.96	383.75	376.53	352.55	348.44	367.40	366.23	374.48
1977	338.75	310.88	279.19	280.25	289.01	294.34	286.15	273.39	251.86	241.57	233.04	279.86
1978	264.48	273.48	288.37	279.41	285.23	272.42	289.25	319.73	316.48	319.17	315.52	293.05
1979	316.79	325.93	327.79	323.83	318.35	322.00	325.15	327.93	362.10	427.37	450.13	347.94
1980	441.75	463.53	449.02	456.21	459.16	469.31	437.80	405.10	417.16	408.82	431.13	439.91
1981	516.92	533.55	534.18	490.44	487.76	466.63	437.24	443.61	419.44	396.19	389.70	465.06
1982	455.63	464.17	458.24	412.26	402.15	388.75	372.12	381.51	361.90	343.24	338.02	398.00
1983	372.06	343.44	355.16	347.45	350.51	357.16	352.01	362.74	355.95	346.89	341.15	353.14
1984	401.17	366.85	348.11	342.08	339.64	327.98	342.91	350.70	352.34	353.04	342.55	351.58
1985	341.46	342.26	342.57	333.39	332.49	333.37	331.33	333.82	319.64	323.43	308.43	331.11

	Sep	Oct	Nov	Dec	Jan	Feb	Mar	Apr	May	Jun	Jul
AVERAGE MOVE											
All Years		-0.66	-6.52	-4.23	-0.12	-0.77	-8.96	-4.53	-6.76	6.33	4.11
Less Extremes		-2.02	-5.21	-7.36	0.75	-2.09	-7.90	-2.11	-6.71	4.07	3.38
Ave Up - All Years		12.07	6.81	24.81	7.92	12.45	10.17	8.09	19.57	21.87	20.59
Ave Down - All Years		-26.12	-18.18	-18.74	-12.17	-12.33	-15.92	-29.76	-16.33	-11.44	-6.88
COUNT											
Number Up		10	7	5	9	7	4	10	4	8	6
Number Down		5	8	10	6	8	11	5	11	7	9
Pct Up		66.7%	46.7%	33.3%	60.0%	46.7%	26.7%	66.7%	26.7%	53.3%	40.0%
Pct Down		33.3%	53.3%	66.7%	40.0%	53.3%	73.3%	33.3%	73.3%	46.7%	60.0%
EXTREMES											
Greatest Up		50.65	15.51	78.27	39.96	36.72	16.83	30.48	34.18	65.27	32.66
Greatest Down		-34.32	-45.51	-45.98	-51.42	-21.13	-48.57	-71.02	-48.25	-23.25	-14.99
SEASONAL INDEX : AVERAGE PERCENTAGE METHOD											
All Years	103.6	103.2	101.7	100.9	101.0	100.3	98.3	97.6	96.0	98.2	99.2
Less Extremes	103.9	103.0	101.2	100.6	100.7	99.2	97.9	97.3	96.0	97.7	98.1
SEASONAL INDEX : LINK RELATIVE METHOD											
All Years		101.6	100.6	100.7	101.1	100.6	99.1	98.7	97.3	99.6	100.9
Less Extremes		101.7	100.9	100.2	101.0	100.6	99.1	99.1	97.5	99.3	100.6

WHEAT - JULY - MONTH OF HIGH AND LOW

Year of Expiration	Sep	Oct	Nov	Dec	Jan	Feb	Mar	Apr	May	Jun	Jul
1971			H						L		
1972	L										H
1973	L										H
1974						H			L		
1975		H								L	
1976	H								L		
1977	H										L
1978	L							H			
1979	L										H
1980						H		L			
1981			H								L
1982		H									L
1983	H										L
1984	H					L					
1985			H								L

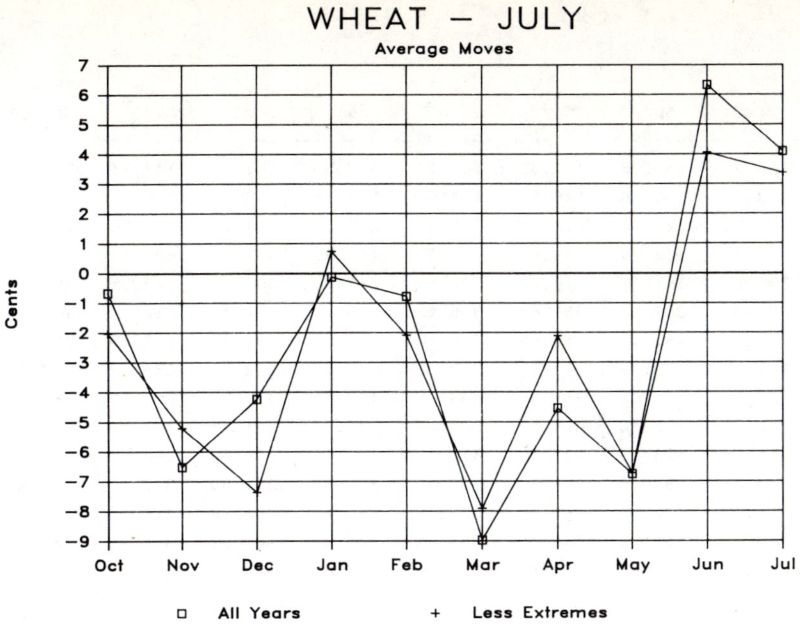
WHEAT — JULY
Average Moves
Cents
7
6
5
4
3
2
1
0
-1
-2
-3
-4
-5
-6
-7
-8
-9
Oct
Nov
Dec
Jan
Feb
Mar
Apr
May
Jun
Jul
□ All Years
+ Less Extremes

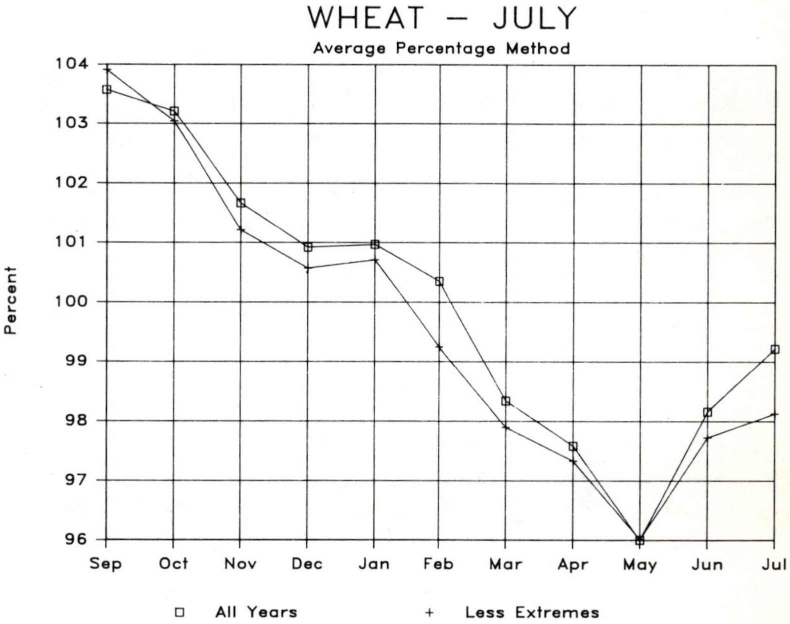
WHEAT — JULY
Average Percentage Method
Percent
104
103
102
101
100
99
98
97
96
Sep
Oct
Nov
Dec
Jan
Feb
Mar
Apr
May
Jun
Jul
□ All Years
+ Less Extremes

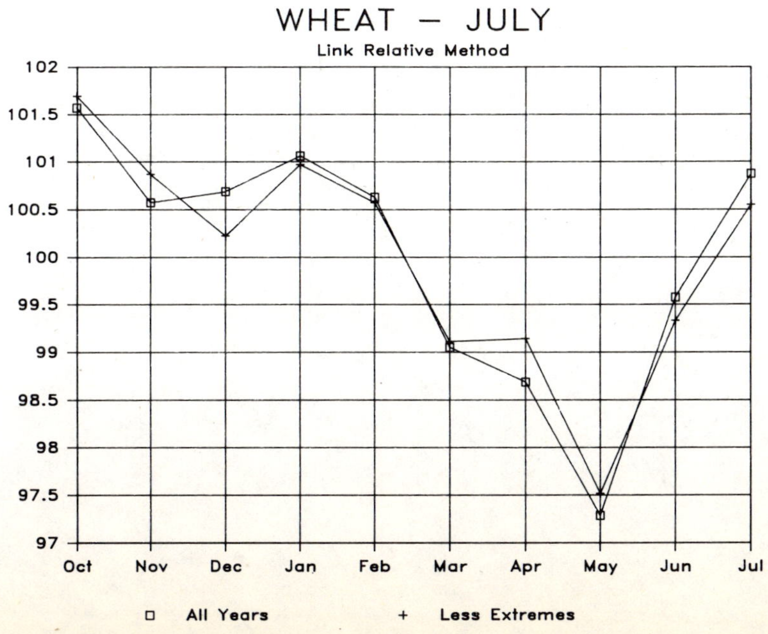
WHEAT — JULY
Link Relative Method
102
101.5
101
100.5
100
99.5
99
98.5
98
97.5
97
Oct
Nov
Dec
Jan
Feb
Mar
Apr
May
Jun
Jul
□ All Years
+ Less Extremes

WHEAT - SEPTEMBER - MONTHLY AVERAGE PRICE

Year of Expiration	Nov	Dec	Jan	Feb	Mar	Apr	May	Jun	Jul	Aug	Sep	Nov-Sep Average
1971	164.96	161.12	163.34	159.33	155.43	155.98	152.47	161.22	152.55	144.56	147.23	156.20
1972	141.07	146.39	147.06	144.07	150.08	150.16	146.58	144.07	153.65	178.78	201.95	154.90
1973	207.34	238.15	235.79	216.26	213.73	223.09	253.92	276.63	299.00	467.91	504.56	285.13
1974	363.21	441.71	479.39	513.58	469.48	402.39	356.41	406.38	447.25	437.17	427.79	431.34
1975	483.66	445.05	394.52	378.36	360.06	351.84	319.49	312.01	351.96	406.87	415.91	383.61
1976	377.00	357.18	366.20	389.95	382.36	359.92	356.64	376.13	365.36	322.46	312.96	360.56
1977	284.33	286.19	295.38	301.53	293.32	281.16	258.96	249.13	235.11	221.35	232.50	267.18
1978	293.42	284.52	290.91	276.63	294.18	323.30	319.86	322.00	317.63	322.32	335.87	307.33
1979	329.76	327.95	322.48	324.55	328.33	331.00	364.68	433.16	443.56	430.03	431.56	369.73
1980	459.87	468.47	471.38	481.01	450.49	419.16	430.55	420.87	445.83	451.45	471.45	451.87
1981	542.01	501.07	500.42	480.57	451.58	458.80	436.39	414.52	406.66	398.50	398.96	453.59
1982	469.39	423.23	413.54	403.99	385.47	394.89	376.84	358.32	349.67	341.89	327.23	385.86
1983	362.51	356.45	360.33	366.83	361.52	372.78	365.49	357.56	357.15	384.54	375.93	365.55
1984	354.81	348.68	346.58	332.78	345.72	351.43	353.59	358.83	347.57	347.16	344.25	348.31
1985	346.75	336.58	333.47	333.46	331.20	333.36	320.88	325.33	307.81	284.61	279.33	321.16

	Nov	Dec	Jan	Feb	Mar	Apr	May	Jun	Jul	Aug	Sep
AVERAGE MOVE											
All Years		-3.82	-0.13	-1.19	-8.66	-4.25	-6.43	6.89	4.31	10.59	4.52
Less Extremes		-6.90	0.84	-2.48	-7.95	-1.98	-6.48	4.37	3.17	2.53	3.53
Ave Up - All Years		25.02	8.99	13.72	10.07	7.75	19.52	22.65	24.69	47.78	13.13
Ave Down - All Years		-18.25	-10.56	-11.13	-15.48	-28.25	-15.87	-11.12	-9.28	-14.20	-8.39
COUNT											
Number Up		5	8	6	4	10	4	8	6	6	9
Number Down		10	7	9	11	5	11	7	9	9	6
Pct Up		33.3%	53.3%	40.0%	26.7%	66.7%	26.7%	53.3%	40.0%	40.0%	60.0%
Pct Down		66.7%	46.7%	60.0%	73.3%	33.3%	73.3%	46.7%	60.0%	60.0%	40.0%
EXTREMES											
Greatest Up		78.50	37.68	34.20	17.55	29.12	33.68	68.47	40.88	168.91	36.65
Greatest Down		-46.16	-50.52	-19.85	-44.11	-67.08	-45.98	-21.86	-17.52	-42.90	-14.65
SEASONAL INDEX : AVERAGE PERCENTAGE METHOD											
All Years	101.8	100.9	100.9	100.3	98.3	97.5	95.8	97.9	98.8	102.9	105.0
Less Extremes	102.2	101.1	101.5	100.7	99.2	98.4	96.1	97.6	98.0	99.7	101.0
SEASONAL INDEX : LINK RELATIVE METHOD											
All Years		102.3	102.1	100.9	98.8	97.9	96.0	97.9	98.6	102.1	103.4
Less Extremes		101.6	102.0	101.1	99.3	99.0	97.0	98.6	99.4	100.4	101.6

WHEAT - SEPTEMBER - MONTH OF HIGH AND LOW

Year of Expiration	Nov	Dec	Jan	Feb	Mar	Apr	May	Jun	Jul	Aug	Sep
1971	H									L	
1972	L										H
1973	L										H
1974				H			L				
1975	H							L			
1976				H							L
1977				H						L	
1978				L							H
1979			L						H		
1980				H		L					
1981	H									L	
1982	H										L
1983		L								H	
1984				L				H			
1985	H										L

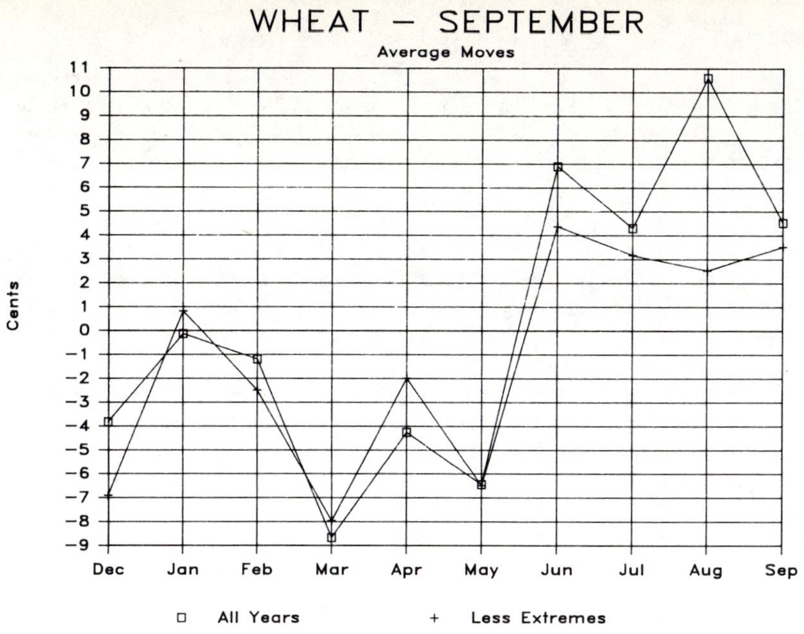
WHEAT – SEPTEMBER
Average Moves
Cents
11
10
9
8
7
6
5
4
3
2
1
0
-1
-2
-3
-4
-5
-6
-7
-8
-9
Dec
Jan
Feb
Mar
Apr
May
Jun
Jul
Aug
Sep
All Years
Less Extremes

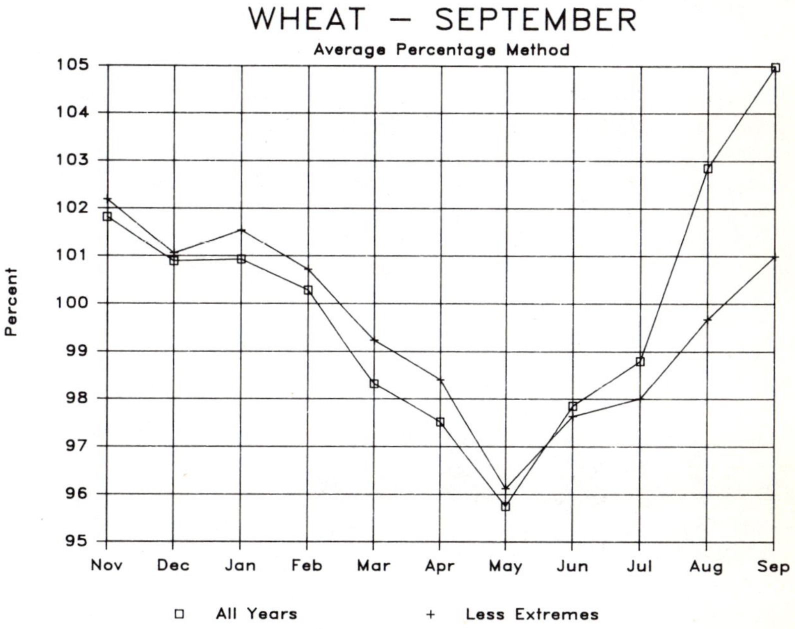
WHEAT – SEPTEMBER
Average Percentage Method
Percent
105
104
103
102
101
100
99
98
97
96
95
Nov
Dec
Jan
Feb
Mar
Apr
May
Jun
Jul
Aug
Sep
All Years
Less Extremes

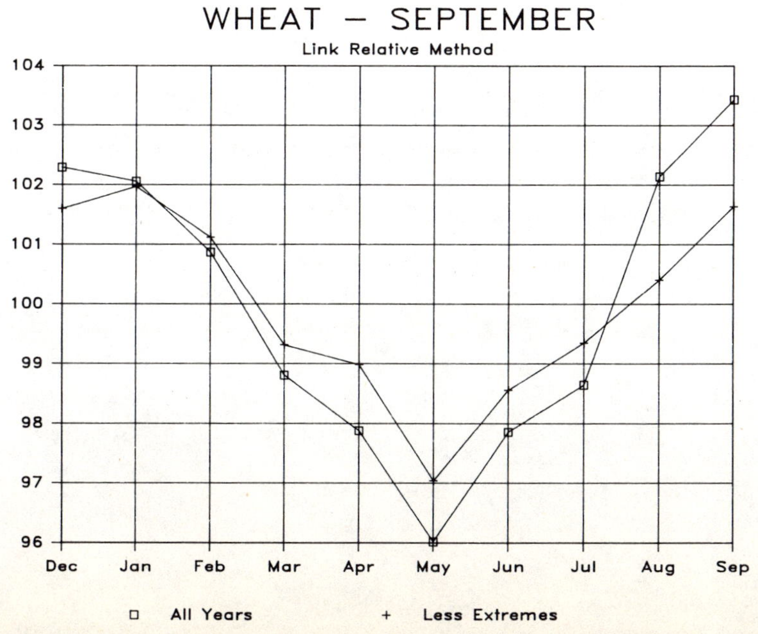
WHEAT – SEPTEMBER
Link Relative Method
104
103
102
101
100
99
98
97
96
Dec
Jan
Feb
Mar
Apr
May
Jun
Jul
Aug
Sep
All Years
Less Extremes

WHEAT - DECEMBER - MONTHLY AVERAGE PRICE

Year of Expiration	Feb	Mar	Apr	May	Jun	Jul	Aug	Sep	Oct	Nov	Dec	Feb-Dec Average
1971	164.17	160.36	160.39	156.48	165.30	156.18	147.68	147.13	154.54	163.04	173.19	158.95
1972	147.99	154.27	154.31	151.05	148.46	158.61	185.01	210.74	215.92	229.71	259.64	183.25
1973	217.27	214.45	224.02	253.39	273.42	293.42	450.89	501.11	452.43	465.55	534.50	352.77
1974	514.71	471.43	406.77	364.90	414.96	453.94	451.31	451.70	515.44	492.53	468.07	455.07
1975	386.37	368.83	361.02	328.31	322.29	364.49	423.26	429.60	404.49	354.61	335.36	370.78
1976	399.84	392.58	371.76	367.81	388.90	379.74	336.63	316.52	288.38	263.09	261.34	342.42
1977	311.70	303.24	291.39	267.63	259.47	245.96	232.05	245.16	252.29	270.94	258.43	267.11
1978	284.12	301.64	329.29	325.76	327.50	322.04	319.28	335.00	349.19	364.00	362.90	329.16
1979	335.42	338.56	341.70	375.09	446.13	454.43	441.17	444.90	443.29	427.69	425.00	406.67
1980	498.78	467.69	437.56	448.17	439.01	463.76	472.51	496.20	520.95	517.76	470.79	475.74
1981	502.95	472.33	482.33	461.91	439.86	436.21	429.20	426.07	432.49	427.75	392.65	445.80
1982	424.88	403.98	413.35	397.86	379.76	371.94	363.90	341.67	312.32	333.51	319.38	369.32
1983	382.68	376.59	387.26	379.71	371.76	374.26	404.17	388.07	365.50	347.07	342.93	374.55
1984	345.01	358.84	365.11	367.91	373.80	363.27	363.01	351.83	353.15	358.91	346.94	358.89
1985	343.41	341.45	343.79	331.27	332.04	315.22	297.10	292.44	308.67	332.31	343.38	325.55

	Feb	Mar	Apr	May	Jun	Jul	Aug	Sep	Oct	Nov	Dec
AVERAGE MOVE											
All Years		-8.87	-3.74	-6.19	7.03	4.72	10.91	4.06	-0.60	-1.37	-3.60
Less Extremes		-8.25	-1.47	-6.49	4.34	3.50	3.80	2.54	-1.86	0.43	-5.84
Ave Up - All Years		10.19	7.91	19.04	22.43	20.99	56.26	17.36	16.26	14.93	30.02
Ave Down - All Years		-15.80	-27.05	-15.36	-10.58	-9.51	-11.76	-11.14	-25.91	-20.01	-15.82
COUNT											
Number Up		4	10	4	8	7	5	8	9	8	4
Number Down		11	5	11	7	8	10	7	6	7	11
Pct Up		26.7%	66.7%	26.7%	53.3%	46.7%	33.3%	53.3%	60.0%	53.3%	26.7%
Pct Down		73.3%	33.3%	73.3%	46.7%	53.3%	66.7%	46.7%	40.0%	46.7%	73.3%
EXTREMES											
Greatest Up		17.52	27.65	33.39	71.04	42.20	157.47	50.21	63.73	23.64	68.95
Greatest Down		-43.28	-64.65	-41.88	-22.05	-16.82	-43.11	-22.23	-48.67	-49.88	-46.98
SEASONAL INDEX : AVERAGE PERCENTAGE METHOD											
All Years	100.1	98.1	97.3	95.4	97.3	98.2	101.3	102.9	102.8	103.2	103.4
Less Extremes	101.8	99.7	98.8	96.3	97.6	98.3	100.4	100.9	102.2	103.0	101.7
SEASONAL INDEX : LINK RELATIVE METHOD											
All Years		99.3	98.2	96.2	97.9	98.5	101.8	102.7	102.2	102.0	101.1
Less Extremes		99.9	99.5	97.4	98.7	99.4	100.5	101.4	101.0	101.6	100.6

WHEAT - DECEMBER - MONTH OF HIGH AND LOW

Year of Expiration	Feb	Mar	Apr	May	Jun	Jul	Aug	Sep	Oct	Nov	Dec
1971								L			H
1972	L										H
1973		L									H
1974				L					H		
1975					L			H			
1976	H										L
1977	H						L				
1978	L										H
1979	L					H					
1980			L						H		
1981	H										L
1982	H								L		
1983							H				L
1984	L				H						
1985			H					L			

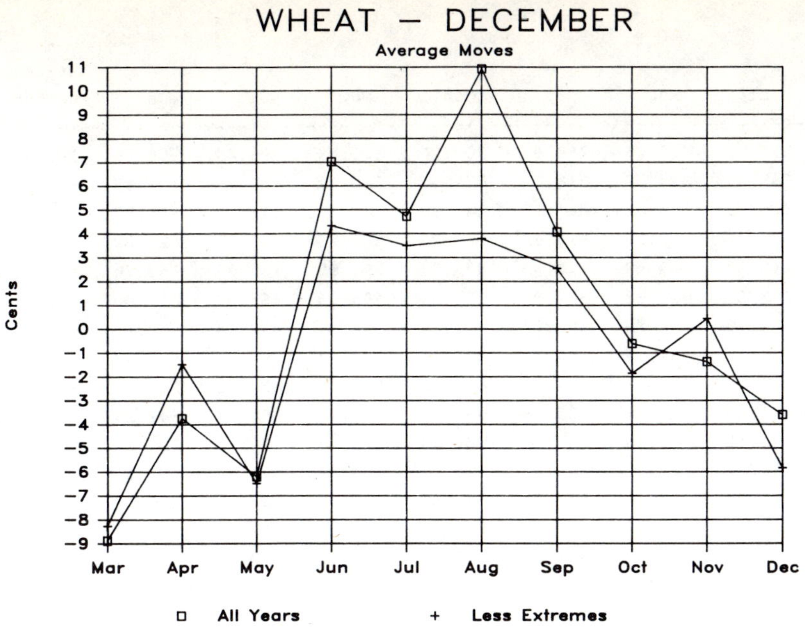
WHEAT – DECEMBER
Average Moves
Cents
11
10
9
8
7
6
5
4
3
2
1
0
–1
–2
–3
–4
–5
–6
–7
–8
–9
Mar
Apr
May
Jun
Jul
Aug
Sep
Oct
Nov
Dec
All Years
Less Extremes

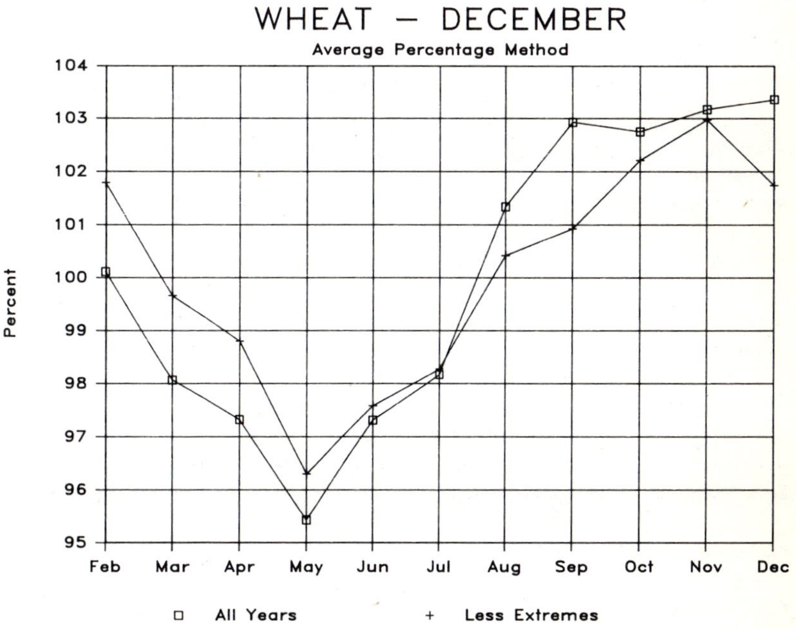
WHEAT – DECEMBER
Average Percentage Method
Percent
104
103
102
101
100
99
98
97
96
95
Feb
Mar
Apr
May
Jun
Jul
Aug
Sep
Oct
Nov
Dec
All Years
Less Extremes

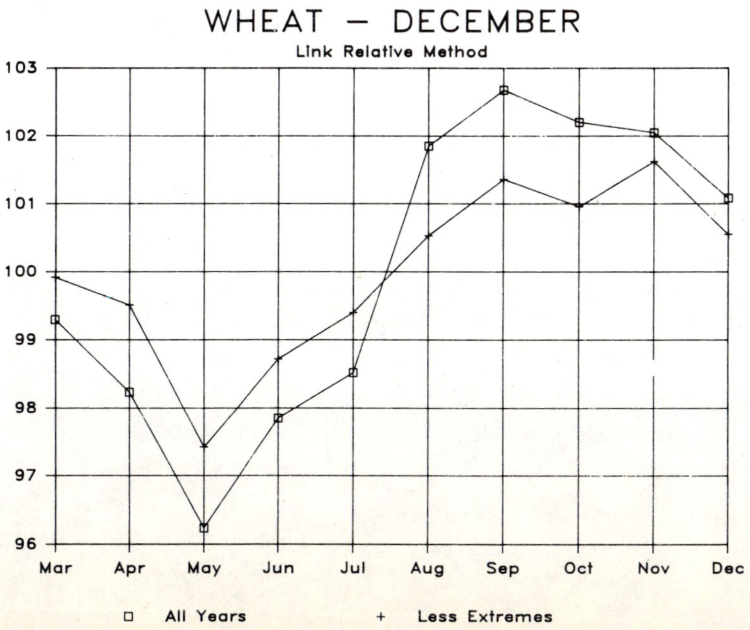
WHEAT – DECEMBER
Link Relative Method
103
102
101
100
99
98
97
96
Mar
Apr
May
Jun
Jul
Aug
Sep
Oct
Nov
Dec
All Years
Less Extremes

SOYBEANS - JANUARY - MONTHLY AVERAGE PRICE

Year of Expiration	Mar	Apr	May	Jun	Jul	Aug	Sep	Oct	Nov	Dec	Jan	Mar-Jan Average
1971	257.54	262.46	262.80	276.93	297.92	289.06	289.86	302.70	305.89	295.49	300.36	285.55
1972	291.02	287.84	296.19	316.70	333.66	324.03	318.10	321.64	313.72	313.28	307.42	311.24
1973	317.06	325.24	323.25	325.79	325.90	335.42	344.11	343.90	368.17	417.29	446.07	352.02
1974	406.50	429.12	503.79	615.88	676.52	769.51	645.99	586.25	567.76	600.82	616.00	583.47
1975	618.91	540.61	540.00	549.41	710.63	782.59	774.83	873.24	791.95	736.93	650.70	688.16
1976	563.13	558.66	504.80	500.77	563.57	620.13	583.20	535.35	486.05	463.54	472.00	531.93
1977	509.14	511.95	549.90	653.17	702.20	658.06	687.19	648.76	668.31	692.74	712.11	635.78
1978	720.89	732.49	735.86	724.28	600.55	536.63	534.00	538.13	598.13	595.83	580.38	627.02
1979	618.13	623.40	635.55	637.72	614.19	629.48	657.80	691.53	679.89	683.83	684.88	650.58
1980	717.71	711.96	728.68	787.81	765.88	727.76	728.75	691.72	677.35	663.61	642.29	713.05
1981	707.96	669.19	669.92	679.27	782.40	795.56	858.50	881.80	925.43	798.10	791.29	778.13
1982	827.43	858.94	809.53	766.83	781.40	722.62	685.07	677.13	654.49	628.65	630.52	731.14
1983	659.37	687.71	685.06	655.86	633.71	592.07	563.04	546.57	573.06	567.17	576.98	612.78
1984	652.71	690.09	665.18	633.17	701.66	877.77	915.05	859.02	827.02	787.19	758.25	760.65
1985	744.25	734.95	743.38	738.06	651.07	649.09	622.26	624.70	622.33	590.65	580.88	663.78

	Mar	Apr	May	Jun	Jul	Aug	Sep	Oct	Nov	Dec	Jan
AVERAGE MOVE											
All Years		0.86	1.95	13.85	18.64	11.23	-6.80	-5.69	-4.19	-14.96	-5.66
Less Extremes		4.14	0.65	10.65	18.62	4.33	-3.19	-9.54	-3.20	-11.25	-2.12
Ave Up - All Years		16.96	18.08	36.96	55.79	62.23	24.02	25.48	29.52	27.63	11.18
Ave Down - All Years		-23.29	-22.24	-20.80	-55.67	-33.39	-33.77	-32.96	-26.67	-30.45	-24.91
COUNT											
Number Up		9	9	9	10	7	7	7	6	4	8
Number Down		6	6	6	5	8	8	8	9	11	7
Pct Up		60.0%	60.0%	60.0%	66.7%	46.7%	46.7%	46.7%	40.0%	26.7%	53.3%
Pct Down		40.0%	40.0%	40.0%	33.3%	53.3%	53.3%	53.3%	60.0%	73.3%	46.7%
EXTREMES											
Greatest Up		37.38	74.67	112.09	161.21	176.11	62.94	98.41	60.00	49.12	28.78
Greatest Down		-78.30	-53.86	-42.69	-123.73	-63.92	-123.52	-59.74	-81.29	-127.34	-86.23
SEASONAL INDEX : AVERAGE PERCENTAGE METHOD											
All Years	96.0	96.3	96.7	99.4	102.6	104.1	102.7	101.9	101.4	99.7	99.2
Less Extremes	96.5	96.4	96.5	99.7	102.3	103.4	102.7	101.2	100.9	99.3	98.1
SEASONAL INDEX : LINK RELATIVE METHOD											
All Years		96.3	96.7	99.3	102.9	104.1	102.5	101.3	100.6	98.6	97.6
Less Extremes		97.1	97.3	99.4	102.8	103.3	102.5	101.0	100.4	98.4	97.9

SOYBEANS - JANUARY - MONTH OF HIGH AND LOW

Year of Expiration	Mar	Apr	May	Jun	Jul	Aug	Sep	Oct	Nov	Dec	Jan
1971	L								H		
1972		L			H						
1973	L										H
1974	L					H					
1975			L					H			
1976						H				L	
1977	L										H
1978			H				L				
1979					L			H			
1980				H							L
1981		L							H		
1982		H								L	
1983		H						L			
1984				L			H				
1985	H										L

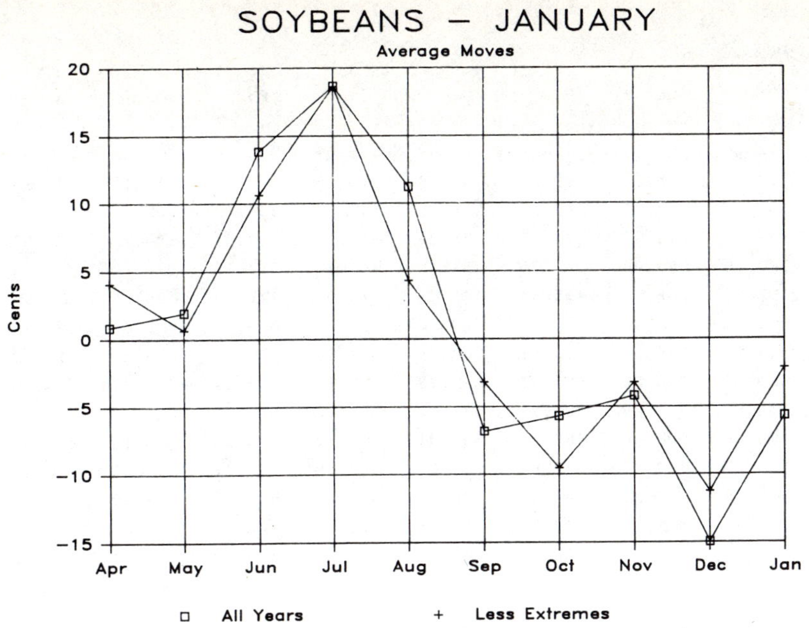
SOYBEANS – JANUARY
Average Moves
Cents
20
15
10
5
0
−5
−10
−15
Apr
May
Jun
Jul
Aug
Sep
Oct
Nov
Dec
Jan
All Years
Less Extremes

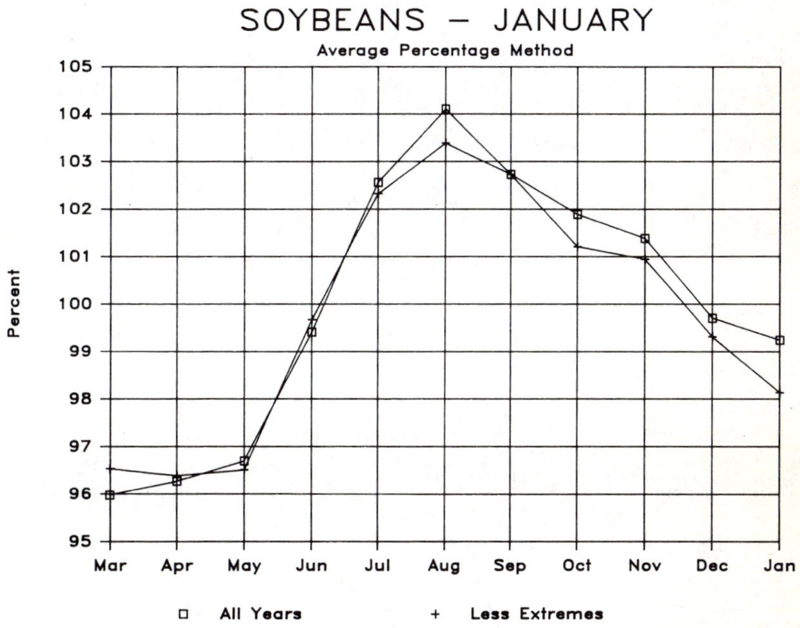
SOYBEANS – JANUARY
Average Percentage Method
Percent
105
104
103
102
101
100
99
98
97
96
95
Mar
Apr
May
Jun
Jul
Aug
Sep
Oct
Nov
Dec
Jan
All Years
Less Extremes

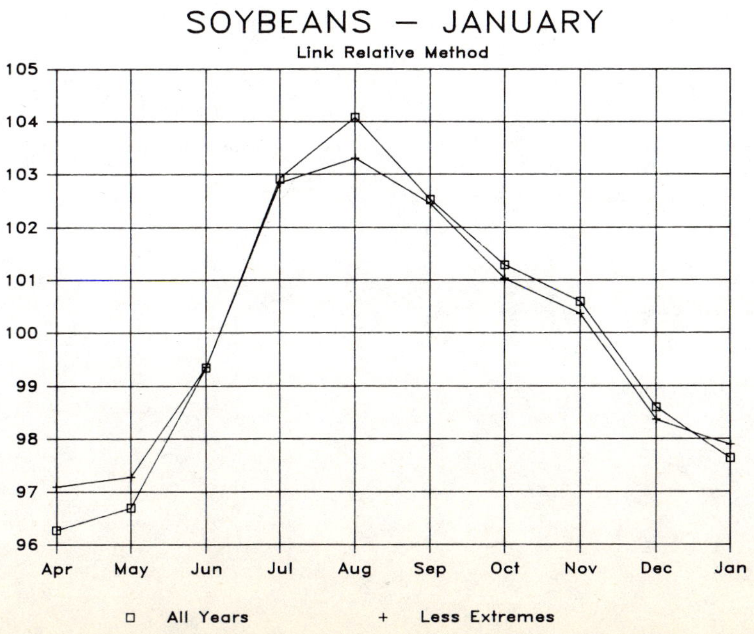
SOYBEANS – JANUARY
Link Relative Method
105
104
103
102
101
100
99
98
97
96
Apr
May
Jun
Jul
Aug
Sep
Oct
Nov
Dec
Jan
All Years
Less Extremes

SOYBEANS - MARCH - MONTHLY AVERAGE PRICE

Year of Expiration	May	Jun	Jul	Aug	Sep	Oct	Nov	Dec	Jan	Feb	Mar	May-Mar Average
1971	266.59	280.88	302.38	293.91	294.27	306.71	309.81	299.95	305.89	305.54	301.83	297.07
1972	299.57	320.22	336.46	327.90	322.26	325.69	318.61	318.64	313.16	319.58	337.10	321.74
1973	326.93	329.97	330.20	339.93	348.89	348.35	369.54	416.55	452.80	583.99	650.38	408.87
1974	502.90	611.03	674.74	769.67	651.99	591.93	570.37	606.82	626.25	644.04	632.21	625.63
1975	544.51	555.58	714.19	786.68	782.89	884.84	807.95	753.10	648.58	568.20	537.10	689.42
1976	511.89	509.01	572.02	629.37	592.06	545.37	495.34	473.31	475.30	479.67	475.80	523.56
1977	556.04	658.92	708.08	664.23	691.63	655.46	671.94	697.08	720.66	739.91	830.81	690.43
1978	741.36	730.00	608.08	544.35	541.88	546.57	605.80	603.95	582.60	570.95	653.48	611.73
1979	642.00	644.48	620.95	637.36	665.60	700.00	692.10	697.23	698.94	745.34	745.47	680.86
1980	739.80	799.43	776.12	740.72	744.82	713.09	700.32	686.22	662.05	656.84	624.21	713.06
1981	684.99	694.92	796.09	808.76	878.07	906.60	955.39	831.31	786.12	750.18	726.18	801.69
1982	830.80	787.76	802.85	744.42	708.06	699.13	672.84	641.85	642.26	629.47	610.33	706.34
1983	699.69	672.50	650.62	608.05	578.08	560.32	583.90	576.67	589.70	590.37	579.69	608.14
1984	678.10	645.02	715.35	887.13	926.31	871.99	843.21	803.95	761.13	722.48	773.85	784.41
1985	754.65	750.56	664.68	663.51	635.63	638.70	636.68	604.10	593.96	581.99	579.61	645.82
AVERAGE MOVE												
All Years		14.03	18.84	11.54	-5.57	-4.51	-4.06	-14.87	-10.09	1.94	11.30	
Less Extremes		11.18	18.91	5.01	-2.70	-8.43	-3.33	-11.23	-6.39	-1.67	8.56	
Ave Up - All Years		36.90	55.91	62.19	25.37	26.93	28.73	22.75	12.79	32.30	51.48	
Ave Down - All Years		-20.27	-55.30	-32.77	-32.64	-32.03	-25.92	-33.68	-36.24	-24.62	-15.48	
COUNT												
Number Up		9	10	7	7	7	6	5	8	7	6	
Number Down		6	5	8	8	8	9	10	7	8	9	
Pct Up		60.0%	66.7%	46.7%	46.7%	46.7%	40.0%	33.3%	53.3%	46.7%	40.0%	
Pct Down		40.0%	33.3%	53.3%	53.3%	53.3%	60.0%	66.7%	46.7%	53.3%	60.0%	
EXTREMES												
Greatest Up		108.13	158.62	171.78	69.31	101.95	59.23	47.01	36.25	131.18	90.90	
Greatest Down		-43.04	-121.92	-63.73	-117.69	-60.05	-76.89	-124.08	-104.52	-80.38	-32.62	
SEASONAL INDEX : AVERAGE PERCENTAGE METHOD												
All Years	96.1	98.6	101.6	103.1	101.8	101.2	100.6	98.8	97.7	99.1	101.3	
Less Extremes	95.5	98.4	102.3	103.1	101.9	100.4	100.0	98.7	97.3	97.0	98.7	
SEASONAL INDEX : LINK RELATIVE METHOD												
All Years		98.3	101.9	103.3	102.0	101.0	100.4	98.6	97.3	97.9	99.4	
Less Extremes		98.5	102.1	102.8	102.2	101.0	100.5	98.7	97.8	97.6	98.9	

SOYBEANS - MARCH - MONTH OF HIGH AND LOW

Year of Expiration	May	Jun	Jul	Aug	Sep	Oct	Nov	Dec	Jan	Feb	Mar
1971	L						H				
1972	L										H
1973	L										H
1974	L			H							
1975						H					L
1976				H				L			
1977	L										H
1978	H				L						
1979			L								H
1980		H									L
1981	L						H				
1982	H										L
1983	H					L					
1984		L			H						
1985	H										L

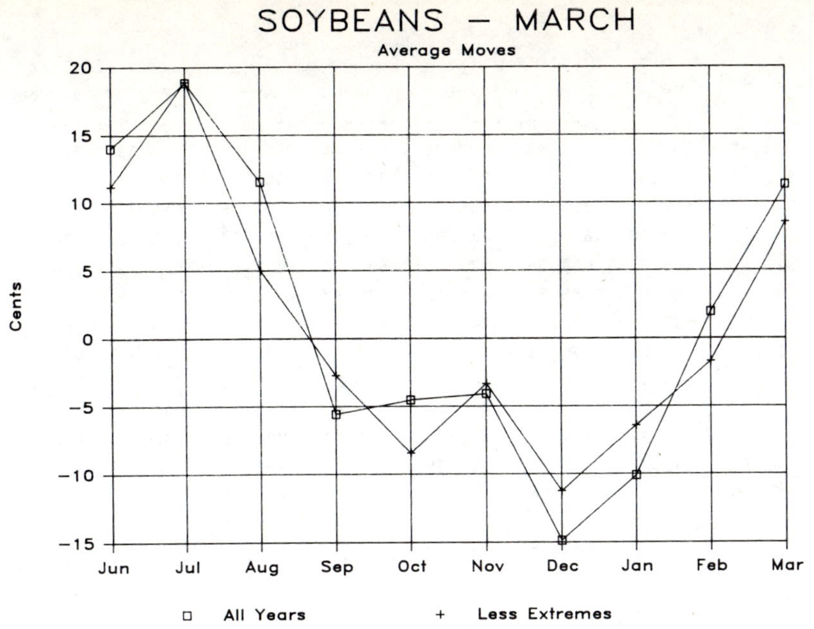
SOYBEANS — MARCH
Average Moves
Cents
20
15
10
5
0
−5
−10
−15
Jun
Jul
Aug
Sep
Oct
Nov
Dec
Jan
Feb
Mar
All Years
Less Extremes

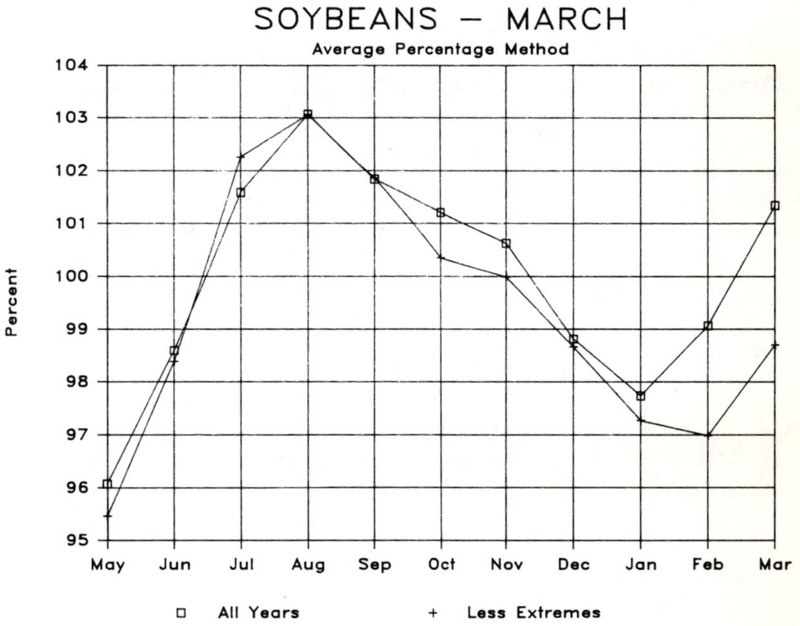
SOYBEANS — MARCH
Average Percentage Method
Percent
104
103
102
101
100
99
98
97
96
95
May
Jun
Jul
Aug
Sep
Oct
Nov
Dec
Jan
Feb
Mar
All Years
Less Extremes

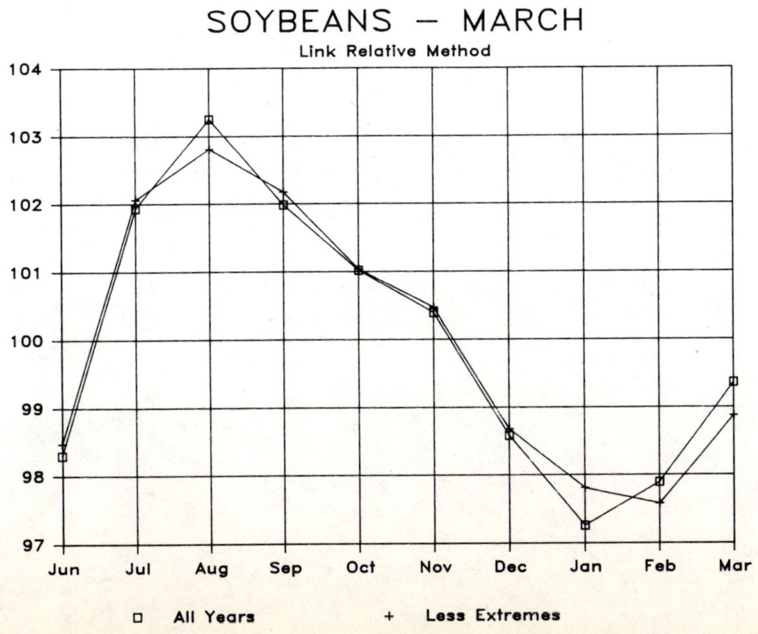
SOYBEANS — MARCH
Link Relative Method
104
103
102
101
100
99
98
97
Jun
Jul
Aug
Sep
Oct
Nov
Dec
Jan
Feb
Mar
All Years
Less Extremes

SOYBEANS - MAY - MONTHLY AVERAGE PRICE

Year of Expiration	Jul	Aug	Sep	Oct	Nov	Dec	Jan	Feb	Mar	Apr	May	Jul-May Average
1971	305.69	297.86	298.01	309.44	313.35	304.33	310.23	309.26	305.14	291.90	296.39	303.78
1972	338.61	330.34	325.29	328.93	322.77	322.92	317.84	324.25	341.64	352.02	350.27	332.26
1973	333.89	343.22	351.88	351.15	371.01	412.88	436.57	555.22	602.58	633.75	851.29	476.67
1974	668.74	767.22	655.66	596.98	572.32	610.58	632.30	651.26	631.77	559.74	541.38	626.18
1975	714.48	787.50	788.80	891.82	820.55	765.33	660.56	579.25	559.84	572.67	523.79	696.78
1976	579.18	636.80	598.94	552.80	502.80	481.39	483.73	488.13	480.37	480.31	507.06	526.50
1977	709.05	666.31	691.98	656.57	666.75	692.58	721.55	745.15	845.90	988.54	973.73	759.83
1978	614.13	550.70	548.36	553.95	612.99	609.96	590.14	579.42	676.92	703.83	723.50	614.90
1979	624.89	641.66	669.29	703.56	698.68	705.09	708.56	760.17	765.11	740.44	720.28	703.43
1980	781.01	749.25	757.20	731.04	719.51	706.92	684.10	680.06	631.66	593.79	607.75	694.75
1981	802.93	812.10	885.44	923.42	977.51	860.32	812.45	776.86	755.55	784.46	754.62	831.42
1982	819.50	764.16	729.36	720.17	690.50	656.03	655.16	645.58	627.26	653.32	658.21	692.66
1983	664.26	621.32	590.67	570.98	593.35	585.06	600.56	605.38	605.34	636.21	623.57	608.79
1984	725.16	886.71	928.76	873.69	850.83	813.94	776.01	738.83	789.07	787.38	837.63	818.91
1985	674.86	673.55	645.42	651.50	649.94	616.96	605.61	594.53	593.95	598.50	581.35	626.02

	Jul	Aug	Sep	Oct	Nov	Dec	Jan	Feb	Mar	Apr	May
AVERAGE MOVE											
All Years		11.49	-4.24	-3.27	-3.54	-14.57	-9.93	2.53	11.92	10.98	11.60
Less Extremes		5.71	-1.96	-7.18	-3.15	-11.02	-5.62	0.05	9.72	7.24	0.41
Ave Up - All Years		60.85	23.34	28.86	28.24	22.51	14.51	32.64	53.03	34.92	48.22
Ave Down - All Years		-31.70	-35.77	-31.38	-24.73	-33.11	-31.31	-23.81	-15.49	-24.93	-20.45
COUNT											
Number Up		7	8	7	6	5	7	7	6	9	7
Number Down		8	7	8	9	10	8	8	9	6	8
Pct Up		46.7%	53.3%	46.7%	40.0%	33.3%	46.7%	46.7%	40.0%	60.0%	46.7%
Pct Down		53.3%	46.7%	53.3%	60.0%	66.7%	53.3%	53.3%	60.0%	40.0%	53.3%
EXTREMES											
Greatest Up		161.54	73.35	103.02	59.04	41.88	28.97	118.65	100.76	142.64	217.54
Greatest Down		-63.43	-111.56	-58.68	-71.26	-117.19	-104.78	-81.31	-48.41	-72.04	-48.88
SEASONAL INDEX : AVERAGE PERCENTAGE METHOD											
All Years	100.4	101.9	100.7	100.3	99.7	97.8	96.6	97.7	99.7	101.2	103.9
Less Extremes	101.4	102.6	101.8	100.2	100.0	97.8	96.6	97.4	99.1	100.2	100.4
SEASONAL INDEX : LINK RELATIVE METHOD											
All Years		101.9	101.0	100.4	99.9	98.3	97.1	98.0	99.8	100.9	102.6
Less Extremes		101.5	101.1	100.4	100.0	98.5	98.1	98.3	99.8	101.0	101.3

SOYBEANS - MAY - MONTH OF HIGH AND LOW

Year of Expiration	Jul	Aug	Sep	Oct	Nov	Dec	Jan	Feb	Mar	Apr	May
1971					H					L	
1972							L			H	
1973	L										H
1974		H									L
1975				H							L
1976		H								L	
1977				L						H	
1978			L								H
1979	L								H		
1980	H									L	
1981					H						L
1982	H								L		
1983	H			L							
1984	L		H								
1985	H										L

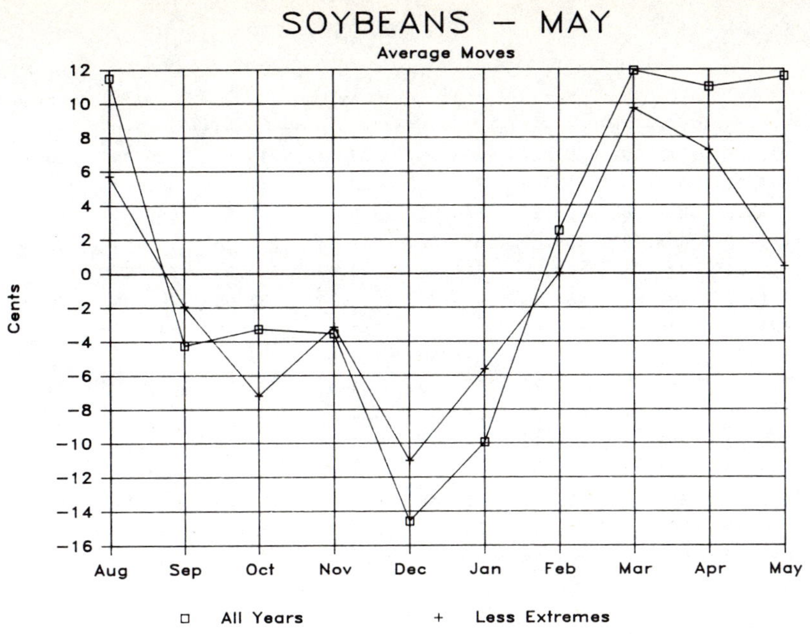
SOYBEANS — MAY
Average Moves
Cents
12
10
8
6
4
2
0
−2
−4
−6
−8
−10
−12
−14
−16
Aug
Sep
Oct
Nov
Dec
Jan
Feb
Mar
Apr
May
□ All Years
+ Less Extremes

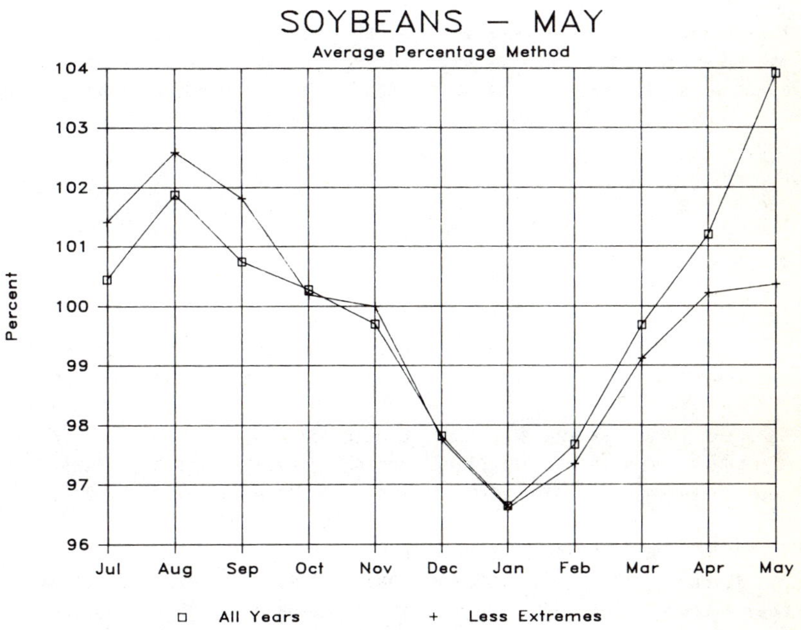
SOYBEANS — MAY
Average Percentage Method
Percent
104
103
102
101
100
99
98
97
96
Jul
Aug
Sep
Oct
Nov
Dec
Jan
Feb
Mar
Apr
May
□ All Years
+ Less Extremes

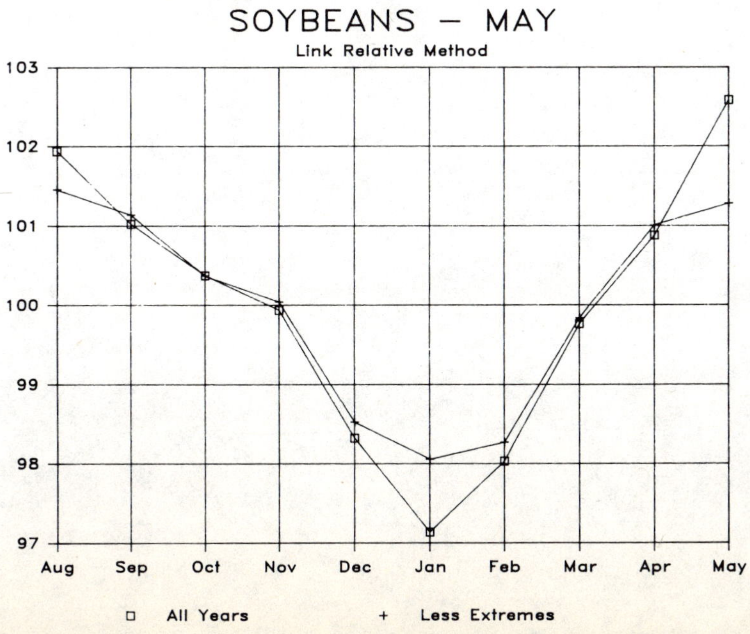
SOYBEANS — MAY
Link Relative Method
103
102
101
100
99
98
97
Aug
Sep
Oct
Nov
Dec
Jan
Feb
Mar
Apr
May
□ All Years
+ Less Extremes

SOYBEANS - JULY - MONTHLY AVERAGE PRICE

Year of Expiration	Sep	Oct	Nov	Dec	Jan	Feb	Mar	Apr	May	Jun	Jul	Sep-Jul Average
1971	299.33	309.86	314.01	306.95	313.18	311.90	308.20	295.38	302.16	319.57	336.85	310.67
1972	326.43	330.12	325.23	325.61	321.12	327.66	345.42	356.78	353.40	347.65	351.63	337.37
1973	353.69	352.74	371.82	409.74	423.14	529.06	565.21	600.96	838.24	1097.53	889.64	584.70
1974	657.09	599.38	572.67	613.80	635.68	655.78	635.49	556.82	547.24	552.26	656.98	607.56
1975	792.05	895.00	826.53	772.00	667.66	586.78	565.53	566.66	510.83	508.81	546.57	658.04
1976	603.38	557.77	508.65	489.81	491.25	495.80	488.54	488.77	531.39	635.05	706.96	545.22
1977	690.42	655.41	658.70	685.35	720.10	746.03	846.09	984.65	954.50	827.76	641.08	764.55
1978	553.31	560.55	618.27	614.13	595.77	584.99	682.05	694.30	714.00	686.94	667.87	633.83
1979	669.78	703.84	701.38	708.84	714.40	769.15	772.76	752.55	736.92	780.71	771.68	734.73
1980	765.51	745.55	735.19	724.63	703.96	702.11	655.80	618.32	624.83	633.08	743.95	695.72
1981	885.62	929.35	989.22	880.62	833.07	800.65	778.77	809.21	770.51	721.08	729.18	829.75
1982	746.64	737.52	705.59	668.82	668.18	661.33	636.99	665.19	663.54	628.69	618.09	672.78
1983	600.71	578.19	601.54	593.23	609.79	618.74	619.24	652.85	630.86	602.25	636.44	613.08
1984	923.42	866.35	849.00	817.13	785.50	750.56	798.59	798.53	853.75	782.02	688.00	810.26
1985	650.65	658.14	659.87	626.79	614.82	605.08	603.44	606.21	576.47	576.60	563.68	612.89

	Sep	Oct	Nov	Dec	Jan	Feb	Mar	Apr	May	Jun	Jul
AVERAGE MOVE											
All Years		-2.55	-2.81	-13.35	-9.32	3.20	10.43	9.67	10.76	6.09	-10.09
Less Extremes		-6.42	-2.58	-10.21	-5.40	1.76	7.91	6.55	-1.54	-3.17	-4.18
Ave Up - All Years		29.96	24.17	22.71	14.26	32.39	43.31	29.43	61.35	62.51	48.60
Ave Down - All Years		-31.00	-26.41	-31.38	-29.96	-22.34	-18.33	-29.85	-22.96	-43.27	-77.18
COUNT											
Number Up		7	7	5	7	7	7	10	6	7	8
Number Down		8	8	10	8	8	8	5	9	8	7
Pct Up		46.7%	46.7%	33.3%	46.7%	46.7%	46.7%	66.7%	40.0%	46.7%	53.3%
Pct Down		53.3%	53.3%	66.7%	53.3%	53.3%	53.3%	33.3%	60.0%	53.3%	46.7%
EXTREMES											
Greatest Up		102.95	59.87	41.14	34.75	105.92	100.06	138.56	237.28	259.29	110.87
Greatest Down		-57.72	-68.47	-108.60	-104.34	-80.88	-46.31	-78.67	-55.83	-126.74	-207.88
SEASONAL INDEX : AVERAGE PERCENTAGE METHOD											
All Years	100.5	100.1	99.6	97.7	96.5	97.2	98.8	100.1	102.1	104.1	103.2
Less Extremes	102.0	100.5	100.3	98.4	97.7	97.0	98.9	98.9	100.8	99.7	100.9
SEASONAL INDEX : LINK RELATIVE METHOD											
All Years		100.9	100.3	98.6	97.2	97.9	99.2	99.9	101.4	102.3	102.3
Less Extremes		100.9	100.4	98.9	98.4	98.6	99.7	100.6	100.5	100.6	101.3

SOYBEANS - JULY - MONTH OF HIGH AND LOW

Year of Expiration	Sep	Oct	Nov	Dec	Jan	Feb	Mar	Apr	May	Jun	Jul
1971								L			H
1972					L			H			
1973		L								H	
1974	H								L		
1975		H								L	
1976							L				H
1977								H			L
1978	L								H		
1979	L									H	
1980	H							L			
1981			H							L	
1982	H										L
1983		L						H			
1984	H										L
1985			H								L

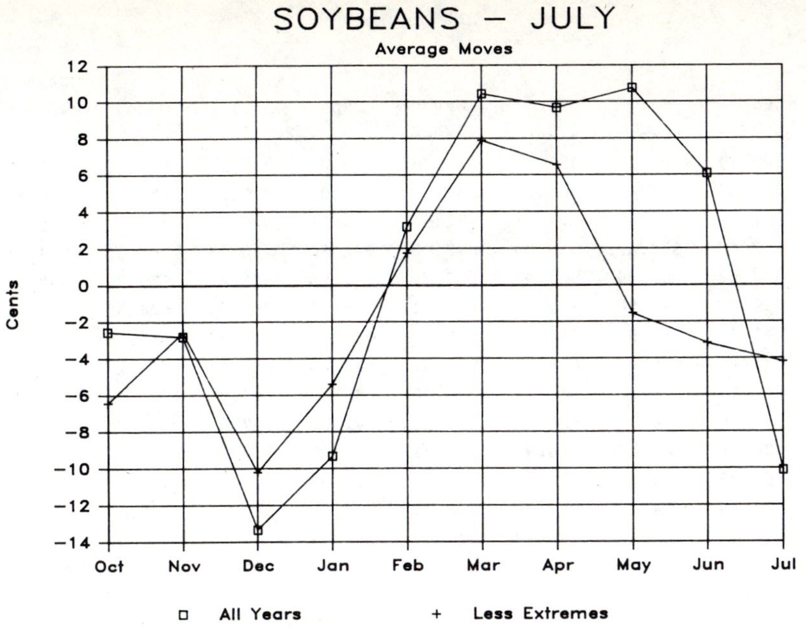
SOYBEANS – JULY
Average Moves
Cents
12
10
8
6
4
2
0
−2
−4
−6
−8
−10
−12
−14
Oct
Nov
Dec
Jan
Feb
Mar
Apr
May
Jun
Jul
□ All Years
+ Less Extremes

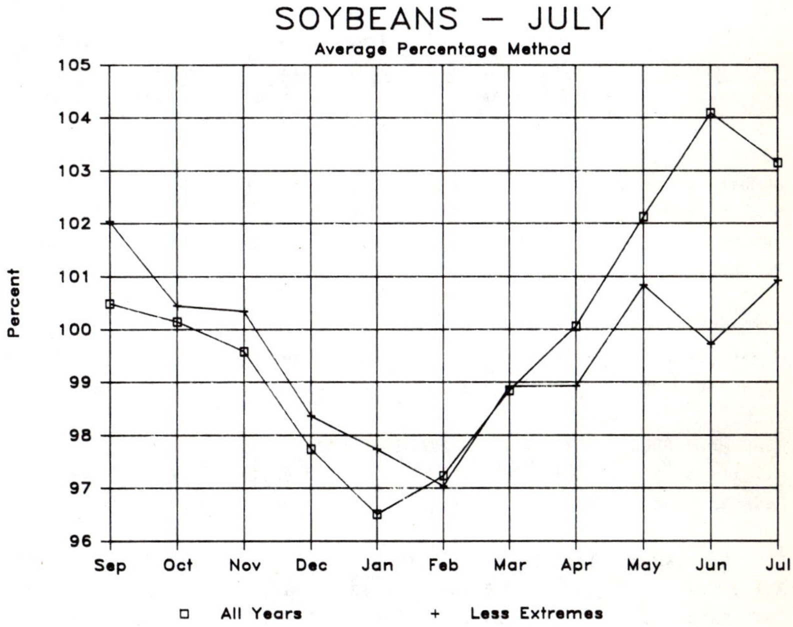
SOYBEANS – JULY
Average Percentage Method
Percent
105
104
103
102
101
100
99
98
97
96
Sep
Oct
Nov
Dec
Jan
Feb
Mar
Apr
May
Jun
Jul
□ All Years
+ Less Extremes

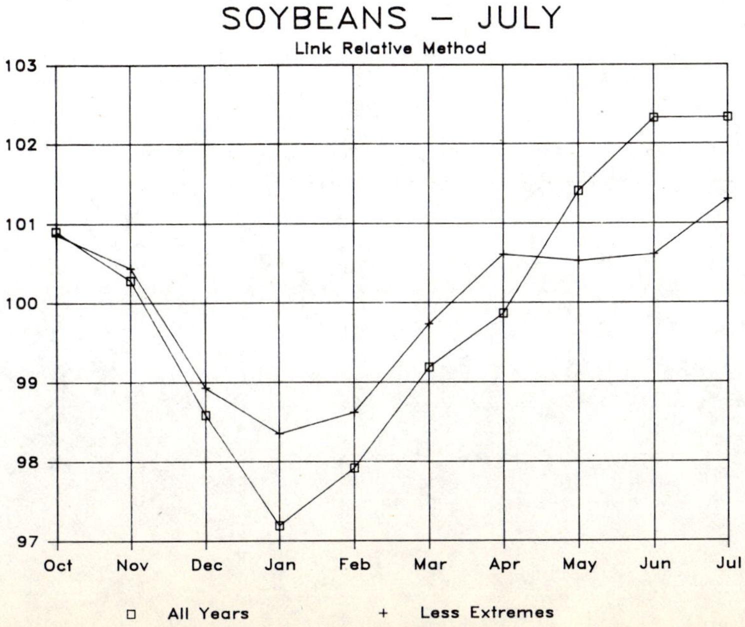
SOYBEANS – JULY
Link Relative Method
103
102
101
100
99
98
97
Oct
Nov
Dec
Jan
Feb
Mar
Apr
May
Jun
Jul
□ All Years
+ Less Extremes

SOYBEANS - AUGUST - MONTHLY AVERAGE PRICE

Year of Expiration	Oct	Nov	Dec	Jan	Feb	Mar	Apr	May	Jun	Jul	Aug	Oct-Aug Average
1971	304.81	310.71	304.13	310.34	308.94	306.19	295.12	301.44	319.89	337.09	330.19	311.71
1972	325.42	323.16	324.65	320.12	326.55	343.87	355.57	352.39	347.07	350.62	359.34	338.98
1973	349.53	368.76	405.43	414.66	511.79	536.61	573.71	787.66	1050.21	940.24	972.50	628.28
1974	597.05	567.12	609.26	633.84	652.68	634.42	553.68	547.85	552.60	710.03	799.30	623.44
1975	887.87	822.13	766.83	666.14	588.67	567.44	564.97	505.39	500.96	555.40	610.32	639.65
1976	558.19	510.05	493.60	494.32	499.37	491.00	492.80	535.01	638.09	682.75	624.80	547.27
1977	755.60	648.28	675.13	714.13	741.30	837.58	964.04	932.48	823.80	635.73	583.58	755.60
1978	562.56	618.32	612.00	595.25	585.91	676.48	676.74	698.06	677.48	650.45	634.14	635.22
1979	695.41	694.63	701.80	709.72	761.57	766.55	749.11	740.98	786.43	763.86	713.69	734.88
1980	750.87	741.73	731.83	712.51	710.50	666.05	628.68	633.36	641.02	747.22	758.05	701.98
1981	914.89	963.07	872.62	836.58	808.26	786.77	818.98	776.51	727.31	733.96	703.39	812.94
1982	741.39	707.95	670.41	670.74	665.97	640.64	668.94	667.39	632.88	616.12	582.63	660.46
1983	578.48	601.58	594.11	611.48	622.49	624.20	658.91	636.69	607.86	661.91	819.69	637.94
1984	838.69	826.25	801.07	778.67	747.33	789.14	790.49	841.19	782.29	665.02	644.97	773.19
1985	658.04	659.85	628.59	616.16	607.25	604.71	607.79	576.48	570.38	551.78	522.98	600.36

	Oct	Nov	Dec	Jan	Feb	Mar	Apr	May	Jun	Jul	Aug
AVERAGE MOVE											
All Years		-10.35	-11.47	-7.12	3.59	8.87	8.52	8.89	8.36	-3.74	3.83
Less Extremes		-7.97	-9.52	-3.47	2.64	6.25	6.32	-1.62	-2.19	-1.96	-3.26
Ave Up - All Years		25.66	22.87	13.17	31.07	39.64	27.70	56.53	73.66	55.52	58.97
Ave Down - All Years		-34.35	-28.65	-30.31	-20.44	-18.05	-29.82	-22.87	-35.17	-71.46	-32.93
COUNT											
Number Up		6	5	8	7	7	10	6	6	8	6
Number Down		9	10	7	8	8	5	9	9	7	9
Pct Up		40.0%	33.3%	53.3%	46.7%	46.7%	66.7%	40.0%	40.0%	53.3%	40.0%
Pct Down		60.0%	66.7%	46.7%	53.3%	53.3%	33.3%	60.0%	60.0%	46.7%	60.0%
EXTREMES											
Greatest Up		55.76	42.14	39.00	97.13	96.27	126.46	213.95	262.55	157.43	157.78
Greatest Down		-107.33	-90.45	-100.70	-77.46	-44.45	-80.74	-59.57	-108.68	-188.07	-57.95
SEASONAL INDEX : AVERAGE PERCENTAGE METHOD											
All Years	100.6	99.1	97.4	96.4	97.0	98.4	99.5	101.1	103.1	103.3	104.0
Less Extremes	101.2	99.9	98.2	98.1	97.7	98.5	98.2	100.9	100.1	101.2	102.2
SEASONAL INDEX : LINK RELATIVE METHOD											
All Years		100.4	98.8	97.5	98.1	99.0	99.4	100.6	101.7	102.3	102.2
Less Extremes		100.2	98.9	98.5	98.8	99.7	100.6	100.5	100.7	101.4	100.7

SOYBEANS - AUGUST - MONTH OF HIGH AND LOW

Year of Expiration	Oct	Nov	Dec	Jan	Feb	Mar	Apr	May	Jun	Jul	Aug
1971							L			H	
1972				L							H
1973	L								H		
1974								L			H
1975	H								L		
1976						L				H	
1977							H				L
1978	L							H			
1979		L							H		
1980							L				H
1981		H									L
1982	H									L	
1983	L									H	
1984								H			L
1985		H									L

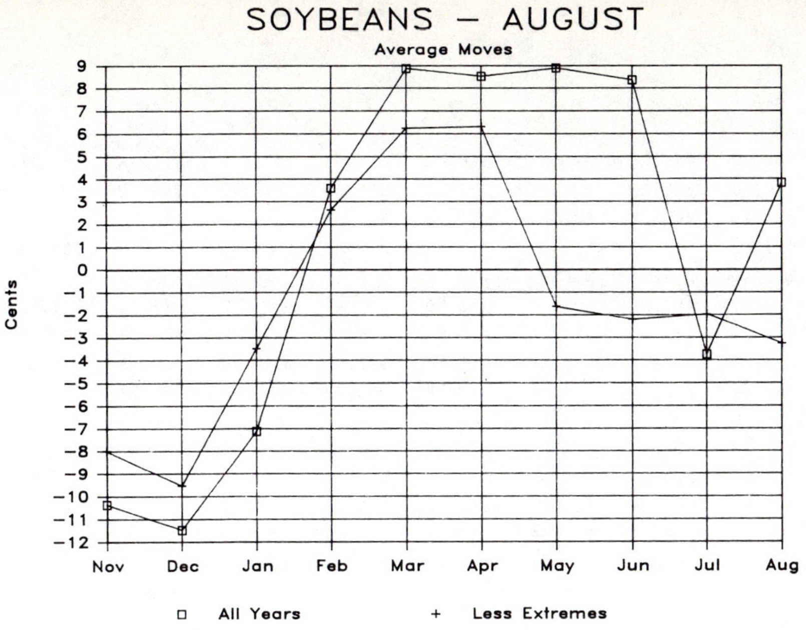
SOYBEANS — AUGUST
Average Moves
Cents
9
8
7
6
5
4
3
2
1
0
−1
−2
−3
−4
−5
−6
−7
−8
−9
−10
−11
−12
Nov
Dec
Jan
Feb
Mar
Apr
May
Jun
Jul
Aug
□ All Years
+ Less Extremes

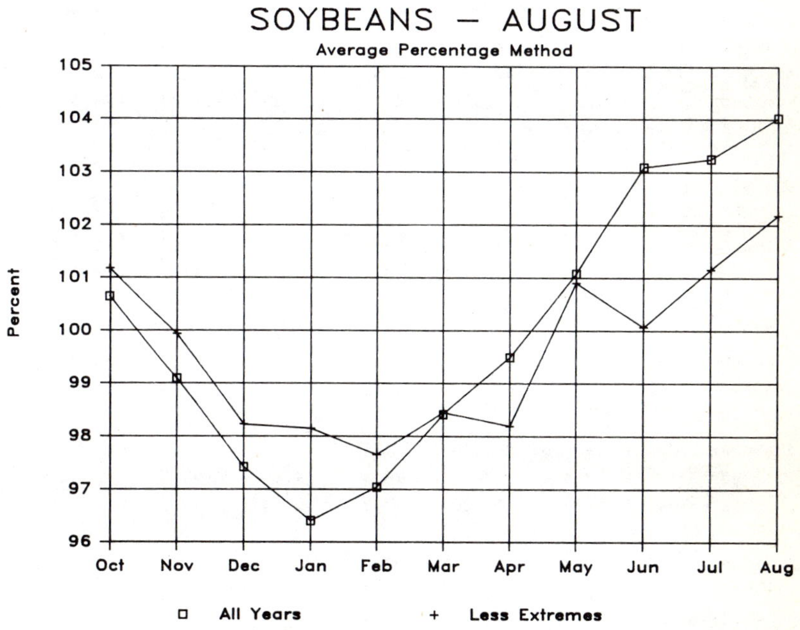
SOYBEANS — AUGUST
Average Percentage Method
Percent
105
104
103
102
101
100
99
98
97
96
Oct
Nov
Dec
Jan
Feb
Mar
Apr
May
Jun
Jul
Aug
□ All Years
+ Less Extremes

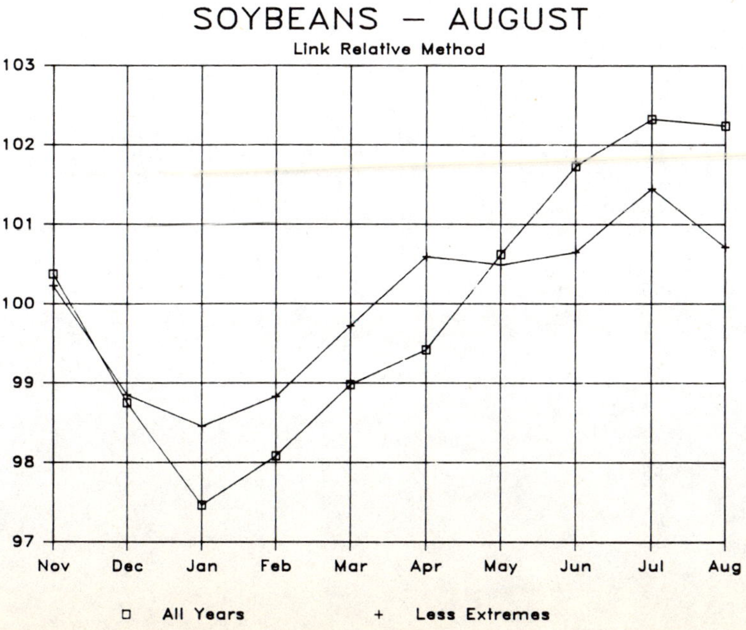
SOYBEANS — AUGUST
Link Relative Method
103
102
101
100
99
98
97
Nov
Dec
Jan
Feb
Mar
Apr
May
Jun
Jul
Aug
□ All Years
+ Less Extremes

SOYBEANS - SEPTEMBER - MONTHLY AVERAGE PRICE

Year of Expiration	Nov	Dec	Jan	Feb	Mar	Apr	May	Jun	Jul	Aug	Sep	Nov-Sep Average
1971	293.07	289.98	296.54	296.65	294.67	289.28	296.71	316.60	335.91	325.88	314.36	304.51
1972	310.39	314.67	308.36	311.59	326.44	338.29	335.99	334.81	337.19	343.92	345.12	327.89
1973	351.98	374.47	385.65	449.65	456.95	492.87	643.42	865.13	821.91	824.35	648.75	574.10
1974	559.33	603.61	628.66	641.92	624.10	545.63	542.90	550.93	710.88	781.39	737.23	629.69
1975	778.32	732.79	644.10	580.40	561.16	556.61	498.76	494.10	553.42	605.56	566.91	597.47
1976	512.21	498.70	499.07	503.18	495.92	496.95	538.11	642.16	687.21	641.23	695.43	564.56
1977	616.85	645.00	686.16	713.86	771.02	811.01	795.24	755.69	606.59	539.02	528.04	678.95
1978	602.95	596.02	580.10	576.50	632.50	642.09	662.99	656.58	625.63	633.48	655.85	624.06
1979	673.03	678.73	684.75	719.13	729.52	721.01	729.08	782.29	761.77	717.53	707.27	718.56
1980	743.69	734.30	718.19	717.89	674.70	637.30	641.30	649.33	755.77	764.52	821.38	714.40
1981	887.22	835.95	830.55	812.95	793.57	824.99	779.61	733.39	742.47	691.50	665.73	781.63
1982	708.95	669.66	670.86	667.25	641.34	670.27	668.00	634.68	614.43	571.27	546.86	642.14
1983	593.90	587.98	610.19	623.74	628.51	665.16	642.00	612.44	670.70	850.07	900.68	671.40
1984	752.39	741.17	742.58	723.94	756.72	754.96	778.11	751.67	650.27	637.79	612.96	718.42
1985	648.39	621.38	609.88	602.63	599.07	605.19	575.75	564.16	549.26	513.99	512.87	582.05

	Nov	Dec	Jan	Feb	Mar	Apr	May	Jun	Jul	Aug	Sep
AVERAGE MOVE											
All Years		-7.22	-1.92	3.04	2.99	4.36	5.09	14.40	5.30	1.21	-12.14
Less Extremes		-7.79	1.44	3.49	2.38	7.99	-1.26	3.11	5.28	-7.21	-4.87
Ave Up - All Years		20.98	12.80	20.04	26.18	22.39	36.47	69.15	57.48	46.83	37.05
Ave Down - All Years		-21.32	-23.99	-16.39	-17.29	-22.68	-22.36	-22.10	-54.34	-38.71	-36.73
COUNT											
Number Up		5	9	8	7	9	7	6	8	7	5
Number Down		10	6	7	8	6	8	9	7	8	10
Pct Up		33.3%	60.0%	53.3%	46.7%	60.0%	46.7%	40.0%	53.3%	46.7%	33.3%
Pct Down		66.7%	40.0%	46.7%	53.3%	40.0%	53.3%	60.0%	46.7%	53.3%	66.7%
EXTREMES											
Greatest Up		44.27	41.15	64.00	57.17	39.99	150.55	221.71	159.95	179.37	56.85
Greatest Down		-51.27	-88.68	-63.71	-43.19	-78.46	-57.85	-46.23	-149.11	-67.57	-175.60
SEASONAL INDEX : AVERAGE PERCENTAGE METHOD											
All Years	98.4	97.3	96.9	97.5	98.1	98.8	99.9	102.8	104.0	104.2	102.1
Less Extremes	98.8	97.8	98.4	98.4	98.3	98.2	99.8	100.7	102.1	103.1	101.5
SEASONAL INDEX : LINK RELATIVE METHOD											
All Years		98.6	98.0	98.4	98.5	98.7	99.5	101.8	103.2	102.8	100.4
Less Extremes		98.7	98.8	99.1	99.3	100.3	100.1	100.9	102.3	100.9	99.5

SOYBEANS - SEPTEMBER - MONTH OF HIGH AND LOW

Year of Expiration	Nov	Dec	Jan	Feb	Mar	Apr	May	Jun	Jul	Aug	Sep
1971						L			H		
1972			H								L
1973	L							H			
1974							L			H	
1975	H							L			
1976					L						H
1977						H					L
1978				L			H				
1979	L							H			
1980						L					H
1981	H										L
1982	H										L
1983		L									H
1984							H				L
1985	H										L

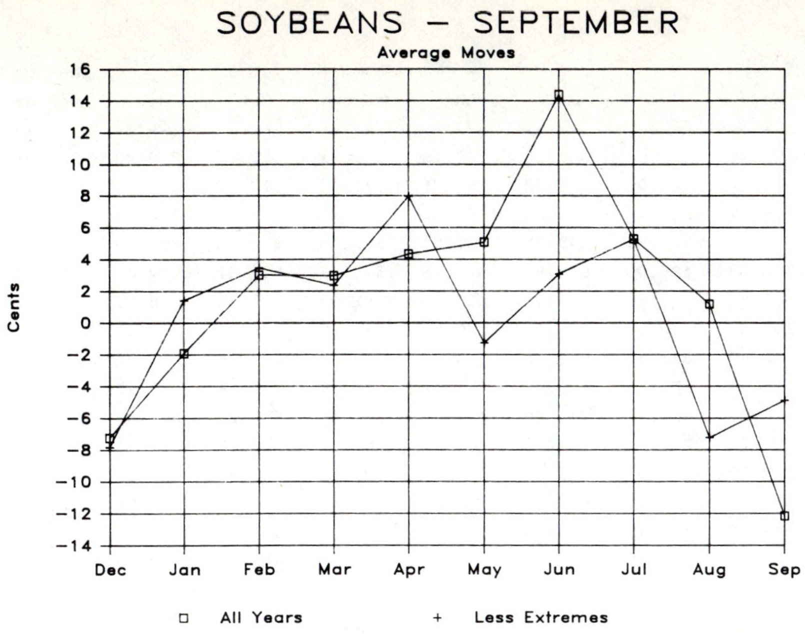
SOYBEANS – SEPTEMBER
Average Moves
Cents
16
14
12
10
8
6
4
2
0
–2
–4
–6
–8
–10
–12
–14
Dec
Jan
Feb
Mar
Apr
May
Jun
Jul
Aug
Sep
All Years
+ Less Extremes

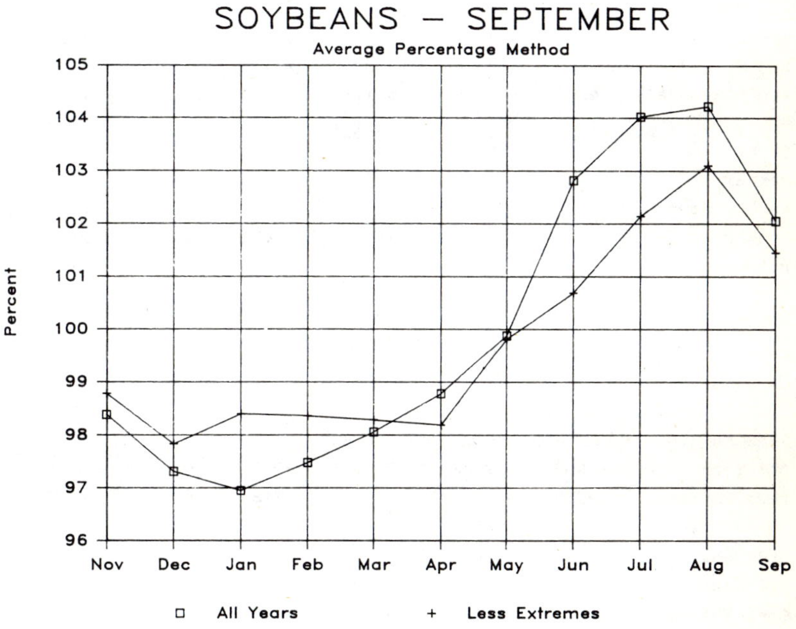
SOYBEANS – SEPTEMBER
Average Percentage Method
Percent
105
104
103
102
101
100
99
98
97
96
Nov
Dec
Jan
Feb
Mar
Apr
May
Jun
Jul
Aug
Sep
All Years
+ Less Extremes

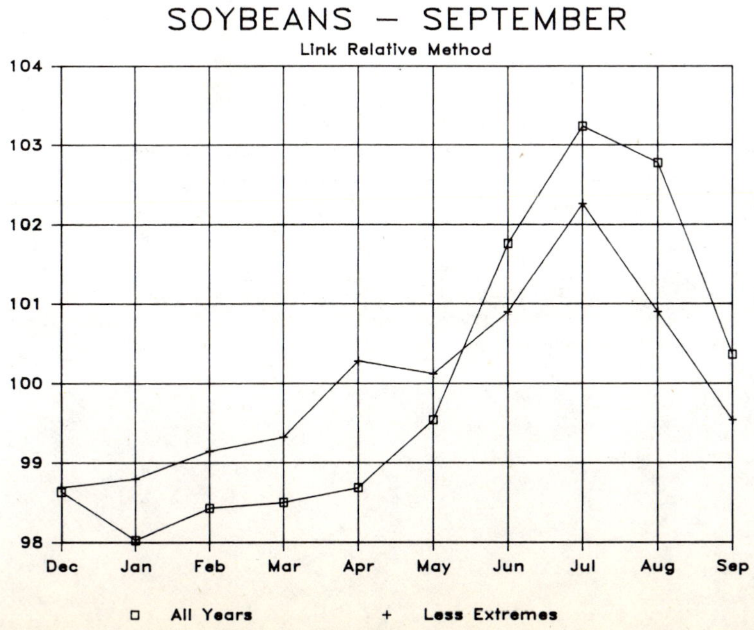
SOYBEANS – SEPTEMBER
Link Relative Method
104
103
102
101
100
99
98
Dec
Jan
Feb
Mar
Apr
May
Jun
Jul
Aug
Sep
All Years
+ Less Extremes

SOYBEANS - NOVEMBER - MONTHLY AVERAGE PRICE

Year of Expiration	Jan	Feb	Mar	Apr	May	Jun	Jul	Aug	Sep	Oct	Nov	Jan-Nov Average
1971	287.66	287.37	286.71	283.63	291.89	312.62	330.25	320.49	314.21	318.40	310.83	304.01
1972	300.80	301.16	312.73	321.27	319.44	321.65	321.73	331.26	339.40	340.47	365.05	325.00
1973	357.87	394.59	407.55	428.43	505.57	631.42	686.64	780.01	644.32	584.57	550.54	542.86
1974	621.57	629.76	616.11	538.02	535.69	545.34	708.25	781.07	768.15	858.83	800.00	672.98
1975	634.15	576.01	557.19	553.24	498.63	494.00	554.92	611.46	573.44	524.57	482.44	550.91
1976	504.67	508.53	502.26	504.45	543.85	648.49	696.94	650.65	681.02	641.25	658.52	594.60
1977	667.60	696.49	715.89	728.94	731.56	720.28	594.15	529.64	526.39	531.08	590.88	639.35
1978	576.27	575.87	611.77	618.53	630.65	633.68	608.43	623.04	650.96	683.74	670.75	625.79
1979	673.18	697.20	708.99	702.80	718.69	777.56	755.87	714.47	713.18	671.84	657.77	708.32
1980	728.89	728.80	690.56	652.49	655.02	664.30	770.86	782.86	838.61	857.23	899.07	751.70
1981	834.68	826.36	809.14	840.08	790.73	748.60	762.60	703.10	663.99	656.48	643.60	752.67
1982	676.39	675.83	646.71	674.93	672.20	640.61	618.16	577.47	548.41	532.45	560.56	620.34
1983	614.63	633.38	640.69	677.50	652.73	622.03	687.79	866.47	901.05	842.88	830.54	724.52
1984	716.89	710.58	732.76	723.35	732.98	726.43	638.56	636.22	610.58	613.84	618.29	678.22
1985	611.48	606.11	601.23	610.39	583.00	567.29	554.10	516.15	512.33	504.89	512.50	561.77

	Jan	Feb	Mar	Apr	May	Jun	Jul	Aug	Sep	Oct	Nov
AVERAGE MOVE											
All Years		2.75	-0.52	1.19	0.31	12.78	15.66	9.01	-9.22	-8.24	-0.75
Less Extremes		4.82	-0.42	4.54	-1.38	8.30	15.24	1.61	-4.49	-11.88	-0.94
Ave Up - All Years		17.26	17.30	17.40	20.95	41.78	59.06	62.51	31.35	22.18	26.23
Ave Down - All Years		-9.94	-16.11	-23.13	-23.29	-20.37	-49.43	-37.81	-29.51	-34.85	-24.35
COUNT											
Number Up		7	7	9	8	8	9	7	5	7	7
Number Down		8	8	6	7	7	6	8	10	8	8
Pct Up		46.7%	46.7%	60.0%	53.3%	53.3%	60.0%	46.7%	33.3%	46.7%	46.7%
Pct Down		53.3%	53.3%	40.0%	46.7%	46.7%	40.0%	53.3%	66.7%	53.3%	53.3%
EXTREMES											
Greatest Up		36.72	35.90	36.82	77.15	125.85	162.91	178.68	55.75	90.68	59.79
Greatest Down		-58.14	-38.24	-78.08	-54.61	-42.12	-126.13	-64.51	-135.69	-59.75	-58.83
SEASONAL INDEX : AVERAGE PERCENTAGE METHOD											
All Years	96.9	97.2	97.3	97.6	97.9	100.4	103.0	104.4	102.7	101.3	101.2
Less Extremes	97.9	98.2	97.9	97.8	98.0	100.7	102.0	103.1	102.6	100.6	101.0
SEASONAL INDEX : LINK RELATIVE METHOD											
All Years		98.2	97.9	97.7	97.8	100.1	103.0	103.8	101.8	100.0	99.7
Less Extremes		98.4	98.2	98.8	98.6	100.1	102.7	102.7	101.6	99.6	99.3

SOYBEANS - NOVEMBER - MONTH OF HIGH AND LOW

Year of Expiration	Jan	Feb	Mar	Apr	May	Jun	Jul	Aug	Sep	Oct	Nov
1971				L			H				
1972	L										H
1973	L							H			
1974					L					H	
1975	H										L
1976			L				H				
1977					H				L		
1978		L								H	
1979						H					L
1980				L							H
1981	H										L
1982	H									L	
1983	L								H		
1984					H				L		
1985	H									L	

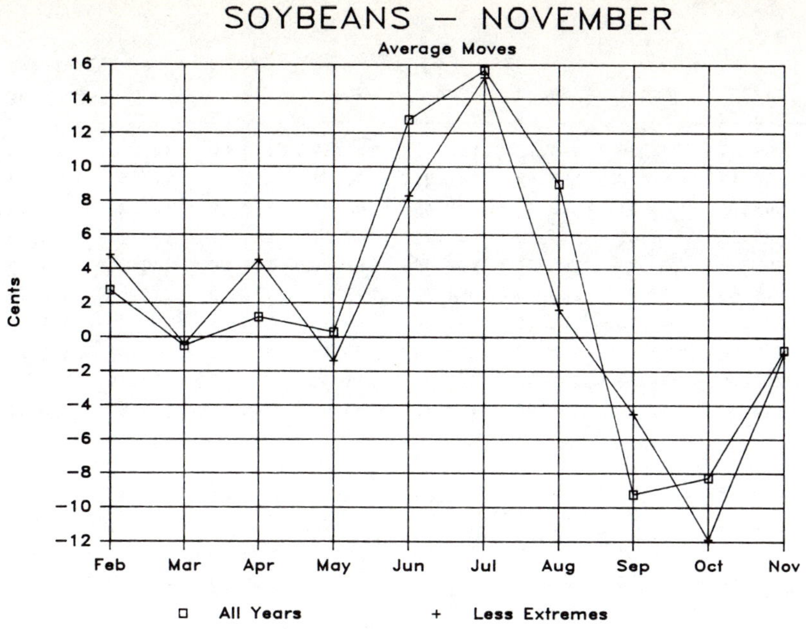
SOYBEANS – NOVEMBER
Average Moves
Cents
16
14
12
10
8
6
4
2
0
−2
−4
−6
−8
−10
−12
Feb
Mar
Apr
May
Jun
Jul
Aug
Sep
Oct
Nov
All Years
Less Extremes

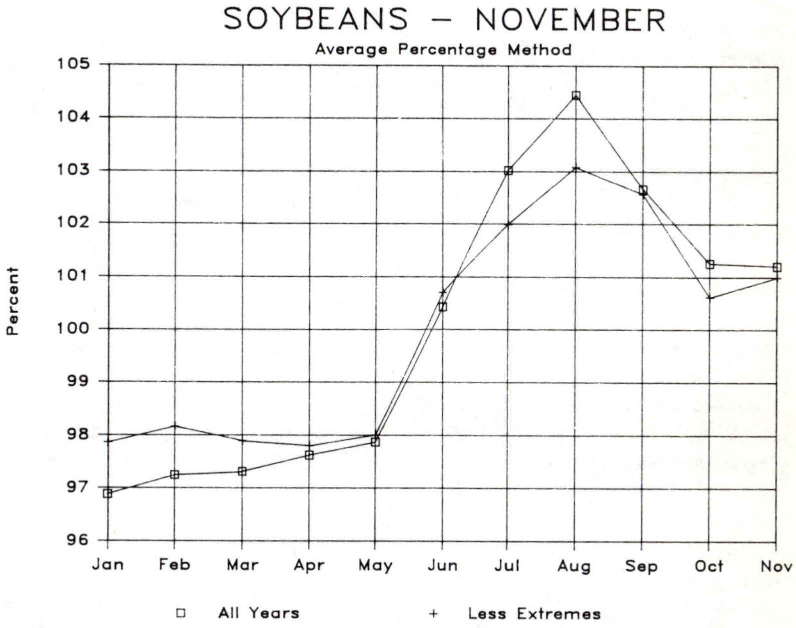
SOYBEANS – NOVEMBER
Average Percentage Method
Percent
105
104
103
102
101
100
99
98
97
96
Jan
Feb
Mar
Apr
May
Jun
Jul
Aug
Sep
Oct
Nov
All Years
Less Extremes

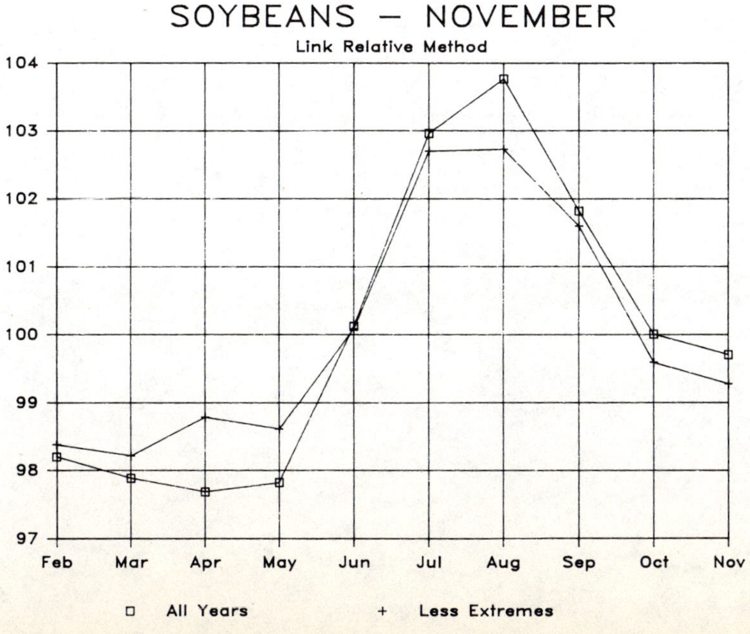
SOYBEANS – NOVEMBER
Link Relative Method
104
103
102
101
100
99
98
97
Feb
Mar
Apr
May
Jun
Jul
Aug
Sep
Oct
Nov
All Years
Less Extremes

SOYBEAN MEAL - JANUARY - MONTHLY AVERAGE PRICE

Year of Expiration	Mar	Apr	May	Jun	Jul	Aug	Sep	Oct	Nov	Dec	Jan	Mar-Jan Average
1976	139.71	140.73	129.10	130.61	139.90	152.96	145.71	137.13	131.12	130.60	132.74	137.30
1977	143.60	143.85	159.30	192.01	204.47	187.72	191.68	184.31	188.74	199.86	210.55	182.37
1978	193.92	193.82	193.03	194.03	163.01	144.01	143.43	146.46	165.44	159.22	159.23	168.69
1979	166.64	169.48	169.03	170.52	165.16	168.02	174.13	185.99	187.53	191.82	189.11	176.13
1980	195.85	193.68	196.89	214.98	207.35	196.76	196.21	190.06	192.46	189.80	182.22	196.02
1981	195.71	187.38	187.91	188.10	214.63	223.52	248.49	264.70	279.61	235.92	229.59	223.23
1982	235.74	247.24	232.94	220.89	221.59	206.98	197.48	194.24	190.60	186.86	190.29	211.35
1983	193.76	200.34	198.58	191.85	185.69	173.76	164.13	159.92	173.16	173.57	178.81	181.23
1984	196.30	204.65	195.41	185.15	202.09	241.30	241.77	235.36	233.91	219.60	204.49	214.55
1985	204.13	198.09	189.71	188.83	174.80	166.92	157.90	157.11	155.61	146.42	140.54	170.91

	Mar	Apr	May	Jun	Jul	Aug	Sep	Oct	Nov	Dec	Jan
AVERAGE MOVE											
All Years		1.39	-2.74	2.51	0.17	-1.67	-0.10	-0.57	4.29	-6.45	-1.61
Less Extremes		1.34	-3.56	0.55	0.77	-4.62	-2.04	-1.66	3.74	-3.99	-1.46
Ave Up - All Years		5.09	6.40	9.17	13.18	16.01	8.88	10.37	9.25	5.27	4.30
Ave Down - All Years		-4.16	-6.65	-7.48	-12.84	-13.46	-6.09	-5.25	-3.15	-11.47	-7.52
COUNT											
Number Up		6	3	6	5	4	4	3	6	3	5
Number Down		4	7	4	5	6	6	7	4	7	5
Pct Up		60.0%	30.0%	60.0%	50.0%	40.0%	40.0%	30.0%	60.0%	30.0%	50.0%
Pct Down		40.0%	70.0%	40.0%	50.0%	60.0%	60.0%	70.0%	40.0%	70.0%	50.0%
EXTREMES											
Greatest Up		11.50	15.45	32.71	26.53	39.21	24.97	16.21	18.98	11.12	10.69
Greatest Down		-8.32	-14.30	-12.04	-31.02	-19.00	-9.63	-8.59	-6.00	-43.69	-15.11
SEASONAL INDEX : AVERAGE PERCENTAGE METHOD											
All Years	100.7	101.4	99.8	101.3	101.0	100.0	99.6	99.1	101.3	98.3	97.6
Less Extremes	101.1	102.3	100.0	101.8	100.5	100.2	99.7	98.2	99.7	98.4	97.3
SEASONAL INDEX : LINK RELATIVE METHOD											
All Years		99.5	98.4	100.4	100.9	100.3	100.0	99.7	102.2	99.6	99.0
Less Extremes		100.7	99.4	100.2	101.4	99.9	99.2	98.9	101.3	99.6	99.3

SOYBEAN MEAL - JANUARY - MONTH OF HIGH AND LOW

Year of Expiration	Mar	Apr	May	Jun	Jul	Aug	Sep	Oct	Nov	Dec	Jan
1976			L			H					
1977	L										H
1978				H			L				
1979					L					H	
1980				H							L
1981		L							H		
1982		H								L	
1983		H						L			
1984				L			H				
1985	H										L

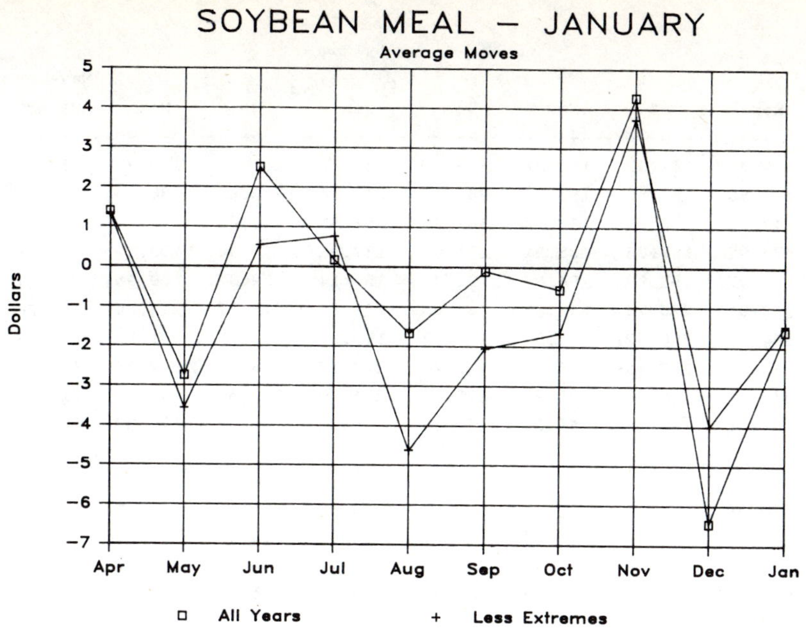
SOYBEAN MEAL — JANUARY
Average Moves
Dollars
5
4
3
2
1
0
−1
−2
−3
−4
−5
−6
−7
Apr
May
Jun
Jul
Aug
Sep
Oct
Nov
Dec
Jan
All Years
Less Extremes

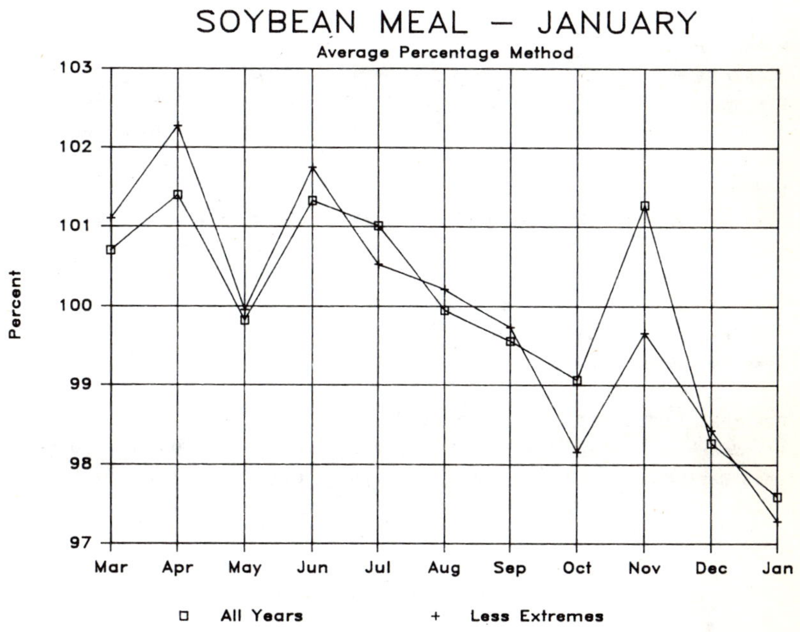
SOYBEAN MEAL — JANUARY
Average Percentage Method
Percent
103
102
101
100
99
98
97
Mar
Apr
May
Jun
Jul
Aug
Sep
Oct
Nov
Dec
Jan
All Years
Less Extremes

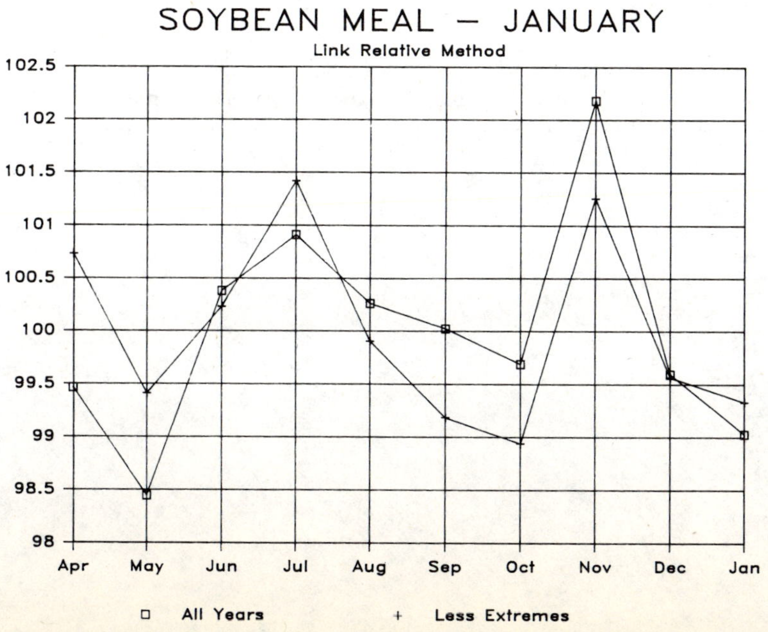
SOYBEAN MEAL — JANUARY
Link Relative Method
102.5
102
101.5
101
100.5
100
99.5
99
98.5
98
Apr
May
Jun
Jul
Aug
Sep
Oct
Nov
Dec
Jan
All Years
Less Extremes

SOYBEAN MEAL - MARCH - MONTHLY AVERAGE PRICE

Year of Expiration	May	Jun	Jul	Aug	Sep	Oct	Nov	Dec	Jan	Feb	Mar	May-Mar Average
1976	132.14	133.13	143.60	157.10	149.25	139.97	133.27	133.23	135.39	137.56	133.21	138.90
1977	160.68	192.35	205.55	188.96	192.86	186.55	190.28	202.47	212.14	212.82	230.98	197.78
1978	194.87	196.46	166.31	147.56	147.32	150.73	168.72	162.05	157.61	150.48	171.81	164.90
1979	171.22	172.70	167.71	170.55	175.97	187.04	188.51	191.05	189.82	196.98	193.89	182.31
1980	199.73	217.25	208.87	199.34	199.97	193.93	194.99	191.47	185.14	179.87	169.96	194.59
1981	192.09	192.27	218.01	225.38	252.01	270.24	286.67	245.05	229.97	215.77	205.65	230.28
1982	239.76	227.70	228.88	213.63	204.21	200.52	195.54	188.88	190.57	187.77	181.82	205.39
1983	202.82	196.32	189.93	177.69	167.36	162.63	174.63	173.77	179.22	176.98	172.24	179.42
1984	200.33	189.12	206.35	241.98	243.65	236.97	235.94	221.26	201.99	190.51	200.41	215.32
1985	192.20	191.85	177.96	169.98	162.21	162.88	161.81	152.25	144.32	132.35	129.33	161.56
AVERAGE MOVE												
All Years		2.33	0.40	-2.10	0.26	-0.33	3.89	-6.89	-3.53	-4.51	0.82	
Less Extremes		0.46	1.05	-4.74	-1.71	-1.54	3.45	-4.93	-3.21	-4.76	-0.37	
Ave Up - All Years		8.90	13.57	14.84	7.65	8.34	8.78	7.37	4.74	3.33	16.46	
Ave Down - All Years		-7.53	-12.76	-13.39	-7.12	-6.12	-3.44	-10.45	-9.05	-7.87	-5.88	
COUNT												
Number Up		6	5	4	5	4	6	2	4	3	3	
Number Down		4	5	6	5	6	4	8	6	7	7	
Pct Up		60.0%	50.0%	40.0%	50.0%	40.0%	60.0%	20.0%	40.0%	30.0%	30.0%	
Pct Down		40.0%	50.0%	60.0%	50.0%	60.0%	40.0%	80.0%	60.0%	70.0%	70.0%	
EXTREMES												
Greatest Up		31.67	25.75	35.63	26.62	18.23	17.99	12.19	9.67	7.16	21.32	
Greatest Down		-12.06	-30.15	-18.75	-10.33	-9.28	-6.70	-41.62	-19.27	-14.20	-10.12	
SEASONAL INDEX : AVERAGE PERCENTAGE METHOD												
All Years	101.6	102.9	102.5	101.3	100.9	100.5	102.5	99.2	97.5	95.3	95.8	
Less Extremes	102.0	103.3	102.8	101.3	100.8	99.7	100.6	99.2	97.3	95.3	95.1	
SEASONAL INDEX : LINK RELATIVE METHOD												
All Years		99.7	100.7	100.1	100.4	100.5	103.0	100.5	99.4	97.4	98.3	
Less Extremes		100.0	101.6	100.3	99.9	100.1	102.4	100.5	99.6	97.8	98.0	

SOYBEAN MEAL - MARCH - MONTH OF HIGH AND LOW

Year of Expiration	May	Jun	Jul	Aug	Sep	Oct	Nov	Dec	Jan	Feb	Mar
1976	L			H							
1977	L										H
1978		H			L						
1979			L							H	
1980		H									L
1981	L						H				
1982	H										L
1983	H					L					
1984		L			H						
1985	H										L

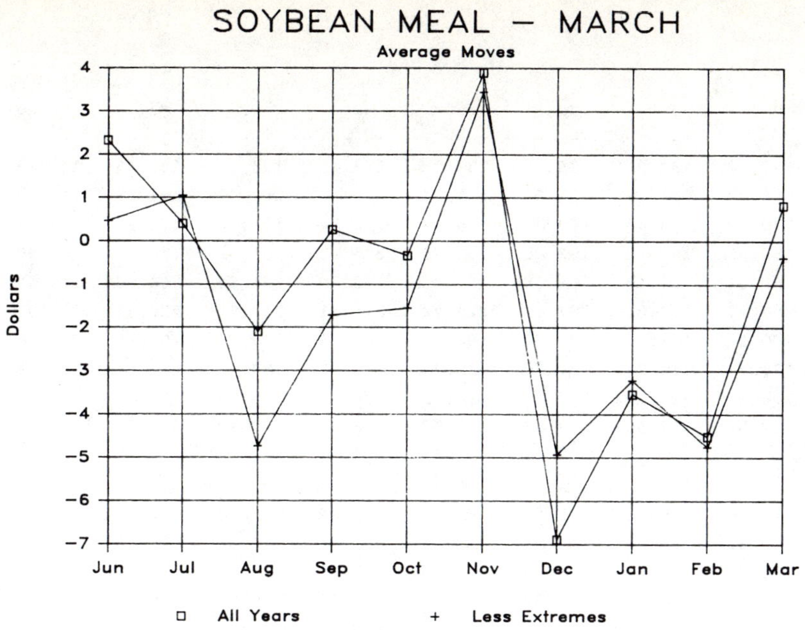
SOYBEAN MEAL — MARCH
Average Moves
Dollars
4
3
2
1
0
−1
−2
−3
−4
−5
−6
−7
Jun
Jul
Aug
Sep
Oct
Nov
Dec
Jan
Feb
Mar
□ All Years
+ Less Extremes

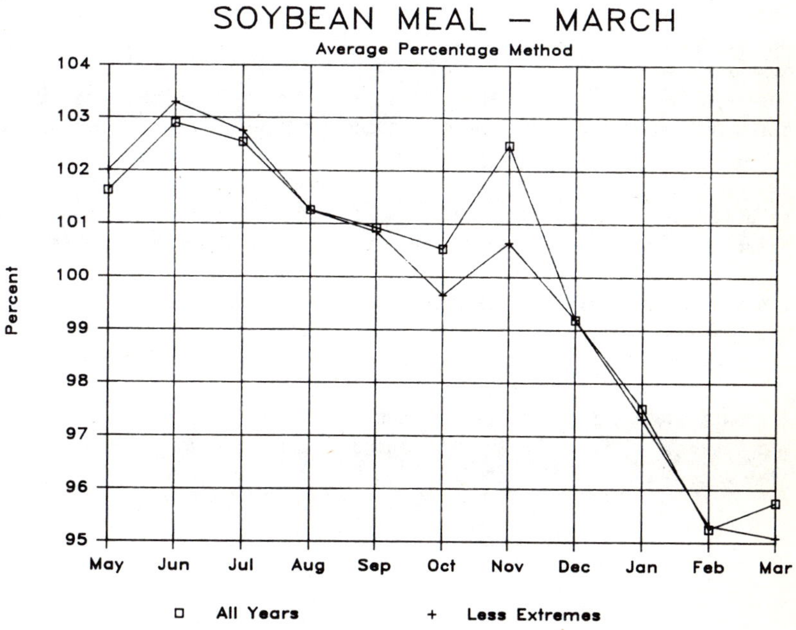
SOYBEAN MEAL — MARCH
Average Percentage Method
Percent
104
103
102
101
100
99
98
97
96
95
May
Jun
Jul
Aug
Sep
Oct
Nov
Dec
Jan
Feb
Mar
□ All Years
+ Less Extremes

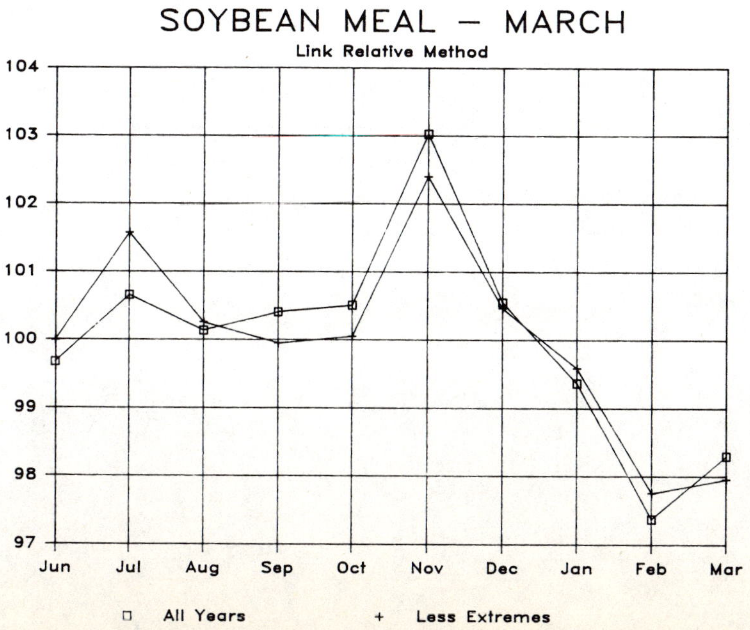
SOYBEAN MEAL — MARCH
Link Relative Method
104
103
102
101
100
99
98
97
Jun
Jul
Aug
Sep
Oct
Nov
Dec
Jan
Feb
Mar
□ All Years
+ Less Extremes

SOYBEAN MEAL - MAY - MONTHLY AVERAGE PRICE

Year of Expiration	Jul	Aug	Sep	Oct	Nov	Dec	Jan	Feb	Mar	Apr	May	Jul-May Average
1976	145.16	159.63	151.38	140.49	132.02	132.03	135.56	137.25	133.41	133.18	147.46	140.69
1977	207.01	190.09	193.31	187.11	188.72	200.76	212.97	215.24	238.15	282.40	264.55	216.39
1978	168.00	150.17	149.80	153.16	170.69	164.44	160.41	154.44	176.34	177.75	176.94	163.83
1979	168.59	172.17	177.17	187.25	187.06	189.45	190.06	200.35	200.41	194.61	188.83	186.90
1980	209.14	201.20	202.79	197.29	197.14	194.45	189.48	185.72	173.35	164.38	168.96	189.45
1981	220.15	226.46	251.78	271.18	288.39	252.83	237.68	224.72	214.71	224.51	220.32	239.34
1982	231.97	218.28	210.28	206.22	200.11	191.38	192.50	188.65	183.79	189.86	191.16	200.38
1983	194.81	182.06	170.87	164.61	175.73	174.75	180.79	180.72	180.63	188.67	181.86	179.59
1984	210.19	242.31	244.63	236.71	234.87	221.29	203.87	194.93	204.91	195.34	189.95	216.27
1985	180.84	174.29	167.17	168.06	167.39	157.60	149.85	138.27	135.62	128.39	121.76	153.57

	Jul	Aug	Sep	Oct	Nov	Dec	Jan	Feb	Mar	Apr	May
AVERAGE MOVE											
All Years		-1.92	0.25	-0.71	3.00	-6.31	-2.58	-3.29	2.10	3.78	-2.73
Less Extremes		-4.19	-1.45	-1.95	2.62	-4.95	-2.58	-3.78	1.31	0.38	-2.96
Ave Up - All Years		14.12	7.49	8.43	11.87	4.82	4.70	4.75	13.71	13.91	6.72
Ave Down - All Years		-12.61	-6.98	-6.80	-2.91	-11.08	-9.87	-6.73	-5.64	-6.36	-6.78
COUNT											
Number Up		4	5	4	4	3	5	3	4	5	3
Number Down		6	5	6	6	7	5	7	6	5	7
Pct Up		40.0%	50.0%	40.0%	40.0%	30.0%	50.0%	30.0%	40.0%	50.0%	30.0%
Pct Down		60.0%	50.0%	60.0%	60.0%	70.0%	50.0%	70.0%	60.0%	50.0%	70.0%
EXTREMES											
Greatest Up		32.13	25.32	19.40	17.53	12.05	12.21	10.29	22.91	44.25	14.28
Greatest Down		-17.84	-11.19	-10.89	-8.47	-35.56	-17.42	-12.95	-12.37	-9.56	-17.85
SEASONAL INDEX : AVERAGE PERCENTAGE METHOD											
All Years	103.3	102.2	101.7	101.1	102.5	99.4	98.2	96.5	97.6	99.2	98.1
Less Extremes	103.1	102.6	101.9	101.4	102.2	99.5	98.3	96.0	97.2	97.2	97.4
SEASONAL INDEX : LINK RELATIVE METHOD											
All Years		100.7	100.8	100.5	102.3	99.8	99.0	97.6	98.9	100.5	99.9
Less Extremes		100.7	100.5	100.3	102.1	100.1	99.6	98.3	99.4	100.0	98.9

SOYBEAN MEAL - MAY - MONTH OF HIGH AND LOW

Year of Expiration	Jul	Aug	Sep	Oct	Nov	Dec	Jan	Feb	Mar	Apr	May
1976		H			L						
1977				L						H	
1978			L							H	
1979	L								H		
1980	H									L	
1981					H				L		
1982	H								L		
1983	H			L							
1984			H								L
1985	H										L

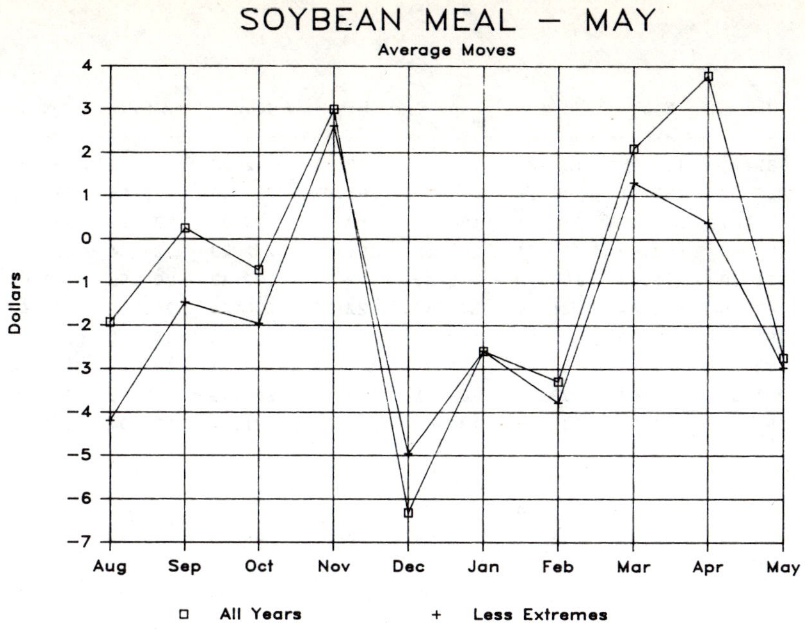
SOYBEAN MEAL — MAY
Average Moves
Dollars
4
3
2
1
0
−1
−2
−3
−4
−5
−6
−7
Aug
Sep
Oct
Nov
Dec
Jan
Feb
Mar
Apr
May
□ All Years
+ Less Extremes

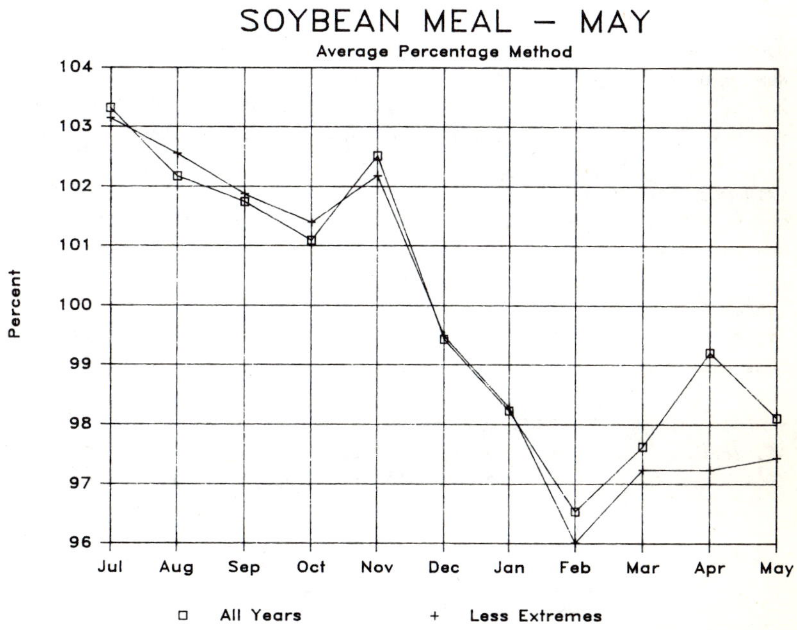
SOYBEAN MEAL — MAY
Average Percentage Method
Percent
104
103
102
101
100
99
98
97
96
Jul
Aug
Sep
Oct
Nov
Dec
Jan
Feb
Mar
Apr
May
□ All Years
+ Less Extremes

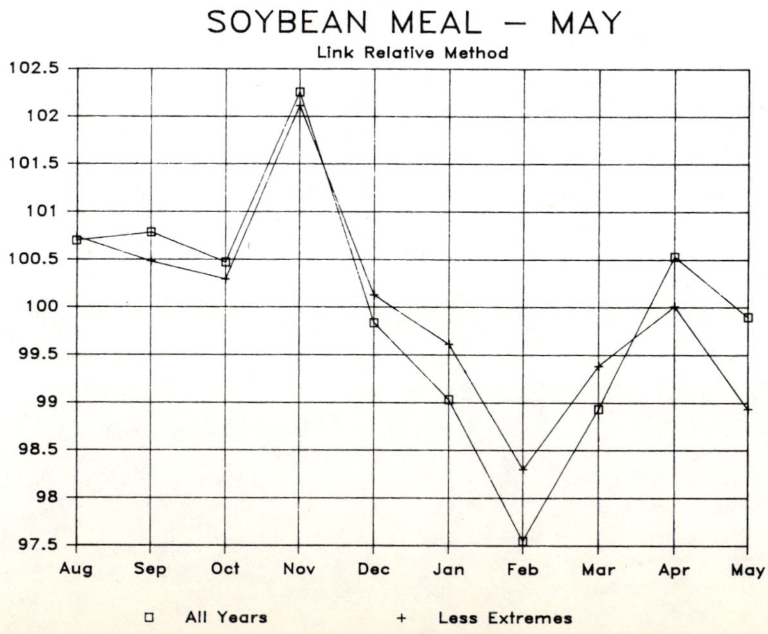
SOYBEAN MEAL — MAY
Link Relative Method
102.5
102
101.5
101
100.5
100
99.5
99
98.5
98
97.5
Aug
Sep
Oct
Nov
Dec
Jan
Feb
Mar
Apr
May
□ All Years
+ Less Extremes

SOYBEAN MEAL - JULY - MONTHLY AVERAGE PRICE

Year of Expiration	Sep	Oct	Nov	Dec	Jan	Feb	Mar	Apr	May	Jun	Jul	Sep-Jul Average
1976	155.09	143.33	134.71	135.08	137.91	139.28	135.80	136.47	158.11	192.90	206.04	152.25
1977	193.54	186.86	186.06	199.06	212.23	215.81	240.37	284.27	264.07	224.46	169.55	216.02
1978	152.11	155.83	172.97	166.94	162.84	157.30	178.44	180.44	180.08	173.97	171.77	168.42
1979	178.32	187.59	187.21	189.05	190.69	202.99	203.64	199.15	194.94	211.29	206.54	195.58
1980	205.74	200.74	200.09	198.25	194.40	191.47	180.15	172.20	173.70	172.42	201.50	190.06
1981	251.65	271.40	289.62	258.71	243.36	231.84	221.74	232.52	222.17	206.06	206.62	239.61
1982	216.08	211.86	204.44	193.84	194.94	192.00	186.68	192.37	190.32	182.55	180.10	195.01
1983	173.98	166.74	176.85	175.66	182.66	184.33	184.55	191.98	184.03	174.71	184.35	179.98
1984	245.49	236.74	233.96	221.09	205.65	198.63	209.33	200.81	197.63	183.99	167.76	209.19
1985	170.96	172.80	172.92	162.60	155.02	144.08	141.43	134.40	124.36	121.77	125.94	147.84
AVERAGE MOVE												
All Years		-0.91	2.49	-5.85	-2.06	-2.20	2.44	4.25	-3.52	-4.53	-2.39	
Less Extremes		-2.13	1.91	-5.08	-2.29	-2.85	1.40	0.89	-4.58	-5.06	0.23	
Ave Up - All Years		8.64	11.40	5.07	5.15	4.73	11.46	11.75	11.57	25.57	11.32	
Ave Down - All Years		-7.27	-3.45	-10.54	-9.26	-6.82	-6.57	-7.00	-7.29	-12.05	-16.11	
COUNT												
Number Up		4	4	3	5	4	5	6	2	2	5	
Number Down		6	6	7	5	6	5	4	8	8	5	
Pct Up		40.0%	40.0%	30.0%	50.0%	40.0%	50.0%	60.0%	20.0%	20.0%	50.0%	
Pct Down		60.0%	60.0%	70.0%	50.0%	60.0%	50.0%	40.0%	80.0%	80.0%	50.0%	
EXTREMES												
Greatest Up		19.75	18.22	13.00	13.17	12.30	24.56	43.90	21.63	34.79	29.08	
Greatest Down		-11.76	-8.63	-30.91	-15.44	-11.52	-11.32	-8.52	-20.20	-39.61	-54.90	
SEASONAL INDEX : AVERAGE PERCENTAGE METHOD												
All Years	102.7	101.9	103.1	100.2	99.1	97.9	99.2	101.0	99.5	98.0	97.4	
Less Extremes	102.5	102.0	103.0	100.4	99.5	98.0	98.9	98.6	98.6	96.3	95.0	
SEASONAL INDEX : LINK RELATIVE METHOD												
All Years		100.2	101.7	99.6	99.1	98.2	99.8	101.7	100.8	99.6	99.4	
Less Extremes		100.6	102.1	100.2	99.9	99.2	100.5	101.5	99.7	97.7	98.6	

SOYBEAN MEAL - JULY - MONTH OF HIGH AND LOW

Year of Expiration	Sep	Oct	Nov	Dec	Jan	Feb	Mar	Apr	May	Jun	Jul
1976			L								H
1977								H			L
1978	L							H			
1979	L										H
1980	H							L			
1981			H							L	
1982	H										L
1983		L						H			
1984	H										L
1985			H							L	

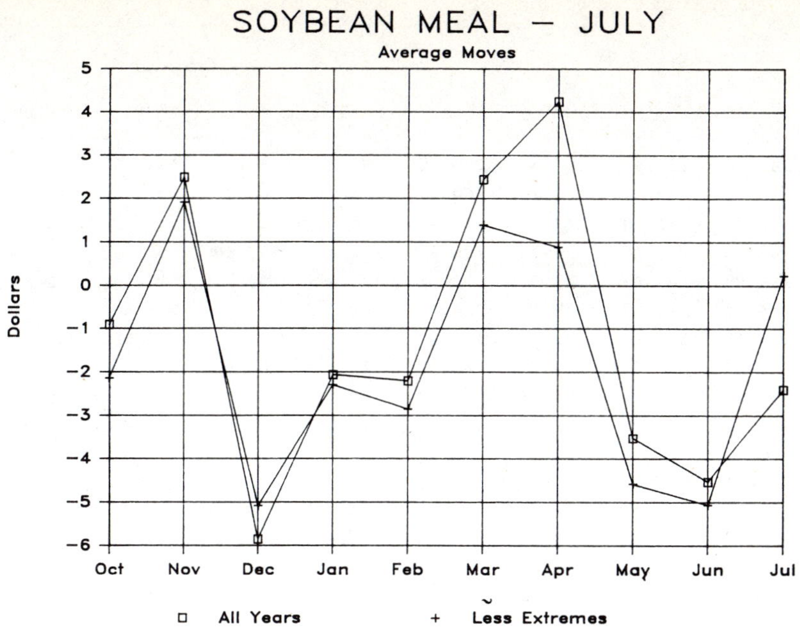
SOYBEAN MEAL — JULY
Average Moves
Dollars
5
4
3
2
1
0
−1
−2
−3
−4
−5
−6
Oct
Nov
Dec
Jan
Feb
Mar
Apr
May
Jun
Jul
All Years
Less Extremes

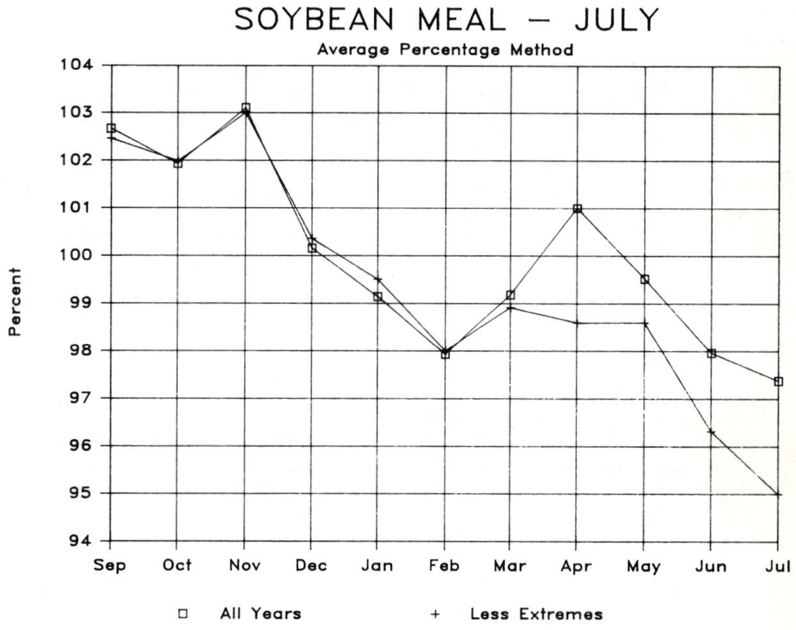
SOYBEAN MEAL — JULY
Average Percentage Method
Percent
104
103
102
101
100
99
98
97
96
95
94
Sep
Oct
Nov
Dec
Jan
Feb
Mar
Apr
May
Jun
Jul
All Years
Less Extremes

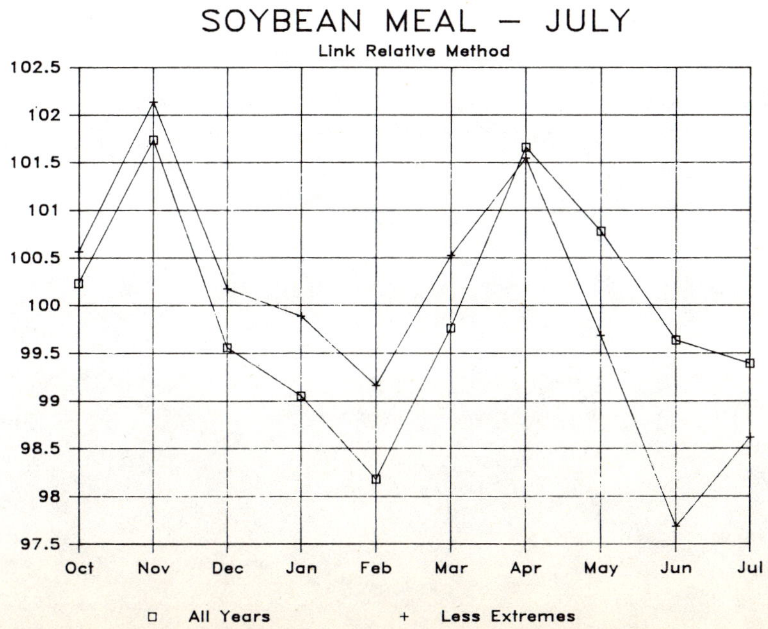
SOYBEAN MEAL — JULY
Link Relative Method
102.5
102
101.5
101
100.5
100
99.5
99
98.5
98
97.5
Oct
Nov
Dec
Jan
Feb
Mar
Apr
May
Jun
Jul
All Years
Less Extremes

SOYBEAN MEAL - AUGUST - MONTHLY AVERAGE PRICE

Year of Expiration	Oct	Nov	Dec	Jan	Feb	Mar	Apr	May	Jun	Jul	Aug	Oct-Aug Average
1976	144.67	136.26	136.51	139.28	140.46	137.33	137.85	158.06	192.67	199.40	178.60	154.64
1977	212.26	184.34	196.40	210.81	215.35	238.30	280.41	260.90	225.51	166.79	143.79	212.26
1978	157.21	174.29	168.16	163.27	158.33	178.32	179.51	179.42	174.89	168.58	163.29	169.57
1979	186.50	186.60	188.50	191.07	202.12	203.46	199.75	196.42	212.41	203.80	190.09	196.43
1980	202.43	202.01	200.55	196.57	194.09	183.29	175.51	176.38	175.47	202.74	210.16	192.65
1981	267.97	281.93	257.17	244.45	234.55	224.67	235.33	223.42	208.21	207.29	201.56	235.14
1982	213.71	205.23	194.22	195.63	193.22	188.10	193.54	191.19	183.16	178.73	168.58	191.39
1983	166.17	176.65	175.61	183.02	185.67	186.53	193.98	185.53	175.87	189.91	232.19	186.46
1984	226.58	224.78	216.34	204.86	199.31	209.82	202.08	198.93	187.05	165.47	156.21	199.22
1985	172.10	173.93	163.91	156.90	146.72	144.23	137.33	127.34	124.64	125.71	122.93	145.07

	Oct	Nov	Dec	Jan	Feb	Mar	Apr	May	Jun	Jul	Aug
AVERAGE MOVE											
All Years		-0.36	-4.87	-1.15	-1.61	2.43	4.12	-3.77	-3.77	-5.15	-4.10
Less Extremes		0.91	-4.50	-1.65	-2.12	1.51	0.86	-4.80	-4.61	-2.50	-7.54
Ave Up - All Years		8.69	4.73	5.71	4.85	11.13	11.23	10.54	25.30	12.28	24.85
Ave Down - All Years		-9.40	-8.98	-8.01	-5.91	-6.28	-6.54	-7.35	-11.04	-16.76	-11.34
COUNT											
Number Up		5	3	5	4	5	6	2	2	4	2
Number Down		5	7	5	6	5	4	8	8	6	8
Pct Up		50.0%	30.0%	50.0%	40.0%	50.0%	60.0%	20.0%	20.0%	40.0%	20.0%
Pct Down		50.0%	70.0%	50.0%	60.0%	50.0%	40.0%	80.0%	80.0%	60.0%	80.0%
EXTREMES											
Greatest Up		17.08	12.06	14.41	11.05	22.96	42.10	20.20	34.61	27.27	42.28
Greatest Down		-27.92	-24.76	-12.71	-10.18	-10.80	-7.78	-19.50	-35.39	-58.72	-23.00
SEASONAL INDEX : AVERAGE PERCENTAGE METHOD											
All Years	103.3	103.2	100.7	100.0	99.1	100.4	102.1	100.5	99.2	96.9	94.7
Less Extremes	103.2	103.2	100.7	100.3	99.6	100.3	100.0	99.2	97.6	95.2	94.3
SEASONAL INDEX : LINK RELATIVE METHOD											
All Years		99.9	98.5	98.7	98.5	100.4	102.6	101.9	101.4	100.0	98.1
Less Extremes		100.1	98.9	99.3	99.4	101.3	102.8	101.3	100.0	99.9	96.9

SOYBEAN MEAL - AUGUST - MONTH OF HIGH AND LOW

Year of Expiration	Oct	Nov	Dec	Jan	Feb	Mar	Apr	May	Jun	Jul	Aug
1976		L								H	
1977							H				L
1978	L						H				
1979	L								H		
1980									L		H
1981		H									L
1982	H										L
1983	L										H
1984	H										L
1985		H									L

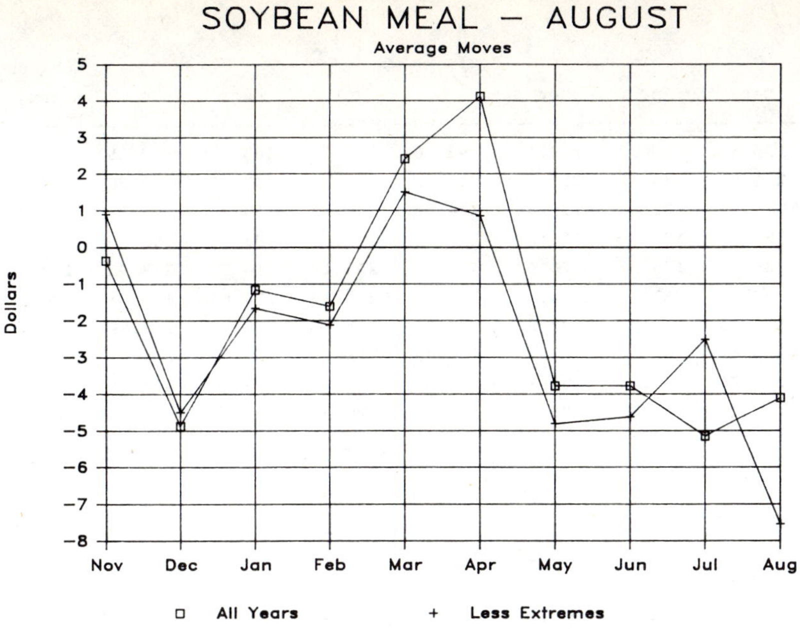
SOYBEAN MEAL — AUGUST
Average Moves
Dollars
5
4
3
2
1
0
−1
−2
−3
−4
−5
−6
−7
−8
Nov
Dec
Jan
Feb
Mar
Apr
May
Jun
Jul
Aug
All Years
+ Less Extremes

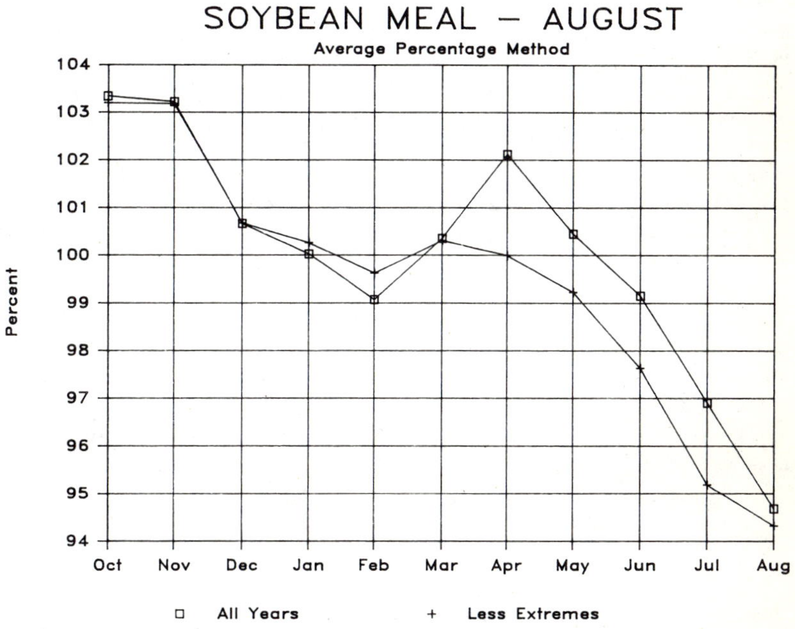
SOYBEAN MEAL — AUGUST
Average Percentage Method
Percent
104
103
102
101
100
99
98
97
96
95
94
Oct
Nov
Dec
Jan
Feb
Mar
Apr
May
Jun
Jul
Aug
All Years
+ Less Extremes

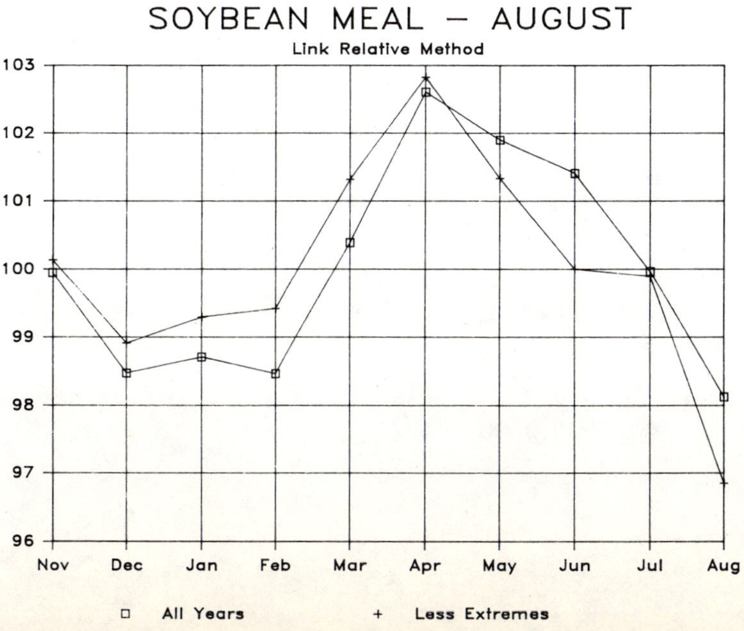
SOYBEAN MEAL — AUGUST
Link Relative Method
103
102
101
100
99
98
97
96
Nov
Dec
Jan
Feb
Mar
Apr
May
Jun
Jul
Aug
All Years
+ Less Extremes

SOYBEAN MEAL - SEPTEMBER - MONTHLY AVERAGE PRICE

Year of Expiration	Nov	Dec	Jan	Feb	Mar	Apr	May	Jun	Jul	Aug	Sep	Nov-Sep Average
1976	136.85	137.45	139.81	141.07	138.61	139.18	158.34	192.46	200.79	183.32	192.59	160.04
1977	177.34	189.91	202.81	207.44	221.06	234.98	226.78	212.11	165.75	142.17	139.80	192.74
1978	171.27	164.79	161.90	158.35	171.15	173.84	175.88	174.95	167.73	165.44	169.99	168.66
1979	185.30	187.34	190.55	198.02	200.24	197.50	195.82	212.72	204.22	191.48	188.70	195.63
1980	204.05	202.98	199.39	197.04	186.38	178.37	178.93	178.35	205.41	214.38	237.93	198.47
1981	263.34	249.18	244.21	237.22	227.67	237.89	224.84	210.61	209.79	196.80	190.20	226.52
1982	206.19	194.93	196.19	194.71	189.05	195.05	192.57	184.46	178.74	166.20	157.92	186.91
1983	177.07	176.19	183.86	186.65	188.42	196.22	187.36	177.43	192.13	236.59	238.67	194.60
1984	212.01	208.21	200.18	196.67	206.54	200.24	194.94	187.89	167.93	156.78	148.68	189.09
1985	174.91	165.27	158.35	149.11	146.25	139.81	130.12	127.34	128.46	124.23	129.85	143.06

AVERAGE MOVE	Nov	Dec	Jan	Feb	Mar	Apr	May	Jun	Jul	Aug	Sep
All Years		-3.21	0.10	-1.10	0.91	1.77	-2.75	-0.73	-3.74	-4.36	1.69
Less Extremes		-3.81	-0.48	-1.15	0.77	1.47	-4.20	-3.34	-2.26	-8.05	0.21
Ave Up - All Years		5.07	5.48	4.04	8.06	6.86	7.25	25.51	12.80	26.72	9.01
Ave Down - All Years		-6.75	-5.28	-4.52	-6.24	-5.87	-7.03	-7.29	-14.76	-12.12	-5.63
COUNT											
Number Up		3	5	4	5	6	3	2	4	2	5
Number Down		7	5	6	5	4	7	8	6	8	5
Pct Up		30.0%	50.0%	40.0%	50.0%	60.0%	30.0%	20.0%	40.0%	20.0%	50.0%
Pct Down		70.0%	50.0%	60.0%	50.0%	40.0%	70.0%	80.0%	60.0%	80.0%	50.0%
EXTREMES											
Greatest Up		12.57	12.91	7.47	13.62	13.91	19.15	34.13	27.06	44.46	23.55
Greatest Down		-14.16	-8.03	-9.24	-10.65	-8.01	-13.05	-14.67	-46.37	-23.58	-8.27
SEASONAL INDEX : AVERAGE PERCENTAGE METHOD											
All Years	102.9	101.1	101.0	100.3	100.9	101.7	100.4	100.4	98.4	95.9	97.0
Less Extremes	102.6	101.2	101.5	100.9	101.0	101.0	99.5	99.3	96.6	95.5	96.9
SEASONAL INDEX : LINK RELATIVE METHOD											
All Years		99.6	100.0	99.7	100.6	101.6	100.9	101.3	100.0	97.7	98.7
Less Extremes		99.5	100.1	100.3	101.5	102.9	101.5	100.4	100.1	96.4	97.3

SOYBEAN MEAL - SEPTEMBER - MONTH OF HIGH AND LOW

Year of Expiration	Nov	Dec	Jan	Feb	Mar	Apr	May	Jun	Jul	Aug	Sep
1976	L								H		
1977						H					L
1978				L			H				
1979	L							H			
1980								L			H
1981	H										L
1982	H										L
1983		L									H
1984	H										L
1985	H									L	

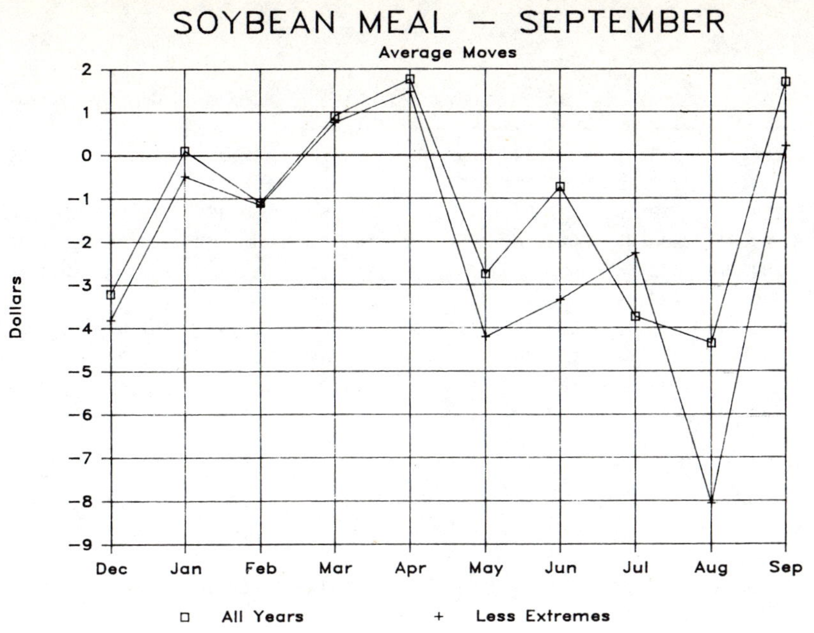

SOYBEAN MEAL — SEPTEMBER
Average Moves
Dollars
2
1
0
−1
−2
−3
−4
−5
−6
−7
−8
−9
Dec
Jan
Feb
Mar
Apr
May
Jun
Jul
Aug
Sep
□ All Years
+ Less Extremes

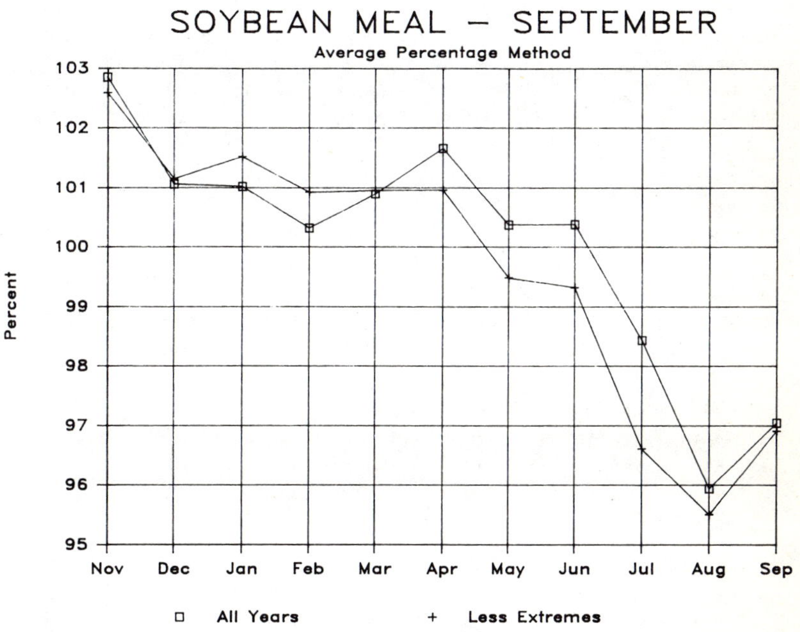

SOYBEAN MEAL — SEPTEMBER
Average Percentage Method
Percent
103
102
101
100
99
98
97
96
95
Nov
Dec
Jan
Feb
Mar
Apr
May
Jun
Jul
Aug
Sep
□ All Years
+ Less Extremes

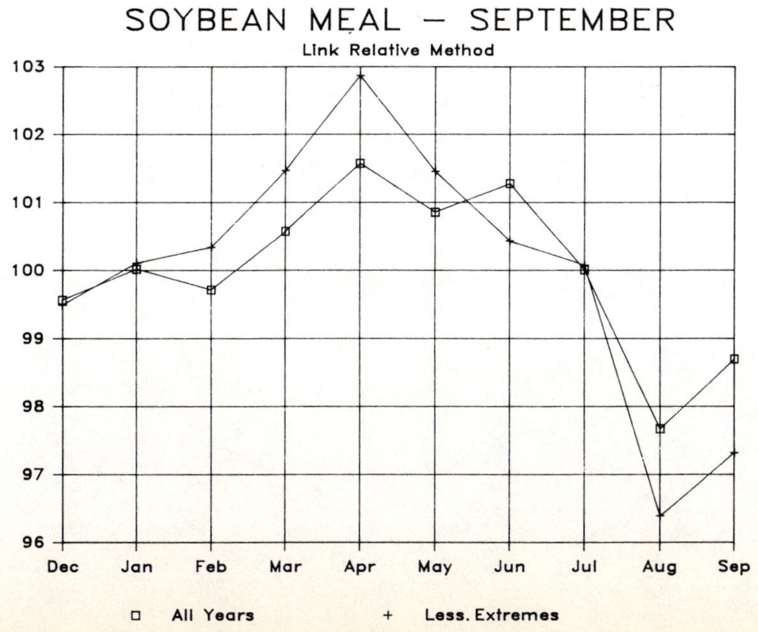

SOYBEAN MEAL — SEPTEMBER
Link Relative Method
103
102
101
100
99
98
97
96
Dec
Jan
Feb
Mar
Apr
May
Jun
Jul
Aug
Sep
□ All Years
+ Less. Extremes

SOYBEAN MEAL - OCTOBER - MONTHLY AVERAGE PRICE

Year of Expiration	Dec	Jan	Feb	Mar	Apr	May	Jun	Jul	Aug	Sep	Oct	Dec-Oct Average
1976	166.09	139.57	141.54	139.63	140.27	157.91	191.82	201.77	184.48	187.35	176.59	166.09
1977	179.29	191.73	197.13	197.08	204.61	201.30	197.57	160.51	140.29	138.29	138.71	176.95
1978	163.65	160.22	157.96	164.98	168.67	170.16	172.76	166.15	165.85	170.23	178.54	167.20
1979	184.28	188.08	192.98	195.79	193.00	194.27	212.44	204.39	192.31	189.99	186.77	194.03
1980	204.95	201.40	199.21	189.32	180.94	181.56	181.18	207.73	217.14	240.26	246.69	204.58
1981	239.34	240.90	237.71	230.08	240.42	225.89	212.29	212.26	197.85	187.65	184.72	219.01
1982	194.78	196.60	195.54	189.75	195.54	193.08	185.25	178.79	166.31	156.90	152.47	182.27
1983	174.82	183.62	187.91	189.86	198.08	188.78	178.70	194.46	237.44	236.81	230.31	200.07
1984	189.00	192.42	193.79	201.47	194.93	187.00	183.83	168.37	159.04	149.02	147.60	178.77
1985	166.32	159.25	151.83	148.89	142.94	132.90	129.92	130.78	125.49	130.02	138.81	141.56

	Dec	Jan	Feb	Mar	Apr	May	Jun	Jul	Aug	Sep	Oct
AVERAGE MOVE											
All Years		-0.87	0.18	-0.87	1.25	-2.66	1.29	-2.06	-3.90	0.03	-0.53
Less Extremes		0.67	0.48	-0.82	1.32	-3.71	-0.92	-1.26	-7.72	-1.58	-0.42
Ave Up - All Years		5.31	3.59	4.86	6.04	5.26	18.23	13.28	26.20	8.73	5.99
Ave Down - All Years		-10.14	-3.22	-4.70	-5.92	-7.93	-5.96	-12.28	-11.42	-5.76	-4.88
COUNT											
Number Up		6	5	4	6	4	3	4	2	4	4
Number Down		4	5	6	4	6	7	6	8	6	6
Pct Up		60.0%	50.0%	40.0%	60.0%	40.0%	30.0%	40.0%	20.0%	40.0%	40.0%
Pct Down		40.0%	50.0%	60.0%	40.0%	60.0%	70.0%	60.0%	80.0%	60.0%	60.0%
EXTREMES											
Greatest Up		12.45	5.40	7.68	10.34	17.63	33.92	26.55	42.98	23.12	8.79
Greatest Down		-26.53	-7.41	-9.88	-8.39	-14.53	-13.60	-37.06	-20.22	-10.20	-10.76
SEASONAL INDEX : AVERAGE PERCENTAGE METHOD											
All Years	102.1	101.3	101.3	100.9	101.5	100.1	101.1	99.7	97.3	97.3	97.2
Less Extremes	102.0	102.1	102.1	101.6	101.9	99.9	100.9	98.1	96.8	97.1	96.6
SEASONAL INDEX : LINK RELATIVE METHOD											
All Years		99.8	100.2	100.1	100.9	100.1	101.5	100.9	98.7	98.8	99.0
Less Extremes		99.8	100.8	101.0	102.4	101.0	101.1	101.1	97.5	97.4	97.8

SOYBEAN MEAL - OCTOBER - MONTH OF HIGH AND LOW

Year of Expiration	Dec	Jan	Feb	Mar	Apr	May	Jun	Jul	Aug	Sep	Oct
1976		L						H			
1977					H					L	
1978			L								H
1979	L						H				
1980					L						H
1981		H									L
1982		H									L
1983	L								H		
1984				H							L
1985	H								L		

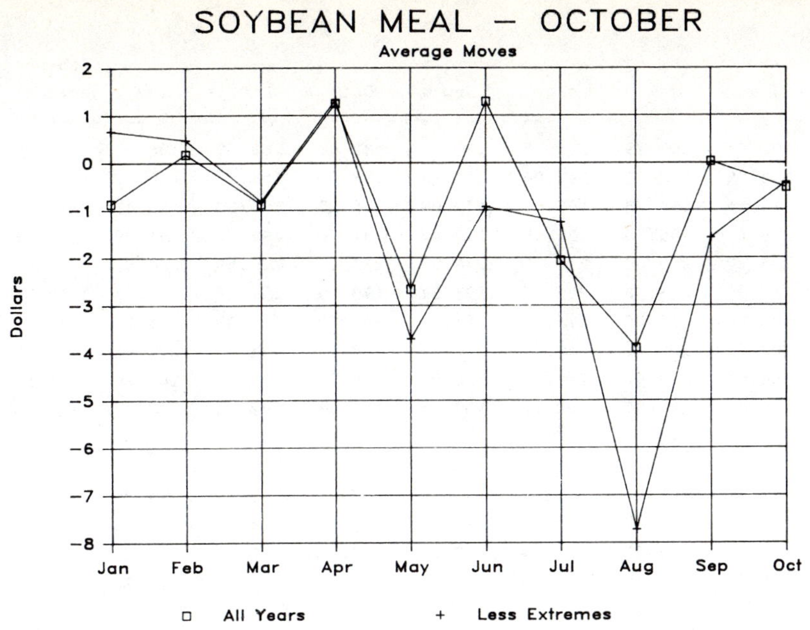
SOYBEAN MEAL — OCTOBER
Average Moves
Dollars
2
1
0
−1
−2
−3
−4
−5
−6
−7
−8
Jan
Feb
Mar
Apr
May
Jun
Jul
Aug
Sep
Oct
All Years
Less Extremes

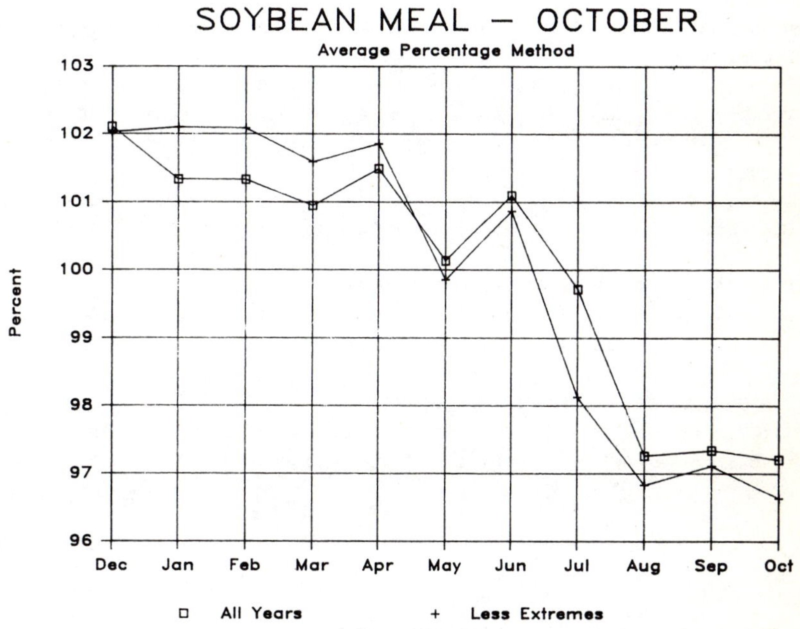
SOYBEAN MEAL — OCTOBER
Average Percentage Method
Percent
103
102
101
100
99
98
97
96
Dec
Jan
Feb
Mar
Apr
May
Jun
Jul
Aug
Sep
Oct
All Years
Less Extremes

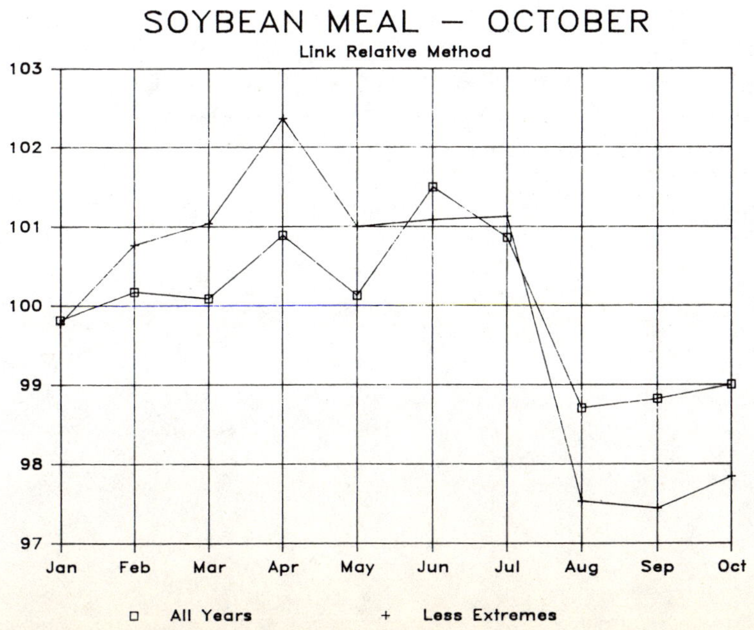
SOYBEAN MEAL — OCTOBER
Link Relative Method
103
102
101
100
99
98
97
Jan
Feb
Mar
Apr
May
Jun
Jul
Aug
Sep
Oct
All Years
Less Extremes

SOYBEAN MEAL - DECEMBER - MONTHLY AVERAGE PRICE

Year of Expiration	Feb	Mar	Apr	May	Jun	Jul	Aug	Sep	Oct	Nov	Dec	Feb-Dec Average
1976	144.92	141.81	142.19	158.43	191.68	203.29	186.75	190.83	182.66	186.59	198.17	175.21
1977	195.64	193.86	194.85	193.29	193.58	161.15	142.04	141.12	143.96	164.15	156.02	170.88
1978	159.85	165.79	168.23	168.16	170.46	164.75	167.07	172.99	185.12	186.00	191.47	172.71
1979	192.57	195.56	192.59	195.45	213.65	205.76	195.05	194.02	187.50	190.67	191.09	195.81
1980	202.90	193.52	185.18	185.71	185.70	212.69	221.80	246.07	261.20	274.58	234.61	218.54
1981	241.28	233.23	244.55	230.32	218.06	218.38	203.56	193.54	190.19	187.18	188.33	213.51
1982	197.91	192.35	198.34	196.36	189.57	183.06	171.07	161.51	157.83	172.38	174.06	181.31
1983	191.84	194.46	202.87	193.45	183.07	199.52	240.71	240.51	234.41	231.97	216.81	211.78
1984	195.39	203.13	196.92	188.40	186.90	172.42	164.29	155.06	154.03	152.38	146.76	174.15
1985	156.99	153.71	148.10	138.26	135.00	135.87	128.77	133.98	141.33	143.68	143.67	141.76

	Feb	Mar	Apr	May	Jun	Jul	Aug	Sep	Oct	Nov	Dec
AVERAGE MOVE											
All Years		-1.19	0.64	-2.60	1.98	-1.08	-3.58	0.85	0.86	5.14	-4.86
Less Extremes		-1.28	0.43	-3.50	-0.14	-0.67	-7.23	-0.72	0.21	4.27	-2.52
Ave Up - All Years		4.82	4.92	6.54	13.51	11.25	17.54	9.87	9.36	8.35	4.06
Ave Down - All Years		-5.19	-5.78	-6.52	-5.70	-13.40	-12.63	-5.16	-4.81	-2.36	-13.78
COUNT											
Number Up		4	6	3	4	5	3	4	4	7	5
Number Down		6	4	7	6	5	7	6	6	3	5
Pct Up		40.0%	60.0%	30.0%	40.0%	50.0%	30.0%	40.0%	40.0%	70.0%	50.0%
Pct Down		60.0%	40.0%	70.0%	60.0%	50.0%	70.0%	60.0%	60.0%	30.0%	50.0%
EXTREMES											
Greatest Up		7.74	11.32	16.24	33.25	26.99	41.19	24.27	15.13	20.19	11.58
Greatest Down		-9.38	-8.34	-14.23	-12.26	-32.43	-19.12	-10.02	-8.17	-3.01	-39.96
SEASONAL INDEX : AVERAGE PERCENTAGE METHOD											
All Years	101.7	101.1	101.3	99.9	101.1	100.0	97.6	98.0	98.6	101.4	99.2
Less Extremes	102.4	101.7	102.2	100.1	101.6	98.8	97.4	98.0	97.8	100.2	99.4
SEASONAL INDEX : LINK RELATIVE METHOD											
All Years		100.3	100.5	99.5	100.9	100.5	98.2	98.6	99.1	102.2	100.3
Less Extremes		101.4	102.0	100.5	100.8	100.9	97.4	97.6	98.4	101.0	100.1

SOYBEAN MEAL - DECEMBER - MONTH OF HIGH AND LOW

Year of Expiration	Feb	Mar	Apr	May	Jun	Jul	Aug	Sep	Oct	Nov	Dec
1976		L				H					
1977	H							L			
1978	L										H
1979					H				L		
1980			L							H	
1981			H							L	
1982			H						L		
1983					L		H				
1984		H									L
1985	H						L				

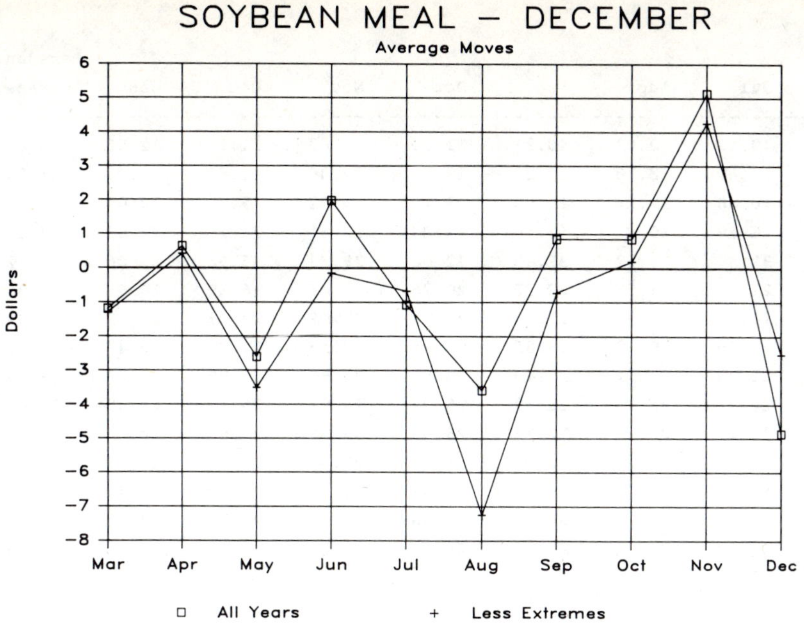
SOYBEAN MEAL – DECEMBER
Average Moves
Dollars
6
5
4
3
2
1
0
−1
−2
−3
−4
−5
−6
−7
−8
Mar
Apr
May
Jun
Jul
Aug
Sep
Oct
Nov
Dec
□ All Years
+ Less Extremes

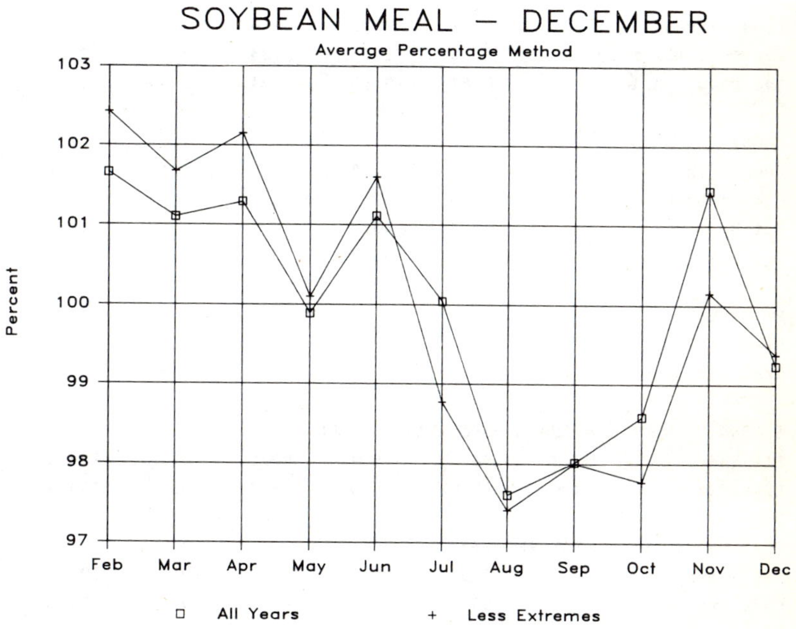
SOYBEAN MEAL – DECEMBER
Average Percentage Method
Percent
103
102
101
100
99
98
97
Feb
Mar
Apr
May
Jun
Jul
Aug
Sep
Oct
Nov
Dec
□ All Years
+ Less Extremes

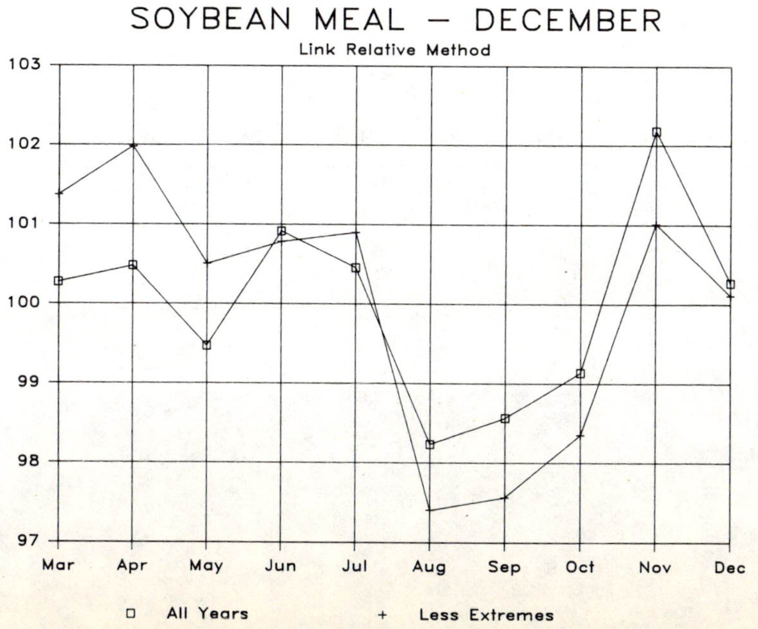
SOYBEAN MEAL – DECEMBER
Link Relative Method
103
102
101
100
99
98
97
Mar
Apr
May
Jun
Jul
Aug
Sep
Oct
Nov
Dec
□ All Years
+ Less Extremes

SOYBEAN OIL - JANUARY - MONTHLY AVERAGE PRICE

Year of Expiration	Mar	Apr	May	Jun	Jul	Aug	Sep	Oct	Nov	Dec	Jan	Mar-Jan Average
1971	8.80	9.44	9.44	9.84	10.13	10.01	10.31	11.99	12.67	11.91	12.05	10.60
1972	10.58	10.29	10.55	11.65	13.00	12.78	12.27	12.68	12.36	11.68	10.90	11.70
1973	11.07	11.21	10.81	10.37	10.08	10.24	10.00	9.79	9.82	9.76	10.04	10.29
1974	11.08	11.64	12.75	14.11	16.49	19.83	17.50	18.23	17.61	23.16	25.96	17.12
1975	20.61	19.80	21.36	23.44	31.39	35.67	37.45	42.06	39.73	36.98	33.86	31.12
1976	22.09	21.71	19.55	18.64	22.03	24.57	22.92	20.78	18.44	16.59	16.65	20.36
1977	17.26	17.01	16.84	19.09	21.53	20.93	22.93	21.27	22.09	21.27	20.72	20.09
1978	25.44	26.56	27.04	25.75	21.45	19.39	18.83	18.44	20.13	21.89	20.47	22.31
1979	21.91	22.09	23.26	23.02	21.87	22.91	24.49	25.56	24.56	24.89	24.89	23.59
1980	25.19	25.12	25.79	27.25	27.29	26.25	26.83	25.97	26.07	25.12	23.40	25.84
1981	24.42	22.56	22.40	23.15	27.16	27.08	27.74	26.63	28.35	25.05	24.56	25.37
1982	26.77	27.03	25.87	24.54	25.49	23.31	22.02	21.91	20.84	19.50	18.89	23.29
1983	20.30	21.35	21.73	20.39	19.49	18.30	17.88	17.32	17.25	16.57	16.44	18.82
1984	18.89	20.49	20.32	19.76	22.14	30.00	34.21	30.36	27.88	27.42	28.32	25.44
1985	25.59	26.17	28.93	28.59	24.34	25.90	25.07	25.46	26.66	25.88	26.22	26.26

	Mar	Apr	May	Jun	Jul	Aug	Sep	Oct	Nov	Dec	Jan
AVERAGE MOVE											
All Years		0.17	0.28	0.20	0.95	0.89	0.22	-0.13	-0.27	-0.45	-0.29
Less Extremes		0.21	0.27	0.16	0.82	0.58	0.11	-0.21	-0.25	-0.69	-0.31
Ave Up - All Years		0.68	1.05	1.34	2.52	2.97	1.58	1.48	0.89	2.55	0.65
Ave Down - All Years		-0.61	-0.60	-0.81	-2.18	-0.94	-0.98	-1.21	-1.28	-1.20	-1.10
COUNT											
Number Up		9	8	7	10	7	7	6	7	3	7
Number Down		6	7	8	5	8	8	9	8	12	8
Pct Up		60.0%	53.3%	46.7%	66.7%	46.7%	46.7%	40.0%	46.7%	20.0%	46.7%
Pct Down		40.0%	46.7%	53.3%	33.3%	53.3%	53.3%	60.0%	53.3%	80.0%	53.3%
EXTREMES											
Greatest Up		1.60	2.76	2.25	7.95	7.86	4.21	4.61	1.71	5.55	2.81
Greatest Down		-1.86	-2.15	-1.34	-4.30	-2.17	-2.33	-3.86	-2.48	-3.30	-3.12
SEASONAL INDEX : AVERAGE PERCENTAGE METHOD											
All Years	93.4	94.5	95.4	96.5	100.8	104.3	104.6	104.3	103.4	101.7	100.9
Less Extremes	94.0	95.0	95.5	96.7	101.0	104.4	103.9	103.6	102.6	100.7	98.6
SEASONAL INDEX : LINK RELATIVE METHOD											
All Years		95.2	95.8	96.8	101.5	104.7	104.1	103.2	101.7	99.4	97.6
Less Extremes		95.3	96.4	97.5	102.2	104.4	104.1	103.2	102.1	98.4	96.5

SOYBEAN OIL - JANUARY - MONTH OF HIGH AND LOW

Year of Expiration	Mar	Apr	May	Jun	Jul	Aug	Sep	Oct	Nov	Dec	Jan
1971	L								H		
1972		L			H						
1973		H								L	
1974	L										H
1975		L						H			
1976						H				L	
1977			L				H				
1978			H					L			
1979					L			H			
1980					H						L
1981			L						H		
1982		H									L
1983			H								L
1984	L						H				
1985			H		L						

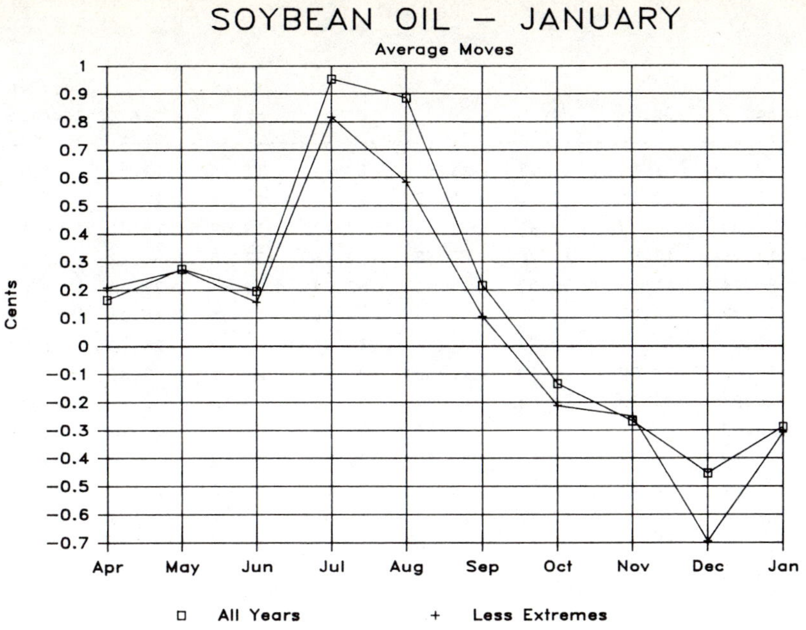
SOYBEAN OIL – JANUARY
Average Moves
Cents
1
0.9
0.8
0.7
0.6
0.5
0.4
0.3
0.2
0.1
0
–0.1
–0.2
–0.3
–0.4
–0.5
–0.6
–0.7
Apr
May
Jun
Jul
Aug
Sep
Oct
Nov
Dec
Jan
All Years
+ Less Extremes

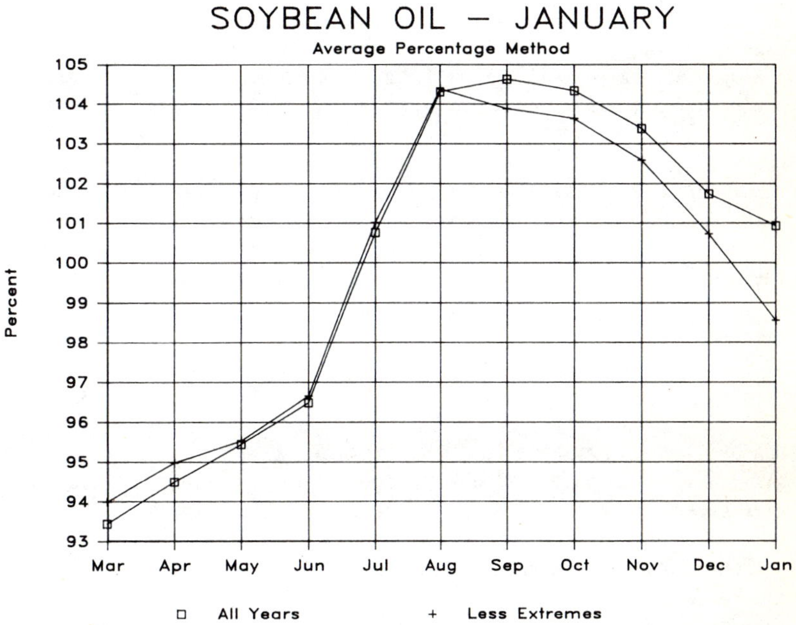
SOYBEAN OIL – JANUARY
Average Percentage Method
Percent
105
104
103
102
101
100
99
98
97
96
95
94
93
Mar
Apr
May
Jun
Jul
Aug
Sep
Oct
Nov
Dec
Jan
All Years
+ Less Extremes

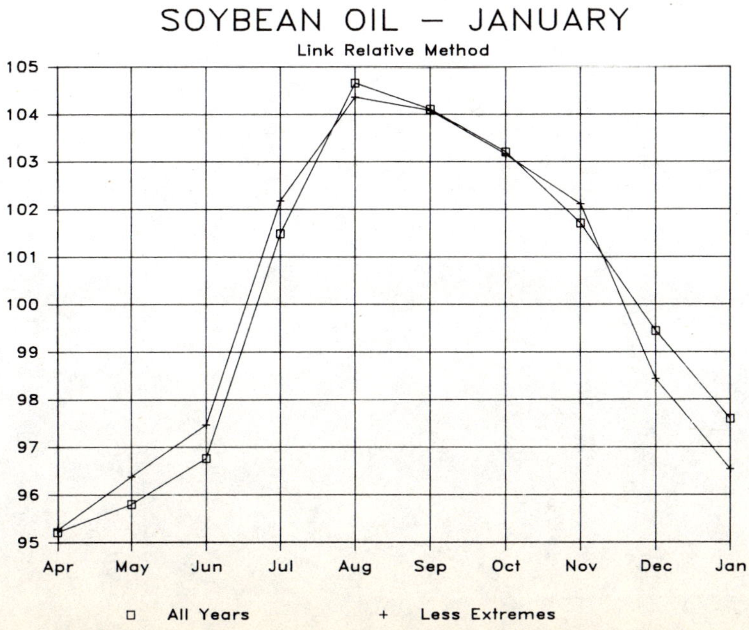
SOYBEAN OIL – JANUARY
Link Relative Method
105
104
103
102
101
100
99
98
97
96
95
Apr
May
Jun
Jul
Aug
Sep
Oct
Nov
Dec
Jan
All Years
+ Less Extremes

SOYBEAN OIL - MARCH - MONTHLY AVERAGE PRICE

Year of Expiration	May	Jun	Jul	Aug	Sep	Oct	Nov	Dec	Jan	Feb	Mar	May-Mar Average
1971	9.34	9.74	10.11	9.97	10.18	11.66	12.31	11.68	12.14	11.96	12.03	11.01
1972	10.47	11.56	12.87	12.68	12.18	12.51	12.24	11.77	11.01	11.08	11.62	11.82
1973	10.79	10.38	10.11	10.29	10.09	9.90	9.96	9.93	10.19	13.02	13.82	10.77
1974	12.51	13.76	16.16	19.30	17.29	17.84	16.70	20.58	24.76	32.45	30.22	20.14
1975	20.99	23.08	30.86	35.06	36.84	41.82	39.09	35.91	32.77	28.57	27.32	32.03
1976	19.16	18.50	21.83	24.34	22.77	20.83	18.47	16.69	16.39	16.51	16.74	19.29
1977	16.96	19.21	21.60	21.02	23.03	21.48	22.29	21.55	21.44	22.89	26.12	21.60
1978	26.78	25.57	21.52	19.48	19.00	18.69	20.10	21.65	20.56	21.07	25.81	21.84
1979	23.11	22.87	21.80	22.79	24.21	25.32	24.65	24.91	25.08	27.30	27.06	24.46
1980	25.84	27.33	27.31	26.28	26.83	25.97	25.81	25.17	23.80	23.53	22.30	25.47
1981	22.77	23.51	27.31	27.33	28.28	27.33	29.18	25.99	24.53	23.82	23.70	25.80
1982	26.43	25.13	26.19	24.08	22.81	22.65	21.45	20.10	19.57	19.00	18.25	22.33
1983	22.07	20.74	19.82	18.64	18.26	17.66	17.57	16.95	16.95	17.21	16.99	18.44
1984	20.65	20.03	22.41	29.97	34.02	30.46	28.31	27.96	28.39	26.79	29.15	27.10
1985	28.72	28.42	24.44	25.92	24.85	25.00	25.61	25.00	25.99	28.06	29.61	26.51

	May	Jun	Jul	Aug	Sep	Oct	Nov	Dec	Jan	Feb	Mar
AVERAGE MOVE											
All Years		0.22	0.97	0.85	0.23	-0.10	-0.36	-0.53	-0.15	0.65	0.50
Less Extremes		0.18	0.83	0.57	0.11	-0.22	-0.35	-0.66	-0.26	0.48	0.38
Ave Up - All Years		1.33	2.76	2.51	1.57	1.44	0.90	1.90	0.93	1.91	1.69
Ave Down - All Years		-0.76	-1.72	-1.04	-0.94	-1.12	-1.20	-1.13	-1.10	-1.25	-0.86
COUNT											
Number Up		7	9	8	7	6	6	3	7	9	8
Number Down		8	6	7	8	9	9	12	8	6	7
Pct Up		46.7%	60.0%	53.3%	46.7%	40.0%	40.0%	20.0%	46.7%	60.0%	53.3%
Pct Down		53.3%	40.0%	46.7%	53.3%	60.0%	60.0%	80.0%	53.3%	40.0%	46.7%
EXTREMES											
Greatest Up		2.25	7.78	7.56	4.05	4.98	1.84	3.88	4.18	7.69	4.74
Greatest Down		-1.33	-4.04	-2.11	-2.02	-3.56	-2.72	-3.18	-3.14	-4.20	-2.22
SEASONAL INDEX : AVERAGE PERCENTAGE METHOD											
All Years	93.9	94.9	99.0	102.1	102.4	102.1	100.8	98.6	98.3	102.7	105.3
Less Extremes	94.1	95.2	99.0	101.2	101.9	101.2	100.5	98.4	97.5	99.6	103.7
SEASONAL INDEX : LINK RELATIVE METHOD											
All Years		96.9	101.4	104.2	103.4	102.2	100.0	97.2	95.9	98.7	100.2
Less Extremes		97.4	101.9	103.9	103.4	102.4	100.8	97.3	95.5	98.0	99.3

SOYBEAN OIL - MARCH - MONTH OF HIGH AND LOW

Year of Expiration	May	Jun	Jul	Aug	Sep	Oct	Nov	Dec	Jan	Feb	Mar
1971	L						H				
1972	L		H								
1973						L					H
1974	L									H	
1975	L					H					
1976				H					L		
1977	L										H
1978	H					L					
1979			L							H	
1980		H									L
1981	L						H				
1982	H										L
1983	H							L			
1984		L			H						
1985			L								H

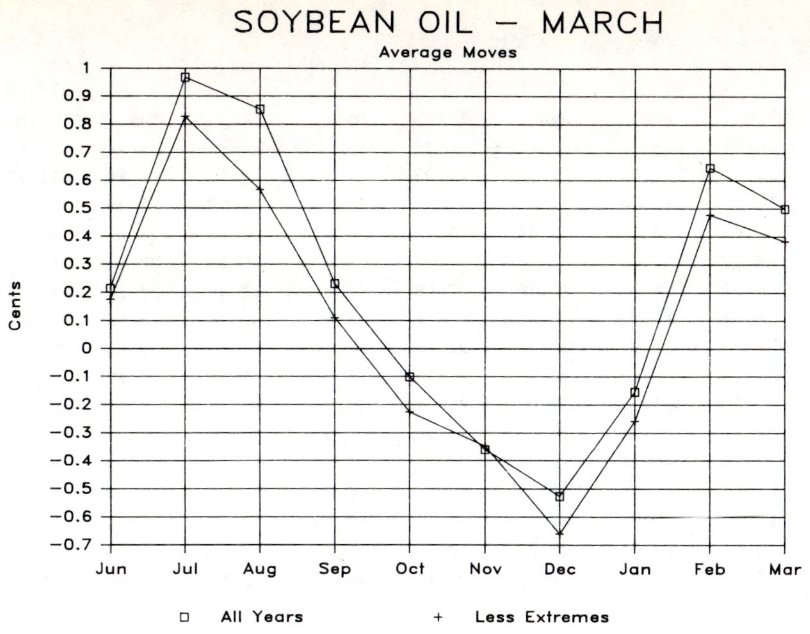

SOYBEAN OIL — MARCH
Average Moves
Cents
1
0.9
0.8
0.7
0.6
0.5
0.4
0.3
0.2
0.1
0
−0.1
−0.2
−0.3
−0.4
−0.5
−0.6
−0.7
Jun
Jul
Aug
Sep
Oct
Nov
Dec
Jan
Feb
Mar
□ All Years
+ Less Extremes

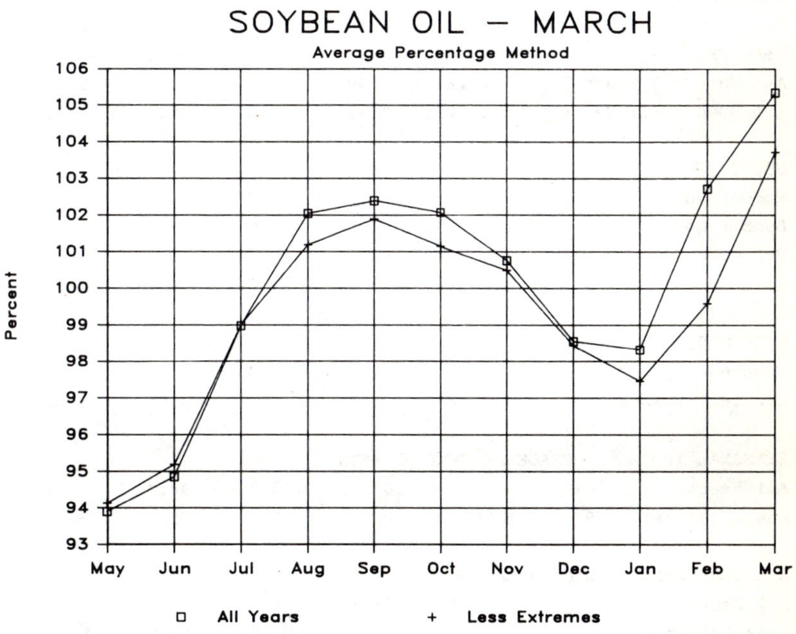

SOYBEAN OIL — MARCH
Average Percentage Method
Percent
106
105
104
103
102
101
100
99
98
97
96
95
94
93
May
Jun
Jul
Aug
Sep
Oct
Nov
Dec
Jan
Feb
Mar
□ All Years
+ Less Extremes

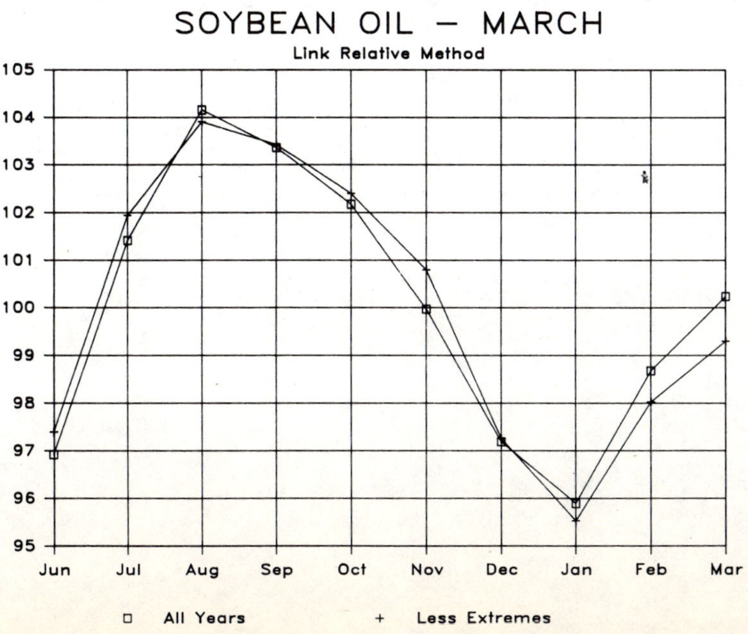

SOYBEAN OIL — MARCH
Link Relative Method
105
104
103
102
101
100
99
98
97
96
95
Jun
Jul
Aug
Sep
Oct
Nov
Dec
Jan
Feb
Mar
□ All Years
+ Less Extremes

SOYBEAN OIL - MAY - MONTHLY AVERAGE PRICE

Year of Expiration	Jul	Aug	Sep	Oct	Nov	Dec	Jan	Feb	Mar	Apr	May	Jul-May Average
1971	10.07	9.94	10.12	11.40	12.12	11.51	12.06	11.92	11.89	10.93	11.10	11.19
1972	12.76	12.58	12.11	12.39	12.16	11.78	11.11	11.22	11.78	11.89	11.48	11.93
1973	10.17	10.36	10.17	9.99	10.07	10.06	10.34	13.11	14.01	14.90	16.25	11.77
1974	16.05	19.02	17.09	17.65	16.33	19.18	22.90	27.96	26.33	26.25	28.54	21.57
1975	30.04	34.45	36.32	41.52	38.52	34.87	31.78	27.79	26.97	27.08	23.26	32.05
1976	21.63	24.10	22.64	20.84	18.51	16.83	16.57	16.70	16.74	16.36	15.96	18.81
1977	21.68	21.06	23.05	21.55	22.31	21.69	21.71	23.19	26.80	29.54	30.86	23.95
1978	21.53	19.52	19.09	18.90	20.14	21.44	20.63	20.92	25.60	26.43	27.77	22.00
1979	21.74	22.70	23.95	25.12	24.64	24.81	25.07	27.48	27.48	26.43	25.83	25.02
1980	27.33	26.30	26.82	26.10	25.76	25.26	24.18	24.14	22.40	20.46	20.60	24.48
1981	27.43	27.45	28.48	27.74	29.74	26.74	25.36	24.66	24.48	24.49	23.10	26.33
1982	26.69	24.68	23.37	23.23	21.95	20.66	20.22	19.74	18.78	19.66	20.17	21.74
1983	20.08	18.96	18.57	17.97	17.86	17.30	17.35	17.63	17.53	19.01	19.40	18.33
1984	22.67	29.65	33.30	30.19	28.55	28.35	28.78	27.12	29.62	31.40	37.17	29.71
1985	24.56	25.94	24.67	24.79	25.18	24.68	25.49	27.18	28.65	32.10	31.64	26.81

	Jul	Aug	Sep	Oct	Nov	Dec	Jan	Feb	Mar	Apr	May
AVERAGE MOVE											
All Years		0.82	0.20	-0.02	-0.37	-0.58	-0.11	0.48	0.55	0.52	0.41
Less Extremes		0.56	0.10	-0.19	-0.35	-0.60	-0.17	0.47	0.41	0.49	0.33
Ave Up - All Years		2.42	1.50	1.43	0.86	1.45	0.76	1.58	1.72	1.23	1.48
Ave Down - All Years		-1.02	-0.93	-1.00	-1.19	-1.08	-1.10	-1.17	-0.78	-0.88	-1.18
COUNT											
Number Up		8	7	6	6	3	8	9	8	10	9
Number Down		7	8	9	9	12	7	6	7	5	6
Pct Up		53.3%	46.7%	40.0%	40.0%	20.0%	53.3%	60.0%	53.3%	66.7%	60.0%
Pct Down		46.7%	53.3%	60.0%	60.0%	80.0%	46.7%	40.0%	46.7%	33.3%	40.0%
EXTREMES											
Greatest Up		6.98	3.65	5.20	2.00	2.86	3.71	5.07	4.68	3.44	5.77
Greatest Down		-2.02	-1.93	-3.11	-3.00	-3.65	-3.09	-3.99	-1.74	-1.94	-3.82
SEASONAL INDEX : AVERAGE PERCENTAGE METHOD											
All Years	97.2	99.9	100.0	100.0	98.7	96.2	96.1	99.4	102.0	104.2	106.3
Less Extremes	97.0	98.7	100.1	99.1	98.8	96.1	95.8	98.0	101.9	104.0	106.5
SEASONAL INDEX : LINK RELATIVE METHOD											
All Years		101.4	101.1	100.7	99.0	96.5	96.0	98.8	101.0	102.3	103.3
Less Extremes		101.9	101.7	101.2	99.9	96.8	95.8	98.3	100.0	101.7	102.8

SOYBEAN OIL - MAY - MONTH OF HIGH AND LOW

Year of Expiration	Jul	Aug	Sep	Oct	Nov	Dec	Jan	Feb	Mar	Apr	May
1971		L					H				
1972	H						L				
1973				L							H
1974	L										H
1975				H							L
1976		H									L
1977		L									H
1978				L							H
1979	L								H		
1980	H									L	
1981					H						L
1982	H								L		
1983	H					L					
1984	L										H
1985	L									H	

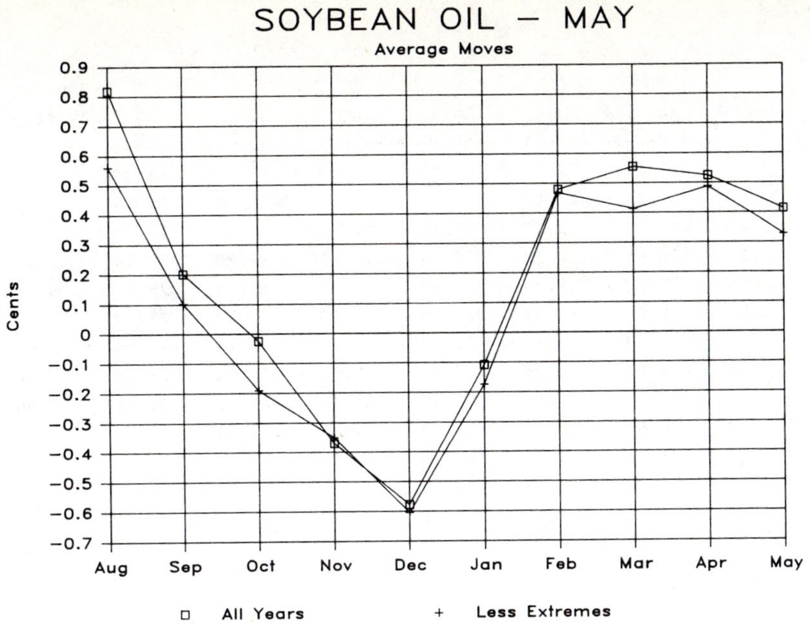
SOYBEAN OIL — MAY
Average Moves
Cents
0.9
0.8
0.7
0.6
0.5
0.4
0.3
0.2
0.1
0
−0.1
−0.2
−0.3
−0.4
−0.5
−0.6
−0.7
Aug
Sep
Oct
Nov
Dec
Jan
Feb
Mar
Apr
May
□ All Years
+ Less Extremes

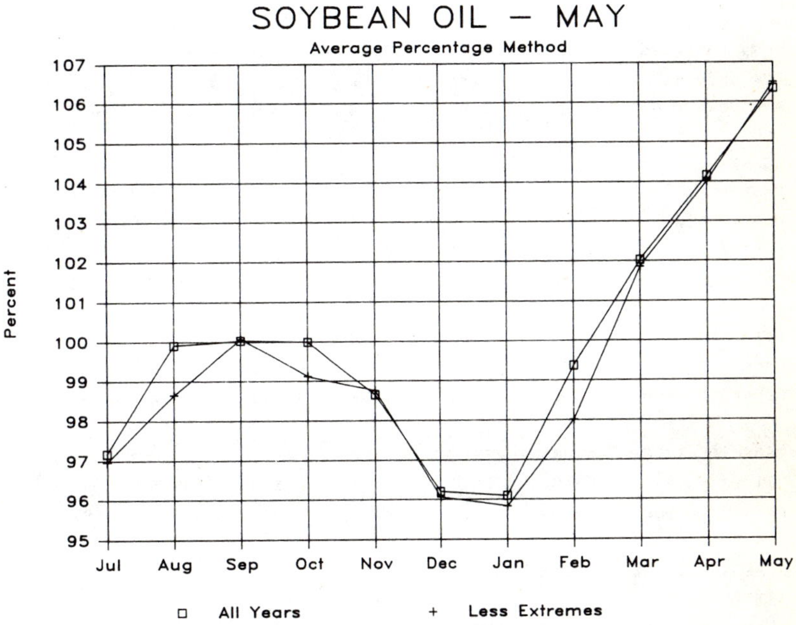
SOYBEAN OIL — MAY
Average Percentage Method
Percent
107
106
105
104
103
102
101
100
99
98
97
96
95
Jul
Aug
Sep
Oct
Nov
Dec
Jan
Feb
Mar
Apr
May
□ All Years
+ Less Extremes

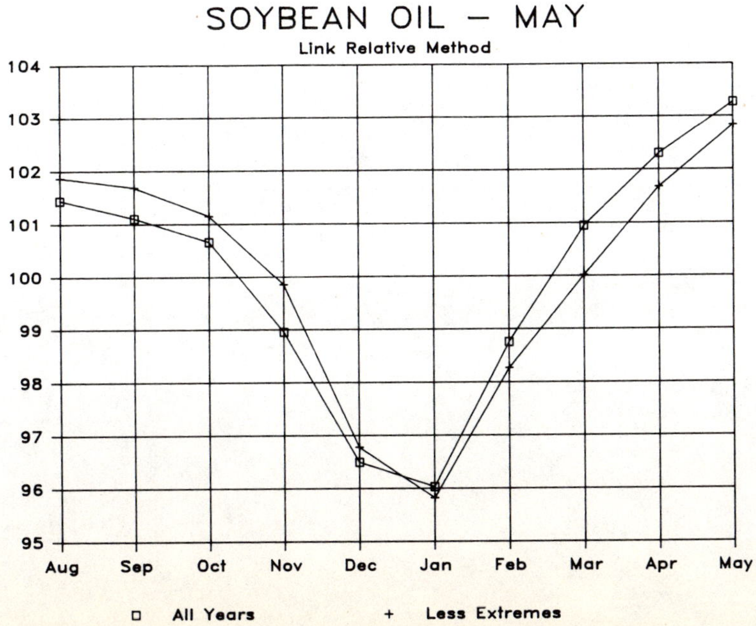
SOYBEAN OIL — MAY
Link Relative Method
104
103
102
101
100
99
98
97
96
95
Aug
Sep
Oct
Nov
Dec
Jan
Feb
Mar
Apr
May
□ All Years
+ Less Extremes

SOYBEAN OIL - JULY - MONTHLY AVERAGE PRICE

Year of Expiration	Sep	Oct	Nov	Dec	Jan	Feb	Mar	Apr	May	Jun	Jul	Sep-Jul Average
1971	10.03	11.17	11.96	11.40	11.97	11.87	11.78	10.83	11.19	12.64	14.24	11.73
1972	12.04	12.29	12.09	11.78	11.19	11.30	11.89	12.02	11.56	10.72	10.40	11.57
1973	10.25	10.07	10.16	10.12	10.45	13.07	13.99	14.86	16.71	18.98	19.66	13.48
1974	16.88	17.45	16.02	18.49	21.83	25.54	24.14	24.24	26.81	29.79	37.04	23.48
1975	35.73	41.16	38.17	34.04	30.80	27.02	25.90	25.72	22.45	21.90	25.07	29.81
1976	22.51	20.86	18.59	17.00	16.76	16.90	16.93	16.55	16.23	18.29	21.92	18.41
1977	23.04	21.59	22.33	21.76	21.92	23.43	27.01	29.82	31.24	28.17	23.19	24.86
1978	19.19	19.09	20.16	21.26	20.68	20.82	25.16	25.69	27.08	25.95	25.24	22.76
1979	23.70	24.87	24.61	24.71	25.04	27.50	27.56	26.66	26.16	27.10	28.81	26.06
1980	26.80	26.25	25.85	25.47	24.52	24.63	22.98	21.13	21.30	22.00	26.36	24.30
1981	28.74	28.23	30.23	27.47	26.16	25.49	25.24	25.29	23.74	22.38	23.32	26.03
1982	23.93	23.81	22.46	21.21	20.83	20.39	19.28	20.25	20.61	19.06	18.61	20.95
1983	19.01	18.32	18.12	17.65	17.74	18.01	17.92	19.39	19.40	18.96	20.28	18.62
1984	32.55	29.74	28.75	28.42	28.87	27.22	29.52	31.32	37.05	34.05	30.23	30.70
1985	24.55	24.63	24.86	24.43	25.06	26.50	27.55	30.62	30.25	30.48	28.68	27.05

	Sep	Oct	Nov	Dec	Jan	Feb	Mar	Apr	May	Jun	Jul
AVERAGE MOVE											
All Years		0.04	-0.35	-0.61	-0.09	0.39	0.48	0.50	0.49	-0.09	0.84
Less Extremes		-0.16	-0.32	-0.58	-0.11	0.46	0.34	0.49	0.38	-0.09	0.79
Ave Up - All Years		1.44	0.82	1.23	0.74	1.25	1.61	1.18	1.54	1.52	2.74
Ave Down - All Years		-0.89	-1.12	-1.07	-1.04	-1.33	-0.82	-0.85	-1.08	-1.49	-2.01
COUNT											
Number Up		6	6	3	8	10	8	10	9	7	9
Number Down		9	9	12	7	5	7	5	6	8	6
Pct Up		40.0%	40.0%	20.0%	53.3%	66.7%	53.3%	66.7%	60.0%	46.7%	60.0%
Pct Down		60.0%	60.0%	80.0%	46.7%	33.3%	46.7%	33.3%	40.0%	53.3%	40.0%
EXTREMES											
Greatest Up		5.44	2.00	2.47	3.34	3.71	4.34	3.07	5.73	2.99	7.24
Greatest Down		-2.80	-2.99	-4.13	-3.24	-3.78	-1.65	-1.85	-3.27	-3.07	-4.98
SEASONAL INDEX : AVERAGE PERCENTAGE METHOD											
All Years	98.8	99.0	97.6	95.0	94.8	97.2	99.4	101.4	103.7	104.3	108.9
Less Extremes	99.0	97.8	97.5	95.0	95.4	97.0	99.5	101.1	104.2	103.9	107.0
SEASONAL INDEX : LINK RELATIVE METHOD											
All Years		101.8	99.8	96.8	96.1	98.1	99.5	100.4	101.4	101.2	104.8
Less Extremes		102.4	100.7	97.3	96.2	97.9	98.8	100.0	101.0	100.8	104.9

SOYBEAN OIL - JULY - MONTH OF HIGH AND LOW

Year of Expiration	Sep	Oct	Nov	Dec	Jan	Feb	Mar	Apr	May	Jun	Jul
1971	L										H
1972		H									L
1973		L									H
1974			L								H
1975		H								L	
1976	H								L		
1977		L							H		
1978		L							H		
1979	L										H
1980	H							L			
1981			H							L	
1982	H										L
1983				L							H
1984						L			H		
1985				L				H			

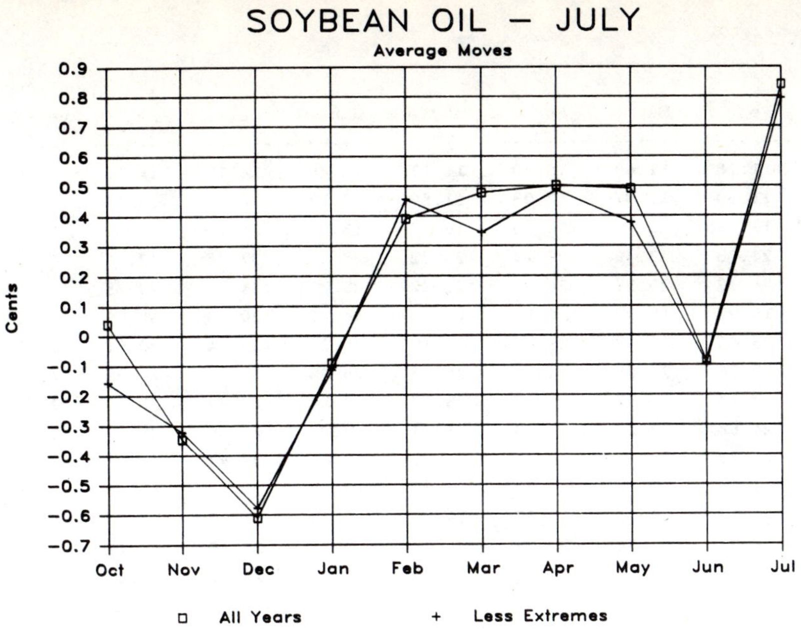
SOYBEAN OIL – JULY
Average Moves
Cents
0.9
0.8
0.7
0.6
0.5
0.4
0.3
0.2
0.1
0
−0.1
−0.2
−0.3
−0.4
−0.5
−0.6
−0.7
Oct
Nov
Dec
Jan
Feb
Mar
Apr
May
Jun
Jul
□ All Years
+ Less Extremes

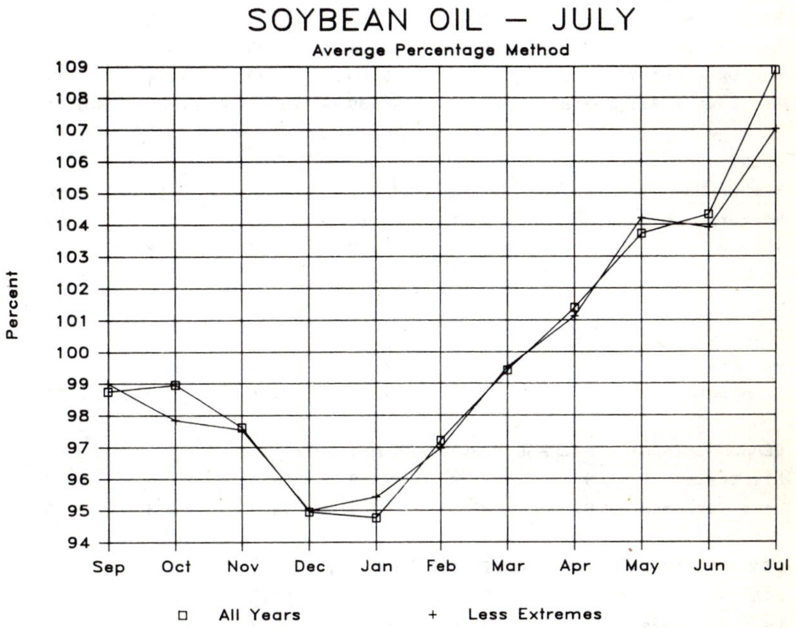
SOYBEAN OIL – JULY
Average Percentage Method
Percent
109
108
107
106
105
104
103
102
101
100
99
98
97
96
95
94
Sep
Oct
Nov
Dec
Jan
Feb
Mar
Apr
May
Jun
Jul
□ All Years
+ Less Extremes

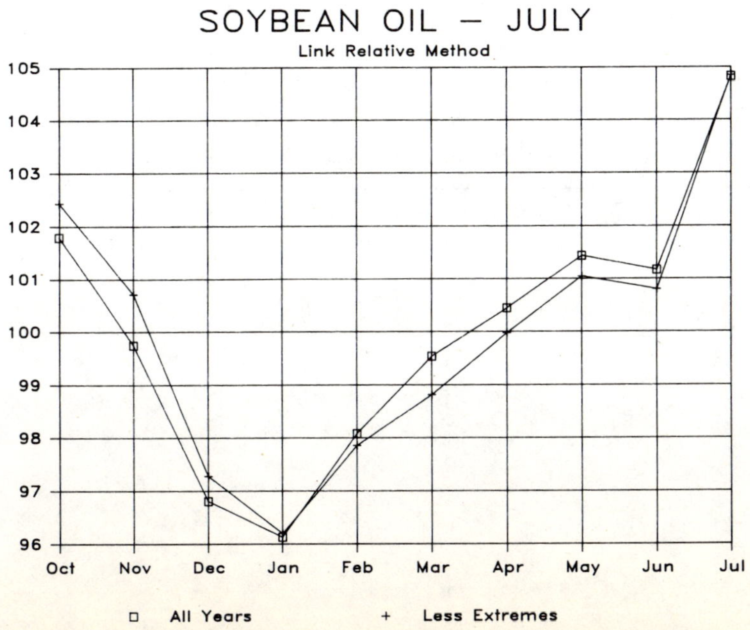
SOYBEAN OIL – JULY
Link Relative Method
105
104
103
102
101
100
99
98
97
96
Oct
Nov
Dec
Jan
Feb
Mar
Apr
May
Jun
Jul
□ All Years
+ Less Extremes

SOYBEAN OIL - AUGUST - MONTHLY AVERAGE PRICE

Year of Expiration	Oct	Nov	Dec	Jan	Feb	Mar	Apr	May	Jun	Jul	Aug	Oct-Aug Average
1971	10.92	11.72	11.17	11.75	11.78	11.68	10.80	11.11	12.40	14.18	14.66	12.01
1972	12.12	11.97	11.72	11.20	11.30	11.87	12.03	11.59	10.77	10.29	10.19	11.37
1973	10.07	10.16	10.14	10.44	12.86	13.75	14.66	16.36	18.52	21.10	33.57	15.60
1974	16.39	15.71	18.06	21.33	24.58	23.46	23.19	25.42	28.12	37.25	43.96	25.22
1975	40.67	37.65	33.09	29.83	26.33	25.15	24.89	21.82	20.82	24.91	28.85	28.55
1976	20.82	18.58	17.02	16.82	16.97	16.99	16.65	16.35	18.43	20.98	19.99	18.15
1977	24.85	21.43	21.58	21.91	23.45	26.98	29.72	31.10	28.26	23.24	20.81	24.85
1978	19.15	20.11	21.14	20.64	20.76	24.65	24.91	26.17	25.36	24.21	24.59	22.88
1979	24.62	24.53	24.62	25.03	27.23	27.37	26.57	26.26	27.24	28.24	28.17	26.35
1980	26.24	25.87	25.53	24.75	24.88	23.29	21.43	21.54	22.24	26.49	26.58	24.44
1981	27.99	29.90	27.57	26.37	25.78	25.52	25.64	24.16	22.81	23.47	21.73	25.54
1982	23.99	22.57	21.29	21.06	20.68	19.48	20.51	20.85	19.32	18.57	17.43	20.52
1983	18.33	18.12	17.75	17.90	18.16	18.07	19.58	19.53	19.13	21.31	28.32	19.65
1984	28.60	28.30	27.96	28.61	26.95	28.54	30.32	35.83	33.11	28.15	27.79	29.47
1985	24.36	24.54	24.12	24.74	25.98	26.85	29.68	29.28	29.30	26.95	23.32	26.28

	Oct	Nov	Dec	Jan	Feb	Mar	Apr	May	Jun	Jul	Aug
AVERAGE MOVE											
All Years		-0.53	-0.56	-0.02	0.35	0.40	0.46	0.45	-0.10	0.90	1.37
Less Extremes		-0.50	-0.48	-0.03	0.43	0.28	0.46	0.33	-0.11	0.72	0.90
Ave Up - All Years		0.79	0.90	0.79	1.04	1.44	1.26	1.60	1.42	3.14	4.44
Ave Down - All Years		-1.19	-1.09	-0.95	-1.54	-0.79	-0.74	-0.86	-1.43	-2.45	-1.31
COUNT											
Number Up		5	4	8	11	8	9	8	7	9	7
Number Down		10	11	7	4	7	6	7	8	6	8
Pct Up		33.3%	26.7%	53.3%	73.3%	53.3%	60.0%	53.3%	46.7%	60.0%	46.7%
Pct Down		66.7%	73.3%	46.7%	26.7%	46.7%	40.0%	46.7%	53.3%	40.0%	53.3%
EXTREMES											
Greatest Up		1.91	2.35	3.28	3.25	3.90	2.84	5.51	2.70	9.14	12.48
Greatest Down		-3.42	-4.56	-3.26	-3.50	-1.58	-1.87	-3.07	-2.84	-5.02	-3.63
SEASONAL INDEX : AVERAGE PERCENTAGE METHOD											
All Years	98.5	96.4	93.9	93.9	95.8	97.7	99.5	101.5	101.7	106.5	114.4
Less Extremes	97.8	96.3	94.4	95.1	96.3	97.6	99.0	101.6	102.7	104.9	109.0
SEASONAL INDEX : LINK RELATIVE METHOD											
All Years		101.5	98.2	97.2	98.4	99.0	99.2	99.5	98.6	102.1	106.3
Less Extremes		101.5	98.1	97.1	98.3	98.6	99.4	100.0	99.2	102.9	104.9

SOYBEAN OIL - AUGUST - MONTH OF HIGH AND LOW

Year of Expiration	Oct	Nov	Dec	Jan	Feb	Mar	Apr	May	Jun	Jul	Aug
1971							L				H
1972	H										L
1973	L										H
1974		L									H
1975	H								L		
1976								L		H	
1977								H			L
1978	L							H			
1979		L								H	
1980							L				H
1981		H									L
1982	H										L
1983			L								H
1984					L			H			
1985							H				L

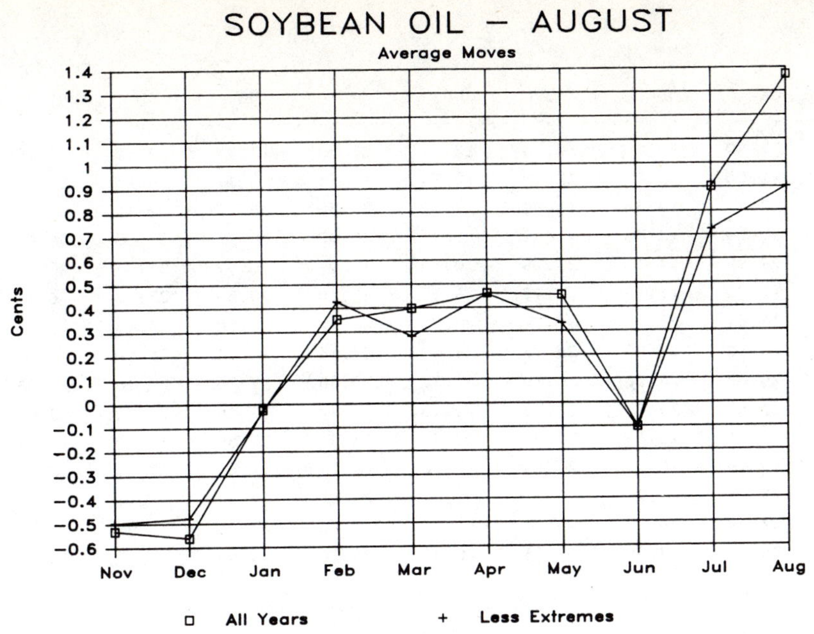
SOYBEAN OIL — AUGUST
Average Moves
Cents
1.4
1.3
1.2
1.1
1
0.9
0.8
0.7
0.6
0.5
0.4
0.3
0.2
0.1
0
−0.1
−0.2
−0.3
−0.4
−0.5
−0.6
Nov
Dec
Jan
Feb
Mar
Apr
May
Jun
Jul
Aug
All Years
Less Extremes

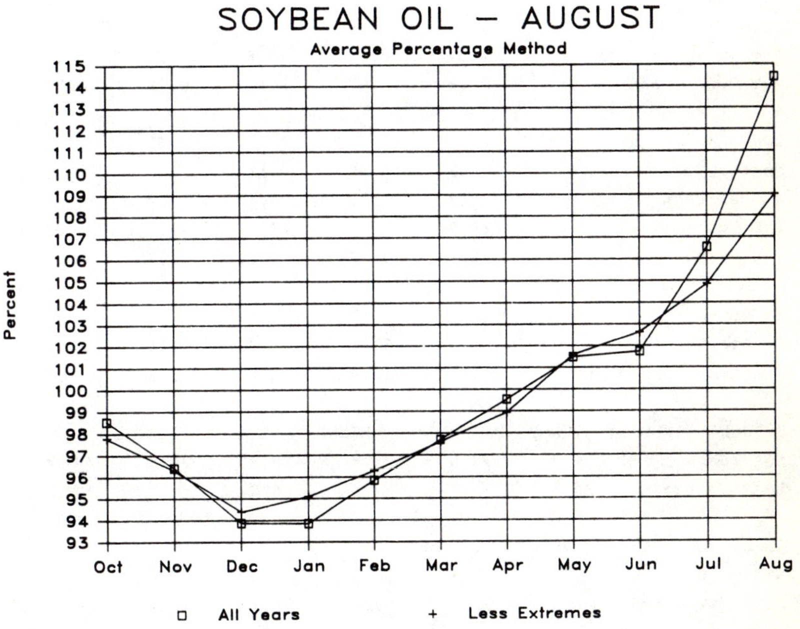
SOYBEAN OIL — AUGUST
Average Percentage Method
Percent
115
114
113
112
111
110
109
108
107
106
105
104
103
102
101
100
99
98
97
96
95
94
93
Oct
Nov
Dec
Jan
Feb
Mar
Apr
May
Jun
Jul
Aug
All Years
Less Extremes

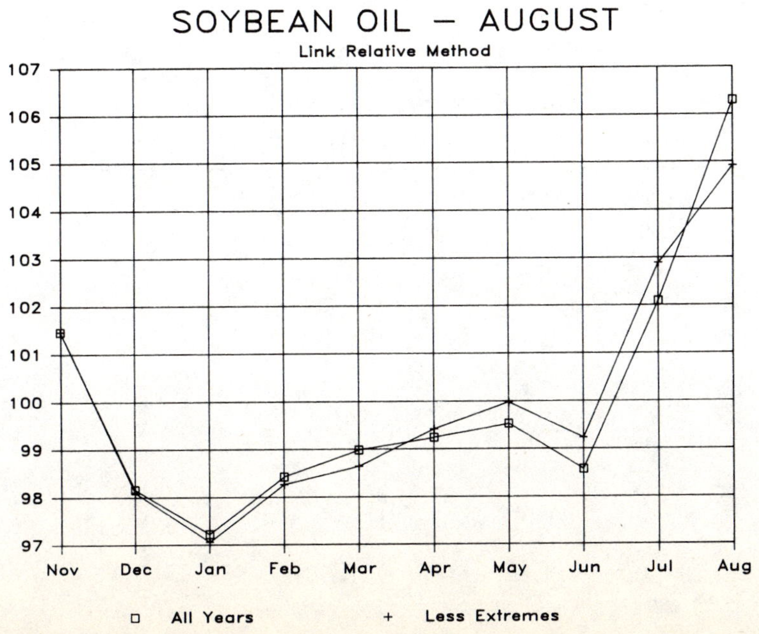
SOYBEAN OIL — AUGUST
Link Relative Method
107
106
105
104
103
102
101
100
99
98
97
Nov
Dec
Jan
Feb
Mar
Apr
May
Jun
Jul
Aug
All Years
Less Extremes

SOYBEAN OIL - SEPTEMBER - MONTHLY AVERAGE PRICE

Year of Expiration	Nov	Dec	Jan	Feb	Mar	Apr	May	Jun	Jul	Aug	Sep	Nov-Sep Average
1971	11.43	10.78	11.31	11.46	11.39	10.69	10.99	12.21	13.83	13.95	12.92	11.90
1972	11.84	11.65	11.12	11.15	11.68	11.89	11.49	10.74	10.33	10.17	9.86	11.08
1973	10.14	10.06	10.29	12.53	13.43	14.38	15.94	17.92	20.56	29.20	22.38	16.07
1974	15.64	17.81	20.81	23.80	22.90	22.44	24.42	26.75	35.45	40.31	37.53	26.17
1975	37.06	32.34	28.77	25.62	24.39	24.13	21.26	20.15	23.97	26.69	24.02	26.22
1976	18.55	17.05	16.89	17.04	17.05	16.73	16.45	18.57	21.10	20.59	23.30	18.48
1977	21.47	21.21	21.92	23.48	26.61	28.75	30.04	27.92	22.96	20.18	18.44	23.91
1978	19.78	20.74	20.29	20.37	23.68	23.80	25.18	24.80	23.44	24.54	26.68	23.03
1979	24.17	24.11	24.34	26.22	26.63	26.08	26.19	27.32	27.96	27.76	29.16	26.36
1980	25.90	25.59	24.96	25.14	23.58	21.70	21.75	22.45	26.72	26.46	27.20	24.68
1981	29.23	27.67	26.62	26.03	25.74	25.93	24.55	23.22	23.93	21.59	20.76	25.02
1982	22.69	21.42	21.28	20.95	19.66	20.73	21.03	19.56	18.73	17.53	17.24	20.07
1983	18.16	17.87	18.04	18.32	18.21	19.75	19.67	19.24	21.47	29.82	34.11	21.33
1984	26.88	26.75	27.69	26.29	27.58	29.23	33.99	31.86	26.92	27.25	26.99	28.31
1985	24.31	23.91	24.55	25.56	26.22	28.86	28.45	28.31	26.28	23.02	21.87	25.57

	Nov	Dec	Jan	Feb	Mar	Apr	May	Jun	Jul	Aug	Sep
AVERAGE MOVE											
All Years		-0.55	.00	0.34	0.32	0.42	0.42	-0.03	0.84	1.03	-0.44
Less Extremes		-0.44	0.04	0.40	0.24	0.43	0.34	-0.05	0.68	0.77	-0.31
Ave Up - All Years		1.57	0.81	0.96	1.28	1.17	1.30	1.58	3.02	3.73	2.26
Ave Down - All Years		-0.88	-0.93	-1.37	-0.78	-0.70	-0.90	-1.10	-2.42	-1.34	-1.79
COUNT											
Number Up		2	8	11	8	9	9	6	9	7	5
Number Down		13	7	4	7	6	6	9	6	8	10
Pct Up		13.3%	53.3%	73.3%	53.3%	60.0%	60.0%	40.0%	60.0%	46.7%	33.3%
Pct Down		86.7%	46.7%	26.7%	46.7%	40.0%	40.0%	60.0%	40.0%	53.3%	66.7%
EXTREMES											
Greatest Up		2.18	3.00	2.99	3.31	2.64	4.76	2.33	8.69	8.64	4.30
Greatest Down		-4.72	-3.56	-3.16	-1.56	-1.88	-2.87	-2.13	-4.95	-3.26	-6.82
SEASONAL INDEX : AVERAGE PERCENTAGE METHOD											
All Years	96.3	93.6	93.6	95.4	97.0	98.7	100.5	100.9	105.2	110.7	108.1
Less Extremes	95.7	93.8	94.6	96.0	96.9	98.1	100.1	101.5	103.9	107.3	106.5
SEASONAL INDEX : LINK RELATIVE METHOD											
All Years		97.9	97.2	98.4	98.8	99.2	99.5	98.9	102.4	105.5	102.1
Less Extremes		98.2	97.4	98.5	98.7	99.4	99.9	99.2	102.6	104.3	101.7

SOYBEAN OIL - SEPTEMBER - MONTH OF HIGH AND LOW

Year of Expiration	Nov	Dec	Jan	Feb	Mar	Apr	May	Jun	Jul	Aug	Sep
1971						L				H	
1972						H					L
1973		L								H	
1974	L									H	
1975	H							L			
1976							L				H
1977							H				L
1978	L										H
1979		L									H
1980						L					H
1981	H										L
1982	H										L
1983		L									H
1984				L			H				
1985						H					L

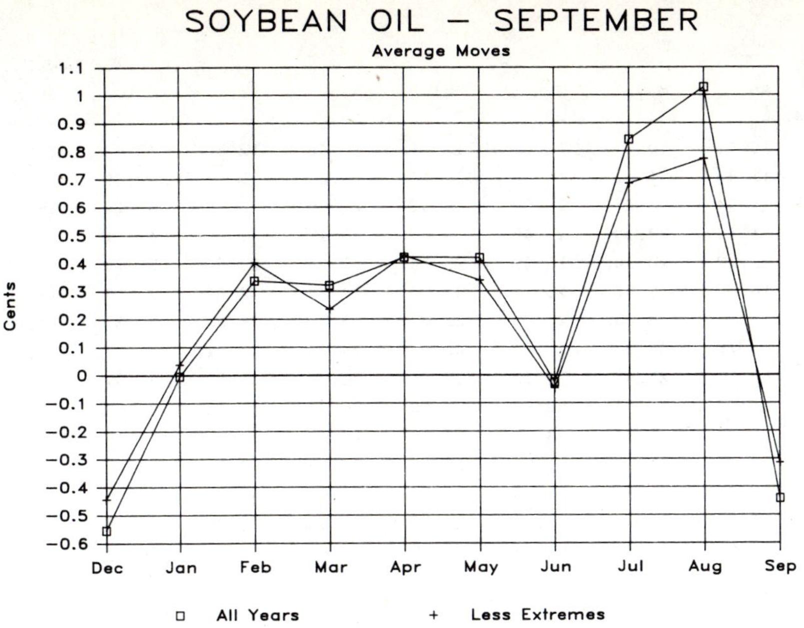
SOYBEAN OIL — SEPTEMBER
Average Moves
Cents
1.1
1
0.9
0.8
0.7
0.6
0.5
0.4
0.3
0.2
0.1
0
−0.1
−0.2
−0.3
−0.4
−0.5
−0.6
Dec
Jan
Feb
Mar
Apr
May
Jun
Jul
Aug
Sep
□ All Years
+ Less Extremes

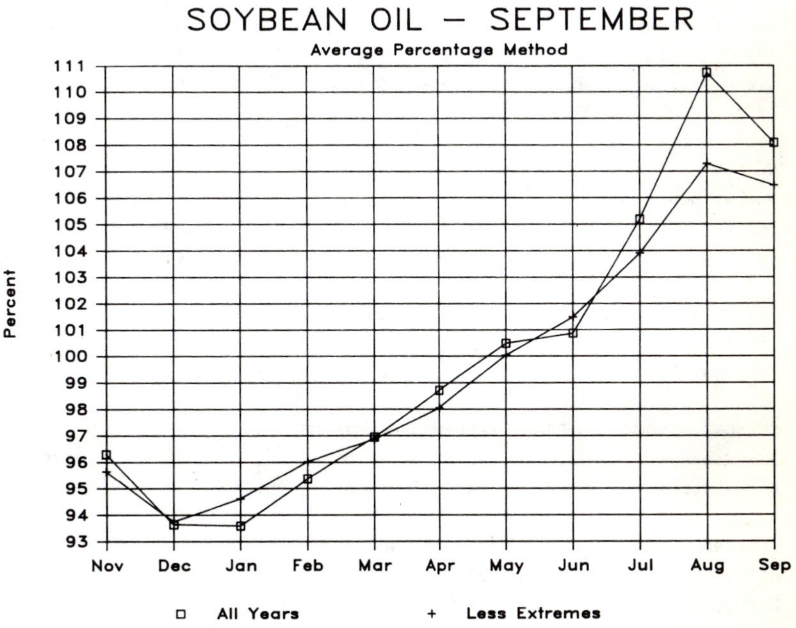
SOYBEAN OIL — SEPTEMBER
Average Percentage Method
Percent
111
110
109
108
107
106
105
104
103
102
101
100
99
98
97
96
95
94
93
Nov
Dec
Jan
Feb
Mar
Apr
May
Jun
Jul
Aug
Sep
□ All Years
+ Less Extremes

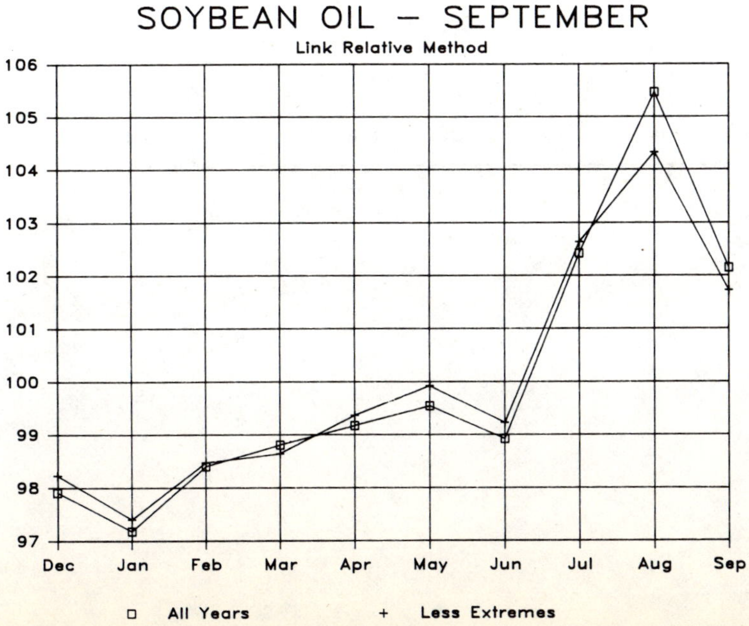
SOYBEAN OIL — SEPTEMBER
Link Relative Method
106
105
104
103
102
101
100
99
98
97
Dec
Jan
Feb
Mar
Apr
May
Jun
Jul
Aug
Sep
□ All Years
+ Less Extremes

SOYBEAN OIL - OCTOBER - MONTHLY AVERAGE PRICE

Year of Expiration	Dec	Jan	Feb	Mar	Apr	May	Jun	Jul	Aug	Sep	Oct	Dec-Oct Average
1971	10.44	10.91	10.98	10.97	10.55	10.81	12.00	13.51	13.46	12.56	12.99	11.74
1972	11.42	10.87	10.83	11.35	11.56	11.17	10.53	10.18	10.20	9.85	9.80	10.71
1973	9.88	9.98	11.43	12.34	12.94	14.23	15.99	18.92	24.60	20.57	23.22	15.83
1974	17.28	20.05	22.46	21.90	21.46	23.30	25.40	33.80	38.40	39.02	43.51	27.87
1975	31.01	27.28	24.67	23.48	23.22	20.70	19.57	23.14	25.74	23.54	21.74	24.01
1976	17.04	16.92	17.08	17.10	16.82	16.57	18.71	21.22	20.70	22.65	20.67	18.68
1977	20.81	21.94	23.51	25.95	27.34	28.33	26.68	22.00	19.70	18.63	18.37	23.02
1978	20.50	19.81	20.00	22.51	22.78	24.28	24.07	22.67	23.74	25.61	26.07	22.91
1979	23.84	23.80	25.24	25.75	25.51	25.97	27.28	27.65	26.94	27.93	27.01	26.08
1980	25.61	25.16	25.36	23.84	21.97	21.96	22.67	26.90	26.70	26.91	25.63	24.79
1981	27.15	26.85	26.28	26.01	26.25	24.94	23.61	24.36	22.05	20.71	21.12	24.49
1982	21.56	21.46	21.20	19.86	20.86	21.19	19.76	18.88	17.69	17.22	17.10	19.71
1983	17.94	18.18	18.45	18.35	19.91	19.79	19.36	21.63	29.91	33.97	30.58	22.55
1984	25.56	26.87	25.51	26.24	27.55	31.08	30.02	25.54	26.46	26.06	28.03	27.17
1985	23.69	24.03	24.87	25.38	27.90	27.55	27.29	25.70	22.87	21.31	20.08	24.61

	Jan	Feb	Mar	Apr	May	Jun	Jul	Aug	Sep	Oct
AVERAGE MOVE										
All Years	0.03	0.25	0.21	0.37	0.35	0.07	0.88	0.87	-0.17	-0.04
Less Extremes	0.10	0.31	0.17	0.38	0.33	0.05	0.73	0.59	-0.20	-0.13
Ave Up - All Years	0.91	0.86	1.02	1.01	1.27	1.54	2.95	3.31	1.62	1.73
Ave Down - All Years	-0.75	-0.97	-0.71	-0.59	-0.71	-0.90	-2.23	-1.26	-1.37	-1.22
COUNT										
Number Up	7	10	8	9	8	6	9	7	6	6
Number Down	8	5	7	6	7	9	6	8	9	9
Pct Up	46.7%	66.7%	53.3%	60.0%	53.3%	40.0%	60.0%	46.7%	40.0%	40.0%
Pct Down	53.3%	33.3%	46.7%	40.0%	46.7%	60.0%	40.0%	53.3%	60.0%	60.0%
EXTREMES										
Greatest Up	2.77	2.41	2.51	2.52	3.53	2.14	8.40	8.28	4.06	4.49
Greatest Down	-3.73	-2.61	-1.51	-1.88	-2.53	-1.65	-4.68	-2.82	-4.03	-3.39

SEASONAL INDEX : AVERAGE PERCENTAGE METHOD	Dec	Jan	Feb	Mar	Apr	May	Jun	Jul	Aug	Sep	Oct
All Years	93.7	93.6	94.8	96.0	97.6	99.0	99.7	104.0	108.3	106.8	106.7
Less Extremes	93.4	94.4	95.5	96.0	97.6	98.4	99.8	103.4	106.4	105.4	104.9

SEASONAL INDEX : LINK RELATIVE METHOD	Jan	Feb	Mar	Apr	May	Jun	Jul	Aug	Sep	Oct
All Years	97.2	97.9	98.0	98.4	98.8	98.7	102.5	105.2	102.4	100.9
Less Extremes	97.1	98.0	98.1	98.8	99.5	99.2	103.0	104.3	101.8	100.3

SOYBEAN OIL - OCTOBER - MONTH OF HIGH AND LOW

Year of Expiration	Dec	Jan	Feb	Mar	Apr	May	Jun	Jul	Aug	Sep	Oct
1971	L							H			
1972					H						L
1973	L								H		
1974	L										H
1975	H						L				
1976						L				H	
1977						H					L
1978		L									H
1979		L								H	
1980						L				H	
1981	L									L	
1982	H										L
1983	L									H	
1984			L			H					
1985					H						L

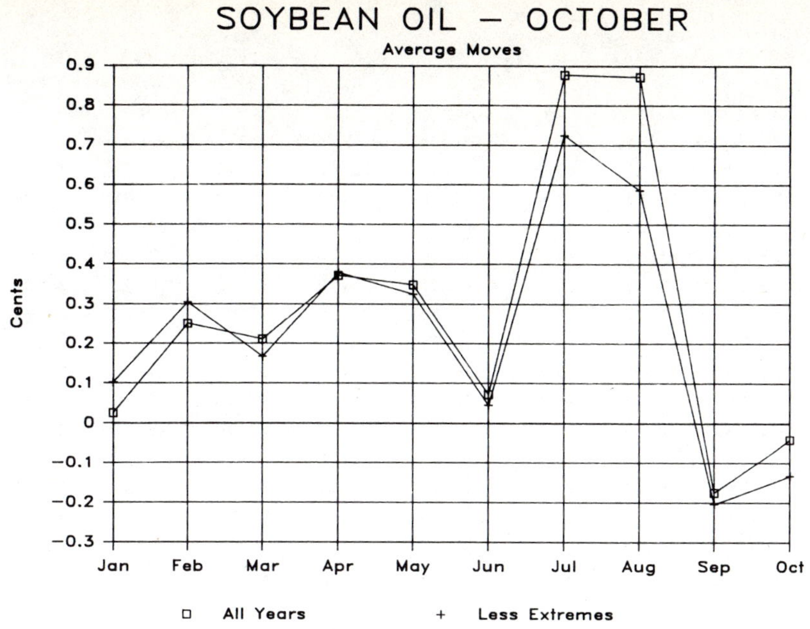
SOYBEAN OIL – OCTOBER
Average Moves
Cents
0.9
0.8
0.7
0.6
0.5
0.4
0.3
0.2
0.1
0
−0.1
−0.2
−0.3
Jan
Feb
Mar
Apr
May
Jun
Jul
Aug
Sep
Oct
□ All Years
+ Less Extremes

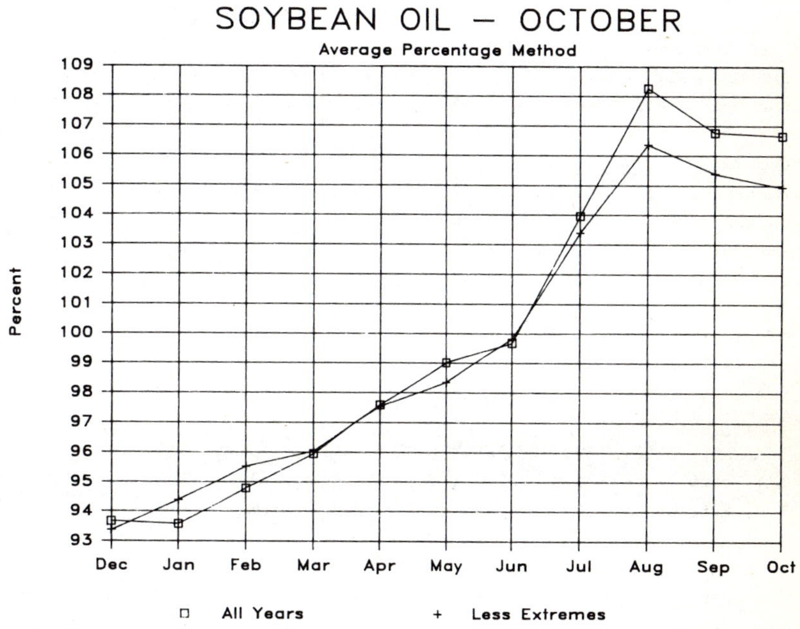
SOYBEAN OIL – OCTOBER
Average Percentage Method
Percent
109
108
107
106
105
104
103
102
101
100
99
98
97
96
95
94
93
Dec
Jan
Feb
Mar
Apr
May
Jun
Jul
Aug
Sep
Oct
□ All Years
+ Less Extremes

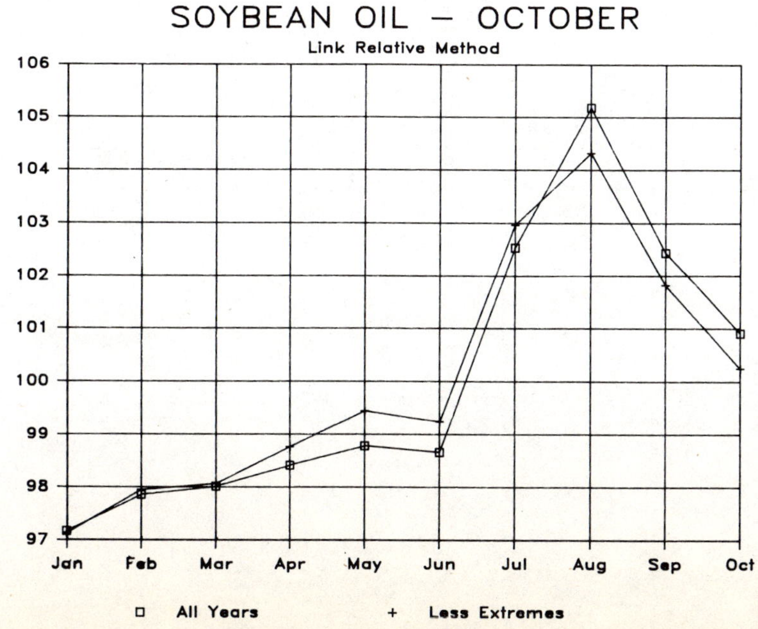
SOYBEAN OIL – OCTOBER
Link Relative Method
106
105
104
103
102
101
100
99
98
97
Jan
Feb
Mar
Apr
May
Jun
Jul
Aug
Sep
Oct
□ All Years
+ Less Extremes

SOYBEAN OIL - DECEMBER - MONTHLY AVERAGE PRICE

Year of Expiration	Feb	Mar	Apr	May	Jun	Jul	Aug	Sep	Oct	Nov	Dec	Feb-Dec Average
1971	10.67	10.68	10.37	10.64	11.73	13.11	12.87	12.35	12.82	12.43	11.69	11.76
1972	10.66	11.11	11.25	10.85	10.36	10.06	10.20	9.95	9.72	9.73	9.81	10.34
1973	10.45	11.28	11.77	12.90	14.38	17.00	20.59	17.96	19.08	18.78	25.37	16.32
1974	21.69	21.31	20.52	22.19	24.19	31.99	36.36	38.00	42.28	40.21	37.26	30.54
1975	23.69	22.56	22.21	20.03	18.95	22.35	24.92	23.06	20.79	18.52	16.92	21.27
1976	17.21	17.20	16.96	16.75	18.99	21.47	20.87	22.85	21.15	21.97	21.27	19.70
1977	23.37	25.47	26.72	27.31	25.92	21.41	19.34	18.76	18.34	20.32	22.29	22.66
1978	19.93	22.05	22.31	23.58	23.30	22.00	23.04	24.81	25.83	24.43	24.76	23.28
1979	24.86	25.32	25.19	25.79	27.26	27.35	26.33	27.05	26.11	26.45	25.75	26.13
1980	25.66	24.26	22.42	22.32	23.04	27.16	27.02	27.53	26.30	27.90	25.02	25.33
1981	26.90	26.61	26.88	25.59	24.26	25.14	22.90	21.59	21.50	20.47	19.57	23.76
1982	21.63	20.15	21.21	21.53	20.13	19.24	18.05	17.63	17.14	17.08	16.64	19.13
1983	18.70	18.71	20.31	20.14	19.61	21.96	30.05	34.26	30.22	27.69	26.76	24.40
1984	25.28	25.71	26.50	29.34	28.75	24.35	25.88	25.23	26.12	28.16	27.24	26.60
1985	24.30	24.73	27.11	26.75	26.39	25.12	22.79	21.24	19.86	19.94	20.67	23.54

	Feb	Mar	Apr	May	Jun	Jul	Aug	Sep	Oct	Nov	Dec
AVERAGE MOVE											
All Years		0.14	0.30	0.27	0.10	0.83	0.77	0.07	-0.34	-0.21	-0.21
Less Extremes		0.12	0.31	0.26	0.05	0.71	0.44	-0.04	-0.41	-0.20	-0.52
Ave Up - All Years		0.76	0.91	1.09	1.50	2.79	3.05	1.80	1.55	0.99	1.94
Ave Down - All Years		-0.78	-0.61	-0.67	-0.83	-2.11	-1.23	-1.09	-1.28	-1.25	-1.28
COUNT											
Number Up		9	9	8	6	9	7	6	5	7	5
Number Down		6	6	7	9	6	8	9	10	8	10
Pct Up		60.0%	60.0%	53.3%	40.0%	60.0%	46.7%	40.0%	33.3%	46.7%	33.3%
Pct Down		40.0%	40.0%	46.7%	60.0%	40.0%	53.3%	60.0%	66.7%	53.3%	66.7%
EXTREMES											
Greatest Up		2.12	2.38	2.84	2.24	7.80	8.09	4.21	4.28	2.04	6.59
Greatest Down		-1.48	-1.84	-2.18	-1.40	-4.50	-2.33	-2.63	-4.04	-2.52	-2.95
SEASONAL INDEX : AVERAGE PERCENTAGE METHOD											
All Years	94.3	95.1	96.5	97.4	98.0	101.8	105.1	104.7	103.0	102.0	102.0
Less Extremes	95.1	95.7	97.1	97.6	98.2	102.0	105.0	103.6	102.0	101.1	99.7
SEASONAL INDEX : LINK RELATIVE METHOD											
All Years		96.5	97.1	97.6	98.1	102.2	105.0	103.6	101.2	99.8	98.9
Less Extremes		96.2	97.2	98.3	98.7	103.0	104.5	103.4	101.2	100.0	97.6

SOYBEAN OIL - DECEMBER - MONTH OF HIGH AND LOW

Year of Expiration	Feb	Mar	Apr	May	Jun	Jul	Aug	Sep	Oct	Nov	Dec
1971			L			H					
1972			H						L		
1973	L										H
1974			L						H		
1975							H				L
1976				L				H			
1977				H					L		
1978	L								H		
1979	L					H					
1980				L						H	
1981	H										L
1982	H										L
1983	L							H			
1984				H		L					
1985			H						L		

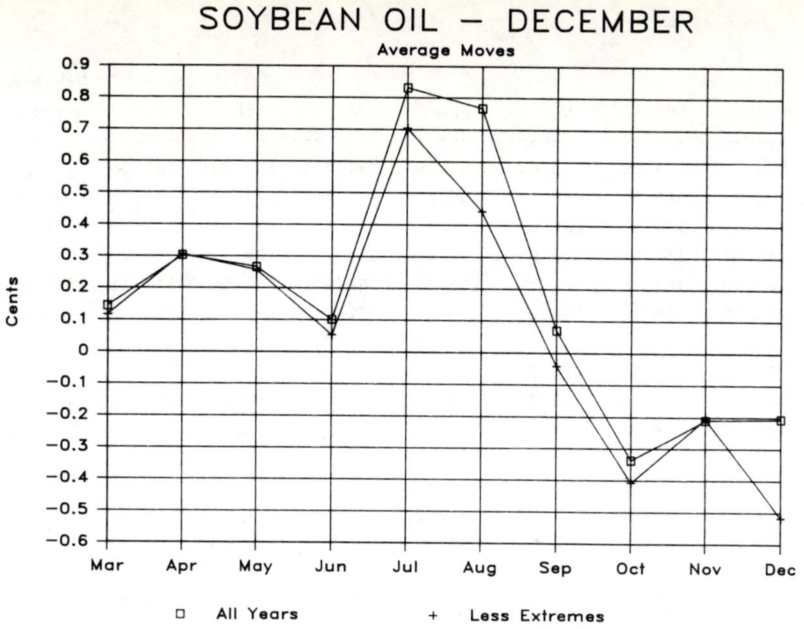
SOYBEAN OIL – DECEMBER
Average Moves
Cents
0.9
0.8
0.7
0.6
0.5
0.4
0.3
0.2
0.1
0
−0.1
−0.2
−0.3
−0.4
−0.5
−0.6
Mar
Apr
May
Jun
Jul
Aug
Sep
Oct
Nov
Dec
□ All Years
+ Less Extremes

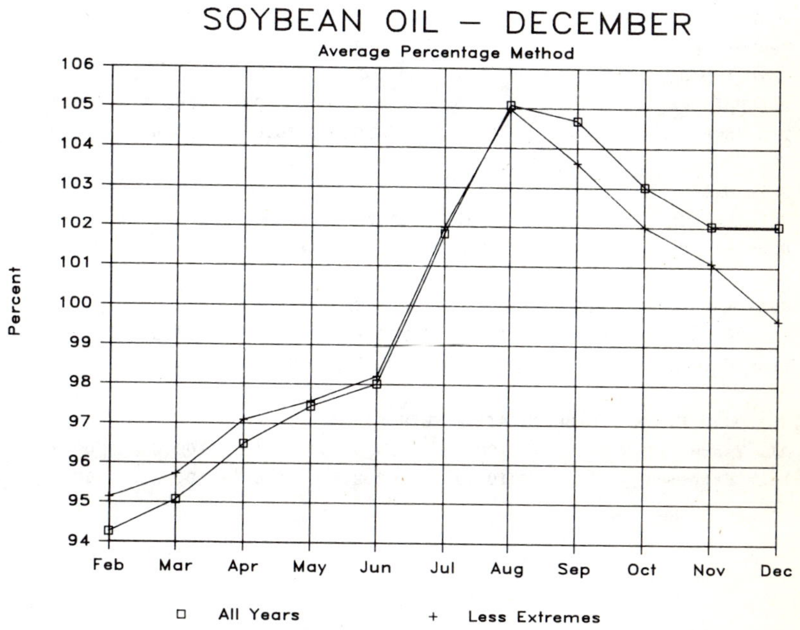
SOYBEAN OIL – DECEMBER
Average Percentage Method
Percent
106
105
104
103
102
101
100
99
98
97
96
95
94
Feb
Mar
Apr
May
Jun
Jul
Aug
Sep
Oct
Nov
Dec
□ All Years
+ Less Extremes

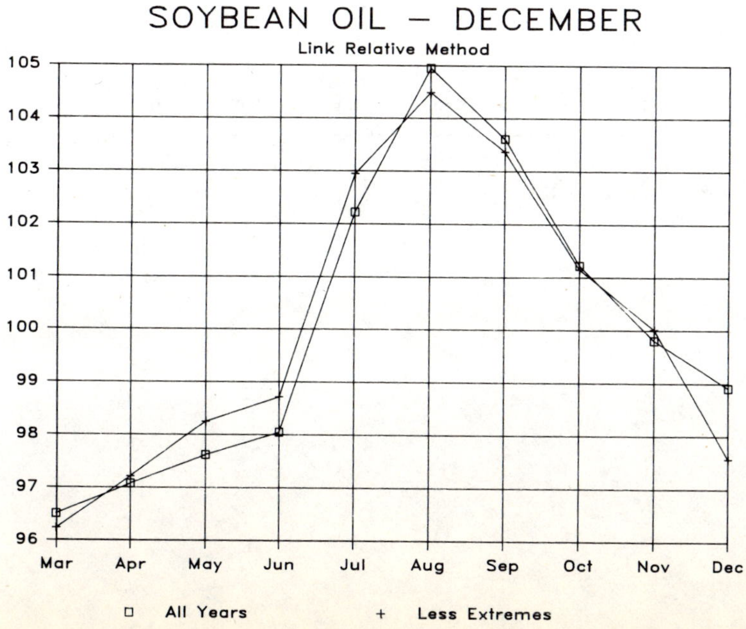
SOYBEAN OIL – DECEMBER
Link Relative Method
105
104
103
102
101
100
99
98
97
96
Mar
Apr
May
Jun
Jul
Aug
Sep
Oct
Nov
Dec
□ All Years
+ Less Extremes

OATS - MARCH - MONTHLY AVERAGE PRICE

Year of Expiration	May	Jun	Jul	Aug	Sep	Oct	Nov	Dec	Jan	Feb	Mar	May-Mar Average
1976	144.80	142.11	152.72	166.92	160.20	154.20	155.04	150.20	154.75	160.32	160.56	154.71
1977	172.26	180.11	178.71	169.09	173.43	165.56	159.41	165.27	176.30	179.90	174.78	172.26
1978	159.53	148.75	128.83	119.19	129.19	131.68	138.98	136.04	131.93	127.41	127.92	134.49
1979	165.06	153.28	144.31	142.33	148.91	152.80	146.09	138.95	135.17	138.29	130.40	145.05
1980	171.22	182.58	177.79	168.30	167.72	164.45	159.13	158.49	146.88	143.55	137.11	161.56
1981	181.93	182.61	203.98	204.51	218.12	216.67	227.06	224.77	222.01	228.33	224.58	212.23
1982	229.31	219.77	212.80	201.85	189.42	203.01	217.83	201.50	209.71	214.29	211.45	210.08
1983	190.70	177.00	174.93	162.76	163.55	158.38	170.28	168.87	168.66	155.74	152.03	167.54
1984	184.31	177.01	183.38	200.87	201.85	196.20	188.91	184.64	182.06	167.93	180.42	186.14
1985	192.40	184.19	180.95	177.19	175.36	179.45	181.83	180.64	176.14	175.80	176.63	180.05

	May	Jun	Jul	Aug	Sep	Oct	Nov	Dec	Jan	Feb	Mar
AVERAGE MOVE											
All Years		-4.41	-0.90	-2.54	1.47	-0.54	2.22	-3.52	-0.58	-1.21	-1.57
Less Extremes		-5.22	-1.31	-3.84	1.70	-1.38	1.83	-3.09	-0.65	-0.53	-2.53
Ave Up - All Years		6.63	12.78	10.74	6.05	6.01	7.94	5.86	7.93	4.64	3.52
Ave Down - All Years		-9.14	-6.77	-8.23	-5.39	-4.90	-6.37	-4.56	-4.22	-7.05	-4.96
COUNT											
Number Up		3	3	3	6	4	6	1	3	5	4
Number Down		7	7	7	4	6	4	9	7	5	6
Pct Up		30.0%	30.0%	30.0%	60.0%	40.0%	60.0%	10.0%	30.0%	50.0%	40.0%
Pct Down		70.0%	70.0%	70.0%	40.0%	60.0%	40.0%	90.0%	70.0%	50.0%	60.0%
EXTREMES											
Greatest Up		11.37	21.37	17.50	13.61	13.59	14.81	5.86	11.02	6.32	12.49
Greatest Down		-13.70	-19.93	-12.17	-12.43	-7.87	-7.30	-16.32	-11.61	-14.13	-7.89
SEASONAL INDEX : AVERAGE PERCENTAGE METHOD											
All Years	104.7	101.9	100.9	99.3	100.3	99.9	101.0	99.0	98.5	97.7	96.7
Less Extremes	105.3	102.5	100.3	99.5	100.6	99.9	101.3	98.6	98.7	97.6	97.1
SEASONAL INDEX : LINK RELATIVE METHOD											
All Years		100.1	99.8	98.7	100.2	100.3	101.8	100.2	100.1	99.7	99.0
Less Extremes		100.3	100.2	98.6	100.2	100.0	101.6	100.1	100.0	100.0	99.0

OATS - MARCH - MONTH OF HIGH AND LOW

Year of Expiration	May	Jun	Jul	Aug	Sep	Oct	Nov	Dec	Jan	Feb	Mar
1976		L		H							
1977		H					L				
1978	H									L	
1979	H										L
1980		H									L
1981	L									H	
1982	H				L						
1983	H										L
1984					H					L	
1985	H				L						

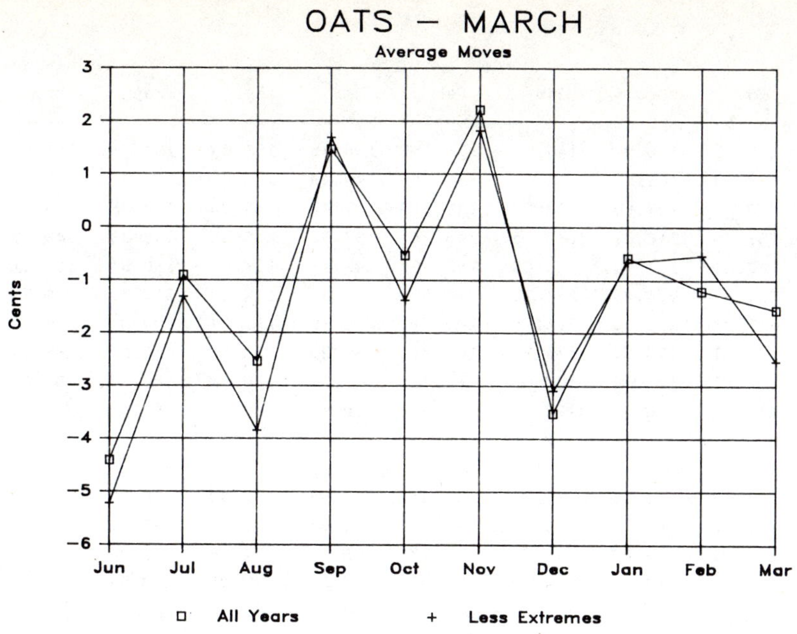
OATS – MARCH
Average Moves
Cents
3
2
1
0
−1
−2
−3
−4
−5
−6
Jun
Jul
Aug
Sep
Oct
Nov
Dec
Jan
Feb
Mar
All Years
Less Extremes

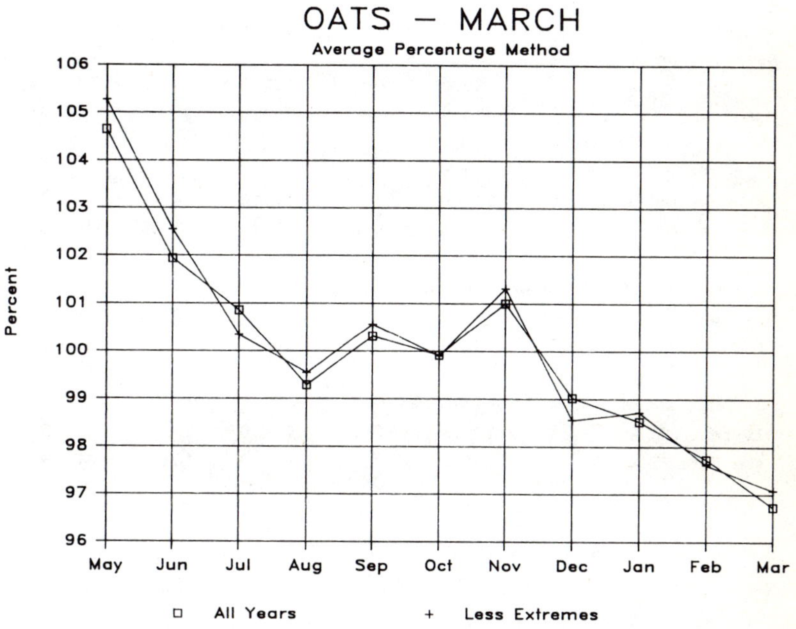
OATS – MARCH
Average Percentage Method
Percent
106
105
104
103
102
101
100
99
98
97
96
May
Jun
Jul
Aug
Sep
Oct
Nov
Dec
Jan
Feb
Mar
All Years
Less Extremes

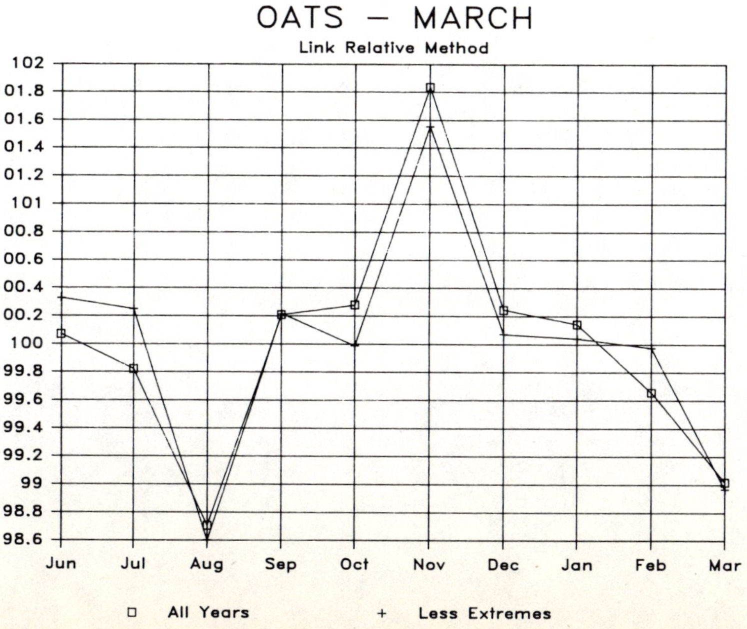
OATS – MARCH
Link Relative Method
102
101.8
101.6
101.4
101.2
101
100.8
100.6
100.4
100.2
100
99.8
99.6
99.4
99.2
99
98.8
98.6
Jun
Jul
Aug
Sep
Oct
Nov
Dec
Jan
Feb
Mar
All Years
Less Extremes

OATS - MAY - MONTHLY AVERAGE PRICE

Year of Expiration	Jul	Aug	Sep	Oct	Nov	Dec	Jan	Feb	Mar	Apr	May	Jul-May Average
1976	152.82	167.17	159.35	152.65	151.15	146.92	149.98	156.05	156.45	153.89	154.98	154.67
1977	177.82	167.88	173.45	165.81	159.53	163.52	172.66	177.25	170.99	176.03	171.87	170.62
1978	135.51	123.68	131.42	134.45	139.99	137.66	134.80	130.82	137.05	144.90	140.35	135.51
1979	145.98	144.59	151.16	156.30	151.74	146.63	142.55	146.54	137.92	139.56	148.33	146.48
1980	180.14	174.02	174.84	171.75	167.21	166.79	156.65	152.59	142.41	139.61	160.54	162.41
1981	206.27	207.37	220.68	221.08	229.43	228.86	224.71	226.88	216.44	219.19	215.77	219.70
1982	216.46	204.41	186.13	197.14	211.33	194.55	201.75	203.79	198.19	211.04	209.37	203.10
1983	175.99	166.68	168.85	166.27	177.21	175.57	176.32	164.74	160.20	162.56	158.61	168.45
1984	188.76	208.85	208.66	200.21	192.71	187.16	183.01	169.54	179.31	180.11	180.77	189.01
1985	180.93	176.51	173.28	177.01	179.20	176.81	173.78	171.50	170.91	167.12	161.40	173.50

AVERAGE MOVE	Jul	Aug	Sep	Oct	Nov	Dec	Jan	Feb	Mar	Apr	May
All Years		-1.95	0.67	-0.51	1.68	-3.50	-0.82	-1.65	-2.99	2.42	0.80
Less Extremes		-3.45	1.45	-0.96	1.27	-2.78	-0.90	-1.14	-3.65	1.89	-0.91
Ave Up - All Years		11.84	6.03	4.66	8.24	4.00	5.04	3.77	5.46	4.76	7.86
Ave Down - All Years		-7.87	-7.38	-5.69	-4.88	-4.34	-4.73	-7.08	-6.61	-3.05	-3.91

COUNT	Jul	Aug	Sep	Oct	Nov	Dec	Jan	Feb	Mar	Apr	May
Number Up		3	6	5	5	1	4	5	3	7	4
Number Down		7	4	5	5	9	6	5	7	3	6
Pct Up		30.0%	60.0%	50.0%	50.0%	10.0%	40.0%	50.0%	30.0%	70.0%	40.0%
Pct Down		70.0%	40.0%	50.0%	50.0%	90.0%	60.0%	50.0%	70.0%	30.0%	60.0%

EXTREMES	Jul	Aug	Sep	Oct	Nov	Dec	Jan	Feb	Mar	Apr	May
Greatest Up		20.09	13.31	11.00	14.19	4.00	9.13	6.08	9.77	12.85	20.93
Greatest Down		-12.05	-18.27	-8.44	-7.50	-16.78	-10.14	-13.47	-10.44	-3.79	-5.72

SEASONAL INDEX : AVERAGE PERCENTAGE METHOD	Jul	Aug	Sep	Oct	Nov	Dec	Jan	Feb	Mar	Apr	May
All Years	102.3	101.0	101.5	101.2	102.0	100.0	99.5	98.5	96.9	98.3	98.9
Less Extremes	102.2	101.0	101.6	101.0	102.7	100.1	99.2	99.0	97.5	98.7	99.0

SEASONAL INDEX : LINK RELATIVE METHOD	Jul	Aug	Sep	Oct	Nov	Dec	Jan	Feb	Mar	Apr	May
All Years		100.3	101.1	101.0	102.0	100.2	99.8	99.0	97.6	99.0	100.0
Less Extremes		99.8	101.2	101.0	101.9	100.4	100.0	99.5	97.9	99.3	99.1

OATS - MAY - MONTH OF HIGH AND LOW

Year of Expiration	Jul	Aug	Sep	Oct	Nov	Dec	Jan	Feb	Mar	Apr	May
1976		H				L					
1977	H				L						
1978		L								H	
1979				H					L		
1980	H									L	
1981	L				H						
1982	H		L								
1983					H						L
1984		H						L			
1985	H										L

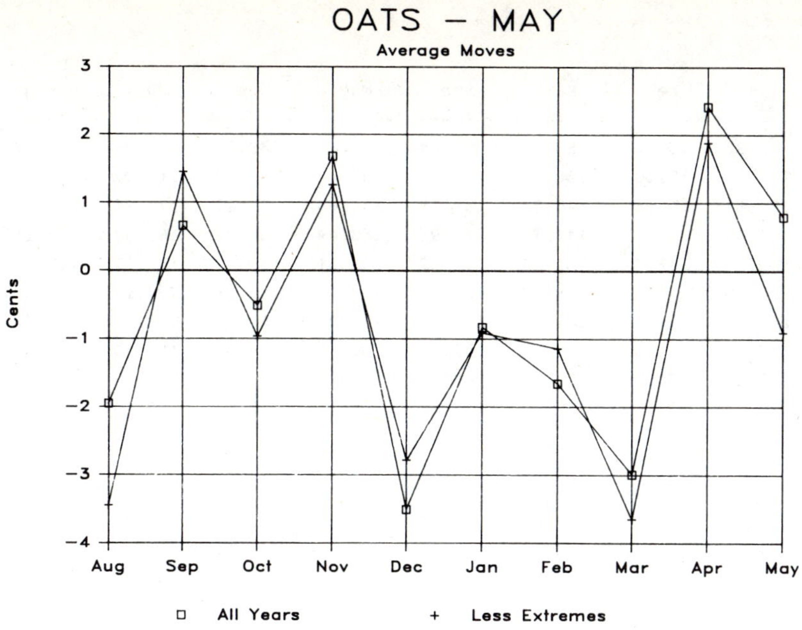
OATS — MAY
Average Moves
Cents
3
2
1
0
−1
−2
−3
−4
Aug
Sep
Oct
Nov
Dec
Jan
Feb
Mar
Apr
May
□ All Years
+ Less Extremes

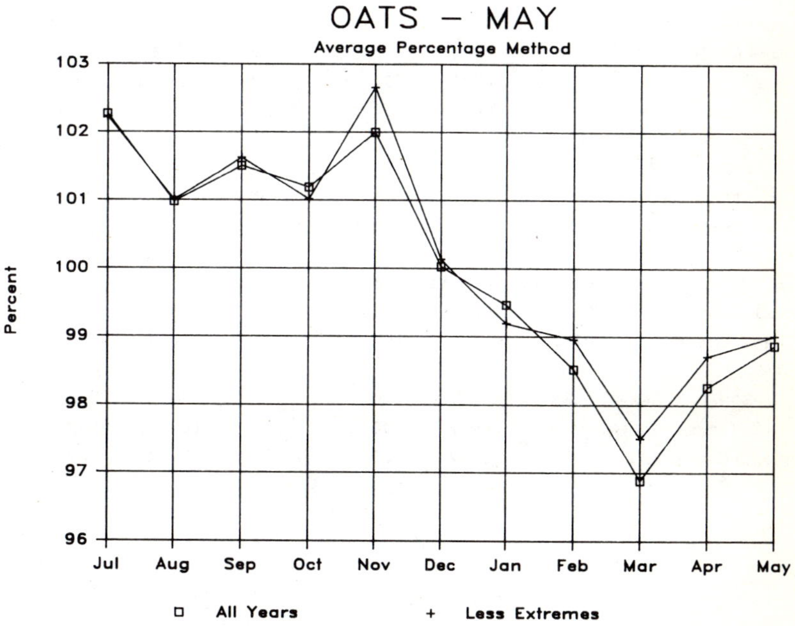
OATS — MAY
Average Percentage Method
Percent
103
102
101
100
99
98
97
96
Jul
Aug
Sep
Oct
Nov
Dec
Jan
Feb
Mar
Apr
May
□ All Years
+ Less Extremes

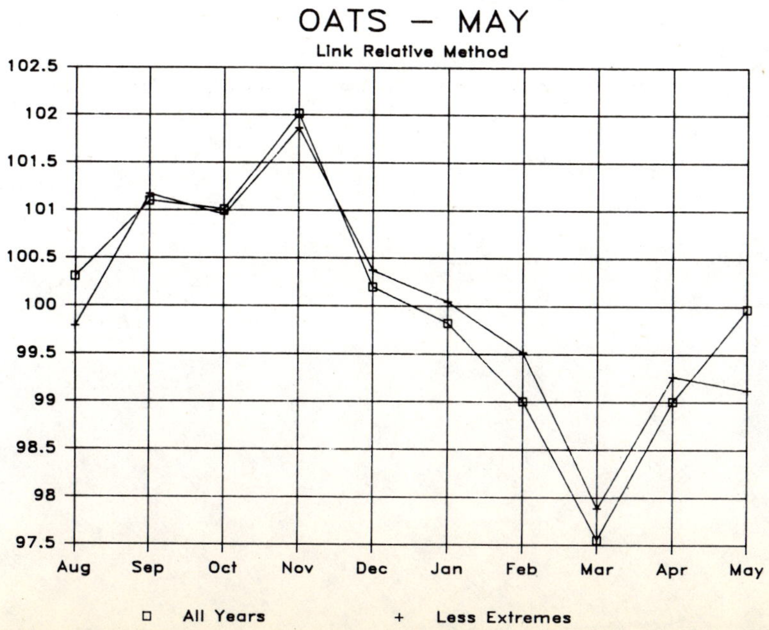
OATS — MAY
Link Relative Method
102.5
102
101.5
101
100.5
100
99.5
99
98.5
98
97.5
Aug
Sep
Oct
Nov
Dec
Jan
Feb
Mar
Apr
May
□ All Years
+ Less Extremes

OATS - JULY - MONTHLY AVERAGE PRICE

Year of Expiration	Sep	Oct	Nov	Dec	Jan	Feb	Mar	Apr	May	Jun	Jul	Sep-Jul Average
1976	159.07	150.16	147.58	142.70	146.32	151.86	153.25	150.04	158.28	188.39	190.05	157.97
1977	170.60	162.18	154.96	158.16	168.10	171.08	164.88	164.84	159.43	136.09	115.92	156.93
1978	131.19	134.87	139.63	138.17	135.68	131.38	140.81	151.38	148.68	136.17	123.96	137.45
1979	151.50	155.80	153.00	151.44	147.66	152.67	145.76	147.95	153.64	161.27	163.54	153.11
1980	177.46	175.84	171.46	171.84	165.14	161.31	151.54	147.87	165.51	169.99	180.17	167.10
1981	218.23	214.55	220.63	226.00	220.49	217.53	208.82	215.77	213.21	209.86	203.15	215.29
1982	181.08	192.26	198.69	185.09	188.85	192.18	183.30	197.77	193.08	186.50	188.50	189.76
1983	170.50	167.89	176.41	176.31	183.48	171.96	166.61	168.64	159.19	154.33	151.48	167.89
1984	212.89	203.19	193.79	187.23	181.17	170.99	177.46	180.31	185.15	183.74	185.45	187.40
1985	171.01	174.41	175.99	173.06	170.28	166.40	166.73	163.41	155.13	151.08	146.10	164.87

	Sep	Oct	Nov	Dec	Jan	Feb	Mar	Apr	May	Jun	Jul
AVERAGE MOVE											
All Years		-1.24	0.10	-2.21	-0.28	-1.98	-2.82	2.88	0.33	-1.39	-2.91
Less Extremes		-1.73	0.23	-1.74	-0.76	-1.73	-3.48	2.25	-0.61	-2.58	-2.39
Ave Up - All Years		5.64	5.47	2.98	6.12	4.22	4.40	6.51	9.10	14.07	3.56
Ave Down - All Years		-5.82	-5.27	-4.44	-4.55	-6.11	-7.64	-2.56	-5.52	-8.01	-9.38
COUNT											
Number Up		4	5	3	4	4	4	6	4	3	5
Number Down		6	5	7	6	6	6	4	6	7	5
Pct Up		40.0%	50.0%	30.0%	40.0%	40.0%	40.0%	60.0%	40.0%	30.0%	50.0%
Pct Down		60.0%	50.0%	70.0%	60.0%	60.0%	60.0%	40.0%	60.0%	70.0%	50.0%
EXTREMES											
Greatest Up		11.18	8.52	5.38	9.94	5.53	9.42	14.47	17.64	30.11	10.18
Greatest Down		-9.70	-9.40	-13.60	-6.71	-11.51	-9.78	-3.67	-9.45	-23.33	-20.17
SEASONAL INDEX : AVERAGE PERCENTAGE METHOD											
All Years	102.6	101.9	101.9	100.6	100.5	99.4	97.9	99.5	99.8	98.9	97.0
Less Extremes	102.1	101.9	102.3	101.3	100.4	99.2	97.9	99.6	99.4	97.9	97.0
SEASONAL INDEX : LINK RELATIVE METHOD											
All Years		100.2	100.6	99.7	100.1	99.4	98.4	100.4	101.3	100.9	99.0
Less Extremes		100.2	100.8	100.3	100.4	100.0	98.6	100.5	100.8	99.8	98.7

OATS - JULY - MONTH OF HIGH AND LOW

Year of Expiration	Sep	Oct	Nov	Dec	Jan	Feb	Mar	Apr	May	Jun	Jul
1976				L							H
1977						H					L
1978								H			L
1979							L				H
1980								L			H
1981				H							L
1982	L		H								
1983					H						L
1984	H					L					
1985			H								L

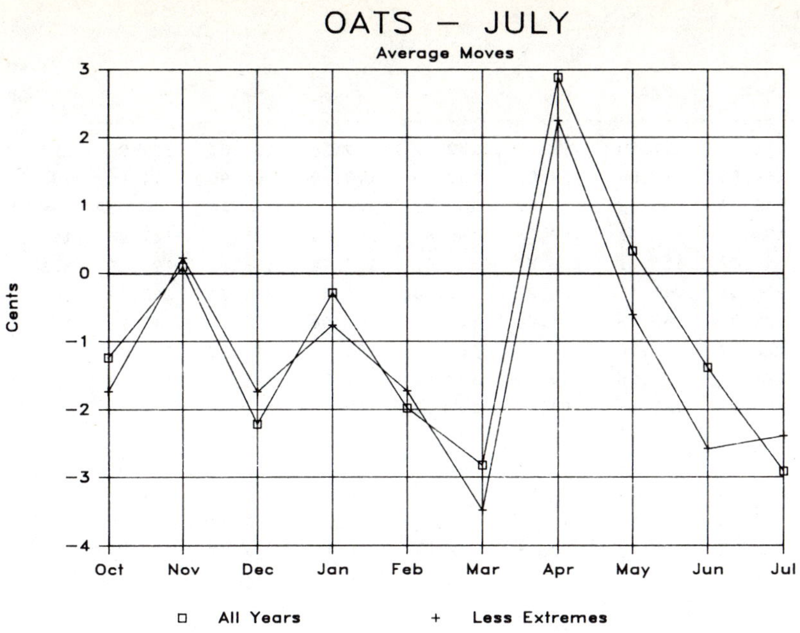
OATS – JULY
Average Moves
3
2
1
0
−1
−2
−3
−4
Cents
Oct
Nov
Dec
Jan
Feb
Mar
Apr
May
Jun
Jul
All Years
Less Extremes

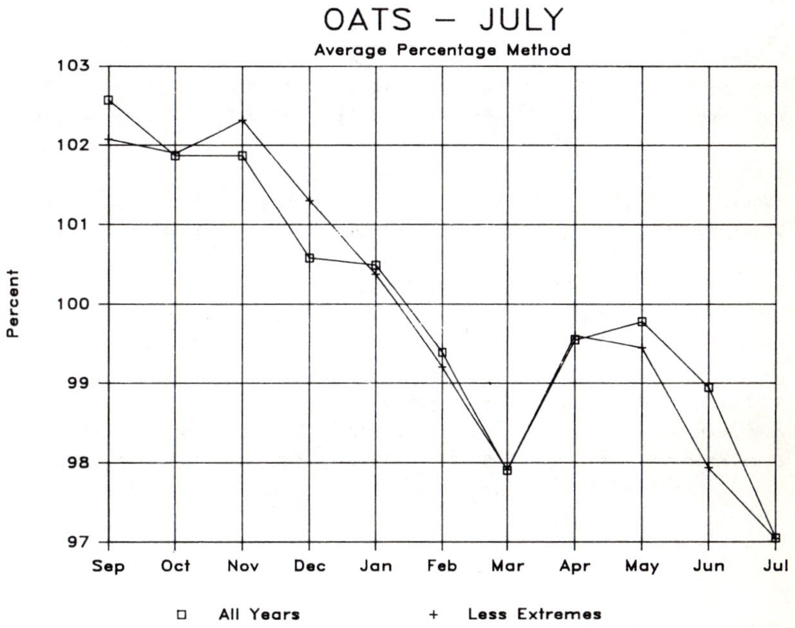
OATS – JULY
Average Percentage Method
103
102
101
100
99
98
97
Percent
Sep
Oct
Nov
Dec
Jan
Feb
Mar
Apr
May
Jun
Jul
All Years
Less Extremes

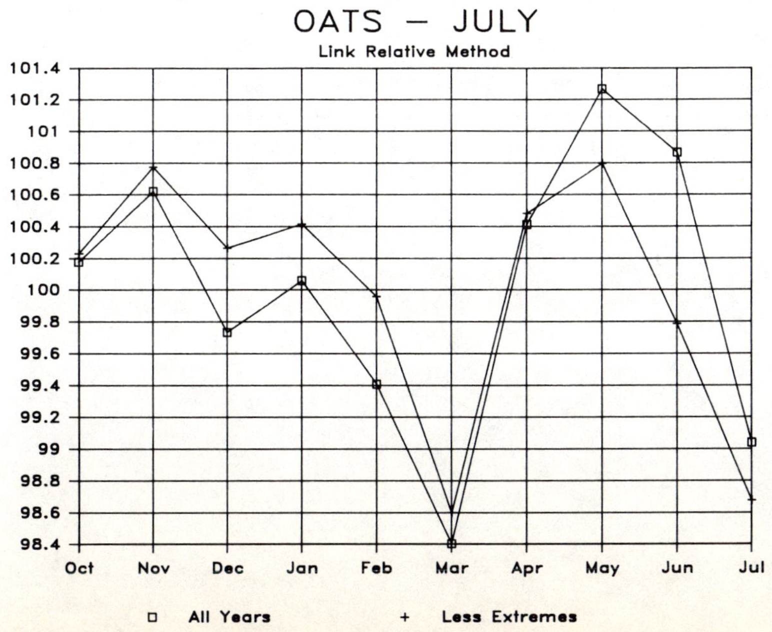
OATS – JULY
Link Relative Method
101.4
101.2
101
100.8
100.6
100.4
100.2
100
99.8
99.6
99.4
99.2
99
98.8
98.6
98.4
Oct
Nov
Dec
Jan
Feb
Mar
Apr
May
Jun
Jul
All Years
Less Extremes

OATS - SEPTEMBER - MONTHLY AVERAGE PRICE

Year of Expiration	Nov	Dec	Jan	Feb	Mar	Apr	May	Jun	Jul	Aug	Sep	Nov-Sep Average
1976	157.78	137.75	145.99	150.50	151.28	147.94	154.98	182.59	179.13	162.67	164.96	157.78
1977	143.85	156.00	163.02	166.63	160.53	159.04	154.03	139.33	118.30	106.90	114.68	143.85
1978	139.41	138.05	137.71	134.00	144.14	155.19	154.17	142.51	128.49	126.16	130.75	139.14
1979	155.69	155.34	152.18	157.30	153.17	153.91	159.08	169.67	163.20	145.23	141.46	155.11
1980	173.19	175.74	171.35	167.85	159.62	155.01	168.86	171.57	186.74	178.86	196.29	173.19
1981	216.57	222.36	217.68	218.03	207.98	216.69	209.21	202.74	194.46	193.43	200.98	209.10
1982	196.60	183.34	184.70	186.84	176.01	188.25	181.24	171.94	168.94	151.10	147.16	176.01
1983	175.16	176.68	187.87	178.25	173.87	174.56	162.69	156.83	160.70	174.92	179.00	172.78
1984	193.21	185.08	177.91	170.04	175.18	179.65	184.43	178.44	176.27	173.02	176.54	179.07
1985	177.34	169.98	166.36	164.22	162.92	160.54	154.25	147.19	137.64	119.61	119.83	152.72

	Nov	Dec	Jan	Feb	Mar	Apr	May	Jun	Jul	Aug	Sep
AVERAGE MOVE											
All Years		-2.85	0.45	-1.11	-2.90	2.61	-0.79	-2.01	-4.89	-8.20	3.97
Less Extremes		-2.58	0.06	-0.83	-3.53	2.31	-1.23	-4.13	-5.39	-9.77	3.28
Ave Up - All Years		5.50	6.95	3.15	5.35	6.32	7.71	13.64	9.52	14.22	5.93
Ave Down - All Years		-8.42	-3.89	-5.37	-6.43	-2.96	-6.45	-8.72	-8.50	-10.69	-3.86
COUNT											
Number Up		4	4	5	3	6	4	3	2	1	8
Number Down		6	6	5	7	4	6	7	8	9	2
Pct Up		40.0%	40.0%	50.0%	30.0%	60.0%	40.0%	30.0%	20.0%	10.0%	80.0%
Pct Down		60.0%	60.0%	50.0%	70.0%	40.0%	60.0%	70.0%	80.0%	90.0%	20.0%
EXTREMES											
Greatest Up		12.15	11.19	5.12	10.14	12.24	13.85	27.62	15.17	14.22	17.43
Greatest Down		-20.03	-7.18	-9.62	-10.83	-4.61	-11.87	-14.69	-21.03	-18.02	-3.94
SEASONAL INDEX : AVERAGE PERCENTAGE METHOD											
All Years	104.1	102.4	102.8	102.2	100.7	102.2	101.7	100.5	97.2	92.0	94.3
Less Extremes	103.1	103.2	102.8	101.4	100.4	102.6	101.5	99.8	97.0	92.7	93.9
SEASONAL INDEX : LINK RELATIVE METHOD											
All Years		99.6	100.7	100.8	100.0	102.2	102.6	102.1	99.4	94.7	97.8
Less Extremes		99.8	101.0	101.5	100.4	102.6	103.1	101.6	99.1	94.0	97.0

OATS - SEPTEMBER - MONTH OF HIGH AND LOW

Year of Expiration	Nov	Dec	Jan	Feb	Mar	Apr	May	Jun	Jul	Aug	Sep
1976		L						H			
1977				H						L	
1978						H				L	
1979								H			L
1980						L					H
1981		H							L		
1982	H										L
1983			H					L			
1984	H			L							
1985	H									L	

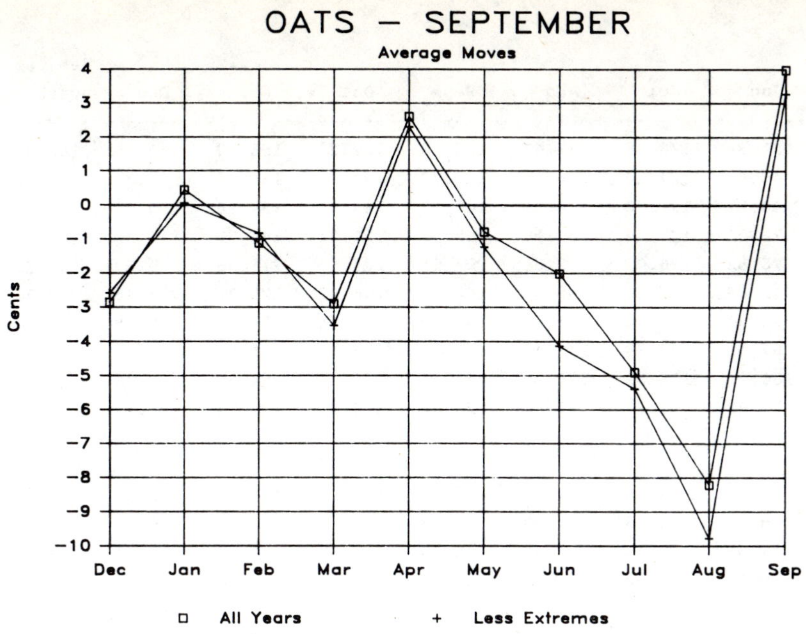
OATS – SEPTEMBER
Average Moves
Cents
4
3
2
1
0
−1
−2
−3
−4
−5
−6
−7
−8
−9
−10
Dec
Jan
Feb
Mar
Apr
May
Jun
Jul
Aug
Sep
All Years
Less Extremes

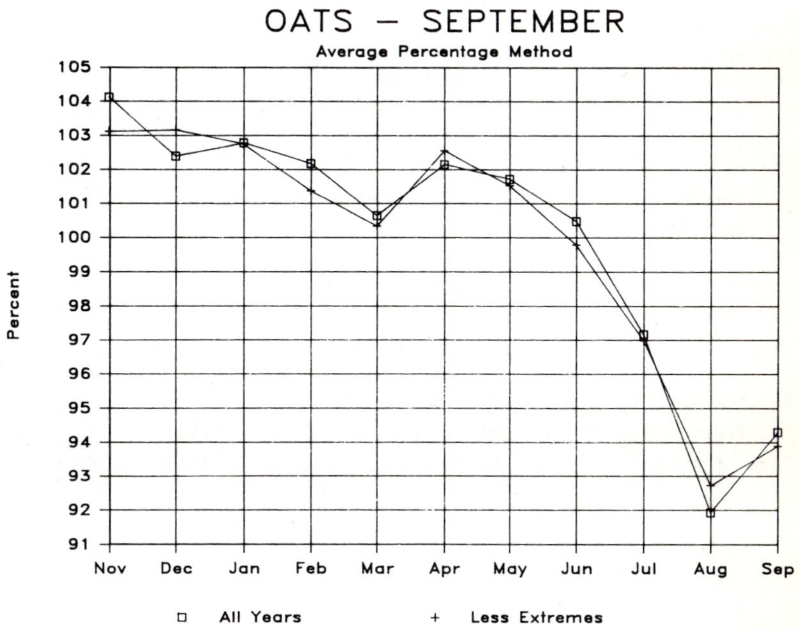
OATS – SEPTEMBER
Average Percentage Method
Percent
105
104
103
102
101
100
99
98
97
96
95
94
93
92
91
Nov
Dec
Jan
Feb
Mar
Apr
May
Jun
Jul
Aug
Sep
All Years
Less Extremes

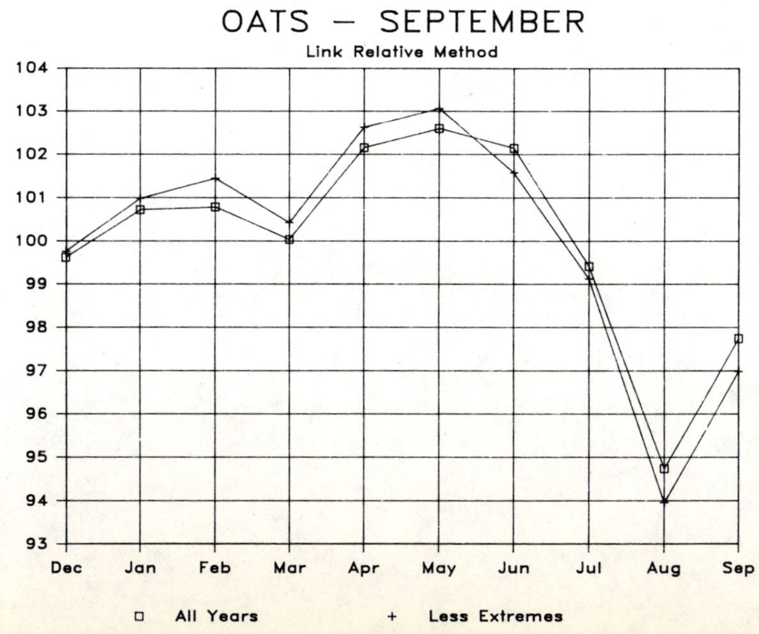
OATS – SEPTEMBER
Link Relative Method
104
103
102
101
100
99
98
97
96
95
94
93
Dec
Jan
Feb
Mar
Apr
May
Jun
Jul
Aug
Sep
All Years
Less Extremes

OATS -DECEMBER - MONTHLY AVERAGE PRICE

Year of Expiration	Feb	Mar	Apr	May	Jun	Jul	Aug	Sep	Oct	Nov	Dec	Feb-Dec Average
1976	163.96	151.55	150.18	156.98	181.33	178.98	167.47	168.69	162.20	156.00	166.25	163.96
1977	169.24	163.35	162.10	157.40	144.89	124.20	114.57	122.79	124.80	136.04	131.82	141.02
1978	139.07	149.13	160.19	160.10	148.57	137.38	134.94	142.13	144.01	134.98	130.08	143.69
1979	162.93	160.18	160.98	165.48	178.31	173.29	159.10	155.09	151.01	144.71	142.65	159.43
1980	177.88	170.35	165.60	176.37	176.83	196.02	193.35	207.63	205.63	213.38	215.59	190.78
1981	225.96	217.18	227.60	219.66	211.09	203.53	195.58	193.27	208.83	225.21	213.78	212.88
1982	191.54	179.26	193.13	185.93	173.61	171.76	157.76	155.39	147.54	159.29	159.68	170.44
1983	187.49	184.74	186.13	173.79	167.59	173.78	188.66	190.66	188.46	181.02	180.66	182.09
1984	174.71	178.82	183.90	188.72	180.75	178.52	176.52	177.43	179.33	184.89	195.76	181.76
1985	167.54	165.81	164.08	158.90	151.38	141.33	127.59	126.00	120.74	124.74	129.23	143.39

	Feb	Mar	Apr	May	Jun	Jul	Aug	Sep	Oct	Nov	Dec
AVERAGE MOVE											
All Years		-4.00	3.35	-1.06	-2.90	-3.56	-6.33	2.36	-0.65	2.77	0.52
Less Extremes		-4.70	3.05	-1.12	-5.10	-4.26	-7.99	1.66	-1.78	2.55	0.73
Ave Up - All Years		7.08	7.10	6.72	12.55	12.69	14.89	5.64	5.34	9.45	5.64
Ave Down - All Years		-6.76	-2.27	-6.24	-9.52	-7.62	-8.68	-2.57	-4.65	-7.24	-4.59
COUNT											
Number Up		2	6	4	3	2	1	6	4	6	5
Number Down		8	4	6	7	8	9	4	6	4	5
Pct Up		20.0%	60.0%	40.0%	30.0%	20.0%	10.0%	60.0%	40.0%	60.0%	50.0%
Pct Down		80.0%	40.0%	60.0%	70.0%	80.0%	90.0%	40.0%	60.0%	40.0%	50.0%
EXTREMES											
Greatest Up		10.06	13.87	10.77	24.36	19.19	14.89	14.29	15.56	16.38	10.87
Greatest Down		-12.41	-4.75	-12.34	-12.51	-20.69	-14.19	-4.01	-7.86	-9.04	-11.43
SEASONAL INDEX : AVERAGE PERCENTAGE METHOD											
All Years	104.7	102.4	104.4	103.7	101.9	99.3	95.3	96.7	96.1	97.6	97.9
Less Extremes	104.2	102.4	105.3	104.2	101.9	99.5	96.0	96.4	96.1	97.1	97.1
SEASONAL INDEX : LINK RELATIVE METHOD											
All Years		101.0	103.2	103.1	101.9	99.7	96.0	97.8	97.6	99.5	100.1
Less Extremes		101.7	104.0	104.1	101.8	99.8	95.5	97.3	96.8	99.1	99.9

OATS - DECEMBER - MONTH OF HIGH AND LOW

Year of Expiration	Feb	Mar	Apr	May	Jun	Jul	Aug	Sep	Oct	Nov	Dec
1976			L		H						
1977	H						L				
1978			H								L
1979					H						L
1980			L								H
1981			H					L			
1982			H						L		
1983					L			H			
1984	L			H							
1985	H								L		

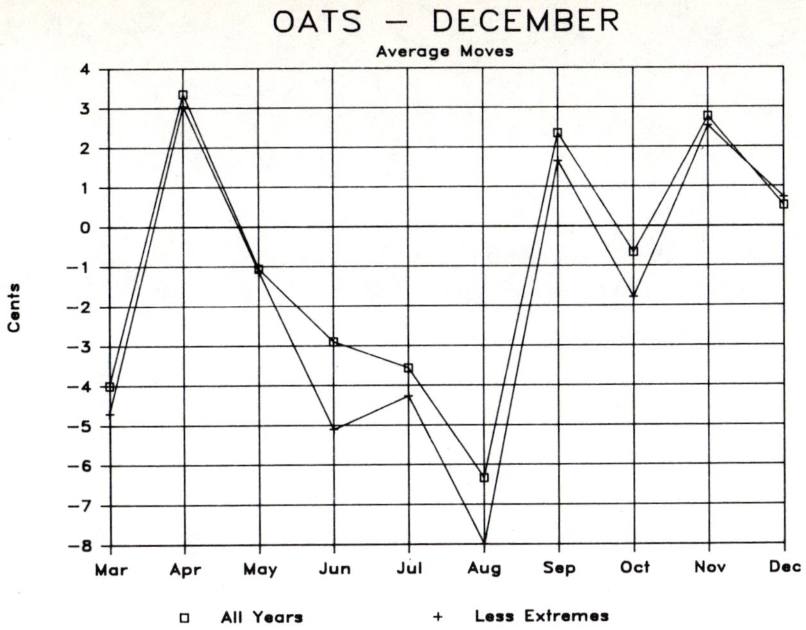
OATS – DECEMBER
Average Moves
Cents
4
3
2
1
0
−1
−2
−3
−4
−5
−6
−7
−8
Mar
Apr
May
Jun
Jul
Aug
Sep
Oct
Nov
Dec
□ All Years
+ Less Extremes

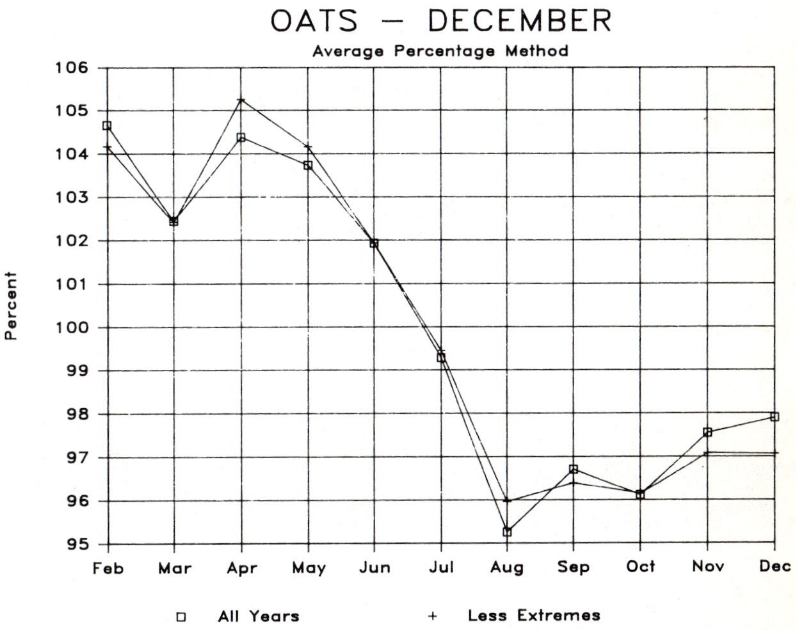
OATS – DECEMBER
Average Percentage Method
Percent
106
105
104
103
102
101
100
99
98
97
96
95
Feb
Mar
Apr
May
Jun
Jul
Aug
Sep
Oct
Nov
Dec
□ All Years
+ Less Extremes

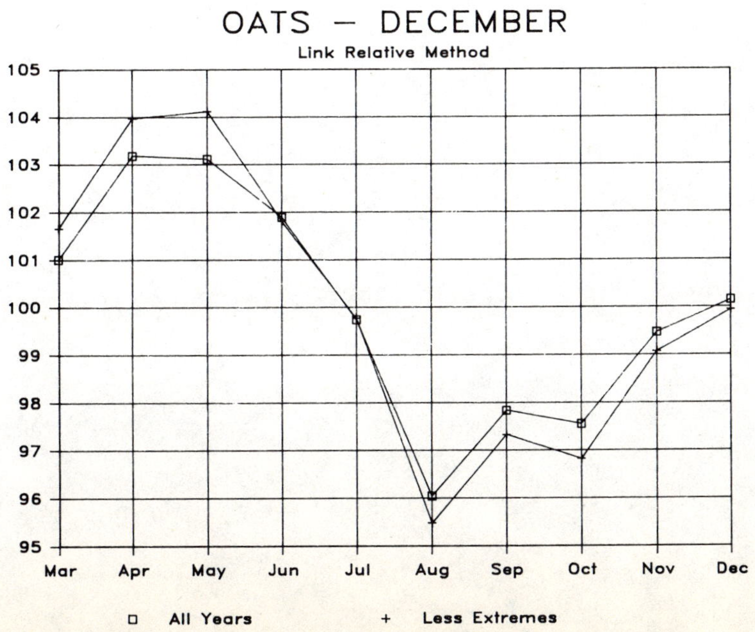
OATS – DECEMBER
Link Relative Method
105
104
103
102
101
100
99
98
97
96
95
Mar
Apr
May
Jun
Jul
Aug
Sep
Oct
Nov
Dec
□ All Years
+ Less Extremes

SEVEN

Meats

Livestock and meat prices have good seasonal price tendencies. This study shows monthly seasonal moves with over 70% reliability. For example, June cattle have rallied 73.3% the last 15 years in January with an average move of $1.37.

CATTLE AND FEEDER CATTLE PRICE SEASONALS

Cattle and feeder cattle are not stellar seasonal performers. The seasonals are not pronounced nor are they particularly strong. The best period for seasonals is probably the upswing in prices in the early summer.

Cattle and feeder cattle have essentially the same seasonality for essentially the same reasons. Feeders have a stronger seasonality primarily because the sources of slack that move cattle away from a strong seasonality are not as strong in the feeders.

The main reason for the lack of strong seasonals in the cattle market is the very long cattle cycle. The cattle cycle describes the periodic rise and fall of the cattle population; the cycle lasts typically 8 to 10 years. It is mainly a function of the life span of cattle (three years from breeding to supermarket), the price of beef, and the investment required to enter the cattle business.

Ranchers usually decide to expand their breeding stock when beef prices are high to fully exploit their rising profit margins. Cows, heifers, and heifer calves are withheld from slaughter to be used to breed more cattle. This reduction in slaughtered cattle decreases the supply of slaughter cattle and further increases the beef price. Calves, yearlings, and steers are fed to an older age and a heavier weight by the ranchers or feedlots to increase the income per animal. The process feeds on itself. As the price of beef rises, ranchers withhold even more animals, particularly the breeding stock composed of cows, heifers, and heifer calves.

Eventually, the offspring of the withheld cattle reach a marketable weight. The economics of cattle raising are essentially the same for all ranchers. This means they tend to expand their herds and bring the offspring to market at the same time. As a result of the increased supply prices drop and profits fall, thus discouraging producers from further expanding their breeding stock and herds. As a result, ranchers sell their breeding stock rather than hang on to cattle they believe will be unprofitable to raise. When the price of beef dips below the cost of raising beef, ranchers dump their remaining stock on the market as fast as possible. They do this rather than wait for the price to drop further and make even less money. Unfortunately, their prophecy of lower prices is largely fulfilled when they dump their stock on the market. Once the herd is reduced to a much lower level, a point of beef scarcity is reached. Prices rise because of the reduced supply and the cattle cycle begins again.

Basically, cattle slaughter and cattle prices are the inverse of each other. In other words, when cattle slaughter is rising, prices are usually declining; when cattle slaughter is decreasing, prices rise.

This long-term cycle, based on the cattle life cycle, tends to obscure the intrayear seasonal price moves of cattle. Nonetheless, the seasons do influence the life cycle of cattle enough to promote some price seasonality.

The seasonal cycle in cattle is the result of the fact that most calves are born within 45 days of April 1, and weaned within 45 days of October 1. The majority of cattle are slaughtered in the fall or winter. Therefore, the demand for beef, which is lowest during the turkey-eating holidays of Thanksgiving and Christmas, occurs at the same time as the heaviest cattle slaughter. As the demand for beef increases through the spring and summer, the supply is decreasing steadily.

Note that heavy cattle slaughter occurs over a period lasting several months. Even though the majority of cattle may be born at about the same time, their slaughter can be spread over many months depending on the weight to which they are fed. The weight will largely be a function of the cattle cycle outlined in the previous paragraphs. Cattle are fed to heavier weights during profitable times and to lighter weights during lean times. This has the effect of spreading the slaughter date through a period of several months depending on the economics of cattle feeding existent at that particular time. This factor is not as pronounced in the feeders. A slaughter steer can be slaughtered at a weight anywhere from 1000 to 1200 pounds, while a feeder will be placed on feed very close to 700 pounds. This ties the feeders to a tighter biological cycle which promotes price seasonality.

HOG PRICE SEASONALS

Hogs are a good seasonal market and the seasonal tendency trader can do very well in this market. Prices are very seasonal because the demand for hogs is highest when production is lowest.

The demand for pork tends to be highest during the summer months because of a corresponding increase in demand for processed luncheon meat and bacon. These products are popular during the summer vacation months because of their ease of preparation. The pattern of consumption for ham, however, is different from that of pork. Ham has two high consumption periods, Christmas and Easter. This firms hog prices during those time periods because ham is an important product of hogs and accounts for much of the value.

Most pigs are born during the months of March, April, and May; the smallest number are born in December, January, and February. Because of this seasonality in births, the production of hogs follows a definite seasonal pattern. It takes roughly five to seven months to fatten a pig for slaughter. Pigs born in the spring are ready for market from August through December. At the same time, there tends to be a shortage of production during the summer because of the shortage of births during the winter months of December, January, and February. This creates a seasonally strong period in the summer.

The seasonality of hogs was more pronounced until the advent of widespread full confinement hog raising in the 1970s. This has reduced the seasonality of production of hogs and, hence, of prices.

PORK BELLY PRICE SEASONALS

The seasonal fluctuation of frozen pork bellies in and out of cold storage, combined with the seasonality of pork belly production, creates many good trading prospects for the seasonal trader. Pork belly demand is steady throughout the year except for a slight increase in demand in the summer. The key factor driving belly prices is the supply, particularly the level of storage stocks.

The supply comes from two sources, fresh and frozen bellies. There tends to be a surplus of pork belly production over demand from October to May because of the seasonal pattern of hog slaughter (see Hog Price Seasonals). This means that the excess pork bellies must be frozen for use during the late May to September period when hog production is lower.

Since the belly contract calls for delivery of frozen, not fresh bellies, the price reflects the relationship between frozen and fresh bellies and the absolute level of storage stocks of frozen pork bellies. The price tends to be weakest in the late fall and early winter since that is the peak period of fresh belly production. The production of fresh pork bellies is smallest during the summer months; this is when frozen pork belly prices are highest.

HIGHEST RELIABLE TRENDS

Commodity	Contract	Month	Position	Reliability	Average Move
Cattle	Jun	Jan	Long	73.3	+1.77
	Jun	Feb	Long	80.0	+1.28
	Aug	Jan	Long	73.3	+1.63
	Oct	Feb	Long	73.3	+1.07
Feeder cattle	Jan	Aug	Long	75.0	+0.84
	Jan	Jan	Long	75.0	+1.66
	Mar	Jan	Long	75.0	+1.84
	Mar	Feb	Long	75.0	+2.79
	Apr	Feb	Long	87.5	+2.44
	May	Feb	Long	75.0	+2.79
	May	May	Short	75.0	−2.42
	Aug	Aug	Long	75.0	+2.37
	Sep	Aug	Long	75.0	+1.75
	Oct	Jul	Long	75.0	+1.62
	Nov	Jul	Long	75.0	+1.63
Hogs	Jun	Jan	Long	73.3	+2.30
	Jul	Jan	Long	73.3	+2.26
	Dec	Dec	Long	73.3	+2.11
Pork bellies	Feb	Sep	Long	73.3	+4.08
	Mar	Sep	Long	73.3	+3.92
	May	Sep	Long	73.3	+3.83
	May	May	Short	73.3	−3.84
	Jul	May	Short	73.3	−4.23
	Aug	May	Short	73.3	−3.98

CATTLE - FEBRUARY - MONTHLY AVERAGE PRICE

Year of Expiration	Apr	May	Jun	Jul	Aug	Sep	Oct	Nov	Dec	Jan	Feb	Apr-Feb Average
1971	29.77	29.57	29.17	29.21	29.02	29.45	29.60	28.46	28.11	30.27	33.74	29.67
1972	30.47	30.55	30.97	31.18	31.57	31.73	32.14	33.12	33.74	35.91	36.77	32.56
1973	32.86	34.43	35.86	35.66	34.78	37.27	37.61	37.41	39.68	42.85	44.47	37.53
1974	43.05	45.35	47.35	52.52	57.06	48.09	48.35	47.41	46.04	51.06	46.58	48.44
1975	46.85	39.11	37.12	45.50	44.84	41.21	44.08	40.58	41.07	37.11	35.08	41.14
1976	38.75	38.78	40.61	40.38	42.68	45.27	41.69	43.47	43.61	39.68	38.77	41.24
1977	45.55	45.28	46.02	44.85	43.86	40.63	41.16	40.28	40.55	37.78	38.40	42.21
1978	45.08	43.31	41.22	39.52	37.35	38.21	38.88	39.19	41.35	42.13	45.48	41.07
1979	50.89	56.28	53.32	54.96	54.11	57.27	56.53	56.70	59.23	62.79	65.11	57.02
1980	71.69	71.62	69.08	68.16	65.94	70.99	70.13	72.96	71.22	66.46	68.38	69.69
1981	64.43	65.44	67.21	70.46	70.68	71.73	72.52	71.22	68.70	65.24	62.23	68.17
1982	70.21	67.65	67.03	64.60	65.11	65.68	64.40	63.68	57.68	60.38	64.79	64.66
1983	63.11	63.83	60.93	61.64	62.52	59.72	59.81	58.72	57.53	60.18	62.97	61.00
1984	62.03	61.24	60.14	60.20	61.42	60.78	59.63	61.55	65.62	69.24	68.44	62.75
1985	63.84	64.13	64.54	64.62	64.52	64.48	64.65	65.77	65.90	65.36	64.99	64.80

	Apr	May	Jun	Jul	Aug	Sep	Oct	Nov	Dec	Jan	Feb
AVERAGE MOVE											
All Years		-0.13	-0.40	0.86	0.13	-0.20	-0.09	-0.04	-0.03	0.43	0.65
Less Extremes		0.03	-0.39	0.53	-0.02	0.07	-0.05	.00	0.11	0.47	0.76
Ave Up - All Years		1.42	1.23	2.17	1.44	1.82	0.63	1.30	1.41	2.87	2.37
Ave Down - All Years		-1.91	-1.83	-1.11	-1.01	-3.22	-1.52	-1.22	-2.19	-3.24	-1.93
COUNT											
Number Up		8	7	9	7	9	10	7	9	9	9
Number Down		7	8	6	8	6	5	8	6	6	6
Pct Up		53.3%	46.7%	60.0%	46.7%	60.0%	66.7%	46.7%	60.0%	60.0%	60.0%
Pct Down		46.7%	53.3%	40.0%	53.3%	40.0%	33.3%	53.3%	40.0%	40.0%	40.0%
EXTREMES											
Greatest Up		5.39	2.00	8.38	4.54	5.05	2.87	2.83	4.07	5.02	4.40
Greatest Down		-7.74	-2.96	-2.43	-2.22	-8.97	-3.58	-3.50	-6.00	-4.76	-4.48
SEASONAL INDEX : AVERAGE PERCENTAGE METHOD											
All Years	99.5	98.9	98.3	100.2	100.4	99.9	99.8	99.5	99.9	101.0	102.6
Less Extremes	99.3	98.8	98.1	99.8	99.8	99.6	99.7	99.4	100.2	100.9	102.7
SEASONAL INDEX : LINK RELATIVE METHOD											
All Years		100.0	99.2	100.8	100.7	100.1	99.8	99.2	99.2	100.0	101.1
Less Extremes		100.5	99.6	100.2	99.8	99.8	99.6	99.2	99.5	100.4	101.6

CATTLE - FEBRUARY - MONTH OF HIGH AND LOW

Year of Expiration	Apr	May	Jun	Jul	Aug	Sep	Oct	Nov	Dec	Jan	Feb
1971					L						H
1972											H
1973											H
1974	L				H						
1975											L
1976	L					H					
1977			H							L	
1978					L						H
1979	L										H
1980					L			H			
1981							H				L
1982	H								L		
1983		H							L		
1984							L			H	
1985	L								H		

CATTLE — FEBRUARY

Average Moves

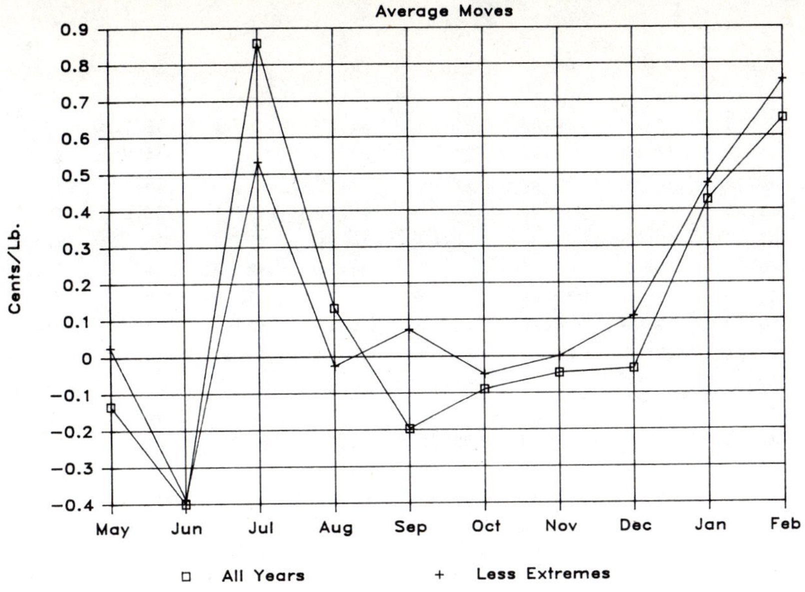

CATTLE — FEBRUARY

Average Percentage Method

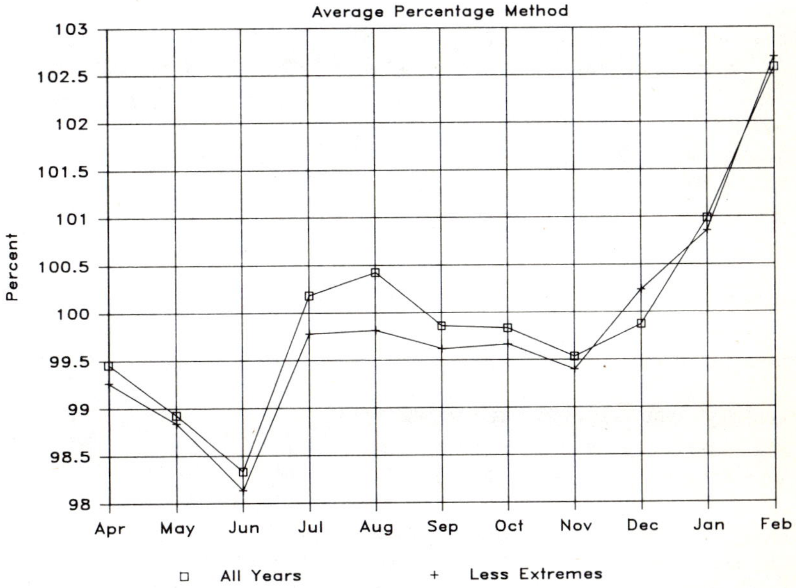

CATTLE — FEBRUARY

Link Relative Method

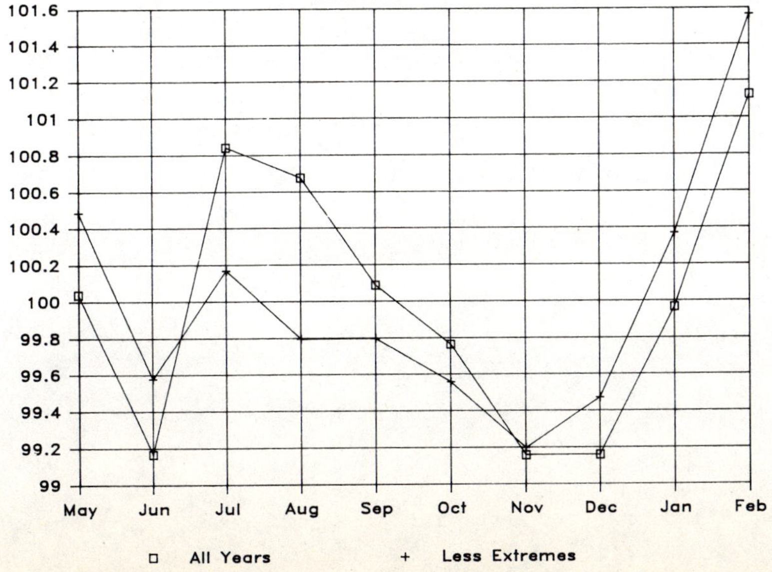

CATTLE - APRIL - MONTHLY AVERAGE PRICE

Year of Expiration	Jun	Jul	Aug	Sep	Oct	Nov	Dec	Jan	Feb	Mar	Apr	Jun-Apr Average
1971	29.17	29.33	29.35	30.07	30.13	29.17	28.83	30.23	32.32	32.21	33.71	30.41
1972	31.12	31.23	31.32	31.25	31.53	32.14	32.55	34.40	34.73	34.60	34.96	32.71
1973	35.65	35.41	34.68	37.03	37.51	37.60	40.03	42.64	43.90	45.94	44.38	39.52
1974	46.97	51.74	56.69	48.31	48.98	48.51	48.02	53.87	48.56	43.15	42.13	48.81
1975	36.71	45.36	45.30	41.80	44.04	41.25	41.82	38.02	36.64	37.96	42.50	41.04
1976	40.14	40.03	42.98	44.48	40.85	41.88	41.62	39.18	38.98	37.63	44.00	41.07
1977	45.93	45.08	44.57	41.85	41.70	39.92	39.76	38.57	38.75	38.73	40.36	41.38
1978	42.04	40.32	37.61	38.12	38.58	39.05	40.78	41.77	45.10	50.60	53.31	42.48
1979	54.01	55.97	54.94	58.19	58.24	58.41	61.41	64.74	67.01	73.35	76.70	62.09
1980	69.90	69.71	67.49	71.30	70.75	73.80	72.87	69.42	70.82	67.40	63.22	69.70
1981	67.74	71.49	72.01	73.67	74.35	73.74	71.10	68.55	66.50	62.58	64.92	69.70
1982	68.02	65.52	65.10	65.56	64.76	63.78	57.43	59.28	63.81	67.08	71.05	64.67
1983	60.70	61.37	62.22	59.84	59.81	58.88	58.26	61.08	63.61	66.87	71.78	62.22
1984	61.20	61.52	63.29	63.06	61.94	63.58	66.31	67.93	67.92	71.10	71.04	65.35
1985	65.27	65.32	65.37	65.72	66.11	67.45	67.49	67.30	67.15	63.61	62.58	65.76

	Jun	Jul	Aug	Sep	Oct	Nov	Dec	Jan	Feb	Mar	Apr
AVERAGE MOVE											
All Years		0.99	0.23	-0.18	-0.07	-0.01	-0.06	0.58	0.59	0.47	1.59
Less Extremes		0.67	0.10	0.15	0.03	-0.03	0.19	0.51	0.74	0.47	1.67
Ave Up - All Years		2.27	1.40	1.62	0.59	1.05	1.56	2.48	1.99	3.56	3.17
Ave Down - All Years		-0.93	-1.10	-2.88	-1.05	-1.22	-1.47	-2.27	-1.52	-2.24	-1.57
COUNT											
Number Up		9	8	9	9	8	7	9	9	7	10
Number Down		6	7	6	6	7	8	6	6	8	5
Pct Up		60.0%	53.3%	60.0%	60.0%	53.3%	46.7%	60.0%	60.0%	46.7%	66.7%
Pct Down		40.0%	46.7%	40.0%	40.0%	46.7%	53.3%	40.0%	40.0%	53.3%	33.3%
EXTREMES											
Greatest Up		8.65	4.95	3.81	2.25	3.05	3.01	5.86	4.54	6.34	6.38
Greatest Down		-2.50	-2.72	-8.37	-3.63	-2.79	-6.35	-3.81	-5.32	-5.40	-4.18
SEASONAL INDEX : AVERAGE PERCENTAGE METHOD											
All Years	97.0	99.0	99.5	98.9	98.8	98.6	98.8	100.1	101.3	102.3	105.8
Less Extremes	96.7	98.9	99.2	98.9	98.8	98.5	99.1	99.9	101.4	102.1	105.7
SEASONAL INDEX : LINK RELATIVE METHOD											
All Years		101.1	100.9	100.0	99.4	98.6	98.3	99.1	99.7	100.0	102.9
Less Extremes		100.7	100.3	99.9	99.4	98.6	98.5	99.2	100.1	100.4	102.8

CATTLE - APRIL - MONTH OF HIGH AND LOW

Year of Expiration	Jun	Jul	Aug	Sep	Oct	Nov	Dec	Jan	Feb	Mar	Apr
1971	H					L					
1972	L										H
1973	L										H
1974		L				H					
1975	H										L
1976	L						H				
1977				H							L
1978		H				L					
1979	L										H
1980						L			H		
1981		L						H			
1982		H								L	
1983			H							L	
1984								L			H
1985		L								H	

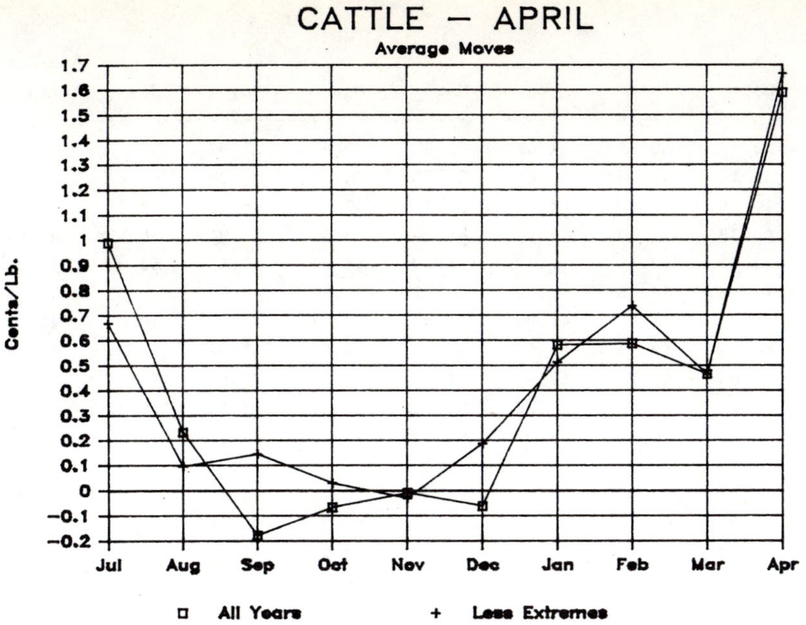
CATTLE – APRIL
Average Moves
Cents/Lb.
1.7
1.6
1.5
1.4
1.3
1.2
1.1
1
0.9
0.8
0.7
0.6
0.5
0.4
0.3
0.2
0.1
0
−0.1
−0.2
Jul
Aug
Sep
Oct
Nov
Dec
Jan
Feb
Mar
Apr
All Years
Less Extremes

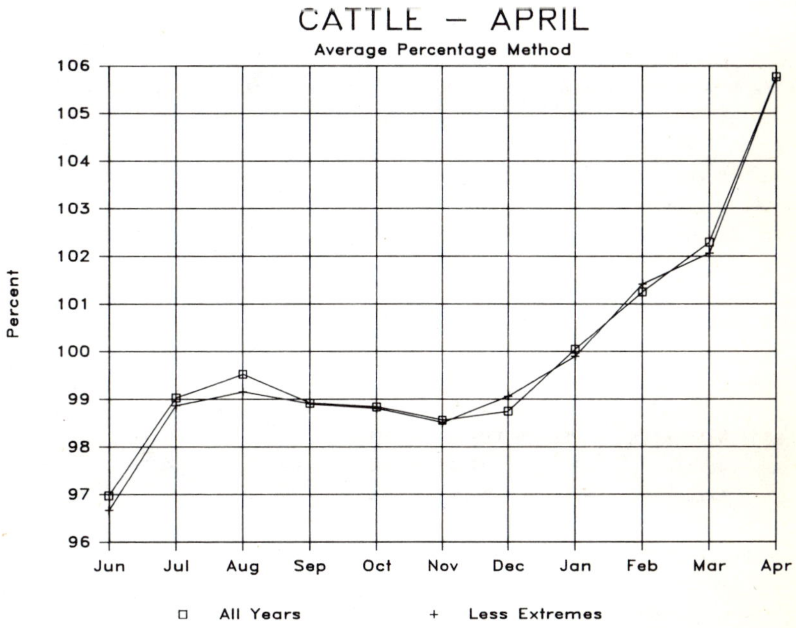
CATTLE – APRIL
Average Percentage Method
Percent
106
105
104
103
102
101
100
99
98
97
96
Jun
Jul
Aug
Sep
Oct
Nov
Dec
Jan
Feb
Mar
Apr
All Years
Less Extremes

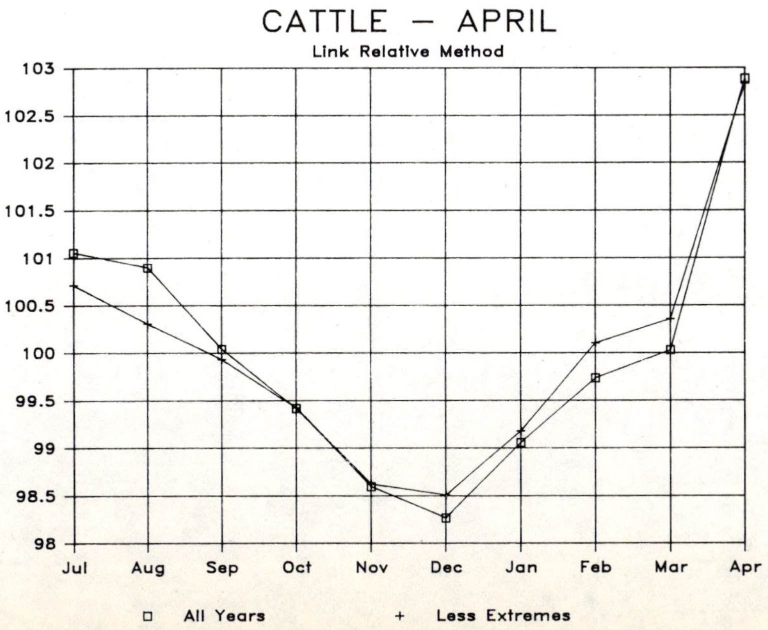
CATTLE – APRIL
Link Relative Method
103
102.5
102
101.5
101
100.5
100
99.5
99
98.5
98
Jul
Aug
Sep
Oct
Nov
Dec
Jan
Feb
Mar
Apr
All Years
Less Extremes

CATTLE - JUNE - MONTHLY AVERAGE PRICE

Year of Expiration	Aug	Sep	Oct	Nov	Dec	Jan	Feb	Mar	Apr	May	Jun	Aug-Jun Average
1971	29.50	30.47	30.53	29.67	29.17	30.38	31.61	31.42	32.60	32.87	32.61	30.98
1972	31.23	31.01	31.25	31.79	32.10	33.68	33.84	33.78	34.39	36.38	37.87	33.39
1973	34.84	37.12	37.57	37.53	40.05	42.70	44.13	45.74	43.25	45.91	47.61	41.49
1974	56.71	48.42	49.15	48.63	48.38	54.24	51.42	46.24	45.58	41.01	36.47	47.84
1975	46.11	43.03	45.28	42.29	42.53	38.67	37.47	38.59	43.30	48.43	53.32	43.55
1976	44.08	44.08	44.08	44.08	44.08	44.08	44.08	42.42	47.38	44.21	42.32	44.08
1977	45.60	43.27	43.14	42.05	41.75	41.08	41.09	41.40	44.31	43.52	40.08	42.48
1978	38.82	39.15	39.58	40.66	42.24	43.15	45.92	49.90	52.09	57.96	57.29	46.07
1979	55.83	58.93	59.93	60.24	63.05	65.81	67.95	71.70	76.03	73.65	70.29	65.76
1980	68.96	72.11	72.27	74.66	74.24	71.64	73.28	69.70	64.27	65.15	66.82	70.28
1981	73.22	74.72	75.21	75.11	72.59	70.88	69.27	66.32	70.01	68.30	69.51	71.38
1982	65.66	66.26	65.63	64.42	58.36	59.33	62.63	65.23	68.20	71.92	71.33	65.36
1983	62.89	60.71	60.43	60.45	60.20	62.72	64.60	66.96	68.46	66.42	66.95	63.71
1984	64.69	64.86	64.09	65.02	66.37	67.01	67.11	68.60	67.29	65.95	65.09	66.01
1985	66.43	66.76	66.64	67.15	67.27	67.58	68.24	66.39	64.23	62.31	59.64	65.69

	Aug	Sep	Oct	Nov	Dec	Jan	Feb	Mar	Apr	May	Jun
AVERAGE MOVE											
All Years		-0.24	0.26	-0.07	-0.09	0.71	0.65	0.12	1.13	0.17	-0.45
Less Extremes		0.11	0.18	-0.03	0.14	0.66	0.71	0.23	1.34	0.10	-0.55
Ave Up - All Years		1.24	0.58	0.72	1.12	1.77	1.28	2.15	2.90	2.93	1.92
Ave Down - All Years		-3.22	-0.39	-0.97	-1.47	-2.21	-1.88	-2.21	-2.41	-2.24	-2.03
COUNT											
Number Up		10	10	8	8	11	12	8	10	7	6
Number Down		5	5	7	7	4	3	7	5	8	9
Pct Up		66.7%	66.7%	53.3%	53.3%	73.3%	80.0%	53.3%	66.7%	46.7%	40.0%
Pct Down		33.3%	33.3%	46.7%	46.7%	26.7%	20.0%	46.7%	33.3%	53.3%	60.0%
EXTREMES											
Greatest Up		3.16	2.25	2.39	2.81	5.86	3.30	3.97	4.96	5.87	4.89
Greatest Down		-8.29	-0.77	-2.98	-6.06	-3.86	-2.82	-5.18	-5.43	-4.56	-4.54
SEASONAL INDEX : AVERAGE PERCENTAGE METHOD											
All Years	98.2	97.4	98.0	97.6	97.7	99.3	100.5	100.7	103.2	104.0	103.3
Less Extremes	97.7	97.8	98.4	97.7	97.7	99.0	101.0	100.9	103.2	103.8	103.8
SEASONAL INDEX : LINK RELATIVE METHOD											
All Years		99.3	99.4	98.6	98.2	99.4	100.1	99.9	102.0	102.2	100.8
Less Extremes		99.2	99.1	98.4	98.2	99.4	100.2	100.1	102.2	102.4	100.9

CATTLE - JUNE - MONTH OF HIGH AND LOW

Year of Expiration	Aug	Sep	Oct	Nov	Dec	Jan	Feb	Mar	Apr	May	Jun
1971					L					H	
1972		L									H
1973	L										H
1974	H										L
1975							L				H
1976									H		L
1977	H										L
1978	L									H	
1979	L								H		
1980				H					L		
1981			H					L			
1982					L					H	
1983					L				H		
1984			L					H			
1985							H				L

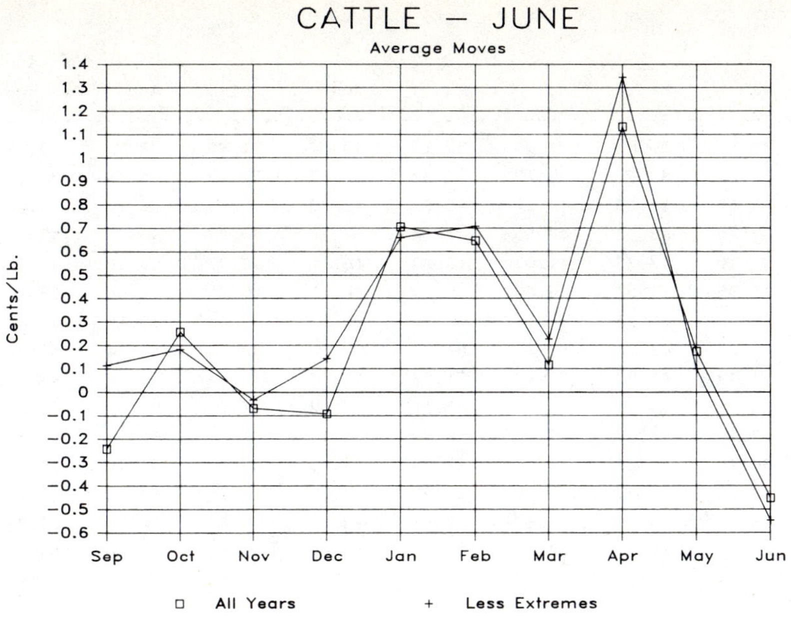
CATTLE – JUNE
Average Moves
Cents/Lb.
1.4
1.3
1.2
1.1
1
0.9
0.8
0.7
0.6
0.5
0.4
0.3
0.2
0.1
0
−0.1
−0.2
−0.3
−0.4
−0.5
−0.6
Sep
Oct
Nov
Dec
Jan
Feb
Mar
Apr
May
Jun
All Years
Less Extremes

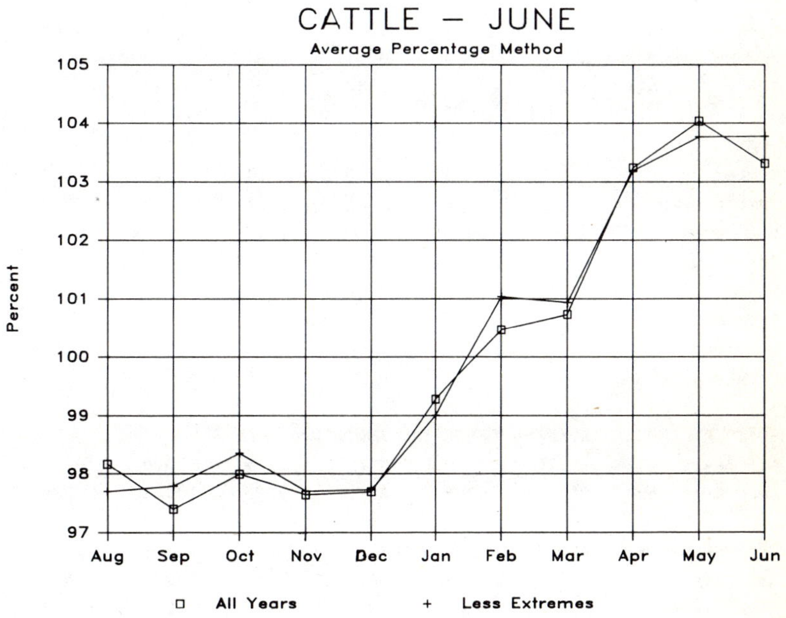
CATTLE – JUNE
Average Percentage Method
Percent
105
104
103
102
101
100
99
98
97
Aug
Sep
Oct
Nov
Dec
Jan
Feb
Mar
Apr
May
Jun
All Years
Less Extremes

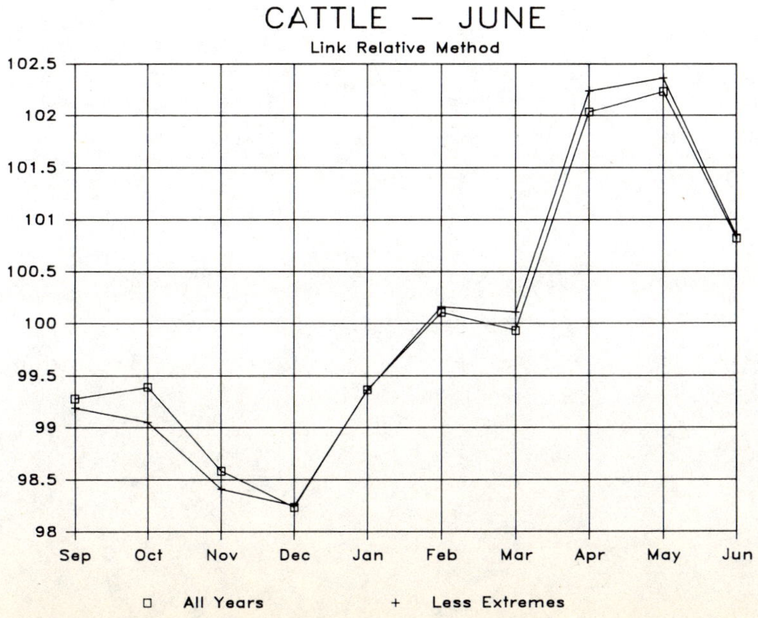
CATTLE – JUNE
Link Relative Method
102.5
102
101.5
101
100.5
100
99.5
99
98.5
98
Sep
Oct
Nov
Dec
Jan
Feb
Mar
Apr
May
Jun
All Years
Less Extremes

CATTLE - AUGUST - MONTHLY AVERAGE PRICE

Year of Expiration	Oct	Nov	Dec	Jan	Feb	Mar	Apr	May	Jun	Jul	Aug	Oct-Aug Average
1971	30.10	29.37	29.02	30.12	30.83	30.63	31.13	31.18	30.92	31.96	33.91	30.83
1972	31.13	31.56	31.83	33.19	33.24	33.20	33.72	35.31	36.97	37.23	35.89	33.93
1973	37.12	36.74	38.80	41.97	43.42	44.89	43.10	45.53	47.28	50.92	56.71	44.23
1974	48.59	47.89	47.59	52.88	52.26	48.35	47.55	41.64	37.18	45.97	48.49	47.13
1975	45.06	42.32	42.63	38.82	37.20	37.65	41.07	43.83	48.61	46.77	46.23	42.74
1976	43.16	43.16	43.16	43.16	43.35	43.31	46.68	45.52	44.85	40.34	38.08	43.16
1977	43.37	42.38	42.38	42.21	41.89	42.21	44.18	43.14	40.82	40.10	40.16	42.08
1978	39.83	40.86	42.35	43.56	46.09	49.24	51.38	57.06	52.54	52.89	51.74	47.96
1979	59.85	60.31	62.28	64.85	66.77	69.53	73.90	71.98	67.34	65.84	61.31	65.82
1980	71.31	73.48	73.40	71.56	72.95	69.32	63.77	65.16	66.68	71.40	73.59	70.24
1981	74.48	74.89	72.61	71.29	69.77	67.00	69.77	66.39	67.83	65.67	67.48	69.74
1982	65.09	64.12	57.79	58.12	60.90	62.45	64.06	66.84	64.00	63.64	66.18	63.02
1983	58.79	59.23	59.21	61.54	63.25	64.42	65.56	63.59	62.66	61.62	63.35	62.11
1984	63.16	63.89	64.80	65.15	64.70	65.39	64.40	63.61	63.24	64.54	64.75	64.33
1985	64.50	65.13	65.41	65.67	66.59	65.78	64.77	63.88	60.91	55.61	54.49	62.98

	Oct	Nov	Dec	Jan	Feb	Mar	Apr	May	Jun	Jul	Aug
AVERAGE MOVE											
All Years		-0.01	-0.14	0.72	0.61	0.01	0.78	-0.03	-0.86	0.18	0.52
Less Extremes		0.03	0.17	0.72	0.61	0.07	0.99	-0.01	-1.00	-0.06	0.51
Ave Up - All Years		0.70	0.91	1.63	1.37	1.45	2.18	2.38	2.23	2.87	2.09
Ave Down - All Years		-1.08	-1.34	-1.79	-0.91	-1.63	-2.03	-2.13	-2.40	-2.18	-1.82
COUNT											
Number Up		9	8	11	10	8	10	7	5	7	9
Number Down		6	7	4	5	7	5	8	10	8	6
Pct Up		60.0%	53.3%	73.3%	66.7%	53.3%	66.7%	46.7%	33.3%	46.7%	60.0%
Pct Down		40.0%	46.7%	26.7%	33.3%	46.7%	33.3%	53.3%	66.7%	53.3%	40.0%
EXTREMES											
Greatest Up		2.17	2.06	5.30	2.78	3.15	4.37	5.69	4.79	8.80	5.78
Greatest Down		-2.74	-6.33	-3.81	-1.62	-3.91	-5.54	-5.91	-4.65	-5.30	-4.53
SEASONAL INDEX : AVERAGE PERCENTAGE METHOD											
All Years	97.7	97.4	97.4	98.9	100.0	100.1	101.9	102.1	100.7	101.3	102.4
Less Extremes	98.1	97.8	97.5	98.5	100.2	100.6	101.9	101.9	101.4	101.2	101.6
SEASONAL INDEX : LINK RELATIVE METHOD											
All Years		98.9	98.5	99.7	100.4	100.1	101.4	101.3	99.5	99.9	100.3
Less Extremes		98.4	98.4	99.7	100.5	100.3	101.9	101.9	99.9	99.4	99.7

CATTLE - AUGUST - MONTH OF HIGH AND LOW

Year of Expiration	Oct	Nov	Dec	Jan	Feb	Mar	Apr	May	Jun	Jul	Aug
1971			L								H
1972	L									H	
1973		L									H
1974				H					L		
1975					L				H		
1976							H				L
1977							H			L	
1978	L							H			
1979	L						H				
1980							L				H
1981		H								L	
1982			L					H			
1983	L						H				
1984	L					H					
1985					H						L

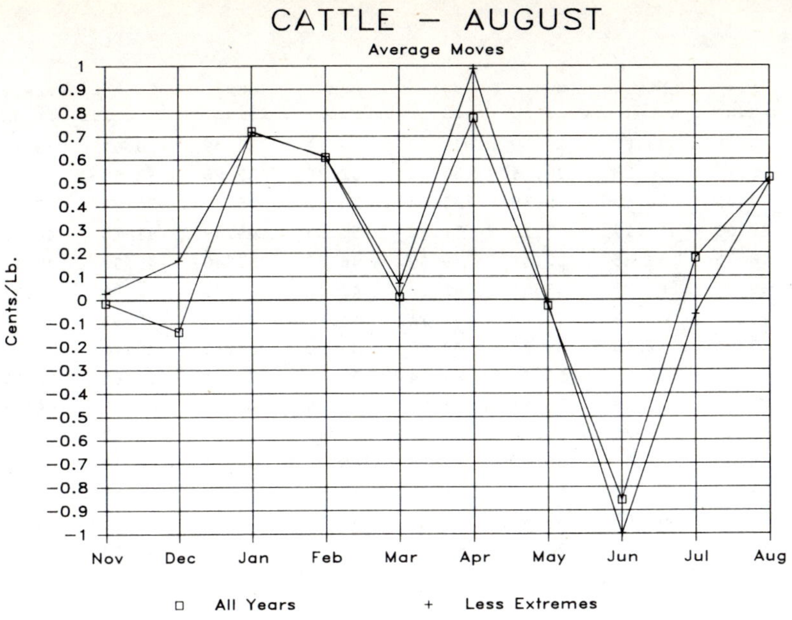

CATTLE – AUGUST
Average Moves
Cents/Lb.
1
0.9
0.8
0.7
0.6
0.5
0.4
0.3
0.2
0.1
0
−0.1
−0.2
−0.3
−0.4
−0.5
−0.6
−0.7
−0.8
−0.9
−1
Nov
Dec
Jan
Feb
Mar
Apr
May
Jun
Jul
Aug
□ All Years
+ Less Extremes

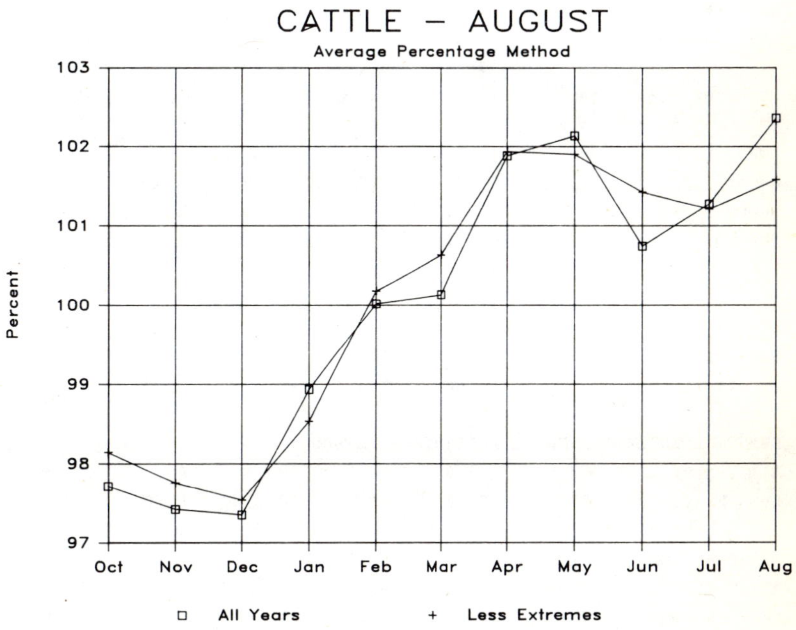

CATTLE – AUGUST
Average Percentage Method
Percent
103
102
101
100
99
98
97
Oct
Nov
Dec
Jan
Feb
Mar
Apr
May
Jun
Jul
Aug
□ All Years
+ Less Extremes

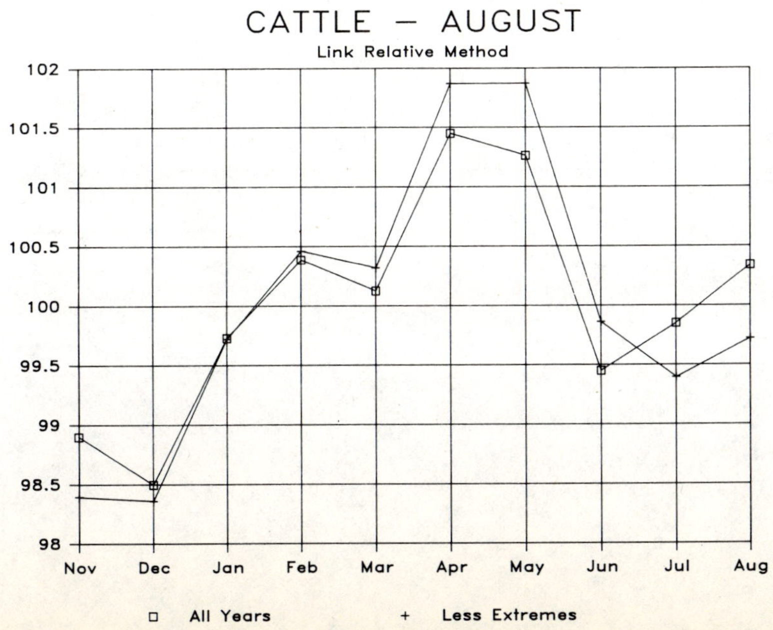

CATTLE – AUGUST
Link Relative Method
102
101.5
101
100.5
100
99.5
99
98.5
98
Nov
Dec
Jan
Feb
Mar
Apr
May
Jun
Jul
Aug
□ All Years
+ Less Extremes

CATTLE - OCTOBER - MONTHLY AVERAGE PRICE

Year of Expiration	Dec	Jan	Feb	Mar	Apr	May	Jun	Jul	Aug	Sep	Oct	Dec-Oct Average
1970	30.04	30.45	30.68	30.78	30.08	29.89	29.59	29.77	29.11	29.29	29.61	29.94
1971	28.70	29.73	30.24	30.02	30.25	30.23	30.24	30.58	32.36	32.26	32.58	30.65
1972	31.39	32.48	32.63	32.48	32.89	34.17	35.39	35.14	33.57	35.07	35.21	33.67
1973	38.04	41.41	42.61	43.79	42.69	45.14	47.13	51.68	55.63	43.49	41.76	44.85
1974	46.88	51.79	52.10	48.79	46.76	39.85	37.49	46.30	46.63	39.40	41.08	45.19
1975	42.35	38.69	36.79	36.78	39.25	40.28	43.51	41.67	42.02	47.79	47.70	41.53
1976	42.84	42.84	43.29	43.60	45.92	45.33	45.72	43.21	41.84	38.61	38.02	42.84
1977	43.00	42.82	42.45	42.60	43.95	42.18	39.77	39.00	38.39	40.15	42.46	41.52
1978	42.21	43.42	45.88	48.60	50.68	55.82	51.19	51.84	51.25	55.31	55.66	50.17
1979	61.78	64.06	65.46	67.85	71.52	70.18	65.76	64.08	62.49	69.46	66.05	66.24
1980	72.09	70.27	71.74	68.19	62.65	63.74	65.12	69.10	69.42	68.45	68.52	68.12
1981	71.47	70.02	68.19	65.48	68.04	64.83	65.05	63.06	65.23	67.29	64.39	66.64
1982	56.75	56.74	59.06	60.50	62.58	64.03	60.74	61.60	63.95	60.02	60.13	60.55
1983	58.20	60.04	61.34	61.77	62.12	60.62	58.86	58.72	59.08	59.09	60.91	60.07
1984	62.68	62.94	62.52	63.49	62.92	62.62	62.52	63.01	63.00	62.48	62.32	62.77

	Dec	Jan	Feb	Mar	Apr	May	Jun	Jul	Aug	Sep	Oct
AVERAGE MOVE											
All Years		0.62	0.49	-0.02	0.51	-0.23	-0.72	0.71	0.35	-0.39	-0.12
Less Extremes		0.62	0.52	0.04	0.73	-0.13	-0.72	0.34	0.22	-0.05	-0.05
Ave Up - All Years		1.64	1.07	1.08	1.75	2.07	1.21	2.48	1.45	2.79	0.79
Ave Down - All Years		-1.42	-1.13	-1.66	-1.99	-1.76	-2.41	-1.31	-0.92	-4.02	-1.48
COUNT											
Number Up		10	11	9	10	6	7	8	8	8	9
Number Down		5	4	6	5	9	8	7	7	7	6
Pct Up		66.7%	73.3%	60.0%	66.7%	40.0%	46.7%	53.3%	53.3%	53.3%	60.0%
Pct Down		33.3%	26.7%	40.0%	33.3%	60.0%	53.3%	46.7%	46.7%	46.7%	40.0%
EXTREMES											
Greatest Up		4.90	2.47	2.71	3.67	5.13	3.23	8.81	3.95	6.97	2.31
Greatest Down		-3.66	-1.90	-3.55	-5.54	-6.90	-4.63	-2.51	-1.60	-12.14	-3.41
SEASONAL INDEX : AVERAGE PERCENTAGE METHOD											
All Years	97.5	98.9	99.8	99.8	100.9	100.5	99.4	100.8	101.4	100.5	100.5
Less Extremes	97.8	98.7	99.5	100.1	101.0	100.6	100.0	100.2	100.4	100.4	100.3
SEASONAL INDEX : LINK RELATIVE METHOD											
All Years		99.2	99.9	99.8	100.7	100.2	98.9	100.5	100.8	100.0	99.9
Less Extremes		99.1	99.9	99.9	101.1	100.9	99.5	99.9	100.1	99.9	99.7

CATTLE - OCTOBER - MONTH OF HIGH AND LOW

Year of Expiration	Dec	Jan	Feb	Mar	Apr	May	Jun	Jul	Aug	Sep	Oct
1970				H					L		
1971	L										H
1972	L						H				
1973	L								H		
1974			H				L				
1975				L						H	
1976					H						L
1977					H				L		
1978	L					H					
1979	L				H						
1980	H				L						
1981	H							L			
1982		L				H					
1983	L				H						
1984				H							L

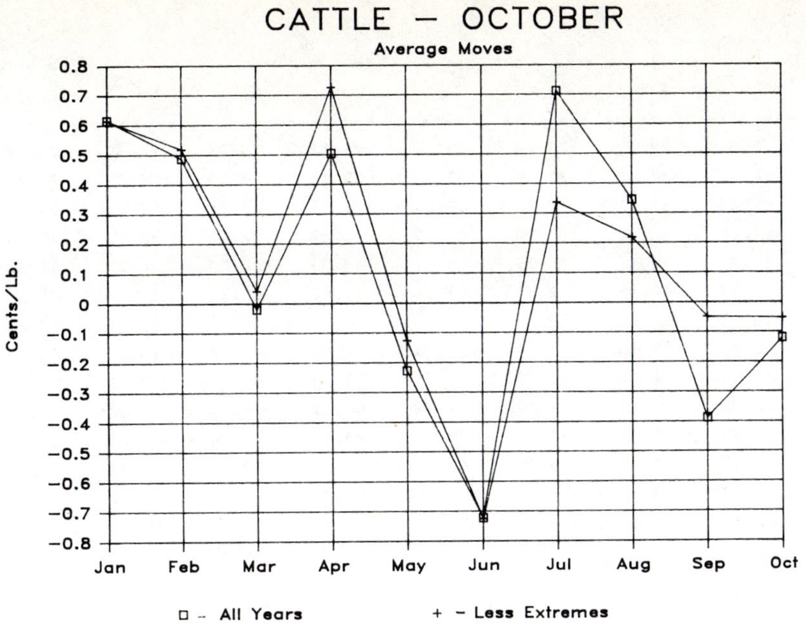
CATTLE — OCTOBER
Average Moves
Cents/Lb.
0.8
0.7
0.6
0.5
0.4
0.3
0.2
0.1
0
−0.1
−0.2
−0.3
−0.4
−0.5
−0.6
−0.7
−0.8
Jan Feb Mar Apr May Jun Jul Aug Sep Oct
□ – All Years
+ – Less Extremes

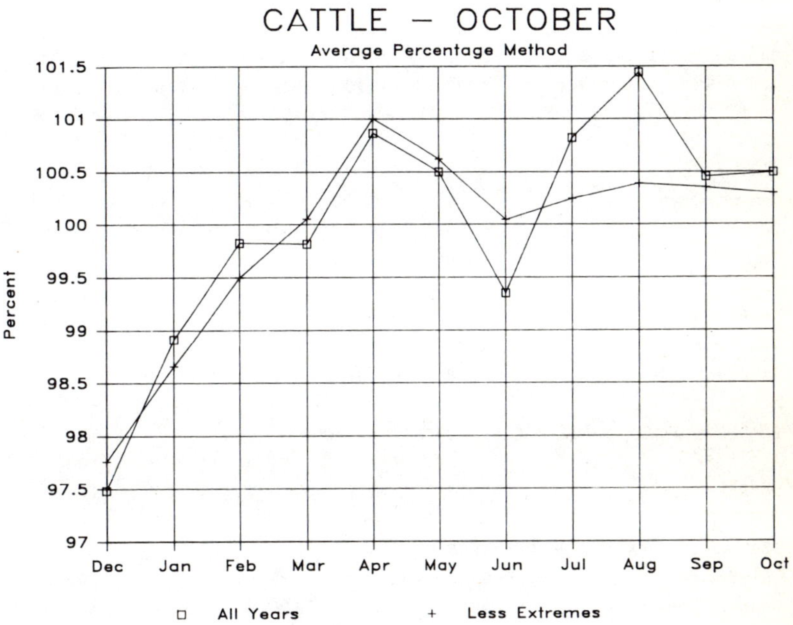
CATTLE — OCTOBER
Average Percentage Method
Percent
101.5
101
100.5
100
99.5
99
98.5
98
97.5
97
Dec Jan Feb Mar Apr May Jun Jul Aug Sep Oct
□ All Years
+ Less Extremes

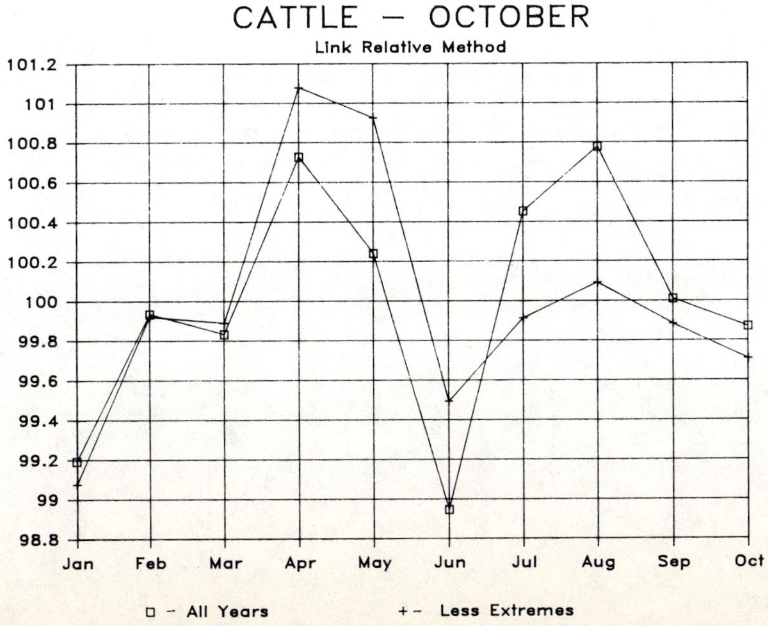
CATTLE — OCTOBER
Link Relative Method
101.2
101
100.8
100.6
100.4
100.2
100
99.8
99.6
99.4
99.2
99
98.8
Jan Feb Mar Apr May Jun Jul Aug Sep Oct
□ – All Years
+ – Less Extremes

CATTLE - DECEMBER - MONTHLY AVERAGE PRICE

Year of Expiration	Feb	Mar	Apr	May	Jun	Jul	Aug	Sep	Oct	Nov	Dec	Feb-Dec Average
1970	30.37	30.42	29.77	29.55	29.09	29.22	28.74	29.07	29.11	28.08	27.30	29.16
1971	30.02	29.87	30.03	29.99	30.21	30.50	31.75	31.95	32.46	34.27	34.97	31.46
1972	32.40	32.29	32.66	34.16	35.43	35.21	33.93	36.21	36.16	35.10	37.13	34.61
1973	42.49	43.38	42.80	45.24	47.25	52.32	56.50	45.40	44.92	42.49	38.65	45.59
1974	52.08	49.33	46.89	39.28	37.41	45.67	45.19	39.92	42.97	38.54	38.13	43.22
1975	36.94	36.89	38.91	39.35	41.69	40.81	42.04	47.20	44.60	45.83	47.05	41.94
1976	43.22	44.03	45.72	45.35	46.15	44.70	43.53	40.02	40.79	40.87	41.08	43.22
1977	43.43	43.79	44.99	43.10	40.79	39.33	37.74	39.24	41.01	41.41	43.05	41.63
1978	46.32	49.03	50.94	56.03	52.41	54.00	52.99	56.69	55.57	55.41	57.39	53.34
1979	66.60	68.44	71.65	70.85	67.38	66.06	64.19	71.38	68.87	69.64	67.13	68.38
1980	72.86	69.48	63.59	64.52	66.24	69.55	69.24	70.12	70.56	67.24	65.82	68.11
1981	69.39	66.71	69.16	66.23	66.10	63.96	65.83	67.67	65.14	63.54	60.43	65.83
1982	59.56	60.82	63.10	64.13	61.09	62.33	63.90	60.86	60.95	60.69	58.84	61.48
1983	62.39	62.76	62.48	61.40	60.02	59.58	59.79	59.59	59.93	61.61	65.29	61.35
1984	63.49	64.19	63.82	63.66	64.12	64.20	64.05	64.07	63.94	66.32	67.16	64.46

	Feb	Mar	Apr	May	Jun	Jul	Aug	Sep	Oct	Nov	Dec
AVERAGE MOVE											
All Years		-0.01	0.34	-0.24	-0.50	0.80	0.13	.00	-0.16	-0.40	-0.11
Less Extremes		0.04	0.60	-0.09	-0.48	0.46	-0.03	0.30	-0.22	-0.30	-0.11
Ave Up - All Years		1.00	1.70	1.91	1.26	2.50	1.72	2.31	0.88	1.19	1.54
Ave Down - All Years		-1.52	-1.70	-1.68	-2.04	-1.13	-0.93	-4.62	-1.35	-1.79	-1.99
COUNT											
Number Up		9	9	6	7	8	6	10	8	7	8
Number Down		6	6	9	8	7	9	5	7	8	7
Pct Up		60.0%	60.0%	40.0%	46.7%	53.3%	40.0%	66.7%	53.3%	46.7%	53.3%
Pct Down		40.0%	40.0%	60.0%	53.3%	46.7%	60.0%	33.3%	46.7%	53.3%	46.7%
EXTREMES											
Greatest Up		2.71	3.21	5.09	2.34	8.26	4.17	7.18	3.05	2.38	3.68
Greatest Down		-3.38	-5.89	-7.61	-3.62	-2.14	-1.87	-11.10	-2.60	-4.43	-3.84
SEASONAL INDEX : AVERAGE PERCENTAGE METHOD											
All Years	99.5	99.5	100.2	99.7	98.9	100.7	100.9	100.6	100.5	99.7	99.8
Less Extremes	98.9	99.3	100.1	99.9	99.3	100.0	99.9	100.3	100.6	99.8	99.9
SEASONAL INDEX : LINK RELATIVE METHOD											
All Years		99.3	100.0	99.6	98.8	100.6	100.7	100.8	100.7	99.8	99.6
Less Extremes		99.4	100.4	100.4	99.5	100.2	99.9	100.6	100.4	99.6	99.7

CATTLE - DECEMBER - MONTH OF HIGH AND LOW

Year of Expiration	Feb	Mar	Apr	May	Jun	Jul	Aug	Sep	Oct	Nov	Dec
1970		H									L
1971		L									H
1972		L									H
1973							H				L
1974	H				L						
1975		L						H			
1976					H			L			
1977			H				L				
1978	L										H
1979			H				L				
1980	H		L								
1981	H										L
1982				H							L
1983						L					H
1984	L										H

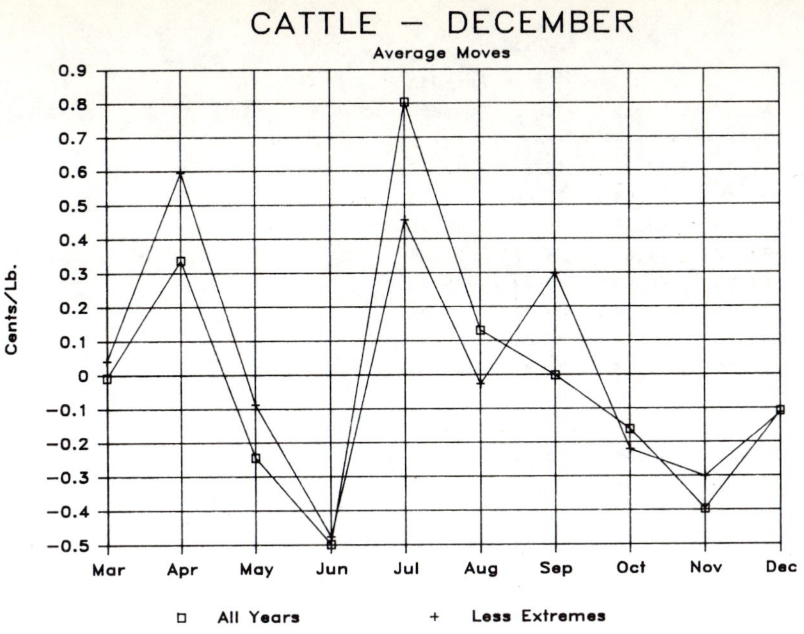
CATTLE — DECEMBER
Average Moves
Cents/Lb.
0.9
0.8
0.7
0.6
0.5
0.4
0.3
0.2
0.1
0
−0.1
−0.2
−0.3
−0.4
−0.5
Mar
Apr
May
Jun
Jul
Aug
Sep
Oct
Nov
Dec
□ All Years
+ Less Extremes

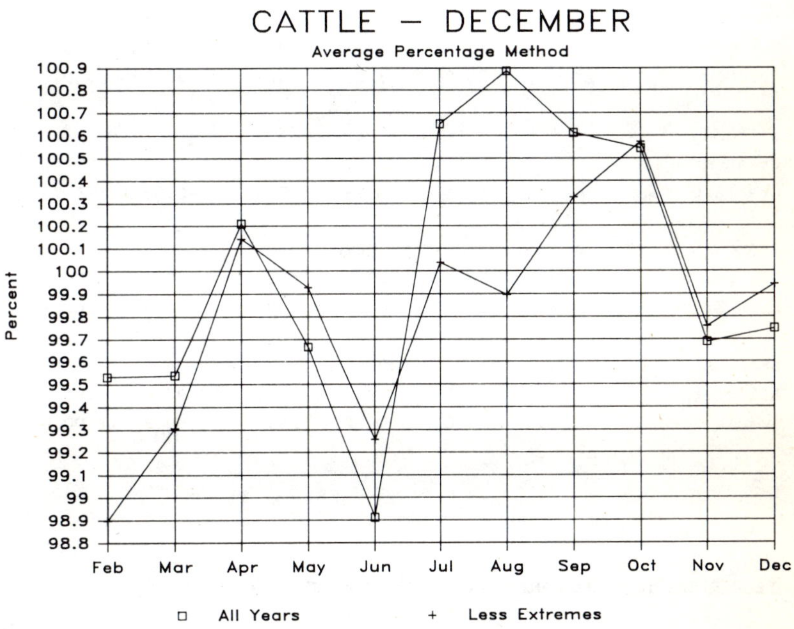
CATTLE — DECEMBER
Average Percentage Method
Percent
100.9
100.8
100.7
100.6
100.5
100.4
100.3
100.2
100.1
100
99.9
99.8
99.7
99.6
99.5
99.4
99.3
99.2
99.1
99
98.9
98.8
Feb
Mar
Apr
May
Jun
Jul
Aug
Sep
Oct
Nov
Dec
□ All Years
+ Less Extremes

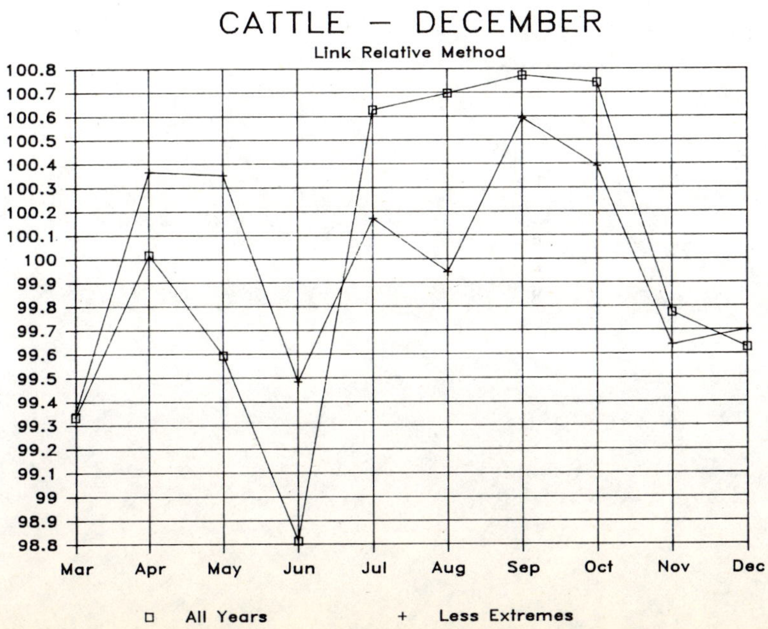
CATTLE — DECEMBER
Link Relative Method
100.8
100.7
100.6
100.5
100.4
100.3
100.2
100.1
100
99.9
99.8
99.7
99.6
99.5
99.4
99.3
99.2
99.1
99
98.9
98.8
Mar
Apr
May
Jun
Jul
Aug
Sep
Oct
Nov
Dec
□ All Years
+ Less Extremes

FEEDER CATTLE - JANUARY - MONTHLY AVERAGE PRICE

Year of Expiration	Jul	Aug	Sep	Oct	Nov	Dec	Jan	Apr-Jan Average
1978	42.99	41.64	41.65	41.76	42.01	43.99	45.33	42.77
1979	65.38	65.68	70.48	69.57	71.46	75.54	77.00	70.73
1980	80.25	80.30	85.38	83.16	86.00	84.33	83.04	83.21
1981	77.67	78.06	79.19	80.10	77.07	74.64	73.30	77.15
1982	65.83	67.26	68.98	67.72	67.20	60.97	62.44	65.77
1983	65.95	68.10	67.13	67.07	66.50	65.38	69.26	67.06
1984	64.13	63.50	63.34	63.26	64.93	68.50	70.04	65.39
1985	68.40	69.12	68.72	68.77	70.00	71.15	71.41	69.65

	Jul	Aug	Sep	Oct	Nov	Dec	Jan
AVERAGE MOVE							
All Years		0.39	1.40	-0.43	0.47	-0.08	0.91
Less Extremes		0.38	1.18	-0.36	0.66	0.25	0.79
Ave Up - All Years		0.84	2.55	0.36	1.58	2.69	1.66
Ave Down - All Years		-0.98	-0.51	-0.91	-1.37	-2.86	-1.31
COUNT							
Number Up		6	5	3	5	4	6
Number Down		2	3	5	3	4	2
Pct Up		75.0%	62.5%	37.5%	62.5%	50.0%	75.0%
Pct Down		25.0%	37.5%	62.5%	37.5%	50.0%	25.0%
EXTREMES							
Greatest Up		2.15	5.08	0.91	2.84	4.08	3.89
Greatest Down		-1.34	-0.96	-2.22	-3.03	-6.23	-1.34
SEASONAL INDEX : AVERAGE PERCENTAGE METHOD							
All Years	98.1	98.5	100.4	99.8	100.5	100.6	102.2
Less Extremes	98.6	98.8	100.2	99.6	100.3	100.9	102.3
SEASONAL INDEX : LINK RELATIVE METHOD							
All Years		99.1	99.1	100.7	99.8	100.1	100.0
Less Extremes		99.0	99.2	100.3	99.4	100.0	100.5

FEEDER CATTLE - JANUARY - MONTH OF HIGH AND LOW

Year of Expiration	Jul	Aug	Sep	Oct	Nov	Dec	Jan
1978			L				H
1979	L						H
1980	L				H		
1981				H			L
1982			H			L	
1983						L	H
1984				L			H
1985	L						H

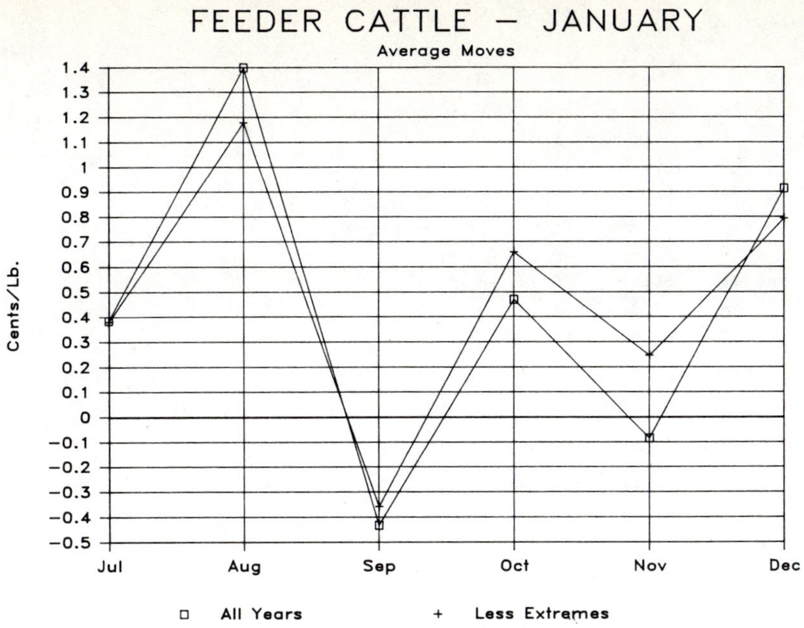
FEEDER CATTLE – JANUARY
Average Moves
Cents/Lb.
1.4
1.3
1.2
1.1
1
0.9
0.8
0.7
0.6
0.5
0.4
0.3
0.2
0.1
0
−0.1
−0.2
−0.3
−0.4
−0.5
Jul
Aug
Sep
Oct
Nov
Dec
□ All Years
+ Less Extremes

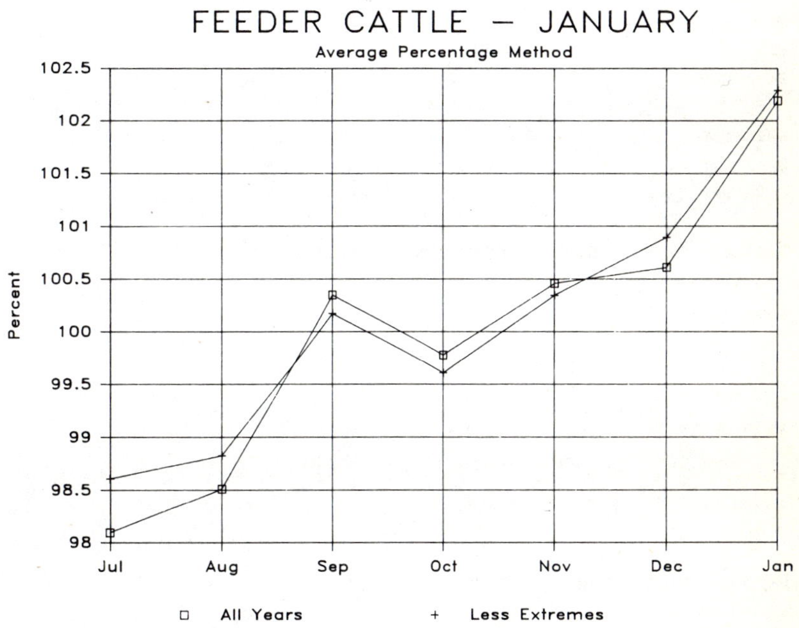
FEEDER CATTLE – JANUARY
Average Percentage Method
Percent
102.5
102
101.5
101
100.5
100
99.5
99
98.5
98
Jul
Aug
Sep
Oct
Nov
Dec
Jan
□ All Years
+ Less Extremes

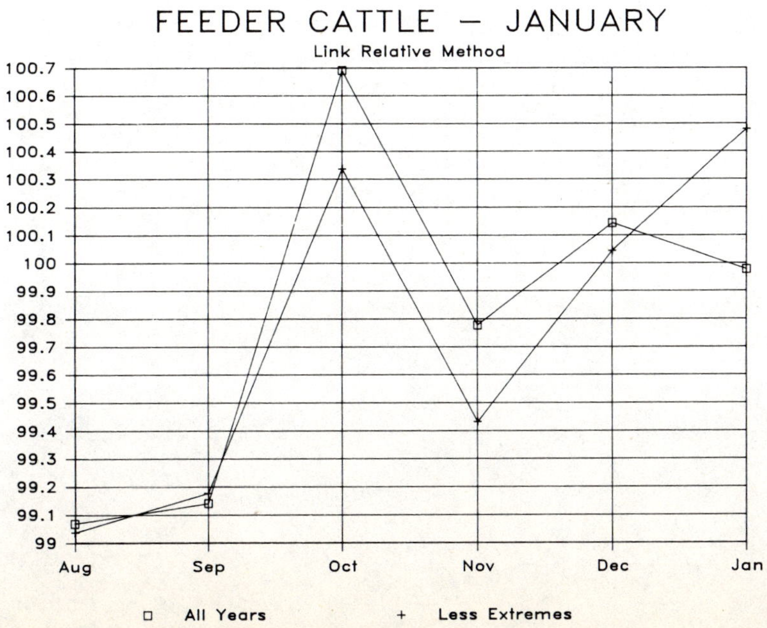
FEEDER CATTLE – JANUARY
Link Relative Method
100.7
100.6
100.5
100.4
100.3
100.2
100.1
100
99.9
99.8
99.7
99.6
99.5
99.4
99.3
99.2
99.1
99
Aug
Sep
Oct
Nov
Dec
Jan
□ All Years
+ Less Extremes

FEEDER CATTLE - MARCH - MONTHLY AVERAGE PRICE

Year of Expiration	Sep	Oct	Nov	Dec	Jan	Feb	Mar	Sep-Mar Average
1978	41.73	41.89	42.15	44.58	46.03	50.40	54.86	45.95
1979	71.28	71.16	72.69	75.62	78.34	81.81	92.07	77.57
1980	86.41	84.08	87.08	85.40	82.74	84.54	80.99	84.46
1981	80.24	81.82	79.22	76.38	74.58	72.68	68.81	76.25
1982	68.92	67.42	66.18	59.68	60.43	64.66	66.72	64.86
1983	66.71	66.44	66.38	65.33	68.68	71.12	71.94	68.09
1984	64.43	64.53	65.95	68.09	69.55	69.97	69.81	67.47
1985	69.16	69.51	70.70	71.85	73.16	72.05	67.82	70.61

	Sep	Oct	Nov	Dec	Jan	Feb	Mar
AVERAGE MOVE							
All Years		-0.25	0.44	-0.43	0.82	1.72	0.73
Less Extremes		-0.21	0.52	0.02	0.98	1.87	-0.04
Ave Up - All Years		0.55	1.48	2.16	1.84	2.79	4.40
Ave Down - All Years		-1.05	-1.30	-3.02	-2.23	-1.51	-2.95
COUNT							
Number Up		4	5	4	6	6	4
Number Down		4	3	4	2	2	4
Pct Up		50.0%	62.5%	50.0%	75.0%	75.0%	50.0%
Pct Down		50.0%	37.5%	50.0%	25.0%	25.0%	50.0%
EXTREMES							
Greatest Up		1.58	2.99	2.93	3.35	4.37	10.26
Greatest Down		-2.33	-2.60	-6.50	-2.66	-1.90	-4.22
SEASONAL INDEX : AVERAGE PERCENTAGE METHOD							
All Years	98.5	98.2	98.7	98.3	99.7	102.6	104.0
Less Extremes	98.5	97.8	99.0	98.8	100.1	102.6	103.8
SEASONAL INDEX : LINK RELATIVE METHOD							
All Years		99.7	99.0	99.1	98.4	99.4	101.8
Less Extremes		99.4	98.6	98.9	98.8	99.9	102.1

FEEDER CATTLE - MARCH - MONTH OF HIGH AND LOW

Year of Expiration	Sep	Oct	Nov	Dec	Jan	Feb	Mar
1978	L						H
1979		L					H
1980			H				L
1981		H					L
1982	H			L			
1983				L			H
1984	L					H	
1985					H		L

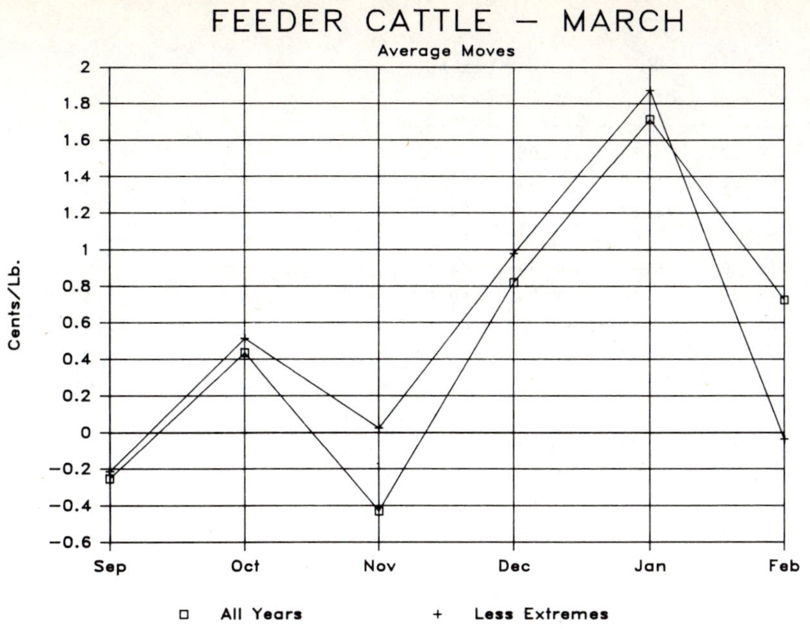
FEEDER CATTLE – MARCH
Average Moves
Cents/Lb.
2
1.8
1.6
1.4
1.2
1
0.8
0.6
0.4
0.2
0
-0.2
-0.4
-0.6
Sep
Oct
Nov
Dec
Jan
Feb
All Years
Less Extremes

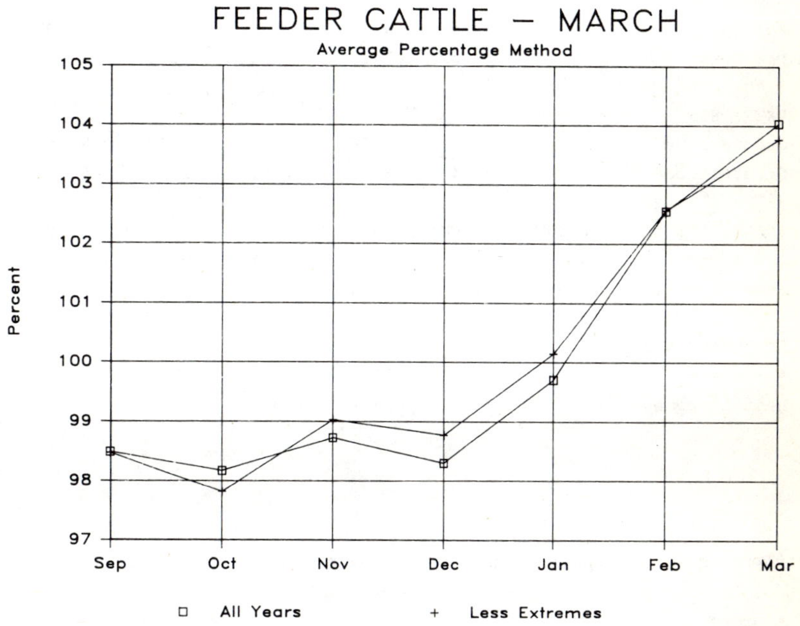
FEEDER CATTLE – MARCH
Average Percentage Method
Percent
105
104
103
102
101
100
99
98
97
Sep
Oct
Nov
Dec
Jan
Feb
Mar
All Years
Less Extremes

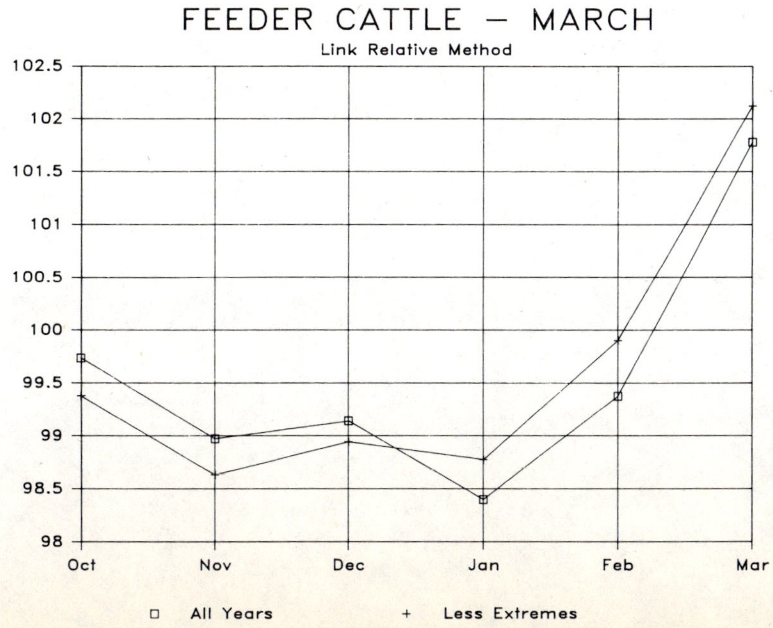
FEEDER CATTLE – MARCH
Link Relative Method
102.5
102
101.5
101
100.5
100
99.5
99
98.5
98
Oct
Nov
Dec
Jan
Feb
Mar
All Years
Less Extremes

FEEDER CATTLE - APRIL - MONTHLY AVERAGE PRICE

Year of Expiration	Oct	Nov	Dec	Jan	Feb	Mar	Apr	Oct-Apr Average
1978	42.08	42.42	44.57	45.92	50.13	55.31	57.05	48.21
1979	71.45	72.81	75.57	78.53	82.51	91.06	91.64	80.51
1980	84.42	87.30	85.90	83.22	85.57	78.62	69.37	82.06
1981	82.04	79.89	77.17	75.51	73.58	68.59	70.11	75.27
1982	67.60	66.35	59.80	59.79	64.16	66.23	67.39	64.47
1983	66.21	66.17	65.35	68.32	70.30	70.16	70.32	68.12
1984	64.71	66.00	67.74	68.93	69.07	69.57	67.97	67.71
1985	69.35	70.09	71.12	72.30	72.35	68.77	66.55	70.08

	Oct	Nov	Dec	Jan	Feb	Mar	Apr
AVERAGE MOVE							
All Years		0.40	-0.48	0.66	1.89	0.08	-0.99
Less Extremes		0.41	-0.01	0.84	2.12	-0.16	-0.07
Ave Up - All Years		1.32	1.92	1.93	2.44	4.08	1.03
Ave Down - All Years		-1.14	-2.87	-1.45	-1.93	-3.91	-4.36
COUNT							
Number Up		5	4	5	7	4	5
Number Down		3	4	3	1	4	3
Pct Up		62.5%	50.0%	62.5%	87.5%	50.0%	62.5%
Pct Down		37.5%	50.0%	37.5%	12.5%	50.0%	37.5%
EXTREMES							
Greatest Up		2.88	2.76	2.97	4.37	8.55	1.74
Greatest Down		-2.14	-6.55	-2.68	-1.93	-6.95	-9.26
SEASONAL INDEX : AVERAGE PERCENTAGE METHOD							
All Years	98.1	98.6	98.0	99.1	102.1	102.7	101.6
Less Extremes	98.0	99.0	97.8	99.4	102.4	102.6	101.7
SEASONAL INDEX : LINK RELATIVE METHOD							
All Years		98.7	99.0	98.3	99.2	101.9	102.2
Less Extremes		98.5	98.7	98.5	99.4	101.9	101.9

FEEDER CATTLE - APRIL - MONTH OF HIGH AND LOW

Year of Expiration	Oct	Nov	Dec	Jan	Feb	Mar	Apr
1978	L						H
1979	L						H
1980		H					L
1981	H					L	
1982	H			L			
1983			L				H
1984	L						H
1985					H		L

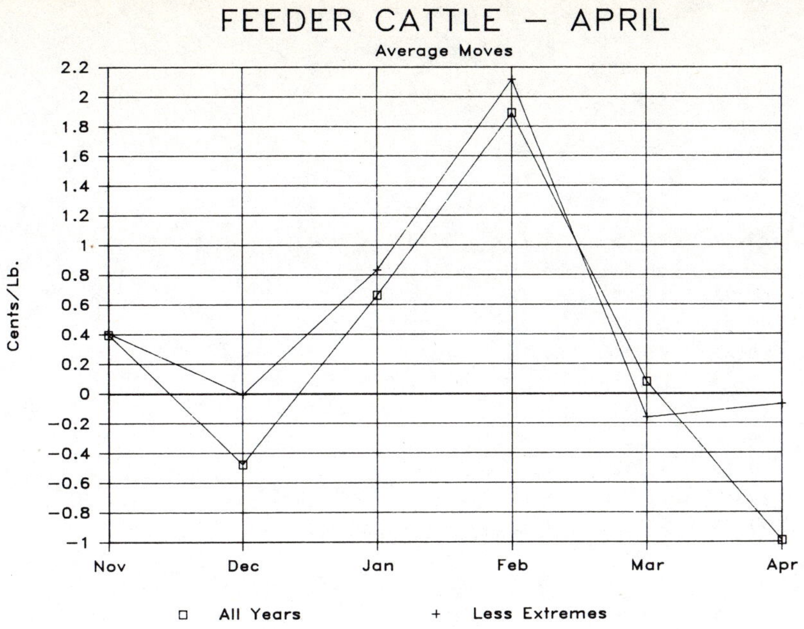
FEEDER CATTLE – APRIL
Average Moves
Cents/Lb.
2.2
2
1.8
1.6
1.4
1.2
1
0.8
0.6
0.4
0.2
0
–0.2
–0.4
–0.6
–0.8
–1
Nov
Dec
Jan
Feb
Mar
Apr
All Years
Less Extremes

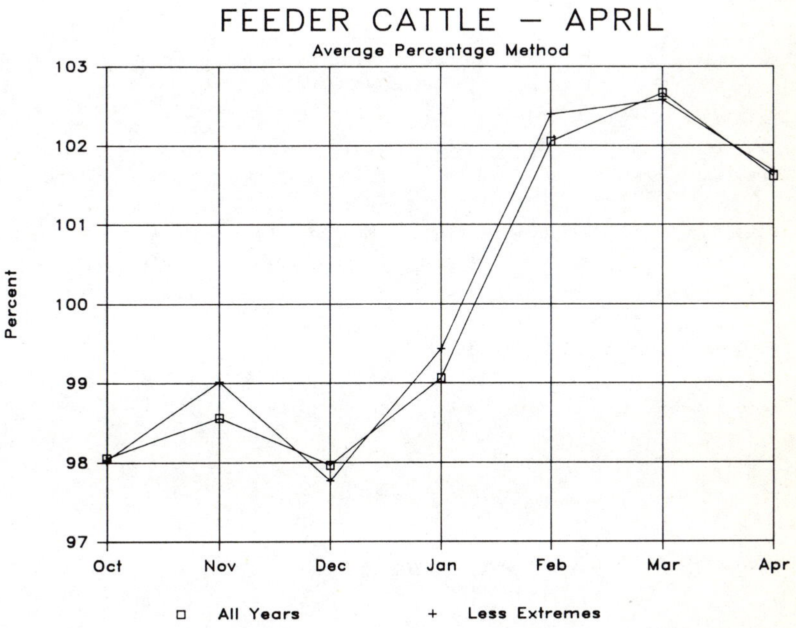
FEEDER CATTLE – APRIL
Average Percentage Method
Percent
103
102
101
100
99
98
97
Oct
Nov
Dec
Jan
Feb
Mar
Apr
All Years
Less Extremes

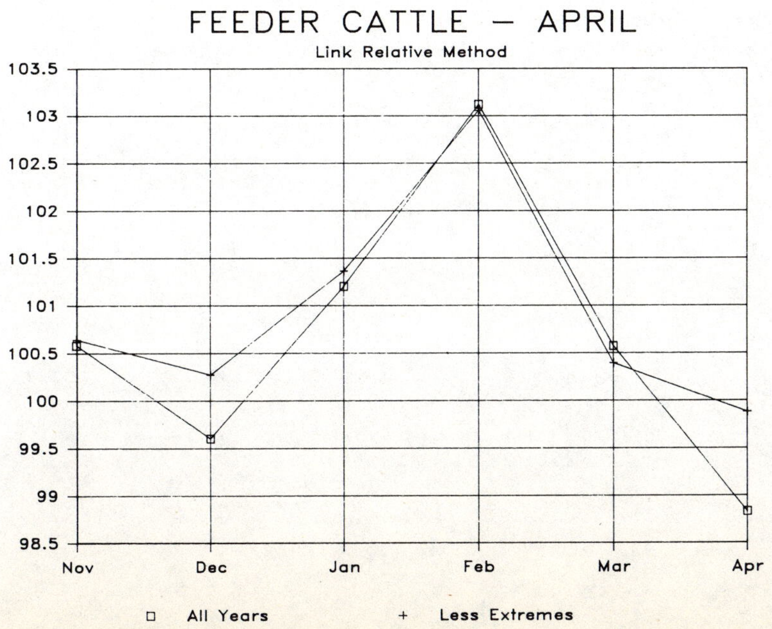
FEEDER CATTLE – APRIL
Link Relative Method
103.5
103
102.5
102
101.5
101
100.5
100
99.5
99
98.5
Nov
Dec
Jan
Feb
Mar
Apr
All Years
Less Extremes

FEEDER CATTLE - MAY - MONTHLY AVERAGE PRICE

Year of Expiration	Nov	Dec	Jan	Feb	Mar	Apr	May	Nov-May Average
1978	42.67	44.46	45.95	50.12	54.52	55.22	60.56	50.50
1979	72.92	75.32	78.40	82.29	88.69	90.32	87.06	82.14
1980	87.21	85.97	83.56	85.87	79.04	69.92	69.12	80.10
1981	80.05	77.33	75.68	73.69	69.49	71.16	65.72	73.30
1982	66.30	59.78	58.99	62.98	65.26	66.51	68.31	64.02
1983	66.00	64.97	66.91	68.39	68.22	66.90	66.47	66.84
1984	65.42	66.77	67.55	67.42	67.98	65.82	62.94	66.27
1985	68.89	69.22	70.36	71.27	69.32	66.51	64.78	68.62

	Dec	Jan	Feb	Mar	Apr	May
AVERAGE MOVE						
All Years	-0.70	0.45	1.83	0.06	-1.27	-0.93
Less Extremes	-0.25	0.48	2.08	0.15	-0.45	-1.22
Ave Up - All Years	1.47	1.68	2.79	3.41	1.31	3.56
Ave Down - All Years	-2.88	-1.62	-1.06	-3.29	-3.85	-2.42
COUNT						
Number Up	4	5	6	4	4	2
Number Down	4	3	2	4	4	6
Pct Up	50.0%	62.5%	75.0%	50.0%	50.0%	25.0%
Pct Down	50.0%	37.5%	25.0%	50.0%	50.0%	75.0%
EXTREMES						
Greatest Up	2.40	3.07	4.17	6.41	1.67	5.33
Greatest Down	-6.52	-2.41	-2.00	-6.84	-9.12	-5.43

SEASONAL INDEX : AVERAGE PERCENTAGE METHOD	Nov	Dec	Jan	Feb	Mar	Apr	May
All Years	99.1	98.1	98.8	101.7	102.1	100.5	99.7
Less Extremes	99.8	98.2	99.2	101.3	102.4	101.1	98.5

SEASONAL INDEX : LINK RELATIVE METHOD	Dec	Jan	Feb	Mar	Apr	May
All Years	99.0	98.1	98.9	101.8	102.3	100.5
Less Extremes	98.4	98.2	98.9	101.7	102.1	101.2

FEEDER CATTLE - MAY - MONTH OF HIGH AND LOW

Year of Expiration	Nov	Dec	Jan	Feb	Mar	Apr	May
1978	L						H
1979	L					H	
1980	H						L
1981	H						L
1982			L				H
1983		L		H			
1984					H		L
1985				H			L

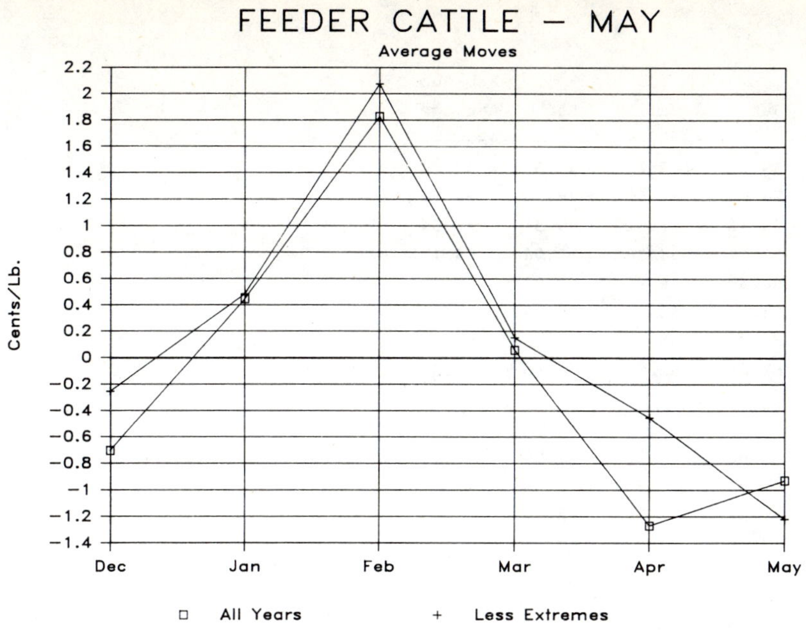
FEEDER CATTLE – MAY
Average Moves
Cents/Lb.
2.2
2
1.8
1.6
1.4
1.2
1
0.8
0.6
0.4
0.2
0
-0.2
-0.4
-0.6
-0.8
-1
-1.2
-1.4
Dec
Jan
Feb
Mar
Apr
May
All Years
Less Extremes

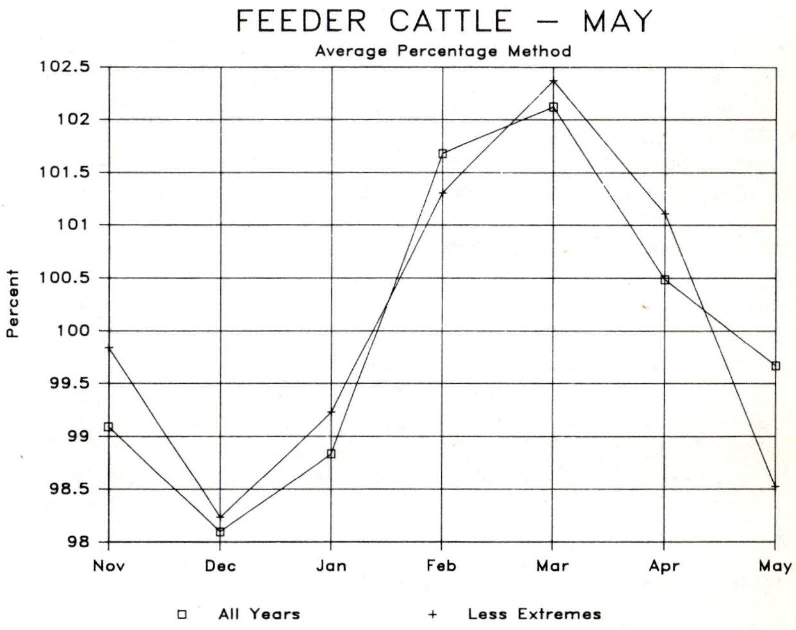
FEEDER CATTLE – MAY
Average Percentage Method
Percent
102.5
102
101.5
101
100.5
100
99.5
99
98.5
98
Nov
Dec
Jan
Feb
Mar
Apr
May
All Years
Less Extremes

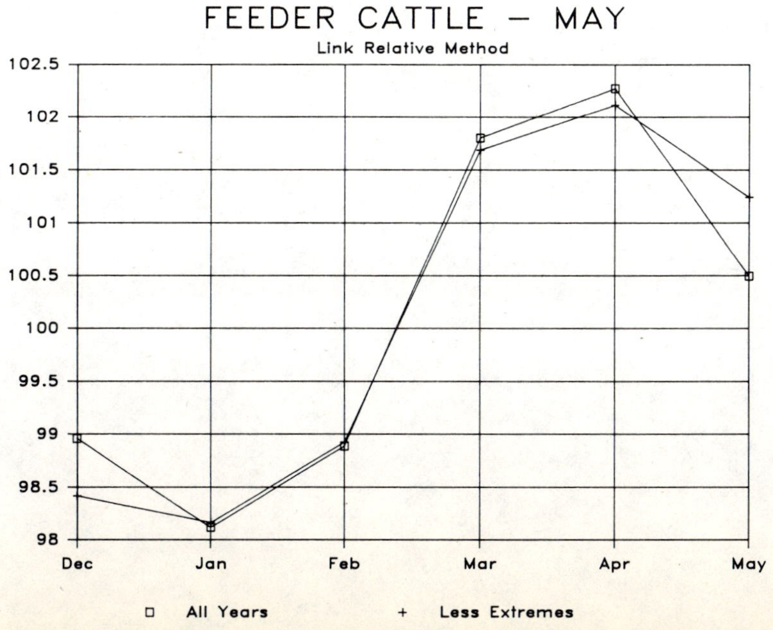
FEEDER CATTLE – MAY
Link Relative Method
102.5
102
101.5
101
100.5
100
99.5
99
98.5
98
Dec
Jan
Feb
Mar
Apr
May
All Years
Less Extremes

FEEDER CATTLE - AUGUST - MONTHLY AVERAGE PRICE

Year of Expiration	Feb	Mar	Apr	May	Jun	Jul	Aug	Feb-Aug Average
1978	50.24	54.63	55.25	63.06	59.01	62.71	62.62	58.22
1979	82.70	87.14	89.53	84.92	76.94	77.90	78.67	82.54
1980	85.77	78.81	70.44	71.30	74.16	76.02	79.31	76.54
1981	74.31	70.17	72.32	66.99	67.67	64.36	68.06	69.12
1982	62.28	64.09	65.66	67.36	64.40	66.75	71.04	65.94
1983	68.57	67.51	65.94	65.49	64.46	62.85	62.94	65.39
1984	67.31	67.67	66.27	65.65	65.74	66.98	66.15	66.54
1985	72.39	70.88	68.83	67.95	67.08	62.93	64.98	67.86

	Feb	Mar	Apr	May	Jun	Jul	Aug
AVERAGE MOVE							
All Years		-0.33	-0.83	-0.19	-1.66	0.13	1.66
Less Extremes		-0.03	-0.11	-0.67	-1.36	0.25	1.64
Ave Up - All Years		2.75	1.68	3.45	1.21	2.03	2.37
Ave Down - All Years		-3.42	-3.34	-2.38	-3.38	-3.02	-0.46
COUNT							
Number Up		4	4	3	3	5	6
Number Down		4	4	5	5	3	2
Pct Up		50.0%	50.0%	37.5%	37.5%	62.5%	75.0%
Pct Down		50.0%	50.0%	62.5%	62.5%	37.5%	25.0%
EXTREMES							
Greatest Up		4.43	2.39	7.81	2.86	3.70	4.29
Greatest Down		-6.96	-8.37	-5.33	-7.98	-4.15	-0.83
SEASONAL INDEX : AVERAGE PERCENTAGE METHOD							
All Years	101.6	101.3	100.2	100.3	97.9	98.2	100.5
Less Extremes	102.5	101.8	100.2	100.1	98.1	97.5	100.2
SEASONAL INDEX : LINK RELATIVE METHOD							
All Years		101.0	101.1	100.0	100.4	98.2	98.4
Less Extremes		101.0	100.9	100.8	100.1	98.0	98.4

FEEDER CATTLE - AUGUST - MONTH OF HIGH AND LOW

Year of Expiration	Feb	Mar	Apr	May	Jun	Jul	Aug
1978	L			H			
1979			H		L		
1980	H		L				
1981	H					L	
1982	L						H
1983	H					L	
1984		H		L			
1985	H					L	

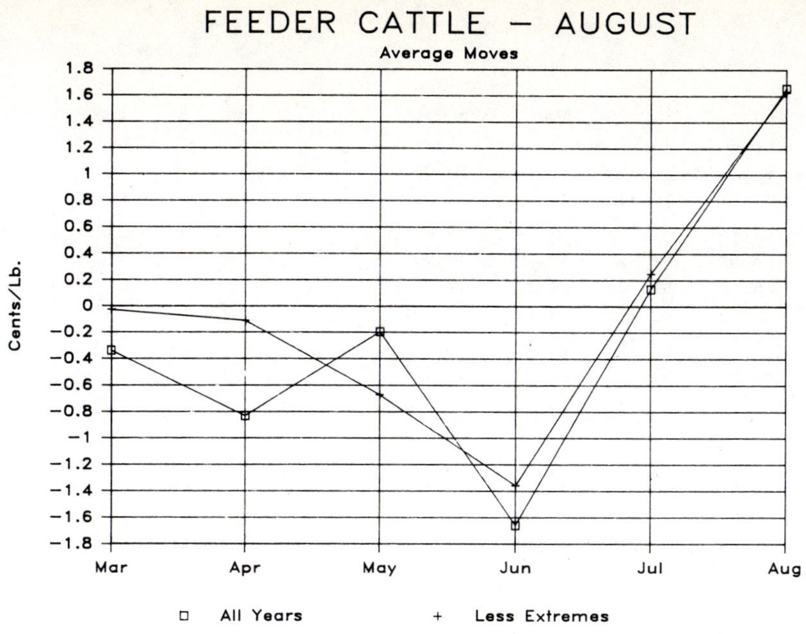
FEEDER CATTLE – AUGUST
Average Moves
Cents/Lb.
1.8
1.6
1.4
1.2
1
0.8
0.6
0.4
0.2
0
-0.2
-0.4
-0.6
-0.8
-1
-1.2
-1.4
-1.6
-1.8
Mar
Apr
May
Jun
Jul
Aug
All Years
Less Extremes

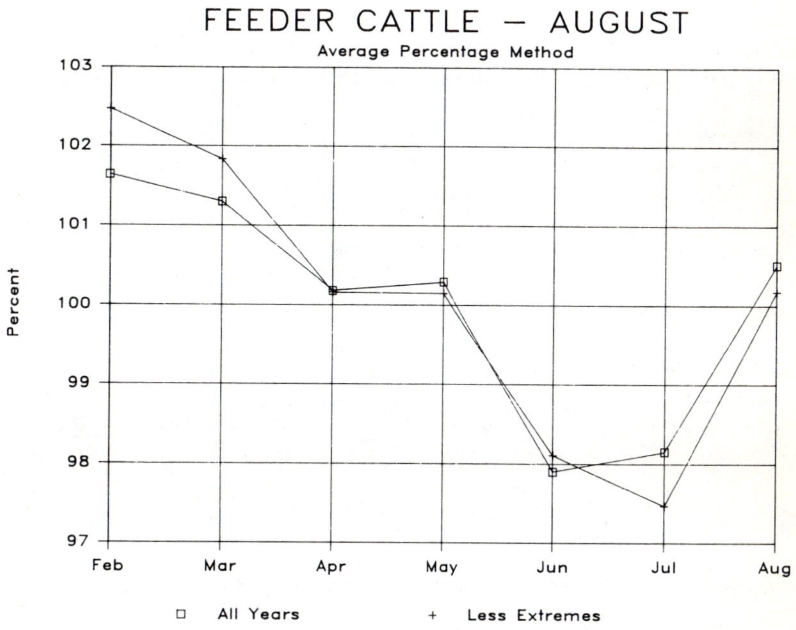
FEEDER CATTLE – AUGUST
Average Percentage Method
Percent
103
102
101
100
99
98
97
Feb
Mar
Apr
May
Jun
Jul
Aug
All Years
Less Extremes

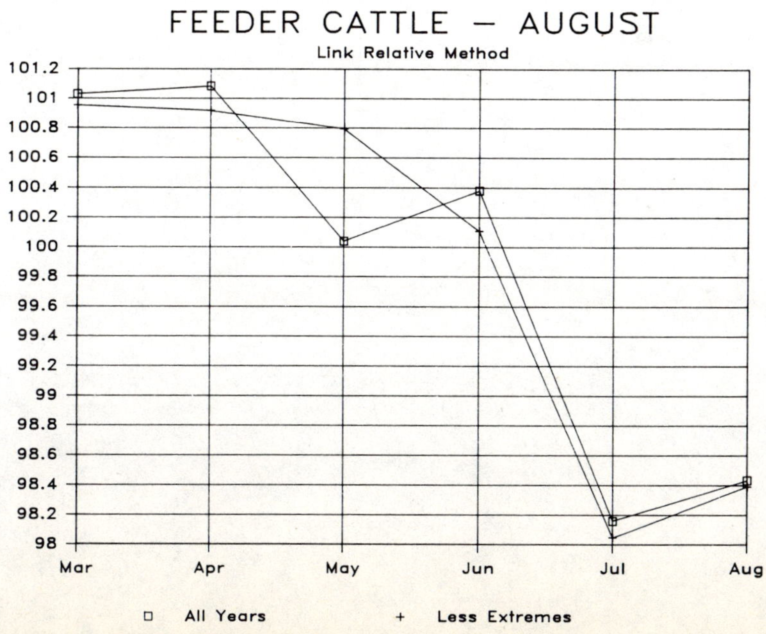
FEEDER CATTLE – AUGUST
Link Relative Method
101.2
101
100.8
100.6
100.4
100.2
100
99.8
99.6
99.4
99.2
99
98.8
98.6
98.4
98.2
98
Mar
Apr
May
Jun
Jul
Aug
All Years
Less Extremes

FEEDER CATTLE - SEPTEMBER - MONTHLY AVERAGE PRICE

Year of Expiration	Mar	Apr	May	Jun	Jul	Aug	Sep	Mar-Sep Average
1978	54.44	54.86	62.48	58.71	62.37	62.68	66.75	60.33
1979	86.47	88.35	84.77	76.77	77.15	78.84	84.79	82.45
1980	78.33	70.31	71.12	73.87	75.72	76.18	76.03	74.51
1981	69.75	72.03	66.72	67.18	63.51	67.29	69.76	68.03
1982	63.16	64.93	66.18	63.93	65.96	69.64	68.71	66.07
1983	66.59	65.39	64.86	63.73	62.21	60.56	58.19	63.07
1984	67.03	65.60	65.18	65.33	66.59	66.45	65.44	65.95
1985	70.45	68.56	67.66	66.89	62.96	63.55	66.68	66.68

	Mar	Apr	May	Jun	Jul	Aug	Sep
AVERAGE MOVE							
All Years		-0.77	-0.13	-1.57	0.01	1.09	1.39
Less Extremes		-0.07	-0.56	-1.22	0.05	1.10	1.26
Ave Up - All Years		1.59	3.22	1.12	1.84	1.75	3.90
Ave Down - All Years		-3.13	-2.15	-3.19	-3.04	-0.89	-1.12
COUNT							
Number Up		4	3	3	5	6	4
Number Down		4	5	5	3	2	4
Pct Up		50.0%	37.5%	37.5%	62.5%	75.0%	50.0%
Pct Down		50.0%	62.5%	62.5%	37.5%	25.0%	50.0%
EXTREMES							
Greatest Up		2.28	7.61	2.75	3.67	3.78	5.96
Greatest Down		-8.02	-5.31	-8.00	-3.93	-1.64	-2.37
SEASONAL INDEX : AVERAGE PERCENTAGE METHOD							
All Years	101.4	100.3	100.4	98.2	98.2	99.8	101.7
Less Extremes	102.6	100.7	100.7	98.6	98.2	99.6	101.8
SEASONAL INDEX : LINK RELATIVE METHOD							
All Years		101.3	100.2	100.5	98.3	98.3	99.8
Less Extremes		101.1	100.9	100.2	98.2	98.2	99.7

FEEDER CATTLE - SEPTEMBER - MONTH OF HIGH AND LOW

Year of Expiration	Mar	Apr	May	Jun	Jul	Aug	Sep
1978	L						H
1979	H			L			
1980	H	L					
1981		H			L		
1982	L					H	
1983	H						L
1984	H		L				
1985	H				L		

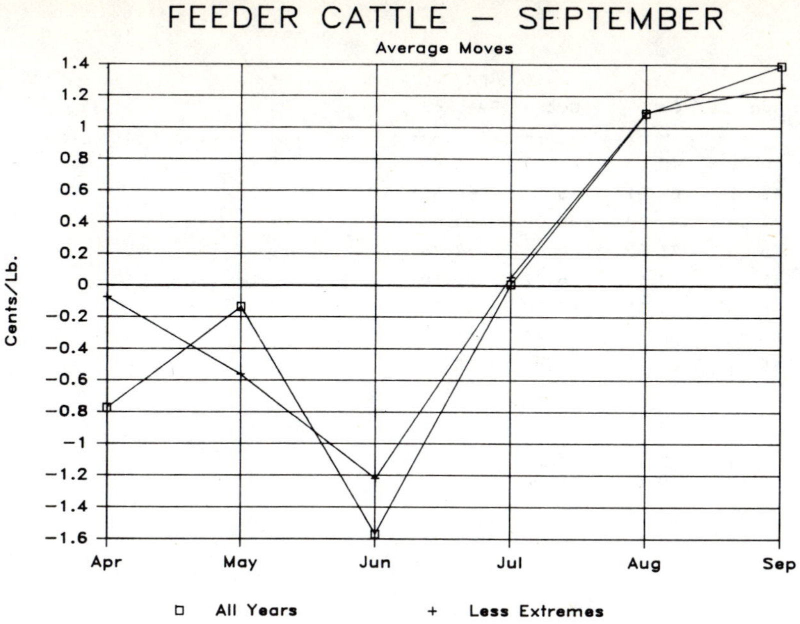
FEEDER CATTLE – SEPTEMBER
Average Moves
Cents/Lb.
1.4
1.2
1
0.8
0.6
0.4
0.2
0
−0.2
−0.4
−0.6
−0.8
−1
−1.2
−1.4
−1.6
Apr
May
Jun
Jul
Aug
Sep
All Years
Less Extremes

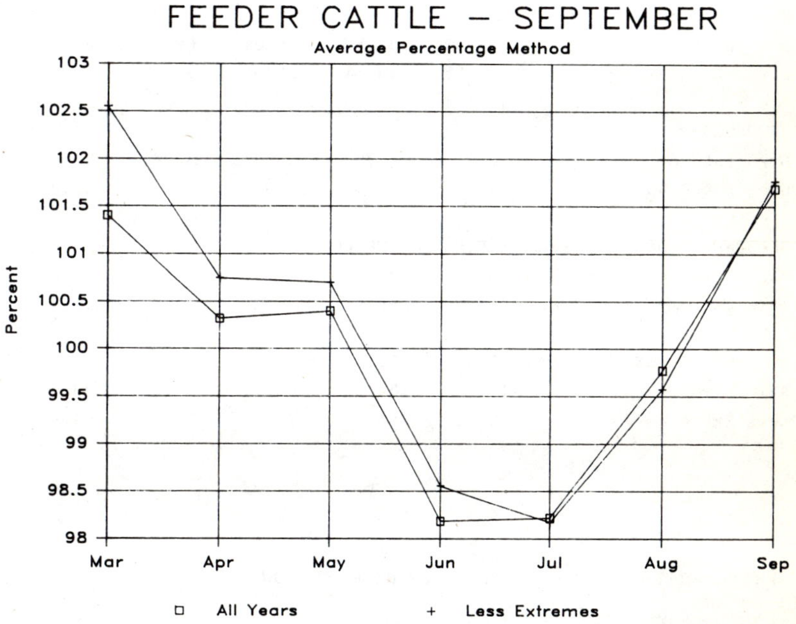
FEEDER CATTLE – SEPTEMBER
Average Percentage Method
Percent
103
102.5
102
101.5
101
100.5
100
99.5
99
98.5
98
Mar
Apr
May
Jun
Jul
Aug
Sep
All Years
Less Extremes

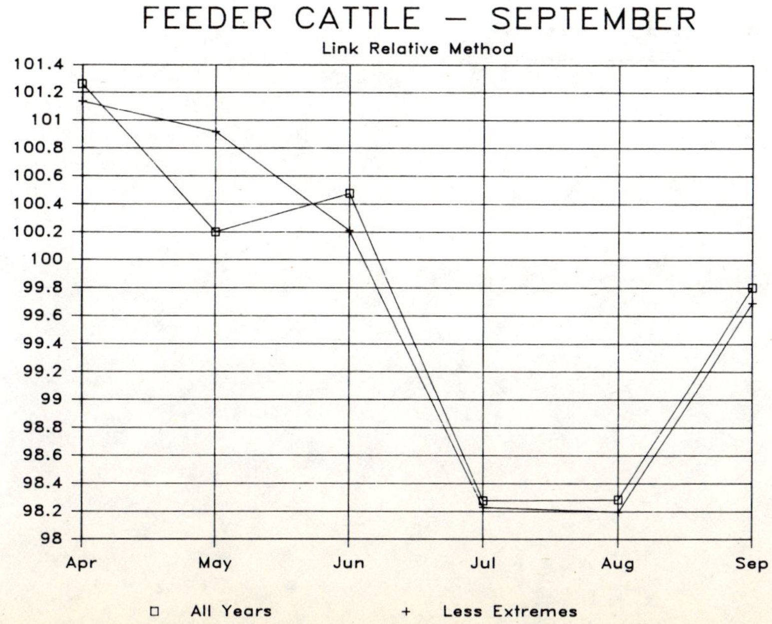
FEEDER CATTLE – SEPTEMBER
Link Relative Method
101.4
101.2
101
100.8
100.6
100.4
100.2
100
99.8
99.6
99.4
99.2
99
98.8
98.6
98.4
98.2
98
Apr
May
Jun
Jul
Aug
Sep
All Years
Less Extremes

FEEDER CATTLE - OCTOBER - MONTHLY AVERAGE PRICE

Year of Expiration	Apr	May	Jun	Jul	Aug	Sep	Oct	Apr-Oct Average
1977	44.45	43.12	41.15	41.56	40.76	40.83	41.07	41.85
1978	54.29	62.20	58.47	62.36	62.62	67.01	65.93	61.84
1979	86.83	83.92	76.13	76.44	77.13	82.40	80.09	80.42
1980	70.08	70.91	73.62	75.50	75.36	76.07	76.31	73.98
1981	71.61	66.71	67.09	63.17	66.15	68.53	66.47	67.10
1982	64.52	65.77	63.12	65.30	68.34	66.35	66.70	65.73
1983	64.75	64.15	63.17	61.58	60.11	58.61	59.65	61.72
1984	65.00	64.77	65.07	66.12	66.82	65.67	65.83	65.61

	Apr	May	Jun	Jul	Aug	Sep	Oct
AVERAGE MOVE							
All Years		.00	-1.71	0.52	0.66	1.02	-0.43
Less Extremes		-0.50	-1.44	0.71	0.62	0.81	-0.36
Ave Up - All Years		3.33	1.13	1.62	1.54	2.56	0.41
Ave Down - All Years		-1.99	-3.42	-2.76	-0.80	-1.55	-1.82
COUNT							
Number Up		3	3	6	5	5	5
Number Down		5	5	2	3	3	3
Pct Up		37.5%	37.5%	75.0%	62.5%	62.5%	62.5%
Pct Down		62.5%	62.5%	25.0%	37.5%	37.5%	37.5%
EXTREMES							
Greatest Up		7.91	2.70	3.89	3.04	5.28	1.04
Greatest Down		-4.90	-7.79	-3.92	-1.46	-2.00	-2.31
SEASONAL INDEX : AVERAGE PERCENTAGE METHOD							
All Years	100.7	100.7	98.1	98.9	99.8	101.2	100.6
Less Extremes	101.6	101.0	98.0	99.2	99.7	101.0	100.3
SEASONAL INDEX : LINK RELATIVE METHOD							
All Years		100.4	100.8	98.1	99.0	99.8	101.2
Less Extremes		101.1	100.3	97.9	99.0	99.9	101.1

FEEDER CATTLE - OCTOBER - MONTH OF HIGH AND LOW

Year of Expiration	Apr	May	Jun	Jul	Aug	Sep	Oct
1977	H				L		
1978	L					H	
1979	H		L				
1980	L						H
1981	H			L			
1982			L		H		
1983	H					L	
1984		L			H		

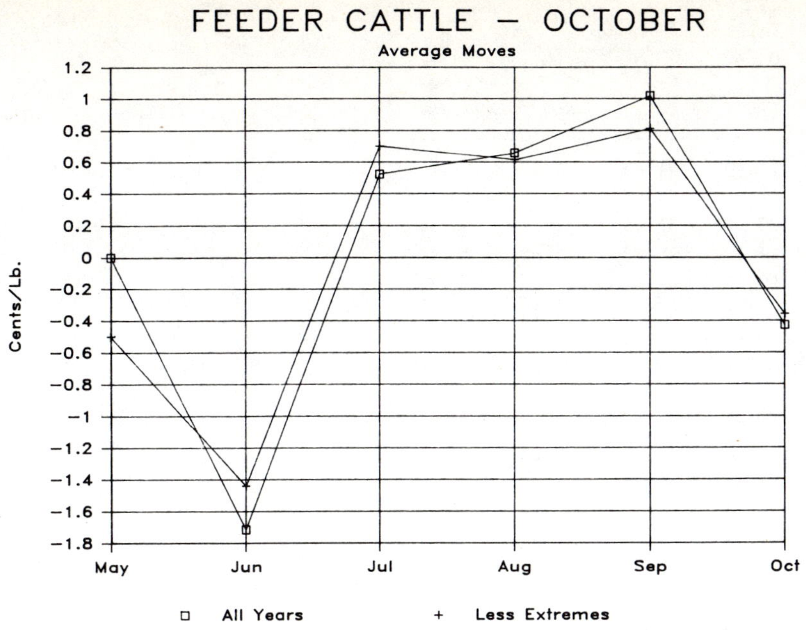
FEEDER CATTLE — OCTOBER
Average Moves
Cents/Lb.
1.2
1
0.8
0.6
0.4
0.2
0
-0.2
-0.4
-0.6
-0.8
-1
-1.2
-1.4
-1.6
-1.8
May
Jun
Jul
Aug
Sep
Oct
All Years
Less Extremes

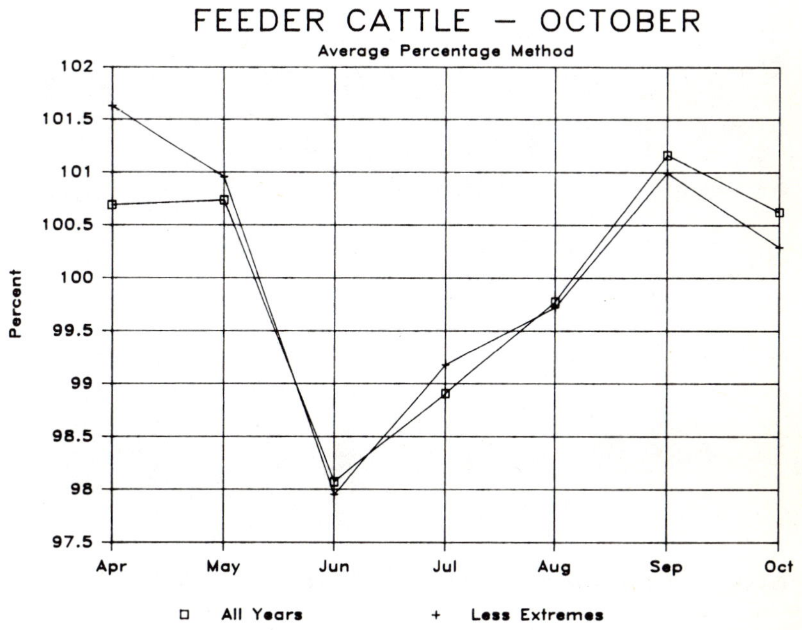
FEEDER CATTLE — OCTOBER
Average Percentage Method
Percent
102
101.5
101
100.5
100
99.5
99
98.5
98
97.5
Apr
May
Jun
Jul
Aug
Sep
Oct
All Years
Less Extremes

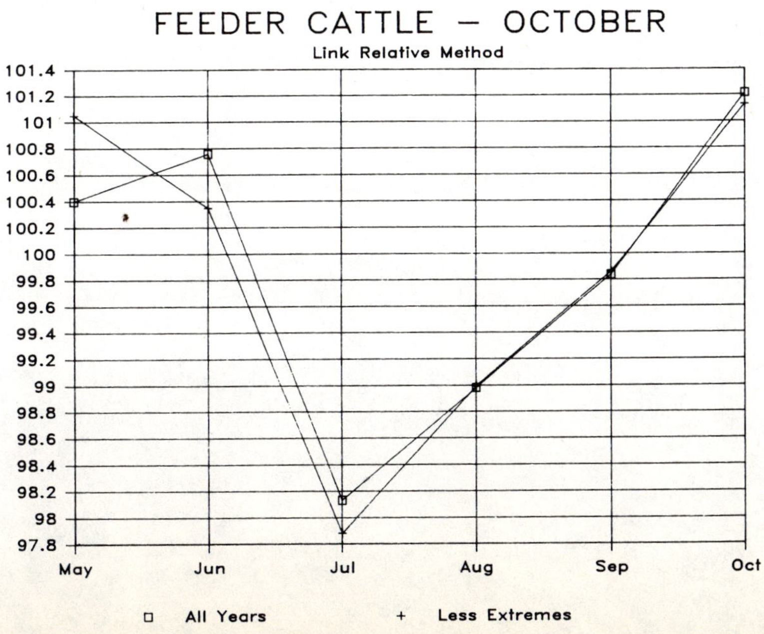
FEEDER CATTLE — OCTOBER
Link Relative Method
101.4
101.2
101
100.8
100.6
100.4
100.2
100
99.8
99.6
99.4
99.2
99
98.8
98.6
98.4
98.2
98
97.8
May
Jun
Jul
Aug
Sep
Oct
All Years
Less Extremes

FEEDER CATTLE - NOVEMBER - MONTHLY AVERAGE PRICE

Year of Expiration	May	Jun	Jul	Aug	Sep	Oct	Nov	May-Nov Average
1977	43.71	41.74	42.09	41.02	41.33	41.23	40.80	41.70
1978	62.61	58.99	63.00	63.87	68.93	66.99	66.52	64.42
1979	84.53	76.87	77.15	78.02	83.68	81.06	81.34	80.38
1980	71.88	74.39	76.41	76.22	77.33	78.07	73.50	75.40
1981	67.59	67.82	64.07	66.66	69.73	67.37	68.09	67.33
1982	66.06	63.43	65.54	68.49	66.95	67.14	65.32	66.13
1983	64.90	63.90	62.40	61.15	59.92	60.57	61.82	62.09
1984	65.66	65.90	66.96	67.72	67.11	67.25	67.77	66.91

	May	Jun	Jul	Aug	Sep	Oct	Nov
AVERAGE MOVE							
All Years		-1.73	0.57	0.69	1.48	-0.66	-0.56
Less Extremes		-1.45	0.72	0.64	1.28	-0.57	-0.20
Ave Up - All Years		1.00	1.63	1.61	3.04	0.43	0.69
Ave Down - All Years		-3.37	-2.63	-0.84	-1.13	-1.76	-1.82
COUNT							
Number Up		3	6	5	5	4	4
Number Down		5	2	3	3	4	4
Pct Up		37.5%	75.0%	62.5%	62.5%	50.0%	50.0%
Pct Down		62.5%	25.0%	37.5%	37.5%	50.0%	50.0%
EXTREMES							
Greatest Up		2.51	4.00	2.95	5.67	0.74	1.25
Greatest Down		-7.66	-3.75	-1.25	-1.55	-2.62	-4.57
SEASONAL INDEX : AVERAGE PERCENTAGE METHOD							
All Years	100.7	98.0	98.9	99.7	101.8	100.9	100.1
Less Extremes	100.8	98.3	99.1	99.5	101.8	100.9	100.0
SEASONAL INDEX : LINK RELATIVE METHOD							
All Years		100.4	97.8	98.8	99.8	101.9	101.0
Less Extremes		100.4	97.9	98.9	99.8	101.7	100.8

FEEDER CATTLE - NOVEMBER - MONTH OF HIGH AND LOW

Year of Expiration	May	Jun	Jul	Aug	Sep	Oct	Nov
1977	H						L
1978		L			H		
1979	H	L					
1980	L					H	
1981			L		H		
1982		L		H			
1983	H				L		
1984	L						H

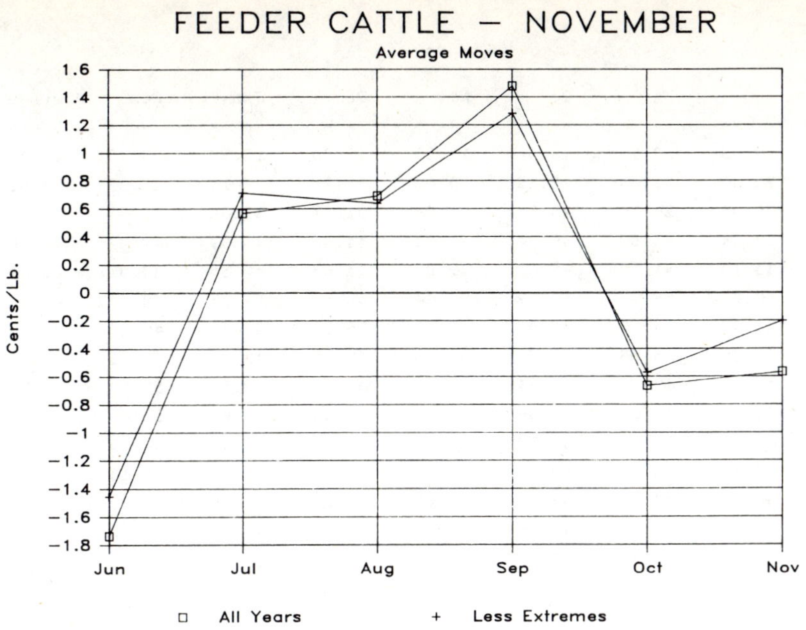
FEEDER CATTLE – NOVEMBER
Average Moves
Cents/Lb.
1.6
1.4
1.2
1
0.8
0.6
0.4
0.2
0
−0.2
−0.4
−0.6
−0.8
−1
−1.2
−1.4
−1.6
−1.8
Jun
Jul
Aug
Sep
Oct
Nov
All Years
Less Extremes

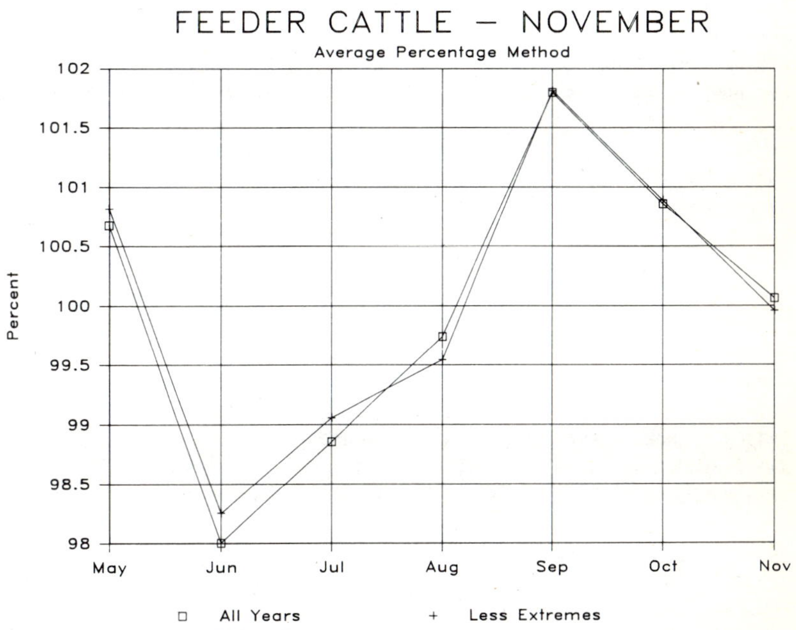
FEEDER CATTLE – NOVEMBER
Average Percentage Method
Percent
102
101.5
101
100.5
100
99.5
99
98.5
98
May
Jun
Jul
Aug
Sep
Oct
Nov
All Years
Less Extremes

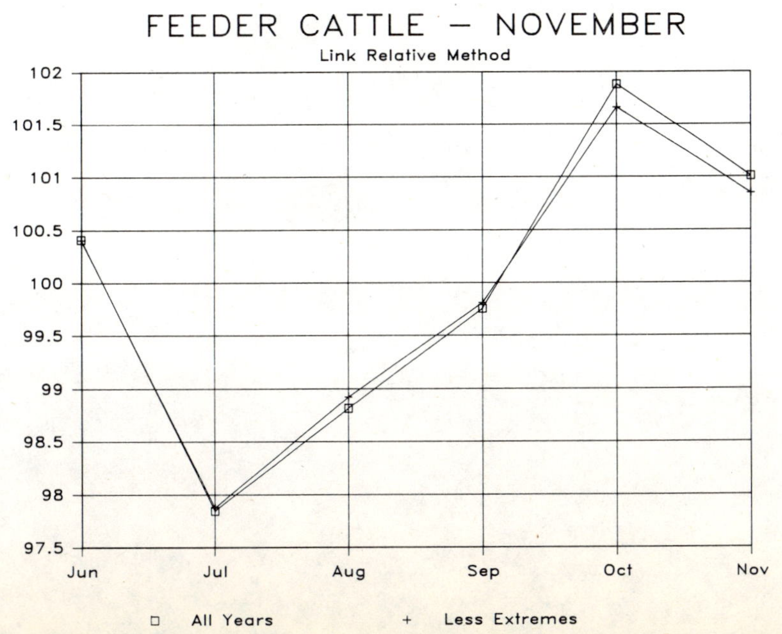
FEEDER CATTLE – NOVEMBER
Link Relative Method
102
101.5
101
100.5
100
99.5
99
98.5
98
97.5
Jun
Jul
Aug
Sep
Oct
Nov
All Years
Less Extremes

HOGS - FEBRUARY - MONTHLY AVERAGE PRICE

Year of Expiration	Apr	May	Jun	Jul	Aug	Sep	Oct	Nov	Dec	Jan	Feb	Apr-Feb Average
1971	19.13	20.92	20.06	19.59	19.83	20.26	18.64	17.23	17.08	17.30	20.39	19.13
1972	24.11	24.07	23.84	21.65	20.60	21.64	22.22	23.02	24.27	27.18	27.32	23.63
1973	26.33	26.77	26.67	27.12	26.95	29.12	28.33	29.34	31.17	33.88	35.31	29.18
1974	32.66	37.13	41.04	50.22	53.64	44.02	45.94	47.74	44.36	46.09	42.27	44.10
1975	39.69	31.56	31.19	41.09	43.10	41.17	45.63	42.85	44.63	40.55	40.81	40.21
1976	44.20	43.76	46.20	47.18	50.83	57.73	54.72	52.64	48.82	47.78	48.48	49.30
1977	41.83	41.35	42.76	40.69	37.49	34.70	32.04	32.13	35.30	37.74	40.30	37.85
1978	39.75	39.39	37.39	35.58	34.06	35.53	35.36	37.53	40.85	45.22	49.01	39.06
1979	45.77	48.32	43.28	43.51	44.78	48.21	51.44	51.24	51.59	52.68	55.59	48.76
1980	43.71	41.27	39.13	37.53	36.96	40.83	38.56	42.87	42.68	40.83	39.00	40.31
1981	42.10	42.18	43.27	47.37	48.60	52.65	54.70	55.04	52.08	46.33	44.65	48.09
1982	57.12	56.27	56.79	53.43	53.84	52.54	49.03	47.90	42.27	47.38	51.16	51.61
1983	53.82	54.76	52.68	54.69	56.17	57.46	56.98	56.11	57.28	58.36	59.00	56.12
1984	47.18	45.99	43.33	43.10	47.87	45.92	45.00	46.76	49.42	52.47	48.12	46.83
1985	54.84	56.44	57.32	53.28	52.08	50.59	49.05	52.24	52.60	52.11	51.24	52.89

	Apr	May	Jun	Jul	Aug	Sep	Oct	Nov	Dec	Jan	Feb
AVERAGE MOVE											
All Years		-0.14	-0.35	0.74	0.72	0.37	-0.31	0.47	-0.02	0.77	0.45
Less Extremes		0.12	-0.32	0.40	0.71	0.64	-0.44	0.42	0.16	0.93	0.56
Ave Up - All Years		1.69	1.71	3.84	2.05	2.74	2.45	1.72	1.77	2.47	1.93
Ave Down - All Years		-1.74	-1.72	-1.97	-1.28	-3.18	-1.70	-1.41	-2.69	-2.64	-2.51
COUNT											
Number Up		7	6	7	9	9	5	9	9	10	10
Number Down		8	9	8	6	6	10	6	6	5	5
Pct Up		46.7%	40.0%	46.7%	60.0%	60.0%	33.3%	60.0%	60.0%	66.7%	66.7%
Pct Down		53.3%	60.0%	53.3%	40.0%	40.0%	66.7%	40.0%	40.0%	33.3%	33.3%
EXTREMES											
Greatest Up		4.47	3.91	9.91	4.76	6.90	4.46	4.31	3.32	5.11	3.79
Greatest Down		-8.12	-5.03	-4.04	-3.20	-9.62	-3.50	-2.77	-5.63	-5.74	-4.35
SEASONAL INDEX : AVERAGE PERCENTAGE METHOD											
All Years	97.9	97.7	96.7	98.1	99.4	100.5	99.5	100.5	101.1	103.4	105.2
Less Extremes	98.7	98.3	96.9	97.6	98.6	99.9	99.6	100.7	101.8	103.4	104.6
SEASONAL INDEX : LINK RELATIVE METHOD											
All Years		99.8	98.2	99.6	100.1	100.8	99.1	99.5	99.4	101.2	102.2
Less Extremes		100.4	98.7	98.9	99.4	100.8	98.8	99.3	99.6	101.7	102.4

HOGS - FEBRUARY - MONTH OF HIGH AND LOW

Year of Expiration	Apr	May	Jun	Jul	Aug	Sep	Oct	Nov	Dec	Jan	Feb
1971		H							L		
1972					L						H
1973	L										H
1974					H						L
1975			L				H				
1976		L				H					
1977			H				L				
1978					L						H
1979			L								H
1980	H				L						
1981	L							H			
1982	H								L		
1983			L								H
1984				L						H	
1985			H				L				

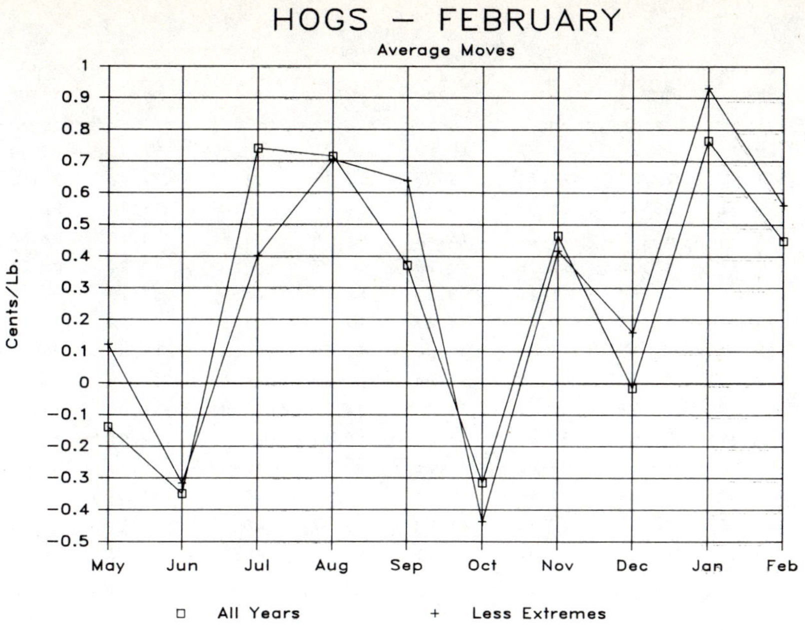
HOGS – FEBRUARY
Average Moves
Cents/Lb.
1
0.9
0.8
0.7
0.6
0.5
0.4
0.3
0.2
0.1
0
−0.1
−0.2
−0.3
−0.4
−0.5
May
Jun
Jul
Aug
Sep
Oct
Nov
Dec
Jan
Feb
All Years
Less Extremes

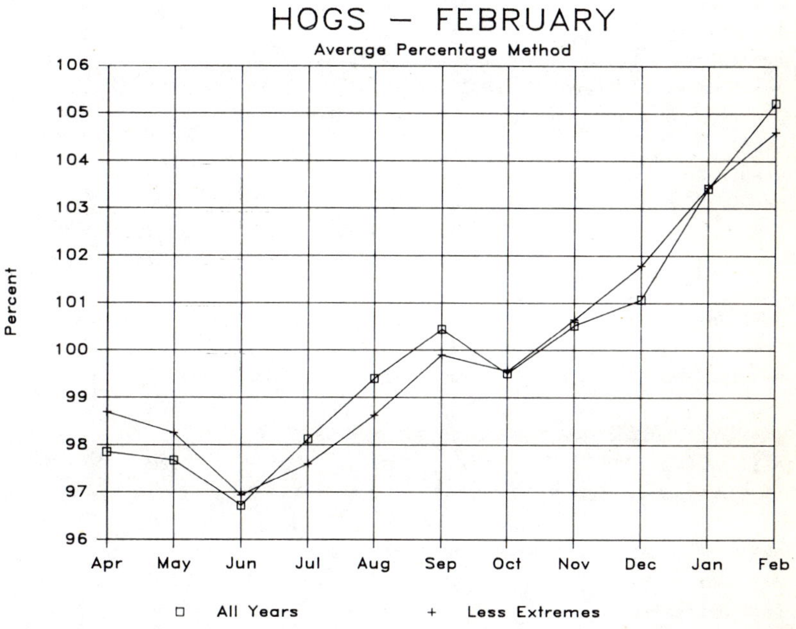
HOGS – FEBRUARY
Average Percentage Method
Percent
106
105
104
103
102
101
100
99
98
97
96
Apr
May
Jun
Jul
Aug
Sep
Oct
Nov
Dec
Jan
Feb
All Years
Less Extremes

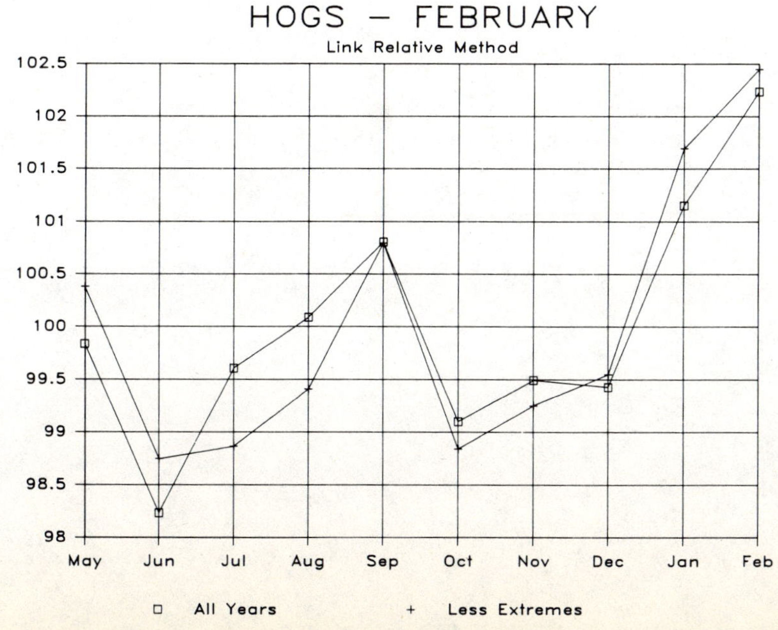
HOGS – FEBRUARY
Link Relative Method
102.5
102
101.5
101
100.5
100
99.5
99
98.5
98
May
Jun
Jul
Aug
Sep
Oct
Nov
Dec
Jan
Feb
All Years
Less Extremes

HOGS - APRIL - MONTHLY AVERAGE PRICE

Year of Expiration	Jun	Jul	Aug	Sep	Oct	Nov	Dec	Jan	Feb	Mar	Apr	Jun-Apr Average
1971	19.05	19.57	20.40	21.49	19.59	18.20	17.75	16.86	18.21	17.71	17.33	18.74
1972	23.48	21.48	20.16	21.11	21.55	22.07	23.61	26.05	25.18	24.70	24.74	23.10
1973	24.81	25.05	24.54	26.30	25.52	26.52	27.92	30.27	32.86	36.77	35.20	28.71
1974	39.42	48.46	51.80	42.62	44.62	46.01	43.21	46.01	41.15	34.95	33.48	42.88
1975	31.01	39.86	42.45	41.20	45.27	42.30	44.16	40.29	40.05	40.09	42.24	40.81
1976	42.88	44.16	47.98	53.58	49.98	47.50	44.16	43.69	43.82	44.35	49.10	46.47
1977	41.16	39.40	36.48	34.14	31.43	30.60	32.45	34.67	36.22	35.30	37.16	35.36
1978	35.59	33.54	31.77	32.86	32.32	33.93	36.31	40.28	44.39	46.31	47.37	37.70
1979	40.91	41.26	42.09	44.88	47.95	47.85	48.07	48.84	52.32	49.47	47.19	46.44
1980	38.72	37.43	36.15	39.78	37.17	40.83	40.51	39.79	37.82	34.96	29.41	37.51
1981	42.39	46.53	47.50	51.65	53.94	54.90	53.47	47.73	47.24	41.67	42.97	48.18
1982	55.37	52.63	51.95	49.58	46.67	45.92	40.81	46.06	47.80	49.80	52.70	49.03
1983	49.65	50.93	51.59	53.72	53.27	52.99	54.19	55.11	53.70	50.53	49.05	52.25
1984	41.95	42.12	47.95	46.89	45.17	46.61	47.89	48.83	45.57	48.09	49.59	46.42
1985	53.06	49.72	48.67	48.12	46.27	48.52	48.74	49.21	47.38	46.08	43.64	48.13

	Jun	Jul	Aug	Sep	Oct	Nov	Dec	Jan	Feb	Mar	Apr
AVERAGE MOVE											
All Years		0.85	0.62	0.43	-0.48	-2.45	-0.10	0.69	.00	-0.86	0.03
Less Extremes		0.54	0.49	0.77	-0.59	-0.14	0.09	0.84	0.06	-0.82	0.09
Ave Up - All Years		2.88	2.36	2.58	2.37	1.31	1.33	2.21	2.14	1.82	1.94
Ave Down - All Years		-2.20	-1.36	-2.79	-1.91	-5.75	-2.24	-2.34	-1.87	-2.65	-2.17
COUNT											
Number Up		9	8	9	5	7	9	10	7	6	8
Number Down		6	7	6	10	8	6	5	8	9	7
Pct Up		60.0%	53.3%	60.0%	33.3%	46.7%	60.0%	66.7%	46.7%	40.0%	53.3%
Pct Down		40.0%	46.7%	40.0%	66.7%	53.3%	40.0%	33.3%	53.3%	60.0%	46.7%
EXTREMES											
Greatest Up		9.04	5.82	5.60	4.07	2.26	2.38	5.25	4.11	3.91	4.75
Greatest Down		-3.34	-2.92	-9.18	-3.60	-37.17	-5.11	-5.74	-4.86	-6.20	-5.55
SEASONAL INDEX : AVERAGE PERCENTAGE METHOD											
All Years	96.6	98.3	99.5	100.8	99.2	99.8	100.0	102.0	102.5	100.7	100.5
Less Extremes	96.6	98.0	99.0	100.7	99.3	99.7	100.5	102.1	102.0	100.1	100.3
SEASONAL INDEX : LINK RELATIVE METHOD											
All Years		98.5	99.4	100.9	99.2	99.6	99.7	101.7	102.0	99.8	99.3
Less Extremes		98.5	99.0	101.1	99.1	99.3	99.7	101.8	102.2	99.8	99.6

HOGS - APRIL - MONTH OF HIGH AND LOW

Year of Expiration	Jun	Jul	Aug	Sep	Oct	Nov	Dec	Jan	Feb	Mar	Apr
1971				H							L
1972			L					H			
1973			L							H	
1974			H								L
1975	L		H								
1976	L			H							
1977	H					L					
1978			L								H
1979	L								H		
1980						H					L
1981						H				L	
1982	H						L				
1983								H			L
1984	L										H
1985	H										L

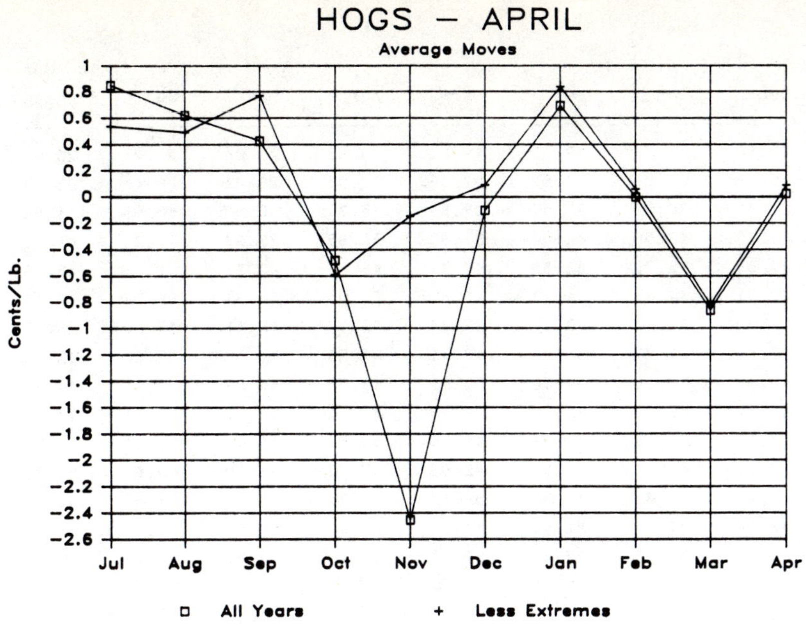

HOGS — APRIL
Average Moves
Cents/Lb.
1
0.8
0.6
0.4
0.2
0
−0.2
−0.4
−0.6
−0.8
−1
−1.2
−1.4
−1.6
−1.8
−2
−2.2
−2.4
−2.6
Jul
Aug
Sep
Oct
Nov
Dec
Jan
Feb
Mar
Apr
□ All Years
+ Less Extremes

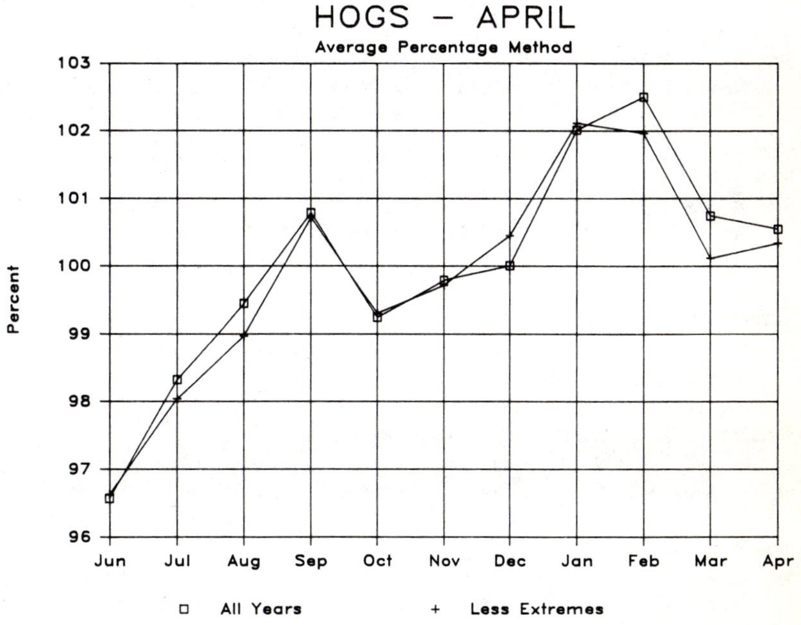

HOGS — APRIL
Average Percentage Method
Percent
103
102
101
100
99
98
97
96
Jun
Jul
Aug
Sep
Oct
Nov
Dec
Jan
Feb
Mar
Apr
□ All Years
+ Less Extremes

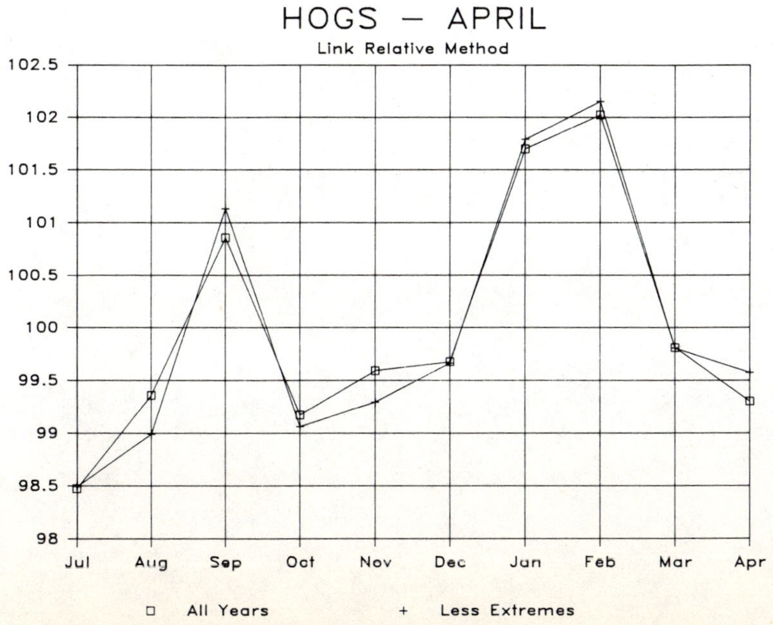

HOGS — APRIL
Link Relative Method
102.5
102
101.5
101
100.5
100
99.5
99
98.5
98
Jul
Aug
Sep
Oct
Nov
Dec
Jan
Feb
Mar
Apr
□ All Years
+ Less Extremes

HOGS - JUNE - MONTHLY AVERAGE PRICE

Year of Expiration	Aug	Sep	Oct	Nov	Dec	Jan	Feb	Mar	Apr	May	Jun	Aug-Jun Average
1971	23.10	23.58	21.95	20.80	20.16	18.75	19.72	19.82	20.31	21.06	20.21	20.86
1972	22.15	23.23	23.41	23.74	25.46	27.76	27.02	27.06	27.65	28.21	28.44	25.83
1973	25.37	27.07	26.29	27.20	28.33	30.91	33.57	37.52	35.30	38.59	40.55	31.88
1974	52.06	43.44	46.56	47.01	44.99	48.08	44.90	37.67	36.65	29.67	27.22	41.66
1975	44.88	43.66	47.41	45.05	47.05	43.29	42.88	42.77	46.46	48.21	51.71	45.76
1976	48.67	53.54	48.80	46.98	43.91	44.65	44.93	45.32	51.04	50.51	51.75	48.19
1977	38.47	37.08	34.39	33.18	34.52	37.14	38.17	37.85	42.07	45.41	45.60	38.53
1978	33.50	34.41	34.07	35.93	37.74	41.71	45.87	48.91	51.58	54.07	52.17	42.72
1979	43.85	46.55	49.94	49.92	49.70	50.13	54.03	51.46	49.55	46.89	42.54	48.59
1980	40.43	43.67	40.69	43.98	43.72	43.32	41.60	39.38	34.51	33.77	35.71	40.07
1981	50.63	55.30	57.19	58.83	57.62	52.13	52.67	46.79	49.87	49.50	51.41	52.90
1982	54.27	51.83	49.15	48.40	43.51	49.05	50.66	53.93	57.72	61.40	60.85	52.79
1983	51.21	53.86	53.86	53.78	55.27	56.40	55.36	53.62	51.21	49.57	48.09	52.93
1984	53.01	52.75	50.59	51.83	52.96	54.04	51.90	54.62	56.08	53.93	52.45	53.10
1985	52.08	51.40	49.57	52.25	52.27	54.11	52.63	51.11	48.12	46.97	48.15	50.79

	Aug	Sep	Oct	Nov	Dec	Jan	Feb	Mar	Apr	May	Jun
AVERAGE MOVE											
All Years		0.51	-0.50	0.33	-0.11	0.95	0.30	-0.54	0.69	-0.03	-0.06
Less Extremes		0.88	-0.50	0.31	0.09	1.09	0.27	-0.37	0.73	0.22	.00
Ave Up - All Years		2.48	2.06	1.55	1.33	2.30	1.89	1.93	2.86	2.27	1.52
Ave Down - All Years		-2.43	-2.20	-1.05	-1.76	-2.76	-1.53	-2.70	-2.57	-2.03	-1.87
COUNT											
Number Up		9	6	8	8	11	8	7	9	7	8
Number Down		6	9	7	7	4	7	8	6	8	7
Pct Up		60.0%	40.0%	53.3%	53.3%	73.3%	53.3%	46.7%	60.0%	46.7%	53.3%
Pct Down		40.0%	60.0%	46.7%	46.7%	26.7%	46.7%	53.3%	40.0%	53.3%	46.7%
EXTREMES											
Greatest Up		4.87	3.76	3.28	2.00	5.54	4.16	3.95	5.73	3.68	3.50
Greatest Down		-8.62	-4.74	-2.36	-4.89	-5.49	-3.18	-7.23	-4.87	-6.98	-4.35
SEASONAL INDEX : AVERAGE PERCENTAGE METHOD											
All Years	97.8	99.0	97.6	98.2	98.2	100.6	101.5	100.5	101.9	102.4	102.3
Less Extremes	97.2	99.4	97.9	98.2	98.6	100.3	101.4	100.1	101.7	102.9	103.2
SEASONAL INDEX : LINK RELATIVE METHOD											
All Years		99.6	98.0	98.4	98.3	100.6	101.4	100.2	101.5	101.2	100.6
Less Extremes		99.8	98.0	98.1	98.1	100.5	101.1	100.0	101.4	101.7	101.2

HOGS - JUNE - MONTH OF HIGH AND LOW

Year of Expiration	Aug	Sep	Oct	Nov	Dec	Jan	Feb	Mar	Apr	May	Jun
1971		H				L					
1972	L										H
1973	L										H
1974	H										L
1975								L			H
1976		H			L						
1977				L							H
1978	L									H	
1979							H				L
1980				H						L	
1981				H				L			
1982					L					H	
1983						H					L
1984			L						H		
1985						H			L		

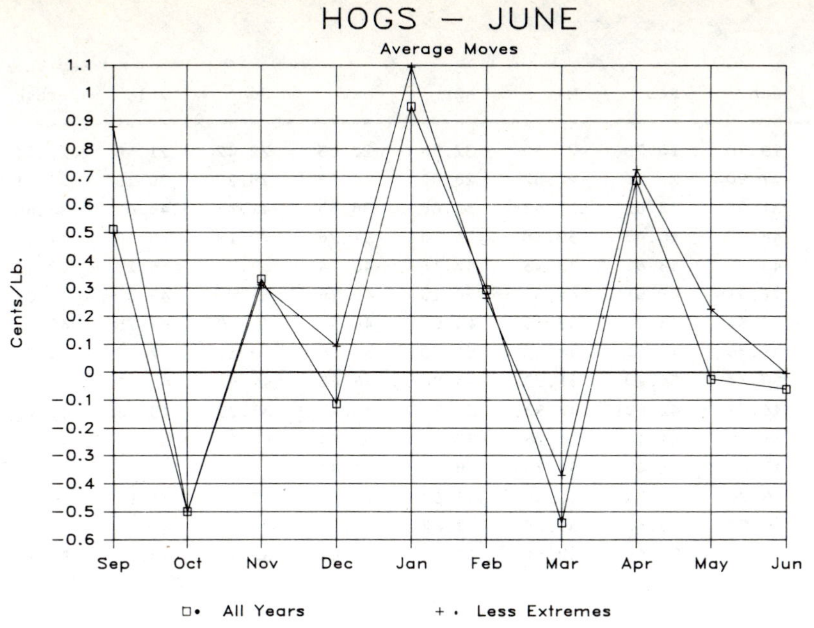
HOGS — JUNE
Average Moves
Cents/Lb.
1.1
1
0.9
0.8
0.7
0.6
0.5
0.4
0.3
0.2
0.1
0
−0.1
−0.2
−0.3
−0.4
−0.5
−0.6
Sep
Oct
Nov
Dec
Jan
Feb
Mar
Apr
May
Jun
All Years
Less Extremes

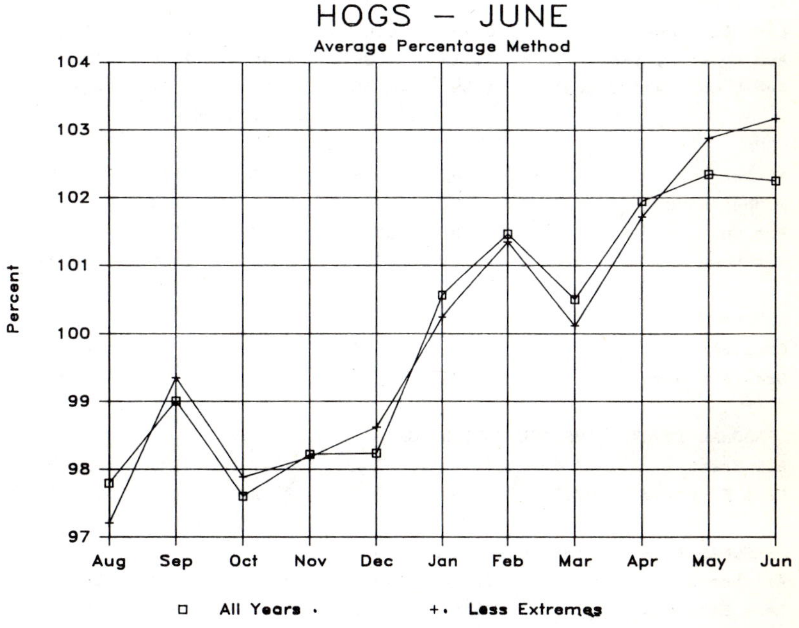
HOGS — JUNE
Average Percentage Method
Percent
104
103
102
101
100
99
98
97
Aug
Sep
Oct
Nov
Dec
Jan
Feb
Mar
Apr
May
Jun
All Years
Less Extremes

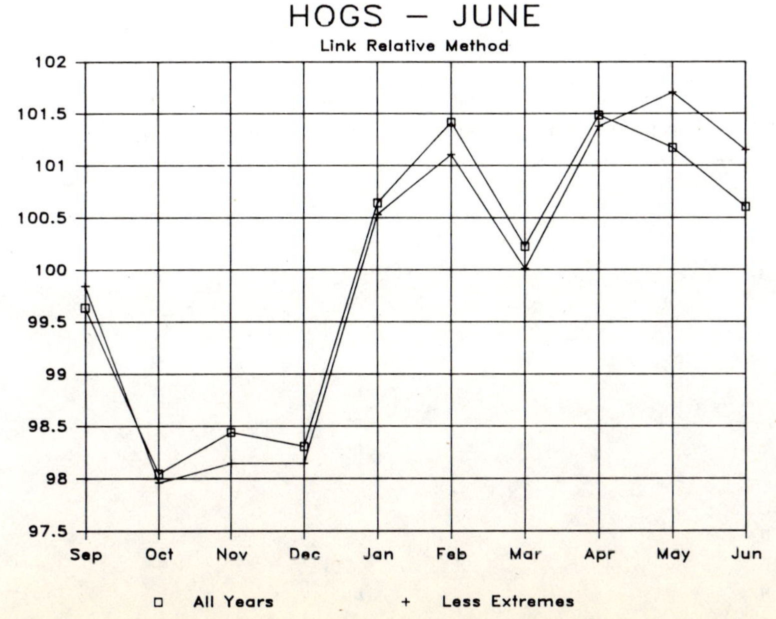
HOGS — JUNE
Link Relative Method
102
101.5
101
100.5
100
99.5
99
98.5
98
97.5
Sep
Oct
Nov
Dec
Jan
Feb
Mar
Apr
May
Jun
All Years
Less Extremes

HOGS - JULY - MONTHLY AVERAGE PRICE

Year of Expiration	Sep	Oct	Nov	Dec	Jan	Feb	Mar	Apr	May	Jun	Jul	Sep-Jul Average
1971	23.80	22.42	21.64	21.18	19.70	20.75	21.30	22.08	22.55	22.02	21.66	21.74
1972	23.31	23.50	23.86	25.56	27.90	27.26	27.52	28.01	28.63	29.22	30.16	26.81
1973	27.02	26.32	27.18	28.22	31.05	33.61	37.43	35.68	38.85	41.37	45.69	33.86
1974	43.47	46.55	47.13	45.68	48.45	46.45	39.88	38.76	31.26	29.19	38.38	41.38
1975	44.92	48.44	45.93	47.63	44.34	43.81	43.83	47.16	48.64	53.24	56.20	47.65
1976	53.33	48.27	46.32	43.81	44.91	45.51	45.59	50.19	49.75	51.27	49.21	48.01
1977	37.34	34.75	34.13	35.23	37.59	38.90	39.76	44.00	46.51	46.30	47.75	40.20
1978	34.52	34.47	36.26	38.05	41.76	45.91	48.92	51.75	54.96	50.12	47.77	44.04
1979	46.71	50.17	50.28	50.13	50.34	54.20	51.93	49.86	46.63	40.99	40.88	48.37
1980	43.89	41.56	44.91	44.68	44.29	42.68	40.93	35.74	35.47	37.72	43.58	41.40
1981	56.27	58.12	59.89	58.78	53.30	54.16	48.26	52.58	52.54	55.13	53.08	54.74
1982	52.08	49.45	49.05	44.52	49.87	51.49	54.70	58.50	61.87	59.07	60.64	53.75
1983	52.76	53.33	53.30	55.00	56.28	55.31	54.05	51.60	49.57	47.32	46.15	52.24
1984	54.20	52.53	53.39	53.89	54.94	53.57	56.25	58.67	57.73	56.47	54.74	55.13
1985	52.13	50.62	53.12	52.66	54.52	53.48	52.51	50.21	49.53	50.41	49.53	51.70
AVERAGE MOVE												
All Years		-0.35	0.40	-0.09	0.95	0.52	-0.28	0.79	-0.02	-0.31	1.04	
Less Extremes		-0.29	0.39	0.11	1.10	0.44	-0.11	0.96	0.29	-0.28	0.67	
Ave Up - All Years		2.11	1.36	1.36	2.26	2.00	1.61	2.98	2.12	2.14	3.76	
Ave Down - All Years		-1.99	-1.05	-1.36	-2.66	-1.16	-3.12	-2.48	-1.89	-2.45	-1.34	
COUNT												
Number Up		6	9	7	11	8	9	9	7	7	7	
Number Down		9	6	8	4	7	6	6	8	8	8	
Pct Up		40.0%	60.0%	46.7%	73.3%	53.3%	60.0%	60.0%	46.7%	46.7%	46.7%	
Pct Down		60.0%	40.0%	53.3%	26.7%	46.7%	40.0%	40.0%	53.3%	53.3%	53.3%	
EXTREMES												
Greatest Up		3.52	3.36	1.78	5.35	4.15	3.83	4.60	3.36	4.61	9.19	
Greatest Down		-5.07	-2.51	-4.53	-5.47	-1.99	-6.57	-5.19	-7.50	-5.64	-2.34	
SEASONAL INDEX : AVERAGE PERCENTAGE METHOD												
All Years	97.4	96.4	97.2	97.2	99.5	100.8	100.5	102.1	102.4	101.8	104.7	
Less Extremes	97.8	96.6	97.2	97.3	98.8	100.7	100.7	102.2	102.7	102.7	103.9	
SEASONAL INDEX : LINK RELATIVE METHOD												
All Years		99.0	99.1	98.5	100.4	101.1	100.1	101.1	100.3	98.9	101.4	
Less Extremes		98.6	98.6	98.2	100.2	100.7	100.0	101.3	101.3	100.1	101.0	

HOGS - JULY - MONTH OF HIGH AND LOW

Year of Expiration	Sep	Oct	Nov	Dec	Jan	Feb	Mar	Apr	May	Jun	Jul
1971	H				L						
1972	L										H
1973		L									H
1974					H				L		
1975						L					H
1976	H			L							
1977			L								H
1978		L							H		
1979						H					L
1980			H						L		
1981			H				L				
1982				L					H		
1983					H						L
1984		L						H			
1985					H				L		

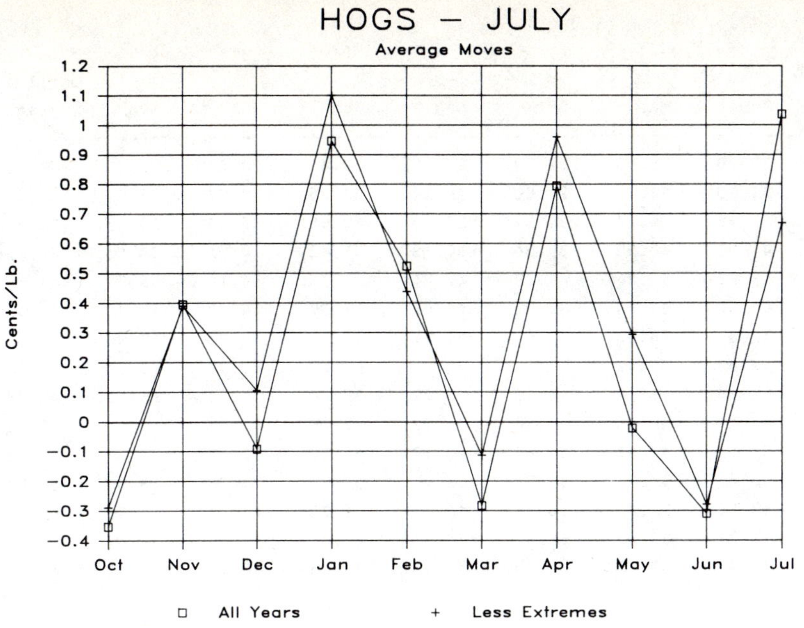
HOGS – JULY
Average Moves
Cents/Lb.
1.2
1.1
1
0.9
0.8
0.7
0.6
0.5
0.4
0.3
0.2
0.1
0
−0.1
−0.2
−0.3
−0.4
Oct
Nov
Dec
Jan
Feb
Mar
Apr
May
Jun
Jul
□ All Years
+ Less Extremes

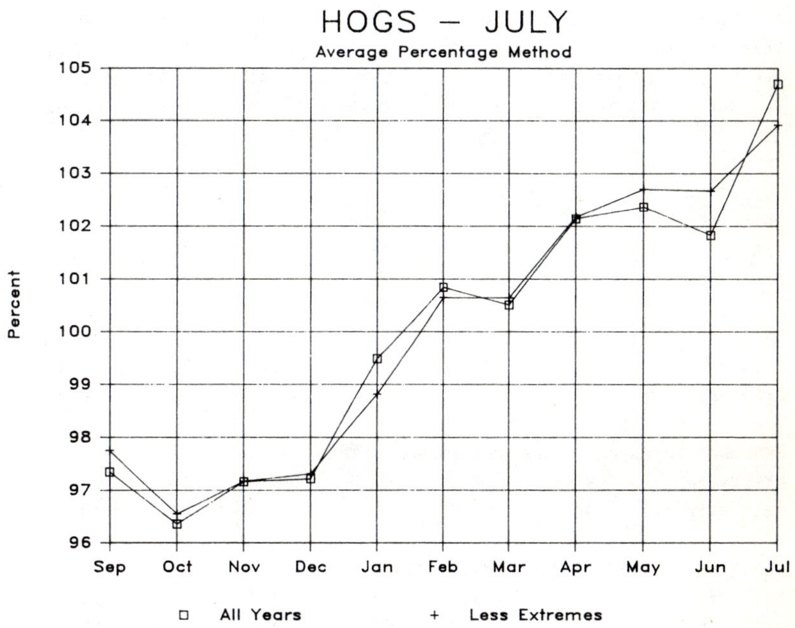
HOGS – JULY
Average Percentage Method
Percent
105
104
103
102
101
100
99
98
97
96
Sep
Oct
Nov
Dec
Jan
Feb
Mar
Apr
May
Jun
Jul
□ All Years
+ Less Extremes

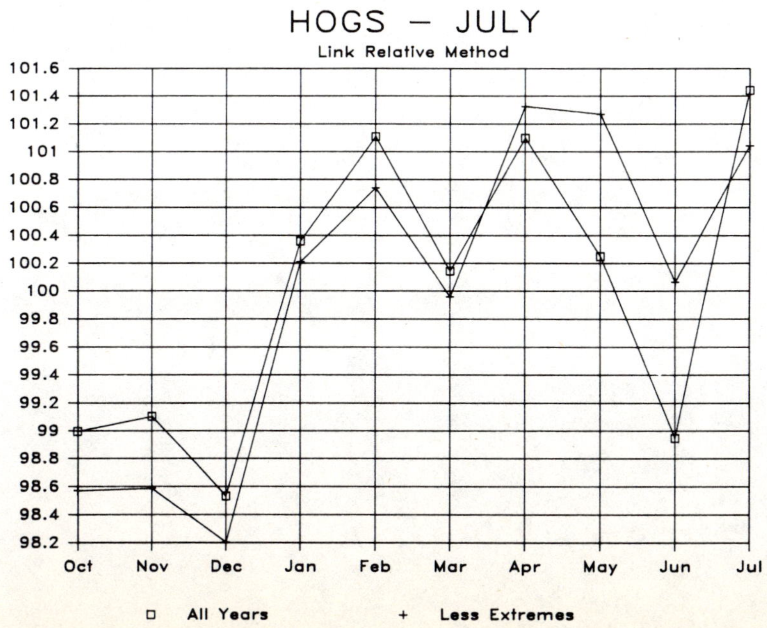
HOGS – JULY
Link Relative Method
101.6
101.4
101.2
101
100.8
100.6
100.4
100.2
100
99.8
99.6
99.4
99.2
99
98.8
98.6
98.4
98.2
Oct
Nov
Dec
Jan
Feb
Mar
Apr
May
Jun
Jul
□ All Years
+ Less Extremes

HOGS - AUGUST - MONTHLY AVERAGE PRICE

Year of Expiration	Oct	Nov	Dec	Jan	Feb	Mar	Apr	May	Jun	Jul	Aug	Oct-Aug Average
1971	22.41	21.82	21.23	19.74	20.76	21.46	22.20	22.67	22.43	20.80	20.23	21.43
1972	22.60	22.77	24.60	27.23	26.39	26.78	27.60	28.14	28.35	28.77	29.31	26.59
1973	25.04	25.32	26.85	29.16	31.38	35.74	34.32	37.95	40.68	49.23	58.63	35.85
1974	45.18	45.29	44.26	46.95	46.51	40.23	38.34	30.13	27.42	38.21	38.86	40.12
1975	47.35	44.54	46.37	43.20	42.83	42.86	46.29	47.34	51.78	54.18	56.22	47.54
1976	45.83	44.28	41.43	43.36	43.62	43.34	47.03	46.01	47.87	44.78	43.35	44.63
1977	33.60	33.40	34.21	35.91	37.47	38.90	42.88	44.47	42.81	42.98	42.96	39.05
1978	32.82	34.47	36.08	39.03	42.86	46.42	50.19	52.82	47.37	45.37	48.88	43.30
1979	48.12	48.05	48.01	48.00	51.46	49.11	46.80	43.37	37.80	37.05	36.38	44.92
1980	40.75	44.03	43.57	43.32	42.11	40.45	35.30	35.09	37.08	42.51	48.49	41.15
1981	56.76	58.37	57.98	52.69	53.17	47.51	52.89	53.17	55.60	51.10	51.66	53.72
1982	48.26	47.84	43.61	48.76	50.45	53.84	57.71	61.06	57.65	59.70	63.96	53.89
1983	50.83	51.01	53.07	54.42	53.59	51.82	48.99	46.77	44.72	44.43	49.56	49.93
1984	51.69	52.88	53.55	54.30	53.37	55.82	58.83	58.31	57.80	53.58	53.36	54.86
1985	48.83	50.74	50.30	53.47	52.43	52.11	50.29	49.55	49.65	46.28	43.92	49.78

	Oct	Nov	Dec	Jan	Feb	Mar	Apr	May	Jun	Jul	Aug
AVERAGE MOVE											
All Years		0.31	0.02	0.96	0.59	-0.14	0.89	-0.19	-0.52	0.66	1.79
Less Extremes		0.33	0.19	1.12	0.48	-0.01	1.00	0.14	-0.51	0.28	1.52
Ave Up - All Years		1.15	1.48	2.46	1.81	2.04	3.19	1.69	1.97	4.26	3.56
Ave Down - All Years		-0.94	-1.25	-2.04	-0.81	-2.62	-2.57	-2.34	-2.70	-2.48	-0.88
COUNT											
Number Up		9	7	10	8	8	9	8	7	7	9
Number Down		6	8	5	7	7	6	7	8	8	6
Pct Up		60.0%	46.7%	66.7%	53.3%	53.3%	60.0%	53.3%	46.7%	46.7%	60.0%
Pct Down		40.0%	53.3%	33.3%	46.7%	46.7%	40.0%	46.7%	53.3%	53.3%	40.0%
EXTREMES											
Greatest Up		3.27	2.06	5.15	3.83	4.35	5.38	3.63	4.44	10.79	9.40
Greatest Down		-2.81	-4.23	-5.29	-1.21	-6.28	-5.15	-8.21	-5.57	-4.50	-2.36
SEASONAL INDEX : AVERAGE PERCENTAGE METHOD											
All Years	95.4	96.1	96.3	98.6	100.1	100.1	101.9	101.6	100.5	102.5	106.8
Less Extremes	96.1	96.7	96.9	98.5	99.9	100.2	102.1	102.1	102.0	101.4	104.4
SEASONAL INDEX : LINK RELATIVE METHOD											
All Years		99.1	98.6	100.3	101.0	100.3	101.3	99.9	97.8	99.6	102.1
Less Extremes		98.5	98.2	100.2	100.8	100.2	101.7	101.1	99.2	99.1	101.2

HOGS - AUGUST - MONTH OF HIGH AND LOW

Year of Expiration	Oct	Nov	Dec	Jan	Feb	Mar	Apr	May	Jun	Jul	Aug
1971				L				H			
1972	L										H
1973	L										H
1974				H					L		
1975					L						H
1976			L						H		
1977		L						H			
1978	L							H			
1979					H						L
1980								L			H
1981		H				L					
1982			L								H
1983				H						L	
1984	L						H				
1985				H							L

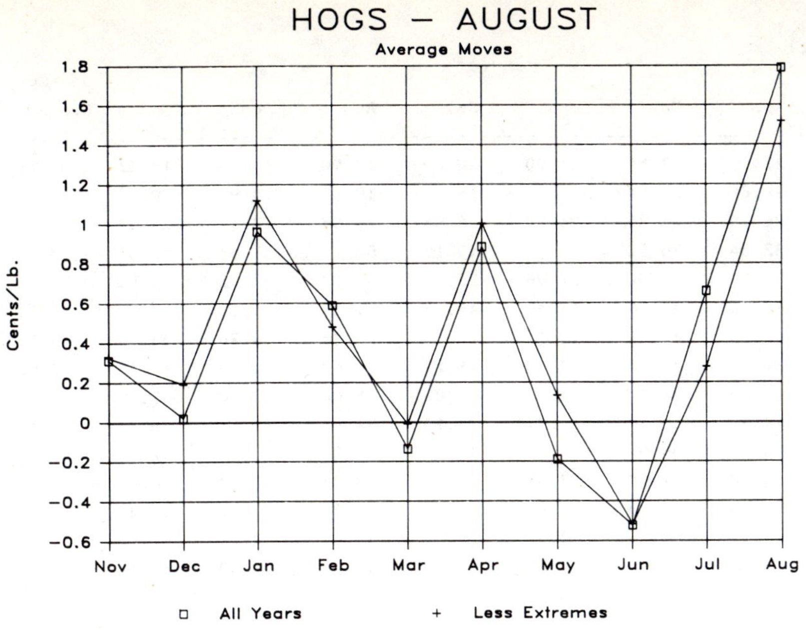
HOGS — AUGUST
Average Moves
Cents/Lb.
1.8
1.6
1.4
1.2
1
0.8
0.6
0.4
0.2
0
−0.2
−0.4
−0.6
Nov
Dec
Jan
Feb
Mar
Apr
May
Jun
Jul
Aug
□ All Years
+ Less Extremes

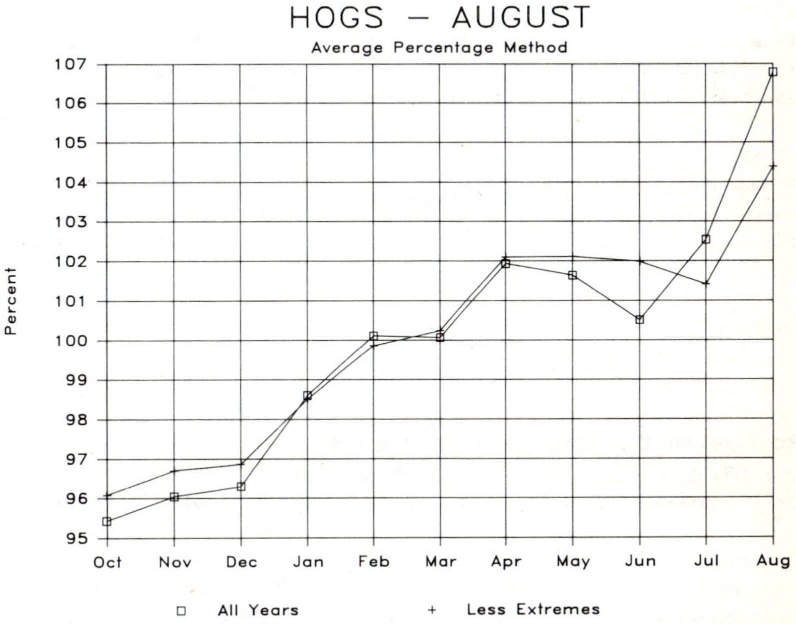
HOGS — AUGUST
Average Percentage Method
Percent
107
106
105
104
103
102
101
100
99
98
97
96
95
Oct
Nov
Dec
Jan
Feb
Mar
Apr
May
Jun
Jul
Aug
□ All Years
+ Less Extremes

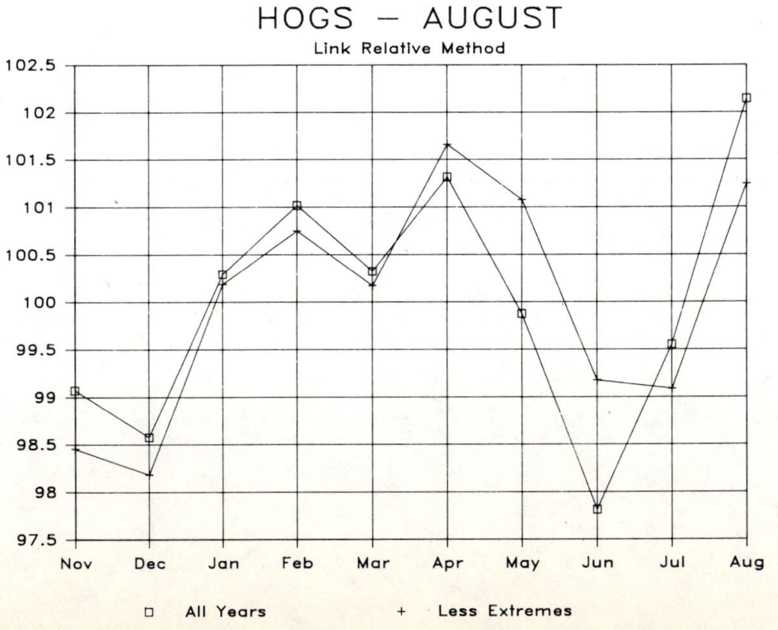
HOGS — AUGUST
Link Relative Method
102.5
102
101.5
101
100.5
100
99.5
99
98.5
98
97.5
Nov
Dec
Jan
Feb
Mar
Apr
May
Jun
Jul
Aug
□ All Years
+ Less Extremes

HOGS - OCTOBER - MONTHLY AVERAGE PRICE

Year of Expiration	Dec	Jan	Feb	Mar	Apr	May	Jun	Jul	Aug	Sep	Oct	Dec-Oct Average
1970	22.11	25.01	25.07	24.53	23.41	22.56	21.00	20.60	19.90	19.68	19.31	22.11
1971	20.87	19.75	20.76	21.23	21.88	22.08	21.75	19.65	18.80	18.99	20.82	20.60
1972	24.02	25.57	24.24	24.84	26.19	26.85	26.60	26.66	26.98	29.21	29.24	26.40
1973	25.17	26.87	28.38	33.32	32.54	36.52	39.92	49.16	52.21	41.35	43.57	37.18
1974	42.63	45.24	45.84	40.51	37.50	28.94	27.06	37.06	37.27	34.91	39.59	37.87
1975	45.37	42.66	42.22	41.82	44.80	44.66	47.49	48.48	51.47	60.45	61.84	48.30
1976	39.41	41.26	41.18	40.43	42.86	42.51	44.16	40.95	38.78	36.76	33.74	40.19
1977	33.28	33.80	35.49	36.89	39.07	39.12	37.40	36.77	36.67	38.55	40.18	37.02
1978	34.08	36.41	39.02	42.54	46.62	48.87	43.57	43.02	45.68	49.10	52.78	43.79
1979	46.21	45.69	49.01	46.52	43.67	40.17	35.31	34.19	34.55	37.86	35.42	40.78
1980	42.80	42.35	41.67	40.13	35.98	35.91	37.31	41.22	44.08	46.33	47.80	41.42
1981	56.76	51.74	52.12	47.11	52.90	52.08	53.67	49.08	50.44	50.59	46.90	51.22
1982	42.84	46.93	48.13	51.20	55.57	57.78	54.86	57.28	60.86	61.34	57.40	54.02
1983	48.90	50.21	49.55	47.53	45.17	43.46	40.89	39.51	43.15	42.19	41.49	44.73
1984	51.71	51.87	50.80	53.08	55.82	56.16	56.65	50.27	48.22	46.50	44.76	51.44

	Dec	Jan	Feb	Mar	Apr	May	Jun	Jul	Aug	Sep	Oct
AVERAGE MOVE											
All Years		0.61	0.54	-0.12	0.82	-0.42	-0.67	0.42	1.01	0.32	0.07
Less Extremes		0.78	0.47	-0.11	0.82	-0.13	-0.63	0.20	1.05	0.51	0.02
Ave Up - All Years		1.90	1.38	2.33	2.95	1.39	1.89	4.43	2.10	2.55	2.12
Ave Down - All Years		-1.97	-0.71	-2.26	-2.38	-2.00	-2.38	-2.26	-1.17	-3.02	-2.27
COUNT											
Number Up		10	9	7	9	7	6	6	10	9	8
Number Down		5	6	8	6	8	9	9	5	6	7
Pct Up		66.7%	60.0%	46.7%	60.0%	46.7%	40.0%	40.0%	66.7%	60.0%	53.3%
Pct Down		33.3%	40.0%	53.3%	40.0%	53.3%	60.0%	60.0%	33.3%	40.0%	46.7%
EXTREMES											
Greatest Up		4.10	3.32	4.94	5.79	3.98	3.40	10.00	3.64	8.99	4.68
Greatest Down		-5.02	-1.33	-5.34	-4.15	-8.55	-5.30	-6.38	-2.17	-10.86	-3.94
SEASONAL INDEX : AVERAGE PERCENTAGE METHOD											
All Years	96.5	98.4	99.8	99.5	101.0	99.7	97.8	99.0	101.0	101.6	102.4
Less Extremes	97.4	98.8	100.0	99.2	101.6	100.7	98.9	97.8	99.4	100.8	101.9
SEASONAL INDEX : LINK RELATIVE METHOD											
All Years		99.3	100.3	100.3	101.5	99.9	97.6	98.9	100.3	100.8	101.0
Less Extremes		99.3	100.5	100.1	101.6	100.7	98.4	98.2	99.7	100.7	100.6

HOGS - OCTOBER - MONTH OF HIGH AND LOW

Year of Expiration	Dec	Jan	Feb	Mar	Apr	May	Jun	Jul	Aug	Sep	Oct
1970			H								L
1971						H			L		
1972	L										H
1973	L								H		
1974			H			L					
1975				L							H
1976							H				L
1977	L										H
1978	L										H
1979			H					L			
1980						L					H
1981	H										L
1982	L									H	
1983		H						L			
1984							H				L

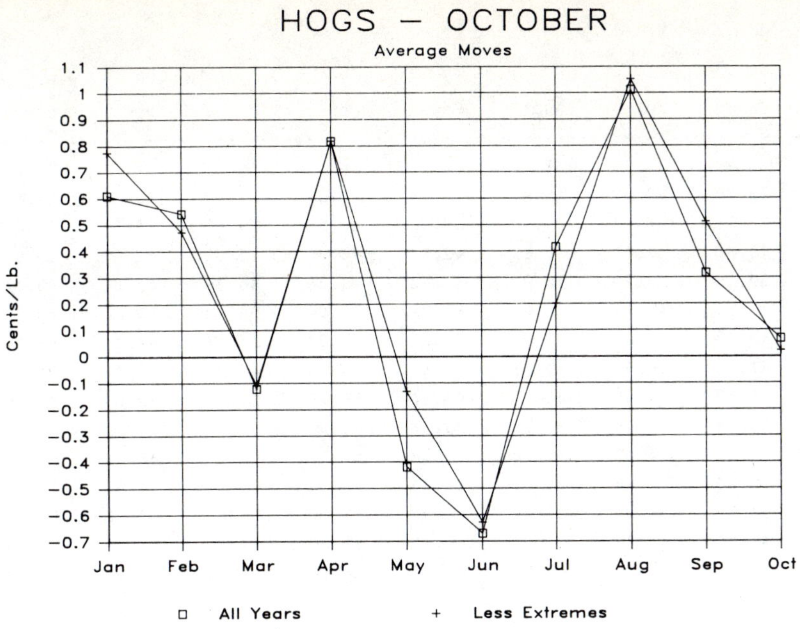
HOGS — OCTOBER
Average Moves
Cents/Lb.
1.1
1
0.9
0.8
0.7
0.6
0.5
0.4
0.3
0.2
0.1
0
-0.1
-0.2
-0.3
-0.4
-0.5
-0.6
-0.7
Jan
Feb
Mar
Apr
May
Jun
Jul
Aug
Sep
Oct
□ All Years
+ Less Extremes

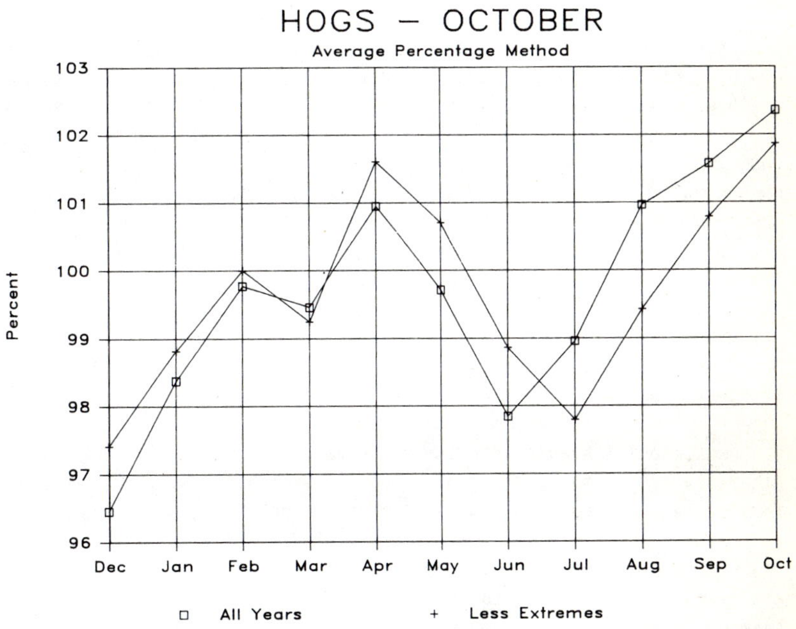
HOGS — OCTOBER
Average Percentage Method
Percent
103
102
101
100
99
98
97
96
Dec
Jan
Feb
Mar
Apr
May
Jun
Jul
Aug
Sep
Oct
□ All Years
+ Less Extremes

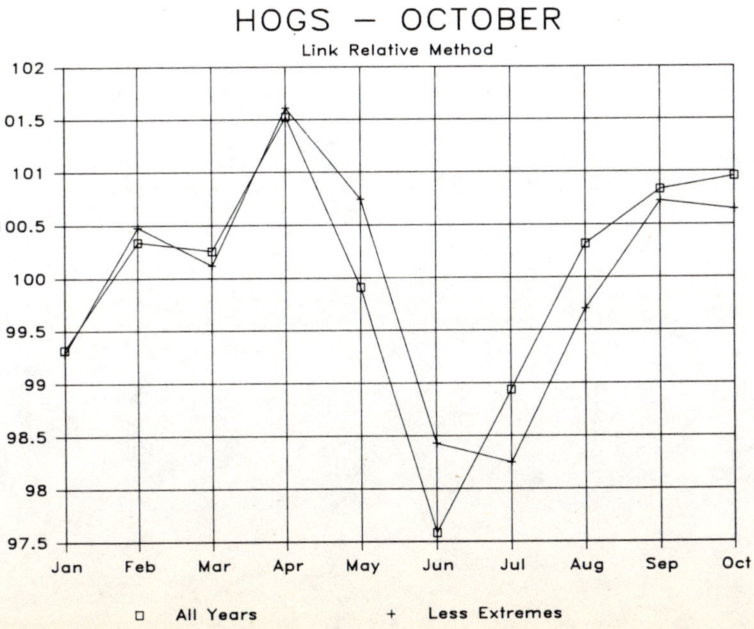
HOGS — OCTOBER
Link Relative Method
102
101.5
101
100.5
100
99.5
99
98.5
98
97.5
Jan
Feb
Mar
Apr
May
Jun
Jul
Aug
Sep
Oct
□ All Years
+ Less Extremes

HOGS - DECEMBER - MONTHLY AVERAGE PRICE

Year of Expiration	Feb	Mar	Apr	May	Jun	Jul	Aug	Sep	Oct	Nov	Dec	Feb-Dec Average
1970	24.00	23.67	22.95	22.18	20.28	20.01	19.64	19.46	18.14	16.63	17.01	20.36
1971	21.18	22.01	23.16	23.30	22.78	20.00	19.25	19.98	21.27	21.97	22.65	21.60
1972	23.58	24.65	26.55	27.11	27.31	27.33	26.99	29.15	28.95	29.85	32.34	27.62
1973	28.43	32.96	32.55	36.70	40.60	50.31	53.57	42.74	44.66	45.51	42.62	40.97
1974	46.47	42.15	38.89	30.24	29.19	39.29	40.09	37.73	43.28	40.36	42.56	39.11
1975	42.49	41.97	45.02	44.52	47.20	48.12	51.21	60.31	58.00	54.93	52.41	49.65
1976	41.96	40.46	42.43	41.90	43.40	40.88	37.96	35.22	32.34	33.18	37.48	38.84
1977	36.77	37.41	39.18	39.43	37.82	36.59	35.65	37.61	38.09	40.27	44.61	38.49
1978	39.29	42.86	47.60	49.84	44.83	44.66	46.33	49.84	52.46	51.70	52.63	47.46
1979	49.64	47.17	44.10	41.06	36.94	35.45	35.14	38.68	36.27	40.80	41.51	40.61
1980	44.34	43.08	39.06	39.14	40.51	44.50	46.08	49.38	50.95	50.39	48.16	45.05
1981	55.00	50.56	55.62	54.22	55.80	51.89	53.06	52.76	48.86	46.14	41.36	51.39
1982	49.02	51.83	55.92	57.78	54.58	57.06	59.01	59.92	57.00	55.61	57.72	55.95
1983	49.11	47.54	45.66	43.91	41.70	40.73	44.17	42.31	41.90	42.40	46.22	44.15
1984	51.99	54.01	56.19	56.37	56.90	51.70	49.95	48.26	46.98	51.30	52.53	52.38

	Feb	Mar	Apr	May	Jun	Jul	Aug	Sep	Oct	Nov	Dec
AVERAGE MOVE											
All Years		-0.06	0.84	-0.48	-0.52	0.58	0.64	0.35	-0.28	0.13	0.72
Less Extremes		-0.08	0.89	-0.21	-0.52	0.29	0.70	0.54	-0.45	0.03	0.86
Ave Up - All Years		2.21	2.88	1.18	1.68	4.53	2.12	3.15	2.24	1.85	2.11
Ave Down - All Years		-2.05	-2.22	-2.38	-2.45	-2.06	-1.05	-2.85	-1.96	-1.85	-3.11
COUNT											
Number Up		7	9	8	7	6	8	8	6	8	11
Number Down		8	6	7	8	9	7	7	9	7	4
Pct Up		46.7%	60.0%	53.3%	46.7%	40.0%	53.3%	53.3%	40.0%	53.3%	73.3%
Pct Down		53.3%	40.0%	46.7%	53.3%	60.0%	46.7%	46.7%	60.0%	46.7%	26.7%
EXTREMES											
Greatest Up		4.52	5.06	4.15	3.90	10.10	3.44	9.10	5.56	4.53	4.34
Greatest Down		-4.45	-4.01	-8.65	-5.01	-5.20	-2.92	-10.83	-3.90	-3.07	-4.78
SEASONAL INDEX : AVERAGE PERCENTAGE METHOD											
All Years	99.1	99.0	100.7	99.4	97.8	99.0	100.0	100.8	100.4	100.7	103.0
Less Extremes	99.7	99.1	101.5	100.3	98.5	98.0	98.7	100.0	100.4	101.3	103.6
SEASONAL INDEX : LINK RELATIVE METHOD											
All Years		100.0	101.5	99.9	98.0	99.4	99.9	100.6	99.7	99.7	101.6
Less Extremes		100.0	101.8	100.8	98.7	98.8	99.5	100.7	99.3	99.2	101.3

HOGS - DECEMBER - MONTH OF HIGH AND LOW

Year of Expiration	Feb	Mar	Apr	May	Jun	Jul	Aug	Sep	Oct	Nov	Dec
1970	H									L	
1971				H			L				
1972	L										H
1973	L						H				
1974	H				L						
1975		L						H			
1976					H				L		
1977							L				H
1978	L										H
1979	H						L				
1980			L						H		
1981					H						L
1982	L							H			
1983	H					L					
1984					H				L		

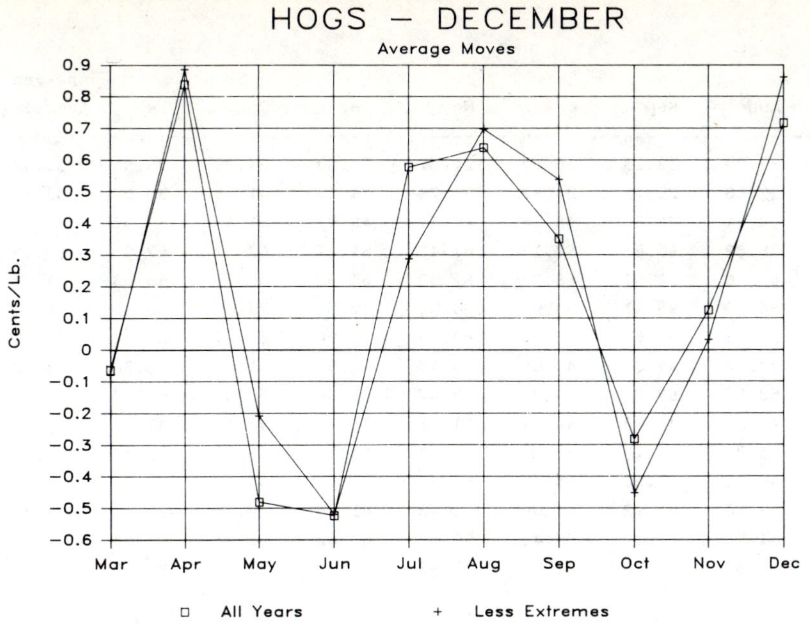
HOGS — DECEMBER
Average Moves
Cents/Lb.
0.9
0.8
0.7
0.6
0.5
0.4
0.3
0.2
0.1
0
-0.1
-0.2
-0.3
-0.4
-0.5
-0.6
Mar
Apr
May
Jun
Jul
Aug
Sep
Oct
Nov
Dec
□ All Years
+ Less Extremes

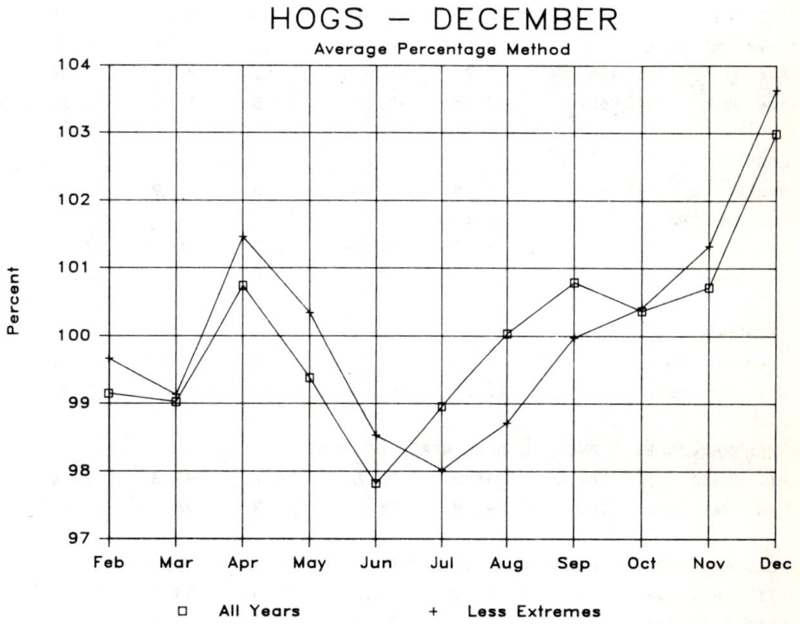
HOGS — DECEMBER
Average Percentage Method
Percent
104
103
102
101
100
99
98
97
Feb
Mar
Apr
May
Jun
Jul
Aug
Sep
Oct
Nov
Dec
□ All Years
+ Less Extremes

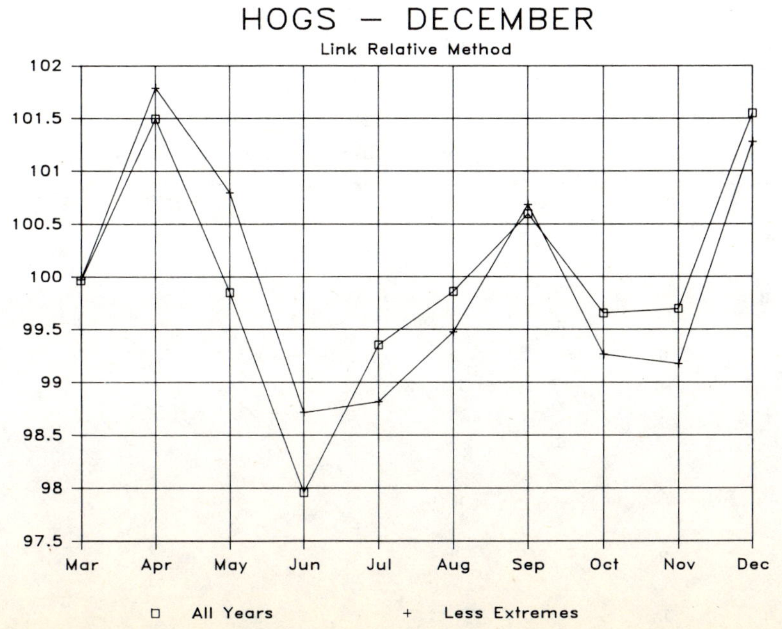
HOGS — DECEMBER
Link Relative Method
102
101.5
101
100.5
100
99.5
99
98.5
98
97.5
Mar
Apr
May
Jun
Jul
Aug
Sep
Oct
Nov
Dec
□ All Years
+ Less Extremes

PORK BELLIES - FEBRUARY - MONTHLY AVERAGE PRICE

Year of Expiration	Apr	May	Jun	Jul	Aug	Sep	Oct	Nov	Dec	Jan	Feb	Apr-Feb Average
1971	35.74	34.74	32.59	31.59	32.00	33.13	30.87	29.67	26.93	24.20	25.95	30.67
1972	35.45	34.98	34.35	29.31	27.88	29.71	31.62	31.79	34.57	41.04	39.03	33.61
1973	41.56	41.66	40.39	43.03	42.81	46.34	46.14	47.69	48.91	51.69	49.56	45.43
1974	49.12	54.11	57.98	71.76	78.82	66.89	67.18	67.42	61.27	62.57	57.95	63.19
1975	52.51	42.29	39.95	54.31	57.76	59.91	68.77	62.93	66.91	61.99	65.58	57.54
1976	67.47	68.70	74.62	77.78	84.20	95.41	93.68	84.34	72.52	72.52	68.32	78.14
1977	62.01	62.61	65.95	61.45	57.03	54.84	50.09	48.89	52.00	54.14	55.44	56.77
1978	57.23	56.10	50.30	48.83	47.20	49.30	47.69	50.10	52.83	61.18	68.80	53.60
1979	68.03	66.47	56.98	55.40	58.56	62.93	68.78	65.83	61.60	59.34	67.07	62.82
1980	52.83	51.26	46.38	42.56	41.50	46.83	44.31	51.53	48.71	43.45	40.07	46.31
1981	48.23	46.95	47.27	57.25	61.22	67.18	69.25	69.73	63.16	53.90	56.34	58.22
1982	71.38	66.63	69.48	64.09	66.33	67.50	65.48	65.92	57.17	64.87	70.58	66.31
1983	72.92	75.83	72.79	74.56	79.80	85.92	81.00	80.46	81.55	83.89	79.63	78.94
1984	63.47	62.58	57.93	57.76	64.53	61.31	59.48	60.92	62.62	65.72	62.83	61.74
1985	76.73	76.19	78.32	68.39	66.60	63.78	64.73	70.83	73.91	72.96	70.99	71.22

	Apr	May	Jun	Jul	Aug	Sep	Oct	Nov	Dec	Jan	Feb
AVERAGE MOVE											
All Years		-0.90	-1.06	0.85	1.88	1.65	-0.13	-0.07	-1.56	0.59	0.31
Less Extremes		-0.64	-0.94	0.65	1.96	1.96	-0.45	0.08	-1.20	0.75	0.12
Ave Up - All Years		1.97	3.07	7.62	4.30	4.08	3.32	2.23	2.46	4.27	4.30
Ave Down - All Years		-2.34	-3.81	-3.65	-1.76	-5.04	-2.43	-3.51	-6.15	-3.62	-3.18
COUNT											
Number Up		5	6	6	9	11	6	9	8	8	7
Number Down		10	9	9	6	4	9	6	7	7	8
Pct Up		33.3%	40.0%	40.0%	60.0%	73.3%	40.0%	60.0%	53.3%	53.3%	46.7%
Pct Down		66.7%	60.0%	60.0%	40.0%	26.7%	60.0%	40.0%	46.7%	46.7%	53.3%
EXTREMES											
Greatest Up		4.99	5.92	14.35	7.06	11.21	8.86	7.22	3.98	8.35	7.72
Greatest Down		-10.22	-9.49	-9.92	-4.42	-11.93	-4.92	-9.35	-11.82	-9.25	-4.62
SEASONAL INDEX : AVERAGE PERCENTAGE METHOD											
All Years	100.0	98.2	95.8	96.7	99.3	102.4	102.1	102.3	100.1	101.2	101.9
Less Extremes	100.5	98.9	96.2	96.2	98.6	101.9	101.8	102.2	99.9	101.3	101.1
SEASONAL INDEX : LINK RELATIVE METHOD											
All Years		98.9	96.2	97.9	99.9	102.7	102.0	102.1	99.5	100.3	100.5
Less Extremes		99.2	96.7	97.3	99.5	103.1	102.0	101.8	99.5	100.3	100.4

PORK BELLIES - FEBRUARY - MONTH OF HIGH AND LOW

Year of Expiration	Apr	May	Jun	Jul	Aug	Sep	Oct	Nov	Dec	Jan	Feb
1971	H									L	
1972					L					H	
1973			L							H	
1974	L				H						
1975			L				H				
1976	L					H					
1977			H					L			
1978					L						H
1979				L			H				
1980	H										L
1981		L						H			
1982	H								L		
1983			L			H					
1984				L						H	
1985			H			L					

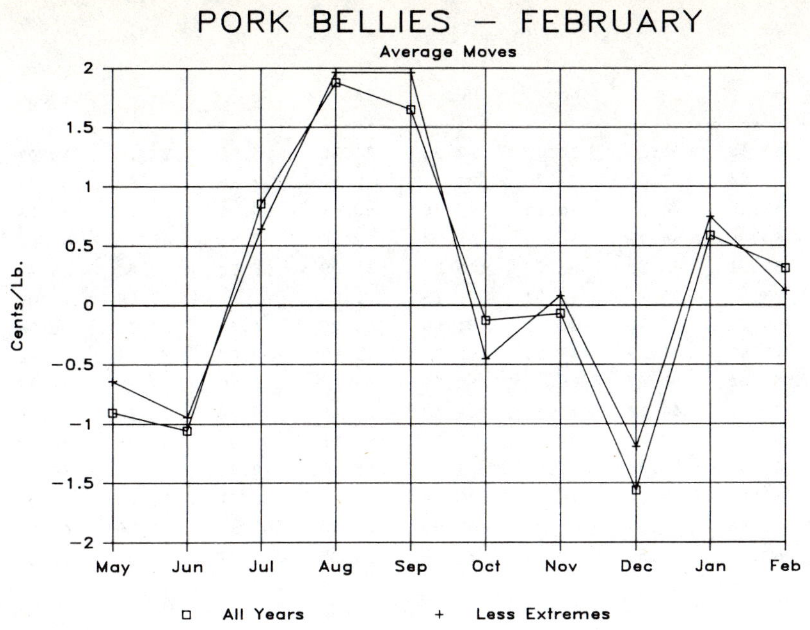
PORK BELLIES — FEBRUARY
Average Moves
Cents/Lb.
2
1.5
1
0.5
0
−0.5
−1
−1.5
−2
May
Jun
Jul
Aug
Sep
Oct
Nov
Dec
Jan
Feb
All Years
Less Extremes

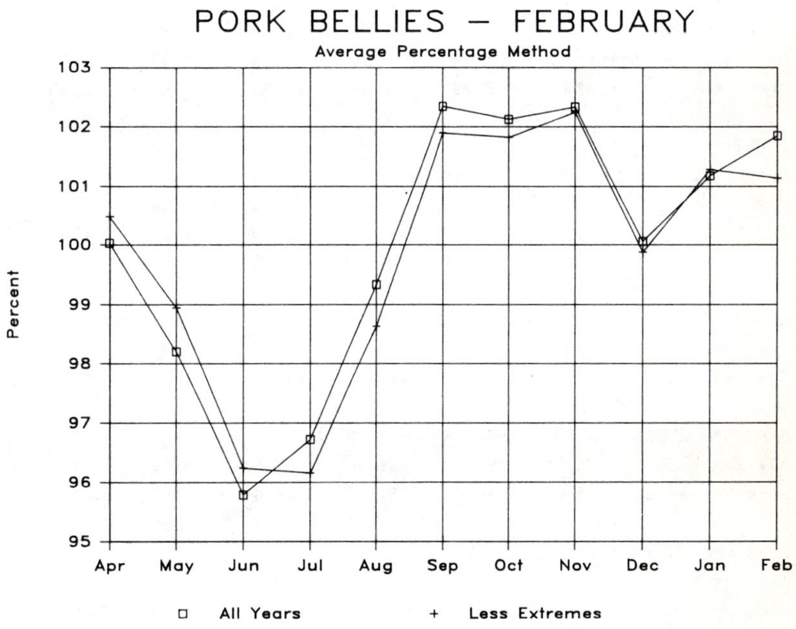
PORK BELLIES — FEBRUARY
Average Percentage Method
Percent
103
102
101
100
99
98
97
96
95
Apr
May
Jun
Jul
Aug
Sep
Oct
Nov
Dec
Jan
Feb
All Years
Less Extremes

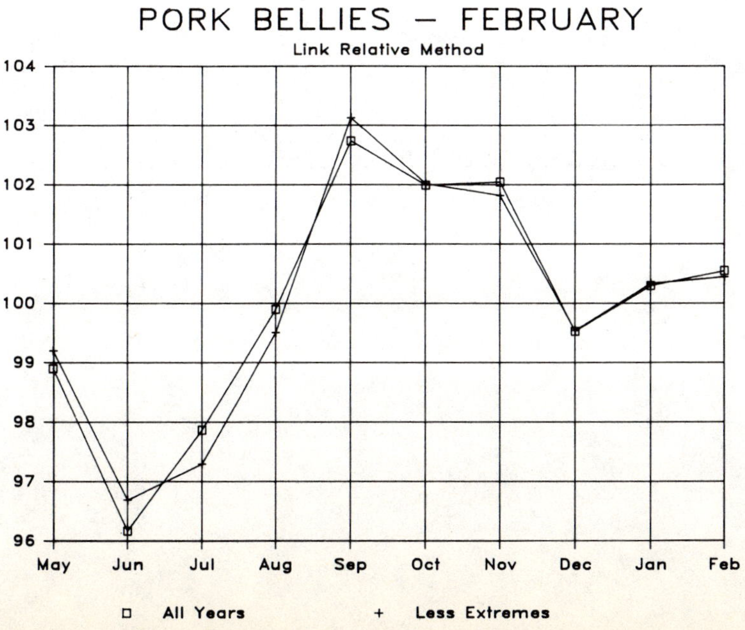
PORK BELLIES — FEBRUARY
Link Relative Method
104
103
102
101
100
99
98
97
96
May
Jun
Jul
Aug
Sep
Oct
Nov
Dec
Jan
Feb
All Years
Less Extremes

PORK BELLIES - MARCH - MONTHLY AVERAGE PRICE

Year of Expiration	May	Jun	Jul	Aug	Sep	Oct	Nov	Dec	Jan	Feb	Mar	May-Mar Average
1971	34.73	32.55	31.63	32.25	33.48	31.19	30.00	27.25	24.30	25.81	27.10	30.03
1972	34.68	34.10	29.31	27.83	29.84	31.60	31.76	34.32	40.30	37.96	39.83	33.78
1973	41.21	39.93	42.45	42.02	45.35	44.56	46.15	47.86	50.66	50.91	56.71	46.16
1974	53.74	57.49	70.96	77.49	65.80	66.72	66.72	61.13	62.76	57.36	48.62	62.62
1975	41.94	39.29	53.85	57.40	59.71	68.38	62.67	66.81	61.99	65.18	63.54	58.25
1976	67.61	73.42	76.02	82.62	93.59	90.97	82.04	71.13	71.87	67.54	70.66	77.04
1977	62.20	65.76	61.34	56.62	54.41	49.78	48.61	51.56	54.26	54.97	52.72	55.66
1978	55.61	49.95	48.48	46.43	47.92	46.39	49.19	51.82	59.57	69.05	79.27	54.88
1979	65.75	56.32	54.62	57.75	61.84	68.02	65.22	60.79	58.60	66.50	62.95	61.67
1980	50.77	46.38	43.02	41.92	47.02	44.54	51.88	49.12	44.18	40.34	42.26	45.59
1981	46.97	47.25	57.35	61.11	67.11	69.27	70.02	63.84	54.85	56.08	45.25	58.10
1982	66.95	69.70	64.29	66.51	67.46	65.44	65.91	57.27	65.43	70.66	73.22	66.62
1983	76.23	73.02	74.03	78.01	83.68	79.80	79.44	80.42	82.70	78.21	73.23	78.07
1984	62.71	57.98	57.72	64.55	61.46	59.64	61.24	62.99	66.04	62.33	63.26	61.81
1985	75.39	77.76	67.76	65.60	63.03	64.52	70.77	73.68	73.35	70.07	73.38	70.48

	May	Jun	Jul	Aug	Sep	Oct	Nov	Dec	Jan	Feb	Mar
AVERAGE MOVE											
All Years		-1.04	0.80	1.69	1.57	-0.06	0.05	-1.44	0.73	0.14	-0.06
Less Extremes		-0.92	0.57	1.78	1.87	-0.38	0.19	-1.15	0.90	-0.15	-0.02
Ave Up - All Years		3.09	7.38	4.13	3.92	3.53	2.33	2.45	3.90	3.68	3.45
Ave Down - All Years		-3.79	-3.59	-1.99	-4.89	-2.45	-3.36	-5.89	-4.04	-3.91	-5.33
COUNT											
Number Up		6	6	9	11	6	9	8	9	8	9
Number Down		9	9	6	4	9	6	7	6	7	6
Pct Up		40.0%	40.0%	60.0%	73.3%	40.0%	60.0%	53.3%	60.0%	53.3%	60.0%
Pct Down		60.0%	60.0%	40.0%	26.7%	60.0%	40.0%	46.7%	40.0%	46.7%	40.0%
EXTREMES											
Greatest Up		5.81	14.56	6.83	10.97	8.68	7.34	4.14	8.17	9.48	10.21
Greatest Down		-9.44	-10.00	-4.72	-11.69	-4.64	-8.93	-10.90	-8.99	-5.40	-10.83
SEASONAL INDEX : AVERAGE PERCENTAGE METHOD											
All Years	98.1	95.7	96.6	99.0	101.9	101.7	102.1	100.0	101.2	101.6	102.1
Less Extremes	98.8	96.2	96.1	98.4	101.5	101.7	101.8	99.9	101.3	100.9	100.7
SEASONAL INDEX : LINK RELATIVE METHOD											
All Years		97.0	98.5	100.1	102.6	101.8	101.8	99.2	100.0	99.8	99.2
Less Extremes		97.6	98.0	99.7	103.0	101.8	101.5	99.2	100.1	99.6	99.5

PORK BELLIES - MARCH - MONTH OF HIGH AND LOW

Year of Expiration	May	Jun	Jul	Aug	Sep	Oct	Nov	Dec	Jan	Feb	Mar
1971	H								L		
1972				L					H		
1973		L									H
1974				H							L
1975		L				H					
1976					H					L	
1977		H					L				
1978						L					H
1979			L			H					
1980							H			L	
1981							H				L
1982								L			H
1983		L			H						
1984			L						H		
1985		H			L						

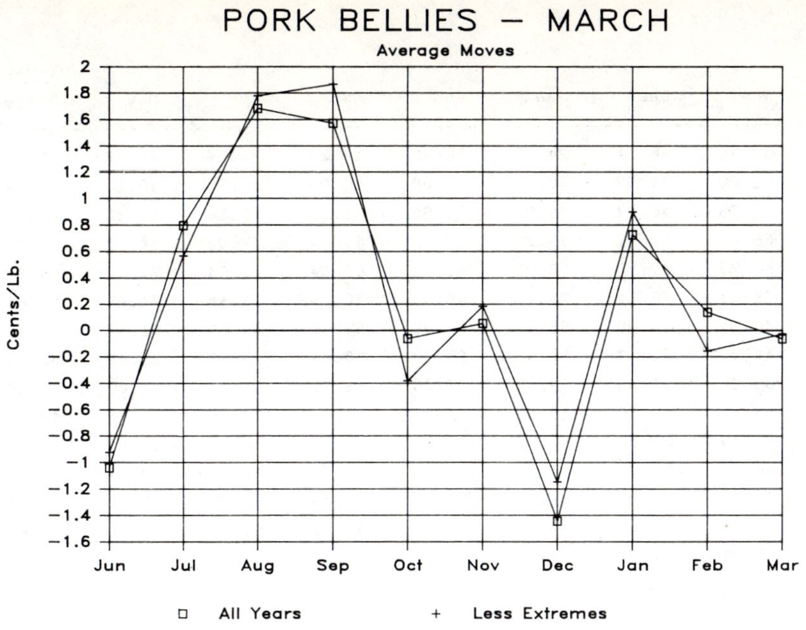
PORK BELLIES – MARCH
Average Moves
Cents/Lb.
2
1.8
1.6
1.4
1.2
1
0.8
0.6
0.4
0.2
0
−0.2
−0.4
−0.6
−0.8
−1
−1.2
−1.4
−1.6
Jun
Jul
Aug
Sep
Oct
Nov
Dec
Jan
Feb
Mar
All Years
Less Extremes

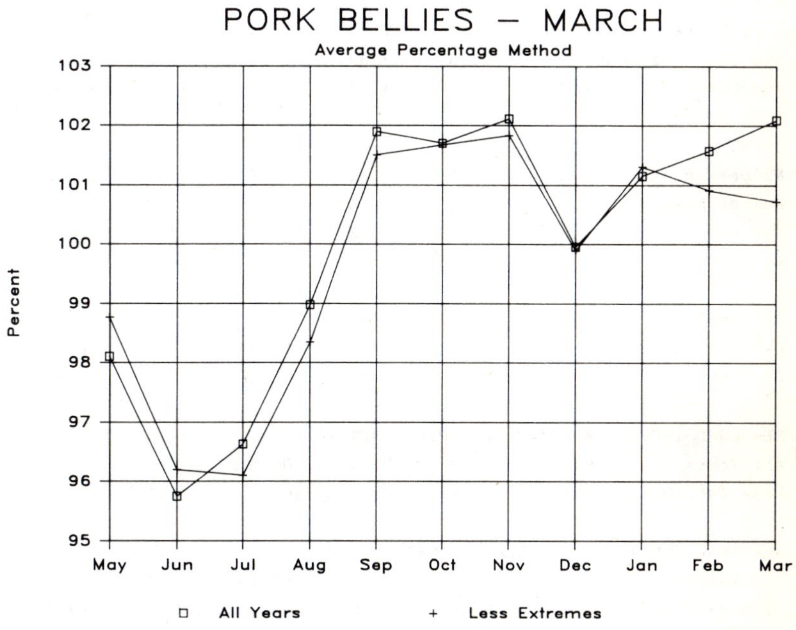
PORK BELLIES – MARCH
Average Percentage Method
Percent
103
102
101
100
99
98
97
96
95
May
Jun
Jul
Aug
Sep
Oct
Nov
Dec
Jan
Feb
Mar
All Years
Less Extremes

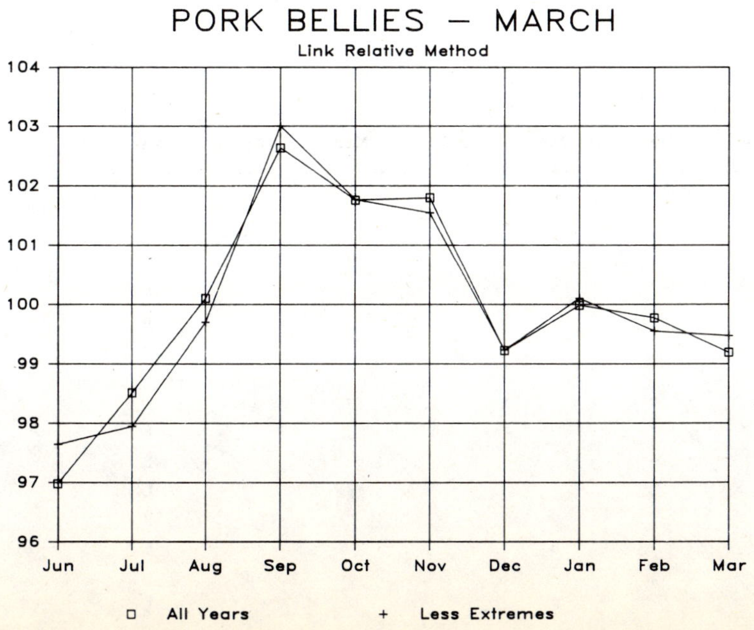
PORK BELLIES – MARCH
Link Relative Method
104
103
102
101
100
99
98
97
96
Jun
Jul
Aug
Sep
Oct
Nov
Dec
Jan
Feb
Mar
All Years
Less Extremes

PORK BELLIES - MAY - MONTHLY AVERAGE PRICE

Year of Expiration	Jul	Aug	Sep	Oct	Nov	Dec	Jan	Feb	Mar	Apr	May	Jul-May Average
1971	32.15	33.07	34.39	32.11	30.96	28.11	24.95	26.28	27.29	26.20	25.97	29.22
1972	30.01	28.51	30.49	31.88	32.00	34.57	40.51	38.08	40.09	40.76	40.18	35.19
1973	42.00	41.41	44.35	43.74	45.33	46.97	49.98	50.96	55.87	52.36	55.38	48.03
1974	70.09	76.24	65.34	66.60	66.60	61.72	63.28	58.22	49.14	47.94	38.01	60.29
1975	54.63	58.36	60.82	69.44	63.72	67.90	63.21	66.23	65.84	71.94	72.66	64.98
1976	74.85	81.30	91.75	85.43	78.42	70.14	71.81	68.00	70.45	76.68	74.65	76.68
1977	61.81	57.28	55.20	50.57	49.30	52.08	55.11	55.92	53.46	59.76	61.37	55.62
1978	49.12	46.79	47.21	46.99	49.35	51.57	58.73	69.08	80.62	75.79	71.65	58.81
1979	54.59	57.27	61.23	67.59	65.46	61.33	59.20	67.26	61.21	58.45	53.40	60.64
1980	43.92	43.08	48.06	45.61	53.12	50.65	45.85	41.97	42.13	33.25	32.12	43.61
1981	57.89	61.75	68.35	70.76	71.79	66.26	56.86	58.14	48.03	56.61	47.40	60.35
1982	65.21	67.59	68.42	66.38	66.72	58.29	66.71	71.55	74.23	80.33	88.07	70.32
1983	71.46	75.05	81.29	79.20	78.52	79.81	82.03	78.58	73.19	71.22	67.65	76.18
1984	58.92	66.36	63.26	61.29	62.98	64.60	67.58	64.03	65.87	69.84	66.70	64.67
1985	69.16	66.71	63.81	65.77	71.91	74.53	74.82	70.78	73.27	66.10	62.86	69.06
AVERAGE MOVE												
All Years		1.67	1.55	-0.04	0.19	-1.17	0.80	0.30	-0.30	0.44	-1.94	
Less Extremes		1.70	1.82	-0.22	0.18	-1.03	1.00	-0.06	-0.45	0.53	-2.08	
Ave Up - All Years		4.13	3.83	3.67	2.60	2.37	3.63	3.83	3.23	5.42	3.27	
Ave Down - All Years		-2.04	-4.75	-2.51	-2.56	-5.22	-4.84	-3.74	-5.58	-3.92	-3.84	
COUNT												
Number Up		9	11	6	8	8	10	8	9	7	4	
Number Down		6	4	9	7	7	5	7	6	8	11	
Pct Up		60.0%	73.3%	40.0%	53.3%	53.3%	66.7%	53.3%	60.0%	46.7%	26.7%	
Pct Down		40.0%	26.7%	60.0%	46.7%	46.7%	33.3%	46.7%	40.0%	53.3%	73.3%	
EXTREMES												
Greatest Up		7.44	10.45	8.62	7.51	4.18	8.42	10.35	11.53	8.58	7.74	
Greatest Down		-4.53	-10.90	-6.32	-7.01	-8.43	-9.40	-5.06	-10.11	-8.88	-9.94	
SEASONAL INDEX : AVERAGE PERCENTAGE METHOD												
All Years	96.0	98.3	101.1	100.8	101.5	99.6	100.8	101.3	101.2	101.3	98.1	
Less Extremes	95.4	97.6	101.3	101.2	101.3	99.6	100.9	101.0	100.1	101.1	98.7	
SEASONAL INDEX : LINK RELATIVE METHOD												
All Years		97.2	100.2	100.1	100.9	99.3	100.8	101.5	101.1	101.4	97.6	
Less Extremes		97.4	101.0	100.4	100.7	99.2	100.8	100.9	100.5	101.2	97.7	

PORK BELLIES - MAY - MONTH OF HIGH AND LOW

Year of Expiration	Jul	Aug	Sep	Oct	Nov	Dec	Jan	Feb	Mar	Apr	May
1971			H				L				
1972		L								H	
1973		L							H		
1974		H									L
1975	L										H
1976			H					L			
1977	H				L						
1978		L							H		
1979				H							L
1980						H					L
1981					H						L
1982	L										H
1983							H				L
1984	L									H	
1985							H				L

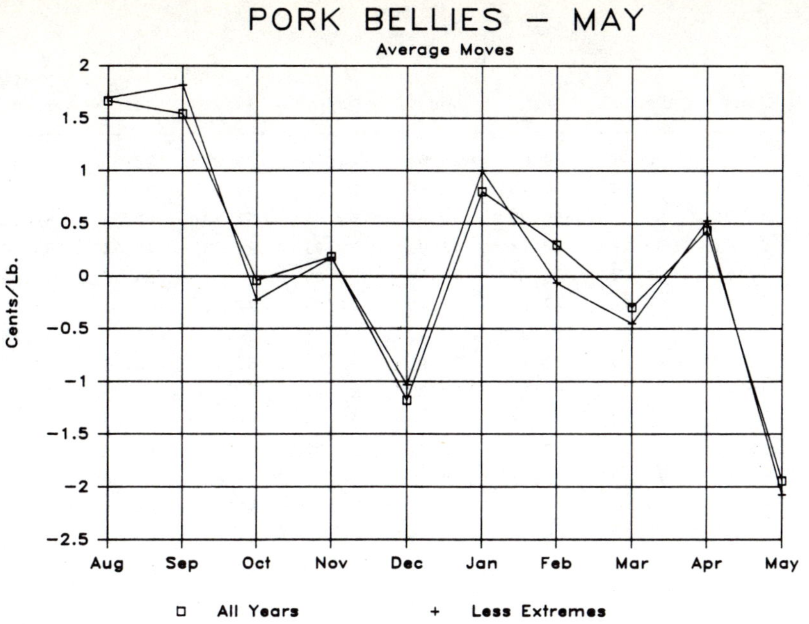

PORK BELLIES – MAY
Average Moves
Cents/Lb.
2
1.5
1
0.5
0
−0.5
−1
−1.5
−2
−2.5
Aug
Sep
Oct
Nov
Dec
Jan
Feb
Mar
Apr
May
□ All Years
+ Less Extremes

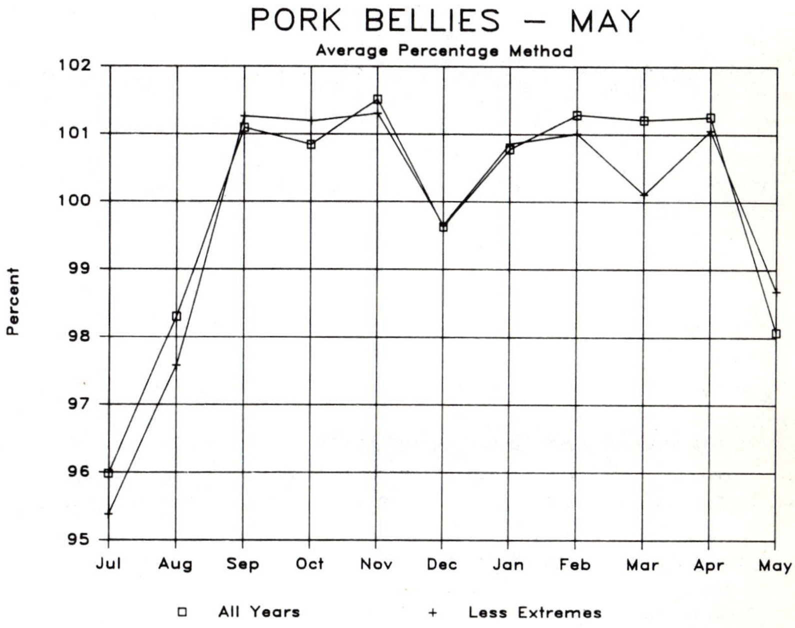

PORK BELLIES – MAY
Average Percentage Method
Percent
102
101
100
99
98
97
96
95
Jul
Aug
Sep
Oct
Nov
Dec
Jan
Feb
Mar
Apr
May
□ All Years
+ Less Extremes

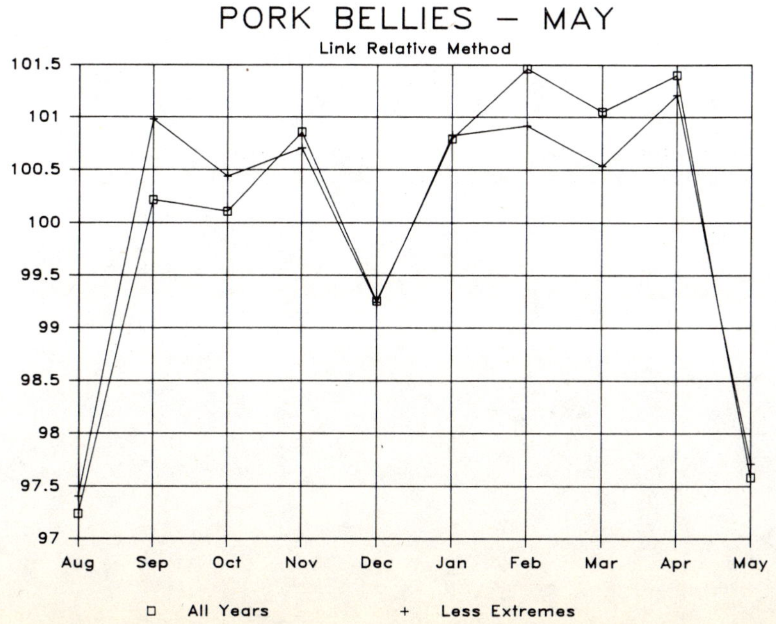

PORK BELLIES – MAY
Link Relative Method
101.5
101
100.5
100
99.5
99
98.5
98
97.5
97
Aug
Sep
Oct
Nov
Dec
Jan
Feb
Mar
Apr
May
□ All Years
+ Less Extremes

PORK BELLIES - JULY - MONTHLY AVERAGE PRICE

Year of Expiration	Sep	Oct	Nov	Dec	Jan	Feb	Mar	Apr	May	Jun	Jul	Sep-Jul Average
1971	34.95	32.82	31.70	28.96	25.69	26.77	27.61	26.64	26.48	25.07	22.35	27.41
1972	31.06	32.01	32.09	34.63	40.01	37.24	39.24	40.66	39.49	36.18	37.82	36.94
1973	42.69	42.47	44.14	45.22	48.25	50.10	55.27	52.39	55.84	57.34	60.23	51.12
1974	64.89	66.37	65.91	61.70	63.91	59.11	50.14	48.91	38.43	33.73	48.21	53.64
1975	61.12	69.67	64.25	68.27	64.06	66.67	66.42	72.36	73.69	79.04	84.73	70.92
1976	89.77	81.91	75.22	69.08	71.59	68.42	70.42	76.20	74.83	77.90	69.15	73.47
1977	55.09	50.92	49.70	52.34	55.50	56.49	54.30	60.36	60.93	54.53	56.40	55.15
1978	47.41	46.24	49.64	51.46	58.22	68.60	80.38	75.91	69.61	55.77	50.11	60.59
1979	61.06	67.38	65.49	61.60	59.47	67.28	61.11	57.32	50.91	41.37	35.73	56.77
1980	49.14	46.73	54.24	51.86	47.52	43.42	43.48	34.58	32.69	31.09	41.63	42.72
1981	68.85	71.93	73.79	68.52	58.90	59.91	49.56	57.82	50.02	53.51	48.82	59.28
1982	69.13	67.27	67.61	59.38	67.81	71.40	74.23	79.63	86.48	75.62	79.00	72.84
1983	77.10	77.41	76.48	78.03	80.57	77.90	72.99	69.76	64.92	60.45	54.83	71.33
1984	64.26	61.87	63.75	65.16	67.92	65.16	66.65	69.88	66.27	67.54	57.95	65.21
1985	64.96	66.78	72.59	74.69	75.42	70.80	73.28	67.20	64.69	66.30	56.34	68.81

	Sep	Oct	Nov	Dec	Jan	Feb	Mar	Apr	May	Jun	Jul
AVERAGE MOVE											
All Years		0.02	0.32	-1.05	0.93	0.30	-0.28	0.30	-2.29	-2.66	-0.81
Less Extremes		-0.03	0.31	-0.88	1.16	-0.09	-0.43	0.40	-2.36	-2.41	-1.28
Ave Up - All Years		3.22	2.82	2.14	3.75	3.67	3.18	5.16	3.05	2.71	5.78
Ave Down - All Years		-2.78	-2.53	-4.69	-4.72	-3.56	-5.47	-3.94	-4.23	-6.24	-6.58
COUNT											
Number Up		7	8	8	10	8	9	7	4	6	7
Number Down		8	7	7	5	7	6	8	11	9	8
Pct Up		46.7%	53.3%	53.3%	66.7%	53.3%	60.0%	46.7%	26.7%	40.0%	46.7%
Pct Down		53.3%	46.7%	46.7%	33.3%	46.7%	40.0%	53.3%	73.3%	60.0%	53.3%
EXTREMES											
Greatest Up		8.55	7.51	4.01	8.43	10.38	11.78	8.26	6.85	5.35	14.48
Greatest Down		-7.86	-6.69	-8.23	-9.62	-4.80	-10.35	-8.91	-10.49	-13.84	-9.96
SEASONAL INDEX : AVERAGE PERCENTAGE METHOD											
All Years	102.5	102.3	103.1	101.2	102.3	102.7	102.3	102.2	98.1	93.1	92.6
Less Extremes	102.4	102.6	102.9	101.2	102.0	102.2	101.5	102.0	98.5	94.0	92.8
SEASONAL INDEX : LINK RELATIVE METHOD											
All Years		98.2	99.8	99.0	101.4	102.6	103.0	103.8	100.0	95.6	96.6
Less Extremes		98.0	99.3	98.7	101.4	102.3	102.7	104.1	100.8	96.7	95.9

PORK BELLIES - JULY - MONTH OF HIGH AND LOW

Year of Expiration	Sep	Oct	Nov	Dec	Jan	Feb	Mar	Apr	May	Jun	Jul
1971	H										L
1972	L							H			
1973		L									H
1974		H								L	
1975	L										H
1976	H					L					
1977			L						H		
1978		L					H				
1979		H									L
1980			H							L	
1981			H								L
1982				L					H		
1983					H						L
1984								H			L
1985					H						L

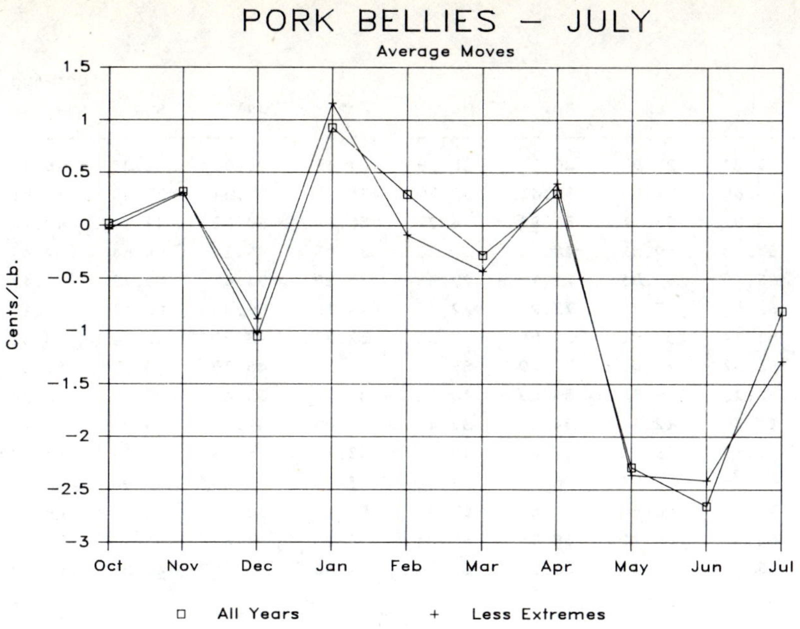
PORK BELLIES — JULY
Average Moves
Cents/Lb.
1.5
1
0.5
0
−0.5
−1
−1.5
−2
−2.5
−3
Oct
Nov
Dec
Jan
Feb
Mar
Apr
May
Jun
Jul
All Years
Less Extremes

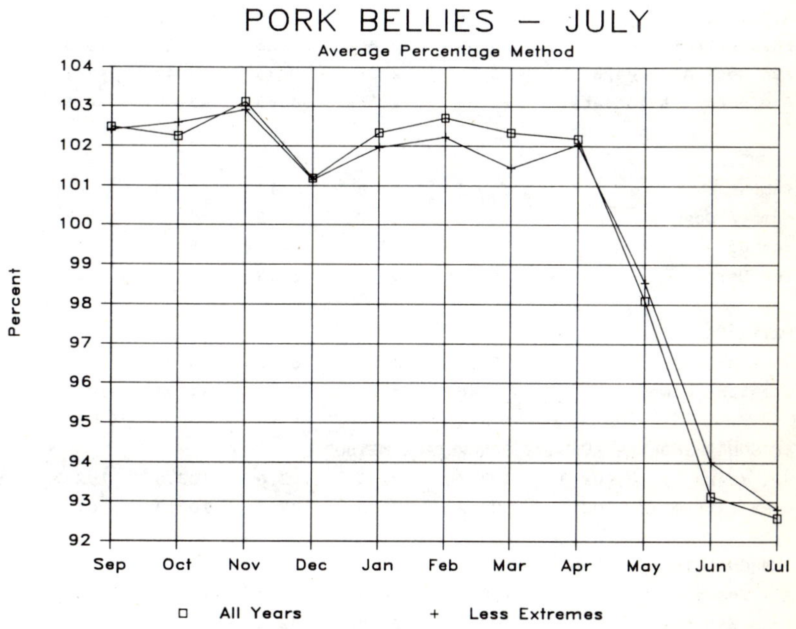
PORK BELLIES — JULY
Average Percentage Method
Percent
104
103
102
101
100
99
98
97
96
95
94
93
92
Sep
Oct
Nov
Dec
Jan
Feb
Mar
Apr
May
Jun
Jul
All Years
Less Extremes

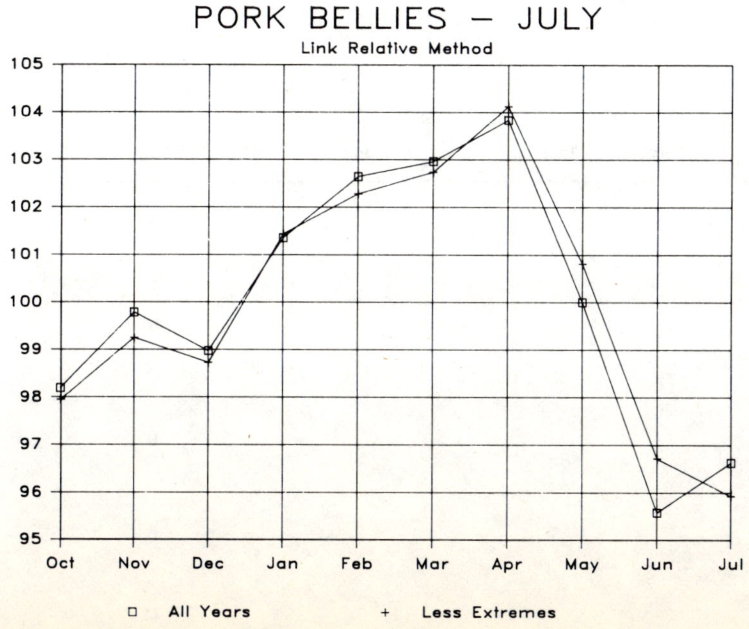
PORK BELLIES — JULY
Link Relative Method
105
104
103
102
101
100
99
98
97
96
95
Oct
Nov
Dec
Jan
Feb
Mar
Apr
May
Jun
Jul
All Years
Less Extremes

PORK BELLIES - AUGUST - MONTHLY AVERAGE PRICE

Year of Expiration	Oct	Nov	Dec	Jan	Feb	Mar	Apr	May	Jun	Jul	Aug	Oct-Aug Average
1971	32.28	31.24	28.54	25.22	26.27	27.06	26.18	25.79	24.41	21.06	21.35	26.31
1972	30.98	31.01	33.48	38.51	35.65	37.53	39.41	38.20	35.26	37.54	37.40	35.91
1973	40.47	41.89	43.16	46.08	48.01	53.51	51.83	55.22	56.91	60.32	49.74	49.74
1974	64.74	64.59	60.27	62.01	57.98	49.53	48.14	37.50	33.05	49.26	54.64	52.88
1975	68.29	63.27	67.21	62.99	65.60	65.04	71.12	72.38	77.95	84.67	98.17	72.43
1976	77.47	71.48	66.09	69.30	66.06	67.88	73.26	72.34	75.16	66.36	66.45	70.17
1977	49.35	48.30	50.51	53.66	54.74	52.91	58.86	59.31	52.83	53.26	52.84	53.32
1978	44.27	47.62	49.20	55.84	65.87	78.01	73.70	67.37	54.19	48.30	50.21	57.69
1979	65.11	63.19	59.52	58.07	65.41	59.05	54.69	48.71	39.29	32.40	30.76	52.38
1980	45.55	53.03	50.74	47.05	42.89	42.46	34.01	32.45	31.09	41.16	49.25	42.70
1981	70.87	72.91	67.97	58.22	59.15	48.83	57.44	49.88	53.37	48.19	54.32	58.29
1982	66.62	66.92	58.74	67.08	69.46	72.04	76.80	84.34	73.72	77.25	91.98	73.18
1983	75.29	73.81	75.06	77.64	75.70	70.88	66.57	62.36	57.81	52.44	64.01	68.33
1984	60.57	62.29	63.83	66.25	63.52	65.21	68.38	65.04	66.32	54.87	56.22	62.95
1985	64.50	70.22	71.99	73.30	68.77	71.23	65.83	64.16	65.86	55.45	49.36	65.52

	Oct	Nov	Dec	Jan	Feb	Mar	Apr	May	Jun	Jul	Aug
AVERAGE MOVE											
All Years		0.36	-1.03	0.99	0.26	-0.26	0.34	-2.08	-2.52	-0.98	2.94
Less Extremes		0.30	-0.86	1.26	-0.13	-0.44	0.38	-2.16	-2.32	-1.50	3.08
Ave Up - All Years		2.76	2.00	3.73	3.42	3.61	5.12	3.16	2.76	6.09	6.30
Ave Down - All Years		-2.38	-4.50	-4.48	-3.36	-4.68	-3.85	-3.98	-6.04	-7.17	-3.77
COUNT											
Number Up		8	8	10	8	8	7	4	6	7	10
Number Down		7	7	5	7	7	8	11	9	8	5
Pct Up		53.3%	53.3%	66.7%	53.3%	53.3%	46.7%	26.7%	40.0%	46.7%	66.7%
Pct Down		46.7%	46.7%	33.3%	46.7%	46.7%	53.3%	73.3%	60.0%	53.3%	33.3%
EXTREMES											
Greatest Up		7.48	3.94	8.33	10.03	12.14	8.61	7.54	5.58	16.21	14.73
Greatest Down		-5.98	-8.17	-9.74	-4.54	-10.33	-8.45	-10.64	-13.18	-11.45	-10.58
SEASONAL INDEX : AVERAGE PERCENTAGE METHOD											
All Years	102.3	103.3	101.3	102.6	103.0	102.7	102.6	98.6	93.8	92.6	97.1
Less Extremes	102.6	103.2	101.6	102.7	102.3	101.6	102.5	99.4	94.6	92.8	97.1
SEASONAL INDEX : LINK RELATIVE METHOD											
All Years		100.7	99.5	101.7	102.6	102.7	103.4	99.4	94.8	95.2	100.0
Less Extremes		100.3	99.5	102.1	102.5	102.6	103.7	100.2	95.8	94.0	99.3

PORK BELLIES - AUGUST - MONTH OF HIGH AND LOW

Year of Expiration	Oct	Nov	Dec	Jan	Feb	Mar	Apr	May	Jun	Jul	Aug
1971	H									L	
1972	L						H				
1973	L									H	
1974	H								L		
1975				L							H
1976	H				L						
1977		L						H			
1978	L					H					
1979					H						L
1980		H							L		
1981		H								L	
1982			L								H
1983				H						L	
1984							H			L	
1985				H							L

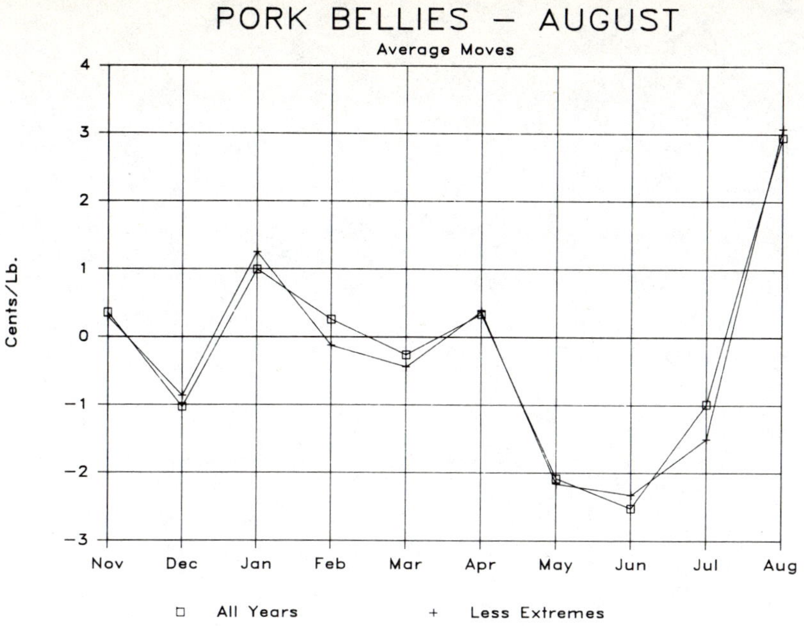

PORK BELLIES – AUGUST
Average Moves
Cents/Lb.
4
3
2
1
0
–1
–2
–3
Nov
Dec
Jan
Feb
Mar
Apr
May
Jun
Jul
Aug
All Years
Less Extremes

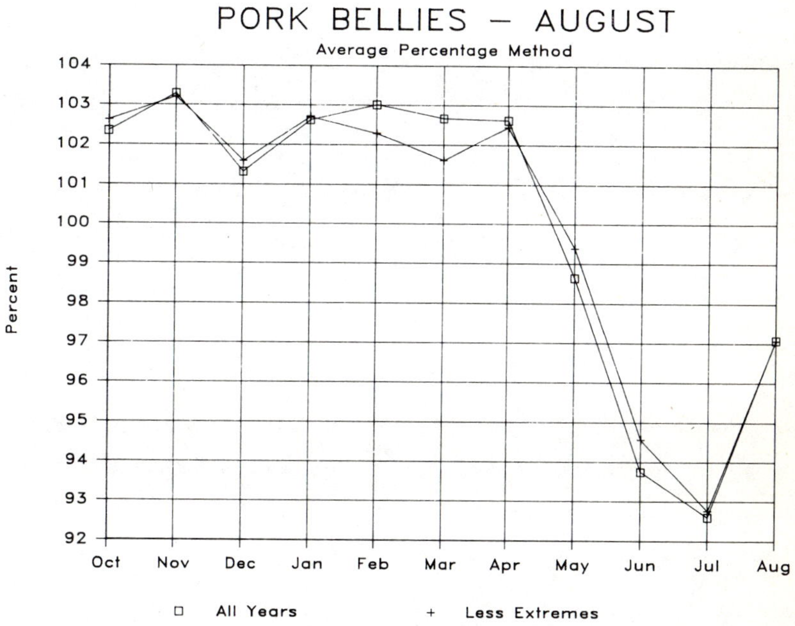

PORK BELLIES – AUGUST
Average Percentage Method
Percent
104
103
102
101
100
99
98
97
96
95
94
93
92
Oct
Nov
Dec
Jan
Feb
Mar
Apr
May
Jun
Jul
Aug
All Years
Less Extremes

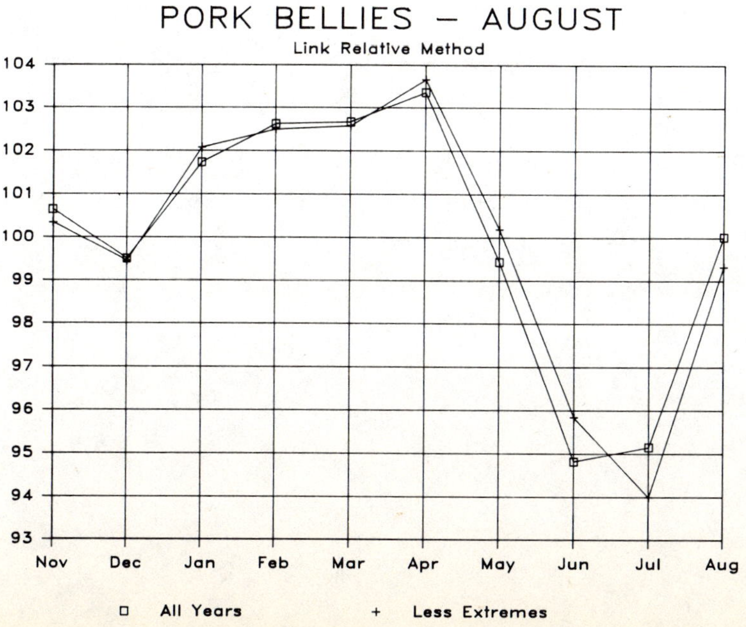

PORK BELLIES – AUGUST
Link Relative Method
104
103
102
101
100
99
98
97
96
95
94
93
Nov
Dec
Jan
Feb
Mar
Apr
May
Jun
Jul
Aug
All Years
Less Extremes

EIGHT

Softs

COCOA

Cocoa seasonality has been drastically distorted by several explosive moves over the last decade. However, there still remain several months of good seasonal consistency.

The cocoa crop year runs from October to September. There is a main crop, from October to March, and a second, or midcrop, from May to June. The main crop accounts for about 80% of the world's output. Only in Brazil is the midcrop greater than the main crop.

Cocoa prices tend to be depressed during the harvest periods of November and May because cocoa is usually harvested and immediately shipped. The main cocoa growing areas in West Africa lack processing facilities and the market becomes glutted. It is during the harvest that manufacturers do the bulk of their buying. Since they can handle in their inventories and in processing a limited amount of cocoa, the demand slackens very quickly, leading to price weakness in near November and March.

Fall is the time of the heaviest grindings by manufacturers. They reduce the cocoa beans into the components with which they make such goods as chocolate bars. The summer months are typified by a sharp price rise due to the markets discounting the fall grindings. On the supply side, the main crops are virtually sold out. Only the midcrop from Brazil prevents an even more drastic price climb.

In autumn, the price weakens because the processors have already purchased the beans needed for fall grinding. It is also late in the summer when the size of the new crop becomes available. Typically, this is considered a bearish factor. Occasionally, there will be a rapid price rise in the October to November period as a result of a lack of information over the main crop size.

COFFEE

Coffee is a another commodity which has had its seasonality distorted by several years of explosive price action. Actually, the reliabilities of coffee seasonality are fairly high even though there is little reason to expect a seasonal variation. This is because coffee is grown around the world and is harvested virtually every month of the year. It is also extremely easy to store green coffee beans. As a result, this supply can often tide over the market during periods of low production.

Not only can crops be harvested throughout the year, but in some areas, several harvests occur in one year. Coffee plants can also withstand greater extremes of climate than most tropical plants, and therefore are less susceptible to frost, flood, or drought damage.

There is also little change in the demand for coffee from one year to the next. People drink coffee no matter what the price or supply. There is a slight seasonal variation in demand through a given year: Consumers tend to drink more coffee in the cold winter months than during the hot summer months.

SUGAR

Sugar is not a stellar seasonal performer. Reliabilities are decent but the strength of moves tends to be low.

Sugar comes from two sources: sugar beet and sugar cane. Sugar cane is grown in tropical and semitropical regions where it is harvested virtually every month of the year. On the other hand, sugar beets grow in temperate zones such as the United States, Europe, and the Soviet Union, where it follows a regular crop pattern of spring planting and fall harvesting.

The primary crop which dominates world sugar prices is currently the sugar beet crop of Western Europe. This is harvested in the fall and creates the dip in prices into September in the following seasonal charts.

ORANGE JUICE

Orange juice has many highly reliable seasonal periods. Its seasonality is dominated by concern over the upcoming crop and the potential for freezing.

The summer rally is caused by anticipation of problems with the crop. The market peaks at about the same time the U.S. Department of Agriculture issues its crop estimate in October and dampens speculative enthusiasm. The interesting seasonal feature is the sharp decline in December as the market adjusts to a lack of a freeze.

HIGHEST RELIABLE TRENDS

Commodity	Contract	Month	Position	Reliability	Average Move
Cocoa	Mar	Sep	Long	90.0	+130.31
	Mar	Oct	Short	70.0	−120.93
	May	Aug	Short	70.0	−101.17
	May	Sep	Long	80.0	+140.14
	May	Oct	Short	70.0	−127.50
	May	Nov	Short	70.0	−83.22
	Jul	Oct	Short	70.0	−127.86
	Jul	Nov	Short	70.0	−86.16
	Sep	Sep	Long	80.0	+185.58
	Dec	Sep	Long	90.0	+153.13
	Dec	Oct	Short	80.0	−93.45
Coffee	Mar	Aug	Long	70.0	+8.69
	Mar	Jan	Long	70.0	+7.35
	May	Aug	Long	70.0	+8.46

Commodity	Contract	Month	Position	Reliability	Average Move
Coffee	May	Jan	Long	70.0	+7.57
	May	Apr	Long	70.0	+9.95
	May	May	Long	80.0	+5.46
	Jul	Jan	Long	70.0	+7.23
	Jul	Mar	Long	70.0	+13.45
	Jul	Apr	Long	70.0	+9.89
	Jul	May	Long	80.0	+6.62
	Sep	Jan	Long	70.0	+7.23
	Sep	Mar	Long	70.0	+13.75
	Sep	Apr	Long	70.0	+8.40
	Sep	May	Long	80.0	+7.15
	Sep	Jul	Short	70.0	−16.55
	Sep	Sep	Long	70.0	+8.58
	Dec	Mar	Long	70.0	+13.00
	Dec	Apr	Long	70.0	+7.64
	Dec	May	Long	70.0	+7.98
	Dec	Jul	Short	70.0	−17.33
	Dec	Oct	Long	70.0	+9.34
	Dec	Nov	Long	70.0	+12.27
	Dec	Dec	Long	70.0	+11.87
Sugar	Jan	May	Short	70.0	−1.36
	Jan	Sep	Short	70.0	−1.55
	Jan	Dec	Short	70.0	−1.93
	Mar	May	Short	70.0	−1.27
	Mar	Nov	Short	70.0	−0.93
	Mar	Dec	Short	70.0	−1.82
	May	Nov	Short	70.0	−0.80
	May	Dec	Short	70.0	−1.83
	May	Mar	Short	80.0	−1.40
	May	Apr	Short	70.0	−1.27
	Jul	Nov	Short	70.0	−0.70
	Jul	Dec	Short	70.0	−1.72
	Jul	Feb	Short	70.0	−0.82
	Jul	Mar	Short	80.0	−1.31
	Jul	Apr	Short	70.0	−1.20
	Jul	May	Short	70.0	−1.08
	Sep	Nov	Short	70.0	−0.74
	Sep	Dec	Short	70.0	−1.51
	Sep	Feb	Short	70.0	−0.77
	Sep	Mar	Short	80.0	−1.15
	Sep	Apr	Short	70.0	−1.10
	Sep	May	Short	70.0	−1.04
	Sep	Jul	Short	70.0	−1.27
	Oct	Dec	Short	70.0	−1.40
	Oct	Feb	Short	70.0	−0.77
	Oct	Mar	Short	80.0	−1.08

(*Continued on next page.*)

Commodity	Contract	Month	Position	Reliability	Average Move
Sugar	Oct	Apr	Short	70.0	−1.06
	Oct	May	Short	70.0	−1.02
Orange juice	Jan	May	Long	80.0	+2.79
	Jan	Jul	Long	70.0	+2.53
	Jan	Aug	Long	80.0	+3.38
	Jan	Sep	Long	70.0	+3.08
	Jan	Oct	Short	70.0	−3.26
	Jan	Nov	Short	70.0	−2.78
	Jan	Dec	Short	70.0	−6.42
	Mar	Jul	Long	70.0	+2.38
	Mar	Aug	Long	80.0	+3.22
	Mar	Sep	Long	70.0	+2.95
	Mar	Oct	Short	70.0	−3.05
	Mar	Dec	Short	70.0	−5.68
	May	Aug	Long	90.0	+2.84
	May	Sep	Long	70.0	+2.77
	May	Oct	Short	70.0	−2.94
	May	Dec	Short	70.0	−5.13
	Jul	Oct	Short	70.0	−2.77
	Jul	Dec	Short	80.0	−4.16
	Jul	Jun	Short	70.0	−5.53
	Sep	Dec	Short	80.0	−8.29
	Sep	Jun	Short	70.0	−6.29
	Sep	Aug	Long	70.0	+4.94
	Sep	Sep	Long	70.0	+2.96
	Nov	Mar	Short	70.0	−5.90
	Nov	Jun	Short	70.0	−5.66
	Nov	Aug	Long	70.0	+4.56

COCOA - MARCH - MONTHLY AVERAGE PRICE

Year of Expiration	May	Jun	Jul	Aug	Sep	Oct	Nov	Dec	Jan	Feb	Mar	May-Mar Average
1976	1057.29	962.64	1122.88	1126.01	1138.21	1244.95	1244.96	1373.46	1473.10	1543.72	1556.76	1258.54
1977	1577.54	1742.17	1885.71	2098.36	2408.95	2634.62	3033.96	3119.71	3582.87	3966.83	4296.01	2758.79
1978	3395.72	3828.65	4000.26	3712.41	3723.10	3491.59	3519.88	3305.09	3133.15	3076.09	3570.18	3523.28
1979	2914.13	2869.88	3065.41	3307.24	3747.03	3822.12	4032.18	3925.52	3631.51	3440.49	3315.66	3461.01
1980	3448.60	3543.82	3311.07	3149.10	3203.25	3021.49	2968.14	3133.07	3091.28	3188.08	3018.88	3188.80
1981	2625.67	2529.05	2453.91	2264.48	2327.10	2235.22	2076.39	1993.76	1979.80	1891.74	1983.60	2214.61
1982	2007.95	1713.23	2068.46	2224.52	2286.71	2100.14	1950.60	2019.67	2100.95	1942.00	1896.88	2028.28
1983	1741.35	1583.91	1558.57	1520.00	1623.38	1574.19	1440.50	1526.33	1678.14	1815.11	1756.85	1619.85
1984	2042.86	2258.59	2247.05	2223.39	2064.05	2014.48	2140.81	2482.14	2561.19	2497.95	2535.00	2278.86
1985	2494.77	2321.81	2126.48	2118.04	2235.26	2179.26	2185.38	2078.74	2154.86	2184.68	2103.27	2198.42

	May	Jun	Jul	Aug	Sep	Oct	Nov	Dec	Jan	Feb	Mar
AVERAGE MOVE											
All Years		4.79	48.60	-9.62	101.35	-43.90	27.47	36.47	42.94	15.98	48.64
Less Extremes		-11.29	45.45	-6.28	91.63	-54.14	4.28	29.77	32.53	-4.14	20.19
Ave Up - All Years		227.13	205.23	153.42	130.31	135.83	128.36	145.90	158.51	143.63	193.04
Ave Down - All Years		-143.44	-108.02	-118.32	-159.34	-120.93	-123.85	-127.68	-130.42	-111.67	-95.76
COUNT											
Number Up		4	5	4	9	3	6	6	6	5	5
Number Down		6	5	6	1	7	4	4	4	5	5
Pct Up		40.0%	50.0%	40.0%	90.0%	30.0%	60.0%	60.0%	60.0%	50.0%	50.0%
Pct Down		60.0%	50.0%	60.0%	10.0%	70.0%	40.0%	40.0%	40.0%	50.0%	50.0%
EXTREMES											
Greatest Up		432.93	355.23	241.83	439.78	225.67	399.33	341.33	463.16	383.97	494.09
Greatest Down		-294.72	-232.75	-287.84	-159.34	-231.51	-158.83	-214.79	-294.01	-191.03	-169.20
SEASONAL INDEX : AVERAGE PERCENTAGE METHOD											
All Years	95.8	94.4	96.8	96.5	100.2	98.8	99.1	101.5	104.5	105.5	107.0
Less Extremes	97.8	95.8	98.2	97.4	100.3	98.6	98.1	101.4	103.2	103.3	103.0
SEASONAL INDEX : LINK RELATIVE METHOD											
All Years		97.5	99.8	99.0	101.9	99.5	98.6	100.0	101.6	101.0	101.1
Less Extremes		97.8	99.9	99.0	102.3	99.8	98.6	99.7	101.4	101.0	100.4

COCOA - MARCH - MONTH OF HIGH AND LOW

Year of Expiration	May	Jun	Jul	Aug	Sep	Oct	Nov	Dec	Jan	Feb	Mar
1976		L									H
1977	L										H
1978			H							L	
1979		L					H				
1980		H					L				
1981	H									L	
1982		L			H						
1983							L			H	
1984						L			H		
1985	H							L			

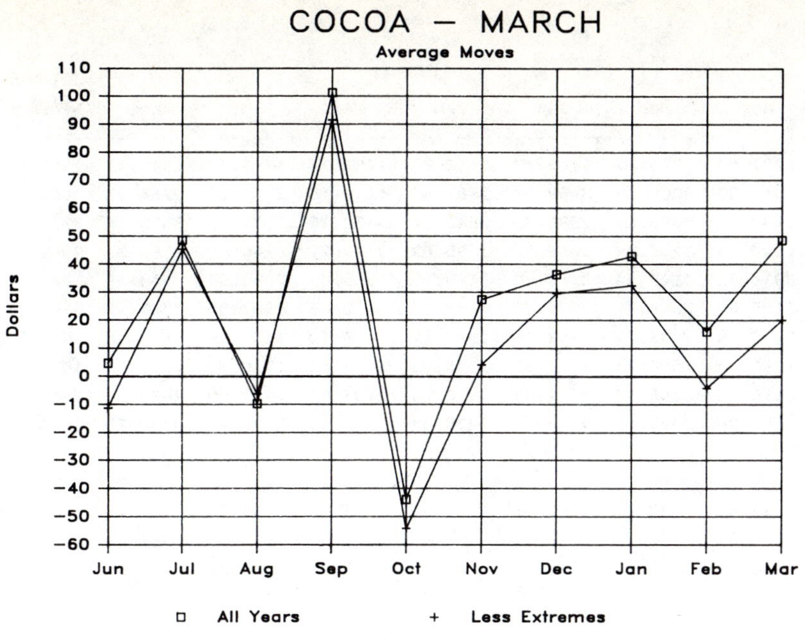
COCOA — MARCH
Average Moves
Dollars
110
100
90
80
70
60
50
40
30
20
10
0
−10
−20
−30
−40
−50
−60
Jun
Jul
Aug
Sep
Oct
Nov
Dec
Jan
Feb
Mar
All Years
Less Extremes

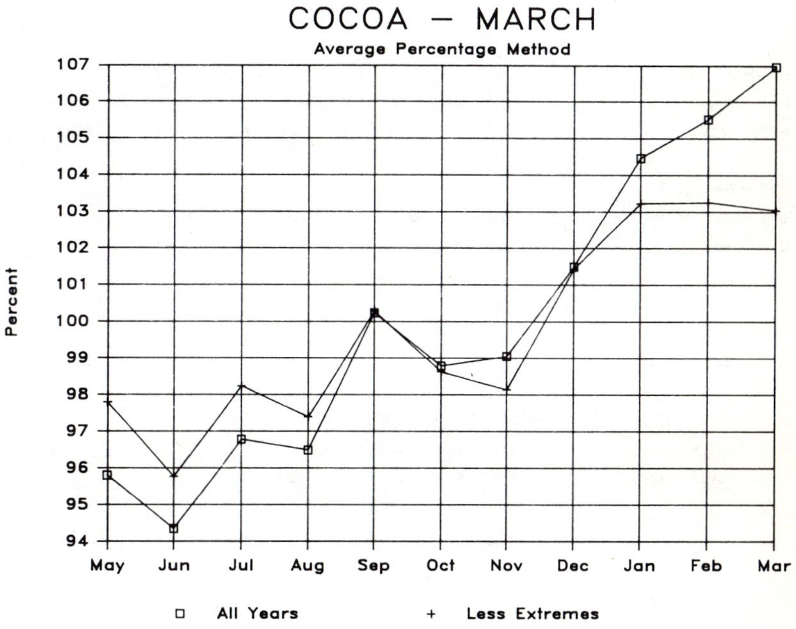
COCOA — MARCH
Average Percentage Method
Percent
107
106
105
104
103
102
101
100
99
98
97
96
95
94
May
Jun
Jul
Aug
Sep
Oct
Nov
Dec
Jan
Feb
Mar
All Years
Less Extremes

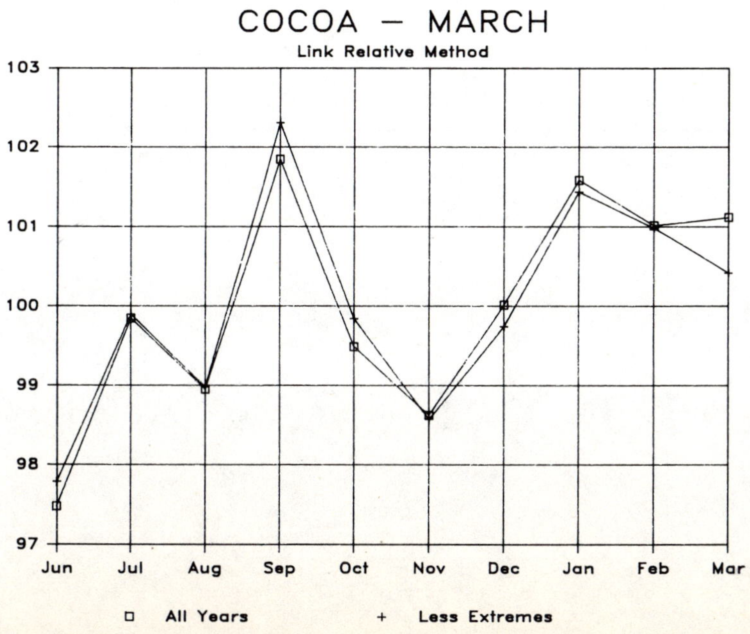
COCOA — MARCH
Link Relative Method
103
102
101
100
99
98
97
Jun
Jul
Aug
Sep
Oct
Nov
Dec
Jan
Feb
Mar
All Years
Less Extremes

COCOA - MAY - MONTHLY AVERAGE PRICE

Year of Expiration	Jul	Aug	Sep	Oct	Nov	Dec	Jan	Feb	Mar	Apr	May	Jul-May Average
1976	1119.20	1105.18	1115.67	1202.04	1201.04	1315.37	1405.47	1466.82	1492.77	1789.33	1943.21	1377.83
1977	1822.48	2026.12	2317.11	2533.23	2911.00	3000.03	3469.53	3887.87	4170.15	3746.58	3784.65	3060.79
1978	3856.40	3587.63	3580.08	3280.97	3193.76	3093.60	2896.33	2846.61	3472.10	3537.35	3316.75	3332.87
1979	3011.12	3246.39	3692.35	3807.65	4025.39	3927.09	3652.62	3495.62	3326.71	3140.89	3184.37	3500.93
1980	3362.23	3203.33	3244.16	3072.64	3014.61	3149.54	3115.60	3196.58	3065.07	2880.98	2653.58	3087.12
1981	2505.91	2314.62	2374.00	2283.57	2125.61	2038.71	2026.60	1958.95	2022.05	1957.95	1781.77	2126.34
1982	2102.59	2262.57	2328.62	2139.73	1993.70	2033.71	2102.45	1977.11	1828.52	1647.00	1646.85	2005.71
1983	1601.95	1565.96	1663.10	1619.38	1491.55	1566.24	1712.81	1856.53	1755.65	1760.55	1862.55	1677.84
1984	2255.30	2230.87	2086.10	2035.57	2156.71	2466.62	2537.48	2430.70	2483.64	2469.60	2600.00	2341.14
1985	2144.24	2129.48	2239.79	2191.48	2187.00	2090.11	2178.46	2220.58	2257.19	2395.43	2340.75	2215.86

	Jul	Aug	Sep	Oct	Nov	Dec	Jan	Feb	Mar	Apr	May
AVERAGE MOVE											
All Years		-10.93	96.88	-47.47	13.41	38.06	41.63	24.00	53.65	-54.82	-21.12
Less Extremes		-9.47	83.46	-48.97	-10.71	21.36	27.66	-2.67	9.99	-52.65	-17.21
Ave Up - All Years		199.63	140.14	139.26	238.89	127.15	155.69	149.30	181.06	126.24	93.56
Ave Down - All Years		-101.17	-76.16	-127.50	-83.22	-95.56	-129.45	-101.30	-137.47	-175.52	-135.80
COUNT											
Number Up		3	8	3	3	6	6	5	6	4	5
Number Down		7	2	7	7	4	4	5	4	6	5
Pct Up		30.0%	80.0%	30.0%	30.0%	60.0%	60.0%	50.0%	60.0%	40.0%	50.0%
Pct Down		70.0%	20.0%	70.0%	70.0%	40.0%	40.0%	50.0%	40.0%	60.0%	50.0%
EXTREMES											
Greatest Up		235.26	445.96	216.12	377.77	309.91	469.50	418.34	625.49	296.57	153.87
Greatest Down		-268.78	-144.78	-299.11	-157.95	-100.16	-274.47	-157.00	-168.91	-423.57	-227.41
SEASONAL INDEX : AVERAGE PERCENTAGE METHOD											
All Years	96.3	95.7	99.2	97.3	97.0	99.1	101.6	102.8	104.2	103.4	103.5
Less Extremes	98.2	97.2	100.0	97.7	96.0	98.2	102.0	101.9	101.8	102.8	101.4
SEASONAL INDEX : LINK RELATIVE METHOD											
All Years		97.5	100.6	98.6	97.8	99.4	101.4	101.6	102.4	100.9	99.8
Less Extremes		97.8	101.4	99.4	98.3	99.7	101.7	101.9	101.8	99.3	98.7

COCOA - MAY - MONTH OF HIGH AND LOW

Year of Expiration	Jul	Aug	Sep	Oct	Nov	Dec	Jan	Feb	Mar	Apr	May
1976		L									H
1977	L								H		
1978	H							L			
1979	L				H						
1980	H										L
1981	H										L
1982			H								L
1983					L						H
1984				L							H
1985						L				H	

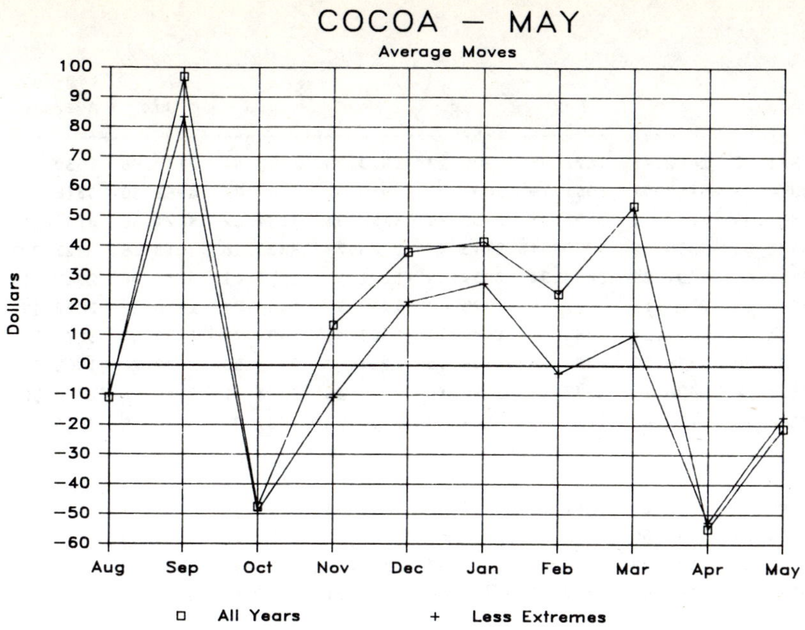
COCOA — MAY
Average Moves
Dollars
100
90
80
70
60
50
40
30
20
10
0
−10
−20
−30
−40
−50
−60
Aug
Sep
Oct
Nov
Dec
Jan
Feb
Mar
Apr
May
□ All Years
+ Less Extremes

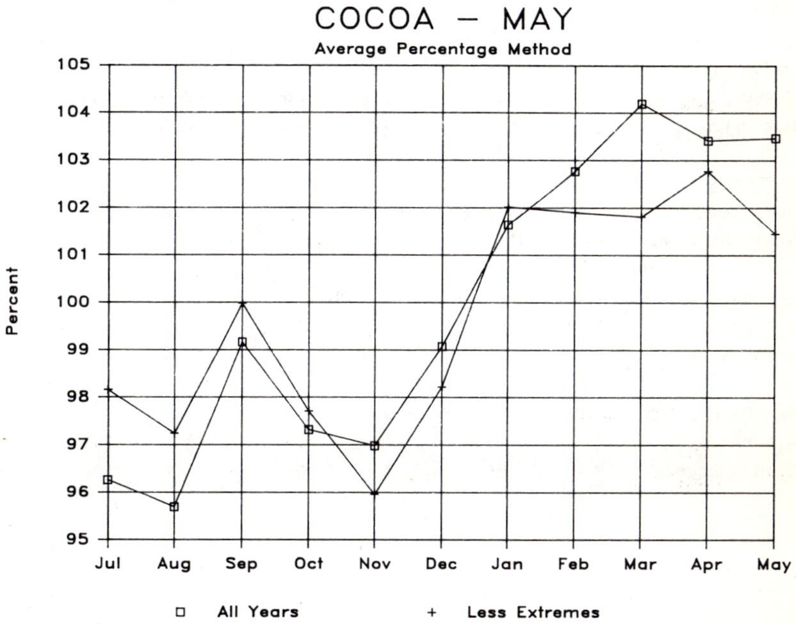
COCOA — MAY
Average Percentage Method
Percent
105
104
103
102
101
100
99
98
97
96
95
Jul
Aug
Sep
Oct
Nov
Dec
Jan
Feb
Mar
Apr
May
□ All Years
+ Less Extremes

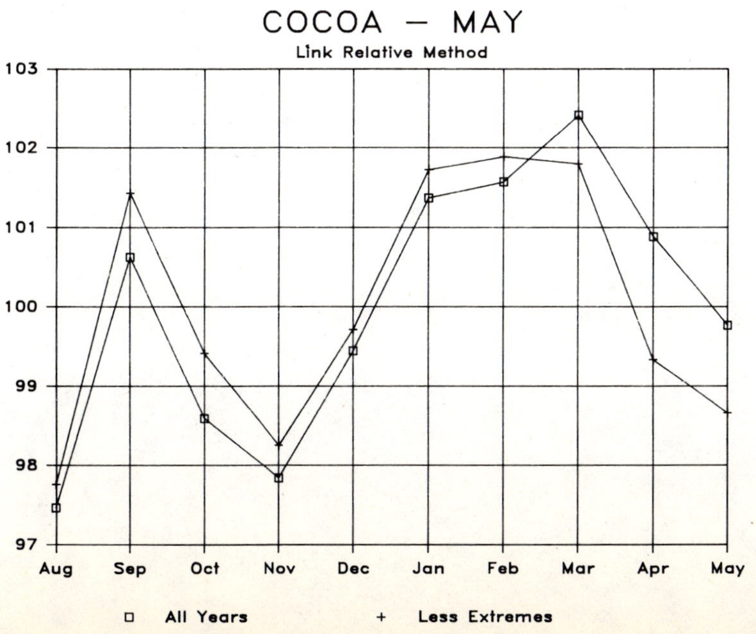
COCOA — MAY
Link Relative Method
103
102
101
100
99
98
97
Aug
Sep
Oct
Nov
Dec
Jan
Feb
Mar
Apr
May
□ All Years
+ Less Extremes

COCOA - JULY - MONTHLY AVERAGE PRICE

Year of Expiration	Sep	Oct	Nov	Dec	Jan	Feb	Mar	Apr	May	Jun	Jul	Sep-Jul Average
1976	1103.39	1172.57	1171.14	1282.25	1361.72	1412.71	1421.85	1700.17	1913.93	2156.04	2137.86	1530.33
1977	2231.55	2437.79	2797.43	2882.80	3344.13	3769.57	4061.79	3637.24	3910.51	4664.81	4963.30	3518.27
1978	3449.51	3138.08	3031.65	2997.73	2800.33	2763.11	3351.43	3433.72	3180.94	3124.22	3271.63	3140.21
1979	3641.43	3783.08	4005.60	3920.25	3671.33	3538.12	3375.54	3195.39	3283.73	3320.58	3018.16	3523.02
1980	3286.48	3123.16	3064.49	3176.10	3151.64	3197.29	3054.34	2839.86	2501.69	2370.41	2326.08	2917.41
1981	2418.24	2328.91	2168.44	2080.91	2074.30	2023.11	2071.59	2025.00	1792.95	1445.73	1818.27	2022.49
1982	2359.62	2160.27	2025.25	2052.05	2115.90	2004.16	1863.65	1640.24	1583.75	1407.23	1398.57	1873.70
1983	1701.19	1659.38	1528.30	1595.48	1738.86	1878.00	1786.78	1799.05	1964.00	2152.50	2030.20	1803.07
1984	2101.86	2055.19	2168.86	2459.91	2520.14	2406.15	2477.46	2499.15	2639.46	2384.91	2146.80	2350.90
1985	2245.42	2202.30	2192.29	2091.16	2166.73	2204.63	2145.00	2182.29	2090.73	2034.30	2061.18	2146.91

	Sep	Oct	Nov	Dec	Jan	Feb	Mar	Apr	May	Jun	Jul
AVERAGE MOVE											
All Years		-47.79	9.27	38.52	40.65	25.18	41.26	-65.73	-9.04	19.90	11.13
Less Extremes		-46.59	-13.31	24.41	24.26	-5.06	-1.65	-63.89	-3.19	-26.01	5.15
Ave Up - All Years		139.02	231.94	115.52	147.31	139.83	201.89	86.37	176.12	305.44	211.33
Ave Down - All Years		-127.86	-86.16	-76.99	-119.34	-89.47	-119.38	-217.84	-194.21	-170.45	-122.33
COUNT											
Number Up		3	3	6	6	5	5	5	5	4	4
Number Down		7	7	4	4	5	5	5	5	6	6
Pct Up		30.0%	30.0%	60.0%	60.0%	50.0%	50.0%	50.0%	50.0%	40.0%	40.0%
Pct Down		70.0%	70.0%	40.0%	40.0%	50.0%	50.0%	50.0%	50.0%	60.0%	60.0%
EXTREMES											
Greatest Up		206.24	359.64	291.05	461.33	425.45	588.32	278.32	273.27	754.31	372.54
Greatest Down		-311.43	-160.47	-101.13	-248.92	-133.21	-162.58	-424.55	-338.17	-347.22	-302.42
SEASONAL INDEX : AVERAGE PERCENTAGE METHOD											
All Years	99.5	97.3	96.6	98.4	100.5	101.4	102.2	100.7	100.8	101.1	101.5
Less Extremes	100.7	98.5	96.9	98.9	100.4	102.0	101.7	101.1	99.8	99.8	99.9
SEASONAL INDEX : LINK RELATIVE METHOD											
All Years		98.0	97.5	99.2	101.3	101.9	102.5	100.8	100.2	99.0	99.5
Less Extremes		98.7	97.9	99.8	102.0	102.5	102.2	99.8	99.8	99.0	98.4

COCOA - JULY - MONTH OF HIGH AND LOW

Year of Expiration	Sep	Oct	Nov	Dec	Jan	Feb	Mar	Apr	May	Jun	Jul
1976	L									H	
1977	L										H
1978	H					L					
1979			H								L
1980	H										L
1981	H									L	
1982	H										L
1983			L							H	
1984		L							H		
1985	H									L	

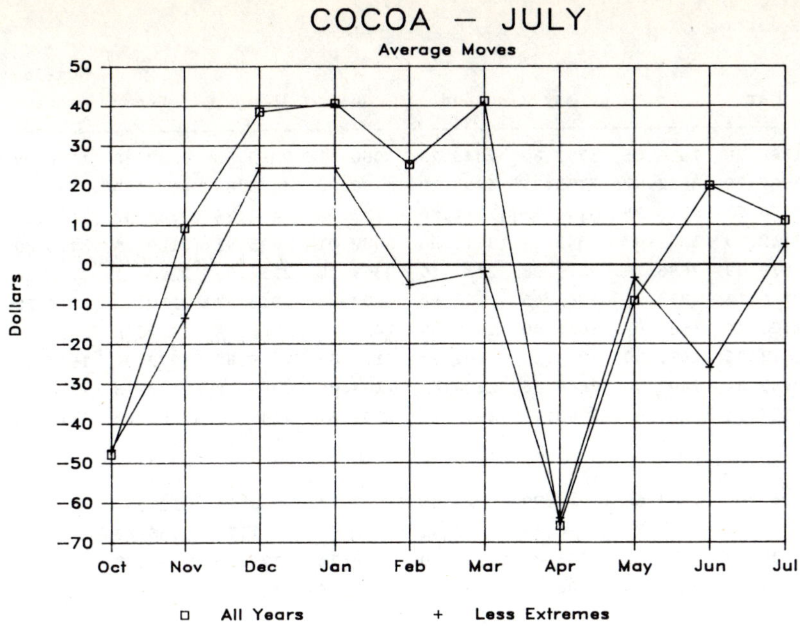
COCOA — JULY
Average Moves
Dollars
50
40
30
20
10
0
−10
−20
−30
−40
−50
−60
−70
Oct
Nov
Dec
Jan
Feb
Mar
Apr
May
Jun
Jul
All Years
Less Extremes

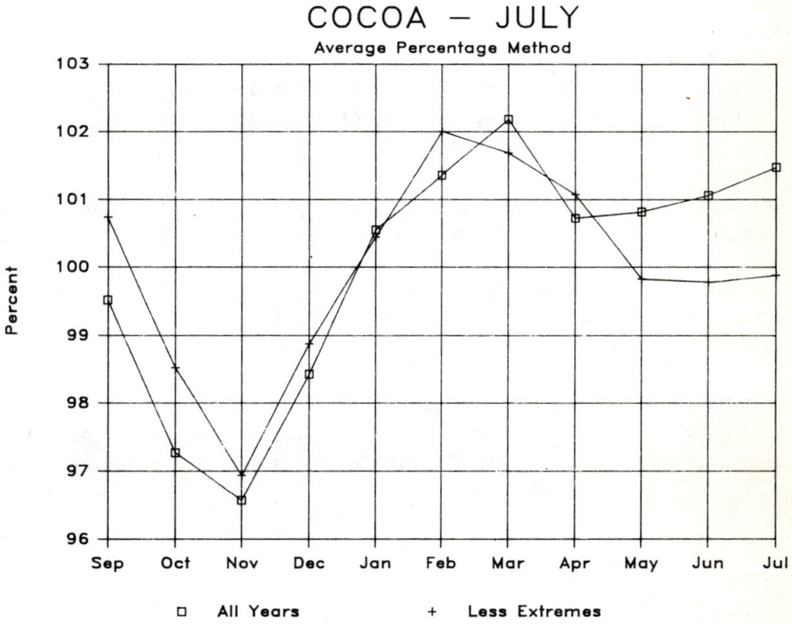
COCOA — JULY
Average Percentage Method
Percent
103
102
101
100
99
98
97
96
Sep
Oct
Nov
Dec
Jan
Feb
Mar
Apr
May
Jun
Jul
All Years
Less Extremes

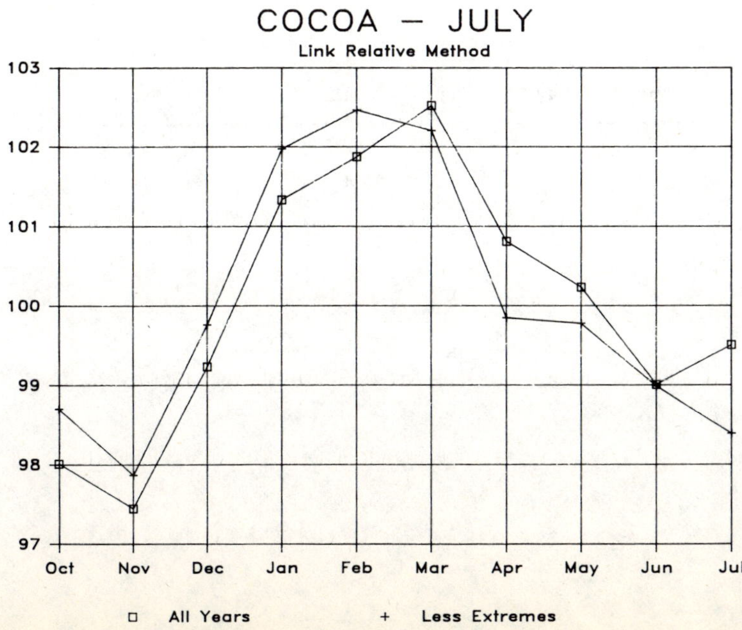
COCOA — JULY
Link Relative Method
103
102
101
100
99
98
97
Oct
Nov
Dec
Jan
Feb
Mar
Apr
May
Jun
Jul
All Years
Less Extremes

COCOA - SEPTEMBER - MONTHLY AVERAGE PRICE

Year of Expiration	Nov	Dec	Jan	Feb	Mar	Apr	May	Jun	Jul	Aug	Sep	Nov-Sep Average
1976	1147.72	1253.11	1327.10	1366.86	1368.29	1616.85	1792.80	2043.73	2060.51	2260.58	2583.30	1710.99
1977	2684.51	2779.88	3218.73	3660.13	3967.78	3532.92	3755.31	4435.10	4688.83	4438.88	4527.60	3789.97
1978	2948.19	2934.44	2743.13	2711.65	3278.73	3356.95	3102.35	3024.60	3233.02	3462.36	3834.82	3148.20
1979	3959.39	3881.78	3683.87	3577.43	3417.20	3251.47	3343.12	3413.56	3082.01	2945.91	3129.11	3425.89
1980	3104.81	3201.66	3191.31	3211.63	3079.39	2886.76	2549.38	2433.49	2369.32	2154.03	2247.51	2766.30
1981	2214.56	2127.48	2123.25	2077.79	2116.14	2077.91	1863.65	1525.96	1903.46	2013.57	2112.43	2014.20
1982	2050.75	2075.29	2133.60	2046.37	1908.44	1685.67	1626.40	1453.59	1427.19	1388.14	1472.36	1751.62
1983	1564.50	1623.95	1763.14	1893.11	1813.96	1821.50	1994.19	2202.64	2172.65	2159.87	1972.00	1907.41
1984	2185.14	2452.86	2509.48	2389.20	2465.32	2491.70	2648.36	2429.43	2164.86	2265.78	2506.78	2409.90
1985	2197.43	2095.00	2157.50	2188.16	2122.91	2139.81	2063.09	2015.40	2102.67	2109.00	2107.40	2118.03

	Nov	Dec	Jan	Feb	Mar	Apr	May	Jun	Jul	Aug	Sep
AVERAGE MOVE											
All Years		36.84	42.57	27.12	41.58	-67.66	-12.29	23.88	22.70	-0.64	129.52
Less Extremes		25.40	23.09	-6.24	1.12	-61.29	-0.99	-12.91	22.63	1.78	138.83
Ave Up - All Years		108.22	138.24	132.42	198.12	75.52	163.87	302.40	188.74	129.35	185.58
Ave Down - All Years		-70.22	-100.95	-78.18	-114.96	-210.84	-188.45	-161.79	-143.34	-130.63	-94.73
COUNT											
Number Up		6	6	5	5	5	5	4	5	5	8
Number Down		4	4	5	5	5	5	6	5	5	2
Pct Up		60.0%	60.0%	50.0%	50.0%	50.0%	50.0%	40.0%	50.0%	50.0%	80.0%
Pct Down		40.0%	40.0%	50.0%	50.0%	50.0%	50.0%	60.0%	50.0%	50.0%	20.0%
EXTREMES											
Greatest Up		267.71	438.85	441.40	567.08	248.57	222.38	679.79	377.50	229.33	372.46
Greatest Down		-102.43	-197.91	-120.28	-160.24	-434.86	-337.38	-337.70	-331.55	-249.94	-187.87
SEASONAL INDEX : AVERAGE PERCENTAGE METHOD											
All Years	96.3	97.9	99.8	100.5	101.2	99.3	98.9	99.0	100.1	100.9	106.1
Less Extremes	97.3	98.4	99.9	101.0	102.5	99.1	98.4	99.4	99.5	99.9	103.6
SEASONAL INDEX : LINK RELATIVE METHOD											
All Years		99.6	101.4	101.6	101.9	99.8	98.8	97.8	98.5	98.2	102.3
Less Extremes		101.0	102.7	102.5	101.7	98.8	98.3	97.6	97.4	97.5	102.5

COCOA - SEPTEMBER - MONTH OF HIGH AND LOW

Year of Expiration	Nov	Dec	Jan	Feb	Mar	Apr	May	Jun	Jul	Aug	Sep
1976	L										H
1977	L								H		
1978				L							H
1979	H									L	
1980				H						L	
1981	H							L			
1982			H							L	
1983	L							H			
1984							H		L		
1985	H							L			

COCOA — SEPTEMBER

Average Moves

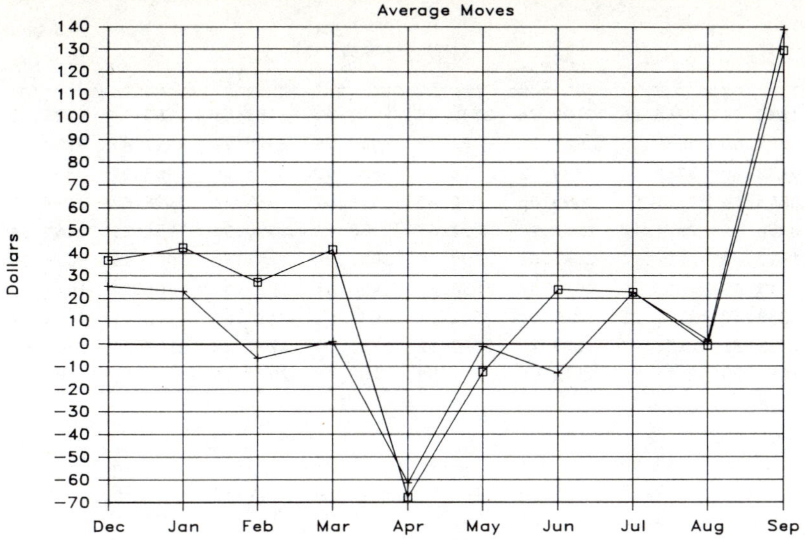

□ All Years + Less Extremes

COCOA — SEPTEMBER

Average Percentage Method

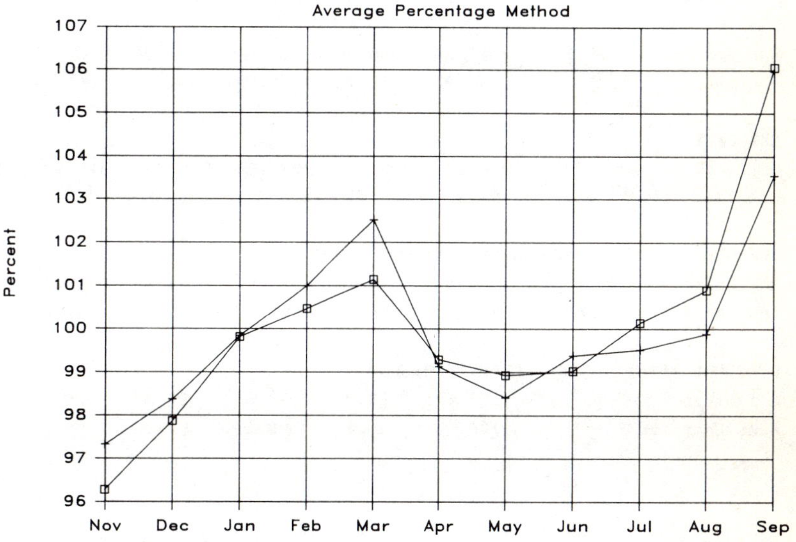

□ All Years + Less Extremes

COCOA — SEPTEMBER

Link Relative Method

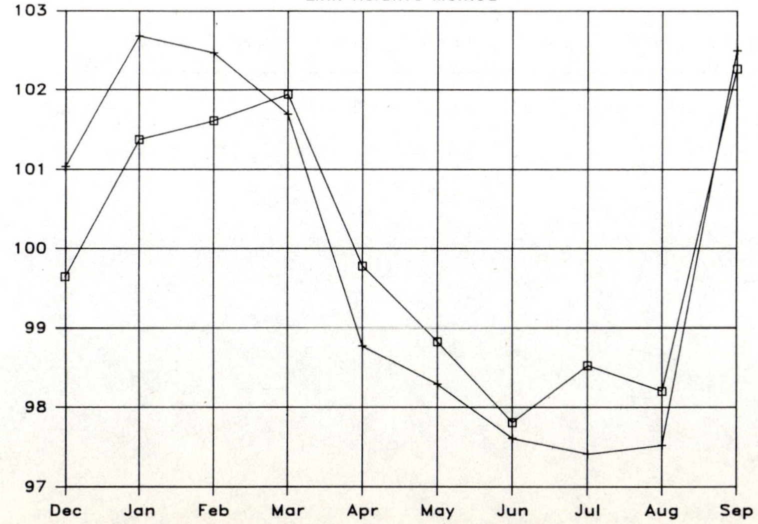

□ All Years + Less Extremes

COCOA - DECEMBER - MONTHLY AVERAGE PRICE

Year of Expiration	Feb	Mar	Apr	May	Jun	Jul	Aug	Sep	Oct	Nov	Dec	Feb-Dec Average
1976	1307.72	1307.34	1508.06	1644.91	1844.58	1965.16	2190.38	2530.99	2755.75	3158.51	3189.27	2127.52
1977	3378.12	3722.71	3321.96	3509.21	4034.66	4230.35	3941.84	4051.77	3962.76	4079.71	3927.47	3832.78
1978	2652.94	3163.31	3227.75	2991.57	2933.20	3136.74	3389.31	3794.47	3828.90	4026.80	3965.87	3373.71
1979	3625.37	3482.40	3329.19	3413.78	3503.44	3221.50	3059.82	3146.45	2975.07	2858.44	2996.67	3237.47
1980	3184.63	3058.62	2888.33	2559.95	2456.19	2377.68	2183.95	2262.67	2158.09	1990.33	1954.29	2461.34
1981	2150.32	2172.41	2135.86	1941.95	1632.32	2002.59	2141.62	2199.10	2027.96	1892.25	2012.29	2028.06
1982	2076.05	1952.04	1742.95	1684.35	1519.41	1492.29	1459.82	1558.33	1490.81	1355.40	1405.91	1612.49
1983	1912.37	1843.04	1853.75	2021.24	2238.50	2229.35	2212.04	2041.81	1987.95	2123.67	2363.18	2075.17
1984	2366.00	2438.64	2430.75	2527.73	2339.91	2128.67	2129.78	2292.32	2228.09	2278.24	2223.11	2307.57
1985	2073.21	2063.19	2093.33	2030.91	1995.25	2121.91	2175.96	2214.58	2188.68	2077.95	2156.60	2108.32

	Feb	Mar	Apr	May	Jun	Jul	Aug	Sep	Oct	Nov	Dec
AVERAGE MOVE											
All Years		47.70	-67.18	-20.63	17.19	40.88	-2.17	120.80	-48.84	23.72	35.34
Less Extremes		13.70	-58.97	-8.15	-5.50	40.06	1.78	121.63	-67.73	0.28	33.26
Ave Up - All Years		237.42	76.50	134.63	258.01	203.35	134.40	153.13	129.60	180.69	109.62
Ave Down - All Years		-78.79	-162.96	-175.90	-143.36	-121.59	-138.74	-170.23	-93.45	-133.25	-76.08
COUNT											
Number Up		4	4	5	4	5	5	9	2	5	6
Number Down		6	6	5	6	5	5	1	8	5	4
Pct Up		40.0%	40.0%	50.0%	40.0%	50.0%	50.0%	90.0%	20.0%	50.0%	60.0%
Pct Down		60.0%	60.0%	50.0%	60.0%	50.0%	50.0%	10.0%	80.0%	50.0%	40.0%
EXTREMES											
Greatest Up		510.37	200.72	187.25	525.45	370.27	252.57	405.16	224.76	402.76	239.51
Greatest Down		-142.97	-400.75	-328.38	-309.63	-281.93	-288.51	-170.23	-171.38	-167.75	-152.23
SEASONAL INDEX : AVERAGE PERCENTAGE METHOD											
All Years	99.7	100.5	98.1	97.0	96.6	98.3	98.8	103.4	101.5	102.0	104.1
Less Extremes	100.8	102.4	99.1	98.0	97.1	97.6	99.1	102.9	99.7	98.9	101.4
SEASONAL INDEX : LINK RELATIVE METHOD											
All Years		100.6	98.7	97.8	97.3	99.3	99.4	103.6	100.9	100.4	102.0
Less Extremes		100.9	98.4	98.0	97.9	99.1	99.3	104.0	100.9	100.0	101.5

COCOA - DECEMBER - MONTH OF HIGH AND LOW

Year of Expiration	Feb	Mar	Apr	May	Jun	Jul	Aug	Sep	Oct	Nov	Dec
1976		L									H
1977			L			H					
1978	L									H	
1979	H									L	
1980	H										L
1981					L			H			
1982	H									L	
1983		L									H
1984				H		L					
1985					L			H			

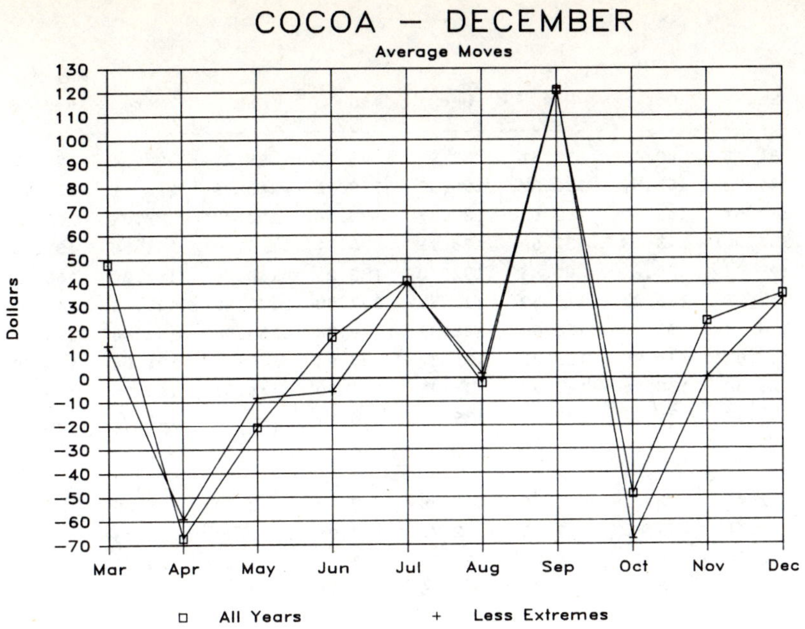
COCOA — DECEMBER
Average Moves
Dollars
130
120
110
100
90
80
70
60
50
40
30
20
10
0
−10
−20
−30
−40
−50
−60
−70
Mar
Apr
May
Jun
Jul
Aug
Sep
Oct
Nov
Dec
□ All Years
+ Less Extremes

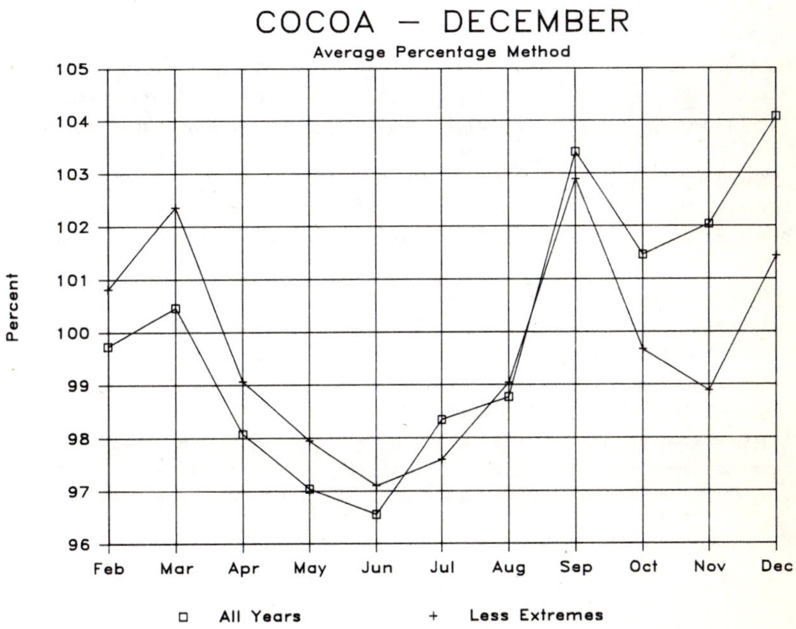
COCOA — DECEMBER
Average Percentage Method
Percent
105
104
103
102
101
100
99
98
97
96
Feb
Mar
Apr
May
Jun
Jul
Aug
Sep
Oct
Nov
Dec
□ All Years
+ Less Extremes

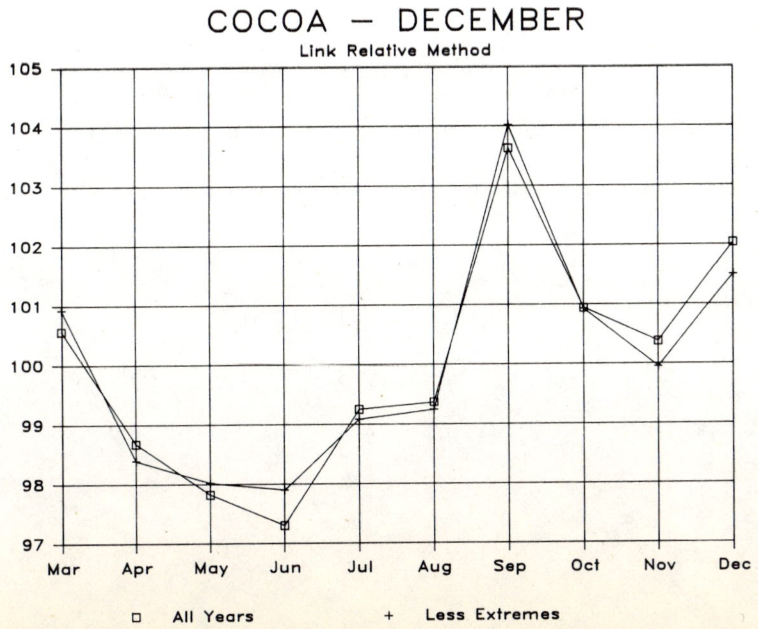
COCOA — DECEMBER
Link Relative Method
105
104
103
102
101
100
99
98
97
Mar
Apr
May
Jun
Jul
Aug
Sep
Oct
Nov
Dec
□ All Years
+ Less Extremes

COFFEE - MARCH - MONTHLY AVERAGE PRICE

Year of Expiration	May	Jun	Jul	Aug	Sep	Oct	Nov	Dec	Jan	Feb	Mar	May-Mar Average
1976	55.11	58.17	64.17	83.67	81.16	80.42	77.61	83.97	93.16	99.29	98.54	79.57
1977	126.89	140.07	129.95	140.87	149.02	165.54	180.37	206.32	218.96	243.99	298.91	181.90
1978	275.13	223.67	185.60	175.48	163.61	141.80	163.63	183.37	195.38	190.77	177.02	188.68
1979	130.84	139.89	111.80	122.42	138.96	143.83	137.59	128.11	130.07	126.07	131.78	131.03
1980	151.75	190.86	199.79	189.36	199.04	200.11	200.84	192.50	172.26	168.90	184.04	186.31
1981	190.58	184.34	160.28	147.76	137.98	130.07	118.69	122.38	127.80	120.58	120.46	141.90
1982	118.69	94.67	100.28	110.28	113.13	129.59	136.90	136.33	140.28	153.98	152.44	126.05
1983	114.02	119.17	112.48	116.24	127.02	135.90	135.31	131.87	127.94	125.37	124.04	124.49
1984	121.87	124.22	124.24	126.37	129.38	138.14	142.70	145.25	142.00	144.81	150.35	135.39
1985	143.59	142.11	136.93	140.80	138.18	134.17	137.68	139.83	146.11	145.25	142.01	140.61

	May	Jun	Jul	Aug	Sep	Oct	Nov	Dec	Jan	Feb	Mar
AVERAGE MOVE											
All Years		-1.13	-9.16	2.77	2.42	2.21	3.18	3.86	2.40	2.50	6.06
Less Extremes		0.13	-7.81	2.59	2.44	3.42	2.66	2.77	3.96	0.90	2.43
Ave Up - All Years		11.98	5.14	8.69	8.50	9.43	8.80	10.08	7.35	11.92	20.33
Ave Down - All Years		-20.80	-18.70	-11.02	-6.70	-8.62	-5.25	-5.46	-9.14	-3.77	-3.45
COUNT											
Number Up		6	4	7	6	6	6	6	7	4	4
Number Down		4	6	3	4	4	4	4	3	6	6
Pct Up		60.0%	40.0%	70.0%	60.0%	60.0%	60.0%	60.0%	70.0%	40.0%	40.0%
Pct Down		40.0%	60.0%	30.0%	40.0%	40.0%	40.0%	40.0%	30.0%	60.0%	60.0%
EXTREMES											
Greatest Up		39.11	8.93	19.50	16.54	16.52	21.83	25.96	12.63	25.03	54.92
Greatest Down		-51.47	-38.07	-12.53	-11.87	-21.81	-11.38	-9.49	-20.24	-7.22	-13.75
SEASONAL INDEX : AVERAGE PERCENTAGE METHOD											
All Years	97.8	97.1	91.5	94.9	96.6	98.5	100.0	102.4	104.6	106.5	109.9
Less Extremes	95.4	96.0	91.3	95.8	97.2	100.1	101.0	103.1	104.4	105.7	106.2
SEASONAL INDEX : LINK RELATIVE METHOD											
All Years		100.2	94.4	97.7	98.5	99.3	99.9	101.4	102.3	102.4	104.0
Less Extremes		100.5	95.1	97.1	97.8	99.2	99.8	101.2	102.9	102.9	103.5

COFFEE - MARCH - MONTH OF HIGH AND LOW

Year of Expiration	May	Jun	Jul	Aug	Sep	Oct	Nov	Dec	Jan	Feb	Mar
1976	L									H	
1977	L										H
1978	H					L					
1979			L			H					
1980	L						H				
1981	H						L				
1982		L								H	
1983			L			H					
1984	L										H
1985						L			H		

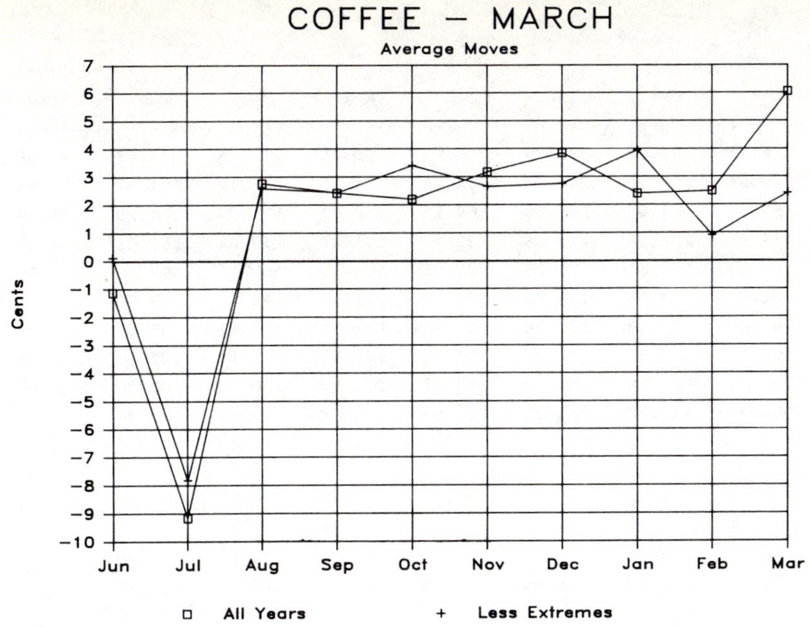
COFFEE — MARCH
Average Moves
Cents
7
6
5
4
3
2
1
0
-1
-2
-3
-4
-5
-6
-7
-8
-9
-10
Jun
Jul
Aug
Sep
Oct
Nov
Dec
Jan
Feb
Mar
□ All Years
+ Less Extremes

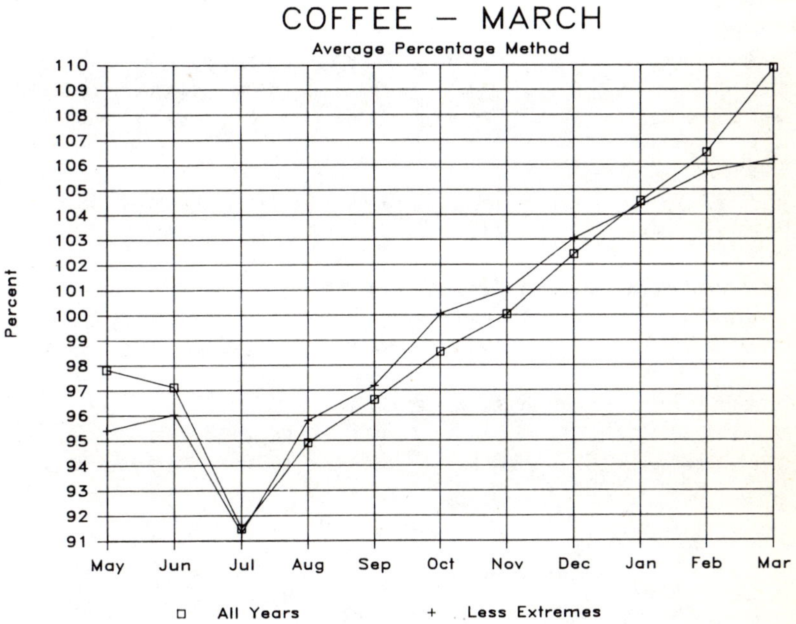
COFFEE — MARCH
Average Percentage Method
Percent
110
109
108
107
106
105
104
103
102
101
100
99
98
97
96
95
94
93
92
91
May
Jun
Jul
Aug
Sep
Oct
Nov
Dec
Jan
Feb
Mar
□ All Years
+ Less Extremes

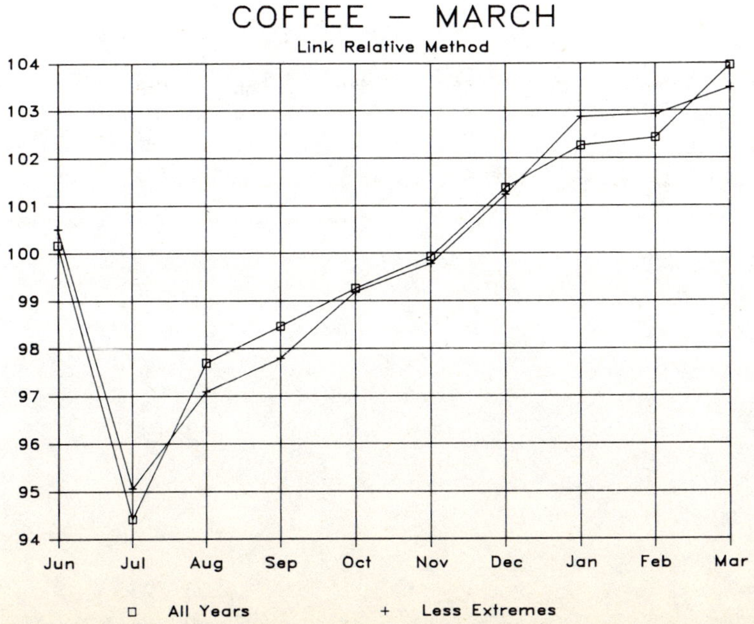
COFFEE — MARCH
Link Relative Method
104
103
102
101
100
99
98
97
96
95
94
Jun
Jul
Aug
Sep
Oct
Nov
Dec
Jan
Feb
Mar
□ All Years
+ Less Extremes

COFFEE - MAY - MONTHLY AVERAGE PRICE

Year of Expiration	Jul	Aug	Sep	Oct	Nov	Dec	Jan	Feb	Mar	Apr	May	Jul-May Average
1976	64.68	84.39	81.65	80.90	78.21	84.26	92.72	98.93	100.16	122.66	135.08	93.06
1977	129.78	140.78	146.95	163.42	179.24	207.15	219.48	242.38	300.29	317.17	284.32	211.91
1978	180.86	172.55	161.09	140.30	152.26	164.67	181.00	169.99	158.61	173.73	175.28	166.39
1979	109.36	119.21	133.26	139.08	133.95	124.94	126.56	125.17	133.86	142.04	152.04	130.86
1980	197.82	188.44	196.04	194.89	193.23	183.41	175.25	174.05	189.30	183.01	192.30	187.98
1981	161.50	149.53	141.53	130.98	121.60	123.95	130.59	125.10	123.92	125.95	123.83	132.59
1982	99.98	111.01	113.21	126.68	131.46	130.49	132.90	141.48	137.38	136.42	139.67	127.33
1983	109.21	111.31	121.68	128.51	130.05	126.95	124.04	120.99	123.09	123.42	127.63	122.44
1984	122.18	124.43	127.22	134.45	138.28	140.10	137.35	139.62	146.28	150.90	152.30	137.55
1985	135.62	138.91	136.97	133.16	136.41	137.79	143.01	143.93	143.58	143.28	144.80	139.77

	Jul	Aug	Sep	Oct	Nov	Dec	Jan	Feb	Mar	Apr	May
AVERAGE MOVE											
All Years		2.96	1.91	1.27	2.23	2.90	3.92	1.87	7.48	6.21	0.87
Less Extremes		2.73	2.06	2.13	1.99	1.37	3.88	0.86	3.54	5.74	3.64
Ave Up - All Years		8.46	7.20	9.96	6.86	8.66	7.57	8.17	15.31	9.95	5.46
Ave Down - All Years		-9.89	-6.03	-7.41	-4.71	-5.73	-4.61	-4.43	-4.25	-2.52	-17.49
COUNT											
Number Up		7	6	5	6	6	7	5	6	7	8
Number Down		3	4	5	4	4	3	5	4	3	2
Pct Up		70.0%	60.0%	50.0%	60.0%	60.0%	70.0%	50.0%	60.0%	70.0%	80.0%
Pct Down		30.0%	40.0%	50.0%	40.0%	40.0%	30.0%	50.0%	40.0%	30.0%	20.0%
EXTREMES											
Greatest Up		19.71	14.05	16.47	15.81	27.91	16.33	22.90	57.91	22.50	12.42
Greatest Down		-11.97	-11.46	-20.79	-9.37	-9.83	-8.16	-11.01	-11.38	-6.29	-32.86
SEASONAL INDEX : AVERAGE PERCENTAGE METHOD											
All Years	90.4	93.3	94.6	95.5	96.5	98.0	100.8	102.0	105.9	110.7	112.5
Less Extremes	90.1	94.2	96.2	96.4	96.8	98.3	100.8	101.6	102.9	107.8	110.8
SEASONAL INDEX : LINK RELATIVE METHOD											
All Years		98.8	98.8	98.5	98.1	98.5	99.7	99.1	101.0	103.7	103.9
Less Extremes		98.6	98.6	99.0	98.9	98.9	100.3	99.7	100.6	102.3	103.1

COFFEE - MAY - MONTH OF HIGH AND LOW

Year of Expiration	Jul	Aug	Sep	Oct	Nov	Dec	Jan	Feb	Mar	Apr	May
1976	L										H
1977	L									H	
1978				L			H				
1979	L										H
1980	H							L			
1981	H										L
1982	L							H			
1983	L				H						
1984	L										H
1985				L							H

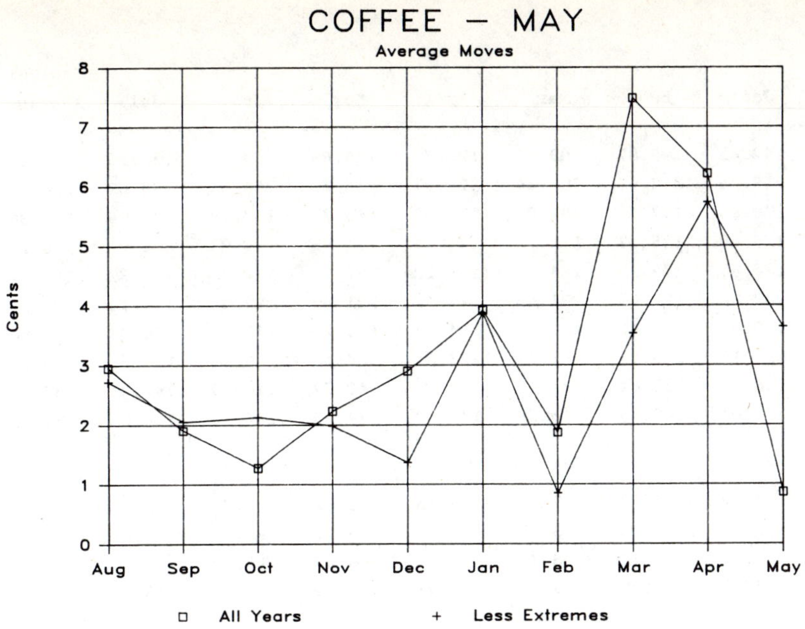
COFFEE — MAY
Average Moves
Cents
8
7
6
5
4
3
2
1
0
Aug
Sep
Oct
Nov
Dec
Jan
Feb
Mar
Apr
May
All Years
Less Extremes

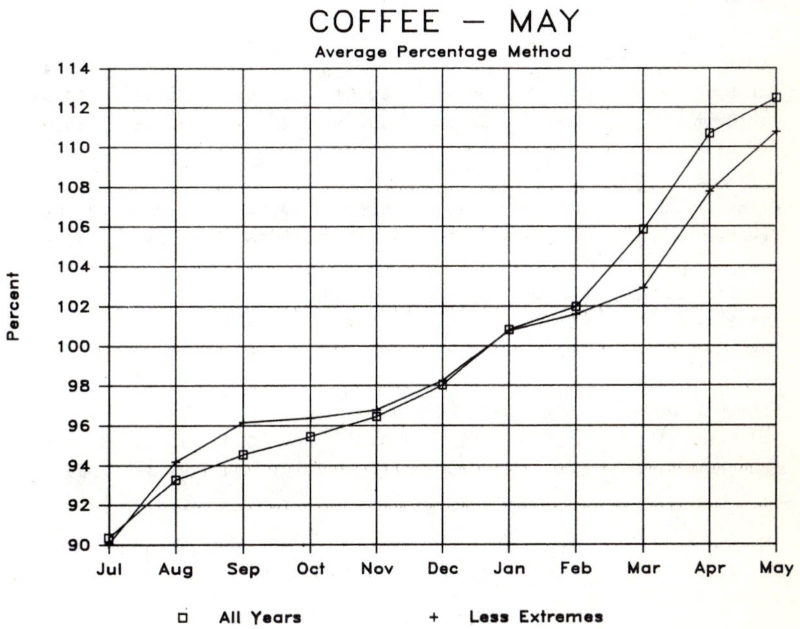
COFFEE — MAY
Average Percentage Method
Percent
114
112
110
108
106
104
102
100
98
96
94
92
90
Jul
Aug
Sep
Oct
Nov
Dec
Jan
Feb
Mar
Apr
May
All Years
Less Extremes

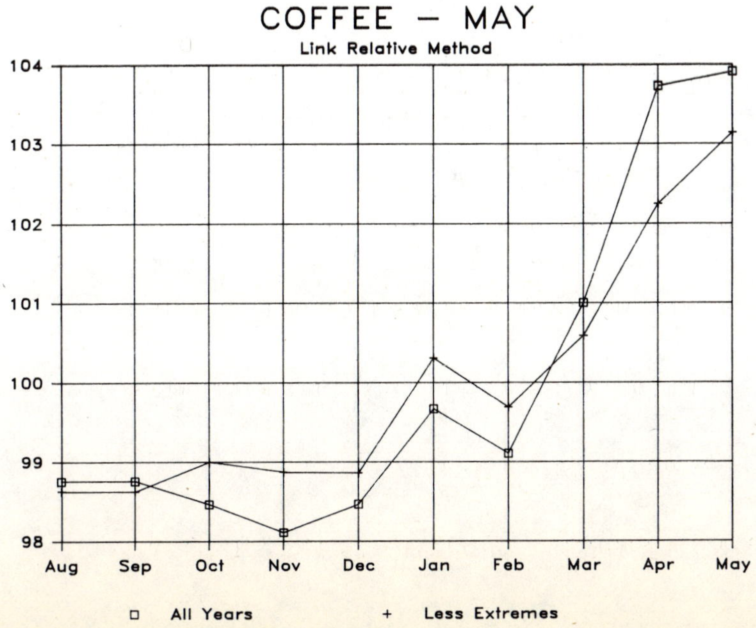
COFFEE — MAY
Link Relative Method
104
103
102
101
100
99
98
Aug
Sep
Oct
Nov
Dec
Jan
Feb
Mar
Apr
May
All Years
Less Extremes

COFFEE - JULY - MONTHLY AVERAGE PRICE

Year of Expiration	Sep	Oct	Nov	Dec	Jan	Feb	Mar	Apr	May	Jun	Jul	Sep-Jul Average
1976	82.27	81.62	78.90	85.09	92.85	98.87	100.15	120.72	135.66	148.91	136.90	105.63
1977	146.10	162.49	179.07	207.81	219.85	242.65	301.84	321.93	286.75	266.65	253.09	235.29
1978	157.73	137.32	145.38	154.43	170.36	157.40	142.02	153.52	160.75	167.38	140.88	153.38
1979	130.19	135.52	131.57	124.01	125.80	125.39	135.78	144.69	154.95	194.93	205.01	146.17
1980	194.87	193.73	191.70	181.54	177.40	179.18	194.27	190.22	197.71	184.37	163.33	186.21
1981	143.02	131.76	123.51	125.04	132.06	127.62	124.65	125.92	121.32	97.24	104.13	123.30
1982	113.70	125.76	129.37	128.62	130.02	134.46	129.90	124.74	126.76	138.04	136.06	128.86
1983	118.08	124.07	125.95	124.05	121.17	119.47	121.77	123.35	128.44	126.00	127.55	123.63
1984	125.58	131.44	135.56	137.22	134.81	135.04	139.90	145.24	149.32	146.90	147.91	138.99
1985	136.09	132.25	135.36	136.33	141.01	142.53	143.59	143.12	144.95	144.10	136.63	139.63

	Sep	Oct	Nov	Dec	Jan	Feb	Mar	Apr	May	Jun	Jul
AVERAGE MOVE											
All Years		0.83	2.04	2.78	4.12	1.73	7.13	5.96	1.32	0.79	-6.30
Less Extremes		1.54	1.51	1.15	3.67	0.93	3.43	5.52	4.18	-1.00	-5.83
Ave Up - All Years		9.13	6.22	8.02	7.23	6.13	13.45	9.89	6.62	17.79	4.88
Ave Down - All Years		-7.46	-4.24	-5.09	-3.15	-4.88	-7.63	-3.23	-19.89	-10.54	-13.76
COUNT											
Number Up		5	6	6	7	6	7	7	8	4	4
Number Down		5	4	4	3	4	3	3	2	6	6
Pct Up		50.0%	60.0%	60.0%	70.0%	60.0%	70.0%	70.0%	80.0%	40.0%	40.0%
Pct Down		50.0%	40.0%	40.0%	30.0%	40.0%	30.0%	30.0%	20.0%	60.0%	60.0%
EXTREMES											
Greatest Up		16.39	16.57	28.74	15.93	22.81	59.19	20.57	14.94	39.98	10.07
Greatest Down		-20.41	-8.25	-10.16	-4.15	-12.96	-15.38	-5.16	-35.18	-24.08	-26.50
SEASONAL INDEX : AVERAGE PERCENTAGE METHOD											
All Years	92.4	92.7	93.5	95.0	97.8	98.5	101.7	105.8	107.9	109.3	105.4
Less Extremes	93.3	93.8	94.7	96.0	97.6	99.4	99.5	103.1	106.5	109.1	103.7
SEASONAL INDEX : LINK RELATIVE METHOD											
All Years		96.3	96.3	97.0	98.8	98.5	100.6	103.5	104.6	104.5	99.8
Less Extremes		97.0	97.0	97.3	99.1	99.0	100.3	102.5	104.2	103.9	99.8

COFFEE - JULY - MONTH OF HIGH AND LOW

Year of Expiration	Sep	Oct	Nov	Dec	Jan	Feb	Mar	Apr	May	Jun	Jul
1976			L							H	
1977	L							H			
1978		L			H						
1979				L							H
1980									H		L
1981	H									L	
1982	L									H	
1983	L								H		
1984	L								H		
1985		L							H		

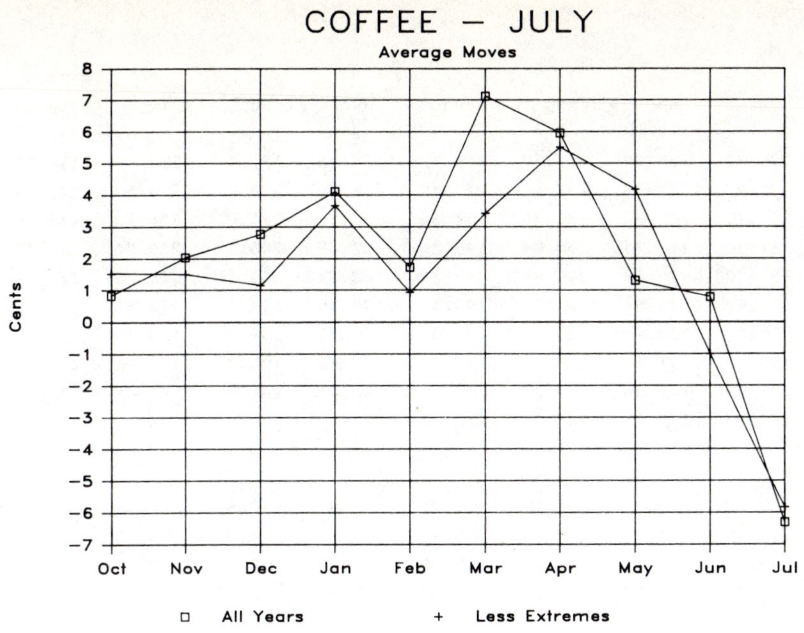
COFFEE – JULY
Average Moves
Cents
Oct
Nov
Dec
Jan
Feb
Mar
Apr
May
Jun
Jul
All Years
Less Extremes

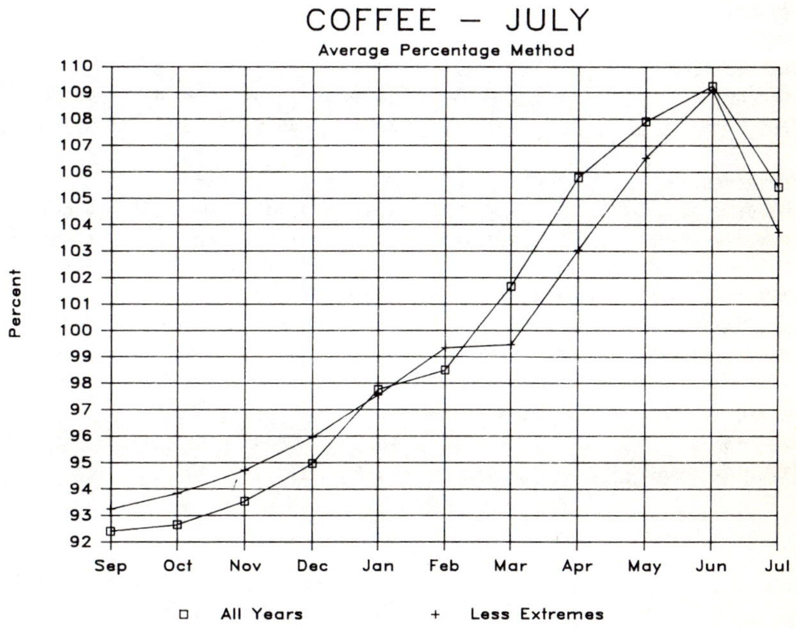
COFFEE – JULY
Average Percentage Method
Percent
Sep
Oct
Nov
Dec
Jan
Feb
Mar
Apr
May
Jun
Jul
All Years
Less Extremes

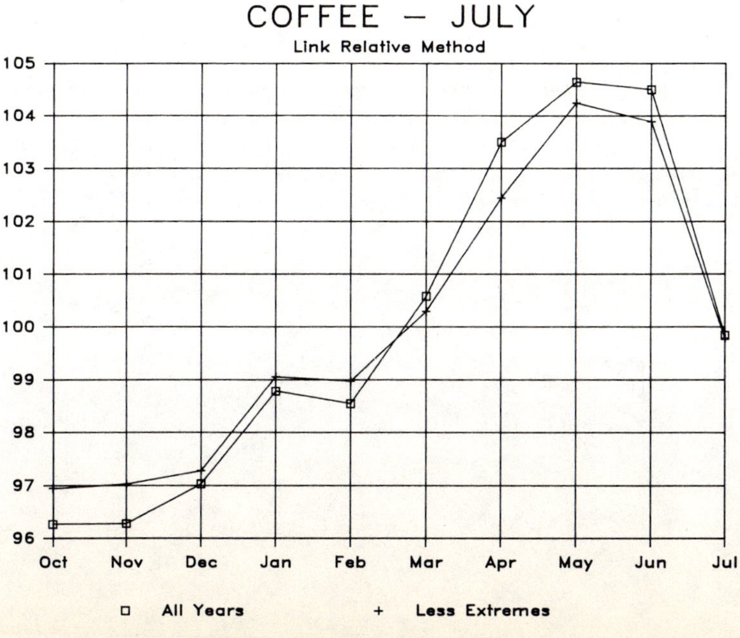
COFFEE – JULY
Link Relative Method
Oct
Nov
Dec
Jan
Feb
Mar
Apr
May
Jun
Jul
All Years
Less Extremes

COFFEE - SEPTEMBER - MONTHLY AVERAGE PRICE

Year of Expiration	Nov	Dec	Jan	Feb	Mar	Apr	May	Jun	Jul	Aug	Sep	Nov-Sep Average
1976	79.62	85.89	92.90	98.79	100.20	119.69	133.80	149.19	136.33	155.43	167.51	119.94
1977	178.67	207.97	220.21	243.23	303.47	323.12	287.16	248.40	223.34	202.49	204.13	240.20
1978	142.10	149.59	166.11	151.15	135.71	137.31	148.86	157.60	126.39	139.83	158.59	146.66
1979	129.62	123.19	125.49	125.79	137.38	147.78	158.04	195.30	207.67	206.14	219.74	161.47
1980	191.22	180.67	178.94	183.80	198.62	196.18	205.23	192.83	162.21	139.16	128.78	177.97
1981	124.55	125.97	133.35	130.18	125.47	125.54	121.27	98.38	108.16	114.00	114.62	120.13
1982	128.05	126.85	127.58	130.21	126.09	120.46	120.57	129.08	124.38	131.14	139.02	127.58
1983	123.18	121.31	119.06	117.96	120.76	121.98	126.10	126.29	127.69	128.95	134.44	124.34
1984	133.11	134.87	132.70	132.06	135.69	142.06	147.33	143.86	141.41	146.05	143.45	139.33
1985	133.86	134.78	139.22	141.03	142.77	142.75	145.46	145.72	136.80	134.94	134.46	139.25

	Nov	Dec	Jan	Feb	Mar	Apr	May	Jun	Jul	Aug	Sep
AVERAGE MOVE											
All Years		2.71	4.44	1.87	7.20	5.07	1.70	-0.72	-9.23	0.37	4.66
Less Extremes		1.05	3.77	1.32	3.40	4.58	4.85	-0.71	-9.18	0.96	4.78
Ave Up - All Years		7.86	7.23	6.42	13.75	8.40	7.15	11.72	7.85	8.51	8.58
Ave Down - All Years		-5.01	-2.05	-4.97	-8.09	-2.70	-20.11	-19.38	-16.55	-11.82	-4.49
COUNT											
Number Up		6	7	6	7	7	8	6	3	6	7
Number Down		4	3	4	3	3	2	4	7	4	3
Pct Up		60.0%	70.0%	60.0%	70.0%	70.0%	80.0%	60.0%	30.0%	60.0%	70.0%
Pct Down		40.0%	30.0%	40.0%	30.0%	30.0%	20.0%	40.0%	70.0%	40.0%	30.0%
EXTREMES											
Greatest Up		29.30	16.52	23.03	60.24	19.65	14.11	37.26	12.37	19.10	18.76
Greatest Down		-10.54	-2.25	-14.96	-15.44	-5.63	-35.96	-38.76	-31.22	-23.04	-10.38
SEASONAL INDEX : AVERAGE PERCENTAGE METHOD											
All Years	92.0	93.3	96.3	96.9	99.9	103.1	105.3	105.7	100.3	101.8	105.3
Less Extremes	93.3	94.6	96.5	97.9	98.7	100.6	104.9	106.4	98.5	101.3	105.2
SEASONAL INDEX : LINK RELATIVE METHOD											
All Years		96.4	98.4	98.3	100.4	102.7	104.3	103.9	97.7	98.0	99.8
Less Extremes		97.1	98.9	99.0	100.3	101.8	104.0	103.3	97.4	98.1	100.1

COFFEE - SEPTEMBER - MONTH OF HIGH AND LOW

Year of Expiration	Nov	Dec	Jan	Feb	Mar	Apr	May	Jun	Jul	Aug	Sep
1976	L										H
1977	L					H					
1978			H						L		
1979		L									H
1980							H				L
1981			H					L			
1982						L					H
1983				L							H
1984				L			H				
1985	L							H			

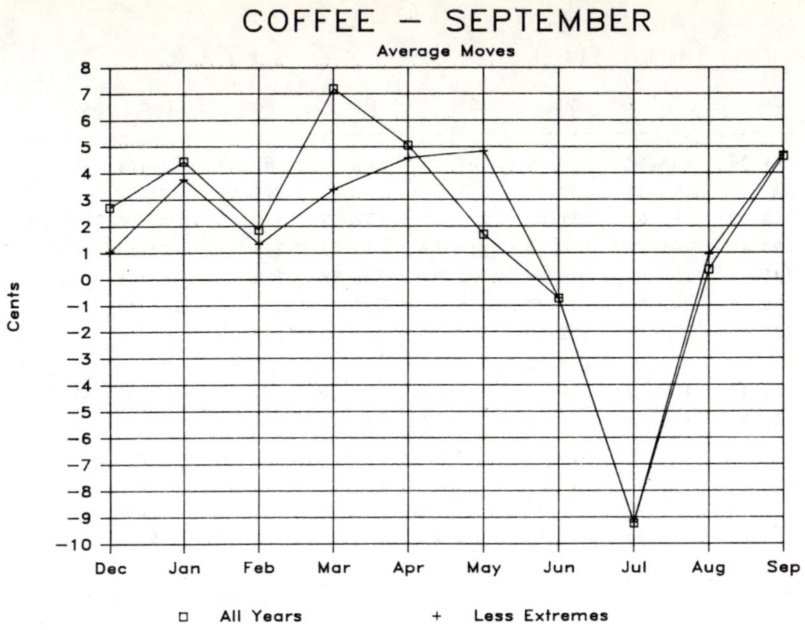
COFFEE — SEPTEMBER
Average Moves
8
7
6
5
4
3
2
1
0
−1
−2
−3
−4
−5
−6
−7
−8
−9
−10
Cents
Dec
Jan
Feb
Mar
Apr
May
Jun
Jul
Aug
Sep
All Years
Less Extremes

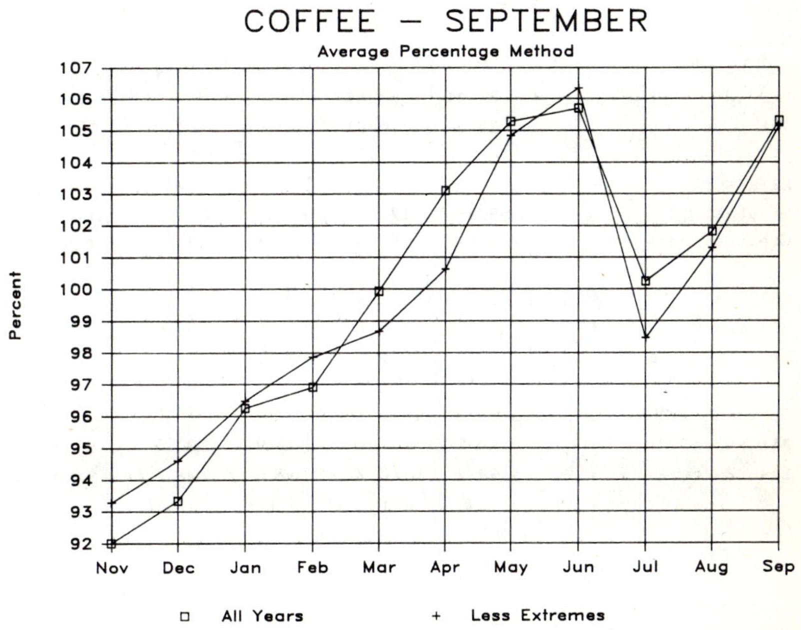
COFFEE — SEPTEMBER
Average Percentage Method
107
106
105
104
103
102
101
100
99
98
97
96
95
94
93
92
Percent
Nov
Dec
Jan
Feb
Mar
Apr
May
Jun
Jul
Aug
Sep
All Years
Less Extremes

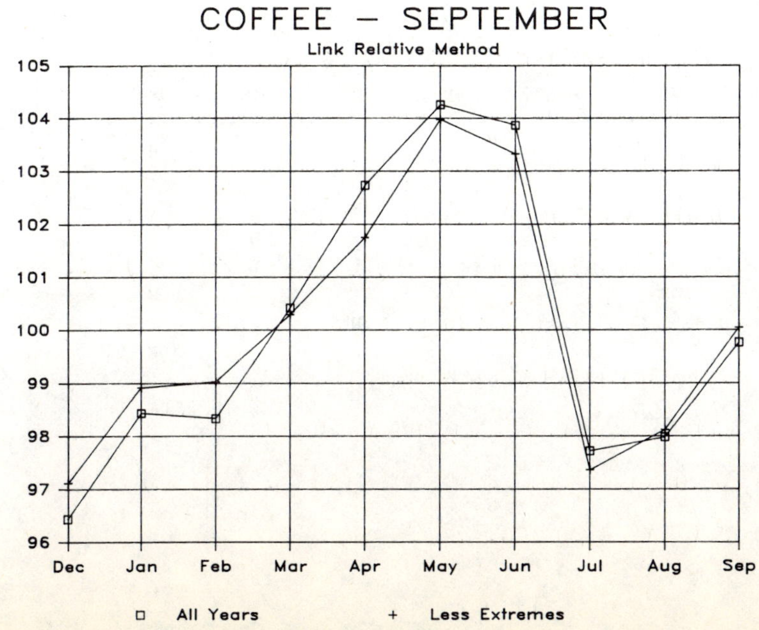
COFFEE — SEPTEMBER
Link Relative Method
105
104
103
102
101
100
99
98
97
96
Dec
Jan
Feb
Mar
Apr
May
Jun
Jul
Aug
Sep
All Years
Less Extremes

COFFEE - DECEMBER - MONTHLY AVERAGE PRICE

Year of Expiration	Feb	Mar	Apr	May	Jun	Jul	Aug	Sep	Oct	Nov	Dec	Feb-Dec Average
1976	98.37	99.62	116.68	129.18	144.36	133.53	145.90	157.09	173.61	182.48	202.76	143.96
1977	240.03	299.97	317.33	279.68	230.91	196.36	188.19	177.61	161.26	201.64	228.32	229.21
1978	137.57	123.96	124.21	137.78	148.30	117.69	131.03	149.24	152.82	146.43	135.96	136.82
1979	125.26	137.39	147.77	155.43	192.93	204.57	196.14	211.72	213.73	216.47	213.45	183.17
1980	182.06	191.37	189.47	198.33	191.54	165.27	146.96	132.97	128.59	113.22	115.16	159.54
1981	129.53	124.23	122.98	119.77	95.96	102.66	110.35	116.46	135.00	144.69	145.84	122.50
1982	126.26	122.77	117.74	117.02	123.52	116.87	123.13	134.28	140.98	137.75	134.35	126.79
1983	115.32	118.45	120.81	124.60	125.82	126.20	128.51	132.15	142.14	147.63	153.43	130.46
1984	129.56	132.69	138.74	145.37	143.16	138.52	143.07	139.77	135.60	140.72	142.35	139.05
1985	139.82	141.93	141.96	144.81	146.31	138.58	137.99	137.13	145.14	158.73	184.35	146.98

	Feb	Mar	Apr	May	Jun	Jul	Aug	Sep	Oct	Nov	Dec
AVERAGE MOVE											
All Years		6.86	4.53	1.43	-0.92	-10.26	1.10	3.71	4.05	6.09	6.62
Less Extremes		2.78	4.12	4.79	0.27	-9.96	2.00	4.11	4.78	4.48	6.25
Ave Up - All Years		13.00	7.64	7.98	12.07	6.24	7.75	10.98	9.34	12.27	11.87
Ave Down - All Years		-7.47	-2.73	-13.86	-20.40	-17.33	-8.87	-7.19	-8.30	-8.33	-5.63
COUNT											
Number Up		7	7	7	6	3	6	6	7	7	7
Number Down		3	3	3	4	7	4	4	3	3	3
Pct Up		70.0%	70.0%	70.0%	60.0%	30.0%	60.0%	60.0%	70.0%	70.0%	70.0%
Pct Down		30.0%	30.0%	30.0%	40.0%	70.0%	40.0%	40.0%	30.0%	30.0%	30.0%
EXTREMES											
Greatest Up		59.93	17.36	13.57	37.50	11.64	13.34	18.21	18.54	40.38	26.68
Greatest Down		-13.61	-5.03	-37.65	-48.77	-34.55	-18.30	-14.00	-16.35	-15.37	-10.47
SEASONAL INDEX : AVERAGE PERCENTAGE METHOD											
All Years	93.8	96.7	99.2	101.0	101.0	94.6	96.1	99.1	102.7	106.0	109.9
Less Extremes	94.5	95.8	96.6	100.1	101.4	93.9	96.5	99.7	104.4	107.8	110.7
SEASONAL INDEX : LINK RELATIVE METHOD											
All Years		99.9	101.6	102.9	102.5	95.3	95.8	97.3	99.2	101.5	103.9
Less Extremes		99.8	100.7	102.8	102.1	95.3	96.2	97.9	99.8	101.5	103.7

COFFEE - DECEMBER - MONTH OF HIGH AND LOW

Year of Expiration	Feb	Mar	Apr	May	Jun	Jul	Aug	Sep	Oct	Nov	Dec
1976	L										H
1977			H						L		
1978						L			H		
1979	L									H	
1980				H						L	
1981						L					H
1982						L			H		
1983	L										H
1984	L			H							
1985								L			H

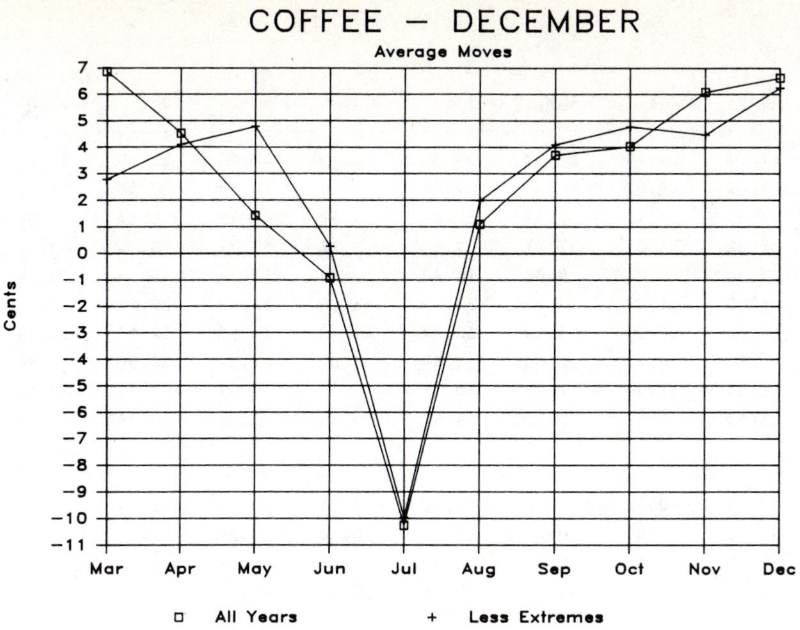
COFFEE – DECEMBER
Average Moves
Cents
7
6
5
4
3
2
1
0
–1
–2
–3
–4
–5
–6
–7
–8
–9
–10
–11
Mar
Apr
May
Jun
Jul
Aug
Sep
Oct
Nov
Dec
All Years
Less Extremes

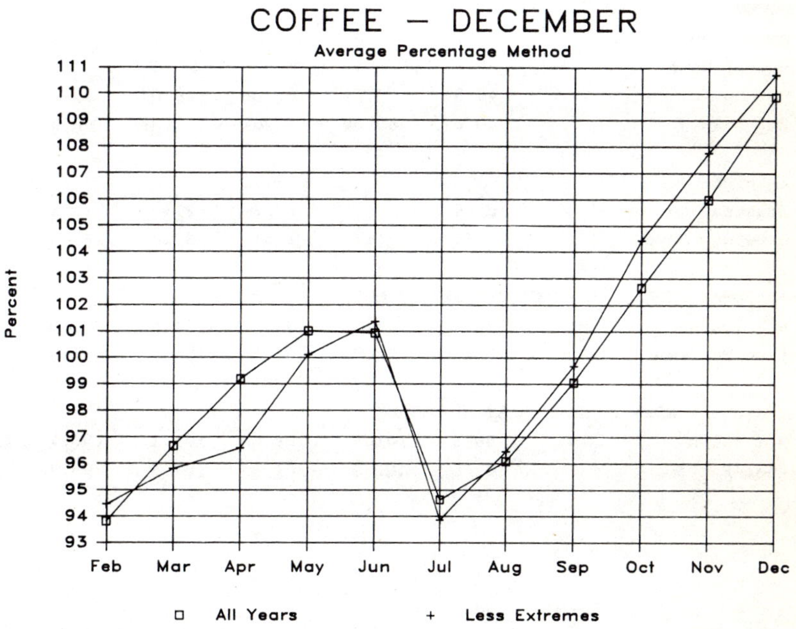
COFFEE – DECEMBER
Average Percentage Method
Percent
111
110
109
108
107
106
105
104
103
102
101
100
99
98
97
96
95
94
93
Feb
Mar
Apr
May
Jun
Jul
Aug
Sep
Oct
Nov
Dec
All Years
Less Extremes

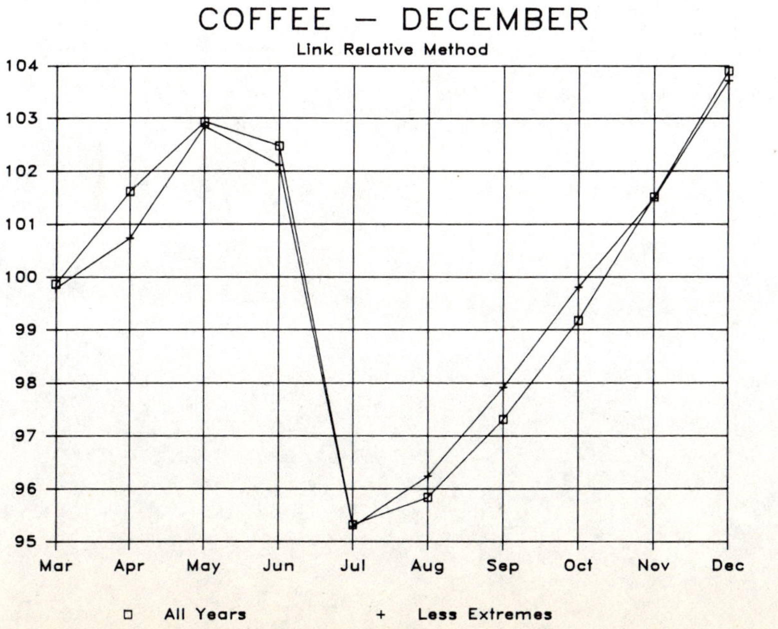
COFFEE – DECEMBER
Link Relative Method
104
103
102
101
100
99
98
97
96
95
Mar
Apr
May
Jun
Jul
Aug
Sep
Oct
Nov
Dec
All Years
Less Extremes

SUGAR - JANUARY - MONTHLY AVERAGE PRICE

Year of Expiration	Feb	Mar	Apr	May	Jun	Jul	Aug	Sep	Oct	Nov	Dec	Feb-Dec Average
1976	15.29	15.29	19.30	15.79	12.56	16.00	17.82	15.09	14.25	13.67	13.18	15.29
1977	13.58	14.43	13.94	14.56	13.83	14.03	11.75	9.14	8.18	8.08	7.50	11.73
1978	9.04	9.43	10.22	9.70	8.95	8.41	8.54	8.24	8.09	8.28	8.64	8.87
1979	10.06	9.11	8.71	8.25	7.92	6.87	7.43	8.61	9.11	8.31	8.14	8.41
1980	9.56	9.55	9.11	9.07	9.40	9.81	9.84	10.48	12.74	15.13	16.09	10.98
1981	25.28	24.73	24.80	33.64	36.10	31.28	34.29	37.09	42.18	38.91	29.64	32.54
1982	23.40	20.47	18.30	16.08	16.93	16.64	14.93	12.07	11.82	11.95	12.97	15.96
1983	14.03	12.32	10.82	9.22	8.14	8.72	7.84	6.90	6.37	7.03	6.50	8.90
1984	10.12	7.93	8.79	11.14	12.12	11.60	11.90	10.51	10.36	9.09	7.79	10.12
1985	8.57	8.61	8.08	6.93	6.63	5.37	4.91	4.90	5.34	5.04	3.88	6.20

AVERAGE MOVE	Feb	Mar	Apr	May	Jun	Jul	Aug	Sep	Oct	Nov	Dec
All Years		-0.70	0.02	0.23	-0.18	-0.38	0.05	-0.62	0.54	-0.29	-1.12
Less Extremes		-0.62	-0.21	-0.38	-0.13	-0.31	-0.03	-0.77	0.16	-0.26	-0.36
Ave Up - All Years		0.32	1.43	3.94	1.16	1.16	0.98	1.54	2.07	0.84	0.78
Ave Down - All Years		-1.39	-0.92	-1.36	-1.07	-1.41	-1.33	-1.55	-0.48	-1.05	-1.93

COUNT	Feb	Mar	Apr	May	Jun	Jul	Aug	Sep	Oct	Nov	Dec
Number Up		4	4	3	4	4	6	3	4	4	3
Number Down		6	6	7	6	6	4	7	6	6	7
Pct Up		40.0%	40.0%	30.0%	40.0%	40.0%	60.0%	30.0%	40.0%	40.0%	30.0%
Pct Down		60.0%	60.0%	70.0%	60.0%	60.0%	40.0%	70.0%	60.0%	60.0%	70.0%

EXTREMES	Feb	Mar	Apr	May	Jun	Jul	Aug	Sep	Oct	Nov	Dec
Greatest Up		0.85	4.01	8.84	2.47	3.45	3.01	2.80	5.09	2.39	1.03
Greatest Down		-2.93	-2.17	-3.51	-3.23	-4.83	-2.28	-2.86	-0.96	-3.27	-9.28

SEASONAL INDEX : AVERAGE PERCENTAGE METHOD	Feb	Mar	Apr	May	Jun	Jul	Aug	Sep	Oct	Nov	Dec
All Years	114.4	108.5	107.6	104.7	101.6	99.0	97.5	91.7	94.2	93.3	87.6
Less Extremes	113.6	108.7	108.7	105.0	101.7	98.5	97.3	91.0	92.8	90.8	83.3

SEASONAL INDEX : LINK RELATIVE METHOD	Feb	Mar	Apr	May	Jun	Jul	Aug	Sep	Oct	Nov	Dec
All Years		99.8	101.6	102.6	101.1	100.7	100.9	96.8	100.1	100.8	95.8
Less Extremes		101.6	102.2	101.5	101.3	99.9	100.9	96.8	99.8	100.0	96.0

SUGAR - JANUARY - MONTH OF HIGH AND LOW

Year of Expiration	Feb	Mar	Apr	May	Jun	Jul	Aug	Sep	Oct	Nov	Dec
1976			H		L						
1977				H							L
1978			H						L		
1979	H					L					
1980				L							H
1981		L							H		
1982	H								L		
1983	H								L		
1984					H						L
1985		H									L

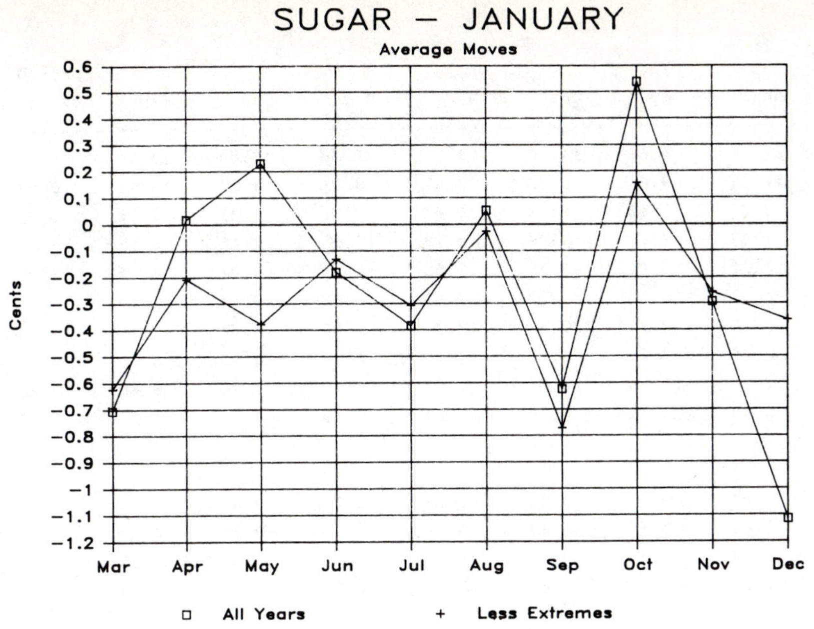
SUGAR — JANUARY
Average Moves
Cents
0.6
0.5
0.4
0.3
0.2
0.1
0
-0.1
-0.2
-0.3
-0.4
-0.5
-0.6
-0.7
-0.8
-0.9
-1
-1.1
-1.2
Mar
Apr
May
Jun
Jul
Aug
Sep
Oct
Nov
Dec
All Years
Less Extremes

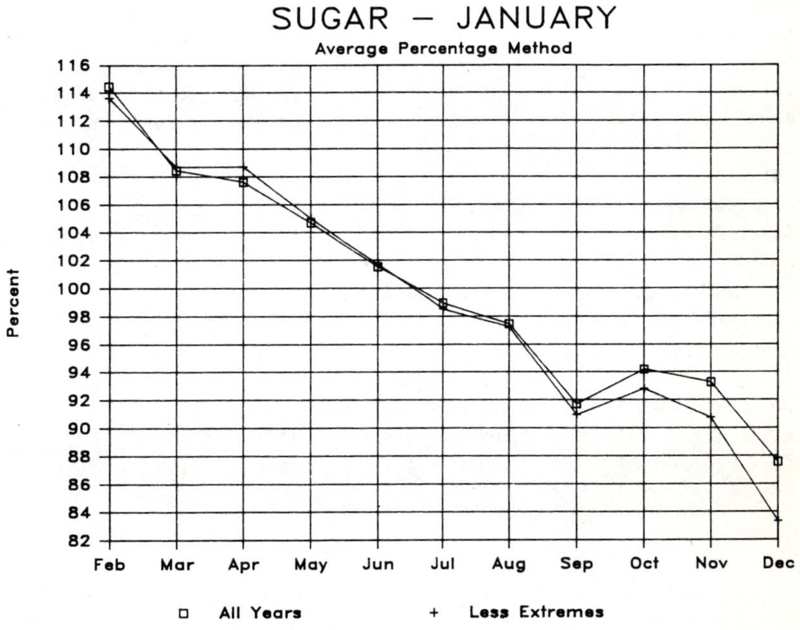
SUGAR — JANUARY
Average Percentage Method
Percent
116
114
112
110
108
106
104
102
100
98
96
94
92
90
88
86
84
82
Feb
Mar
Apr
May
Jun
Jul
Aug
Sep
Oct
Nov
Dec
All Years
Less Extremes

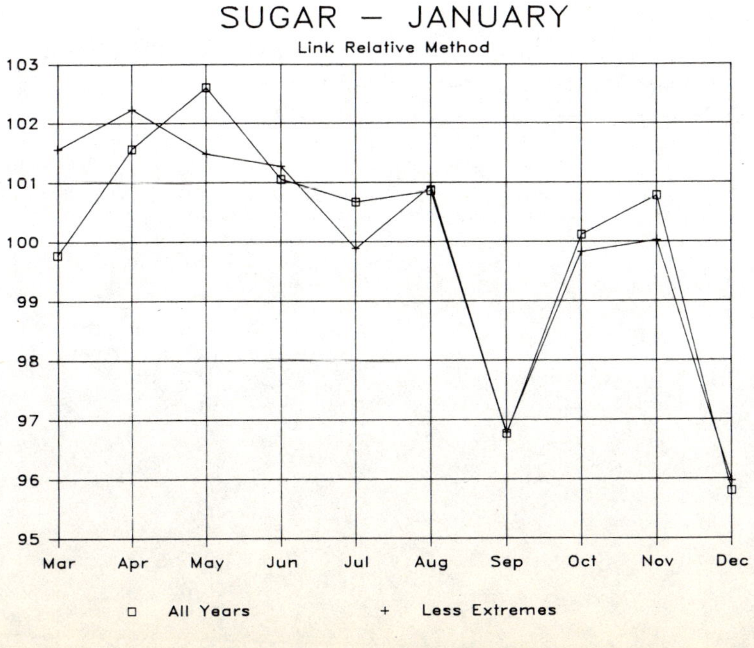
SUGAR — JANUARY
Link Relative Method
103
102
101
100
99
98
97
96
95
Mar
Apr
May
Jun
Jul
Aug
Sep
Oct
Nov
Dec
All Years
Less Extremes

SUGAR - MARCH - MONTHLY AVERAGE PRICE

Year of Expiration	Apr	May	Jun	Jul	Aug	Sep	Oct	Nov	Dec	Jan	Feb	Apr-Feb Average
1976	19.09	15.79	12.56	15.72	17.39	14.83	14.16	13.70	13.28	13.89	13.51	14.90
1977	13.87	14.49	13.88	14.21	12.12	9.49	8.69	8.61	8.11	8.53	8.60	10.97
1978	10.22	9.71	9.08	8.55	8.71	8.58	8.54	8.82	9.31	9.37	8.84	9.07
1979	9.13	8.63	8.20	7.12	7.67	8.78	9.36	8.78	8.61	8.18	8.37	8.44
1980	9.48	9.46	9.75	10.21	10.39	10.98	13.17	15.50	16.31	18.01	23.25	13.32
1981	25.57	33.92	36.89	32.29	34.83	38.33	43.53	39.81	30.53	29.44	25.40	33.69
1982	18.42	16.42	17.17	16.86	15.23	12.75	12.45	12.35	13.26	13.34	13.34	14.69
1983	11.38	9.88	8.71	9.33	8.40	7.49	7.08	7.75	7.18	6.40	6.65	8.20
1984	9.25	11.54	12.47	12.06	12.46	11.16	10.82	9.55	8.72	7.70	6.86	10.23
1985	8.58	7.51	7.22	5.96	5.46	5.48	5.87	5.57	4.59	4.36	4.03	5.88

	May	Jun	Jul	Aug	Sep	Oct	Nov	Dec	Jan	Feb
AVERAGE MOVE										
All Years	0.24	-0.14	-0.36	0.04	-0.48	0.58	-0.32	-1.05	-0.07	-0.03
Less Extremes	-0.33	-0.15	-0.27	-0.01	-0.71	0.17	-0.23	-0.27	-0.16	-0.19
Ave Up - All Years	3.76	1.23	1.15	0.92	1.30	2.09	1.09	0.74	0.57	1.15
Ave Down - All Years	-1.27	-1.06	-1.36	-1.29	-1.67	-0.43	-0.93	-1.82	-0.71	-1.22
COUNT										
Number Up	3	4	4	6	4	4	3	3	5	5
Number Down	7	6	6	4	6	6	7	7	5	5
Pct Up	30.0%	40.0%	40.0%	60.0%	40.0%	40.0%	30.0%	30.0%	50.0%	50.0%
Pct Down	70.0%	60.0%	60.0%	40.0%	60.0%	60.0%	70.0%	70.0%	50.0%	50.0%
EXTREMES										
Greatest Up	8.35	2.97	3.16	2.55	3.50	5.20	2.33	0.91	1.70	5.25
Greatest Down	-3.30	-3.23	-4.61	-2.09	-2.63	-0.80	-3.73	-9.28	-1.09	-4.03

SEASONAL INDEX : AVERAGE PERCENTAGE METHOD

	Apr	May	Jun	Jul	Aug	Sep	Oct	Nov	Dec	Jan	Feb
All Years	112.3	109.2	105.9	103.4	101.6	96.1	98.4	97.3	92.2	91.2	92.3
Less Extremes	113.2	111.1	107.4	103.5	102.1	95.6	97.0	97.0	90.7	87.8	85.2

SEASONAL INDEX : LINK RELATIVE METHOD

	May	Jun	Jul	Aug	Sep	Oct	Nov	Dec	Jan	Feb
All Years	102.4	100.9	100.7	101.0	97.7	101.2	101.8	98.0	97.8	98.6
Less Extremes	102.1	101.7	100.4	101.3	98.1	101.1	101.1	98.4	98.3	97.4

SUGAR - MARCH - MONTH OF HIGH AND LOW

Year of Expiration	Apr	May	Jun	Jul	Aug	Sep	Oct	Nov	Dec	Jan	Feb
1976	H		L								
1977		H							L		
1978	H							L			
1979				L			H				
1980		L									H
1981							H				L
1982	H							L			
1983	H									L	
1984			H								L
1985	H										L

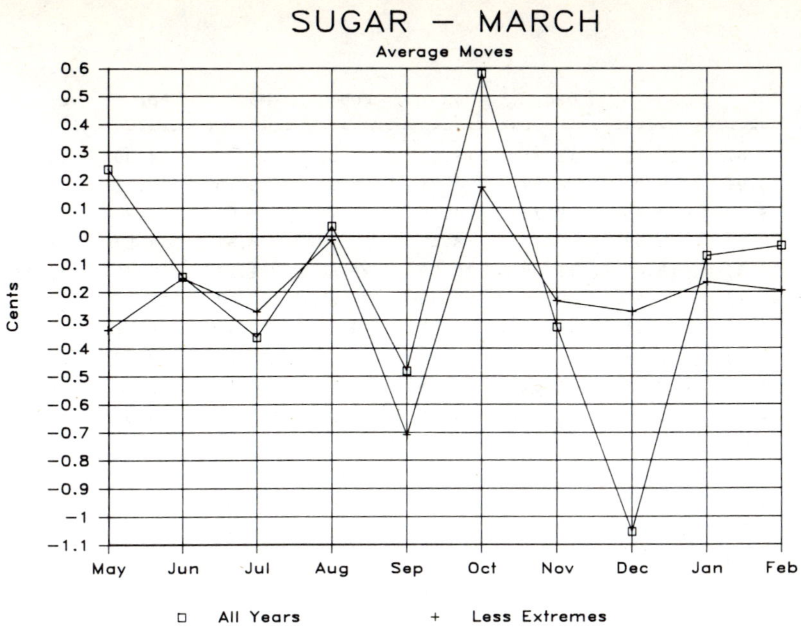
SUGAR – MARCH
Average Moves
Cents
0.6
0.5
0.4
0.3
0.2
0.1
0
−0.1
−0.2
−0.3
−0.4
−0.5
−0.6
−0.7
−0.8
−0.9
−1
−1.1
May
Jun
Jul
Aug
Sep
Oct
Nov
Dec
Jan
Feb
All Years
Less Extremes

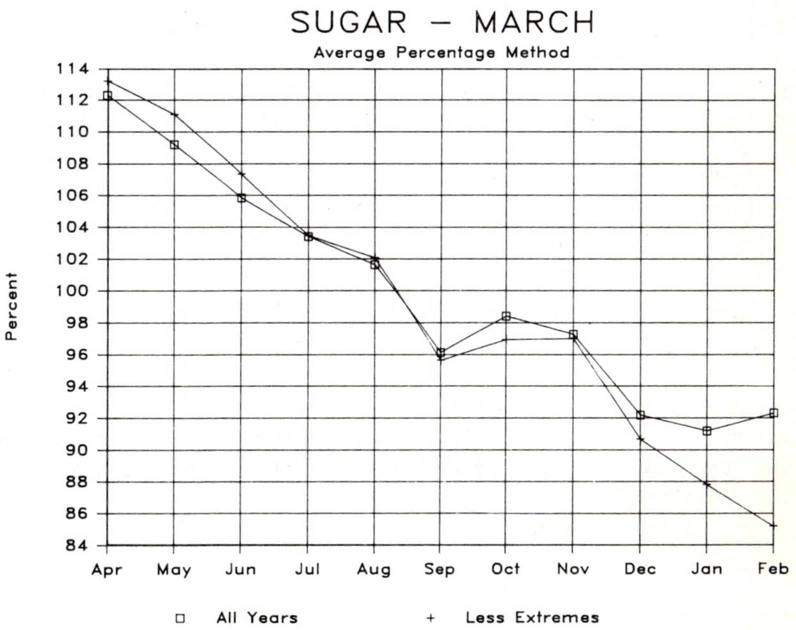
SUGAR – MARCH
Average Percentage Method
Percent
114
112
110
108
106
104
102
100
98
96
94
92
90
88
86
84
Apr
May
Jun
Jul
Aug
Sep
Oct
Nov
Dec
Jan
Feb
All Years
Less Extremes

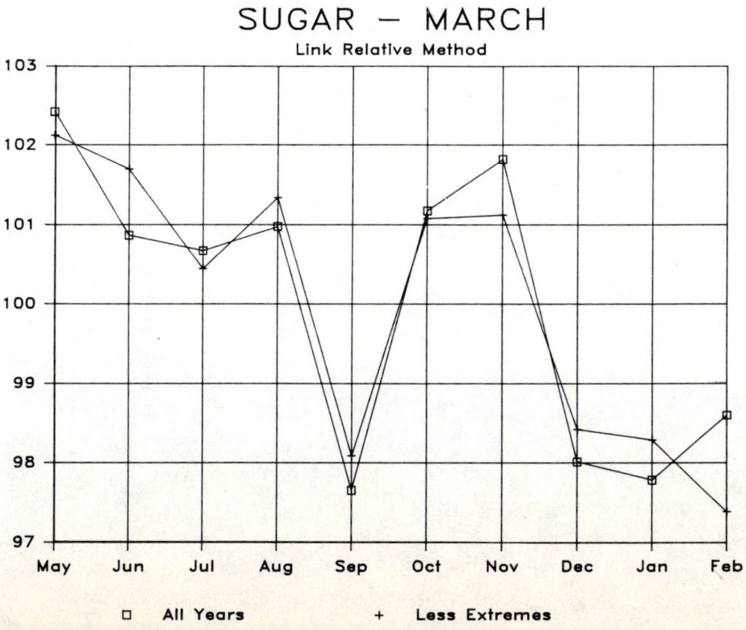
SUGAR – MARCH
Link Relative Method
103
102
101
100
99
98
97
May
Jun
Jul
Aug
Sep
Oct
Nov
Dec
Jan
Feb
All Years
Less Extremes

SUGAR - MAY - MONTHLY AVERAGE PRICE

Year of Expiration	Jun	Jul	Aug	Sep	Oct	Nov	Dec	Jan	Feb	Mar	Apr	Jun-Apr Average
1976	12.47	15.68	17.14	14.67	14.07	13.71	13.31	13.87	13.57	14.71	14.00	14.29
1977	13.89	14.20	12.36	9.74	8.96	8.83	8.52	8.84	8.86	9.10	10.11	10.31
1978	9.17	8.73	8.86	8.98	9.00	9.25	9.74	9.74	9.19	8.03	7.73	8.95
1979	8.39	7.29	7.83	8.97	9.52	8.97	8.83	8.42	8.77	8.61	7.94	8.50
1980	9.96	10.44	10.67	11.25	13.34	15.47	16.29	18.09	24.60	21.13	22.36	15.78
1981	36.20	31.85	34.05	37.98	43.12	40.32	30.69	29.55	25.88	22.18	17.85	31.79
1982	17.32	17.06	15.45	13.08	12.75	12.61	13.39	13.52	13.43	11.47	9.78	13.62
1983	8.95	9.58	8.66	7.81	7.36	8.04	7.49	6.77	6.85	6.62	7.33	7.77
1984	12.66	12.30	12.74	11.50	11.18	9.85	9.04	8.04	7.22	6.96	6.18	9.79
1985	7.50	6.26	5.75	5.82	6.20	5.90	4.92	4.72	4.27	3.99	3.57	5.35

	Jun	Jul	Aug	Sep	Oct	Nov	Dec	Jan	Feb	Mar	Apr
AVERAGE MOVE											
All Years		-0.31	0.01	-0.37	0.57	-0.25	-1.07	-0.07	0.11	-0.98	-0.60
Less Extremes		-0.25	-0.03	-0.62	0.17	-0.23	-0.24	-0.17	-0.22	-0.91	-0.36
Ave Up - All Years		1.16	0.83	1.17	1.63	1.02	0.69	0.70	1.74	0.69	0.98
Ave Down - All Years		-1.29	-1.22	-1.91	-0.50	-0.80	-1.83	-0.58	-0.98	-1.40	-1.27
COUNT											
Number Up		4	6	5	5	3	3	4	4	2	3
Number Down		6	4	5	5	7	7	6	6	8	7
Pct Up		40.0%	60.0%	50.0%	50.0%	30.0%	30.0%	40.0%	40.0%	20.0%	30.0%
Pct Down		60.0%	40.0%	50.0%	50.0%	70.0%	70.0%	60.0%	60.0%	80.0%	70.0%
EXTREMES											
Greatest Up		3.21	2.19	3.93	5.14	2.14	0.81	1.80	6.51	1.14	1.23
Greatest Down		-4.35	-1.84	-2.62	-0.78	-2.80	-9.63	-1.14	-3.67	-3.70	-4.33
SEASONAL INDEX : AVERAGE PERCENTAGE METHOD											
All Years	111.2	108.8	106.8	101.7	103.6	102.2	96.7	95.5	96.4	90.1	86.9
Less Extremes	113.6	110.5	108.8	103.2	102.0	101.2	97.0	94.8	91.8	87.2	84.0
SEASONAL INDEX : LINK RELATIVE METHOD											
All Years		99.8	100.5	98.5	102.3	103.4	100.2	100.5	102.3	97.8	94.9
Less Extremes		99.6	100.9	99.1	102.5	103.3	101.6	101.9	101.1	96.2	93.7

SUGAR - MAY - MONTH OF HIGH AND LOW

Year of Expiration	Jun	Jul	Aug	Sep	Oct	Nov	Dec	Jan	Feb	Mar	Apr
1976	L		H								
1977		H					L				
1978							H				L
1979		L			H						
1980	L								H		
1981					H						L
1982	H										L
1983		H								L	
1984			H								L
1985	H										L

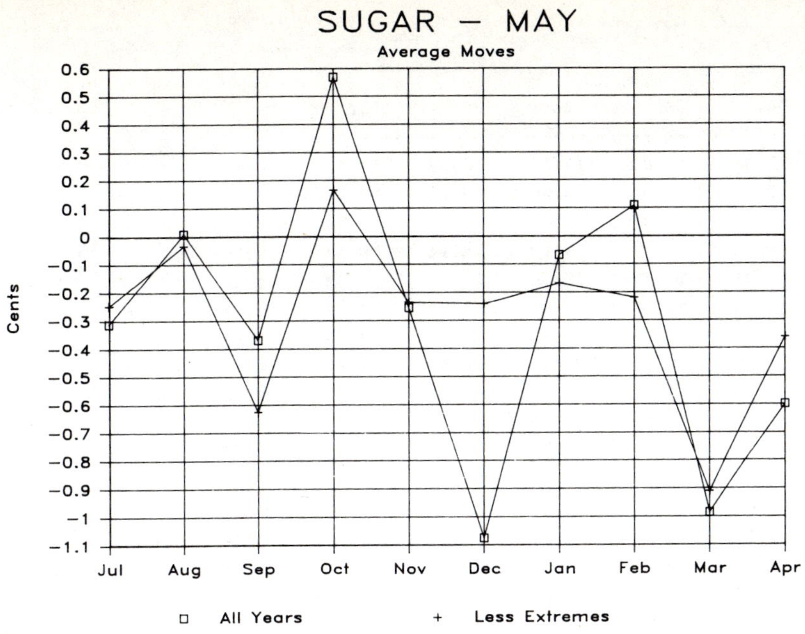
SUGAR — MAY
Average Moves
Cents
0.6
0.5
0.4
0.3
0.2
0.1
0
−0.1
−0.2
−0.3
−0.4
−0.5
−0.6
−0.7
−0.8
−0.9
−1
−1.1
Jul
Aug
Sep
Oct
Nov
Dec
Jan
Feb
Mar
Apr
□ All Years
+ Less Extremes

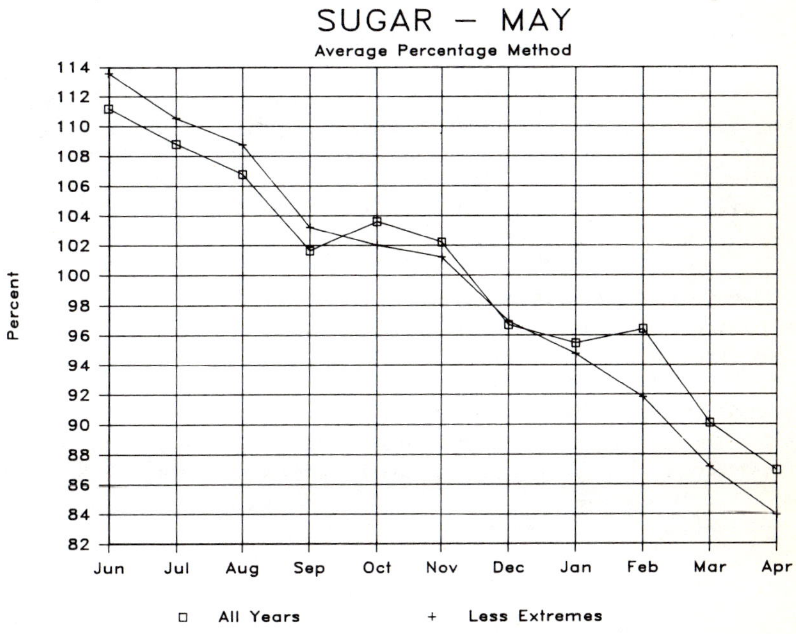
SUGAR — MAY
Average Percentage Method
Percent
114
112
110
108
106
104
102
100
98
96
94
92
90
88
86
84
82
Jun
Jul
Aug
Sep
Oct
Nov
Dec
Jan
Feb
Mar
Apr
□ All Years
+ Less Extremes

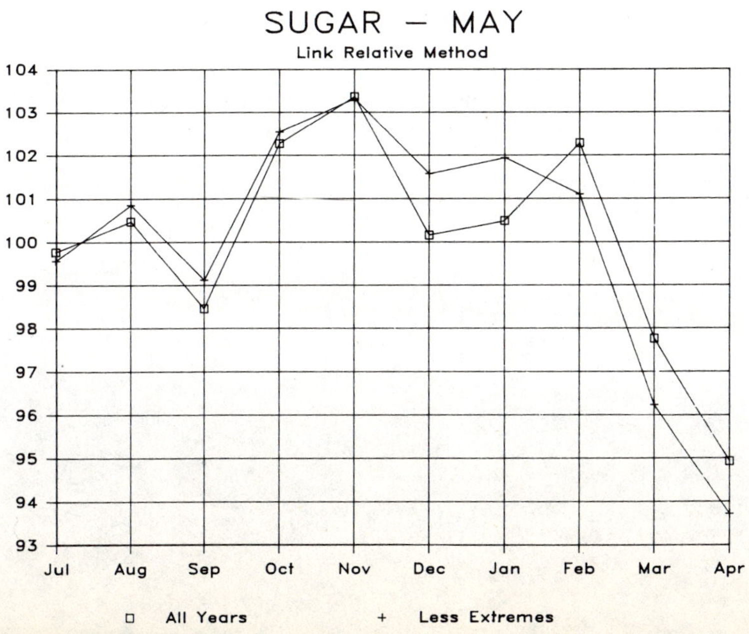
SUGAR — MAY
Link Relative Method
104
103
102
101
100
99
98
97
96
95
94
93
Jul
Aug
Sep
Oct
Nov
Dec
Jan
Feb
Mar
Apr
□ All Years
+ Less Extremes

SUGAR - JULY - MONTHLY AVERAGE PRICE

Year of Expiration	Aug	Sep	Oct	Nov	Dec	Jan	Feb	Mar	Apr	May	Jun	Aug-Jun Average
1976	16.92	14.56	14.03	13.71	13.34	13.84	13.59	14.64	14.13	14.45	12.94	14.20
1977	12.51	9.98	9.14	8.99	8.81	8.96	8.88	9.19	10.17	9.22	8.12	9.45
1978	9.00	9.28	9.38	9.56	9.96	9.92	9.40	8.36	8.00	7.44	7.16	8.86
1979	8.02	9.18	9.67	9.17	9.06	8.66	9.03	8.94	8.33	8.09	8.31	8.77
1980	10.96	11.52	13.53	15.42	16.26	18.17	25.26	22.56	23.22	32.45	32.64	20.18
1981	33.03	37.18	41.78	39.61	30.56	29.57	26.09	22.20	18.13	15.47	16.46	28.19
1982	15.68	13.36	13.03	12.86	13.58	13.71	13.55	11.70	10.00	8.39	7.06	12.08
1983	8.88	8.06	7.61	8.24	7.71	7.11	7.18	6.90	7.67	9.93	10.94	8.20
1984	12.96	11.77	11.48	10.15	9.35	8.35	7.57	7.40	6.69	5.81	5.53	8.82
1985	6.04	6.13	6.48	6.19	5.22	5.09	4.62	4.21	3.77	3.11	2.81	4.88

	Aug	Sep	Oct	Nov	Dec	Jan	Feb	Mar	Apr	May	Jun
AVERAGE MOVE											
All Years		-0.30	0.51	-0.22	-1.01	-0.05	0.18	-0.91	-0.60	0.42	-0.24
Less Extremes		-0.57	0.17	-0.24	-0.23	-0.17	-0.23	-0.78	-0.36	-0.29	-0.24
Ave Up - All Years		1.25	1.51	0.90	0.65	0.68	2.52	0.68	0.81	3.93	0.60
Ave Down - All Years		-1.84	-0.49	-0.70	-1.72	-0.53	-0.82	-1.31	-1.20	-1.08	-0.80
COUNT											
Number Up		5	5	3	3	4	3	2	3	3	4
Number Down		5	5	7	7	6	7	8	7	7	6
Pct Up		50.0%	50.0%	30.0%	30.0%	40.0%	30.0%	20.0%	30.0%	30.0%	40.0%
Pct Down		50.0%	50.0%	70.0%	70.0%	60.0%	70.0%	80.0%	70.0%	70.0%	60.0%
EXTREMES											
Greatest Up		4.15	4.60	1.88	0.84	1.91	7.09	1.05	0.98	9.23	1.00
Greatest Down		-2.53	-0.84	-2.17	-9.05	-1.00	-3.47	-3.89	-4.07	-2.66	-1.51
SEASONAL INDEX : AVERAGE PERCENTAGE METHOD											
All Years	112.5	107.4	109.0	107.0	101.1	99.7	99.7	93.8	90.1	91.1	88.5
Less Extremes	115.4	110.5	109.4	106.6	102.3	99.6	98.2	93.5	90.2	87.0	83.2
SEASONAL INDEX : LINK RELATIVE METHOD											
All Years		99.5	103.0	103.9	100.9	101.4	103.4	99.3	96.5	97.1	95.0
Less Extremes		99.6	103.1	104.1	102.9	103.6	103.0	98.9	96.6	94.9	93.2

SUGAR - JULY - MONTH OF HIGH AND LOW

Year of Expiration	Aug	Sep	Oct	Nov	Dec	Jan	Feb	Mar	Apr	May	Jun
1976	H										L
1977	H										L
1978						H					L
1979			H							L	
1980	L										H
1981			H							L	
1982	H										L
1983								L			H
1984	H										L
1985			H								L

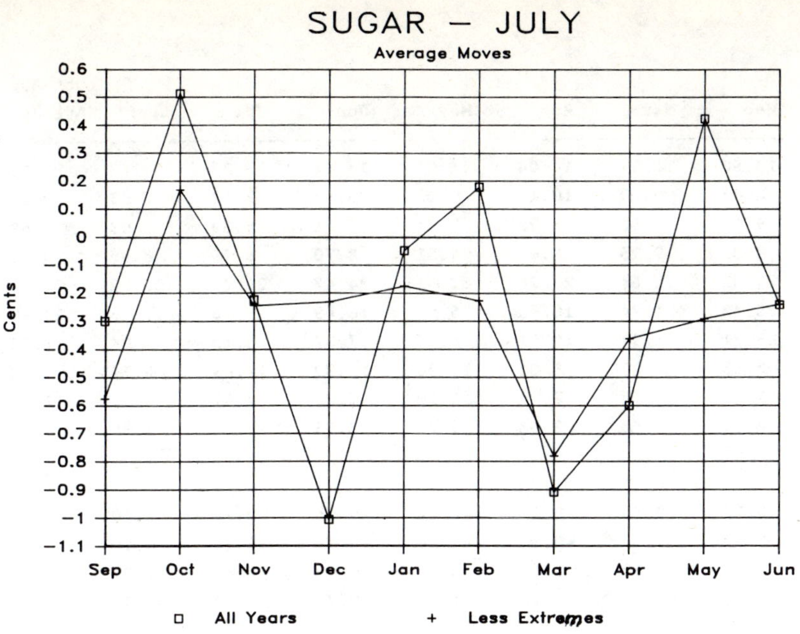
SUGAR – JULY
Average Moves
Cents
0.6
0.5
0.4
0.3
0.2
0.1
0
-0.1
-0.2
-0.3
-0.4
-0.5
-0.6
-0.7
-0.8
-0.9
-1
-1.1
Sep
Oct
Nov
Dec
Jan
Feb
Mar
Apr
May
Jun
All Years
Less Extremes

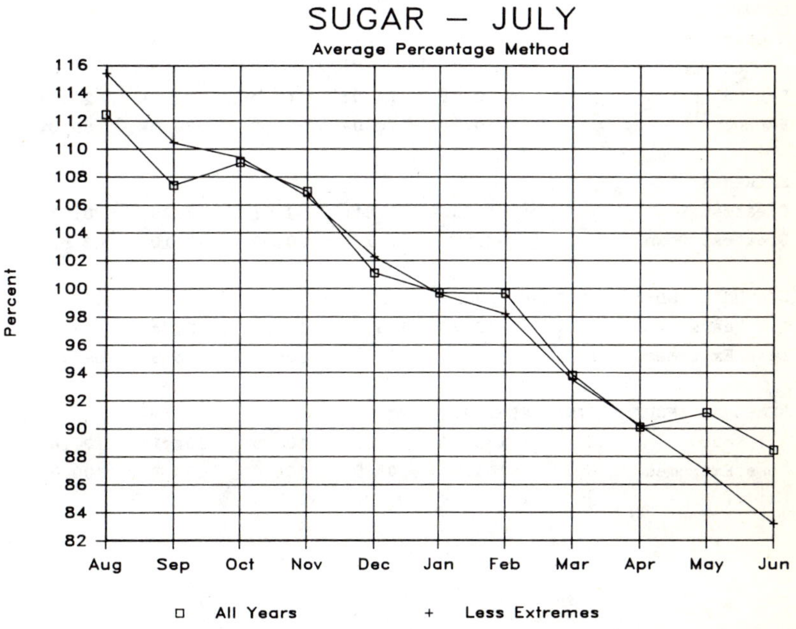
SUGAR – JULY
Average Percentage Method
Percent
116
114
112
110
108
106
104
102
100
98
96
94
92
90
88
86
84
82
Aug
Sep
Oct
Nov
Dec
Jan
Feb
Mar
Apr
May
Jun
All Years
Less Extremes

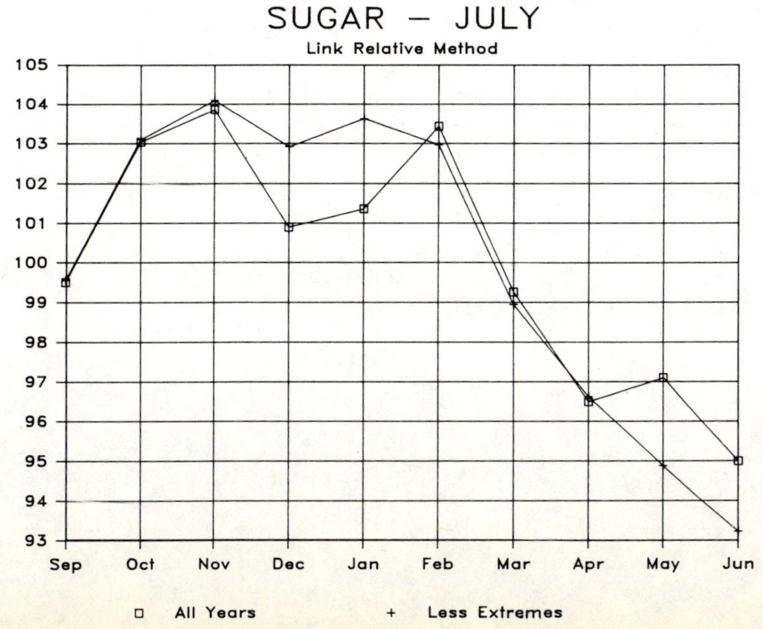
SUGAR – JULY
Link Relative Method
105
104
103
102
101
100
99
98
97
96
95
94
93
Sep
Oct
Nov
Dec
Jan
Feb
Mar
Apr
May
Jun
All Years
Less Extremes

SUGAR - SEPTEMBER - MONTHLY AVERAGE PRICE

Year of Expiration	Oct	Nov	Dec	Jan	Feb	Mar	Apr	May	Jun	Jul	Aug	Oct-Aug Average
1976	13.98	13.72	13.36	13.84	13.60	14.54	14.04	14.61	13.41	13.37	10.43	13.54
1977	9.23	9.04	8.95	9.00	8.87	9.20	10.16	9.40	8.49	7.63	7.68	8.88
1978	9.63	9.80	10.15	10.10	9.58	8.60	8.22	7.71	7.31	6.39	7.03	8.59
1979	9.82	9.38	9.30	8.89	9.23	9.15	8.63	8.51	8.70	8.79	8.95	9.03
1980	13.77	15.41	16.22	18.23	25.51	23.54	23.78	32.61	34.47	29.25	32.72	24.14
1981	39.51	37.01	29.24	28.56	25.45	21.94	18.35	15.80	16.69	16.45	14.76	23.98
1982	13.28	13.12	13.79	13.91	13.71	11.94	10.31	8.66	7.37	8.13	7.04	11.02
1983	7.93	8.53	8.01	7.44	7.55	7.22	8.04	10.30	11.29	10.81	10.74	8.90
1984	11.70	10.38	9.57	8.59	7.83	7.74	7.12	6.12	5.81	4.67	4.14	7.61
1985	6.74	6.44	5.47	5.33	4.91	4.40	3.93	3.26	2.93	3.32	4.36	4.64

	Oct	Nov	Dec	Jan	Feb	Mar	Apr	May	Jun	Jul	Aug
AVERAGE MOVE											
All Years		-0.27	-0.88	-0.02	0.24	-0.80	-0.57	0.44	-0.05	-0.77	-0.10
Less Extremes		-0.24	-0.23	-0.15	-0.23	-0.68	-0.38	-0.24	-0.14	-0.40	-0.19
Ave Up - All Years		0.81	0.61	0.66	2.58	0.63	0.67	3.89	0.98	0.41	1.07
Ave Down - All Years		-0.74	-1.51	-0.47	-0.77	-1.15	-1.10	-1.04	-0.74	-1.27	-1.27
COUNT											
Number Up		3	3	4	3	2	3	3	4	3	5
Number Down		7	7	6	7	8	7	7	6	7	5
Pct Up		30.0%	30.0%	40.0%	30.0%	20.0%	30.0%	30.0%	40.0%	30.0%	50.0%
Pct Down		70.0%	70.0%	60.0%	70.0%	80.0%	70.0%	70.0%	60.0%	70.0%	50.0%
EXTREMES											
Greatest Up		1.65	0.81	2.01	7.28	0.93	0.96	8.83	1.86	0.76	3.47
Greatest Down		-2.50	-7.77	-0.98	-3.10	-3.51	-3.59	-2.55	-1.29	-5.22	-2.94
SEASONAL INDEX : AVERAGE PERCENTAGE METHOD											
All Years	115.8	112.9	106.9	105.2	104.4	98.7	94.7	94.4	92.2	87.4	87.5
Less Extremes	117.1	113.9	109.4	106.3	104.3	99.7	94.5	92.8	89.5	86.4	85.6
SEASONAL INDEX : LINK RELATIVE METHOD											
All Years		103.1	100.7	101.5	104.1	100.6	98.4	99.5	98.2	96.2	97.7
Less Extremes		103.7	103.0	104.0	103.8	100.5	98.6	97.7	97.0	95.4	96.4

SUGAR - SEPTEMBER - MONTH OF HIGH AND LOW

Year of Expiration	Oct	Nov	Dec	Jan	Feb	Mar	Apr	May	Jun	Jul	Aug
1976								H			L
1977							H			L	
1978			H							L	
1979	H							L			
1980	L								H		
1981	H										L
1982				H							L
1983						L			H		
1984	H										L
1985	H								L		

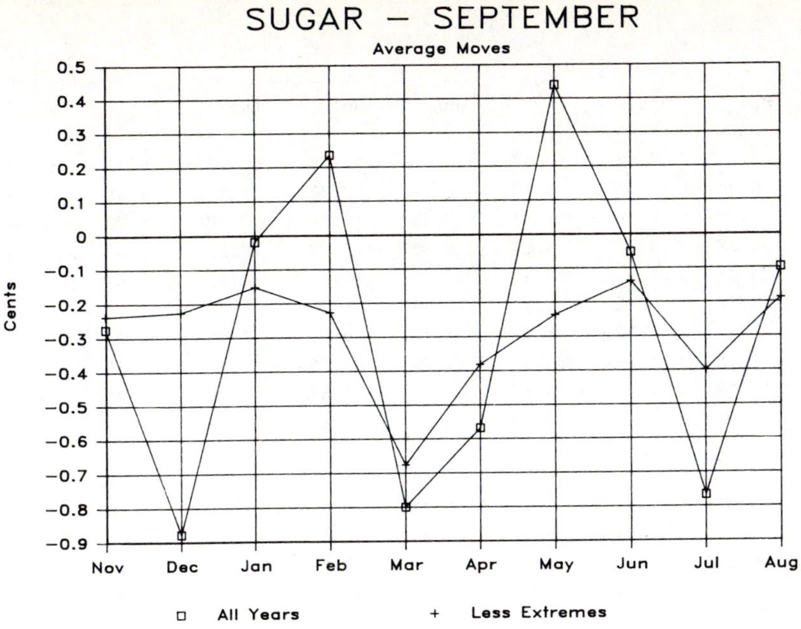
SUGAR — SEPTEMBER
Average Moves
Cents
0.5
0.4
0.3
0.2
0.1
0
−0.1
−0.2
−0.3
−0.4
−0.5
−0.6
−0.7
−0.8
−0.9
Nov
Dec
Jan
Feb
Mar
Apr
May
Jun
Jul
Aug
All Years
Less Extremes

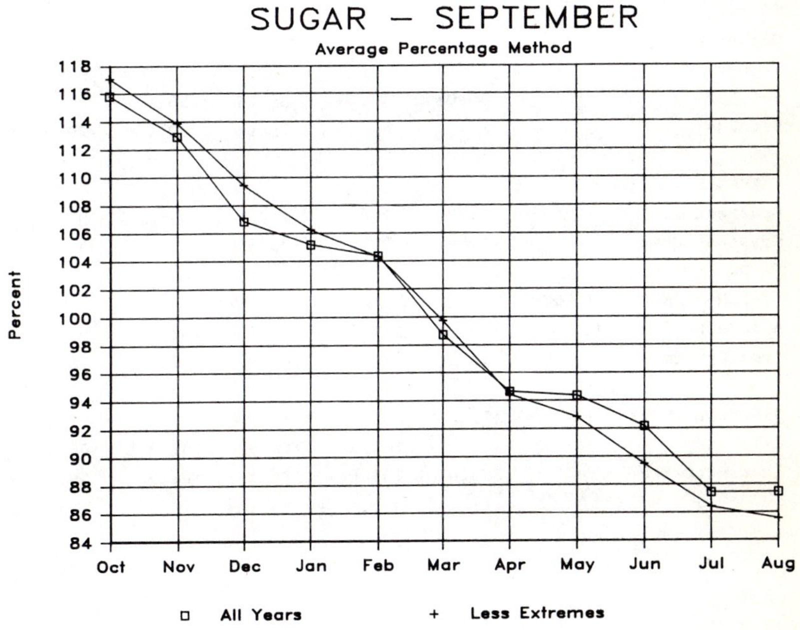
SUGAR — SEPTEMBER
Average Percentage Method
Percent
118
116
114
112
110
108
106
104
102
100
98
96
94
92
90
88
86
84
Oct
Nov
Dec
Jan
Feb
Mar
Apr
May
Jun
Jul
Aug
All Years
Less Extremes

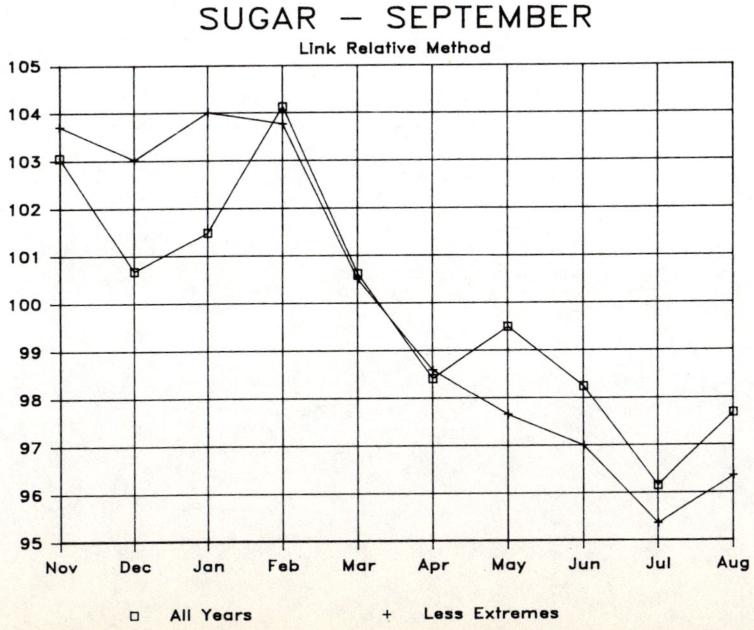
SUGAR — SEPTEMBER
Link Relative Method
105
104
103
102
101
100
99
98
97
96
95
Nov
Dec
Jan
Feb
Mar
Apr
May
Jun
Jul
Aug
All Years
Less Extremes

SUGAR - OCTOBER - MONTHLY AVERAGE PRICE

Year of Expiration	Nov	Dec	Jan	Feb	Mar	Apr	May	Jun	Jul	Aug	Sep	Nov-Sep Average
1976	13.72	13.37	13.84	13.59	14.51	14.03	14.67	13.66	13.75	10.90	8.42	13.13
1977	9.06	9.02	9.04	8.89	9.20	10.13	9.49	8.72	7.87	7.86	7.36	8.79
1978	9.92	10.27	10.22	9.69	8.72	8.34	7.83	7.43	6.50	7.10	8.22	8.57
1979	9.48	9.41	9.00	9.34	9.27	8.76	8.69	8.95	9.09	9.25	9.89	9.19
1980	15.43	16.20	18.22	25.50	24.01	24.09	32.97	35.26	30.32	33.42	35.81	26.47
1981	35.76	28.70	28.28	25.24	21.78	18.41	15.88	16.76	16.56	14.87	11.70	21.27
1982	13.31	14.00	14.10	13.87	12.11	10.52	8.85	7.48	8.30	7.25	6.22	10.55
1983	8.74	8.23	7.67	7.80	7.46	8.30	10.53	11.57	11.09	11.17	9.85	9.31
1984	10.56	9.74	8.76	8.01	7.98	7.37	6.35	6.05	4.87	4.38	4.21	7.12
1985	6.64	5.68	5.51	5.07	4.56	4.06	3.39	3.02	3.45	4.52	5.27	4.65

	Nov	Dec	Jan	Feb	Mar	Apr	May	Jun	Jul	Aug	Sep
AVERAGE MOVE											
All Years		-0.80	.00	0.23	-0.74	-0.56	0.46	0.02	-0.71	-0.11	-0.38
Less Extremes		-0.21	-0.13	-0.24	-0.61	-0.39	-0.22	-0.09	-0.37	-0.17	-0.37
Ave Up - All Years		0.60	0.65	2.58	0.61	0.62	3.91	1.12	0.37	1.00	1.23
Ave Down - All Years		-1.40	-0.43	-0.77	-1.08	-1.06	-1.02	-0.70	-1.43	-1.22	-1.44
COUNT											
Number Up		3	4	3	2	3	3	4	4	5	4
Number Down		7	6	7	8	7	7	6	6	5	6
Pct Up		30.0%	40.0%	30.0%	20.0%	30.0%	30.0%	40.0%	40.0%	50.0%	40.0%
Pct Down		70.0%	60.0%	70.0%	80.0%	70.0%	70.0%	60.0%	60.0%	50.0%	60.0%
EXTREMES											
Greatest Up		0.77	2.02	7.28	0.92	0.93	8.87	2.29	0.82	3.10	2.39
Greatest Down		-7.06	-0.98	-3.05	-3.46	-3.37	-2.53	-1.37	-4.94	-2.85	-3.17
SEASONAL INDEX : AVERAGE PERCENTAGE METHOD											
All Years	116.4	110.3	108.5	107.1	101.6	97.2	96.4	94.4	90.2	89.9	87.9
Less Extremes	117.2	113.1	110.3	107.0	102.6	96.3	95.8	93.3	89.3	89.0	86.1
SEASONAL INDEX : LINK RELATIVE METHOD											
All Years		101.5	102.2	104.6	101.3	98.9	100.0	98.9	97.1	98.6	96.8
Less Extremes		103.6	104.5	104.1	101.2	99.1	98.3	98.0	96.8	97.7	96.6

SUGAR - OCTOBER - MONTH OF HIGH AND LOW

Year of Expiration	Nov	Dec	Jan	Feb	Mar	Apr	May	Jun	Jul	Aug	Sep
1976							H				L
1977						H					L
1978		H							L		
1979							L				H
1980	L										H
1981	H										L
1982			H								L
1983					L			H			
1984	H										L
1985	H							L			

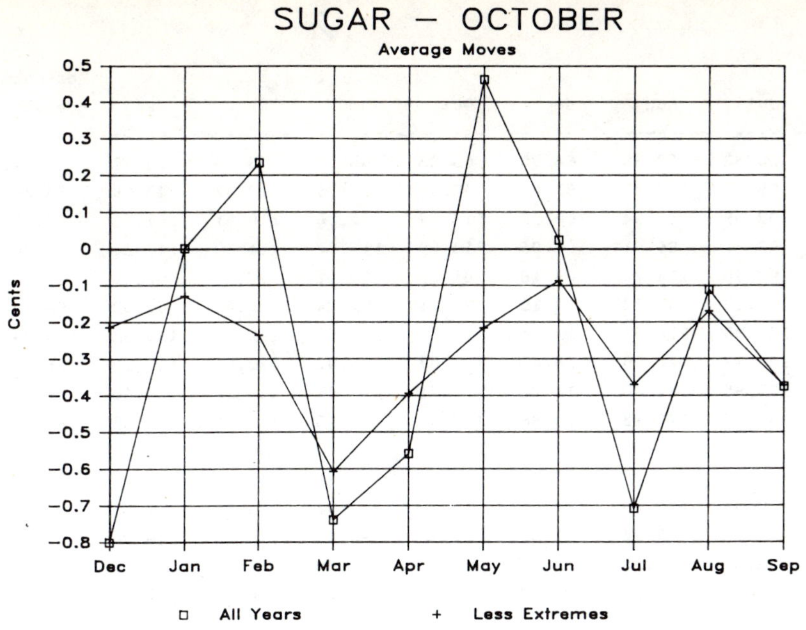
SUGAR – OCTOBER
Average Moves
Cents
0.5
0.4
0.3
0.2
0.1
0
-0.1
-0.2
-0.3
-0.4
-0.5
-0.6
-0.7
-0.8
Dec
Jan
Feb
Mar
Apr
May
Jun
Jul
Aug
Sep
All Years
Less Extremes

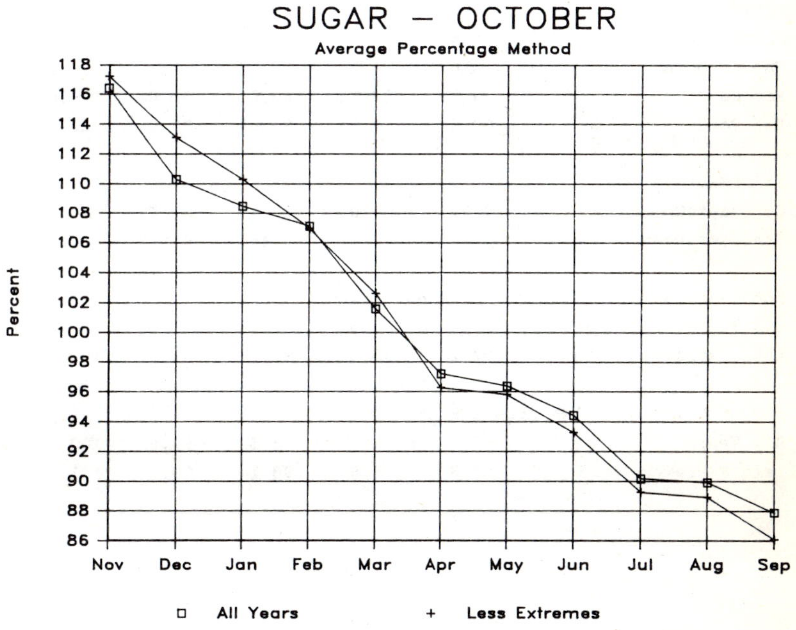
SUGAR – OCTOBER
Average Percentage Method
Percent
118
116
114
112
110
108
106
104
102
100
98
96
94
92
90
88
86
Nov
Dec
Jan
Feb
Mar
Apr
May
Jun
Jul
Aug
Sep
All Years
Less Extremes

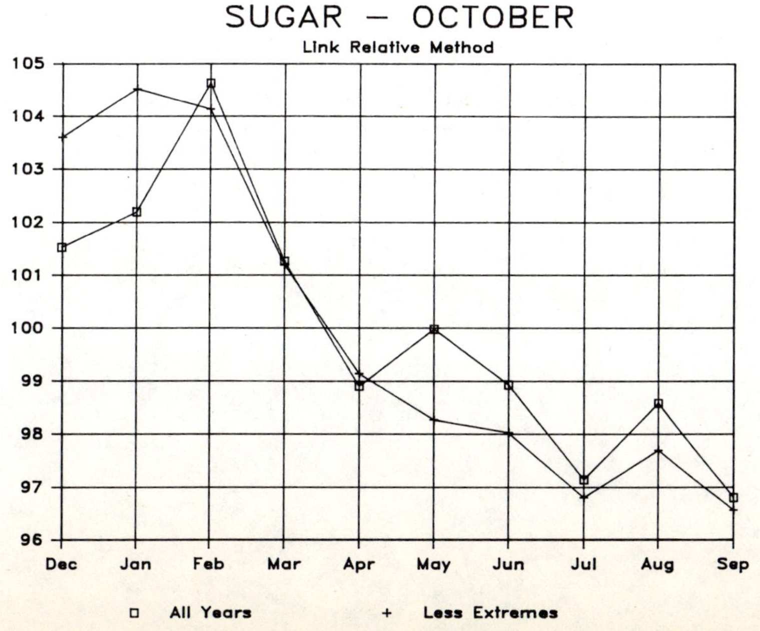
SUGAR – OCTOBER
Link Relative Method
105
104
103
102
101
100
99
98
97
96
Dec
Jan
Feb
Mar
Apr
May
Jun
Jul
Aug
Sep
All Years
Less Extremes

ORANGE JUICE - JANUARY - MONTHLY AVERAGE PRICE

Year of Expiration	Mar	Apr	May	Jun	Jul	Aug	Sep	Oct	Nov	Dec	Jan	Mar-Jan Average
1976	54.70	54.74	57.16	58.11	60.82	62.98	64.50	63.23	63.02	59.68	58.21	59.74
1977	68.29	65.20	61.83	57.33	55.72	52.32	51.60	48.98	47.34	43.47	40.38	53.86
1978	71.07	74.70	81.02	88.34	92.09	96.94	100.53	118.72	127.86	110.51	107.14	97.17
1979	93.73	90.50	86.36	90.75	93.35	96.01	100.06	113.09	117.92	114.10	117.31	101.20
1980	98.79	98.78	99.29	95.35	98.26	104.79	104.48	101.29	95.91	97.35	92.84	98.83
1981	101.55	91.79	92.69	90.29	91.13	93.72	98.15	96.01	91.24	82.94	89.92	92.67
1982	139.68	144.73	147.15	142.06	135.88	134.84	132.64	124.75	121.80	122.76	130.83	134.28
1983	131.03	123.50	125.56	122.99	126.42	128.08	128.47	125.87	125.02	123.96	114.50	125.03
1984	104.56	102.83	103.82	107.50	108.95	111.40	113.26	118.71	123.81	126.26	145.60	115.16
1985	159.41	172.32	179.01	172.53	165.96	170.13	175.86	172.75	169.13	161.96	158.35	168.85

	Mar	Apr	May	Jun	Jul	Aug	Sep	Oct	Nov	Dec	Jan
AVERAGE MOVE											
All Years		-0.37	1.48	-0.87	0.34	2.26	1.84	1.39	-0.04	-4.00	1.21
Less Extremes		-0.86	1.53	-1.19	0.77	2.44	1.85	0.45	-0.52	-3.15	0.28
Ave Up - All Years		5.41	2.79	4.08	2.53	3.38	3.08	12.22	6.35	1.62	9.40
Ave Down - All Years		-4.23	-3.75	-4.17	-4.78	-2.22	-1.08	-3.26	-2.78	-6.42	-4.25
COUNT											
Number Up		4	8	4	7	8	7	3	3	3	4
Number Down		6	2	6	3	2	3	7	7	7	6
Pct Up		40.0%	80.0%	40.0%	70.0%	80.0%	70.0%	30.0%	30.0%	30.0%	40.0%
Pct Down		60.0%	20.0%	60.0%	30.0%	20.0%	30.0%	70.0%	70.0%	70.0%	60.0%
EXTREMES											
Greatest Up		12.91	6.70	7.31	3.76	6.52	5.73	18.19	9.14	2.46	19.34
Greatest Down		-9.76	-4.14	-6.48	-6.56	-3.41	-2.20	-7.89	-5.38	-17.35	-9.45
SEASONAL INDEX : AVERAGE PERCENTAGE METHOD											
All Years	98.8	97.6	98.6	97.8	98.5	100.5	102.2	103.6	103.5	99.1	99.9
Less Extremes	98.5	97.2	98.5	97.7	98.7	100.5	102.2	102.8	102.0	99.6	99.7
SEASONAL INDEX : LINK RELATIVE METHOD											
All Years		97.9	98.9	98.3	98.9	100.7	102.1	103.3	102.7	98.4	98.7
Less Extremes		97.8	98.8	98.1	99.0	101.3	103.0	103.1	102.3	98.5	98.2

ORANGE JUICE - JANUARY - MONTH OF HIGH AND LOW

Year of Expiration	Mar	Apr	May	Jun	Jul	Aug	Sep	Oct	Nov	Dec	Jan
1976	L						H				
1977	H										L
1978	L								H		
1979			L						H		
1980						H					L
1981	H									L	
1982			H						L		
1983	H										L
1984		L									H
1985			H								L

ORANGE JUICE — JANUARY
Average Moves

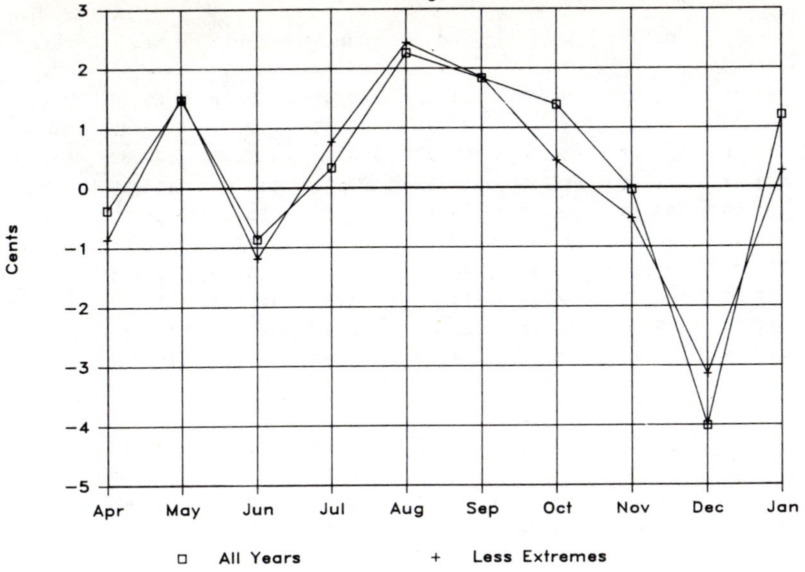

ORANGE JUICE — JANUARY
Average Percentage Method

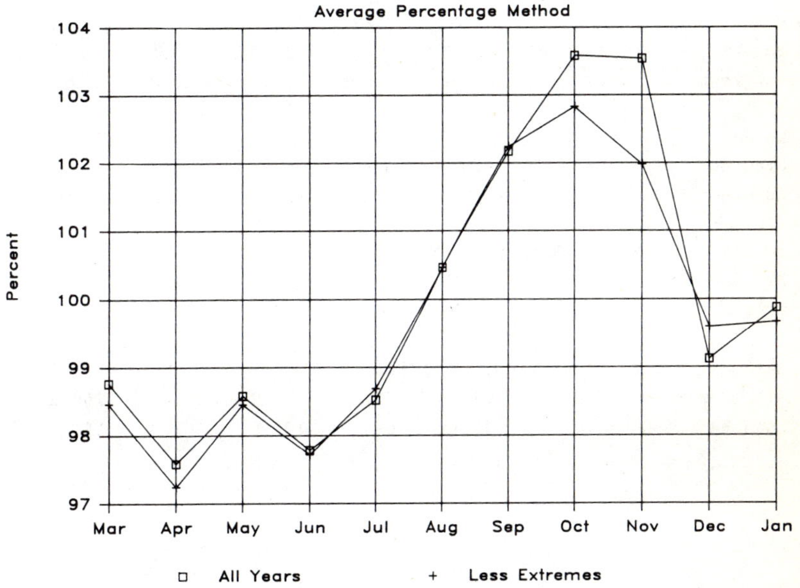

ORANGE JUICE — JANUARY
Link Relative Method

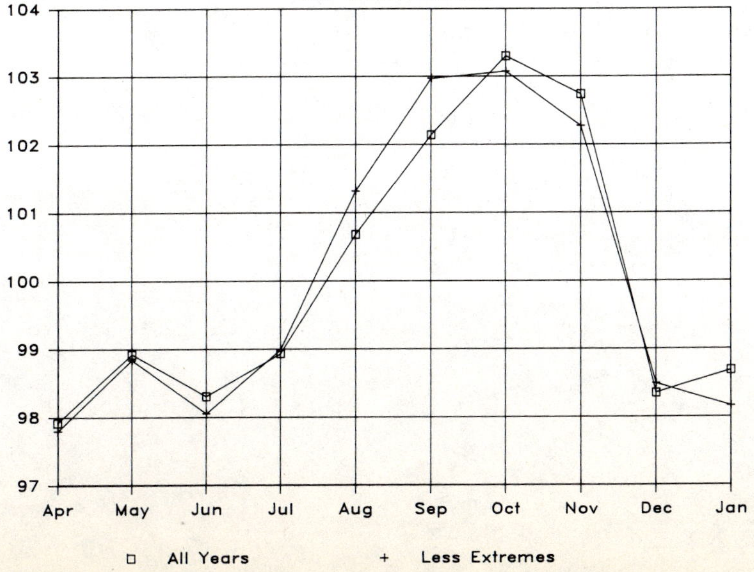

ORANGE JUICE - MARCH - MONTHLY AVERAGE PRICE

Year of Expiration	May	Jun	Jul	Aug	Sep	Oct	Nov	Dec	Jan	Feb	Mar	May-Mar Average
1976	58.55	59.60	61.93	64.10	65.49	64.41	64.49	61.46	60.33	62.31	61.13	62.16
1977	62.78	58.39	56.78	53.59	53.04	50.30	48.41	44.31	48.55	72.13	76.87	56.83
1978	79.13	85.94	89.43	94.06	97.18	115.43	126.56	109.97	106.40	121.09	120.85	104.18
1979	84.51	89.23	91.57	94.21	98.07	111.75	118.55	116.33	120.75	113.06	104.15	103.83
1980	99.79	96.21	99.10	105.40	105.05	102.13	96.82	98.43	91.17	85.50	96.42	97.82
1981	93.62	91.26	92.07	94.64	98.76	96.84	93.09	85.88	105.89	137.13	133.04	102.02
1982	147.96	143.46	137.55	137.23	135.06	127.13	123.49	124.56	139.23	133.39	123.38	133.86
1983	126.97	124.55	127.59	128.76	129.51	127.20	126.13	125.23	111.94	107.57	113.13	122.60
1984	103.07	106.55	108.27	110.35	112.47	116.45	122.14	126.31	151.40	161.28	166.78	125.92
1985	178.42	172.40	166.10	170.29	175.59	173.10	169.90	164.19	167.68	170.16	164.50	170.21
AVERAGE MOVE												
All Years		-0.72	0.28	2.22	1.76	1.45	0.49	-3.29	4.67	6.03	-0.34	
Less Extremes		-1.00	0.70	2.39	1.81	0.53	-0.12	-2.56	4.36	4.59	-0.54	
Ave Up - All Years		4.01	2.38	3.22	2.95	11.97	5.93	2.28	11.99	13.98	6.68	
Ave Down - All Years		-3.88	-4.61	-1.76	-1.02	-3.05	-3.14	-5.68	-6.31	-5.89	-5.02	
COUNT												
Number Up		4	7	8	7	3	4	3	6	6	4	
Number Down		6	3	2	3	7	6	7	4	4	6	
Pct Up		40.0%	70.0%	80.0%	70.0%	30.0%	40.0%	30.0%	60.0%	60.0%	40.0%	
Pct Down		60.0%	30.0%	20.0%	30.0%	70.0%	60.0%	70.0%	40.0%	40.0%	60.0%	
EXTREMES												
Greatest Up		6.81	3.49	6.30	5.31	18.25	11.13	4.17	25.09	31.24	10.93	
Greatest Down		-6.02	-6.31	-3.19	-2.16	-7.93	-5.30	-16.59	-13.29	-7.69	-10.01	
SEASONAL INDEX : AVERAGE PERCENTAGE METHOD												
All Years	95.7	95.0	95.6	97.4	99.0	100.3	100.7	97.1	101.2	109.0	109.2	
Less Extremes	96.3	95.0	95.7	97.3	99.1	100.4	100.0	97.7	100.8	108.5	108.1	
SEASONAL INDEX : LINK RELATIVE METHOD												
All Years		99.7	99.2	99.9	100.2	100.5	99.4	94.8	98.0	104.7	103.7	
Less Extremes		99.1	99.1	100.6	101.4	100.8	99.6	95.7	98.9	102.9	101.9	

ORANGE JUICE - MARCH - MONTH OF HIGH AND LOW

Year of Expiration	May	Jun	Jul	Aug	Sep	Oct	Nov	Dec	Jan	Feb	Mar
1976	L				H						
1977								L			H
1978	L						H				
1979	L								H		
1980				H						L	
1981								L		H	
1982	H										L
1983					H					L	
1984	L										H
1985	H							L			

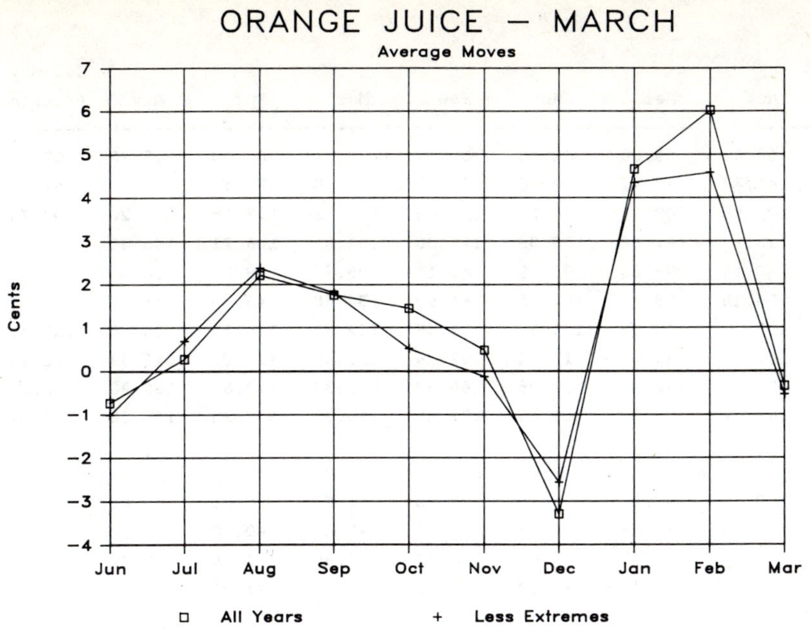
ORANGE JUICE – MARCH
Average Moves
Cents
7
6
5
4
3
2
1
0
−1
−2
−3
−4
Jun
Jul
Aug
Sep
Oct
Nov
Dec
Jan
Feb
Mar
□ All Years
+ Less Extremes

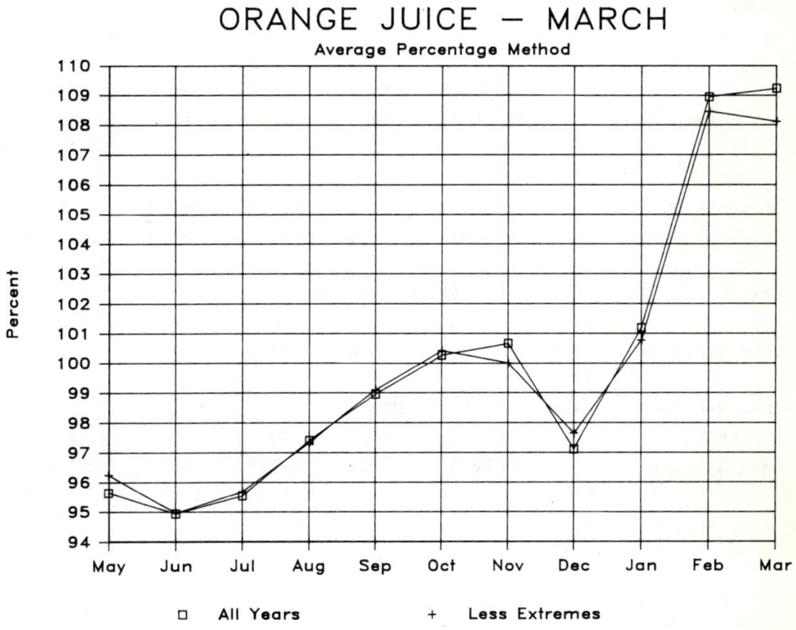
ORANGE JUICE – MARCH
Average Percentage Method
Percent
110
109
108
107
106
105
104
103
102
101
100
99
98
97
96
95
94
May
Jun
Jul
Aug
Sep
Oct
Nov
Dec
Jan
Feb
Mar
□ All Years
+ Less Extremes

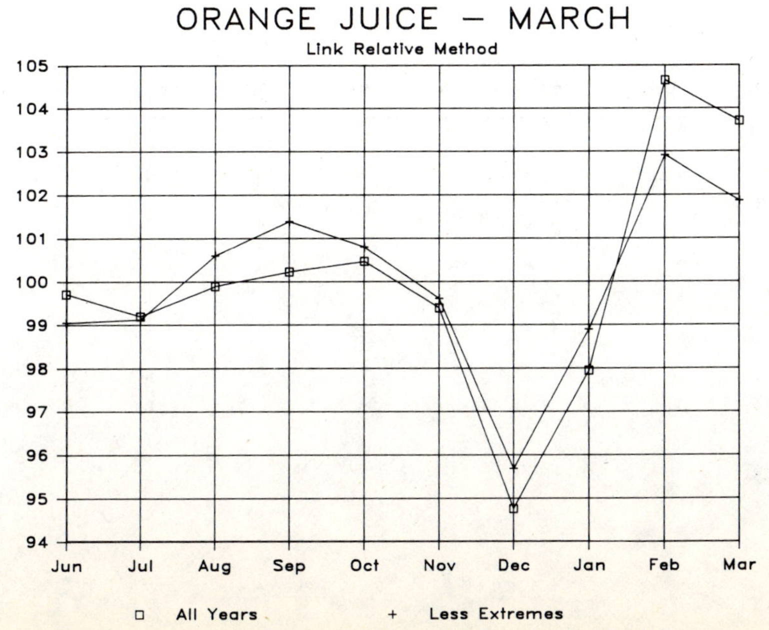
ORANGE JUICE – MARCH
Link Relative Method
105
104
103
102
101
100
99
98
97
96
95
94
Jun
Jul
Aug
Sep
Oct
Nov
Dec
Jan
Feb
Mar
□ All Years
+ Less Extremes

ORANGE JUICE - MAY - MONTHLY AVERAGE PRICE

Year of Expiration	Jul	Aug	Sep	Oct	Nov	Dec	Jan	Feb	Mar	Apr	May	Jul-May Average
1976	62.94	65.23	66.45	65.48	65.69	63.00	62.08	64.21	62.76	60.15	58.28	63.30
1977	57.87	55.10	54.48	51.59	49.47	45.41	49.58	72.70	77.30	79.49	80.70	61.25
1978	89.32	93.96	96.81	114.94	125.58	109.71	106.65	119.83	117.83	117.18	115.20	109.73
1979	91.25	93.92	97.89	111.56	118.94	117.86	123.03	114.86	104.65	106.21	103.41	107.60
1980	99.76	105.81	105.59	103.15	98.10	99.64	92.39	86.11	95.75	89.13	88.10	96.68
1981	93.04	95.58	99.39	97.50	94.15	88.16	108.36	141.92	138.68	143.35	141.00	112.83
1982	139.15	139.57	137.46	129.47	125.47	125.98	141.53	136.88	122.22	115.15	116.05	129.90
1983	128.83	129.73	130.59	128.38	127.28	126.27	112.74	107.76	111.46	114.37	116.34	121.25
1984	108.29	110.38	112.27	115.63	121.22	126.41	152.95	160.89	166.32	179.80	186.80	140.09
1985	166.40	170.36	175.14	172.95	169.74	164.52	168.63	172.28	165.28	157.36	156.38	167.19
AVERAGE MOVE												
All Years		2.28	1.64	1.46	0.50	-2.87	5.10	5.95	-1.52	-0.01	0.01	
Less Extremes		2.44	1.72	0.55	-0.08	-2.25	4.75	4.26	-1.27	-0.70	-0.52	
Ave Up - All Years		2.84	2.77	11.72	5.95	2.41	12.62	13.93	5.85	4.96	2.77	
Ave Down - All Years		-2.77	-0.98	-2.94	-3.14	-5.13	-6.19	-6.02	-6.43	-4.97	-1.84	
COUNT												
Number Up		9	7	3	4	3	6	6	4	5	4	
Number Down		1	3	7	6	7	4	4	6	5	6	
Pct Up		90.0%	70.0%	30.0%	40.0%	30.0%	60.0%	60.0%	40.0%	50.0%	40.0%	
Pct Down		10.0%	30.0%	70.0%	60.0%	70.0%	40.0%	40.0%	60.0%	50.0%	60.0%	
EXTREMES												
Greatest Up		6.05	4.78	18.12	10.64	5.19	26.54	33.56	9.64	13.47	7.00	
Greatest Down		-2.77	-2.11	-7.99	-5.05	-15.86	-13.53	-8.16	-14.66	-7.92	-2.79	
SEASONAL INDEX : AVERAGE PERCENTAGE METHOD												
All Years	93.6	95.5	96.9	98.1	98.4	95.4	99.4	106.3	105.6	105.5	105.3	
Less Extremes	93.9	95.9	97.4	98.9	98.6	96.3	99.9	106.1	104.7	104.6	103.8	
SEASONAL INDEX : LINK RELATIVE METHOD												
All Years		98.1	98.6	99.3	98.6	94.7	98.5	105.3	103.7	102.3	101.0	
Less Extremes		98.7	99.7	99.5	98.8	95.6	99.6	103.9	102.6	101.4	100.3	

ORANGE JUICE - MAY - MONTH OF HIGH AND LOW

Year of Expiration	Jul	Aug	Sep	Oct	Nov	Dec	Jan	Feb	Mar	Apr	May
1976			H								L
1977						L					H
1978	L				H						
1979	L						H				
1980		H						L			
1981						L				H	
1982							H			L	
1983			H					L			
1984	L										H
1985			H								L

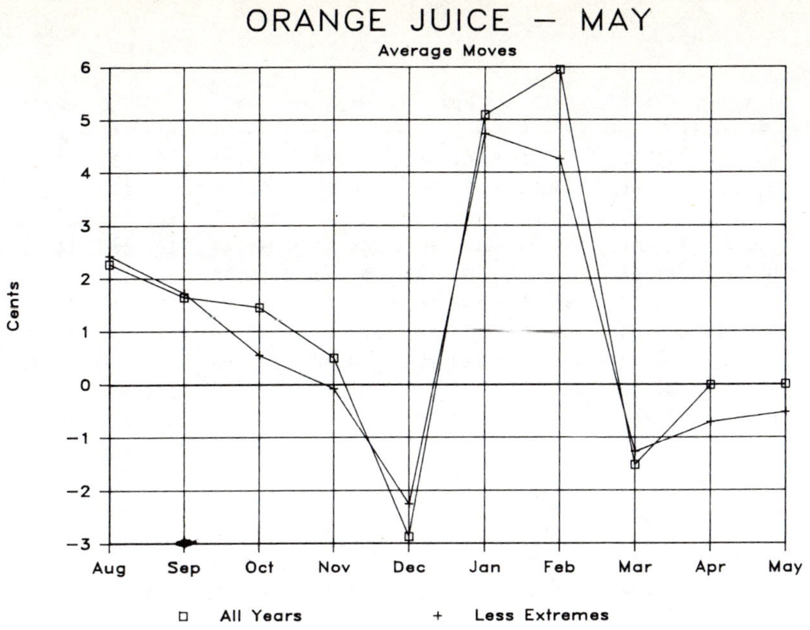
ORANGE JUICE — MAY
Average Moves
Cents
6
5
4
3
2
1
0
−1
−2
−3
Aug
Sep
Oct
Nov
Dec
Jan
Feb
Mar
Apr
May
All Years
Less Extremes

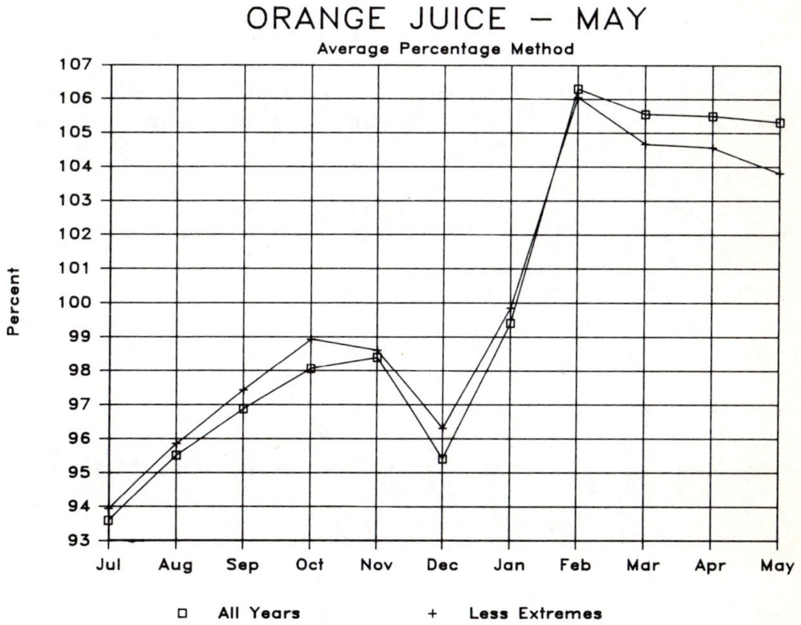
ORANGE JUICE — MAY
Average Percentage Method
Percent
107
106
105
104
103
102
101
100
99
98
97
96
95
94
93
Jul
Aug
Sep
Oct
Nov
Dec
Jan
Feb
Mar
Apr
May
All Years
Less Extremes

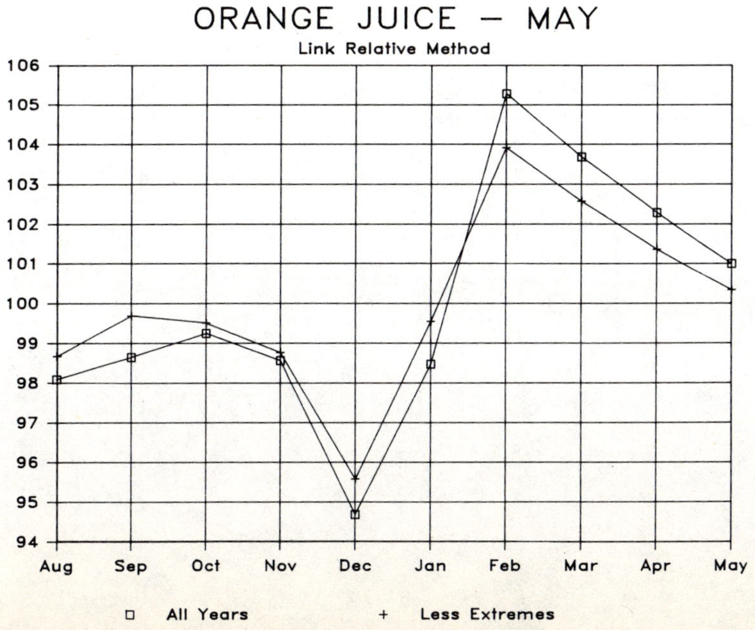
ORANGE JUICE — MAY
Link Relative Method
106
105
104
103
102
101
100
99
98
97
96
95
94
Aug
Sep
Oct
Nov
Dec
Jan
Feb
Mar
Apr
May
All Years
Less Extremes

ORANGE JUICE - JULY - MONTHLY AVERAGE PRICE

Year of Expiration	Sep	Oct	Nov	Dec	Jan	Feb	Mar	Apr	May	Jun	Jul	Sep-Jul Average
1976	67.55	66.55	67.01	64.71	63.91	65.89	64.51	61.81	59.08	55.07	53.73	62.71
1977	55.75	52.91	50.56	46.58	50.59	73.41	76.84	79.75	84.12	96.50	99.91	69.72
1978	96.87	114.36	125.49	109.71	106.68	118.48	116.70	115.05	110.92	118.09	123.90	114.20
1979	97.66	111.24	119.54	119.14	124.66	116.14	105.39	106.45	104.29	97.44	100.81	109.34
1980	106.12	104.22	99.26	100.80	93.76	87.48	96.94	89.93	89.29	86.65	87.62	94.73
1981	99.92	98.20	95.21	90.38	110.51	145.27	140.90	146.16	142.88	134.21	124.01	120.70
1982	139.81	131.82	127.34	127.27	143.87	139.85	125.19	117.91	119.10	116.05	123.63	128.35
1983	131.61	129.59	128.44	127.35	113.83	108.49	110.39	113.20	114.97	117.03	119.36	119.48
1984	112.20	115.46	120.53	126.36	153.77	160.39	164.62	178.36	184.10	178.17	172.53	151.50
1985	174.72	172.80	169.58	164.75	169.33	173.44	166.36	157.26	150.10	142.57	139.47	161.85

	Sep	Oct	Nov	Dec	Jan	Feb	Mar	Apr	May	Jun	Jul
AVERAGE MOVE											
All Years		1.49	0.58	-2.59	5.38	5.79	-2.10	-0.20	-0.70	-1.71	0.32
Less Extremes		0.68	-0.04	-1.99	4.99	3.96	-1.97	-0.82	-0.70	-2.60	0.73
Ave Up - All Years		11.44	6.24	3.69	13.04	13.68	4.76	5.16	3.27	7.20	3.91
Ave Down - All Years		-2.77	-3.19	-4.16	-6.10	-6.04	-6.67	-5.55	-3.35	-5.53	-5.07
COUNT											
Number Up		3	4	2	6	6	4	5	4	3	6
Number Down		7	6	8	4	4	6	5	6	7	4
Pct Up		30.0%	40.0%	20.0%	60.0%	60.0%	40.0%	50.0%	40.0%	30.0%	60.0%
Pct Down		70.0%	60.0%	80.0%	40.0%	40.0%	60.0%	50.0%	60.0%	70.0%	40.0%
EXTREMES											
Greatest Up		17.49	11.13	5.83	27.41	34.77	9.46	13.74	5.73	12.38	7.58
Greatest Down		-7.99	-4.97	-15.77	-13.52	-8.52	-14.66	-9.10	-7.16	-8.67	-10.20
SEASONAL INDEX : AVERAGE PERCENTAGE METHOD											
All Years	95.8	96.9	97.3	94.7	98.6	104.6	103.2	102.9	102.3	101.5	102.1
Less Extremes	96.5	97.9	98.9	96.4	99.9	104.3	102.9	102.0	101.1	98.7	99.0
SEASONAL INDEX : LINK RELATIVE METHOD											
All Years		97.7	97.5	94.3	98.5	105.4	103.6	102.5	101.2	99.6	99.6
Less Extremes		98.4	98.1	95.5	100.1	104.6	103.0	102.0	100.9	98.4	99.1

ORANGE JUICE - JULY - MONTH OF HIGH AND LOW

Year of Expiration	Sep	Oct	Nov	Dec	Jan	Feb	Mar	Apr	May	Jun	Jul
1976	H										L
1977			L								H
1978	L		H								
1979					H					L	
1980	H									L	
1981				L				H			
1982					H					L	
1983	H					L					
1984	L								H		
1985	H										L

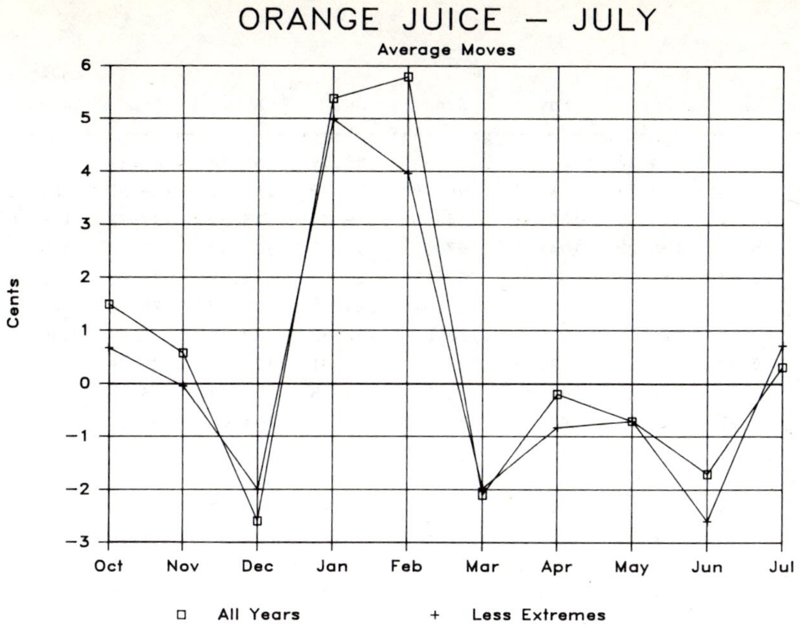
ORANGE JUICE – JULY
Average Moves
Cents
6
5
4
3
2
1
0
−1
−2
−3
Oct
Nov
Dec
Jan
Feb
Mar
Apr
May
Jun
Jul
All Years
Less Extremes

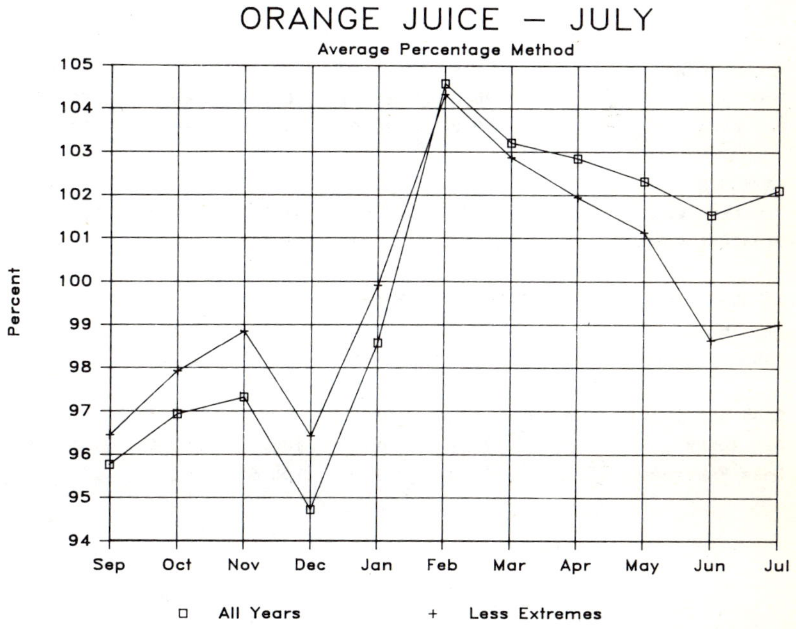
ORANGE JUICE – JULY
Average Percentage Method
Percent
105
104
103
102
101
100
99
98
97
96
95
94
Sep
Oct
Nov
Dec
Jan
Feb
Mar
Apr
May
Jun
Jul
All Years
Less Extremes

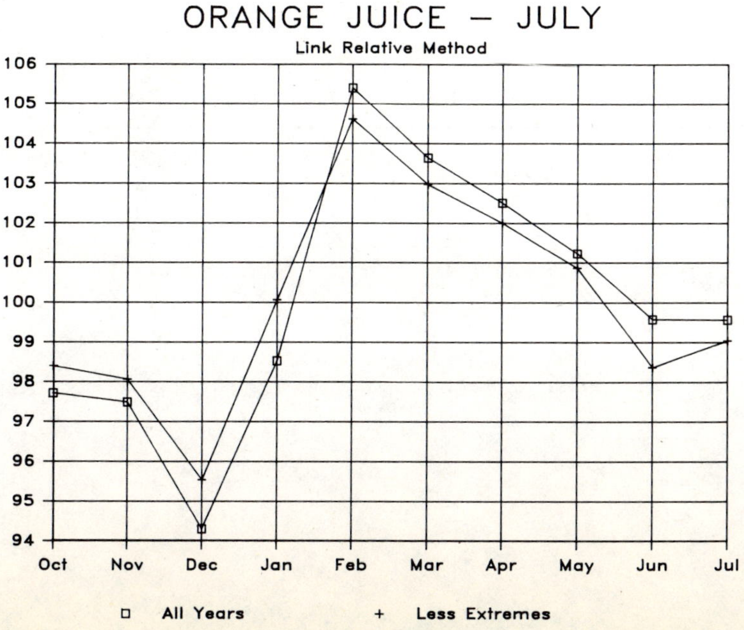
ORANGE JUICE – JULY
Link Relative Method
106
105
104
103
102
101
100
99
98
97
96
95
94
Oct
Nov
Dec
Jan
Feb
Mar
Apr
May
Jun
Jul
All Years
Less Extremes

ORANGE JUICE - SEPTEMBER - MONTHLY AVERAGE PRICE

Year of Expiration	Nov	Dec	Jan	Feb	Mar	Apr	May	Jun	Jul	Aug	Sep	Nov-Sep Average
1976	67.69	65.62	65.01	67.22	66.07	63.38	60.17	55.48	53.58	50.38	49.17	60.34
1977	84.94	46.41	51.84	73.92	76.56	79.72	84.92	96.39	103.92	116.44	119.32	84.94
1978	124.52	109.12	106.71	117.03	116.04	113.99	109.24	114.65	119.82	123.22	127.77	116.56
1979	120.14	120.12	125.52	116.92	105.91	106.22	104.91	97.07	99.90	106.97	107.52	110.11
1980	100.46	102.01	95.15	89.00	98.67	91.14	90.25	87.17	88.38	91.92	96.03	93.65
1981	96.01	92.55	112.64	147.25	142.86	146.60	145.70	137.44	129.10	126.32	125.38	127.44
1982	128.98	128.20	145.47	142.17	127.45	120.12	122.11	118.65	125.85	129.18	128.04	128.75
1983	129.71	128.19	114.57	109.11	109.87	111.90	113.80	115.58	117.31	118.71	122.08	117.35
1984	120.07	126.46	154.44	159.99	163.76	177.11	182.92	174.73	168.65	171.98	175.10	161.38
1985	167.50	162.93	166.88	171.96	165.91	156.55	147.96	139.44	134.98	134.08	136.24	153.13

	Nov	Dec	Jan	Feb	Mar	Apr	May	Jun	Jul	Aug	Sep
AVERAGE MOVE											
All Years		-5.84	5.66	5.63	-2.15	-0.64	-0.48	-2.54	0.49	2.77	1.74
Less Extremes		-3.28	5.28	3.79	-2.05	-1.29	-0.25	-3.54	0.71	2.30	1.76
Ave Up - All Years		3.97	13.35	13.31	4.22	4.52	3.72	6.22	4.28	4.94	2.96
Ave Down - All Years		-8.29	-5.88	-5.88	-6.39	-5.79	-3.27	-6.29	-5.19	-2.29	-1.10
COUNT											
Number Up		2	6	6	4	5	4	3	6	7	7
Number Down		8	4	4	6	5	6	7	4	3	3
Pct Up		20.0%	60.0%	60.0%	40.0%	50.0%	40.0%	30.0%	60.0%	70.0%	70.0%
Pct Down		80.0%	40.0%	40.0%	60.0%	50.0%	60.0%	70.0%	40.0%	30.0%	30.0%
EXTREMES											
Greatest Up		6.39	27.97	34.61	9.68	13.35	5.80	11.46	7.53	12.52	4.54
Greatest Down		-38.53	-13.62	-8.60	-14.72	-9.37	-8.58	-8.53	-8.34	-3.20	-1.21
SEASONAL INDEX : AVERAGE PERCENTAGE METHOD											
All Years	100.5	94.1	98.0	103.0	101.5	100.6	100.1	98.3	99.1	101.6	103.1
Less Extremes	102.3	97.2	100.6	103.5	101.6	99.7	99.1	97.7	97.5	99.5	101.1
SEASONAL INDEX : LINK RELATIVE METHOD											
All Years		95.7	99.9	106.1	103.8	101.9	100.4	97.6	97.3	98.5	98.8
Less Extremes		97.0	101.6	105.6	103.3	101.6	100.2	96.7	96.8	98.2	98.9

ORANGE JUICE - SEPTEMBER - MONTH OF HIGH AND LOW

Year of Expiration	Nov	Dec	Jan	Feb	Mar	Apr	May	Jun	Jul	Aug	Sep
1976	H										L
1977		L									H
1978			L								H
1979			H					L			
1980		H						L			
1981		L		H							
1982			H					L			
1983	H			L							
1984	L						H				
1985				H						L	

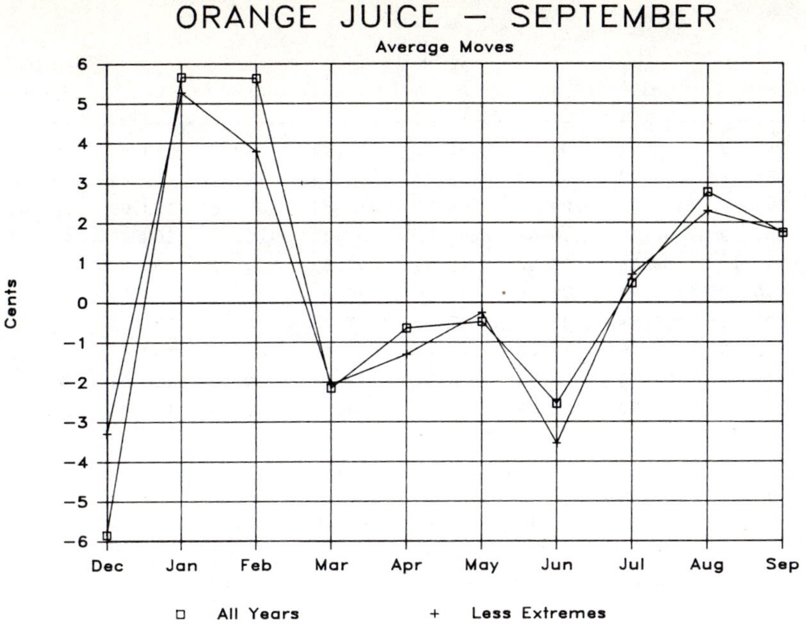
ORANGE JUICE — SEPTEMBER
Average Moves
Cents
6
5
4
3
2
1
0
−1
−2
−3
−4
−5
−6
Dec
Jan
Feb
Mar
Apr
May
Jun
Jul
Aug
Sep
All Years
Less Extremes

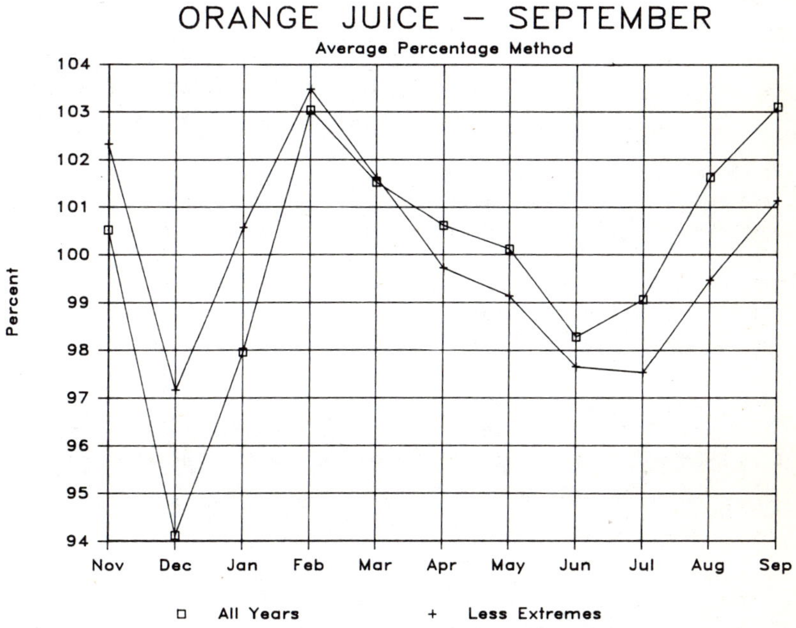
ORANGE JUICE — SEPTEMBER
Average Percentage Method
Percent
104
103
102
101
100
99
98
97
96
95
94
Nov
Dec
Jan
Feb
Mar
Apr
May
Jun
Jul
Aug
Sep
All Years
Less Extremes

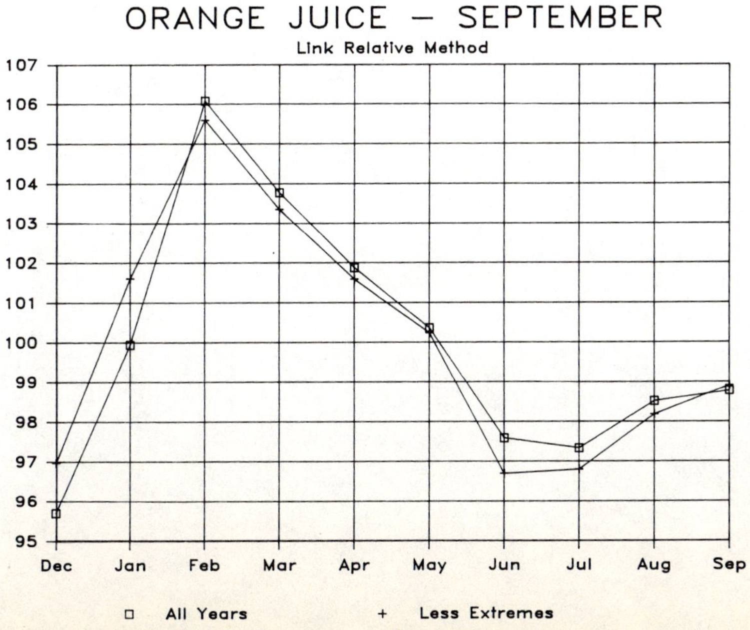
ORANGE JUICE — SEPTEMBER
Link Relative Method
107
106
105
104
103
102
101
100
99
98
97
96
95
Dec
Jan
Feb
Mar
Apr
May
Jun
Jul
Aug
Sep
All Years
Less Extremes

ORANGE JUICE - NOVEMBER - MONTHLY AVERAGE PRICE

Year of Expiration	Jan	Feb	Mar	Apr	May	Jun	Jul	Aug	Sep	Oct	Nov	Jan-Nov Average
1976	57.00	68.51	67.30	64.38	61.03	56.41	54.51	51.12	50.25	48.53	48.01	57.00
1977	53.06	73.62	75.54	79.64	85.31	95.22	100.63	111.75	116.23	125.52	132.82	95.39
1978	105.37	113.03	110.14	107.68	103.34	107.85	109.72	113.11	112.83	121.66	123.05	111.62
1979	120.37	112.33	102.10	102.21	102.29	96.10	98.84	105.13	105.00	106.25	105.10	105.06
1980	94.00	89.79	100.12	91.70	91.10	88.25	89.28	92.38	97.33	94.10	89.74	92.53
1981	112.98	146.59	141.92	145.60	146.60	139.51	132.52	130.56	129.25	121.21	118.52	133.20
1982	146.25	143.46	129.23	121.93	123.84	120.94	125.66	127.82	127.78	125.06	125.72	128.88
1983	115.09	108.94	107.14	107.93	109.83	113.08	114.88	116.22	118.15	123.89	132.53	115.24
1984	153.26	158.03	162.09	174.42	179.91	172.64	166.36	170.88	175.85	169.99	164.63	168.01
1985	165.86	170.63	164.33	155.08	146.41	137.70	132.32	130.36	132.26	121.03	113.88	142.72

	Jan	Feb	Mar	Apr	May	Jun	Jul	Aug	Sep	Oct	Nov
AVERAGE MOVE											
All Years		6.17	-2.50	-0.94	-0.09	-2.20	-0.30	2.46	1.56	-0.77	-0.32
Less Extremes		4.51	-2.64	-1.55	0.26	-2.89	-0.17	2.11	1.49	-0.72	-0.59
Ave Up - All Years		13.81	5.44	4.20	2.67	5.89	2.93	4.56	3.65	6.28	4.50
Ave Down - All Years		-5.30	-5.90	-6.07	-4.24	-5.66	-5.14	-2.43	-0.53	-5.47	-3.54
COUNT											
Number Up		6	3	5	6	3	6	7	5	4	4
Number Down		4	7	5	4	7	4	3	5	6	6
Pct Up		60.0%	30.0%	50.0%	60.0%	30.0%	60.0%	70.0%	50.0%	40.0%	40.0%
Pct Down		40.0%	70.0%	50.0%	40.0%	70.0%	40.0%	30.0%	50.0%	60.0%	60.0%
EXTREMES											
Greatest Up		33.61	10.33	12.34	5.67	9.91	5.42	11.12	4.97	9.29	8.64
Greatest Down		-8.04	-14.23	-9.25	-8.67	-8.71	-6.99	-3.39	-1.32	-11.23	-7.15
SEASONAL INDEX : AVERAGE PERCENTAGE METHOD											
All Years	97.2	103.2	101.3	99.9	99.6	97.8	97.8	99.9	101.2	101.0	101.0
Less Extremes	100.0	104.3	101.9	100.4	99.6	97.7	97.5	99.0	100.3	99.2	98.9
SEASONAL INDEX : LINK RELATIVE METHOD											
All Years		101.4	100.0	99.2	99.2	97.9	98.1	100.2	101.6	101.2	101.0
Less Extremes		102.0	100.2	99.4	99.4	97.4	97.8	100.0	101.5	101.2	101.0

ORANGE JUICE - NOVEMBER - MONTH OF HIGH AND LOW

Year of Expiration	Jan	Feb	Mar	Apr	May	Jun	Jul	Aug	Sep	Oct	Nov
1976		H									L
1977	L										H
1978					L						H
1979	H					L					
1980			H			L					
1981	L				H						
1982	H					L					
1983			L								H
1984	L				H						
1985		H									L

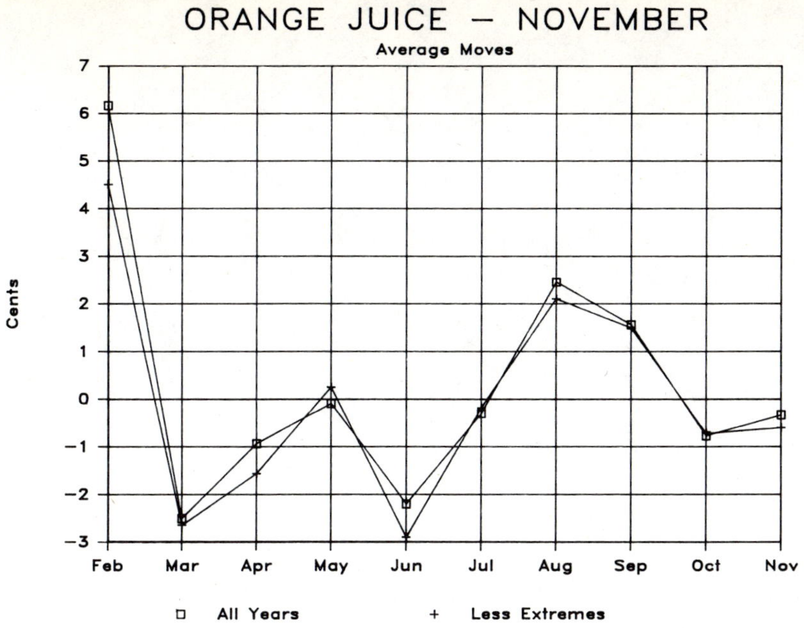
ORANGE JUICE — NOVEMBER
Average Moves
Cents
7
6
5
4
3
2
1
0
−1
−2
−3
Feb
Mar
Apr
May
Jun
Jul
Aug
Sep
Oct
Nov
All Years
Less Extremes

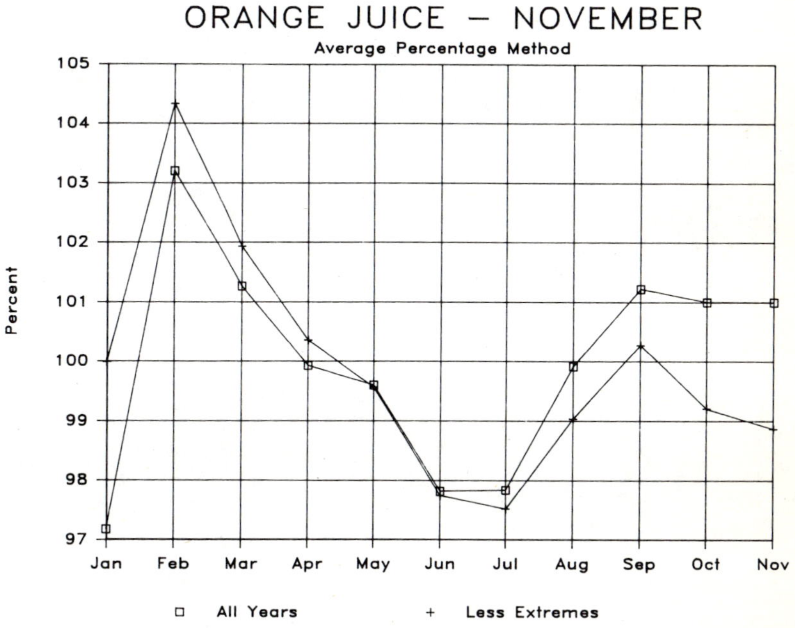
ORANGE JUICE — NOVEMBER
Average Percentage Method
Percent
105
104
103
102
101
100
99
98
97
Jan
Feb
Mar
Apr
May
Jun
Jul
Aug
Sep
Oct
Nov
All Years
Less Extremes

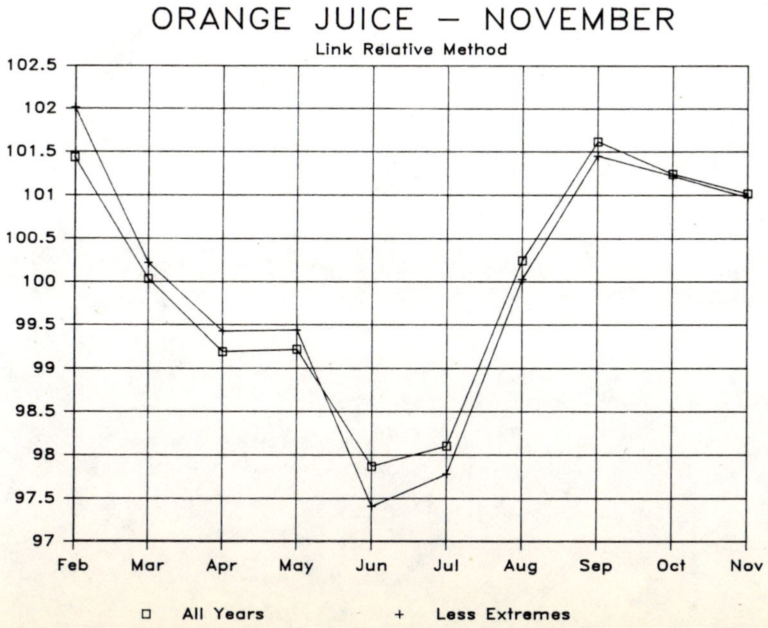
ORANGE JUICE — NOVEMBER
Link Relative Method
102.5
102
101.5
101
100.5
100
99.5
99
98.5
98
97.5
97
Feb
Mar
Apr
May
Jun
Jul
Aug
Sep
Oct
Nov
All Years
Less Extremes

NINE

Miscellaneous Commodities

COTTON

Cotton is a reasonable vehicle for seasonal tendency traders. There are several key months of good seasonality. Generally, cotton follows the usual price pattern of harvest lows and late season highs.

Most cotton in the United States is planted by May 31 and harvested around October. The deep south area—Mississippi, Arkansas, Tennessee, Louisiana, and Missouri—produces a little more than 30% of the domestic cotton crop. The harvest period is from late September to mid-November. North Carolina, South Carolina, Georgia, and Alabama produce slightly less than 15% of the crop. Harvesting takes place from the beginning of October to the first week in November. Texas and Oklahoma produce more than 30% of the total crop. Harvest in this area can take place, depending on the location, from July to October, with the bulk of it in September.

It is this harvest period that takes the price from its July highs down to the late fall lows. The period immediately after harvest is typified by heavy mill consumption and exports. This is a common occurrence in many commodities. The users of a commodity like to take advantage of harvest lows to do their purchasing. In cotton, this causes a short rally during the winter. Once the buying spurt is over, prices slowly move higher during the summer as supplies dwindle, but demand stays steady.

Cotton prices tend to be very sensitive toward weather. The ideal climate for cotton growth is hot and humid. Too much or too little rainfall creates problems. The summer price surge is largely based on uncertainty about the weather.

LUMBER

Lumber has some superb seasonal tendencies. Every serious seasonality trader should examine closely the charts in this chapter.

The lumber seasonal charts are dominated by a strong upswing that starts in October and ends in February followed by a long decline back to October. The major determinant of the price of lumber is the demand because lumber can be stored for an indefinate period of time.

The largest use of lumber is in the housing industry with its peak construction season in the summer. In most of North America, winter is unsuitable for building; therefore, construction companies and wholesalers ensure themselves of adequate lumber supplies by prepurchasing. These winter purchases create the large price hike found during the cold months.

The spring and summer periods are typified by working from inventories accumulated during the prvious winter. One should watch out for a sharp summer price rise around August and September because of low inventories of lumber.

HIGHEST RELIABLE TRENDS

Commodity	Contract	Month	Position	Reliability	Average Move
Cotton	Mar	Oct	Short	70.0	−0.64
	May	Oct	Short	70.0	−0.69
	Jul	Oct	Short	70.0	−0.76
	Jul	Apr	Short	70.0	−1.29
	Jul	Jun	Short	70.0	−3.67
	Oct	Jun	Short	70.0	−3.42
	Oct	Jul	Short	70.0	−2.36
	Oct	Aug	Short	70.0	−4.40
	Oct	Sep	Short	80.0	−2.03
	Oct	Oct	Long	70.0	+1.51
	Dec	Jun	Short	70.0	−2.58
	Dec	Jul	Short	70.0	−1.70
	Dec	Sep	Short	70.0	−1.90
	Dec	Dec	Short	80.0	−1.07
Lumber	Jan	Jun	Short	70.0	−3.56
	Mar	Aug	Short	70.0	−8.68
	Mar	Nov	Long	70.0	+8.73
	Mar	Dec	Long	70.0	+7.15
	Mar	Jan	Long	70.0	+5.52
	Mar	Mar	Short	100.0	−8.93
	May	Nov	Long	70.0	+8.51
	May	Dec	Long	70.0	+5.91
	May	Mar	Short	90.0	−11.17
	Jul	Nov	Long	70.0	+7.46
	Jul	Mar	Short	90.0	−10.24
	Sep	Mar	Short	90.0	−9.11
	Sep	Jul	Short	70.0	−8.36
	Nov	Mar	Short	80.0	−8.91
	Nov	Jun	Short	70.0	−4.31
	Nov	Jul	Short	70.0	−7.96

COTTON - MARCH - MONTHLY AVERAGE PRICE

Year of Expiration	May	Jun	Jul	Aug	Sep	Oct	Nov	Dec	Jan	Feb	Mar	May-Mar Average
1976	48.34	48.35	49.98	52.41	55.18	54.76	55.63	59.17	61.11	60.51	61.53	55.18
1977	64.78	74.18	79.86	76.38	76.80	82.19	81.18	77.48	70.98	75.85	78.81	76.23
1978	67.71	62.64	59.18	55.24	53.73	53.36	51.68	52.30	55.01	55.47	55.82	56.56
1979	64.50	64.37	63.49	66.30	66.86	70.20	71.47	68.47	65.58	63.71	60.67	65.96
1980	63.76	65.20	65.05	66.43	66.35	66.13	69.52	72.15	77.87	85.84	83.40	71.06
1981	74.95	72.52	79.39	87.32	92.40	91.04	90.06	92.61	91.53	88.97	87.42	86.20
1982	81.25	79.12	78.67	73.32	68.57	68.18	65.31	63.38	65.23	63.54	63.45	70.00
1983	73.76	71.22	74.93	70.37	67.62	66.25	65.39	65.81	66.01	66.71	71.76	69.08
1984	75.98	80.56	79.98	81.54	79.95	79.63	80.95	79.04	75.50	76.14	78.96	78.93
1985	78.20	75.40	71.50	68.63	67.01	67.93	66.55	66.03	66.04	64.23	64.59	68.74

AVERAGE MOVE	May	Jun	Jul	Aug	Sep	Oct	Nov	Dec	Jan	Feb	Mar
All Years		0.03	0.85	-0.41	-0.35	0.52	-0.19	-0.13	-0.16	0.61	0.54
Less Extremes		-0.50	0.69	-0.83	-0.48	0.15	-0.30	-0.14	-0.10	0.09	0.43
Ave Up - All Years		3.86	4.47	3.22	2.21	3.22	1.71	1.95	2.07	2.93	2.09
Ave Down - All Years		-2.52	-1.57	-4.04	-2.05	-0.64	-1.46	-2.21	-3.50	-1.71	-1.78

COUNT	May	Jun	Jul	Aug	Sep	Oct	Nov	Dec	Jan	Feb	Mar
Number Up		4	4	5	4	3	4	5	6	5	6
Number Down		6	6	5	6	7	6	5	4	5	4
Pct Up		40.0%	40.0%	50.0%	40.0%	30.0%	40.0%	50.0%	60.0%	50.0%	60.0%
Pct Down		60.0%	60.0%	50.0%	60.0%	70.0%	60.0%	50.0%	40.0%	50.0%	40.0%

EXTREMES	May	Jun	Jul	Aug	Sep	Oct	Nov	Dec	Jan	Feb	Mar
Greatest Up		9.39	6.88	7.93	5.08	5.39	3.38	3.54	5.72	7.97	5.05
Greatest Down		-5.08	-3.90	-5.35	-4.75	-1.38	-2.87	-3.70	-6.51	-2.56	-3.04

SEASONAL INDEX : AVERAGE PERCENTAGE METHOD	May	Jun	Jul	Aug	Sep	Oct	Nov	Dec	Jan	Feb	Mar
All Years	100.0	99.7	100.6	99.8	99.2	100.0	99.7	99.6	99.7	100.5	101.3
Less Extremes	99.4	100.0	100.4	100.0	99.0	99.8	99.6	99.8	99.1	99.2	100.6

SEASONAL INDEX : LINK RELATIVE METHOD	May	Jun	Jul	Aug	Sep	Oct	Nov	Dec	Jan	Feb	Mar
All Years		100.0	101.0	100.3	99.6	100.1	99.6	99.4	99.4	99.9	100.6
Less Extremes		100.3	101.3	100.3	99.8	100.0	99.6	99.3	99.5	99.6	100.3

COTTON - MARCH - MONTH OF HIGH AND LOW

Year of Expiration	May	Jun	Jul	Aug	Sep	Oct	Nov	Dec	Jan	Feb	Mar
1976	L										H
1977	L					H					
1978	H						L				
1979							H				L
1980	L									H	
1981				L				H			
1982	H							L			
1983			H				L				
1984				H					L		
1985	H									L	

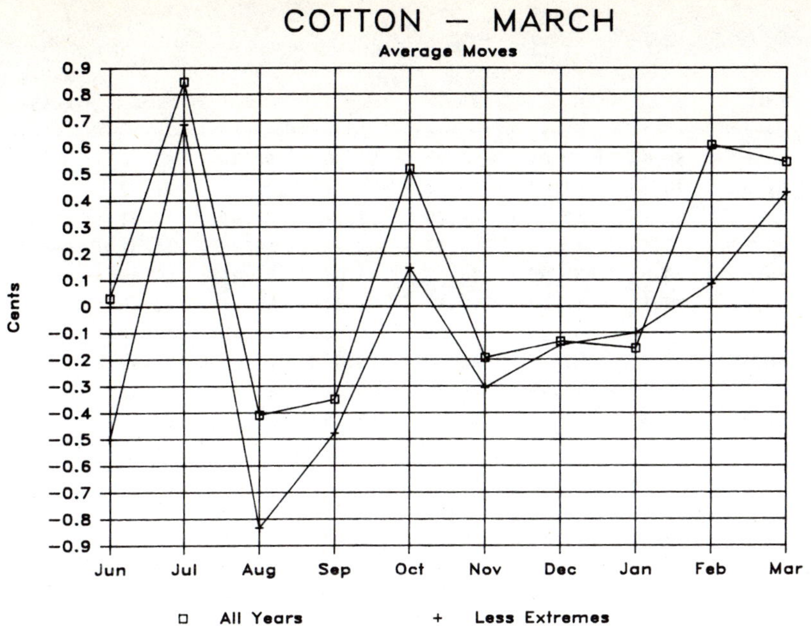
COTTON — MARCH
Average Moves
Cents
0.9
0.8
0.7
0.6
0.5
0.4
0.3
0.2
0.1
0
-0.1
-0.2
-0.3
-0.4
-0.5
-0.6
-0.7
-0.8
-0.9
Jun
Jul
Aug
Sep
Oct
Nov
Dec
Jan
Feb
Mar
□ All Years
+ Less Extremes

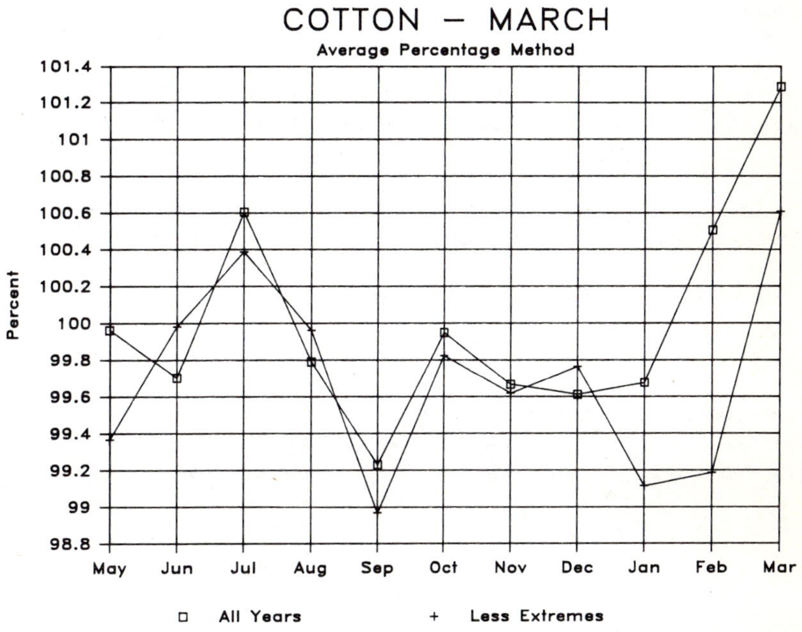
COTTON — MARCH
Average Percentage Method
Percent
101.4
101.2
101
100.8
100.6
100.4
100.2
100
99.8
99.6
99.4
99.2
99
98.8
May
Jun
Jul
Aug
Sep
Oct
Nov
Dec
Jan
Feb
Mar
□ All Years
+ Less Extremes

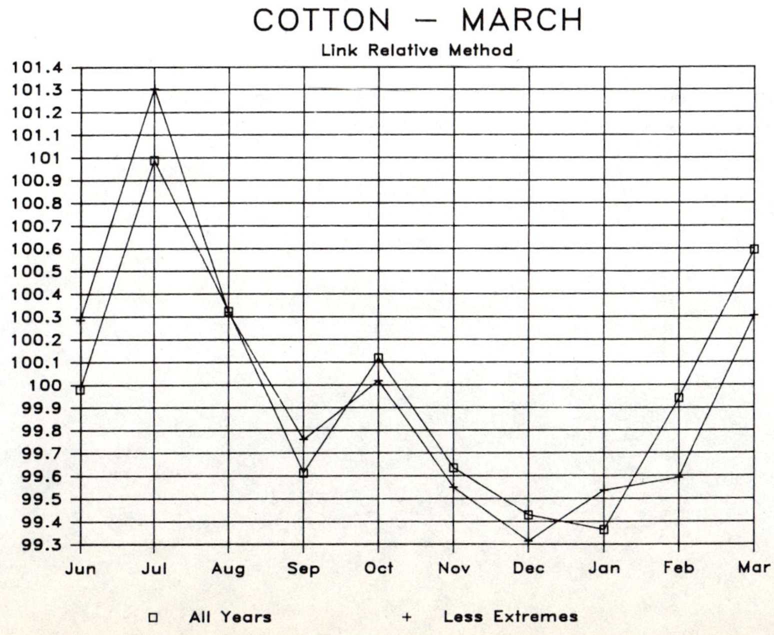
COTTON — MARCH
Link Relative Method
101.4
101.3
101.2
101.1
101
100.9
100.8
100.7
100.6
100.5
100.4
100.3
100.2
100.1
100
99.9
99.8
99.7
99.6
99.5
99.4
99.3
Jun
Jul
Aug
Sep
Oct
Nov
Dec
Jan
Feb
Mar
□ All Years
+ Less Extremes

COTTON - MAY - MONTHLY AVERAGE PRICE

Year of Expiration	Jul	Aug	Sep	Oct	Nov	Dec	Jan	Feb	Mar	Apr	May	Jul-May Average
1976	50.56	52.97	55.63	55.42	56.50	59.79	62.01	61.44	59.40	60.59	63.98	58.03
1977	78.42	76.47	77.53	82.26	81.32	78.10	71.62	75.64	79.54	77.03	76.67	77.69
1978	59.70	55.82	54.39	54.10	52.44	53.13	56.08	56.78	57.66	56.62	57.38	55.83
1979	64.45	67.15	67.80	71.41	73.13	70.39	67.70	66.07	62.21	59.38	61.51	66.47
1980	65.82	67.56	67.66	67.22	70.89	73.64	79.25	86.12	84.01	83.24	82.64	75.28
1981	80.09	87.41	92.45	91.16	90.36	93.12	92.69	90.14	87.33	86.14	82.19	88.46
1982	80.19	75.17	70.41	69.91	66.94	64.83	67.00	65.78	65.43	66.69	67.95	69.12
1983	76.18	71.96	69.12	67.51	66.81	67.31	67.35	68.00	73.02	71.80	70.31	69.94
1984	80.42	81.84	80.78	80.31	81.95	80.21	76.29	76.40	80.24	80.44	82.91	80.16
1985	72.35	69.56	68.16	69.13	67.84	66.87	67.05	65.26	65.96	67.91	68.02	68.01

	Jul	Aug	Sep	Oct	Nov	Dec	Jan	Feb	Mar	Apr	May
AVERAGE MOVE											
All Years		-0.23	-0.20	0.45	-0.02	-0.08	-0.04	0.46	0.32	-0.50	0.37
Less Extremes		-0.57	-0.28	0.17	-0.12	-0.11	0.06	0.03	0.25	-0.51	0.54
Ave Up - All Years		3.12	1.90	3.10	2.03	2.00	2.20	2.47	2.87	1.15	1.69
Ave Down - All Years		-3.57	-2.30	-0.69	-1.39	-2.16	-3.38	-1.55	-2.23	-1.59	-1.60
COUNT											
Number Up		5	5	3	4	5	6	5	5	4	6
Number Down		5	5	7	6	5	4	5	5	6	4
Pct Up		50.0%	50.0%	30.0%	40.0%	50.0%	60.0%	50.0%	50.0%	40.0%	60.0%
Pct Down		50.0%	50.0%	70.0%	60.0%	50.0%	40.0%	50.0%	50.0%	60.0%	40.0%
EXTREMES											
Greatest Up		7.32	5.04	4.72	3.67	3.29	5.61	6.87	5.01	1.95	3.39
Greatest Down		-5.02	-4.77	-1.61	-2.97	-3.21	-6.48	-2.55	-3.86	-2.82	-3.95
SEASONAL INDEX : AVERAGE PERCENTAGE METHOD											
All Years	100.2	99.5	99.1	99.8	99.7	99.6	99.8	100.4	100.8	100.2	100.9
Less Extremes	99.8	99.6	99.6	100.1	99.1	99.6	99.9	99.3	100.4	100.2	100.8
SEASONAL INDEX : LINK RELATIVE METHOD											
All Years		100.0	99.5	100.0	99.8	99.7	99.8	100.3	100.6	99.8	100.4
Less Extremes		100.2	99.9	100.1	99.9	99.6	100.0	100.0	100.3	99.6	100.4

COTTON - MAY - MONTH OF HIGH AND LOW

Year of Expiration	Jul	Aug	Sep	Oct	Nov	Dec	Jan	Feb	Mar	Apr	May
1976	L										H
1977				H			L				
1978	H				L						
1979					H					L	
1980	L							H			
1981	L					H					
1982	H					L					
1983	H				L						
1984							L				H
1985	H							L			

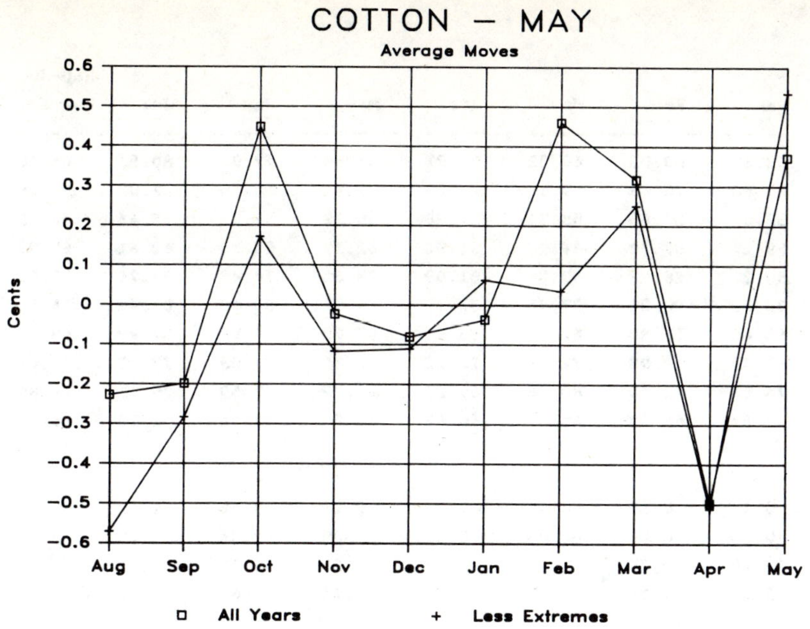
COTTON – MAY
Average Moves
Cents
0.6
0.5
0.4
0.3
0.2
0.1
0
−0.1
−0.2
−0.3
−0.4
−0.5
−0.6
Aug
Sep
Oct
Nov
Dec
Jan
Feb
Mar
Apr
May
All Years
Less Extremes

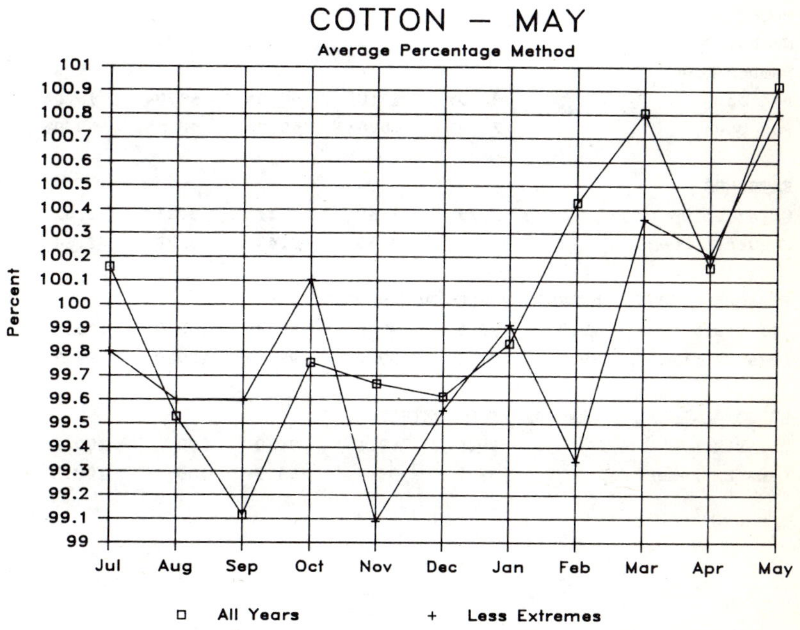
COTTON – MAY
Average Percentage Method
Percent
101
100.9
100.8
100.7
100.6
100.5
100.4
100.3
100.2
100.1
100
99.9
99.8
99.7
99.6
99.5
99.4
99.3
99.2
99.1
99
Jul
Aug
Sep
Oct
Nov
Dec
Jan
Feb
Mar
Apr
May
All Years
Less Extremes

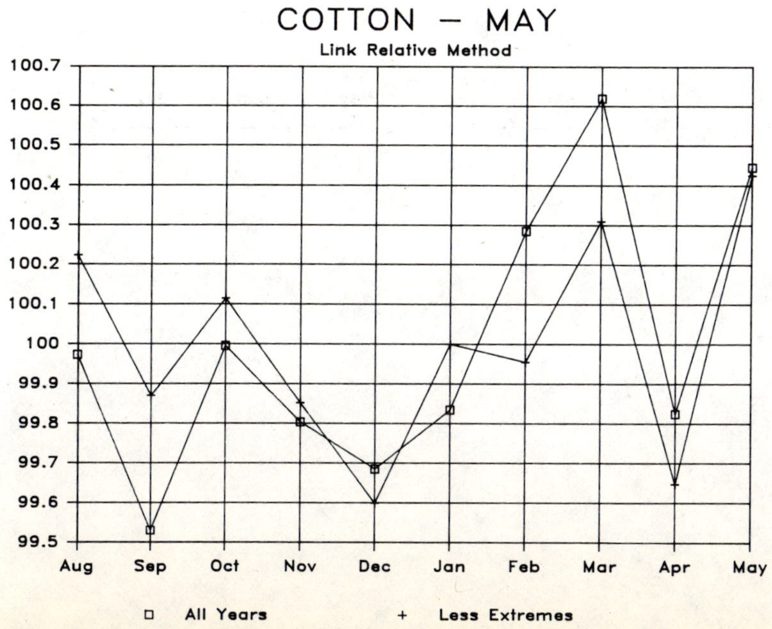
COTTON – MAY
Link Relative Method
100.7
100.6
100.5
100.4
100.3
100.2
100.1
100
99.9
99.8
99.7
99.6
99.5
Aug
Sep
Oct
Nov
Dec
Jan
Feb
Mar
Apr
May
All Years
Less Extremes

COTTON - JULY - MONTHLY AVERAGE PRICE

Year of Expiration	Sep	Oct	Nov	Dec	Jan	Feb	Mar	Apr	May	Jun	Jul	Sep-Jul Average
1976	56.09	55.87	56.92	60.09	62.31	62.02	60.02	61.37	65.86	77.03	88.58	64.20
1977	76.54	80.27	79.39	77.66	71.88	75.66	79.45	77.23	73.44	63.95	67.07	74.78
1978	55.00	54.70	53.22	53.93	57.07	57.85	58.84	57.98	60.39	59.22	56.44	56.78
1979	68.06	71.61	73.57	71.38	69.27	67.79	64.20	61.04	62.17	65.83	62.61	67.05
1980	68.70	68.34	71.89	74.87	80.21	86.22	83.08	81.09	79.83	74.46	78.78	77.04
1981	92.12	90.81	90.28	92.87	92.85	90.01	87.78	87.37	83.91	83.48	82.40	88.54
1982	72.02	71.48	68.63	66.23	68.66	67.89	67.43	68.51	67.75	64.88	67.98	68.31
1983	70.66	68.66	67.93	68.36	68.40	68.98	72.38	72.21	73.36	77.63	77.62	71.47
1984	81.27	80.65	82.30	80.91	76.64	76.40	80.48	80.27	83.72	79.59	76.41	79.88
1985	69.29	70.18	69.03	67.86	67.87	66.08	65.37	66.62	64.60	62.34	61.19	66.40

	Sep	Oct	Nov	Dec	Jan	Feb	Mar	Apr	May	Jun	Jul
AVERAGE MOVE											
All Years		0.28	0.06	0.10	0.10	0.37	0.01	-0.53	0.13	-0.66	1.07
Less Extremes		0.14	-0.01	0.03	0.18	0.07	-0.04	-0.44	0.08	-1.04	0.29
Ave Up - All Years		2.72	2.05	1.97	2.20	2.79	3.07	1.23	2.53	6.37	5.52
Ave Down - All Years		-0.76	-1.27	-1.78	-3.04	-1.24	-2.02	-1.29	-2.26	-3.67	-1.90
COUNT											
Number Up		3	4	5	6	4	4	3	5	3	4
Number Down		7	6	5	4	6	6	7	5	7	6
Pct Up		30.0%	40.0%	50.0%	60.0%	40.0%	40.0%	30.0%	50.0%	30.0%	40.0%
Pct Down		70.0%	60.0%	50.0%	40.0%	60.0%	60.0%	70.0%	50.0%	70.0%	60.0%
EXTREMES											
Greatest Up		3.73	3.55	3.17	5.34	6.02	4.07	1.35	4.49	11.17	11.55
Greatest Down		-2.01	-2.85	-2.40	-5.78	-2.84	-3.59	-3.16	-3.79	-9.50	-3.22
SEASONAL INDEX : AVERAGE PERCENTAGE METHOD											
All Years	99.2	99.6	99.6	99.7	100.0	100.5	100.5	99.8	100.2	99.6	101.2
Less Extremes	99.9	100.2	99.7	99.6	100.0	99.7	100.5	100.2	100.4	98.8	98.0
SEASONAL INDEX : LINK RELATIVE METHOD											
All Years		99.9	99.8	99.9	100.2	100.6	100.5	99.6	99.9	99.2	100.4
Less Extremes		99.7	99.7	99.7	100.4	100.5	100.6	100.1	100.4	99.2	99.6

COTTON - JULY - MONTH OF HIGH AND LOW

Year of Expiration	Sep	Oct	Nov	Dec	Jan	Feb	Mar	Apr	May	Jun	Jul
1976		L									H
1977		H								L	
1978			L						H		
1979			H					L			
1980		L				L					
1981				H							L
1982	H									L	
1983			L							H	
1984						L			H		
1985		H									L

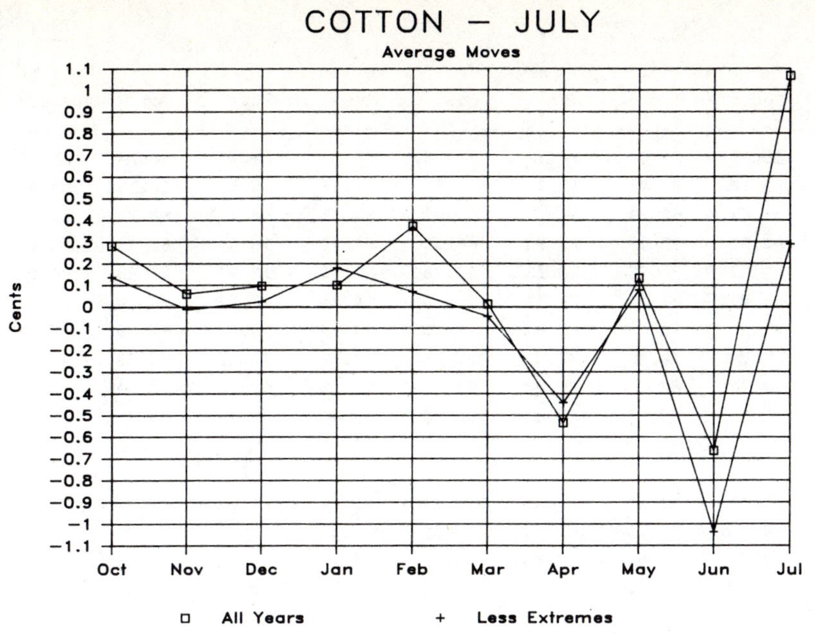
COTTON – JULY
Average Moves
Cents
1.1
1
0.9
0.8
0.7
0.6
0.5
0.4
0.3
0.2
0.1
0
−0.1
−0.2
−0.3
−0.4
−0.5
−0.6
−0.7
−0.8
−0.9
−1
−1.1
Oct
Nov
Dec
Jan
Feb
Mar
Apr
May
Jun
Jul
□ All Years
+ Less Extremes

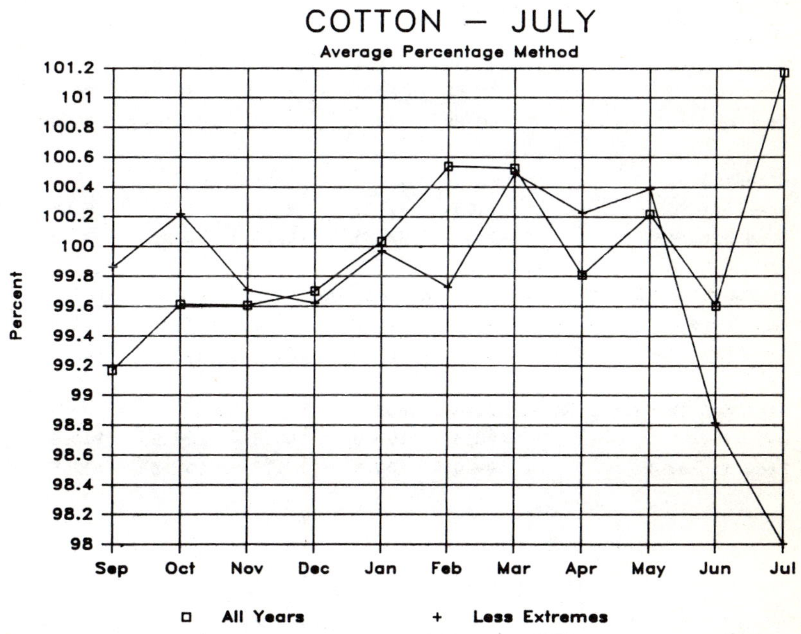
COTTON – JULY
Average Percentage Method
Percent
101.2
101
100.8
100.6
100.4
100.2
100
99.8
99.6
99.4
99.2
99
98.8
98.6
98.4
98.2
98
Sep
Oct
Nov
Dec
Jan
Feb
Mar
Apr
May
Jun
Jul
□ All Years
+ Less Extremes

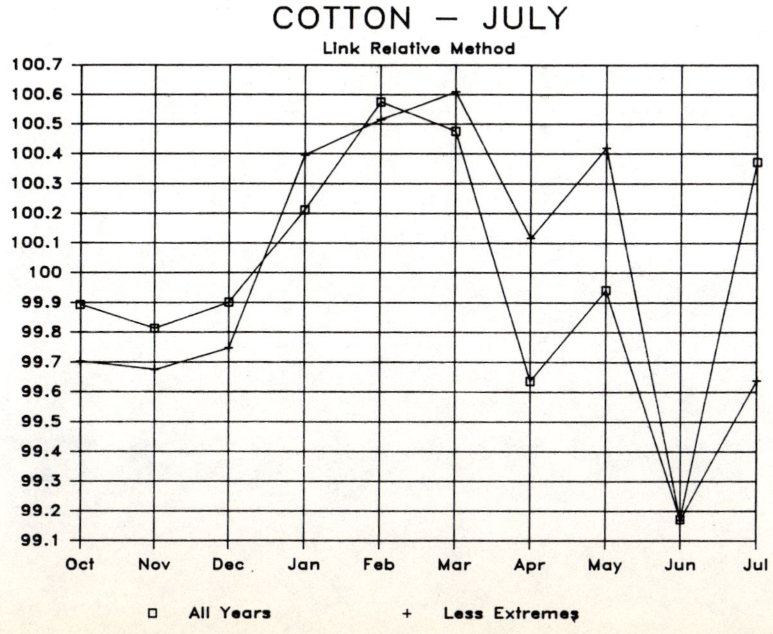
COTTON – JULY
Link Relative Method
100.7
100.6
100.5
100.4
100.3
100.2
100.1
100
99.9
99.8
99.7
99.6
99.5
99.4
99.3
99.2
99.1
Oct
Nov
Dec
Jan
Feb
Mar
Apr
May
Jun
Jul
□ All Years
+ Less Extremes

COTTON - OCTOBER - MONTHLY AVERAGE PRICE

Year of Expiration	Dec	Jan	Feb	Mar	Apr	May	Jun	Jul	Aug	Sep	Oct	Dec-Oct Average
1976	58.02	59.94	60.62	59.12	60.96	66.04	77.41	83.32	77.17	75.73	80.24	68.96
1977	71.73	68.18	72.03	75.42	73.19	70.91	63.42	60.05	54.31	51.57	52.15	64.81
1978	54.91	57.96	58.92	60.14	59.81	62.31	61.71	60.02	62.58	62.39	64.22	60.45
1979	66.69	65.70	66.04	64.86	62.57	63.46	65.92	64.55	64.19	63.95	65.20	64.83
1980	73.71	76.40	80.52	79.47	77.32	76.78	72.13	80.98	89.10	91.97	88.33	80.61
1981	87.44	88.15	85.80	85.20	85.01	81.53	79.51	77.15	69.28	64.17	65.10	78.94
1982	68.05	70.85	70.53	70.05	71.32	70.57	67.80	70.76	65.69	63.43	61.78	68.26
1983	67.26	67.70	67.69	70.88	72.29	74.49	78.49	77.56	79.67	77.15	75.53	73.52
1984	75.57	73.00	73.78	76.81	77.32	80.03	75.71	69.67	66.00	64.27	64.33	72.41
1985	68.21	67.82	66.35	65.11	65.33	63.52	61.44	60.64	58.72	59.28	60.71	63.37

	Dec	Jan	Feb	Mar	Apr	May	Jun	Jul	Aug	Sep	Oct
AVERAGE MOVE											
All Years		0.41	0.66	0.48	-0.19	0.45	-0.61	0.12	-1.80	-1.28	0.37
Less Extremes		0.58	0.60	0.36	-0.19	0.36	-1.25	-0.20	-2.28	-1.32	0.35
Ave Up - All Years		1.93	1.79	2.71	1.05	2.68	5.95	5.91	4.26	1.71	1.51
Ave Down - All Years		-1.88	-1.03	-1.01	-1.44	-1.77	-3.42	-2.36	-4.40	-2.03	-2.30
COUNT											
Number Up		6	6	4	5	5	3	3	3	2	7
Number Down		4	4	6	5	5	7	7	7	8	3
Pct Up		60.0%	60.0%	40.0%	50.0%	50.0%	30.0%	30.0%	30.0%	20.0%	70.0%
Pct Down		40.0%	40.0%	60.0%	50.0%	50.0%	70.0%	70.0%	70.0%	80.0%	30.0%
EXTREMES											
Greatest Up		3.05	4.12	3.39	1.84	5.08	11.37	8.84	8.12	2.87	4.50
Greatest Down		-3.55	-2.35	-1.50	-2.29	-3.48	-7.49	-6.04	-7.87	-5.10	-3.64
SEASONAL INDEX : AVERAGE PERCENTAGE METHOD											
All Years	99.4	99.9	100.9	101.6	101.3	102.0	101.2	101.2	98.5	96.7	97.4
Less Extremes	99.9	100.1	101.2	101.7	101.5	101.8	101.2	99.8	98.7	96.6	97.1
SEASONAL INDEX : LINK RELATIVE METHOD											
All Years		98.8	100.0	100.8	100.8	101.9	101.4	101.7	99.2	97.4	98.2
Less Extremes		99.0	100.3	101.3	101.5	102.5	101.3	101.2	98.3	96.8	97.8

COTTON - OCTOBER - MONTH OF HIGH AND LOW

Year of Expiration	Dec	Jan	Feb	Mar	Apr	May	Jun	Jul	Aug	Sep	Oct
1976	L							H			
1977				H						L	
1978	L										H
1979	H				L						
1980							L			H	
1981		H								L	
1982					H						L
1983	L								H		
1984						H				L	
1985	H								L		

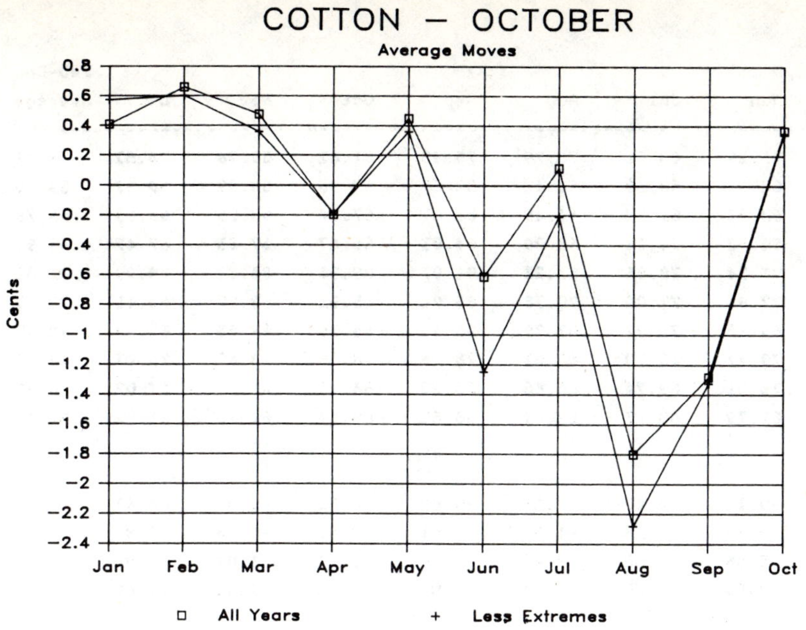
COTTON – OCTOBER
Average Moves
Cents
0.8
0.6
0.4
0.2
0
−0.2
−0.4
−0.6
−0.8
−1
−1.2
−1.4
−1.6
−1.8
−2
−2.2
−2.4
Jan
Feb
Mar
Apr
May
Jun
Jul
Aug
Sep
Oct
All Years
Less Extremes

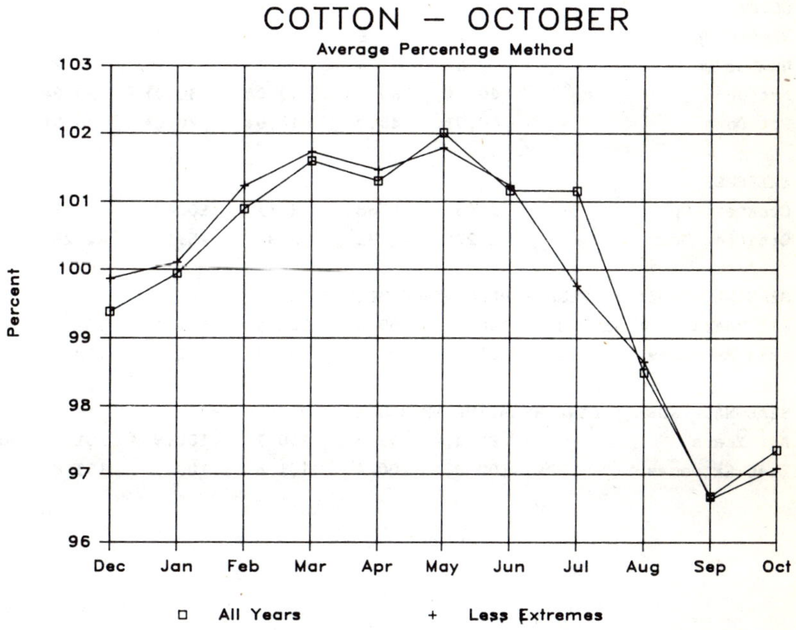
COTTON – OCTOBER
Average Percentage Method
Percent
103
102
101
100
99
98
97
96
Dec
Jan
Feb
Mar
Apr
May
Jun
Jul
Aug
Sep
Oct
All Years
Less Extremes

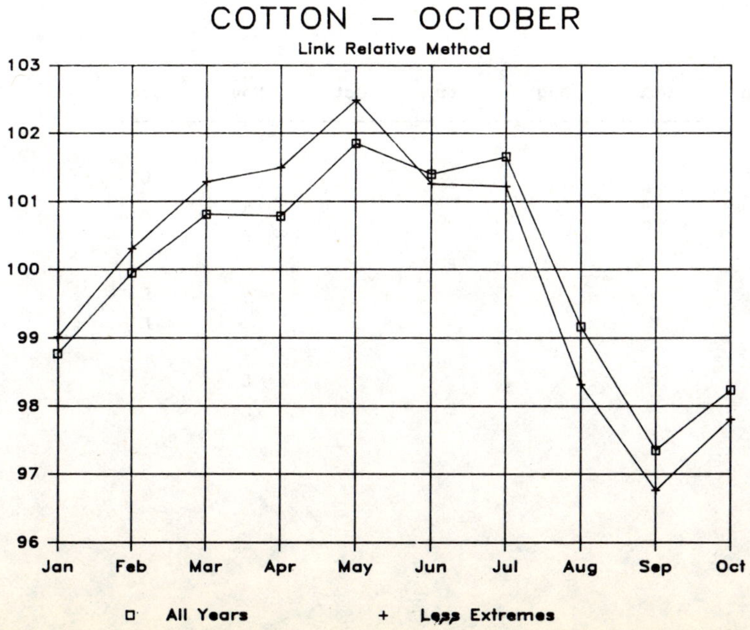
COTTON – OCTOBER
Link Relative Method
103
102
101
100
99
98
97
96
Jan
Feb
Mar
Apr
May
Jun
Jul
Aug
Sep
Oct
All Years
Less Extremes

COTTON - DECEMBER - MONTHLY AVERAGE PRICE

Year of Expiration	Feb	Mar	Apr	May	Jun	Jul	Aug	Sep	Oct	Nov	Dec	Feb-Dec Average
1976	58.70	58.12	59.99	64.51	75.19	80.51	75.79	75.95	81.42	80.24	78.52	71.72
1977	68.23	70.89	68.79	67.28	62.09	58.59	54.42	52.67	52.35	50.99	50.37	59.70
1978	59.31	60.75	60.74	63.52	63.22	61.93	64.49	64.67	67.74	68.05	66.99	63.76
1979	64.86	64.59	62.52	62.90	64.53	64.13	65.09	64.81	65.47	67.85	67.47	64.93
1980	77.36	76.16	73.85	74.00	71.24	78.96	87.23	91.97	89.94	88.82	88.29	81.62
1981	82.61	82.46	82.59	79.74	77.65	77.00	70.78	65.94	65.91	62.87	60.81	73.49
1982	71.69	71.21	72.50	71.93	69.15	72.92	67.79	65.49	64.35	62.68	62.38	68.37
1983	67.92	70.47	72.25	74.80	79.47	78.70	80.61	78.58	78.35	78.87	76.97	76.09
1984	72.36	74.83	75.13	77.09	74.01	69.74	66.86	65.20	66.26	65.17	67.02	70.33
1985	66.48	65.21	65.38	63.65	61.79	60.77	59.04	58.61	60.19	61.15	61.22	62.14

	Feb	Mar	Apr	May	Jun	Jul	Aug	Sep	Oct	Nov	Dec
AVERAGE MOVE											
All Years		0.52	-0.10	0.57	-0.11	0.49	-1.11	-0.82	0.81	-0.53	-0.67
Less Extremes		0.47	-0.07	0.50	-0.82	0.18	-1.65	-1.01	0.58	-0.58	-0.81
Ave Up - All Years		2.28	0.92	2.06	5.66	5.60	3.43	1.70	2.37	1.04	0.96
Ave Down - All Years		-0.66	-1.62	-1.66	-2.58	-1.70	-4.14	-1.90	-0.75	-1.58	-1.07
COUNT											
Number Up		4	6	6	3	3	4	3	5	4	2
Number Down		6	4	4	7	7	6	7	5	6	8
Pct Up		40.0%	60.0%	60.0%	30.0%	30.0%	40.0%	30.0%	50.0%	40.0%	20.0%
Pct Down		60.0%	40.0%	40.0%	70.0%	70.0%	60.0%	70.0%	50.0%	60.0%	80.0%
EXTREMES											
Greatest Up		2.65	1.88	4.51	10.69	7.71	8.27	4.74	5.47	2.38	1.85
Greatest Down		-1.27	-2.31	-2.84	-5.19	-4.28	-6.22	-4.84	-2.03	-3.04	-2.06
SEASONAL INDEX : AVERAGE PERCENTAGE METHOD											
All Years	100.0	100.8	100.6	101.4	101.1	101.5	99.7	98.4	99.6	98.9	98.0
Less Extremes	100.5	101.0	100.9	101.4	102.2	100.7	99.8	97.9	99.4	99.0	98.5
SEASONAL INDEX : LINK RELATIVE METHOD											
All Years		99.4	99.5	100.7	100.9	101.6	100.1	98.9	100.3	99.7	98.9
Less Extremes		100.0	100.4	101.6	100.9	101.4	99.5	98.4	99.8	99.4	98.7

COTTON - DECEMBER - MONTH OF HIGH AND LOW

Year of Expiration	Feb	Mar	Apr	May	Jun	Jul	Aug	Sep	Oct	Nov	Dec
1976		L							H		
1977		H									L
1978	L									H	
1979			L							H	
1980					L			H			
1981	H										L
1982						H					L
1983	L						H				
1984				H						L	
1985	H							L			

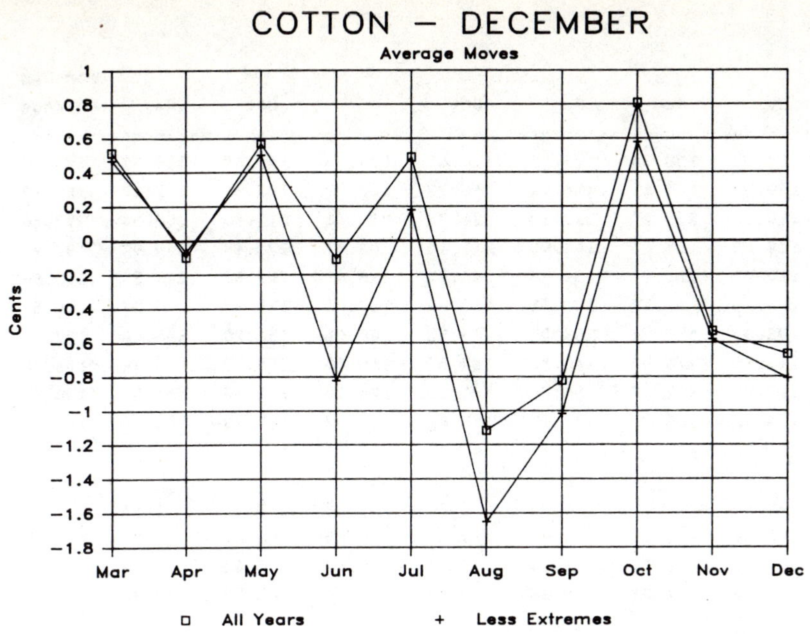
COTTON — DECEMBER
Average Moves
Cents
1
0.8
0.6
0.4
0.2
0
−0.2
−0.4
−0.6
−0.8
−1
−1.2
−1.4
−1.6
−1.8
Mar
Apr
May
Jun
Jul
Aug
Sep
Oct
Nov
Dec
All Years
Less Extremes

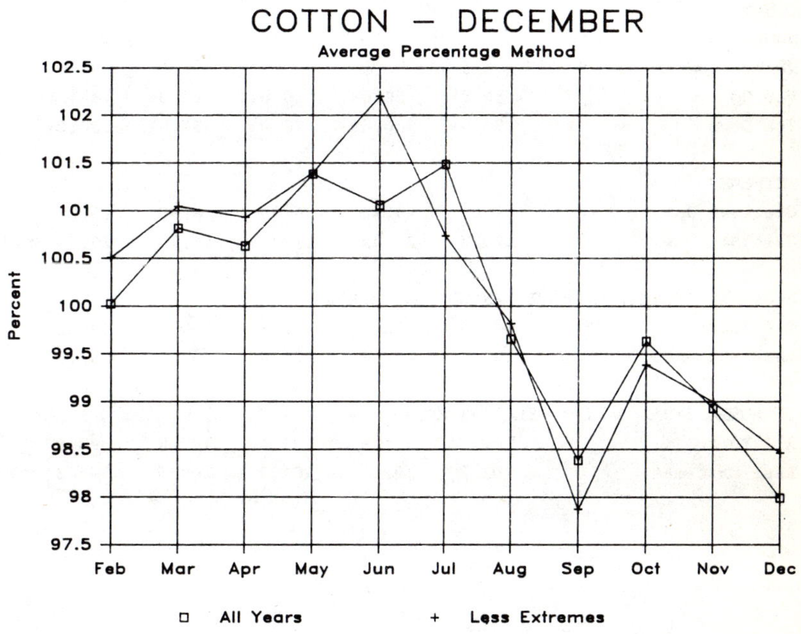
COTTON — DECEMBER
Average Percentage Method
Percent
102.5
102
101.5
101
100.5
100
99.5
99
98.5
98
97.5
Feb
Mar
Apr
May
Jun
Jul
Aug
Sep
Oct
Nov
Dec
All Years
Less Extremes

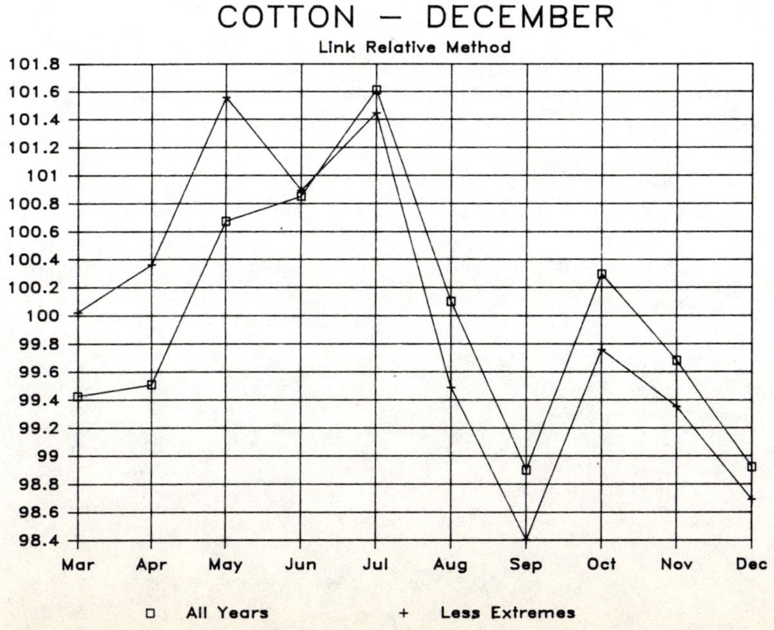
COTTON — DECEMBER
Link Relative Method
101.8
101.6
101.4
101.2
101
100.8
100.6
100.4
100.2
100
99.8
99.6
99.4
99.2
99
98.8
98.6
98.4
Mar
Apr
May
Jun
Jul
Aug
Sep
Oct
Nov
Dec
All Years
Less Extremes

LUMBER - JANUARY - MONTHLY AVERAGE PRICE

Year of Expiration	Mar	Apr	May	Jun	Jul	Aug	Sep	Oct	Nov	Dec	Jan	Mar-Jan Average
1976	145.27	156.27	151.55	155.16	153.94	138.26	129.27	126.49	143.38	147.49	150.87	145.27
1977	169.22	173.40	169.26	167.38	159.32	156.15	164.64	166.23	176.09	182.61	177.17	169.22
1978	198.10	202.27	206.57	206.10	210.08	225.27	239.18	224.72	215.61	213.86	208.54	213.66
1979	189.45	181.25	181.97	181.43	184.80	187.60	196.90	211.10	202.91	220.48	239.98	197.99
1980	198.10	202.27	206.57	206.10	210.08	225.27	239.18	224.72	215.61	213.86	208.54	213.66
1981	189.32	174.40	193.70	202.28	208.79	197.77	183.51	180.62	180.21	160.57	170.33	185.59
1982	213.18	209.67	201.33	201.43	195.39	178.34	159.01	145.82	148.01	151.20	146.48	177.26
1983	171.00	163.75	160.16	148.46	148.91	146.95	146.63	152.58	165.00	165.53	175.94	158.63
1984	217.46	222.36	227.24	225.34	212.57	192.37	185.00	186.73	178.24	172.86	164.07	198.57
1985	209.10	191.33	167.01	159.06	143.92	146.77	139.09	142.81	151.37	151.29	158.84	160.05

	Mar	Apr	May	Jun	Jul	Aug	Sep	Oct	Nov	Dec	Jan
AVERAGE MOVE											
All Years		-2.33	-1.16	-1.26	-2.50	-3.30	-1.23	-2.06	1.46	0.33	2.10
Less Extremes		-2.06	-0.82	-1.19	-2.04	-3.51	-0.87	-2.54	0.85	0.67	1.29
Ave Up - All Years		5.68	6.70	4.10	3.65	9.01	11.40	5.44	9.98	6.38	10.12
Ave Down - All Years		-10.33	-9.02	-3.56	-8.64	-11.52	-9.66	-9.55	-7.06	-5.72	-5.92
COUNT											
Number Up		5	5	3	5	4	4	5	5	5	5
Number Down		5	5	7	5	6	6	5	5	5	5
Pct Up		50.0%	50.0%	30.0%	50.0%	40.0%	40.0%	50.0%	50.0%	50.0%	50.0%
Pct Down		50.0%	50.0%	70.0%	50.0%	60.0%	60.0%	50.0%	50.0%	50.0%	50.0%
EXTREMES											
Greatest Up		11.00	19.30	8.59	6.50	15.20	13.91	14.20	16.89	17.57	19.50
Greatest Down		-17.77	-24.33	-11.70	-15.14	-20.20	-19.33	-14.46	-9.11	-19.64	-8.79
SEASONAL INDEX : AVERAGE PERCENTAGE METHOD											
All Years	105.1	103.8	102.7	101.9	100.4	98.1	97.1	96.1	97.6	97.9	99.2
Less Extremes	103.5	103.4	102.6	101.8	100.2	97.9	96.5	96.6	98.6	97.8	98.5
SEASONAL INDEX : LINK RELATIVE METHOD											
All Years		102.3	101.9	101.4	100.2	98.6	97.8	97.3	99.3	99.8	101.4
Less Extremes		102.0	101.7	101.3	100.5	98.8	98.2	97.6	99.0	99.8	101.2

LUMBER - JANUARY - MONTH OF HIGH AND LOW

Year of Expiration	Mar	Apr	May	Jun	Jul	Aug	Sep	Oct	Nov	Dec	Jan
1976		H						L			
1977						H					H
1978								L			H
1979		L									H
1980	L						H				
1981					H					L	
1982	H							L			
1983							L				H
1984			H								L
1985	H						L				

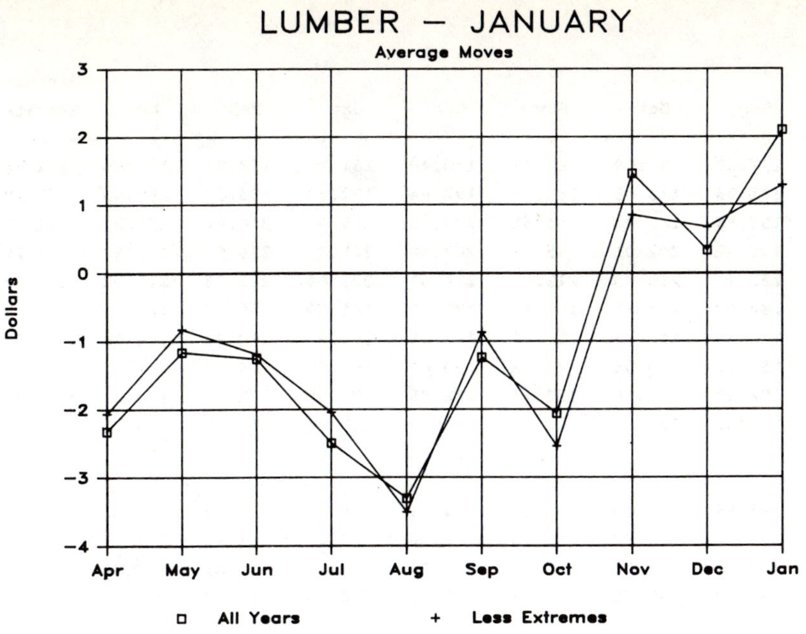
LUMBER — JANUARY
Average Moves
Dollars
3
2
1
0
−1
−2
−3
−4
Apr
May
Jun
Jul
Aug
Sep
Oct
Nov
Dec
Jan
All Years
Less Extremes

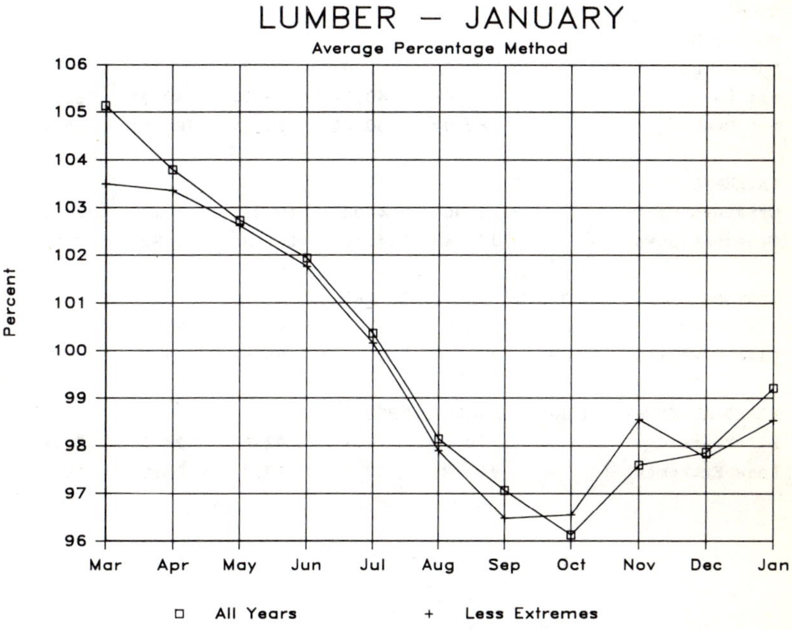
LUMBER — JANUARY
Average Percentage Method
Percent
106
105
104
103
102
101
100
99
98
97
96
Mar
Apr
May
Jun
Jul
Aug
Sep
Oct
Nov
Dec
Jan
All Years
Less Extremes

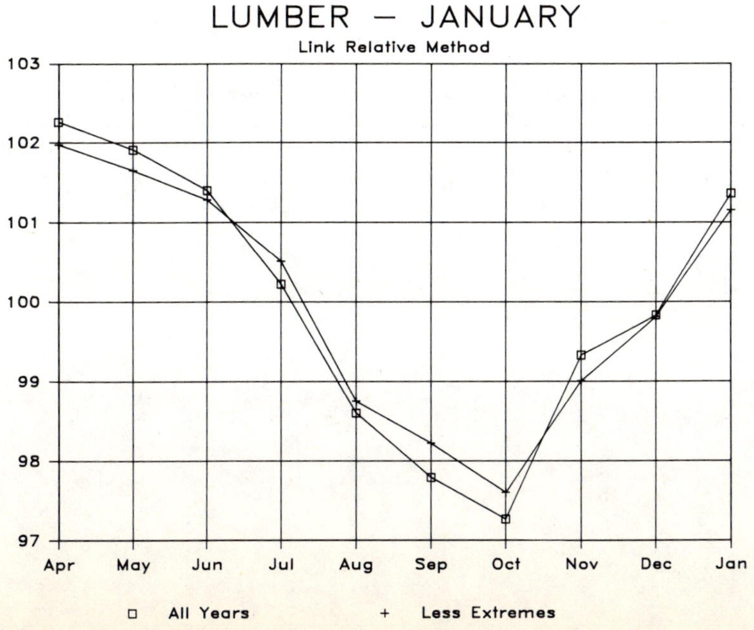
LUMBER — JANUARY
Link Relative Method
103
102
101
100
99
98
97
Apr
May
Jun
Jul
Aug
Sep
Oct
Nov
Dec
Jan
All Years
Less Extremes

LUMBER - MARCH - MONTHLY AVERAGE PRICE

Year of Expiration	May	Jun	Jul	Aug	Sep	Oct	Nov	Dec	Jan	Feb	Mar	May-Mar Average
1976	152.56	159.18	158.57	147.35	137.59	135.09	150.77	155.40	161.79	163.97	155.95	152.56
1977	177.20	173.15	164.90	162.21	171.06	173.65	185.63	192.44	182.82	185.20	180.90	177.20
1978	199.92	199.35	195.91	193.59	192.68	189.93	194.61	209.58	209.92	216.64	214.33	201.50
1979	183.03	183.80	186.16	189.34	198.22	207.01	195.68	207.56	221.25	236.60	221.97	202.78
1980	209.26	209.71	211.59	221.82	232.95	219.03	212.26	218.61	222.64	223.75	213.02	217.69
1981	204.71	211.67	215.69	204.47	194.99	195.22	197.94	178.65	181.30	166.27	149.33	190.93
1982	211.32	211.15	204.38	187.56	170.63	158.75	162.16	164.01	151.96	140.92	134.85	172.51
1983	167.86	155.32	155.64	154.75	155.97	163.04	177.12	180.67	191.25	184.37	177.08	169.37
1984	231.32	228.70	218.17	202.55	196.98	201.18	192.41	186.85	177.39	181.87	180.33	199.79
1985	171.04	166.34	152.16	155.63	148.83	153.80	162.34	160.06	161.04	146.88	129.45	155.23

	May	Jun	Jul	Aug	Sep	Oct	Nov	Dec	Jan	Feb	Mar
AVERAGE MOVE											
All Years		-0.98	-3.52	-4.39	-1.94	-0.32	3.42	2.29	0.75	-1.49	-8.93
Less Extremes		-0.53	-3.13	-4.66	-1.70	0.24	3.73	3.40	0.74	-1.90	-8.79
Ave Up - All Years		3.70	2.14	5.63	7.52	4.64	8.73	7.15	5.52	5.37	NONE
Ave Down - All Years		-4.11	-7.30	-8.68	-8.24	-7.76	-8.96	-9.04	-10.38	-11.77	-8.93
COUNT											
Number Up		4	4	3	4	6	7	7	7	6	0
Number Down		6	6	7	6	4	3	3	3	4	10
Pct Up		40.0%	40.0%	30.0%	40.0%	60.0%	70.0%	70.0%	70.0%	60.0%	0.0%
Pct Down		60.0%	60.0%	70.0%	60.0%	40.0%	30.0%	30.0%	30.0%	40.0%	100.0%
EXTREMES											
Greatest Up		6.96	4.02	10.23	11.13	8.79	15.68	14.97	13.69	15.35	0.00
Greatest Down		-12.54	-14.18	-16.82	-16.92	-13.92	-11.33	-19.29	-12.05	-15.03	-17.44
SEASONAL INDEX : AVERAGE PERCENTAGE METHOD											
All Years	104.0	103.5	101.4	98.8	97.5	97.4	99.7	100.9	101.3	100.2	95.3
Less Extremes	103.5	102.7	100.4	98.5	97.2	97.9	99.8	100.9	101.5	100.5	95.6
SEASONAL INDEX : LINK RELATIVE METHOD											
All Years		100.4	99.1	97.5	97.0	97.6	100.7	102.6	103.6	103.0	98.5
Less Extremes		100.2	99.2	97.3	96.8	97.6	100.5	102.8	103.9	103.1	98.7

LUMBER - MARCH - MONTH OF HIGH AND LOW

Year of Expiration	May	Jun	Jul	Aug	Sep	Oct	Nov	Dec	Jan	Feb	Mar
1976						L				H	
1977				L				H			
1978						L				H	
1979	L									H	
1980	L				H						
1981			H								L
1982	H										L
1983				L					H		
1984	H								L		
1985	H										L

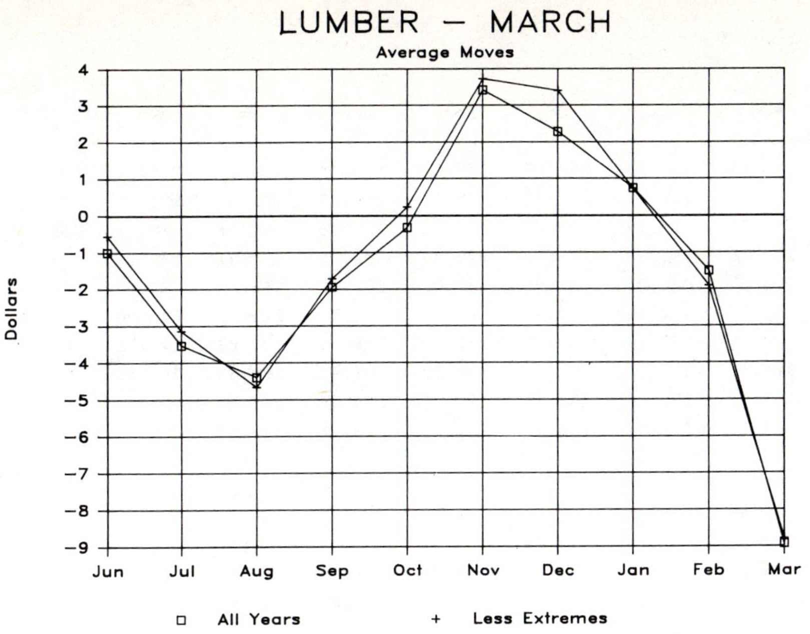
LUMBER — MARCH
Average Moves
Dollars
4
3
2
1
0
−1
−2
−3
−4
−5
−6
−7
−8
−9
Jun
Jul
Aug
Sep
Oct
Nov
Dec
Jan
Feb
Mar
All Years
Less Extremes

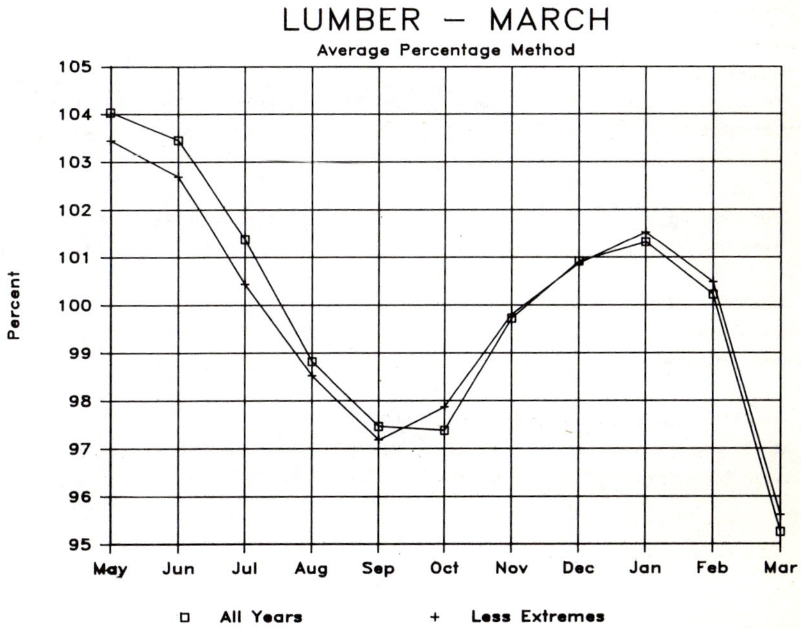
LUMBER — MARCH
Average Percentage Method
Percent
105
104
103
102
101
100
99
98
97
96
95
May
Jun
Jul
Aug
Sep
Oct
Nov
Dec
Jan
Feb
Mar
All Years
Less Extremes

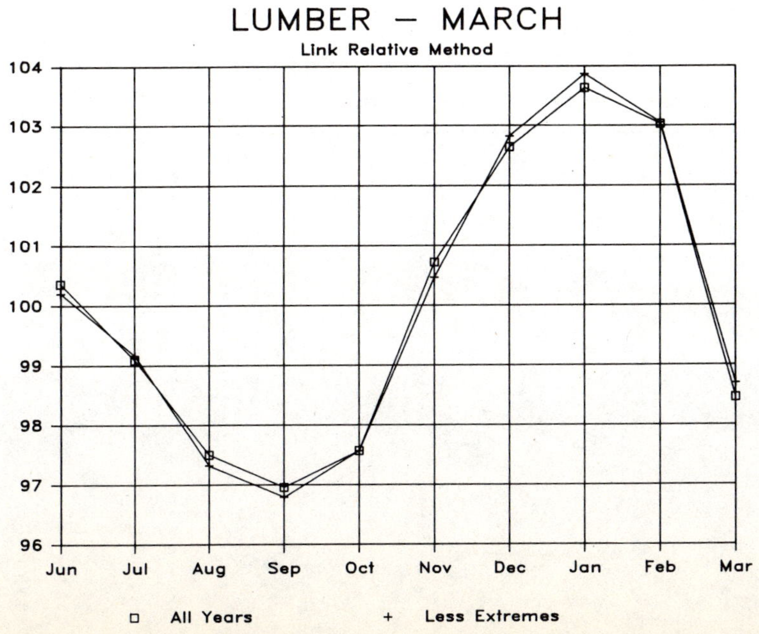
LUMBER — MARCH
Link Relative Method
104
103
102
101
100
99
98
97
96
Jun
Jul
Aug
Sep
Oct
Nov
Dec
Jan
Feb
Mar
All Years
Less Extremes

LUMBER - MAY - MONTHLY AVERAGE PRICE

Year of Expiration	Jul	Aug	Sep	Oct	Nov	Dec	Jan	Feb	Mar	Apr	May	Jul-May Average
1976	161.32	151.16	143.47	141.44	154.68	158.13	168.69	173.14	163.74	158.90	145.56	156.38
1977	183.84	163.00	176.38	178.52	191.90	198.27	190.20	195.74	192.22	181.54	170.67	183.84
1978	201.04	197.67	197.89	195.26	197.74	210.19	209.74	215.41	211.22	208.44	218.17	205.71
1979	187.34	190.88	199.41	205.46	192.70	197.95	209.71	226.92	217.16	218.97	232.16	207.15
1980	213.06	219.47	229.15	218.29	213.67	224.06	227.91	229.08	202.91	165.98	154.79	208.94
1981	222.06	212.76	204.83	206.95	212.12	191.86	195.06	183.11	172.23	175.53	173.26	195.43
1982	208.44	191.21	174.61	166.83	170.33	170.33	157.96	147.82	143.74	133.87	123.31	162.59
1983	160.88	161.96	164.56	171.98	185.66	189.11	201.41	196.03	187.92	188.63	204.40	182.96
1984	221.54	209.55	205.04	209.94	202.72	195.16	188.95	191.91	194.68	169.35	134.17	193.00
1985	158.27	162.87	157.05	161.47	169.60	166.99	169.03	156.51	132.11	136.20	144.06	155.83

	Jul	Aug	Sep	Oct	Nov	Dec	Jan	Feb	Mar	Apr	May
AVERAGE MOVE											
All Years		-5.72	-0.81	0.37	3.50	1.09	1.66	-0.30	-9.77	-8.05	-3.69
Less Extremes		-5.35	-0.62	0.90	4.26	2.34	2.09	-0.96	-9.29	-5.96	-2.18
Ave Up - All Years		3.91	6.88	4.51	8.51	5.91	7.29	6.17	2.78	2.48	11.64
Ave Down - All Years		-12.15	-8.51	-5.83	-8.20	-10.14	-6.77	-10.00	-11.17	-15.07	-13.90
COUNT											
Number Up		4	5	6	7	7	6	6	1	4	4
Number Down		6	5	4	3	3	4	4	9	6	6
Pct Up		40.0%	50.0%	60.0%	70.0%	70.0%	60.0%	60.0%	10.0%	40.0%	40.0%
Pct Down		60.0%	50.0%	40.0%	30.0%	30.0%	40.0%	40.0%	90.0%	60.0%	60.0%
EXTREMES											
Greatest Up		6.40	13.38	7.42	13.68	12.45	12.30	17.21	2.78	4.09	15.77
Greatest Down		-20.84	-16.60	-10.86	-12.76	-20.26	-12.38	-12.52	-26.17	-36.93	-35.18
SEASONAL INDEX : AVERAGE PERCENTAGE METHOD											
All Years	103.9	100.7	99.9	100.1	102.3	102.9	103.7	103.3	97.9	93.7	91.6
Less Extremes	102.9	100.1	99.9	100.2	102.7	103.1	103.7	103.9	98.6	94.0	91.8
SEASONAL INDEX : LINK RELATIVE METHOD											
All Years		97.2	97.5	98.5	101.6	103.0	104.7	105.1	100.4	96.9	95.1
Less Extremes		97.4	97.4	98.2	101.3	103.0	104.7	104.6	100.1	97.3	96.0

LUMBER - MAY - MONTH OF HIGH AND LOW

Year of Expiration	Jul	Aug	Sep	Oct	Nov	Dec	Jan	Feb	Mar	Apr	May
1976				L				H			
1977		L				H					
1978				L							H
1979	L										H
1980			H								L
1981	H								L		
1982	H										L
1983	L										H
1984	H										L
1985							H		L		

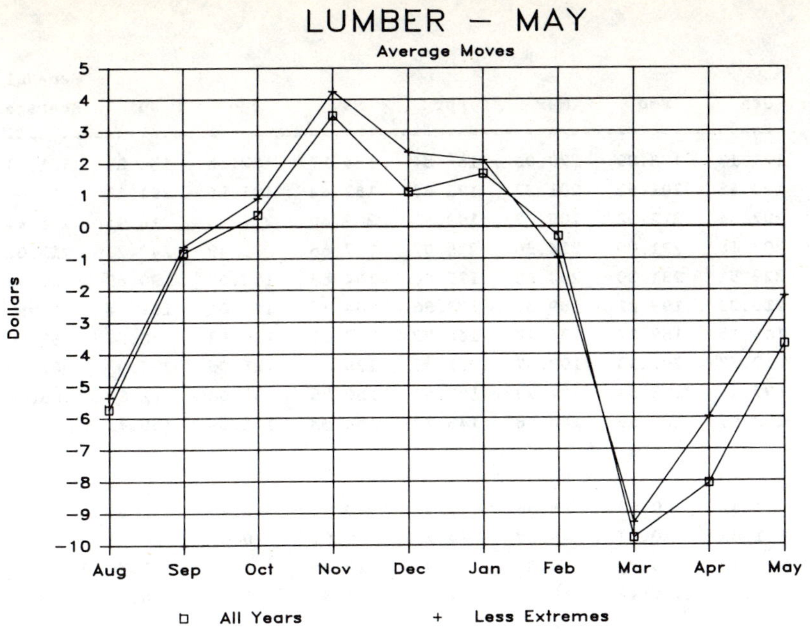
LUMBER — MAY
Average Moves
Dollars
5
4
3
2
1
0
−1
−2
−3
−4
−5
−6
−7
−8
−9
−10
Aug
Sep
Oct
Nov
Dec
Jan
Feb
Mar
Apr
May
All Years
Less Extremes

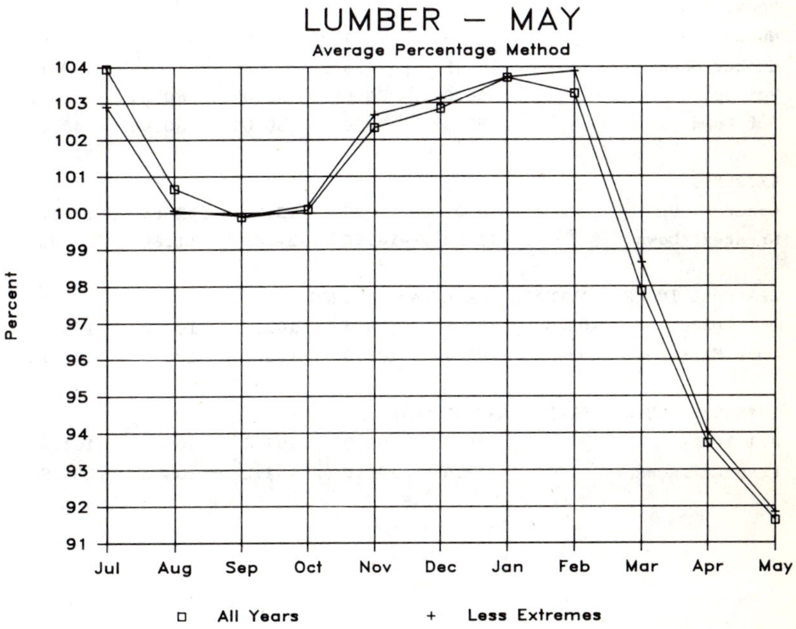
LUMBER — MAY
Average Percentage Method
Percent
104
103
102
101
100
99
98
97
96
95
94
93
92
91
Jul
Aug
Sep
Oct
Nov
Dec
Jan
Feb
Mar
Apr
May
All Years
Less Extremes

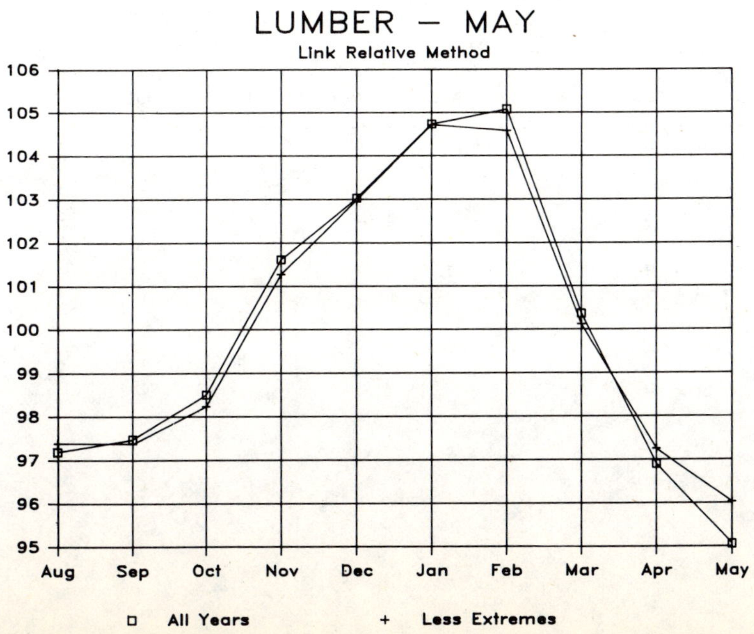
LUMBER — MAY
Link Relative Method
106
105
104
103
102
101
100
99
98
97
96
95
Aug
Sep
Oct
Nov
Dec
Jan
Feb
Mar
Apr
May
All Years
Less Extremes

LUMBER - JULY - MONTHLY AVERAGE PRICE

Year of Expiration	Sep	Oct	Nov	Dec	Jan	Feb	Mar	Apr	May	Jun	Jul	Sep-Jul Average
1976	161.63	149.89	156.72	161.32	171.17	178.09	170.09	168.34	154.17	152.15	154.38	161.63
1977	192.00	185.53	197.19	202.30	193.65	201.52	201.37	192.83	182.44	181.86	181.33	192.00
1978	202.27	198.83	201.08	210.69	207.34	212.02	205.77	199.51	209.40	207.00	216.91	206.44
1979	200.86	204.89	190.33	192.69	203.18	221.00	214.36	215.97	227.66	231.49	240.78	213.02
1980	224.77	216.63	212.20	226.13	229.51	231.30	204.68	175.86	184.86	190.90	190.69	207.96
1981	217.79	221.76	228.07	206.63	210.23	199.21	189.56	193.36	184.77	185.01	181.14	201.59
1982	183.19	175.79	180.14	179.82	168.15	159.17	154.18	146.02	139.63	136.93	138.54	160.14
1983	172.41	180.41	193.77	197.93	210.77	207.13	199.97	203.93	226.34	228.06	205.93	202.42
1984	214.84	217.00	211.13	202.36	197.41	198.57	204.93	182.54	150.55	135.08	121.03	185.04
1985	166.43	169.19	176.69	171.30	173.91	163.59	140.88	145.23	154.53	151.09	150.41	160.30

	Sep	Oct	Nov	Dec	Jan	Feb	Mar	Apr	May	Jun	Jul
AVERAGE MOVE											
All Years		-1.63	2.74	0.39	1.42	0.63	-8.58	-6.22	-0.93	-1.48	-1.84
Less Extremes		-1.57	3.57	1.42	1.62	-0.07	-8.19	-4.72	0.04	-0.67	-0.77
Ave Up - All Years		4.19	7.46	6.63	7.13	6.70	6.37	3.43	12.46	2.96	5.76
Ave Down - All Years		-7.44	-8.29	-8.98	-7.15	-8.49	-10.24	-12.65	-14.31	-4.44	-6.91
COUNT											
Number Up		5	7	6	6	6	1	4	5	4	4
Number Down		5	3	4	4	4	9	6	5	6	6
Pct Up		50.0%	70.0%	60.0%	60.0%	60.0%	10.0%	40.0%	50.0%	40.0%	40.0%
Pct Down		50.0%	30.0%	40.0%	40.0%	40.0%	90.0%	60.0%	50.0%	60.0%	60.0%
EXTREMES											
Greatest Up		8.01	13.35	13.93	12.84	17.82	6.37	4.35	22.41	6.04	9.91
Greatest Down		-11.74	-14.56	-21.43	-11.68	-11.02	-26.61	-28.82	-32.00	-15.47	-22.13
SEASONAL INDEX : AVERAGE PERCENTAGE METHOD											
All Years	102.8	101.8	103.4	103.5	104.2	104.3	99.7	96.4	95.6	94.7	93.7
Less Extremes	103.3	101.4	103.8	104.1	104.5	104.1	99.7	96.9	95.4	95.1	94.8
SEASONAL INDEX : LINK RELATIVE METHOD											
All Years		98.7	101.0	102.0	103.5	104.4	100.4	97.9	97.8	97.3	96.8
Less Extremes		98.5	101.0	102.2	103.5	103.9	99.9	97.8	98.0	97.8	97.5

LUMBER - JULY - MONTH OF HIGH AND LOW

Year of Expiration	Sep	Oct	Nov	Dec	Jan	Feb	Mar	Apr	May	Jun	Jul
1976		L				H					
1977				H							L
1978		L									H
1979			L								H
1980						H		L			
1981			H								L
1982	H									L	
1983	L									H	
1984		H									L
1985			H				L				

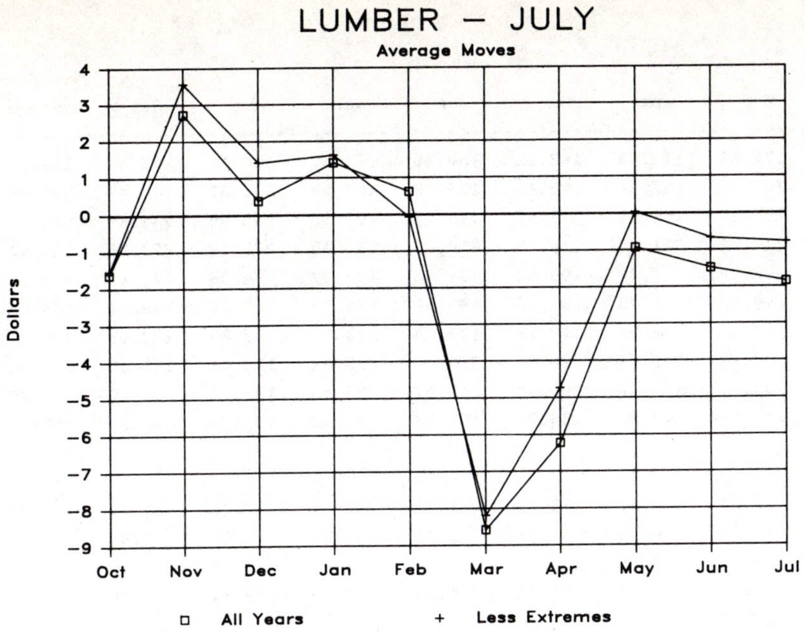
LUMBER – JULY
Average Moves
Dollars
4
3
2
1
0
–1
–2
–3
–4
–5
–6
–7
–8
–9
Oct
Nov
Dec
Jan
Feb
Mar
Apr
May
Jun
Jul
All Years
Less Extremes

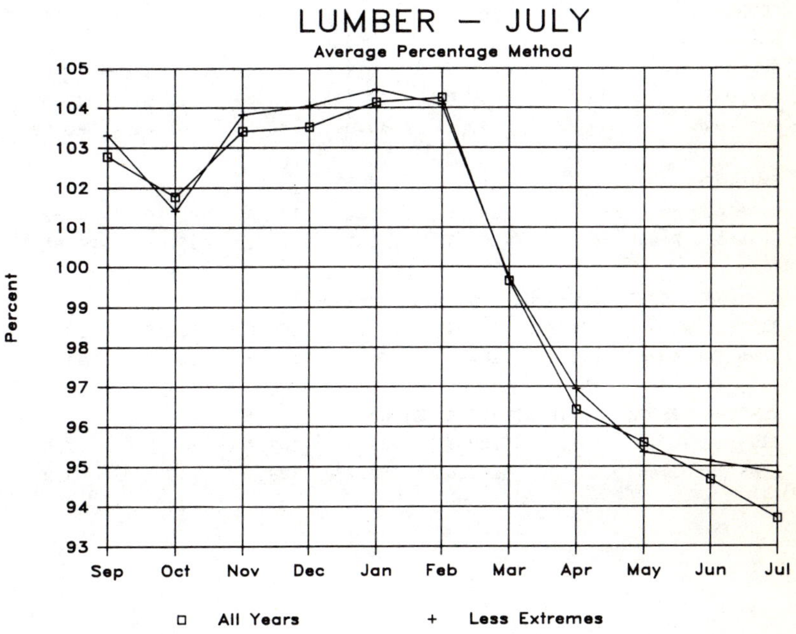
LUMBER – JULY
Average Percentage Method
Percent
105
104
103
102
101
100
99
98
97
96
95
94
93
Sep
Oct
Nov
Dec
Jan
Feb
Mar
Apr
May
Jun
Jul
All Years
Less Extremes

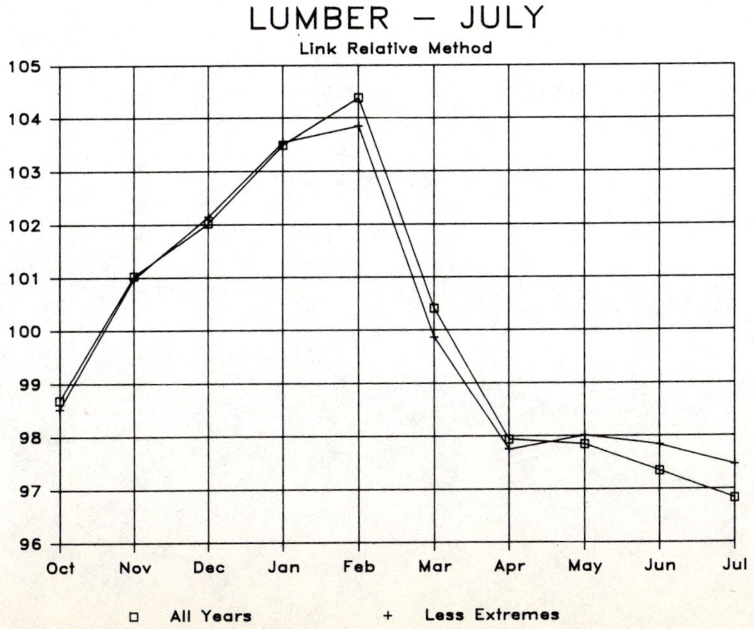
LUMBER – JULY
Link Relative Method
105
104
103
102
101
100
99
98
97
96
Oct
Nov
Dec
Jan
Feb
Mar
Apr
May
Jun
Jul
All Years
Less Extremes

LUMBER - SEPTEMBER - MONTHLY AVERAGE PRICE

Year of Expiration	Nov	Dec	Jan	Feb	Mar	Apr	May	Jun	Jul	Aug	Sep	Nov-Sep Average
1976	166.11	163.48	172.14	178.92	172.06	172.44	162.51	160.35	153.65	160.00	165.53	166.11
1977	198.49	202.19	194.41	201.48	201.42	197.56	188.41	189.03	185.99	205.67	204.46	197.19
1978	202.58	207.89	201.54	203.83	198.23	191.51	198.92	195.71	207.05	215.96	233.45	205.15
1979	186.44	188.57	198.55	215.80	210.86	211.60	218.38	219.03	235.30	271.77	273.56	220.90
1980	208.44	225.42	228.66	233.47	207.58	187.07	196.61	204.66	207.29	194.96	175.67	206.35
1981	233.47	214.37	216.46	206.73	198.97	198.48	191.74	193.57	188.36	160.84	148.64	195.60
1982	185.90	188.01	176.70	167.67	162.38	154.86	149.13	139.19	138.54	132.03	132.83	157.02
1983	197.96	201.51	214.73	212.10	207.49	211.81	226.09	226.86	210.84	174.14	155.49	203.55
1984	215.64	202.51	200.92	201.01	206.71	186.46	158.90	145.37	126.56	129.39	121.42	172.26
1985	179.09	173.61	176.96	167.69	146.69	149.88	155.77	153.54	145.42	133.78	141.17	156.69

	Nov	Dec	Jan	Feb	Mar	Apr	May	Jun	Jul	Aug	Sep
AVERAGE MOVE											
All Years		-0.66	1.35	0.76	-7.63	-5.07	-1.52	-1.91	-2.83	-2.05	-2.63
Less Extremes		-0.55	1.45	0.01	-7.02	-4.32	-0.24	-1.71	-3.22	-2.53	-3.06
Ave Up - All Years		5.63	6.76	6.38	5.70	2.16	8.78	2.39	10.08	14.85	6.60
Ave Down - All Years		-10.08	-6.76	-7.67	-9.11	-9.89	-11.82	-6.21	-8.36	-18.94	-11.86
COUNT											
Number Up		6	6	6	1	4	5	5	3	5	5
Number Down		4	4	4	9	6	5	5	7	5	5
Pct Up		60.0%	60.0%	60.0%	10.0%	40.0%	50.0%	50.0%	30.0%	50.0%	50.0%
Pct Down		40.0%	40.0%	40.0%	90.0%	60.0%	50.0%	50.0%	70.0%	50.0%	50.0%
EXTREMES											
Greatest Up		16.98	13.22	17.26	5.70	4.32	14.28	8.05	16.27	36.47	17.49
Greatest Down		-19.11	-11.31	-9.73	-25.89	-20.51	-27.56	-13.53	-18.81	-36.71	-19.29
SEASONAL INDEX : AVERAGE PERCENTAGE METHOD											
All Years	105.9	105.4	105.9	106.0	101.9	99.2	98.0	96.8	94.9	93.6	92.4
Less Extremes	106.2	106.1	106.6	105.8	100.7	99.1	97.1	96.5	96.1	92.2	91.2
SEASONAL INDEX : LINK RELATIVE METHOD											
All Years		100.6	102.4	103.9	100.9	99.5	99.6	99.3	98.4	98.0	97.4
Less Extremes		100.4	102.2	103.2	100.4	99.2	100.0	99.8	98.9	98.4	97.6

LUMBER - SEPTEMBER - MONTH OF HIGH AND LOW

Year of Expiration	Nov	Dec	Jan	Feb	Mar	Apr	May	Jun	Jul	Aug	Sep
1976				H					L		
1977									L	H	
1978						L					H
1979	L										H
1980				H							L
1981	H										L
1982		H								L	
1983								H			L
1984	H										L
1985	H									L	

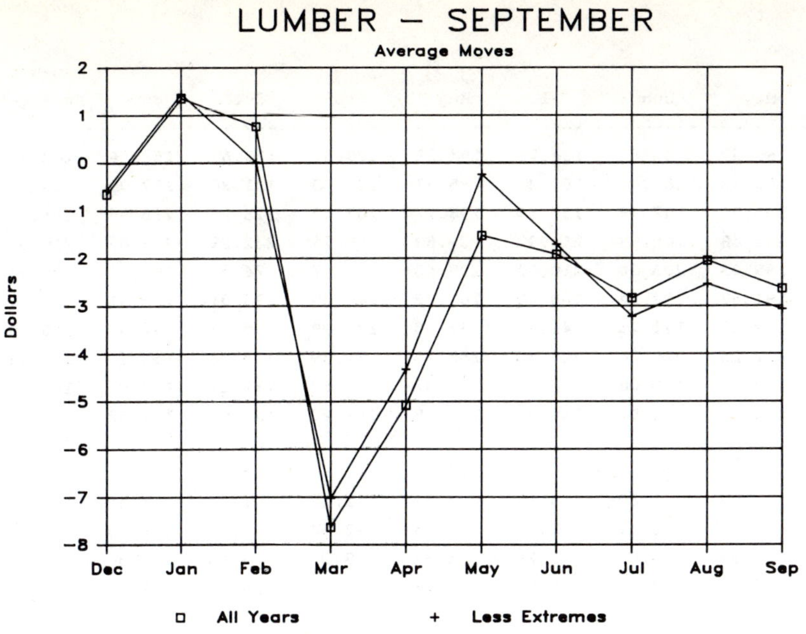
LUMBER — SEPTEMBER
Average Moves
Dollars
2
1
0
−1
−2
−3
−4
−5
−6
−7
−8
Dec
Jan
Feb
Mar
Apr
May
Jun
Jul
Aug
Sep
All Years
Less Extremes

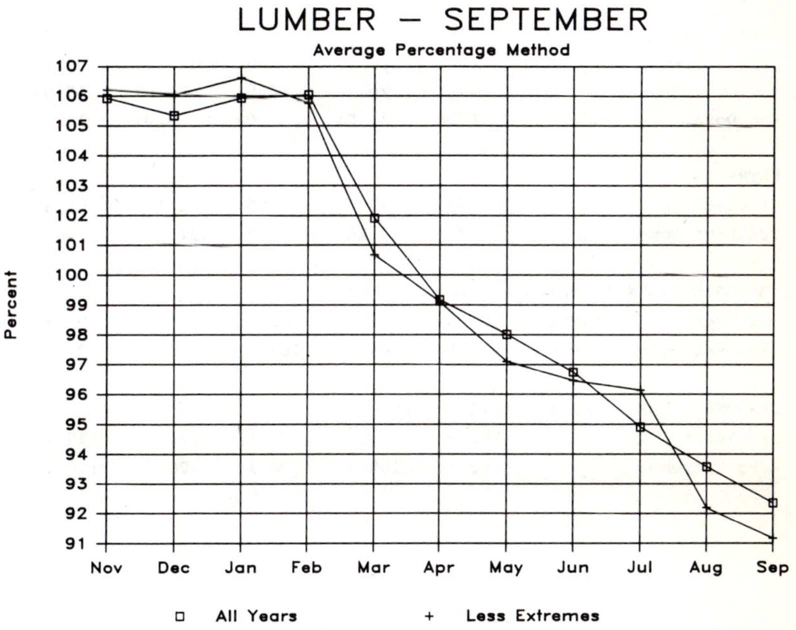
LUMBER — SEPTEMBER
Average Percentage Method
Percent
107
106
105
104
103
102
101
100
99
98
97
96
95
94
93
92
91
Nov
Dec
Jan
Feb
Mar
Apr
May
Jun
Jul
Aug
Sep
All Years
Less Extremes

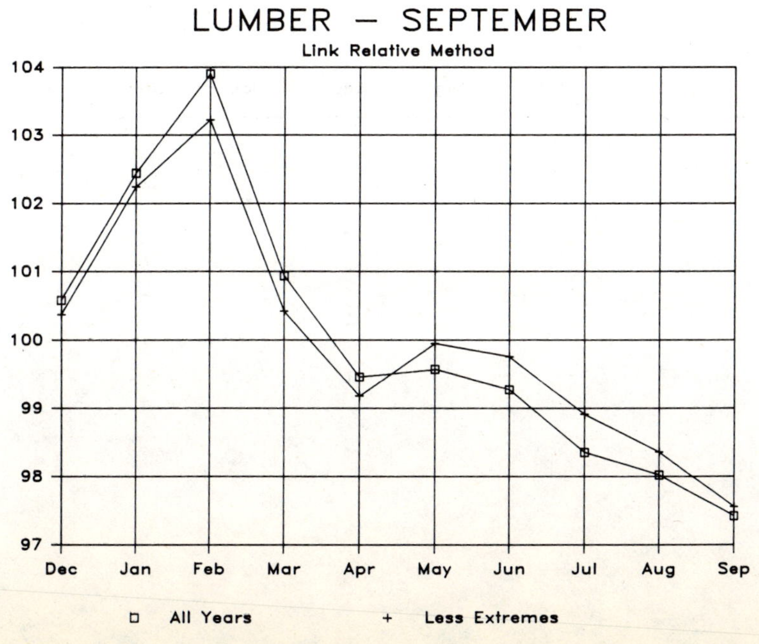
LUMBER — SEPTEMBER
Link Relative Method
104
103
102
101
100
99
98
97
Dec
Jan
Feb
Mar
Apr
May
Jun
Jul
Aug
Sep
All Years
Less Extremes

LUMBER - NOVEMBER - MONTHLY AVERAGE PRICE

Year of Expiration	Jan	Feb	Mar	Apr	May	Jun	Jul	Aug	Sep	Oct	Nov	Jan-Nov Average
1976	163.47	175.90	169.32	170.18	165.59	162.81	154.26	154.29	160.67	158.61	163.06	163.47
1977	188.51	195.56	197.31	198.15	188.48	187.49	184.23	195.41	188.73	181.36	182.09	189.76
1978	194.73	194.55	189.71	182.82	186.00	182.98	189.48	194.27	207.33	225.27	215.96	196.64
1979	190.99	203.74	200.92	201.94	206.48	206.52	214.92	236.83	250.28	242.29	231.87	216.98
1980	225.87	229.60	204.40	186.38	199.03	208.56	210.90	199.63	184.17	174.51	165.54	198.96
1981	217.39	207.58	205.39	201.39	191.52	194.14	188.20	167.02	148.25	135.01	133.91	180.89
1982	176.81	168.79	163.51	156.11	152.68	141.26	141.16	137.65	135.99	138.61	146.00	150.78
1983	215.16	214.03	210.49	214.39	222.25	220.24	208.55	183.25	171.39	173.28	163.26	199.66
1984	204.78	201.84	204.64	183.96	159.39	150.06	132.29	135.97	127.82	131.24	138.04	160.91
1985	178.32	168.85	148.02	150.70	155.69	155.07	146.63	132.99	137.20	138.97	143.62	150.55

	Jan	Feb	Mar	Apr	May	Jun	Jul	Aug	Sep	Oct	Nov
AVERAGE MOVE											
All Years		0.44	-6.67	-4.77	-1.89	-1.80	-3.85	-3.33	-2.55	-1.27	-1.58
Less Extremes		0.18	-5.54	-3.87	-0.87	-2.01	-3.64	-3.74	-2.52	-2.17	-1.60
Ave Up - All Years		8.99	2.28	1.86	6.65	4.06	5.75	8.32	9.28	5.53	4.80
Ave Down - All Years		-5.26	-8.91	-11.40	-10.43	-4.31	-7.96	-14.98	-10.43	-8.06	-7.96
COUNT											
Number Up		4	2	5	5	3	3	5	4	5	5
Number Down		6	8	5	5	7	7	5	6	5	5
Pct Up		40.0%	20.0%	50.0%	50.0%	30.0%	30.0%	50.0%	40.0%	50.0%	50.0%
Pct Down		60.0%	80.0%	50.0%	50.0%	70.0%	70.0%	50.0%	60.0%	50.0%	50.0%
EXTREMES											
Greatest Up		12.75	2.80	3.90	12.65	9.53	8.40	21.91	13.45	17.94	7.39
Greatest Down		-9.81	-25.20	-20.68	-24.57	-11.43	-17.77	-25.30	-18.77	-13.24	-10.41
SEASONAL INDEX : AVERAGE PERCENTAGE METHOD											
All Years	109.1	109.0	105.2	102.5	101.1	99.9	97.5	95.4	94.0	93.4	92.9
Less Extremes	109.4	108.9	104.1	102.2	100.7	99.5	98.3	95.0	93.1	93.1	93.2
SEASONAL INDEX : LINK RELATIVE METHOD											
All Years		103.6	101.3	100.1	100.3	100.4	99.2	98.6	98.2	98.7	99.7
Less Extremes		102.8	100.9	100.1	100.7	100.6	99.7	98.7	98.3	98.6	99.4

LUMBER - NOVEMBER - MONTH OF HIGH AND LOW

Year of Expiration	Jan	Feb	Mar	Apr	May	Jun	Jul	Aug	Sep	Oct	Nov
1976		H					L				
1977				H			L				
1978				L						H	
1979	L								H		
1980		H									L
1981	H										L
1982	H								L		
1983					H						L
1984	H								L		
1985	H							L			

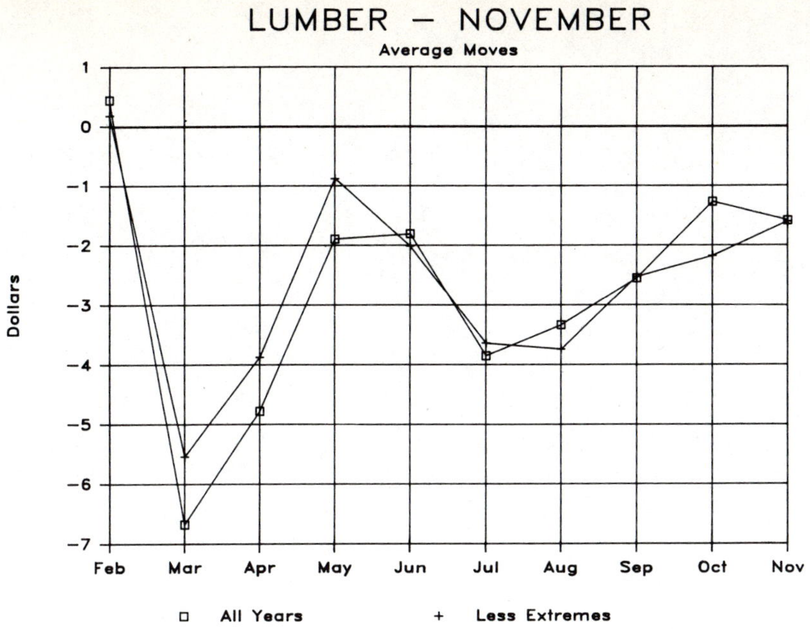
LUMBER – NOVEMBER
Average Moves
Dollars
1
0
−1
−2
−3
−4
−5
−6
−7
Feb
Mar
Apr
May
Jun
Jul
Aug
Sep
Oct
Nov
□ All Years
+ Less Extremes

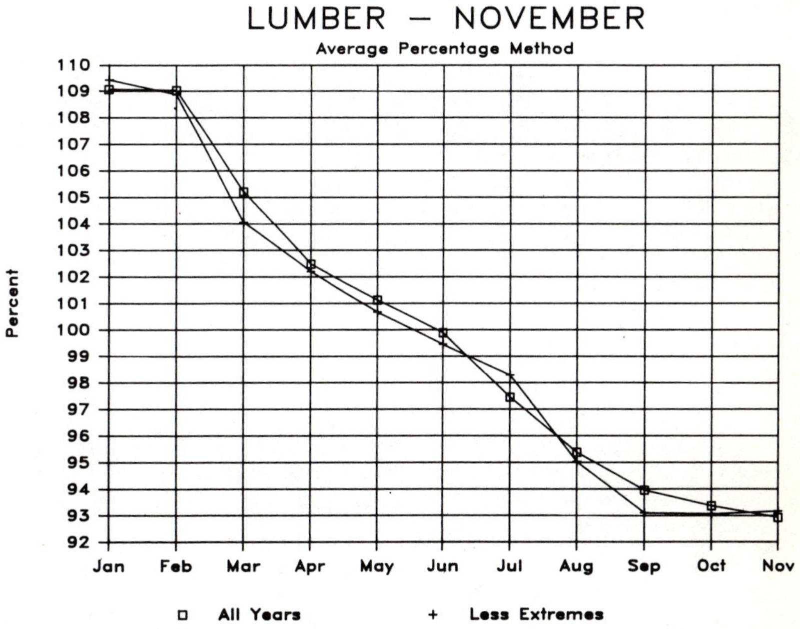
LUMBER – NOVEMBER
Average Percentage Method
Percent
110
109
108
107
106
105
104
103
102
101
100
99
98
97
96
95
94
93
92
Jan
Feb
Mar
Apr
May
Jun
Jul
Aug
Sep
Oct
Nov
□ All Years
+ Less Extremes

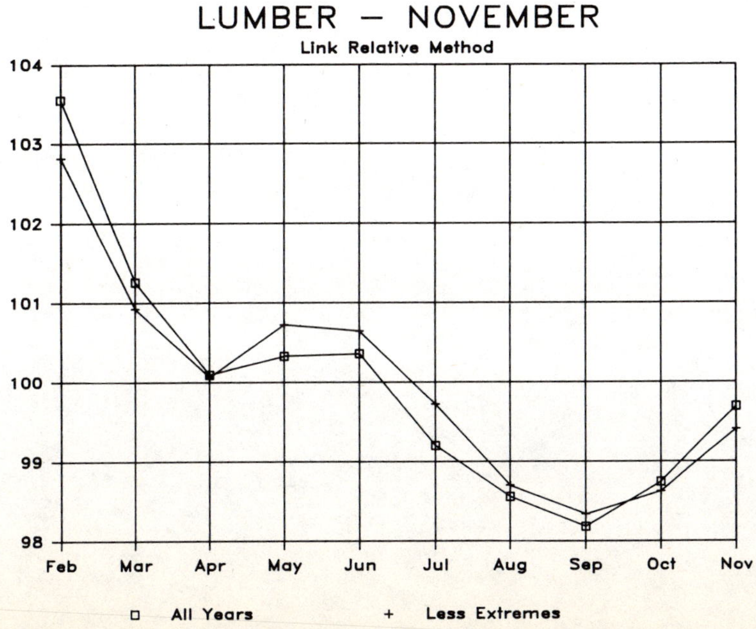
LUMBER – NOVEMBER
Link Relative Method
104
103
102
101
100
99
98
Feb
Mar
Apr
May
Jun
Jul
Aug
Sep
Oct
Nov
□ All Years
+ Less Extremes

TEN

Seasonal Calendar

The following is a list of all seasonal trends with over 70% reliability sorted by month and by commodity. Following that is a list of seasonal trends of greater than 80% sorted by reliability. The average move is the average for all years in the direction of the seasonal trend. For example, if the seasonal tendency is for prices to drop in February then the average move column will show the average move for only those months that the commodity dropped.

JANUARY

Commodity	Contract	Position	Reliability	Average Move
Canadian dollar	March	Short	75.0	−0.28
Swiss franc	March	Short	70.0	−1.02
Swiss franc	June	Short	70.0	−0.99
Swiss franc	September	Short	70.0	−1.02
Platinum	January	Short	70.0	−39.49
Copper	January	Long	70.0	+4.36
Oats	March	Short	70.0	−4.22
Cattle	June	Long	73.3	+1.77
Cattle	August	Long	73.3	+1.63
Feeder cattle	January	Long	75.0	+1.66
Feeder cattle	March	Long	75.0	+1.84
Hogs	June	Long	73.3	+2.30
Hogs	July	Long	73.3	+2.26
Coffee	March	Long	70.0	+7.35
Coffee	May	Long	70.0	+7.57
Coffee	July	Long	70.0	+7.23
Coffee	September	Long	70.0	+7.23
Lumber	March	Long	70.0	+5.52

FEBRUARY

Commodity	Contract	Position	Reliability	Average Move
T-bonds	March	Short	85.7	−2.81
T-bonds	June	Short	85.7	−2.86
T-bonds	September	Short	85.7	−2.88

(Continued on next page.)

Commodity	Contract	Position	Reliability	Average Move
T-bills	March	Short	85.7	−0.65
T-bills	June	Short	85.7	−0.61
T-bills	September	Short	85.7	−0.55
Deutsche mark	March	Short	70.0	−1.27
Deutsche mark	June	Short	70.0	−1.29
Deutsche mark	September	Short	70.0	−1.30
Japanese yen	March	Short	100.0	−0.98
Japanese yen	June	Short	100.0	−1.00
Swiss franc	March	Short	70.0	−1.81
Swiss franc	June	Short	70.0	−1.83
Swiss franc	September	Short	70.0	−1.82
Copper	March	Long	70.0	+4.28
Copper	May	Long	70.0	+4.61
Copper	July	Long	70.0	+4.70
Copper	September	Long	70.0	+4.70
Soybean meal	March	Short	70.0	−7.87
Soybean meal	May	Short	70.0	−6.73
Soybean oil	August	Long	73.3	+1.04
Soybean oil	September	Long	73.3	+0.96
Cattle	June	Long	80.0	+1.28
Cattle	October	Long	73.3	+1.07
Feeder cattle	March	Long	75.0	+2.79
Feeder cattle	April	Long	87.5	+2.44
Feeder cattle	May	Long	75.0	+2.79
Sugar	July	Short	70.0	−0.82
Sugar	September	Short	70.0	−0.77
Sugar	October	Short	70.0	−0.77

MARCH

Commodity	Contract	Position	Reliability	Average Move
T-bills	March	Short	71.4	−0.61
T-bills	June	Short	71.4	−0.62
British pound	March	Short	70.0	−4.17
British pound	December	Short	70.0	−5.72
Japanese yen	March	Short	75.0	−0.69
Swiss franc	March	Short	70.0	−1.08
Swiss franc	June	Short	90.0	−0.87
Platinum	October	Short	70.0	−40.77
Wheat	July	Short	73.3	−15.92
Wheat	September	Short	73.3	−15.48
Wheat	December	Short	73.3	−15.80
Soybean meal	March	Short	70.0	−5.88
Oats	May	Short	70.0	−6.61
Oats	September	Short	70.0	−6.43
Oats	December	Short	80.0	−6.76

Commodity	Contract	Position	Reliability	Average Move
Coffee	July	Long	70.0	+13.45
Coffee	September	Long	70.0	+13.75
Coffee	December	Long	70.0	+13.00
Sugar	May	Short	80.0	−1.40
Sugar	July	Short	80.0	−1.31
Sugar	September	Short	80.0	−1.15
Sugar	October	Short	80.0	−1.08
Orange juice	November	Short	80.0	−5.90
Lumber	March	Short	100.0	−8.93
Lumber	May	Short	90.0	−11.17
Lumber	July	Short	90.0	−10.24
Lumber	September	Short	90.0	−9.11
Lumber	November	Short	80.0	−8.91

APRIL

Commodity	Contract	Position	Reliability	Average Move
T-bills	June	Long	71.4	+0.79
T-bills	September	Long	71.4	+0.76
T-bills	December	Long	71.4	+0.70
Canadian dollar	September	Short	75.0	−0.68
Deutsche mark	June	Short	70.0	−0.88
Deutsche mark	September	Short	70.0	−0.92
Deutsche mark	December	Short	70.0	−0.95
Japanese yen	June	Short	75.0	−0.88
Swiss franc	June	Short	70.0	−1.11
Swiss franc	September	Short	70.0	−1.13
Swiss franc	December	Short	70.0	−1.23
Gold	June	Short	70.0	−13.28
Gold	August	Short	70.0	−13.91
Gold	October	Short	70.0	−14.50
Gold	December	Short	70.0	−15.14
Silver	January	Short	70.0	−238.81
Copper	July	Long	70.0	+2.13
Copper	September	Long	70.0	+2.11
Copper	December	Long	70.0	+2.02
Oats	May	Long	70.0	+4.76
Coffee	May	Long	70.0	+9.95
Coffee	July	Long	70.0	+9.89
Coffee	September	Long	70.0	+8.40
Coffee	December	Long	70.0	+7.64
Sugar	May	Short	70.0	−1.27
Sugar	July	Short	70.0	−1.20
Sugar	September	Short	70.0	−1.10
Sugar	October	Short	70.0	−1.06
Cotton	July	Short	70.0	−1.29

MAY

Commodity	Contract	Position	Reliability	Average Move
T-bills	September	Long	71.4	+0.92
T-bills	December	Long	71.4	+0.81
Deutsche mark	June	Short	70.0	−1.10
Deutsche mark	September	Short	70.0	−1.07
Deutsche mark	December	Short	70.0	−1.05
Swiss franc	June	Short	80.0	−0.99
Swiss franc	September	Short	80.0	−0.99
Swiss franc	December	Short	70.0	−1.13
Gold	February	Short	80.0	−9.85
Gold	June	Short	70.0	−9.99
Gold	August	Short	70.0	−10.73
Gold	October	Short	70.0	−11.42
Gold	December	Short	70.0	−12.09
Silver	May	Short	70.0	−58.30
Silver	July	Short	70.0	−67.87
Silver	September	Short	70.0	−71.39
Silver	December	Short	70.0	−75.64
Copper	January	Short	80.0	−3.16
Copper	May	Short	80.0	−2.57
Copper	July	Short	80.0	−3.10
Copper	September	Short	80.0	−2.98
Copper	December	Short	80.0	−2.83
Corn	May	Short	73.3	−5.40
Corn	July	Short	73.3	−7.42
Wheat	May	Short	73.3	−18.27
Wheat	July	Short	73.3	−16.33
Wheat	September	Short	73.3	−15.87
Wheat	December	Short	73.3	−15.36
Soybean meal	January	Short	70.0	−6.65
Soybean meal	May	Short	70.0	−6.78
Soybean meal	July	Short	80.0	−7.29
Soybean meal	August	Short	80.0	−7.35
Soybean meal	September	Short	70.0	−7.03
Soybean meal	December	Short	70.0	−6.52
Feeder cattle	May	Short	75.0	−2.42
Pork bellies	May	Short	73.3	−3.84
Pork bellies	July	Short	73.3	−4.23
Pork bellies	August	Short	73.3	−3.98
Coffee	May	Long	80.0	+5.46
Coffee	July	Long	80.0	+6.62
Coffee	September	Long	80.0	+7.15
Coffee	December	Long	70.0	+7.98
Sugar	January	Short	70.0	−1.36
Sugar	March	Short	70.0	−1.27
Sugar	July	Short	70.0	−1.08
Sugar	September	Short	70.0	−1.04
Sugar	October	Short	70.0	−1.02
Orange juice	January	Long	80.0	+2.79

JUNE

Commodity	Contract	Position	Reliability	Average Move
T-bonds	June	Long	71.4	+2.79
T-bills	June	Long	71.4	+0.83
T-bills	September	Long	71.4	+0.78
British pound	March	Short	80.0	−4.15
Canadian dollar	June	Short	75.0	−0.64
Canadian dollar	September	Short	75.0	−0.90
Deutsche mark	March	Long	70.0	+0.54
Gold	February	Short	70.0	−14.26
Gold	June	Short	70.0	−10.45
Gold	August	Short	70.0	−13.11
Gold	October	Short	70.0	−13.48
Gold	December	Short	70.0	−13.80
Platinum	January	Short	70.0	−16.13
Platinum	July	Short	70.0	−16.65
Platinum	October	Short	70.0	−16.27
Copper	January	Short	80.0	−4.42
Copper	March	Short	80.0	−4.41
Copper	July	Short	90.0	−3.88
Copper	September	Short	80.0	−4.40
Copper	December	Short	80.0	−4.38
Soybean meal	July	Short	80.0	−12.05
Soybean meal	August	Short	80.0	−11.04
Soybean meal	September	Short	80.0	−7.29
Soybean meal	October	Short	70.0	−5.96
Oats	March	Short	70.0	−9.14
Oats	July	Short	70.0	−8.01
Oats	September	Short	70.0	−8.72
Oats	December	Short	70.0	−9.52
Orange juice	July	Short	70.0	−5.53
Orange juice	September	Short	70.0	−6.29
Orange juice	November	Short	70.0	−5.66
Cotton	July	Short	70.0	−3.67
Cotton	October	Short	70.0	−3.42
Cotton	December	Short	70.0	−2.58
Lumber	January	Short	70.0	−3.56
Lumber	November	Short	70.0	−4.31

JULY

Commodity	Contract	Position	Reliability	Average Move
T-bonds	March	Short	71.4	−2.19
T-bonds	September	Short	71.4	−2.18
T-bonds	December	Short	71.4	−2.16
T-bills	March	Short	71.4	−0.38
Gold	February	Long	70.0	+38.29
Gold	April	Long	70.0	+14.00
Silver	January	Long	70.0	+32.87

(*Continued on next page.*)

Commodity	Contract	Position	Reliability	Average Move
Silver	March	Long	70.0	+33.98
Oats	March	Short	70.0	−6.77
Oats	September	Short	80.0	−8.50
Oats	December	Short	80.0	−7.62
Feeder cattle	October	Long	75.0	+1.62
Feeder cattle	November	Long	75.0	+1.63
Coffee	September	Short	70.0	−16.55
Coffee	December	Short	70.0	−17.33
Sugar	September	Short	70.0	−1.27
Orange juice	January	Long	70.0	+2.53
Orange juice	March	Long	70.0	+2.38
Cotton	October	Short	70.0	−2.36
Cotton	December	Short	70.0	−1.70
Lumber	September	Short	70.0	−8.36
Lumber	November	Short	70.0	−7.96

AUGUST

Commodity	Contract	Position	Reliability	Average Move
T-bonds	September	Short	71.4	−1.85
T-bonds	December	Short	71.4	−1.86
British pound	March	Short	70.0	−2.71
Canadian dollar	September	Short	75.0	−0.50
Deutsche mark	March	Short	80.0	−0.86
Deutsche mark	September	Short	70.0	−0.86
Deutsche mark	December	Short	70.0	−0.83
Japanese yen	September	Short	75.0	−0.52
Japanese yen	December	Short	75.0	−0.52
Swiss franc	March	Short	80.0	−0.94
Swiss franc	September	Short	80.0	−0.86
Swiss franc	December	Short	70.0	−0.96
Soybean meal	August	Short	80.0	−11.34
Soybean meal	September	Short	80.0	−12.12
Soybean meal	October	Short	80.0	−11.42
Soybean meal	December	Short	70.0	−12.63
Oats	March	Short	70.0	−8.23
Oats	May	Short	70.0	−7.87
Oats	September	Short	90.0	−10.69
Oats	December	Short	90.0	−8.68
Feeder cattle	January	Long	75.0	+0.84
Feeder cattle	August	Long	75.0	+2.37
Feeder cattle	September	Long	75.0	+1.75
Cocoa	May	Short	70.0	−101.17
Coffee	March	Long	70.0	+8.69
Coffee	May	Long	70.0	+8.46
Orange juice	January	Long	80.0	+3.38
Orange juice	March	Long	80.0	+3.22

Commodity	Contract	Position	Reliability	Average Move
Orange juice	May	Long	90.0	+2.84
Orange juice	September	Long	70.0	+2.29
Orange juice	November	Long	70.0	+4.56
Cotton	October	Short	70.0	−4.40
Lumber	March	Short	70.0	−8.68

SEPTEMBER

Commodity	Contract	Position	Reliability	Average Move
T-bills	September	Long	71.4	+0.42
British pound	March	Short	70.0	−2.98
British pound	June	Short	70.0	−2.23
British pound	December	Short	70.0	−3.03
Japanese yen	September	Short	75.0	−0.63
Gold	February	Long	70.0	+31.64
Gold	April	Long	70.0	+32.74
Gold	June	Long	70.0	+33.84
Gold	October	Long	70.0	+29.09
Gold	December	Long	70.0	+30.58
Silver	January	Long	70.0	+163.32
Silver	March	Long	70.0	+166.39
Silver	May	Long	70.0	+169.07
Silver	September	Long	70.0	+160.93
Silver	December	Long	70.0	+161.87
Platinum	January	Long	70.0	+25.83
Platinum	April	Long	70.0	+26.77
Platinum	October	Long	70.0	+24.75
Copper	January	Short	70.0	−2.99
Copper	March	Short	70.0	−3.03
Copper	May	Short	70.0	−3.05
Copper	December	Short	70.0	−2.62
Oats	September	Long	80.0	+5.93
Pork bellies	February	Long	73.3	+4.08
Pork bellies	March	Long	73.3	+3.92
Pork bellies	May	Long	73.3	+3.83
Cocoa	March	Long	90.0	+130.31
Cocoa	May	Long	80.0	+140.14
Cocoa	September	Long	80.0	+185.58
Cocoa	December	Long	90.0	+153.13
Coffee	September	Long	70.0	+8.58
Sugar	January	Short	70.0	−1.55
Orange juice	January	Long	70.0	+3.08
Orange juice	March	Long	70.0	+2.95
Orange juice	May	Long	70.0	+2.77
Orange juice	September	Long	70.0	+2.96
Cotton	October	Short	80.0	−2.03
Cotton	December	Short	70.0	−1.90

OCTOBER

Commodity	Contract	Position	Reliability	Average Move
T-bills	June	Long	71.4	+0.66
T-bills	December	Long	71.4	+0.77
British pound	June	Short	70.0	−3.05
Canadian dollar	March	Short	75.0	−0.53
Deutsche mark	March	Long	70.0	+1.22
Soybean meal	January	Short	70.0	−5.25
Cocoa	March	Short	70.0	−120.93
Cocoa	May	Short	70.0	−127.50
Cocoa	July	Short	70.0	−127.86
Cocoa	December	Short	80.0	−93.45
Coffee	December	Long	70.0	+9.34
Orange juice	January	Short	70.0	−3.26
Orange juice	March	Short	70.0	−3.05
Orange juice	May	Short	70.0	−2.94
Orange juice	July	Short	70.0	−2.77
Cotton	March	Short	70.0	−0.64
Cotton	May	Short	70.0	−0.69
Cotton	July	Short	70.0	−0.76
Cotton	October	Long	70.0	+1.51

NOVEMBER

Commodity	Contract	Position	Reliability	Average Move
T-bills	December	Long	71.4	+0.82
Swiss franc	March	Short	70.0	−1.61
Swiss franc	June	Short	70.0	−1.61
Gold	February	Short	80.0	−16.91
Gold	April	Short	80.0	−17.30
Gold	June	Short	80.0	−17.74
Gold	August	Short	80.0	−18.25
Platinum	January	Short	70.0	−15.89
Platinum	April	Short	70.0	−16.35
Platinum	July	Short	70.0	−16.86
Copper	January	Short	80.0	−1.64
Copper	March	Short	80.0	−1.57
Copper	May	Short	80.0	−1.59
Copper	July	Short	80.0	−1.60
Copper	December	Short	80.0	−1.70
Soybean meal	December	Long	70.0	+8.35
Cocoa	May	Short	70.0	−83.22
Cocoa	July	Short	70.0	−86.16
Coffee	December	Long	70.0	+12.27
Sugar	March	Short	70.0	−0.93
Sugar	May	Short	70.0	−0.80
Sugar	July	Short	70.0	−0.70
Sugar	September	Short	70.0	−0.74
Orange juice	January	Short	70.0	−2.78

Commodity	Contract	Position	Reliability	Average Move
Lumber	March	Long	70.0	+8.73
Lumber	May	Long	70.0	+8.51
Lumber	July	Long	70.0	+7.46

DECEMBER

Commodity	Contract	Position	Reliability	Average Move
T-bills	March	Short	71.4	−0.36
Canadian dollar	December	Short	75.0	−0.63
Japanese yen	March	Long	75.0	+1.00
Silver	May	Short	70.0	−58.56
Silver	July	Short	70.0	−59.89
Silver	September	Short	70.0	−61.28
Copper	December	Long	70.0	+2.32
Wheat	March	Short	73.3	−19.18
Wheat	May	Short	73.3	−19.56
Wheat	December	Short	73.3	−15.82
Soybeans	January	Short	73.3	−30.45
Soybean meal	January	Short	70.0	−11.47
Soybean meal	March	Short	80.0	−10.45
Soybean meal	May	Short	70.0	−11.08
Soybean meal	July	Short	70.0	−10.54
Soybean meal	August	Short	70.0	−8.98
Soybean meal	September	Short	70.0	−6.75
Soybean oil	January	Short	80.0	−1.20
Soybean oil	March	Short	80.0	−1.13
Soybean oil	May	Short	80.0	−1.08
Soybean oil	July	Short	80.0	−1.07
Soybean oil	August	Short	73.3	−1.09
Soybean oil	September	Short	86.7	−0.88
Oats	March	Short	90.0	−4.56
Oats	May	Short	90.0	−4.34
Oats	July	Short	70.0	−4.44
Hogs	December	Long	73.3	+2.11
Coffee	December	Long	70.0	+11.87
Sugar	January	Short	70.0	−1.93
Sugar	March	Short	70.0	−1.82
Sugar	May	Short	70.0	−1.83
Sugar	July	Short	70.0	−1.72
Sugar	September	Short	70.0	−1.51
Sugar	October	Short	70.0	−1.40
Orange juice	January	Short	70.0	−6.42
Orange juice	March	Short	70.0	−5.68
Orange juice	May	Short	70.0	−5.13
Orange juice	July	Short	80.0	−4.16
Orange juice	September	Short	80.0	−8.29
Cotton	December	Short	80.0	−1.07
Lumber	March	Long	70.0	+7.15
Lumber	May	Long	70.0	+5.91

HIGHLY RELIABLE SEASONAL PRICE TENDENCIES—100% RELIABLE

Commodity	Contract	Month	Position	Reliability	Average Move
Japanese yen	March	February	Short	100.0	−0.98
Japanese yen	June	February	Short	100.0	−1.00
Lumber	March	March	Short	100.0	−8.93

HIGHLY RELIABLE SEASONAL PRICE TENDENCIES—90%+ RELIABLE

Commodity	Contract	Month	Position	Reliability	Average Move
Swiss franc	June	March	Short	90.0	−0.87
Copper	July	June	Short	90.0	−3.88
Oats	March	December	Short	90.0	−4.56
Oats	May	December	Short	90.0	−4.34
Oats	September	August	Short	90.0	−10.69
Oats	December	August	Short	90.0	−8.68
Cocoa	March	September	Long	90.0	+130.31
Cocoa	December	September	Long	90.0	+153.13
Orange juice	May	August	Long	90.0	+2.84
Lumber	May	March	Short	90.0	−11.17
Lumber	July	March	Short	90.0	−10.24
Lumber	September	March	Short	90.0	−9.11

HIGHLY RELIABLE SEASONAL PRICE TENDENCIES—80%+ RELIABLE

Commodity	Contract	Month	Position	Reliability	Average Move
T-bonds	March	February	Short	85.7	−2.81
T-bonds	June	February	Short	85.7	−2.86
T-bonds	September	February	Short	85.7	−2.88
T-bills	March	February	Short	85.7	−0.65
T-bills	June	February	Short	85.7	−0.61
T-bills	September	February	Short	85.7	−0.55
British pound	March	June	Short	80.0	−4.15
Deutsche mark	March	August	Short	80.0	−0.86
Swiss franc	March	August	Short	80.0	−0.94
Swiss franc	June	May	Short	80.0	−0.99
Swiss franc	September	May	Short	80.0	−0.99
Swiss franc	September	August	Short	80.0	−0.86
Gold	February	May	Short	80.0	−9.85
Gold	February	November	Short	80.0	−16.91
Gold	April	November	Short	80.0	−17.30
Gold	June	November	Short	80.0	−17.74
Gold	August	November	Short	80.0	−18.25
Gold	December	November	Short	80.0	−16.91
Copper	January	May	Short	80.0	−3.16
Copper	January	June	Short	80.0	−4.42
Copper	January	November	Short	80.0	−1.64
Copper	March	June	Short	80.0	−4.41
Copper	March	November	Short	80.0	−1.57

Commodity	Contract	Month	Position	Reliability	Average Move
Copper	May	September	Short	80.0	−1.59
Copper	May	May	Short	80.0	−2.57
Copper	July	November	Short	80.0	−1.60
Copper	July	May	Short	80.0	−3.10
Copper	September	May	Short	80.0	−2.98
Copper	September	June	Short	80.0	−4.40
Copper	December	May	Short	80.0	−2.83
Copper	December	June	Short	80.0	−4.38
Copper	December	November	Short	80.0	−1.70
Soybean meal	March	December	Short	80.0	−10.45
Soybean meal	July	May	Short	80.0	−7.29
Soybean meal	July	June	Short	80.0	−12.05
Soybean meal	August	May	Short	80.0	−7.35
Soybean meal	August	June	Short	80.0	−11.04
Soybean meal	August	August	Short	80.0	−11.34
Soybean meal	September	June	Short	80.0	−7.29
Soybean meal	September	August	Short	80.0	−12.12
Soybean meal	October	August	Short	80.0	−11.42
Soybean oil	January	December	Short	80.0	−1.20
Soybean oil	March	December	Short	80.0	−1.13
Soybean oil	May	December	Short	80.0	−1.08
Soybean oil	July	December	Short	80.0	−1.07
Soybean oil	September	December	Short	86.7	−0.88
Oats	September	July	Short	80.0	−8.50
Oats	September	September	Long	80.0	+5.93
Oats	December	March	Short	80.0	−6.76
Oats	December	July	Short	80.0	−7.62
Cattle	June	February	Long	80.0	+1.28
Feeder cattle	April	February	Long	87.5	+2.44
Cocoa	May	September	Long	80.0	+140.14
Cocoa	September	September	Long	80.0	+185.58
Cocoa	December	October	Short	80.0	−93.45
Coffee	May	May	Long	80.0	+5.46
Coffee	July	May	Long	80.0	+6.62
Coffee	September	May	Long	80.0	+7.15
Sugar	May	March	Short	80.0	−1.40
Sugar	July	March	Short	80.0	−1.31
Sugar	September	March	Short	80.0	−1.15
Sugar	October	March	Short	80.0	−1.08
Orange juice	January	May	Long	80.0	+2.79
Orange juice	January	August	Long	80.0	+3.38
Orange juice	March	August	Long	80.0	+3.22
Orange juice	July	December	Short	80.0	−4.16
Orange juice	September	December	Short	80.0	−8.29
Cotton	October	September	Short	80.0	−2.03
Cotton	December	December	Short	80.0	−1.07
Lumber	November	March	Short	80.0	−8.91

ELEVEN

Further Reading

There are now several good books for seasonal traders. In addition, I would be glad to send you additional information regarding seasonals. Simply write to me at 675 West Hastings, Suite 1614, Vancouver, B.C., Canada V6R 4W3. The software used to generate the tables and charts can be purchased through me. I suggest reading:

Schwager, Jack. *A Complete Guide to the Futures Market*, Wiley New York, 1984.

This is the single best book on commodity futures. If you only have one book on futures, make it this one.

Esserman, Wayne. *The Handbook of Commodity Spreads*, Ewe Publishing, Delphi IN, 1984.

Excellent guide to seasonality of commodity spread prices, particularly the grains.

Bernstein, Jake. *How to Profit from Seasonal Commodity Spreads*, Wiley, New York, 1985.

Excellent companion to the previous book. High quality.